THE LIBRARY OF POLITICAL ECONOMY

POLITICAL ECONOMY is the old name for economics. In the hands of the great classical economists, particularly Smith, Ricardo and Marx, economics was the study of the working and development of the economic system in which men and women lived. Its practitioners were driven by a desire to describe, to explain and to evaluate what they saw around them. No sharp distinction was drawn between economic analysis and economic policy nor between economic behaviour and its interaction with the technical, social and political framework.

The Library of Political Economy has been established to provide widely based explanations of economic behaviour in contemporary society.

In examining the way in which new patterns of social organization and behaviour influence the economic system and policies for combating problems associated with growth, inflation, poverty and the distribution of wealth, contributors stress the link between politics and economics and the importance of institutions in policy formulation.

This 'open-ended' approach to economics implies that there are few laws that can be held to with certainty and, by the same token, there is no generally established body of theory to be applied in all circumstances. Instead economics as presented in this library provides a way of ordering events which has constantly to be updated and modified as new situations develop. This, we believe, is its interest and its challenge.

Editorial Board

Andrew Graham, University of Oxford
Keith Griffin, University of Oxford
Geoffrey Harcourt, University of Cambridge
Roger Opie, University of Oxford
Hugh Stretton, University of Adelaide
Lester Thurow, Massachusetts Institute of Technology

Volumes in the Library

Dangerous Currents: The State of Economics—Lester Thurow
The Political Economy of Nationalism—Dudley Seers
Women's Claims: A Study in Political Economy—Lisa Peattie and Martin Rein
Urban Inequalities under State Socialism—Ivan Szelenyi
Social Innovation and the Division of Labour—Jonathan Gershuny
The Structuring of Labour Markets: The Steel and Construction Industries in Italy—Paola Villa
Monetarism and the Labour Market—Derek Robinson

Monetarism and the Labour Market

Derek Robinson

CLARENDON PRESS · OXFORD
1986

Oxford University Press, Walton Street, Oxford OX2 6DP
Oxford New York Toronto
Delhi Bombay Calcutta Madras Karachi
Kuala Lumpur Singapore Hong Kong Tokyo
Nairobi Dar es Salaam Cape Town
Melbourne Auckland
and associated companies in
Beirut Berlin Ibadan Mexico City Nicosia

Oxford is a trade mark of Oxford University Press

Published in the United States
by Oxford University Press, New York

© Derek Robinson 1986

All rights reserved. No part of this publication may be reproduced, stored in a retrieval system, or transmitted, in any form or by any means, electronic, mechanical, photocopying, recording, or otherwise, without the prior permission of Oxford University Press

This book is sold subject to the condition that it shall not, by way of trade or otherwise, be lent, re-sold, hired out or otherwise circulated without the publisher's prior consent in any form of binding or cover other than that in which it is published and without a similar condition including this condition being imposed on the subsequent purchaser

British Library Cataloguing in Publication Data
Robinson, Derek, 1932 Feb. 9–
Monetarism and the labour market.—(The Library
of political economy)
1. Chicago school of economics
I. Title II. Series
332.4   HB98.3
ISBN 0-19-877191-6
ISBN 0-19-877192-4 Pbk

Library of Congress in Publication Data
Robinson, Derek, 1932 Feb. 9–
Monetarism and the labour market.
(The Library of political economy)
Bibliography: p.
Includes index.
1. Chicago school of economics. 2. Monetary
policy—Great Britain. 3. Labor supply—Great Britain.
I. Title. II. Series.
HB98.3.R63 1986   332.4'941   86-751
ISBN 0-19-877191-6
ISBN 0-19-877192-4 (pbk.)

Set by Downdell Ltd., Oxford
Printed in Great Britain
at the University Printing House, Oxford
by David Stanford
Printer to the University

For Lucy

Preface

INFLATION and unemployment are the two most serious economic problems facing us. For forty years from the mid-thirties there was a growing consensus that economic analysis and policy prescription should be based on Keynesian economics. This consensus has been shattered by the growth of Monetarism. In Britain we have a government which is formally committed to a Monetarist position. It is my belief that Monetarist analysis is misguided and fails to understand the nature of the economic activity it seeks to explain. Nowhere is this more evident than in its treatment of labour markets. The consequences are disastrous. This is not because economic theory is being driven into blind alleys—that is of more importance to economic theorists than the rest of the world—but because these new dogmas are being accepted by policy-makers and leading to immense hardship for many people. This book is an attempt to show how and why Monetarism is wrong.

There is increasingly a division between Monetarists and the rest. For our purpose the rest will be regarded as Keynesians, although there is another main school of Marxist economics. To be a Keynesian does not mean that one accepts every word of Keynes as being the final conclusive statement on an issue. It means that the broad approach set out by Keynes, modified to meet current circumstances, provides the basis of analysis and prescription. Keynes is regarded as providing a guide rather than a tablet of stone. The division of opinion is no mere academic hair-splitting dispute, although some of the individual participants in the debate may bring it down to this. It is an argument about the way in which the economy operates and how people behave and thus provides the foundation for economic policies. It is of direct and crucial concern to all of us as governments will be influenced by some interpretation of economic theory whether they admit it or not.

Two years ago I gave a lecture on 'The Industrial Relations of Monetarism' at the annual conference of the Institute of Personnel Management. Some of my friends suggested I expand this into a book on the labour market and Monetarism which would discuss the assumptions about labour markets which Monetarists make and the way in which labour markets would have to respond if Monetarist policies were to be effective. They and I wanted a book which would be comprehensible to interested laymen who had not studied economics. This volume is therefore directed to those interested in industrial relations, economics, and politics who are not professional economists.

Labour market considerations are often glossed over by Monetarists who are much more interested in the more esoteric aspects of their theory such as the precise definition of money or the ways in which expectations are formed. Yet Monetarism if it has any relevance or validity has so only to the extent that the labour market behaves in the way assumed in Monetarist theories. The behaviour of employers and workers is absolutely central to the Monetarist explanation of inflation and devotees of the more extreme wing in the New Classical School in Britain recognized this.

I have deliberately reversed the priorities and emphasis. There is not much discussion of the wider aspects of Monetarism here and very little treatment is given to some of the important areas of economics relevant to an examination of the full Monetarist position. I am interested in the labour market aspects and have deliberately excluded many other issues. This is not because they are unimportant, but because they are not directly relevant to the subject in hand. Also, if, as I argue, Monetarism has got its labour market analysis wrong in a number of respects, the rest of their arguments might be of less importance. If they do not correctly explain how control of the money supply feeds through and affects wages and so prices the hard-core foundation of their policy prescriptions has gone.

It is recognized that this volume gives unequal treatment of Monetarism in the sense that it concentrates on certain aspects and these aspects are not always, are indeed seldom, seen by many Monertarists as the more important ones. That is their mistake. The labour market comes second in importance only to the basic propositions of the Quantity Theory to the Monetarist case.

Throughout I use a capital M when referring to Monetarism and Monetarists. This is done to emphasize that I regard Monetarism as a broad school of thought which can take on some of the characteristics of a religion. One other stylistic point should be mentioned. I use the masculine form when discussing workers or employers. This is not because I do not realize the importance of women in the labour market, nor is it because I am a complete male chauvinist (although some of my family might not agree). It is more convenient to use a single-gender term and we are more familiar with this being the male form.

In Chapter 1 I set out a brief explanation of Monetarism emphasizing its central tenet that inflation is determined by changes in the money supply. Some variant of the Quantity Theory of Money is central to all Monetarists. There is also a short discussion of the reasons why Monetarism re-emerged as a popular explanation and basis for policy in both economic theory and the real world. Chapter 2 looks at the Quantity Theory of Money and extends it from the usual form of $MV = PT$ to include EW. This allows us to look at the effects on employment and wages. Chapter 3 gives a very short account of some of the elements influencing the demand for and supply of money. This chapter which would be the central theme of a standard work on Monetarism is much abridged and is intended to do two things. First, to sketch out the skeleton of these important issues because no discussion of Monetarism would be complete without some mention of them, and second, to introduce some of the factors such as the definition of money and whether or not the monetary authorities can actually control the money stock, which are relevant to our discussion. Chapter 4 takes up one of the factors which influences the demand for money—the level of income—and considers different definitions and concepts of income. The time-scale over which income is assessed may be particularly important and one version which uses the concept of permanent or lifetime income is examined. The implications that are drawn from this may not be those which a Monetarist would draw. I emphasize fairness and beliefs about the level of future income which individuals, or their trade unions, consider reasonable, or to which they think they are entitled. Such views may influence future behaviour and the levels of wages which are established.

The next part deals with labour market behaviour. Chapter 5 deals with the demand for labour following fairly orthodox economic treatment. In Chapter 6 I look at the supply of labour and while again following fairly orthodox treatment make one important addition. I introduce the notion of acceptable-labour supply whereby the employer decides which of the various people offering to work for him are acceptable to him. This seems to correspond with what happens in the real world where not everyone who applies for a job is acceptable. It has some serious consequences for some economic analysis in that the effective or acceptable labour supply is now determined by the employer, that is from the demand side, as well as by workers from the supply side when they make their labour offers.

Chapter 7 moves the discussion from money wages to real wages. There has long been debate about the importance of money and real wages in economic analysis. An important part of Keynes's contribution was that workers would in certain circumstances accept a reduction in real wages if this was the result of prices rising, although they would resist a similar or an equivalent reduction in real wages caused by a cut in money wages. Monetarists generally conduct all their analysis in terms of real wages. I accept this assumption for purposes of discussion so that we can look at Monetarist arguments in their own terms but it is an assumption that is not necessarily valid in the real world. In Chapter 7 I also look at explanations of unemployment which are currently fashionable and in particular at that which sees unemployment as the voluntary activity of job search.

Chapters 8 and 9 look at the way in which pay and employment might be determined. In Chapter 8 we see how these might be established in what is referred to as a 'free' market composed of individual workers and employers. Here the sort of market forces which provide so much attraction to right-wing politicians are assumed to hold sway, but we should remember that it is only assumed that they so operate. It does not follow that because we assume certain conditions and then postulate certain results that they will ever occur and much less does it follow that they should occur. Chapter 9 looks at what might happen if we introduce trade unions into the analysis. One of the problems we have is that we cannot be sure what it is trade unions are trying to do about wages and employment, and this uncertainty is the greater the more that increases in wages are likely to lead to reductions in employment.

Chapter 10 looks at what we might mean by unemployment. It considers various ways of defining this and of measuring it. There is a key distinction between Monetarists and Keynesians. To many Monetarists all unemployment is voluntary. Keynesians can readily accept the existence of involuntary unemployment which occurs when workers are prepared to work for existing wages but are unable to get jobs. This difference of opinion as to the nature of unemployment leads to crucial departures in policy prescriptions.

The relationship between unemployment and inflation is examined in Chapter 11. This provides the basic analysis of the Monetarists so far as inflation is concerned. It says, essentially, that it is not possible to reduce unemployment by increasing aggregate nominal demand. If this is correct government cannot reduce unemployment by expansionary macro-economic policies and the major contribution put forward by Keynes for reducing unemployment in a recession has to be rejected. We suggest that such dramatic reversal of accepted economic analysis for the past fifty years is not justified.

An important part of the Monetarist explanation of inflation is the role played by expectations of future price and wage levels. This is considered in Chapters 12 and 13. First we look at the role of expectations held by individuals and then at the role of expectations if there are trade unions. In this situation it may be expectations of other things besides the future level of prices which are important. We might regard these as aspirations rather than expectations but they are no less important in determining the behaviour of trade unions and employers.

The Monetarist account of unemployment rest on the concept of the natural rate of unemployment (NRU) which is the level of unemployment which the economy will experience in the long run. Clearly if we wish to reduce unemployment the NRU is of crucial importance. Chapter 14 considers the factors which may determine the NRU and Chapter 15 discusses ways in which we might change it. These options, to a Monetarist, are the only ones available to a government wishing to lower unemployment.

Chapter 16 examines the policies of the Thatcher Government. This Government is committed to Monetarist principles and we consider how well they have stuck to them.

Finally in Chapter 17 I consider counter-inflationary policies which seek to moderate inflation but also try and maintain employment. My own belief that we need to have an incomes policy in order to reconcile high employment and low inflation should be apparent. This is not derived from 'pure objective' economic analysis. Like all policy prescriptions it cannot be so derived. It rests on certain value-judgements.

I would emphasize that all economic analysis which is intended to lead to policy prescription should contain value-judgements. Economic policy necessarily and properly contains social and political value-judgements and all economic policy is intended to change the existing situation. Economists wishing to comment on practical policies are required to make value-judgements. What is important is that we should recognize these for what they are and distinguish them from the analytical parts of their statements. We should certainly not pretend that policy prescriptions are ever value-free. This volume is not value-judgement free. It is based on a Keynesian, or following the current fashion, post-Keynesian view of economics and of the world. It reflects my view that governments not only can but should intervene to influence inflation and unemployment and that aggregate demand policies have a part to play in both areas. Other policies also have parts to play. It reflects the view that it is wicked as well as wasteful to tolerate, much less create, conditions in which there are well over three million unemployed. It reflects the view that there is no need to suffer this massive waste of potential output and resources and that such waste can be avoided by the appropriate combination of policies.

But it also reflects the view that while trade unions are desirable institutions, necessary for the protection of the individual and essential for the correction of the imbalance in the employment relationship, trade unions are important in the generation of inflationary pressures. This should surprise no one, save perhaps those Monetarists who believe that unions can never, or hardly ever, increase wages. I believe that it is part of trade union objectives as they see them to increase the wages of their members in absolute and relative terms and this generates inflationary pressures. I also believe that the preferred way to reconcile this objective and trade union behaviour with the objectives of the rest of society is not to try and smash trade unions or emasculate them but to come to some arrangements whereby they exercise their power differently in pursuit of modified objectives. Trade unions are necessary to protect the interests of their members. Attempts to create an economy in which there are no unions will not lead to some perfect world as might be supposed from the writings of some Monetarists. It will lead to a massively unfair world in which people will once again go through the painful struggles of forming trade unions. Unions exist because people were not prepared to tolerate the conditions that actually existed without them. The results of market forces unrestrained by the countervailing powers of trade unions were unacceptable not only to workers but to prevailing opinion. It is not necessary to share these value-judgements in order to reject the assumptions and conclusions of Monetarism.

Many people have helped in the preparation of this book, although none of them is responsible for the remaining errors. Peter Carr, George Healy, and Sid Kessler encouraged me to write it. Roger Opie and Andrew Graham read the first draft and made many helpful comments. Ken Mayhew read various drafts in addition to giving me the benefit of many conversations. I have long valued his advice. John Power in the Institute's library gave me much more help than his job required and this reflects his keen interest in this subject as well as his good nature. Sybil Owen typed a number of drafts and revisions and she and Caroline Wise typed the final draft with great patience and speed.

Contents

LIST OF ILLUSTRATIONS

LIST OF TABLES

1. WHAT IS MONETARISM?	1
2. THE QUANTITY THEORY, WAGES, AND EMPLOYMENT	18
3. DEMAND AND SUPPLY OF MONEY	33
4. INCOME AND WEALTH	47
5. THE DEMAND FOR LABOUR	65
6. THE SUPPLY OF LABOUR	111
7. REAL WAGES, LABOUR SUPPLY AND UNEMPLOYMENT, AND JOB SEARCH	146
8. DETERMINATION OF PAY AND EMPLOYMENT IN A FREE MARKET	177
9. COLLECTIVE WAGE DETERMINATION, TRADE UNIONS, AND POWER	191
10. UNEMPLOYMENT	228
11. THE MACRO—ECONOMIC VIEW OF INFLATION AND UNEMPLOYMENT	260
12. EXPECTATIONS	289
13. EXPECTATIONS AND TRADE UNIONS	316
14. THE NATURAL RATE OF UNEMPLOYMENT	341

15. CHANGING THE NATURAL RATE OF EMPLOYMENT   368

16. POLICIES OF THE THATCHER GOVERNMENT   415

17. COUNTER-INFLATIONARY POLICIES   460

BIBLIOGRAPHY   481

INDEX   491

List of Illustrations

Fig. 4.1	Monthly Real Pay: Messenger and Principal Maxima	56
Fig. 5.1	Marginal Productivity, Wages, and Employment	67
Fig. 5.2	Supply and Demand for Labour and Wages	93
Fig. 6.1	Individual Labour Supply	113
Fig. 6.2	Adjusted Labour Supply	122
Fig. 6.3	Adjusted Retention Reservation Wage, Demand, and Employment	124
Fig. 6.4	Individual Reservation Wages for Different Occupations	127
Fig. 6.5	Labour-offer and Acceptable-labour Supply Curves	138
Fig. 7.1	Real Reservation Wages, Real Market Wages, and Acceptable Jobs	147
Fig. 7.2	Distribution of Wages and Probability of finding Reservation Wage Jobs	149
Fig. 7.3	Indices of Real Wages of Craftsmen in Two Firms	160
Fig. 11.1	The Phillips Curve	261
Fig. 11.2	Labour Demand and Supply	267
Fig. 11.3	Excess Demand for Labour and Rate of Change of Wages	268
Fig. 11.4	Excess Demand for Labour and the Rate of Unemployment	269
Fig. 11.5	Rate of Change of Wages and the Level of Unemployment	270
Fig. 11.6	Labour Demand and Supply at Expected Rates of Inflation	272
Fig. 11.7	Expectations-augmented Phillips Curve	274
Fig. 15.1	Expectations-augmented Phillips Curve and Revised Reservation Wages	407

List of Tables

Table 3.1	Relationships among the Monetary and Liquidity Aggregates and their Components	34–5
Table 5.1	Overtime Working by Operatives in Manufacturing	107
Table 10.1	Special Employment and Training Measures: Numbers covered December 1984	250
Table 14.1	Estimates of the NRU for the United Kingdom	353
Table 16.1	Target Ranges for Monetary Indicators and Actual Out-turns	419
Table 16.2	Six Monetary Measures	419

CHAPTER ONE

What is Monetarism?

Introduction

MONETARISM is about inflation, its causes, and its cures. Because it is about inflation it is also about the level of output in an economy and the level of employment and unemployment. For present purposes employment and unemployment can be regarded as offsetting movements in a single labour force figure so that if employment goes down unemployment goes up by the same amount, and vice versa. We will also assume at this stage that there is a direct and consistent link between employment and output so that if employment rises so does output. They need not necessarily rise at the same rate but we will assume that they do move together. Of course, neither of these two assumptions is necessarily true in the real world. If employment falls unemployment may also fall, perhaps because some of the unemployed decide to withdraw from labour market activity and so are not classed as unemployed, or perhaps because of demographic factors there is a reduction in the total number of people making up the employed and unemployed. Similarly output may rise even though employment has fallen. More and/or better capital equipment may be used so that a smaller number of workers produce a larger output. The assumed link between employment and output rests upon other assumptions about the rate of productivity growth (i.e. output per worker, or per hour worked) and the rate of change of employment in relation to the amount of change in total output. The level of output is frequently measured in *real* terms to distinguish it from nominal output or the value of output measured at prevailing prices.

Inflation can be regarded as rising prices and Monetarism is a set of economic theories or beliefs which seeks to explain how inflation occurs. It does this by relating the effects of changes in the supply or quantity of money to the real economic activity, that is the output and employment that take place, and seeks to establish that there are certain relationships which will hold in a consistent way. These allow us to determine what the effects will be of doing certain things, and Monetarists concentrate, in particular, on the effects of changing the money supply.

2 What Is Monetarism?

Monetarists say that all inflation is caused by excessive increases in the money supply. They also argue that this is in fact the *only* cause of inflation. Thus, the hard core of Monetarism may be summarized in the statement 'Inflation always and everywhere is a monetary phenomenon'.

However Monetarism is not only about inflation; it is also about employment and unemployment in that it asserts that these can be altered, in the long run certainly, and sometimes also in the short run, by certain actions but not by others. Monetarism is not therefore intended to be a bit of sterile theoretical economic analysis; it is intended to have specific practical policy conclusions. It seeks to tell governments that if they wish to change the rate of inflation they should do certain things and should not do certain other things. In like manner it tells governments that if they wish to change the level of employment or unemployment existing in their economies they may be able to do so by certain policy measures, but that certain other policies, and in particular that of expanding the money supply, either will not achieve this objective, or will do so only for a limited time—the short run—after which there will be additional inflation. Both implicity in its approach, and frequently explicitly in its analysis and assertions, Monetarism specifies certain firm links between inflation and unemployment. When we discuss Monetarism we are therefore discussing a particular approach to the two most important economic issues of our time.

Economics is well known for the supposed inability of economists to agree amongst themselves on almost anything. There are different schools of thought. A great deal of debate, sometimes friendly, sometimes not, sometimes productive and sometimes not, is between Keynesians and Monetarists. We do not intend to go over the full debate between these two main schools of thought, nor do we wish to mislead by 'the absurdity of dividing economists crudely into Keynesians and Monetarists',[1] but there are some differences between the two schools of thought that are sufficiently deep and important to provide a useful demarcation line. The other major school on the international level, the Marxists, is much more distinguishable but is much less involved in these conflicts perhaps because it adopts premises and methods of analysis which are not common to the other two. In one sense both Keynesians and Monetarists use the same type of concepts and methods of analysis, the same terminology, and the same broad framework of economic issues and behaviour, although they differ markedly in their assumptions about the way in which people and businesses behave, and therefore about the causes as well as the cures of economic problems. They may also mean different things when using the same terminology.

This book is about the views associated with Monetarists, and particularly their views about how the labour market operates. A number of other aspects of Monetarist theory, for example the exchange rate, or the determinants of the rate of interest, will not be considered in much detail except where they are directly relevant to labour market aspects. It is not intended therefore to produce a comprehensive account of Monetarism but to concentrate on the labour market issues.

Monetarists themselves have not paid much attention to the labour market. Yet, as we shall see, the working of the labour market is central to Monetarism. Professor Hendry, reviewing the evidence submitted to the House of Commons Treasury and Civil Service Committee said 'Most commentators viewed the labour market as an important intermediate link between monetary policy and its effects on output and inflation'.[2]

Monetarism is a collection of economic doctrines, or a particular approach to economic analysis based on certain views about how people, or economic agents, behave. Its central proposition—that the sole cause of price increases is changes in the supply of money—can be found way back in economic writings. It is not a new idea. Its importance diminished considerably, however, after Keynes had produced his method of analysis in the General Theory. Credit, or otherwise, for the revival of Monetarism is due primarily to Professor Milton Friedman. While Friedmanite Monetarism is now but one of a number of variations within the broad range of Monetarist analyses, the re-emergence of Monetarism as an important explanation of economic developments and as the basis for policy prescription is due more to Friedman than any other individual.

Economic analysis and policy prescription are carried out within a framework of ideas, theories, and views of how people behave. Part of the analysis consists of testing these ideas and assumptions. However, despite the efforts of some economists to produce completely value-free methods of analysis, economic theories are in part accepted because they seem to explain generally what is happening, and they are accepted in part because other theories which had been accepted in the past no longer seem able to explain current events or provide satisfactory policy conclusions. The emergence of an articulate exponent of a new explanation, or the reformulation of an old one restated in new or modern terminology, can lead to the shifting of general perceptions about the way in which an economy behaves. Both Keynes and Friedman exerted great influence on economists and others interested in economic affairs because they challenged the prevailing orthodoxy in economic analysis at times when that orthodoxy appeared incapable of explaining and solving the pressing economic issues of the times. Friedman may be regarded as the leading prophet in the revival of an old fundamentalist religion, but other prophets and disciples have added doctrinal differences.

Like all economic doctrines Monetarism has some tenets which are generally considered central and others which may be accepted by some adherents but not by others. With all schools of thought there is some degree of variation in the beliefs of individual members even thought they share a body of beliefs which differentiate them from others. This is true whether the school of thought be one of economics, or the natural sciences such as Darwinism. The central core of what might be regarded as mainstream Monetarism changes through time and there are important differences of emphasis in different countries.[3]

The main concepts and associated ideas can be summarized:

1. The single most important theme common to all variations of Monetarism is an acceptance of the Quantity Theory of Money. The theory states that fluctuations in the quantity of money are the predominant causes of changes in total money income. Changes in money supply exert the dominant impulse causing changes in aggregate nominal money incomes. The line of causation runs from changes in money supply to changes in aggregate money income and not vice versa.

2. There exists a stable aggregate demand function for money, that is the relationship between the amount of money people wish to hold, and do hold, bears a stable relationship to their money income in aggregate. Laidler (1982) believes this to be 'the *sine qua non* of monetarism', although he also accepts that the last decade has produced a good deal of evidence to suggest that the relationship has shifted in an unpredictable way in a number of countries.

3. In the long run fluctuations in aggregate money incomes (resulting from fluctuations in the money supply) will take the form of variations in prices rather than in output and employment, although in the short run employment and output may be affected by changes in the quantity of money. This has the important consequence that there is no long-run trade-off between inflation and unemployment. There may be a transitory trade-off so that increases in the quantity of money may lead to some rise in employment and output, accompanied by higher inflation, but after a time output and employment will fall back and the overall effect of the increase in money supply will be only on inflation. This is encapsulated in the expectations-augmented Phillips curve discussed in Chapter 11.

4. The private sector is believed to be inherently stable. This means that if it is left alone, free from government intervention, or as Monetarists often refer to it 'free from distortions', the private sector will

tend to operate about the full employment level. There may be departures from full employment but they will be relatively small and temporary. As we shall see, there can be major differences between Keynesians and Monetarists about what is meant by full employment and the Monetarist definition is crucial and controversial.

There are other issues on which not all Monetarists agree or views which they hold either more or less strongly.

5. Markets, including labour markets, 'clear', or, at least, behave 'as if they cleared'. What this means is that prices adjust to the forces of supply and demand in such a way that at the prevailing prices all those who are willing to buy are able to do so, and all those who wish to sell at these prices are able to sell as much as they wish. In other words there are, at the prices established in the market, no unsatisfied buyers or sellers. In labour market terms this means that at the prevailing wage level everyone who wishes to work is employed and every employer is able to hire as much labour as he wishes at the prevailing wage. For this to happen it is necessary that all prices and wages are flexible, that is they can and do move either upward or downward to reflect the changing relative pressures of supply and demand. The assumption that markets clear is important in justifying (3) above for if markets do not always clear it may well be possible that an increase in money supply leads to an increase in output and employment in the long run and not merely to inflation.

6. Expectations about future price levels play a crucial role in determining the current level of inflation and the way in which expectations are formed is central to the Monetarist analysis. One view is that expectations are adaptive; we form our views about the future level of inflation by adapting to our experience of past rates of inflation. The other main view is that expectations are 'rational' so that expectations of future inflation are formed by applying economic theory or analysis to the expected monetary policies.

Non-monetarists may believe expectations to be important, but they do not necessarily place as much importance on expectations about future inflation as do Monetarists, particularly when considering the causes of changes in wage levels and labour market behaviour. Related to the question of expectations is that of the amount of information available to economic agents, particularly information about inflation. Thus economic activity, and more specifically for our purposes, deviations of output and employment from the full employment level, may be seen as the result of voluntary choices by individuals, but individuals who make mistakes in their expectations of future price and wage levels. On this view, the markets might be clearing but are doing so on the basis of errors in expectations or forecasts about inflation.

The commitment to the views that all decisions regarding labour market activity represent the voluntary choices of individuals is a key difference between a Keynesian and a Monetarist view of unemployment and there are some differences of emphasis within the broad Monetarist school.

Both (5) and (6) are difficult and complex issues and will be considered in more detail in later chapters, for example market-clearing in Chapter 11 and rational expectations in Chapter 12.

7. There is antipathy to active stabilization policy which, while not logically implicit in the earlier theoretical analysis, has come to be a view held by Monetarists. This has three important aspects. Firstly, a belief that governments should not interfere in the economy by using fiscal policy to influence the level of output and employment. The previously accepted Keynesian demand-management policies are, therefore, rejected. Secondly, prices and income policies, or various forms of controls on pay and prices, should not be used. This neo-Keynesian supplement to demand-management policy is therefore also rejected. Thirdly, there is support for the adoption by the monetary authorities, the central bank, and/or government of long-term monetary rules or pre-announced targets for the rate of increase in the money supply. This is advocated to provide some constancy in the rate of change of money supply and also to divert attention away from the use of interest rates as the means of influencing the money supply. Interest rates should respond to money-market conditions within a system where the supply of money is controlled rather than be a policy objective in themselves.

Even if most Monetarists would accept all these propositions so that they might be regarded as providing a central statement of the economic theory of Monetarism there is one useful distinction that can be made between two main branches of Monetarism: the New Classical School and the Gradualists.[4]

The New Classical version of Monetarism believes that inflation can be controlled or eliminated quite quickly and without adverse effects on output and employment. Its proponents reach this conclusion because they believe prices and wages to be very flexible, and because the believed expectations are formed 'rationally'. If, therefore, the monetary authorities announce their intention to reduce the money stock, or its rate of increase, and economic agents believe them, then by applying their economic theory to the consequences of such a reduction agents will realize that it is in their own interests to reduce their wages and/or their prices straightaway. What is really important to this view is that people believe that the government will implement their announced policy and that it will work, and for this to occur the policy itself must be credible and government should have a track record of doing what it has said it will do.

Some latter-day New Classical economists complain that prices and wages are not really flexible and how nice things would be if they were. For example some exponents of job-search theories discussed in Chapter 7 adopt this position. Others emphasize the importance of institutional barriers, such as trade unions and collective bargaining, in preventing wage flexibility. Others, perhaps following some version of implicit contracts (discussed in Chapter 5) may come to a pessimistic conclusion that wage inflexibility not only exists but does so for good reasons and is unlikely to be removed easily.

The Gradualists, however, advocate progressively declining monetary targets as they believe that attempts to eliminate inflation very quickly could succeed only with a very high cost in terms of lost output and increased unemployment. Gradualists believe that in the short run the brunt of the effects of controlling the increase in money supply falls on interest rates and real income, and therefore employment, with the price effects coming through later.[5] Prices and wages are not always seen as equally flexible in both upward and downward directions, and wages may be very sticky downwards. Increases in prices and wages following a tight monetary policy may be less than originally expected and the experience of lower inflation may influence expectations about future inflation but all of this may take time.

The classification into these two broad groups hides some other differences. For example International or Global Monetarism was developed during the period of fixed exchanged rates. For a small open economy, such as Britain, the appropriate measure of the money supply was therefore the change in world money supply, with the domestic money supply reacting to changes in the former adjusted for fluctuations in British inflation and output. World money supply and world inflation thus fed through into changes in nominal money income in the UK causing changes in British money supply. The ending of fixed exchange rates and the emergence of floating rates made British inflation a function of British money supply. On this view flexible exchange rates are a necessary condition for the control of domestic inflation through the domestic money supply.

Whether one is a New Classical or a Gradualist the critical point is that the money supply has to be controlled. In order to do this in the UK many Monetarists have maintained that two conditions have to be met. First, there has to be some way of insulating the money supply in the UK from that of the rest of the world. This leads to the conclusion that fixed exchange rates should be abolished. A regime of floating exchange rates would make British inflation a function of British money supply, and flexible exchange rates become a necessary condition for the control of domestic inflation through the domestic money supply.

Second, the government's budget must not add to the money supply. If the government adopts a deficit budgetary position it is necessary to cover the deficit by borrowing. If this is done by the creation of additional bank money through the central bank there will be effects on the money supply. It is argued that even if the deficit is financed by the issuing of additional government bonds or securities there will be inflationary effects as the increase in goverment debt affects the asset markets. The conclusion drawn is that it is essential to control the budget deficit or the Public Sector Borrowing Requirement (PSBR) in order to control the money supply. This provides another plank or reinforcement for a generally conservative position adopted by Monetarists—there should be balanced budgets which, given a general predisposition to oppose higher taxes, means a reduction in government spending. This, of course, contrasts with the Keynesian position that government spending with a budget deficit may be the best way out of a recession and the most effective way of reducing unemployment.

There is a related question of the interactions between control of the money supply, the PSBR, and the rate of interest. These three provide what Terence Higgins MP called the Bermuda Triangle of economics. Put simply, if the first two are controlled, the third will be determined by the demand for money or loans. Attempts to control the rate of interest with a given PSBR means that the money supply must be adjusted to whatever the level of demand for money is in the prevailing circumstances. For any given PSBR it may be possible for the government to control either the quantity of money or the rate of interest, but not both. Whichever of the two monetary variables it goes for it must accept the consequences on the third, and experience suggests that in these circumstances governments respond to the political pressures which build up if interest rates go too high. Just what is 'too high' will vary from time to time and place to place, but there do seem to be limits on what governments think is politically tolerable. For example the perceived importance of the owner-occupier vote, which in this context means the owner-purchaser vote, and its dislike of high interest rates, may well influence government to weaken in its resolve to control the money supply once interest rates start approaching the political backlash zone. Action to reduce the PSBR or moves toward a balanced budget are therefore much more than part of the political rhetoric of a Conservative Monetarist government. They are part of an apparently logically consistent and politically coherent package of economic measures.

Monetarism might be regarded as especially evocative in that it has come to be associated, in practical policy terms, with certain types of measures which are seen by its critics as leading to unnecessarily harsh economic conditions. Public debate about the desirability or otherwise of measures and government policies often leads to the use of emotive terms and the creation of evocative responses. Monetarism, or one particular form of Monetarism, has come to be associated with one particular section of the Conservative Party in this country and with President Reagan in the United States, and with a set of political measures and governmental approach to economic questions. It may not be the case that a belief in Monetarism necessarily leads to support for those particular government policies. This will depend upon the definition of Monetarism that is adopted and the way in which it is thought those theories ought, or can best be, translated into practical policies in the real world.

It is because the different schools of economic thought lead to different policy prescriptions that the debate about Monetarism is far more important than a mere intellectual difference of opinion between academics. Governments, policy-makers, and ultimately the whole economy and society, are influenced by economic doctrines. The debate about Monetarism is also a debate about the type of policies which ought to be introduced. This can be seen as the same thing as a debate about the type of economic policies which *have* to be introduced if certain economic objectives are to be achieved.

Non-Monetarism

Anyone who does not accept the central tenets of Monetarism can be regarded as a non-Monetarist. There is unlikey to be much common ground other than the rejection of Monetarism among the full range of critics. However, as we have suggested, most of these could be described as belonging closely or loosely to either the Keynesian or Marxist schools. We are more interested in the Keynesians, although there are many divisions and subdivisions among them. The important point is not whether every word Keynes wrote is true or valid, but whether the general approach of Keynes, perhaps as subsequently developed, amended, or even corrected by post-Keynesians, offers a better understanding of the way in which the economy and economic agents operate, and therefore a more reliable basis for policy prescription.

There had been widespread agreement between academic economists and politicians from different parties in the post-war period about the main economic objectives and the broad policy measures by which they were to be achieved. Full or high employment, stable prices, economic growth, and improvements in living standards were common objectives. There were disagreements about the relative priority of each objective and about the precise policies to be implemented. Monetary policy, certainly up to the late sixties, was given only a secondary role. 'The primary role for dealing with the domestic economy was assigned to the manipulation of effective demand in relation to estimates of potential output.'[6] Keynesian demand-management policies were generally accepted.

The debate between Keynesians and Monetarists can be seen as a division of opinion on the question of whether demand-management can influence income and output. It is clear that increased government spending can lead to an increase in demand but Monetarists argue that in the long run this is an increase only in money terms and there is no increase in real income and output. However, monetary policy is itself a technique of demand-management. It is an indirect technique; there has to be some mechanism through which it operates. An increase in money supply eases borrowing conditions and reduces interest rates. This is expected to lead to increased spending. Conversely, a tighter monetary policy increases the cost of borrowing and so may lead to a reduction in borrowing, less consumer credit and so reduce aggregate demand. If these mechanisms do not operate there need be no effects on demand resulting from changes in monetary policy. To the extent that economic agents do respond in the way assumed monetary policy is one form of demand-management.

There may be an asymmetry about monetary policy which fiscal policy may not have. Increased interest rates may not lead to a decrease in the demand for finance. Quantitative controls may be necessary. Similarly, a reduction in interest rates may not necessarily lead to an increase in the demand for credit, or if it leads to an increase in demand that demand may be unmet if banks and other financial institutions do not regard the applicants as creditworthy. The use of interest rates to influence the demand for credit and thus the level of aggregate demand for goods and services in order to affect income and output rests on the price elasticity of demand for finance or credit and there is no reason to suppose that this is a smooth continuous function, or stable through time. This is not a Monetarist versus non-Monetarist, or Keynesian versus non-Keynesian issue: essentially it is a question of whether we can rely on market forces alone to influence income and output. In some circumstances they may not be enough.

Put very simply, a Keynesian view is that the levels of output and employment depend upon the aggregate level of demand and that this aggregate can be influenced by government. Both Keynesians and

Monetarists frequently refer to the level of output as also meaning the level of employment in that more output requires more labour and so more employment. It is recognized that output and employment are connected via productivity and if this changes neither output nor employment need change at the same rate or even in the same direction. Output is produced by the private sector when it anticipates the future profitable sale of goods and services. The actual level of sales in the home market will be influenced by incomes and the proportion of those incomes which are spent (the propensity to consume). Thus aggregate demand is crucial. Government can influence aggregate demand by altering the level of public spending through the purchase of goods and services by the public sector, or by increasing incomes received from the state, such as unemployment benefit or employment in the public sector. Fiscal policy can influence aggregate demand if the consumption level changes when taxes are altered. Monetary policy can exert some influence. An expansionary monetary policy can have effects through lowering interest rates which might lead to increased investment. Conversely, tighter monetary policy could lead to a contraction in demand and lower output and employment.

This is, very simply and very crudely, the basis of a Keynesian approach to demand-management. Many refinements can be added to consider the precise effects of different forms of taxation on different types of economic activity and the precise impact of changes in particular interest rates on specific sectors of the economy. Other items, such as hire-purchase regulations and their effects on demand for particular goods at particular times, can be introduced. In the fifties and early sixties it was thought that such measures, in appropriate combinations, could be used to 'fine tune' the economy so that aggregate demand, output, and employment could be kept within very narrow limits in the short run so that government could exert quite sensitive control over the economy.

As we have recently been reminded (Casson 1983) the view that the economy could be controlled in this way had been challenged by some of Keynes's contemporaries. There are two aspects to this argument. The first is whether it is possible to exercise such delicate or precise manipulation of major economic aggregates. Economic agents or decision-takers may react in spurts rather than fine gradations. The second is whether the underlying economic problem to be tackled is amenable to correction by fine tuning. Manipulation of the level of aggregate demand might be expected to have some desirable effects if the economic problem—say the level of inflation or unemployment—arises from the level of aggregate demand. If the underlying problem is due to, say, structural factors in the economy—some industries and sectors are declining as a result of technological change or foreign competition is killing them off—fine tuning might be irrelevant. The first criticism says that fine tuning, rather than being a medicine, is either harmful or, at best, a placebo. The second says that while fine tuning may cure some ailments it is inappropriate in specific circumstances because the economy is suffering from a different disease.

Such belief as there was in the efficiency of fine tuning has generally gone. Whether or not the British economy ever did respond to such measures in the short run in a predictable and sensitive way may be open to doubt, but there is little doubt that even if it once did, it does no longer. Various reasons for the change have been put forward, some of which are relevant to our present discussion.

1. Increases in taxes in order to reduce aggregate demand mean a reduction in living standards as a result of either higher prices (indirect taxes) or lower net disposable incomes (direct taxes). It may be that higher prices from indirect taxes lead to claims for higher wages based on the cost of living. It has also been argued that higher direct taxes lead to claims for higher wage increases to compensate.[7]

2. Higher interest rates lead to higher prices and charges such as rents and mortgages. This increase in living costs generates pressures for higher wages.[8]

3. When the economy is squeezed and unemployment rises, trade unions do not behave as they formerly did. It may be that they once thought of themselves as weaker when there was a restrictionary demand-management policy, but this changed in the sixties so that they began to test whether they were in fact weaker or not. Employers, too, suffer a loss of strength during a squeeze. A loss of income to them during a strike could threaten their viability. It is a difficult question to decide who—unions or employers—becomes relatively weaker during a squeeze. It may well vary from sector to sector and be influenced by the length and severity of the squeeze.

4. Demand-management measures may not impinge directly on the public sector. Separate measures may be needed and those may not be forthcoming, or may be less tight. If wages in the public sector are not subject to the same sort of restraint as in the private sector, there may be pressures in the private sector to emulate the increases obtained in the public sector.

5. Increases in social security benefit levels in relation to net earnings from employment (one measure of the Replacement Ratio) means that there is a smaller loss of income if unemployment rises during a squeeze. The level of demand may therefore fall by less than it would have done previously when unemployment meant a larger reduction in net disposable income. If expectations of obtaining

another job reasonably quickly were high, as they might well be as a result of the general high level of employment in the post-war period, current demand for goods and services might be little affected by what was regarded as but temporary unemployment. Using terminology explained in Chapter 4 permanent income may have been unaffected by the unemployment resulting from the policies to reduce aggregate demand. The increase in the number of wives in paid employment could also allow expenditure to be maintained at high levels.

6. The use of changes in public expenditure to regulate the economy became subject to growing criticism. A very rapid expansion of public spending was thought to have inflationary effects. This led the Expenditure Committee of the House of Commons to conclude that they found 'sharp changes in public expenditure to manage the economy to be partially ineffective and so far as they are effective—damaging'.[9]

If companies base their prices on average costs a reduction in output leads to higher prices. As a result of various factors it appeared that restrictive demand-management policies, rather than reducing prices, increased them. In the stronger version this gives rise to the tag 'all deflationary policies have inflationary consequences'.

The Recent Rise of Monetarism

Governments were attached to demand-management policies because of their prior commitment to full employment. While there were, understandably, disagreements as to what precise figure of unemployment was equivalent to full employment, there was common agreement that there should be no return to the very high levels of unemployment of the thirties. Indeed, Beveridge's figures were regarded as excessively pessimistic. He had assumed an unemployment rate of 3 per cent (1944). From the Korean War of 1950 to the OPEC crisis of 1973 unemployment in Britain was less than Beveridge's optimistic figure.

Full employment was an important policy objective, although temporary increases in unemployment were regarded as necessary on occasions to preserve the fixed exchange rate. For the rest, however, the demand-management policies were generally designed to ensure that the right amount of demand existed to maintain the employment level. This was described as being on a labour standard instead of a gold standard; the main objective of policy being to maintain the employment level (Hicks 1955). It should be noted though that there was also a fixed exchange rate and much government policy was directed towards maintaining the rate of exchange. Usually the level of demand was seen as being primarily influenced by fiscal policy with the quantity of money being adjusted to provide whatever was thought necessary. Monetary policy was generally passive or seen as being directed mainly at influencing interest rates which were regarded as important in influencing investment. Use of the rate of interest to regulate the domestic economy could conflict with the role of relative international interest rates to influence the movement of short-term capital funds. The emphasis was on credit policy affecting interest rates and credit controls rather than monetary policy affecting money supply growth.

The increasing frustration of government policies and the inability to attain the economic objectives led to increasing dissatisfaction with the usual methods of demand-management policies. Both Labour and Conservative governments were led by their inability adequately to control economic developments, and particularly the rate of inflation, to the use of incomes policies and various forms of wage and price controls. Neither of them wanted to do so but felt compelled by the perceived lack of a viable or acceptable alternative.

Governments fell back on incomes policy in an attempt to preserve the level of employment, either because they did not themselves wish to see significantly higher levels of employment or because they thought that such levels as might be necessary to reduce inflation would be politically intolerable. That we are currently experiencing very much higher levels of unemployment than were contemplated then does not alter the point that, at the time, significantly higher levels were thought to be unacceptable.

There was growing disenchantment with prevailing policies. This was true in many countries and various experiments were tested with incomes policies and active manpower policies in order to try and moderate inflation without creating higher unemployment.[10] At the same time increasing attention was focused on the role of changes in the supply of money and its effects on inflation. The International Monetary Fund advocated the use of monetary targets or limits on the growth of domestic credit and conditions about this were part of the terms of an IMF loan to the Labour Government in 1976.

More generally Monetarism began to gain favour. In the academic world Monetarists were becoming more numerous and vociferous. The leading advocate, Professor Milton Friedman, who had long preached Monetarism and was associated with other views generally espousing greater reliance on market forces and a reduced role for government intervention in economic affairs, attracted supporters known as the Chicago School. Others reached similar positions independently. In Britain, Professor Laidler was consistently advocating Monetarist views which differed in some respects from those in the States, being more adjusted to the conditions and institutions of Britain. It is interesting to note that the House of Commons Expenditure Committee in

1974 produced a Report which was critical of a permanent statutory incomes policy and stated that 'we suspect that there should be a greater use of monetary policy' (HC 328). It was, however, somewhat uncertain as to how far monetary policy provided a feasible alternative because a sustained contractionary monetary policy would lead to bankruptcies and 'as companies go bankrupt, so may their employees become unemployed. We do not believe that the public, or therefore their Government, will tolerate this, as the diverse cases of Rolls Royce and Court Lines show.' Interestingly, the economic adviser to this committee was Professor Alan Walters, a leading British Monetarist, who later became special adviser to Mrs Thatcher.

It has been thought that demand-management provided some relatively simply guide-lines but experience had shown that this was not so. As we shall see in Chapter 11 this was one of the attractions of the Phillips curve—it appeared to give a relatively simple choice between inflation and unemployment. Monetarism was to emerge as the new, simple guide-line. Not that Monetarism, either as an economic theory or as the basis for practical policies, is actually simple or necessarily unambiguous, but there was some sense in which it was regarded as such by some of its advocates. The unease felt by policy-makers was shared by academics who provided the theoretical underpinning for the emergence of the new wave of support for Monetarism. To a considerable extent, the time was right; accepted theories and policies were discredited and the new doctrine, at that stage untested and untried by the harsh realities of practical policy measures, appeared to offer relatively simple and straightforward policy guidance. It is often easier to advocate policies based on doctrines which have not been tested recently as the discussion is on a theoretical rather than a practical plane, and most doctrines can get some support on this basis. Doctrines are more likely to be accepted as a basis for policy when other doctrines have become discredited and there is a need to fill an intellectual vacuum. By the end of the seventies the time was ripe for Monetarism.

If it is believed that the private sector of the economy is inherently stable and always at full employment, there is neither room nor need for additional policies associated with demand-management. If the government tries to run the economy with a higher level of employment than the full employment level there will merely be accelerating inflation with no long-term beneficial effects on output or employment. The best that the government can do in addition to controlling the money supply is to help the various markets work more smoothly and effectively. There are at any given time certain wage levels at which the labour markets will clear so that there is full employment. Wages will differ amongst occupations and localities but if they are free to move in response to supply and demand, labour markets will operate so that everyone who wants to work at prevailing wages will get a job, and each employer will be able to recruit and retain the number of workers he needs at prevailing wage rates, i.e. without increasing wage levels. This will require occupational changes and geographical mobility. The government can assist by removing impediments to mobility—some of the 'distortions' so emphasized by Monetarists.

The Monetarist approach rests heavily on the view that restriction of the rate of growth of money stock will reduce inflation by reducing the rate of increase of wages. This is absolutely central to the whole Monetarist position. Monetarism is a policy to affect incomes. By influencing prices it affects profits—capitalists,' income—and by influencing wages it affects workers' incomes. It does not seek to do so by what is known as an incomes policy, but a policy designed to influence incomes it most certainly is.[11] The crucial question which we shall discuss later is whether monetary policy can, or does, affect incomes in the desired way? Second, if it does so, is it only at an extremely high cost in terms of unemployment and possibly industrial unrest? Is a loss of output and employment the means by which reductions in the rate of increase of prices and wages are obtained? We shall argue that whether this is the case depends very much on whether there are changes in attitudes and behaviour. As we shall see, the processes by which changes in the money stock affect wages and prices in the Monetarist analysis are through expectations about future inflation. Expectations provide a crucial link in the transmission mechanism. A fundamental difference between Monetarists and Keynesians is on the question of whether changes in the supply of money affect prices or output and employment. Monetarists believe that in the long run, after some adjustment process in which expectations are changed, and during which output and employment may be altered, the effects will be very heavily concentrated on, if not exclusively confined to, monetary effects on prices. Keynesians believe that if there is 'involuntary' unemployment in the economy the effects of an increase in money supply may well be on output and employment, although some effect may be felt on prices.

In conditions of full employment both schools would agree that the effects will be on prices and so this is not an area of contention although the definition of full employment may differ very considerably. Below full employment, however, there is disagreement, and it is obvious even from this very brief statement of the issue that the question is one of the utmost importance. If changes in the money supply can affect output and employment government has a weapon at hand. If only prices are affected then not only must government use other methods to influence the level of output and employment—assuming that other methods are available to them—but attempts to expand the economy and increase employment by enlarging the money supply, while perhaps having some desirable short-run effects, in the long run will lead only to higher inflation. On this view monetary policy cannot have *real* effects; it cannot in the long run affect the real variables of output and employment but only their money values, that is, prices and wages.

It is therefore important that we have a view of how changes in the supply of money affect labour markets and wages and employment levels. This will require us to have a view as to how labour markets operate, and while there are various economic theories which might help us, there is no obviously correct empirically verifiable theory which satisfactorily explains labour market behaviour and the determination of wages and employment in the real world. We shall have to make the best judgements we can about how labour markets operate, and in particular we shall examine whether it is reasonable to believe that they operate in the way they are assumed to do in Monetarist analysis. For if they do not, it may well be that the Monetarist explanation will have to be rejected.

Notes to Chapter 1

1. J. E. Meade, *Economic Journal*, 91. Accounts of the differences between the two Schools can be found in Morgan 1981, Jackman *et al*. 1981, and *Economic Journal*, 91, Mar. 1981.
2. Third Report from the Treasury and Civil Service Committee, *Monetary Policy* III, HC (1980-1), 163-III, 17.
3. See Laidler 1982; and Purvis 1980.
4. Third Report from the Treasury and Civil Service Committee of the House of Commons, HC (1980-1), 163-I, paras. 4.18 ff.
5. Ninth Report, Evidence, HC 163-II, 158, para. 9. These are the views of Laidler who, although now living in Canada, can be regarded as the leading British Gradualist. Minford is the best-known British exponent of the New Classical version of Monetarism.
6. Lord Croham GCB: Memorandum to Treasury and Civil Service Committee, HC (1979-80), 720, 75, para. 6.
7. D. Jackson, H. A. Turner, and F. Wilkinson, *Do Trade Unions Cause Inflation?* 1972.
8. See Memorandum by the TUC, Ninth Report of Treasury and Civil Service Committee, HC (1979-80), 720, 169.
9. House of Commons, Ninth Report of the Expenditure Committee, 1974, HC 328, para. 54.
10. David C. Smith 1968. Also see Robinson 1979; Chater *et al*. 1981; and Robinson and Mayhew 1983.
11. See Robinson and Mayhew 1983.

CHAPTER TWO

The Quantity Theory, Wages, and Employment

ACCEPTANCE of some form of the Quantity Theory of Money is a necessary condition of Monetarism. The simplest and best-known version of the theory is the Fisher equation (Fisher 1911). This is expressed as $MV = PT$,
where M is the stock of money;
- V is the average transactions-velocity of circulation of money in a specified time-period, i.e. the number of times on average that each unit of money is used;
- P is the average price level in the same time-period;
- T is the number of transactions in the same time-period, i.e. the volume of economic activity as measured by all transactions which involve the use of money. It includes the purchase of existing assets, such as land and houses as well as newly produced goods and services, of which in the short term there is a fairly stable stock. It also includes financial assets such as stock and shares or, say, foreign financial assets like dollar deposits, of which there is no stable stock.

Really this is not a theory, but an identity, in that it must be true by definition. The total money spent during a period, MV, must equal the value of goods, services and financial assets bought with money during that period, PT. We need to know the average velocity of circulation, or how often each unit of money stock is used, in order to quantify the actual amount of purchasing power as each unit of money can be used a number of times in a period. In practice we cannot measure V directly. Instead we calculate it after we have measured M, P, and T.

Classical economists such as Hume, Adam Smith, Ricardo, or Mill, accepted some form of the Quantity Theory although not expressed as formally as the Fisher equation. They also believed that apart from temporary disturbances in the short run, during which adjustments were being made, the economy was in a full employment equilibrium. This means that the level of employment, and so of output, was that which producers, be they employers or workers, wanted to produce at the existing price and wage levels. Everyone who wanted a job at the prevailing wage levels was able to get one and all employers were able to hire as many workers as they wished at the prevailing wage level, and could produce as much as they chose at existing price and cost levels. This view of the long-run equilibrium of the economy, or of the private sector of the economy, is one that is shared by modern Monetarists. There is a tendency for this belief to lead to the conclusion that T is determined by the real factors limiting output, namely the restrictions on output which arise from full employment. Strictly, however, this is not so for T includes a vast number of financial transactions and these may, or may not be a constant function of full employment.

Classical economists believed that both V and T were determined by real factors and not by monetary factors so that they would not be altered by changing the quantity of money. It was assumed that V and T would change only slowly in the long run. If there were a short-run disturbance, say a change in the money supply, either V or T could be affected temporarily, but the economy would quickly return to equilibrium with little alteration in V and T. In the long run, therefore, there was a close relationship between M and P so that changes in the quantity of money were expected to lead to proportionate changes in the average level of prices. Fisher produced a rather more complicated analysis distinguishing between currency and bank deposits, but for present purposes this distinction is unimportant. He concluded that from 'a doubling in the quantity of money . . . it follows necessarily and mathematically that the level of prices must double . . . We may now restate in what causal sense the quantity theory is true. It is true in the sense that one of the normal effects of an increase in the quantity of money is an exactly proportional increase in the general level of prices' (157). This is an important conclusion, because the question of whether an increase in aggregate nominal demand, i.e. the level of demand for goods and services expressed in money (or nominal) terms, leads to a change in prices or in output, is crucial to the way in which changes in the stock of money might affect an economy.

The Fisher equation, however, includes all transactions in T. Since some of these may not be related at all closely to the level of money income, it may be preferable to alter the specification of the relationship to that between changes in the amount of money and changes in the level of output of newly produced goods and services. This excludes the monetary value of financial transactions but includes the money incomes obtained in carrying out those transactions. For example if stocks and shares were bought their value would be excluded but the incomes of the stockbroker and his clerks would be included. This is the same approach as used in measuring national income. If financial transactions are excluded from T their prices should be excluded from

P. An alternative approach is to *assume* that financial transactions are a constant proportion of all transactions.

Henceforth 'transactions' will be used to refer to economic activity involving the buying and selling of goods and services produced in a given time-period, so that $MV = PY$:

V is now the *income*-velocity of circulation in a time-period;
Y is the volume of real income or output in that period;
P is the average level of prices of real output.

This can be rewritten as: $M = 1/V.PY$. This gives us a simple theory of the demand for money saying that it varies directly with the money value of the level of income, i.e. Gross Domestic Product at current prices. This suggests that changes in the stock of money are associated with the same sort of changes in PY or GDP. It is still an accounting identity in that we do not know whether P or Y will change as a result of changes in M, or whether V will be constant. Friedman and Schwartz (1982) claimed to have established a Monetarist explanation of the development of prices in the US and the UK. However, if they established anything—and this is strongly challenged by Hendry and Ericsson (1983)—the best that can be claimed is some relationship between M and PY, and not between M and P. In itself this is not evidence to support a Monetarist position.

Monetarism may offer explanations of two different relationships. It might say that changes in M lead to changes in P. Alternatively it might say that changes in M lead to changes in PY. The first is a strong relationship between money and the average price level. The second actually leaves it open for the effects of a change in M to be felt on Y and is not only acceptable to Keynesians but something which they use to justify an increase in M in certain situations. If the change in PY is expected to be expressed mainly through changes in Y an increase in M will lead to higher output and employment.

The question of whether a change in M affects *only* P is central to Keynesian–Monetarist debate. If a change in the quantity of money affects only prices we say that money is neutral in that it does not affect the level of output of goods and services but only their prices. Money then has only *nominal* effects and the change in money supply, m, determines the rate of change of prices, p, so that $m = p$. If, on the other hand, a change in the quantity of money leads to a change in the level of output, money is non-neutral and there are *real* effects. Note that the neutrality view requires that *all* the effects of a change in the quantity of money be felt on prices whereas the non-neutrality view does not require that all the effects be felt on output with no price effects. The non-neutrality of money does not necessarily mean that increasing the quantity of money will have no inflationary effects. If the effects of an increase in money supply are split between price and output (or nominal and real) effects, then there will be some inflation and some increase in output. We shall consider later whether a change in the quantity of money might have different effects on prices and output at different times so that the initial effects might be on both prices and output, and the long-run effects on prices only. If this is correct then money would be non-neutral in the short run, but neutral in the long run. Then, on the usual assumption that there is a fixed relationship between output and employment, it is not possible to increase the level of employment by increasing the quantity of money or, conversely, to decrease employment by reducing it.

Labour Market Implications of the Quantity Theory

We can apply this simple equation to the labour market. If the quantity of money places an effective constraint on the total demand for goods and services (with a constant V), then we derive a series of possible combinations of employment, E; and wage levels, W, which are consistent with the equation $MV = PT = EW$. Employment and wages (EW) do not make up the whole of total money income; there are other sources of incomes, such as rents and profits, included in MV as an expression of total money income. To the extent that the employment share in total income alters, EW would change even if MV and PT remained constant. If, therefore, we express the relationships as $MV = PT = EW(f)$ where (f) is the employment share in total money income we can apply the basic Fisher equation to the labour market. Omitting (f) simplifies the treatment by assuming that employment income is a constant share of total income.

If V is constant, an increase in W with a fixed M must lead to a reduction in E. This is an important conclusion from this very simplified version of the Quantity Theory. It means that if the quantity of money does not increase, and (assuming that) the velocity of circulation (V) remains constant, any increase in wages must lead to a reduction in employment. Equally, any increase in prices must lead to a reduction in Y, i.e. real output, and, assuming that labour productivity remains constant, a reduction in employment. It does not matter whether wages or prices increase first—an increase in either will lead to a reduction in both output and employment.

In the same way, an increase in M, with a constant V, will lead to an increase in employment or wages, or both, and to an increase in output or prices, or both, and the change will always be such that the increase in M multiplied by the velocity of circulation will equal the increase in PY and EW.

On this very simple version of the Quantity Theory we can see that provided V is a constant we can make some predictions about some variables if we know what happens to some of the other variables. There are certain fixed relationships in the rate of change of the different variables. The equation tells us that changes in M will affect PY and EW in the same proportion, but we do not know whether it will be P and W or Y and E. Similarly, if productivity changes we do not know which of the variables will alter. It is quite possible, of course, that different variables move differently in different sectors of the economy so that in some industries the effects of increases in productivity could lead to reductions in prices with constant employment and higher output, while in other industries productivity growth leads to constant prices and output and reduced employment. Only if we specify that there is always full employment so that E is fixed can we conclude that the effects will be on prices. But the fact that we have specified it for analytical purposes does not mean that it is true in the real world.

Once we allow for changes in productivity so that there is some increase in output per worker it becomes very likely indeed that there will be different effects on prices in different sectors. This means that there will be different consequences for employment in the various sectors. It will be a very unusual situation if the combined effect of all the various output and price decisions in the different industries and firms leads to changes in prices which exactly equal the rate of change in money supply.

Whether the velocity of circulation is stable, or even whether it is known, because a crucial issue if policy is based on some form of the Quantity Theory. As we have seen, the important link between changes in the stock of money and prices rests on an alleged stability in V. Any government seeking to influence the rate of inflation by controlling M must be confident that whatever relationship held in the past will continue in the future, or, that any change in the relationship is known.

The stability of V, both *ex ante* and *ex post*, is essential in order to obtain the conclusions of the Quantity Theory that we have just discussed. Even then we cannot be certain whether P or T, E or W, will be affected, but without the quantification of V, we cannot even conclude that any of those four variables will be affected. If V, is not constant, all the effects of changes in M may be dissipated on V.

The key question is still whether an increase in money supply leads to an increase in output. There is one extreme situation where we can be certain that an increase in M, with a constant V, will lead to changes in P and W. This is where there is physically full employment, i.e. where there are no unemployed resources available. If E is defined in terms of people this would mean that every person capable of working is already in a job, and if productivity is given it is just not possible to obtain a physical increase in output. We could extend the definition of E to include the number of hours each person worked so that, while there were no extra people to bring into employment, those already working might be able to increase the number of hours they worked and so, in effect, increase the number of employment-hours. E could then rise, and W would rise as a result of longer hours of work. It does not necessarily follow that such an increase in W would be inflationary. This would depend upon the relationship between the increase in wages paid for the extra hours, the extra output obtained in those hours, and so the unit labour costs, and the effect of extra output on other costs, such as fixed or overhead costs, related to the pricing decisions of producers.

The definition of full employment used here is an unusually extreme one in that it refers to physical limitations on output—there are just no more people available to enter employment. In Classical and Neoclassical analysis, followed by Monetarists, full employment has a different meaning. It generally means that all those who want to work at the prevailing wage level are in employment. So there is no one not working who is willing and able to work at the prevailing terms and conditions, and employers are able to hire all the workers they wish at the prevailing terms and conditions. Thus, full employment is seen as the same as the level of employment which exists when the economy is in equilibrium. Keynesians do not accept this definition and indeed what is possibly the greatest difference in views between Keynesians and Monetarists is centred on just this issue. We shall consider it in more detail below, but at this point it is relevant in this regard. If there is an increase in aggregate money demand, say following an increase in M, so that people demand more goods and services, is it possible, should producers so decide, actually to increase output of goods and services at prevailing price levels? If it is thought that the labour market is in equilibrium then in order to induce more people to enter the labour force so that output can be increased, it will be necessary to increase wages. This will lead to increased costs and so to increased prices. It is possible, of course, that producers will actually have lower costs if they are able to obtain economies of scale. It may not have been possible to increase sales even at a lower price. This would depend on the price elasticities of demand and the aggregate level of demand. An increase in aggregate demand could lead to an expansion of output and sales at constant or possibly lower costs and prices.

If, however, it is believed that some of those unemployed would be willing to work at the prevailing wage levels, then it is possible that output could be increased without higher costs coming from higher wages. Unit costs might rise because there was insufficient spare capacity but more labour could be available at the prevailing wage levels. We will consider labour markets and whether they are always, or ever, in equilibrium, later. Also, as we shall see, the term 'full employment' may have different meanings.

For the Monetarist approach based on some version of the Quantity Theory to be valid four assumptions are necessary and each of them is highly debatable.

1. The velocity of circulation of money, V, is stable. If V can change, an increase in money supply might have no effects on prices or output, and similarly prices or output might change without there being any change in money supply. The apparent explanatory power of the Quantity Theory is seriously weakened as the area of indeterminacy becomes greater.

Fisher did not assert that V was constant. Rather, he argued that given the structure of an economy, the type of financial institutions it has developed, and the practices which have become established regarding methods and timing of payment for transactions, it might be supposed that there will be some fixed amount of money needed to finance a given level of transactions, so that a fixed amount of money is needed to finance or facilitate each unit of transaction. If changes occur in the structure of the economy, for example firms merge and use bookkeeping entries to record movements of goods and services within the larger organization rather than finance them with money as transactions between different firms, then both the demand for money and its use, and the level of transaction, would change. The internal activity within a firm would not count as transactions of output; only the last stage of external sales would be included. V might well change as a result. Developments in financial institutions and in practices regarding methods or timing of payment for transactions could also take place over a longer time-period; for example more people could be paid monthly rather than weekly, and this would lower V. It is possible for V to change through time, but Fisher believed it would do so only slowly.

The Treasury in its *Economic Progress Report* 123 (July 1980) said that the income velocity of circulation 'has been broadly stable over time'. They went on to note that there had been some fluctuations. In particular, velocity fell sharply in the early 1970s following the introduction of new monetary control arrangements but, 'velocity subsequently rose again to its trend level and, taking account of a moderate secular trend, the relationship has remained steady over the period covered'. Their judgements were based on a diagram which also showed indices of money supply and inflation for the period 1956–79. They concluded that the 'relative stability of velocity is clear'.

The House of Commons Treasury and Civil Service Committee was interested in the stability of the velocity of circulation and questioned the Treasury about their diagram in *EPR* 123. The Committee was not convinced that the evidence showed that the velocity had been stable over the period 1963–79 when the trend rate of growth rose from 2.9 to 3.5[1].

Professor David Hendry, specialist adviser to the Committee, concluded: 'It takes courage to describe the velocity of circulation as "relatively stable"', and went on to say: 'Overall, this aspect is unconvincing and I am left with the contrary impression that velocity is rather adaptable and can accommodate big changes in money supply and/or demand both in the UK and the rest of the world.'[2] This conclusion is reinforced by Hendry and Ericsson (1983) in their powerful criticism of Friedman and Schwartz's (1982) attempts to establish a Monetarist explanation of the development of prices in the US and UK for the period 1867–1975. 'Thus the "model" that velocity is a will-o-the-wisp (or in statistical terms, essentially a random walk) outperforms the best of FS's (Friedman and Schwartz) equations' (69).

The Governor of the Bank of England added support to the view that velocity is not constant.

Dr Bray (MP). Do you know where the long-term velocity of money is?

Mr Richardson. The long-term velocity of money shifts about. Nobody pretends that we have the most perfectly calibrated instruments.

(Q. 457, HC (1980–1), 163-II)

Monetarists now tend to refer to the demand for money being a stable function of a few variables rather than to a constant velocity of circulation. The stability of the demand for money is equivalent to a stable V as a function of the same variables. Thus, if the variables alter so will V. Friedman argued that 'the velocity of circulation is, *as a practical matter*, a stable function of a few arguments' and this makes Monetarism very different from Classical and Neo-classical economics (Laidler 1981, 3). For, while the earlier writers may have assumed a constant V for illustrative purposes they did not claim that it was so on the basis of empirical observation. Indeed, without reliable figures of GNP and the money supply, it is difficult to see how they could have argued about empirical relationships.

Professor Laidler is now less sure about the stability of the demand for money. 'Ten years ago it was possible to argue that this characteristic monetarist belief in a stable demand-for-money function was well supported by empirical evidence as I did in Laidler (1971). However, the last decade has produced a good deal of evidence to suggest that the relationship has shifted in an unpredicted way in a number of countries' (1981, 4).

However, Laidler believes that the shifts in the demand for money 'were, in all probability, real phenomena, and not statistical artefacts, that such shifts were nothing new, and that they were probably to be explained, at least in part, by institutional changes which themselves might plausibly be interpreted as a response to monetary policy' (1981, 23). Thus it is not simply that the particular measurement adopted for the money supply is defective: there is the suggestion that monetary policy itself induces shifts in the demand for money. This, if true, is of importance when considering the desirability of basing government policy on a Monetarist approach.

Finally, Sir Geoffrey Howe, the Chancellor of the Exchequer, testified to the House of Commons Treasury and Civil Service Committee that the velocity of circulation was not constant, although this was during its later hearings on the 1982 Budget. 'Certainly we have acknowledged that there has been a change, as you say, in velocity, . . .' (HC 270 (March 1982), Q. 168). More important perhaps was the admission that an increase in the money supply could in practice be offset by changes in the velocity of circulation.

Mr Eggar. As I understand it, your argument is that although Sterling M3 has been raised and targets have been raised considerably, none the less, monetary conditions have been tight because of the changes in the velocity of circulation, is that right?
Sir Geoffrey Howe. Yes, and because of what one sees happening to the narrower monetary aggregates, because of what one sees happening to the exchange rate, and because of what one sees happening to inflation and to interest rates. . . . (Q 189)
Mr Eggar. But a key one is the velocity of circulation?
Sir Geoffrey Howe. We cannot be confident—you are quite right—that the change in velocity that is taking place recently is something that is likely to be sustained.

(ibid. Q. 189-90)

Sir Geoffrey Howe. We have also secured the monetary growth we were discussing earlier on, which for reasons I have described, we think it necessary to adjust upwards because of the change in the velocity of circulation.

(ibid. Q. 198)

Mr Eggar's first question above exposes the government's view that a failure to control money supply actually operated as successful control would have done *because* the velocity of circulation fell.

2. Income is fixed. The assumption that income or output in real terms is fixed and always at the full employment level seems totally unwarranted unless this is no more than a tautology which equates the prevailing level of activity with full employment. We shall consider the question of whether Y is fixed at various stages later in the book, but it is worth singling out the discussion on the role of rational expectations in Chapter 13 as relevant to the question of whether income is fixed.

3. The causation runs from M to P and not in the reverse direction. Changes in prices are assumed to occur because of changes in the stock of money. It is quite possible that changes in prices cause changes in the stock of money. We shall in Chapters 3 and 4 see that money is difficult to define and control and that Monetarist policy tends to allow the supply of money to be whatever the economy decides. Demand for money then determines its supply. It is by no means obvious that M determines P: it is much more likely that PY determines M.

4. Money is definable, measurable, and controllable. If it is not possible to define and control the money stock then no matter whether the underlying concept of the Quantity Theory is right or wrong, it provides no sound basis for economic policy. If inflation can be controlled only by appropriate monetary action we must be able to define and measure accurately the quantity of money and changes in it. If Monetarism is to have any policy content Monetarists must believe that it is possible to do this. In the real world we find however that the appropriate definition of money can, and does change, and so its measurement and control are not straightforward. We shall discuss this in Chapter 3.

Friedman and other Monetarists see 'the demand for money as part of capital or wealth theory, concerned with the composition of the balance sheet or portfolio of assets' (Friedman 1970). Distinction is made between 'ultimate wealth holders, to whom money is one form in which they choose to hold their wealth, and enterprises to whom money is a producer's good like machinery or inventories'. For ultimate wealth-holders the demand for money is a function of four variables:

(*a*) Total wealth. This is the total that must be divided among various forms of assets. Friedman recognizes that in practice estimates of total wealth are seldom available so that income serves as an index of wealth. However, he rejects the measurement of income over some time-period that is usually provided by statistics as this may be subject to 'erratic year-to-year fluctuations'. Instead he prefers some longer-term concept such as permanent income, which we shall discuss in Chapter 4.

(*b*) The division of wealth between human and non-human forms. 'The major asset of most wealth holders is their personal earning capacity . . .' (Friedman 1970). Transfer of human into non-human wealth, or the reverse, can be done by using non-human wealth to finance the acquisition of skills through education or training. It is, however, limited by institutional constraints and there are considerable limits on the ability to borrow on the collateral of future earning power. The capital market is far from perfect even though many Monetarists assume that it is. The 'fraction of total wealth that is in the form of non-human wealth may be an additional important variable'.

(c) The expected rates of return on money and other assets. The nominal rate of return on money may be zero, negative if there are bank service charges, or positive if interest is paid on current accounts. The nominal rate of return on other types of assets consists of two parts. There is the yield such as dividends or interest, or there may be costs of storage or for the safe keeping of some physical assets. Second, there are changes in the nominal value of assets.

(d) Other variables determining the utility attached to the services rendered by money relative to the services rendered by other assets. This is the same sort of approach as Keynes used in his concept of liquidity preference and relates to the utility or advantages perceived to accrue to the individual from having wealth assets in an easily realizable form. Wealth-holders may prefer liquidity when they expect economic conditions to be uncertain. More liquidity may be desired the greater the number of capital transactions relative to income.

The demand for money for a single wealth-holder is expressed as

$$\frac{M}{P} = f(y, w, r_m, r_b, r_e, \frac{1}{P}\frac{dP}{dt}; u)$$

where: M = the stock of money;
P = the price index implicit in estimating national income at constant prices;
y = national income in constant prices;
w = the fraction of wealth in non-human form;
r_m = the expected nominal rate of return on money;
r_b = the expected nominal rate of return on fixed-value securities including expected changes in their prices;
r_e = the expected nominal rate of return on equities including expected changes in their prices;
$(1/P)(dP/dt)$ = the expected rate of change of prices and goods and so the expected nominal rate of return on real assets;
u = a portmanteau symbol standing for whatever variables other than income may affect the utility attached to the services of money.

Because this equation refers to the demand for money by an individual there are problems of aggregation when seeking to obtain the demand for money of all individual wealth-holders. The distribution of y and w among individuals may well influence the aggregate demand. Also, as Friedman recognizes, the major problems that arise in practice in applying the equation are 'the precise definitions of y and w, the estimation of *expected* rates of return as contrasted with the actual rates of return, and the quantitative specification of the variables designated by u'. A similar equation can be produced for business enterprises except that w would be excluded as irrelevant.

Friedman believes that all the terms in the equation depend on real factors which are assumed by him to be stable. This is the same as arguing that the velocity of circulation is stable as the demand for money and so the extent to which a given stock of M will be used is, according to Friedman, determined by these stable real factors.

The claim that V is empirically stable is, as we have already discussed, not only disputed, but now, in the UK at least, rejected. One reason for this, which is particularly relevant to the Friedman formulation of the demand for money, is that permanent income, or the ratio of human to non-human wealth, might change. This we shall return to in Chapter 3 and discuss more fully in Chapter 4.

There are other formulations of the relationship between the supply of money and prices and output. Some may be regarded as expressing the demand for money which is discussed in Chapter 3, and others put more emphasis on the role of changes in money supply as a cause of price changes. The first type can be regarded as equivalent to $M = 1/V \cdot PY$. As we shall discuss in Chapter 3, it is now usual to add r, the rate of interest, to the right-hand side of this sort of equation. The second type of expression of the Quantity Theory is $P = 1/Y \cdot VM$, where M is exogeneously determined and, with $1/Y$ and V assumed to be constant, P becomes the endogenous variable. It is clearly of the utmost importance whether money determines the level of prices, or whether it determines PY—the Gross Domestic Product expressed in money terms—so that some of the change in GDP can be expressed in changing prices but some, or perhaps all of it, can be expressed in terms of changing output. Work done in the Treasury rejects the view that the second type of formulation, in which money is the cause of movements in prices, provides a satisfactory explanation of British experience. While recognizing that further work needed to be done a Treasury Working Paper concluded

Money appears to be important, but it is certainly not the only variable that may be significant in determining prices, particularly in the short run. Not only do other variables contribute to the explanation, but they also alter the estimated effects of money as a result. Simple "money-only" forms may therefore not only neglect other important determinants of inflation, but may also give a misleading view of the role of money in explaining prices (Wren-Lewis 1982).

This conclusion should not be surprising. If the Quantity Theory is used to establish a causal connection so that M determines P in an aggregate sense there has to be great flexibility of individual prices. If output—or Y—and V are constant, then if there is no change in M any increase in the price of an individual product included in the aggregate P has to be offset by reductions in price elsewhere. This means that the higher the increase in the price of, say, oil, the greater the reduction in all other prices in aggregate. This really does seem to fly in the face of common sense and experience. An increase in the price of oil is expected to lead to an increase in other prices as the cost of an input—oil—has risen. Of course, we might also expect output or Y to fall, but in the Quantity Theory type of approach this is assumed to occur only for a short period, or as a result of a random shock. The fact that other prices did not fall when the price of oil rose does not in itself invalidate the Quantity Theory because the quantity of money was not held constant. But even if it had been it seems too far-fetched to believe that output and employment would have remained constant and other prices and wages would have fallen to maintain a constant P with a constant M.

Conclusions

The Quantity Theory does *not* tell us that prices will move proportionately to the stock of money offset by any productivity changes, but only that on certain assumptions, given V, PY will move in response to changes in M. In labour market terms the most that can be concluded, given the appropriate assumptions, is that a change in the quantity of money will lead to changes in employment and/or wages, but we cannot say that wages will rise at the same rate as the money supply, or even that they will rise at all. If decreases in the money supply are to lead to corresponding reductions in the price level it is essential that at least some prices are reduced, that is that there is downward as well as upward price flexibility. Similarly, if the level of employment is to remain at some full employment, or other constant, level, a decrease in the quantity of money requires that wages, or some wages, are also flexible downwards. If they are not then a reduction in the money supply should lead to less employment. In the same way if wages rise by more than the increase in the money supply there will be a reduction in employment. To the extent that increases in wages lead to increases in prices it is obvious that the determinants of wage changes are crucial factors in any assessment of the effects of controlling the rate of change of money supply. The Quantity Theory does not address this issue and it is in fact indeterminate on the question of whether a reduction in the supply of money will lead to lower wages and constant employment or the same or higher wages and less employment. We have to turn elsewhere for guidance on the determination of wages and wage changes.

In practice many of the policy implications of the Quantity Theory relate not to reductions in the absolute amount of money but to reductions in its rate of growth. In many cases, therefore, it might not be logically necessary that there are actual reductions in all money wage levels. Aggregate money wages can rise, but by a smaller proportion than previously so that as $m_2 > m_1$, so $w_2 > w_1$ and, according to the strict version of the Theory, $w_1 = m_1$ and $w_2 = m_2$. It is possible, of course, that if wages in enough sectors exceed the rate of growth of money supply by a sufficient percentage, it will be necessary for wage levels in some other sectors to fall if the overall aggregate identity relationship is to hold. Flexibility in relative wages might be a necessary condition for the Quantity Theory identity to lead to the conclusion that employment will tend to remain round some constant level so that changes in aggregate money wages are equal to the rate of change in money supply.

The Friedman version of the demand for money by including some notion of human wealth or permanent income introduces labour market factors more directly. These we shall consider in Chapter 4.

Both the Quantity Theory and Friedman's version involve V. If the velocity of circulation is not stable the equations become of little use. The stability or otherwise of V is an empirical question, not something to be established by a priori reasoning or assertion. The evidence does not suggest that V is constant in the UK. Sir Geoffrey apparently tried to argue to the Treasury and Civil Service Committee of the House of Commons that what looks like slack control of the money stock might actually be consistent with a tight control of money *because* V had altered. While one might admire the attempt to have it both ways—the policy analysis rests on an assumption that V is stable and the policy application is defended on the grounds that V has changed—one must accept that there is little empirical support for the claim that V is stable.

Despite the obviously serious limitations on the usefulness of the apparent implications derived from a Quantity Theory approach, some version of the Quantity Theory persists in exercising a pervasive influence. It seems to offer a neat, simple, and understandable explanation of the cause of inflation and the central role played by changes in the money supply. This superficial attraction rests on two key propositions —first, that there is some direct and forecastable relationship between

32 The Quantity Theory, Wages, and Employment

changes in the money supply and the value of total output (PY) and, because physical output (Y) tends always to be at or around its full employment level, this relationship comes down to one between money supply and prices; second, that it is possible to define, measure and control the quantity of money. We have indicated that the first of these is unlikely to be valid and is certainly debatable. We shall discuss the second in Chapter 3.

Notes to Chapter 2

1. See Third Report from the Treasury and Civil Service Committee, *Monetary Policy*, II, HC (1981), 163-II, particularly Q. 288–97 and Annex 2.
2. Third Report from the Treasury and Civil Service Committee, *Monetary Policy*, III, HC 163-III, Appendix 4, 94.

CHAPTER THREE

Demand and Supply of Money

What is money?

IN an economy such as the UK there are a number of different types of money. Cash—coins and bank notes in circulation—is obviously money, but notes in the vaults of the Bank of England which are not yet in circulation are not. Bank deposits are generally equivalent to money in that cheques can be used to pay for transactions or settle debts. There are different sorts of bank deposits. Some are immediately available as they can be withdrawn on demand. These sight deposits, which might, or might not, have interest paid on them, are included in most definitions of money. There are also bank deposits which cannot be withdrawn immediately, and these time deposits are included in some definitions of money but not in others.

We have a narrow definition of money confined to notes and coins plus private sector sight deposits, and a broader definition which also includes bank time deposits in sterling of both the public and private sector. The inclusion of UK residents' deposits in currencies other than sterling is a variation of the broader definition. These are illustrated in Table 3.1, as M0, M1, M2, £M3, and M3.

There are other assets which can be converted into money, quickly and relatively cheaply without great risk of loss of value. For some purposes it may be preferable to have measurements of this even broader range of liquid assets. Table 3.1 also shows two definitions of 'broad' money, PSL_1 (Private Sector Liquidity) and PSL_2.

We cannot produce a single satisfactory definition and measurement of money because people and institutions do not have a constant view of what is acceptable as money. Financial institutions, companies, and individuals adapt their behaviour and modify their view of what is money or 'as good as money'. For example, it is much easier to have cheques accepted now than it was, say, thirty years ago, but, it might now be very difficult to have a cheque accepted without a banker's card.

People and institutions such as companies, trade unions, or a Parent–Teacher Association can choose to hold financial assets in different forms. They can switch from a non-interest current account to

Table 3.1. Relationships among the Monetary and Liquidity Aggregates and their Components

	Notes and coin in circulation with the public	
	plus	Banks' till money
	plus	Banks' operational balances with the Bank of England
	equals	Wide monetary base, M_0
plus	Private sector non-interest-bearing sterling sight bank deposits	
equals	Non-interest-bearing component of M1	
plus	Private sector interest-bearing sterling sight bank deposits	
equals	M1	
	plus	Private sector interest-bearing retail sterling bank deposits
	plus	Private sector holdings of retail building society deposits and national savings bank ordinary accounts
plus	Private sector sterling time bank deposits—original maturity of up to two years	

	Private sector holdings of sterling bank certificates of deposit	
plus		
	Private sector sterling time bank deposits—original maturity of over two years	plus — Private sector holdings of money-market instruments (bank bills, Treasury bills, local authority deposits) and certificates of tax deposit
equals	Sterling M3	equals PSL$_1$
plus	Private sector foreign currency bank deposits	plus — Private sector holdings of building society deposits (excluding term shares and SAYE) and national savings instruments (excluding certificates SAYE and other longer-term deposits)
equals	Total M3	less — Building society holdings of money-market instruments and bank deposits etc
		equals PSL$_2$

Source: Bank of England *Quarterly Bulletin*, December 1982.

an interest-paying deposit account with a bank or building society. This may cause some inconvenience but might be tolerated if interest rates are higher. As interest rates change, or as they are expected to change, there will be switches among the different definitions of money and liquidity. This means that if a government selects one particular definition of money as *the one* to be controlled it may find that this particular monetary indicator no longer measures changes in activity in the way it once did. If people are increasing their demand for money, i.e. their control over liquid resources, and one measure or definition of money is subject to control by the monetary authorities, we ought to expect that other monetary indicators will become of greater importance.

This is sometimes expressed as Goodhart's Law: 'Any observed statistical regularity will tend to collapse once pressure is placed on it for control purposes' (Johnson 1982, 4). This is a particular expression of a more general phenomenon. Whenever government tries to control economic activity and those subject to control do not wish to change their behaviour along the lines indicated by the controls we should expect them to find ways of avoiding, evading, and getting round what are perceived to be irksome restrictions which prevent economic agents from pursuing their own best interests as they see them. We find this with an incomes policy as well as with monetary controls.

It is the same as the penicillin–bacteria syndrome. A type of penicillin is produced to deal with a strain of bacteria. In time the bacteria, or some of them, learn to survive the effects of the penicillin. New types of penicillin are needed, and in time the bacteria will adapt yet again, and so the cycle goes on. When governments introduce policies to influence behaviour they should expect a response from those affected. It may not be possible fully to anticipate the response but the one thing that is certain is that people will not passively accept the constraints and adjust their behaviour to conform fully with the government's intentions.

The Demand for Money

Some version of the Quantity Theory of Money is essential to all forms of Monetarism and as Friedman says, 'The quantity theory is in the first instance a theory of the *demand* for money' (1956, 4). We do not intend to go into a detailed consideration of the demand for money, important though this is, as we are here interested in the labour market implications of Monetarism rather than in Monetarism as a general economic theory.[1] We will therefore do no more than refer briefly to some aspects of the explanations of the demand for money which seem relevant to labour market questions.

People hold money for two main purposes. They hold it for transaction purposes to buy goods and services. They also hold money for speculative purposes as one of the range of assets in which they can keep their wealth.

Money for Transactions Purposes

The demand for money for transactions purposes will be determined by the level of consumption which in turn can be seen as dependent on the level of income or wealth. Wealth may include human capital acquired through education or training and this can influence both current and expected future income. Again we shall discuss this in Chapter 4 but we should note here that human capital differs from some other forms of wealth in that its future realizable value may be very uncertain. It is easier to get a larger loan on the security of £50,000 of fixed interest bonds than it is on the possible insecurity of £50,000 of imputed human capital. As Friedman concludes, for any given total amount of wealth assets, the greater the proportion of total wealth that is in the form of human wealth, the greater the demand for money for the transaction and precautionary motives.

Thus the wealth element of the demand for money is influenced by the form in which wealth is held. But, of course, if the greater part of one's wealth is human wealth, i.e. the expected future flows of income from employment, we should expect a relatively high demand for money as we are saying that one has relatively few assets other than expected future wages and a large part of both current and future income flows will be used mainly to finance consumption expenditure. So in one sense Friedman sees the whole of the demand for money as being a function of the level of wealth, even the transactions or income-consumption demand for money. Moreover, this view is regarded by Friedman as desirable because it allows an important distinction to be made between irregular or unexpected short-term fluctuations in income and the more regular or foreseen and expected *permanent income* which is discussed in Chapter 4.

For many people human capital is their largest component of wealth assets. They are heavily dependent on future expected income from employment and their current income is heavily dependent on their current employment situation. The demand for money for transaction purposes therefore is very much influenced by what is happening in the labour market. Expectations about what might happen in the labour market might also exert considerable influence.

Money for Speculative Reasons

People can choose to hold their assets in cash, which earns no interest but is immediately available, or in other forms of assets, such as deposits in building societies or banks, short-term bills, stocks and shares, property, works of art, jewellery, and so on. Some of these earn interest and some do not. Some of them provide nominal value certainty in that the individual knows the nominal value of the cash amount he will receive when he liquidates the asset. Individuals and institutions such as companies, unions, pension funds, and the local dramatic society decide whether to hold their assets in cash or in some form which can earn a rate of interest but which might have nominal value uncertainty or not be obtainable for a specified period. They have to decide on the liquidity of assets, i.e. the ease and possible cost at which they can be turned into money. Everything with a value can be turned into money—that is what 'value' means in economics—but there may be considerable uncertainty as to how much money it will fetch. The more liquid an asset the greater the ease with which it can be turned into money or the lower the nominal uncertainty.

The speculative demand for money can be seen as a decision about the way in which one's wealth assets are distributed among different types of assets. It can therefore be seen as a choice between money and other items in one's investment portfolio. Keynes emphasized the relevance of financial assets in relation to money and therefore the rate of interest is important in determining the portfolio spread. Friedman believes that the closest substitutes for money are physical assets so the rate of interest is of less importance but asset prices are important.

It is of importance whether higher interest rates lead to a reduction in the demand for money for transactions purposes or for speculative purposes. If transactions are affected there will be less economic activity, lower output, and employment both currently, and as investment is affected, in the future. While there is disagreement about the exact impact of a change in the rate of interest there is much more agreement that interest rates can affect economic activity, and Keynesians would emphasize that the effect can be in real activity and not merely on nominal or monetary variables.

Supply of money

We have seen that money includes things other than cash. Banks and financial institutions can therefore create money as their debts are accepted as money. Banks are profit-making institutions and they make their profits out of lending other people's money or money they have created. Overdrafts are profitable to banks. When people are granted overdraft facilities this means that they can write cheques for more than they have in their bank accounts and the banks will honour the cheques. Recipients of the cheques will deposit them in their bank accounts and in turn write cheques to settle their debts. This explains the banks' tag that every advance creates a deposit. Relatively little of the extra money thus created will lead to a demand for more cash for very long.

The major constraint on the ability of a bank to continually increase the amount of money it creates is prudence; it must ensure that if people decide to convert their bank deposits into cash it has enough cash available to meet their demands. Inability to repay depositors will create a crisis of confidence and a run on the bank. There is therefore a conflict between profitability and prudence.

Banks reconcile these conflicting pressures by holding a variety of different assets of varying liquidity. In addition to cash in their tills and at the Bank of England they lend money to the money-market overnight, and hold bills which are due to mature in a short time. They also hold longer-dated bills and securities which are less liquid. These can always be converted into cash but at an uncertain price.

The monetary authorities are loath to run risks with banks' liquidity. The Bank of England had responsibility for the financial strength and viability of banks before it had responsibility for controlling the money supply and if the two responsibilities seem to conflict it will invariably opt for its earlier responsibility. This means that the Bank of England is disposed to exercise its influence on the supply of money through the demand for money via interest rates. With a Monetarist government such as the Thatcher Administration, this approach raises no conflicts with a government which might be inclined to try direct controls on bank lending.

The burden of controlling the supply of money is therefore passed to interest rates. In short, the supply of money will be whatever is required to meet its demand. If the demand for money rises banks will be free to extend credit to meet the extra demand, subject to the restriction of prudence. If this results in an undesirable increase in the money stock government will allow or encourage interest rates to rise. The higher rates of interest, it is assumed, or hoped, will lead to a reduction in the demand for money and so the undesired increase in the money stock will be avoided. This is a free-market or price-determined view of the determination of the money stock. It is whatever people want it to be, but by manipulating or influencing the price (rate of interest) the authorities hope to influence the demand.

40 Demand and Supply of Money

Given that banks are able to determine the money stock, i.e. it is demand-determined, it is obvious that the state of the labour market influences both the demand for credit and the banks' assessment of the creditworthiness of the applicant for an overdraft. The banks' views of creditworthiness is what turns a desire for an overdraft into effective demand. The more regular the applicant's income and the more secure his job prospects the more likely it is that overdraft facilities will be provided. Those with irregular, albeit large, income receipts, might fare less well, and the shocks or expectations which government policy transmits to the labour market will influence the effective demand for credit as banks assess their customers' future prospects. However, even those with stable jobs and expectations of steadily progressively higher incomes might not find access to credit all that easy. These are the institutional constraints limiting the conversion of human wealth into non-human assets referred to by Friedman and brought out in Chapter 4.

Reliance on interest rates to control the demand for, and so the supply of money, presents obvious problems. There needs to be a 'well-determined and relatively elastic' relationship between the rate of interest and the money variable (Laidler 1982, 188). But the short-run demand for money relationship is according to Laidler ill-understood. 'Because it is so ill-understood, such a relationship might prove less reliable in practice' than empirical tests carried out using data from different policy regimes might suggest. The use of interest rates to control money supply requires the authorities to select a particular monetary aggregate to control. A narrowly defined aggregate means the selection of one whose velocity 'varies relatively much with interest rates', and increases the probability that institutional change in the banking system will undermine the effects of the monetary policy. A disintermediation effect can therefore be expected so that the monetary aggregate being controlled is no longer as important as it was prior to the policy.

The short-run interest-elasticities of demand for money and credit are low. This means that interest rates may have to rise quite a lot before there is an appreciable effect on demand. Higher interest rates can lead to higher prices, thus aggravating inflation.

Politicians may be reluctant to tolerate the political consequences of higher interest rates. Higher mortgages may have significant effect on house purchasers, and the more that government encourages private house ownership the greater may be the potentially disenchanted electorate. If local authority housing costs increase, either through rents or rates, there will be increased expenditure by central government as it needs to finance larger amounts of welfare payments, e.g. the allowance for rents and rates given to those on Supplementary Benefit.

Also, higher interest rates mean a higher payment to service current government borrowing. This may lead to higher taxes, which may be politically unpopular, or to reductions in the level of services provided by government which may be widely or narrowly unpopular depending on the particular services which are cut. Once it is understood that interest rates are being driven up as a result of deliberate policy intervention by the authorities, rather than by the ill-understood but allegedly all-powerful invisible hands of market forces, it could be a reasonable response of the electorate to demand that government cease such intervention. When governments are seen to be able to control an important economic variable and, moreover, are doing so for their own policy ends, it is a relatively short time before public opinion begins to demand that the control be used for other purposes. As Laidler, a Monetarist, points out, 'Other Central Banks which have attempted to use interest control methods have shown themselves less willing, or, perhaps because of political pressures, less able to see those variables fluctuate enough to keep the money supply on track' (1982, 188-9). 'Other' in this context excludes Canada where the central bank kept its money supply growth on target, but this was a very narrow monetary aggregate which was not a very efficient control over inflation. Even so the central bank found itself under acute political pressure on interest rates and exchange rates developments.

The Treasury Triangle

It is argued that there is a three-cornered relationship between the money supply, the rate of interest, and the Public Sector Borrowing Requirement (PSBR). This may not be a completely precise stable relationship but holds in broadish terms so that, for example, with a given money supply, assuming we can define this satisfactorily, and we have seen how difficult that is, it will be necessary to raise the rate of interest if the government increases the PSBR. Similarly, if the government wishes to increase the PSBR but does not wish to have an increase in interest rates it will be necessary to increase the money supply sufficiently so that the increased government borrowing can take place without driving up interest rates. In short the argument holds that with a given money supply and given interest rates there is only a certain amount of new public debt issue that, given their portfolio preferences, the public wishes to hold. If the government seeks to issue a larger amount than this because of an increase in the PSBR it will have to increase the money supply or push up interest rates.

The effective methods of control over the stock of money in the absence of direct controls rely on influencing the demand for money.

This leads to emphasis of the role of interest rates and this is seen as being influenced by the PSBR. The need to issue more government securities requires the government to increase interest rates in order to persuade the market to change its portfolio preference and take up the new issues. The resulting change in asset distribution may lead to a further increase in demand for money. There emerges, in the Treasury view, which is itself a reflection of the government's Monetarist position, a triangular relationship between money supply, rates of interest, and the PSBR, a relationship which has become the 'Bermuda Triangle of economics'. The end-result of a complex and often confusing debate is that it is far from clear whether the government actually can control the quantity of money, assuming that it takes a measure such as £M3. If it seeks to do so there will be some tendencies for people to move into other forms of money. Even if it could control the money supply it might be only at the cost of ever-increasing rates of interest or of causing social, economic, and possibly political disaster by drastic reductions in the PSBR and thus the level of services provided by the government. This is an excessive price to pay for the pursuit of a theoretical position which is by no means established in fact. Control over the money supply may not be the corner-stone of economic policy as asserted by Monetarists. If it is there might still be room to conclude that the application of some forms of direct controls, even though they lead to forms of disintermediation, might well be a better price to pay than ever-rising interest rates or ever-decreasing public expenditure.

A necessary feature of a government policy to impose much tighter control over the money supply by use of interest rates and fiscal policy is an attack on government spending. It is no coincidence that governments pursuing strong Monetarist positions are also anti-government spending, and free market supporters of what is generally regarded as right-wing persuasions. This is for all intents and purposes a *de facto* necessary condition of the Monetarist package for controlling the money supply.

The control of the money supply is not some technical aspect of monetary policy best decided in the inner sanctums of bank parlours. It is inevitably and always a matter of immense political importance. Measures to limit the money supply necessarily require political choices affecting the level of government spending and the type or content of that spending.

It may be that there are, or will be, some effective political constraints, either in reality, or, what is the same thing, believed by politicians to exist, which prevent government introducing or maintaining the appropriate combination of measures necessary to exert enough influence over the demand for money as to lead to the desired reduction in the money supply. We do not know and it is not something capable of determination by Monetarist models. It is a political judgement and the academic areas which might make a contribution are political science, sociology, and industrial relations, and these are not those normally associated with, or regarded as part of a Monetarist's armoury, or even as relevant. What we can say is that while there might be some appropriate combination of fiscal policies and interest rates which would lead to the desired reduction in money supply it may not be possible to implement that combination.

Effective control of the money supply, *to the desired level*, may not therefore be possible.

If, for whatever reason, economic, institutional (disintermediation), or political, it turns out not to be possible to control the money supply, there is little left to Monetarism as a policy prescription.

Can the Money Supply be Controlled?

If direct controls are introduced it may be possible to control the rates of change of those variables or measures of money falling within the scope of the controls. However, as Nigel Lawson MP stated, Monetarism 'consists of two basic propositions' the second of which 'is that government is able to determine the quantity of money' (1980, 4). 'The distinctive feature of our medium-term strategy . . . is that it is confined to charting a course for those variables—notably the quantity of money—which are and must be within the power of government to control' (16). The next year, speaking to the more knowledgeable audience of the Zurich Society of Economists, he admitted that 'for a country as financially advanced as the UK, monetary control is a highly complex matter' (1981, 13). He went on to say that 'the crucial determinant of the Government's success in controlling the growth of broad money must clearly lie, first, in a better control of public sector borrowing . . . and, second, in a better ability to finance in a non-monetary way the public sector borrowing requirement that does emerge—in other words, improvements in funding techniques' (13). The two requirements for *better* control and ability must mean that the government does not yet have sufficient controls or techniques to apply satisfactory control over the money supply or those monetary aggregates which matter, or if they have, they are not prepared to use them. Thus, despite his earlier claim that the quantity of money is one of those variables which *are* within the power of government to control, experience and reality seem to lead to a different conclusion. Because money is an elusive and changing variable, new forms of money created by institutions falling outside the controls will almost certainly develop. Disintermediation resulting from the ingenuity of the banking system in its pursuit of profit can be expected to lead to a constantly changing effective supply of money outside the formal controls. It is the penicillin and bacteria effect. We should expect economic agents to seek ways to avoid, resist, bypass, and overcome those aspects of government control which are seen as irksome or not conducive to the attainment of the objectives of economic agents as they perceive them. At times the controls may be accepted but if the benefits to be obtained from circumventing them are considered sufficiently attractive, new ways of behaviour and carrying out economic activity will develop. This ought to surprise no one. Government should anticipate such responses and seek to prevent the undesirable consequences of their emerging.

The question regarding the use of direct controls over the banking system therefore comes down to whether the expected disintermediation, together with such effects as might result from the controls, are considered more or less harmful than the use of non-direct controls.

Part of the problem for the Thatcher Government is that it is also on the side of the bacteria; it does not wish to harm these important elements of the banking system, opposes putting controls on them, and realizes that trying to coach them into performing the right tricks will be futile as they pursue their own self-interests. Working in the Thatcher Monetarist laboratories is a thankless and hopeless assignment.

It is difficult, and perhaps impossible, to avoid the conclusion that no matter how heated, interesting, or esoteric the academic debates about the theoretical basis of Monetarism might be, for policy purposes Monetarism suffers from one lethal defect. It cannot deliver on one of its basic propositions. We have not yet found ways to exert control over the money supply.

Conclusions

An explanation of the demand for money lies at the heart of the Quantity Theory on which Monetarism is based. The ability to control the supply of money is an essential prerequisite for the successful application of economic policies based on Monetarism.

Money is demanded for transactions purposes, which is closely related to the level of consumption, and for speculative purposes which express preferences for holding wealth assets in different forms, of which money is the most liquid. The consumption decisions on which the transactions demand for money is based are generally believed to be a function of the level of income, but there is no general agreement on the measurement of income, particularly its time-dimension, which is the most appropriate.

Demand and Supply of Money 45

This leads to an emphasis of the desired spread of wealth assets or the portfolio approach. If the money stock is increased so that people are holding more cash assets than they desire they will run down their money balances by increasing their consumption and so aggregate demand. This, on a Quantity Theory view, will then lead to an increase in prices. Of course if the 'excess' money balances are run down by the purchase of other assets which do not lead to an increase in consumption demand, there may not be pressure on prices of consumer goods and therefore no repercussive inflationary pressures. The portfolio approach stresses the importance of the PSBR.

Controlling the supply of money faces the great problem of defining money. Because we change our view of what is money, and more importantly, because there are changes in the ways in which individual definitions of money reflect a stable relationship to economic pressure such as the level of demand, none of the various and increasing number of definitions and measurements of money provides a satisfactory base or measurement. If the key to controlling the money supply is the impact this will have on the aggregate level of nominal demand, we simply do not know what it is we should be controlling. If we find out and are successful in our attempts to control it, economic agents and the banking system in particular will have moved on to some other definition and measurement of money. The financial bacteria have been far more adaptable, ingenious, and successful than the medical ones.

The Thatcher Government has decided in effect to control the money supply through the demand for money. It has forsaken direct controls and the use of reserve asset ratios. It will not let the system have the amount of money it needs at the prevailing price. The rate of interest will therefore determine the supply of money by determining the demand for it. This will be supported by action to control the PSBR.

The Treasury Triangle explanation sees the connections among the money supply, rate of interest, and PSBR as imposing an obligation on government to control the money supply once they have decided the levels of PSBR and interest rates they wish to have. This also provides additional reasons for limiting the PSBR. However, it may mean that the rate of interest will rise to undesirable levels if the demand for money is not very interest-elastic.

Control of the PSBR becomes of vital concern to a government adopting this interpretation of economic relationships. It becomes necessary to control government expenditure in order to avoid having to borrow or raise taxes.

It is by no means clear that a government can control the money supply, assuming we can satisfactorily define and measure this, by ways which prove to be politically acceptable. The increase in interest rates which would accompany such measures would create increasing political rejection by a mortgaged electorate. When, as a result of its own policies, government has to accept an increase in interest rates, it will seek to lay the blame elsewhere. Foreign action will be the most likely candidate; they don't vote in British elections. A Monetarist government will seldom, if ever, have the honesty and courage to inform the electorate that the higher interest rates are the direct results of government's attempts to control the supply of money by influencing the demand for it through interest rates.

Note to Chapter 3

1. Fuller treatment of the Monetarist theory and the difference between the approaches of Monetarists and Keynesians and post-Keynesians can be found in Mayer 1978, Morgan 1978, and Gordon (ed.) 1970.

CHAPTER FOUR

Income and Wealth

WE have just seen that the level of income—in some accounts the level of wealth—is an important factor in determining the level of consumption and therefore the level of demand for goods and services. This will strongly influence the demand for labour and so the level of employment and/or wage levels. In considering the relationships between income and wealth, consumption, and the demand for money, we are getting more directly into labour market issues. The level of demand for goods and services influences the labour market and labour market considerations such as the level of income through wage levels, either current or expected future levels, influence the level of demand. Changes in the money stock may generate processes which lead to changes in demand.

While the connection between the level of income and the demand for goods and so the demand for labour might seem straightforward enough, it is not really quite that simple.

One important question glossed over is the time-scale of income, i.e. over what period does the relationship between income and consumption hold? We would not really expect this to be a simple one-period relationship. People's consumption in this country is not determined by their income on a daily basis. Nor does it seem to be on a single pay-period basis. People do not determine their consumption each week or month on the basis of the income received in the previous week or month, or on that expected in the next pay packet. For example consumption is usually higher at Christmas and holiday periods. Also, some workers have considerable fluctuations in their income from one pay period to another as a result of changes in overtime working, earnings from payment-by-results, or bonuses and commissions. We do not have very good evidence but it seems that their consumption does not vary in the same way. In order to establish some relationship between income, consumption, the demand for money, and employment it is necessary for us to take some view of the appropriate time-period in which income exerts its influence.

There is another reason for considering this issue. People may try to change their level of income. They can do this by changing jobs, working more hours, working harder if they are on payment by results, or by taking a second job. In the case of a household a second member can decide to take a job. But they can also try to increase their income by obtaining a higher rate of pay from their existing job. This might not be very easy for any one individual but may be much easier for a group of people organized in a trade union or professional association. The expected level of income and thus the current level of consumption, might be capable of change by actions of the future income recipients.

As we shall discuss if current consumption is influenced by the expected level of future income the present level of demand may be determined, in part at least, by expectations about future income and these in turn might be influenced by trade union activity. In this chapter therefore we shall try and link up the relationship between the demand for money as determined by transaction needs with a consideration of the determinants of the level of income as seen by individuals influenced perhaps by trade unions.

In theoretical analysis, if there is perfect knowledge of current and future incomes and price levels, and the rate of interest is known, an individual (or consumer unit) can decide to allocate current and future income between current and future expenditure according to personal tastes for immediate versus delayed, but higher, consumption levels (Friedman 1957). This is relatively simple theoretical reasoning because it assumes perfect knowledge of all the important variables, so that everything depends on the individual's preferences for current or future consumption. Friedman simplifies the analysis by pointing out that if we regard future income levels as the current wealth values we can express current consumption in terms of only two variables, the current value of wealth and the rate of interest. We merely discount future income flows by the rate of interest to obtain a current wealth equivalent of the future income flow. If

$$Z_1 = R_1 + \frac{R_2}{1+r} \ldots \frac{R_n}{1+r^{(n)}},$$

where Z_1 is the current value of wealth, R is the receipts or income in each period, and r is the rate of interest, then C_1, the level of consumption expenditure in period 1, can be expressed as

$$C_1 = f(Z_1, r).$$

The actual amount of income or receipts in period 1 is in itself of relatively little importance as it can be offset by changes in R_2 or any period to R_n, or by changes in the rate of interest r. Friedman says: 'This is clearly eminently sensible: if a consumer unit knows that its receipts in any one year are unusually high and if it expects lower receipts subsequently, it will surely tend to adjust its consumption to its "normal" receipts rather than to its current receipts' (1957, 10). Savings would, on this view, depend on current income in relation to the level of consumption based on 'normal' receipts, as they would be the residual between the level of consumption based on (Z_1, r) and R_1. Friedman goes on to say that on 'a theoretical level income is generally defined as the amount a consumer could consume (or believes that it could) while maintaining its wealth intact. On our analysis consumption is a function of income so defined' (10).

While it may be a clearly eminently sensible thing for a 'rational' consumer, seeking to maximize both current and future satisfaction with a given set of preferences, determined before the unexpected unusually high receipts were received, to behave as Friedman suggests, it is clearly not eminently sensible to believe or conclude that this is what all individuals do. Of course it depends on what is meant by 'tend to adjust its consumption to its normal rather than its current receipts', and how far one has to go in not spending all the unexpected or exceptional high receipts before one has stopped *tending* to behave in the way suggested. It certainly seems reasonable to believe, for example, that some individuals, receiving what are regarded as high receipts in one period, which are expected to be followed by lower than usual receipts in others, do not maintain their 'normal' consumption levels, even though they expect lower than usual receipts in the future. There are many stories of individuals receiving redundancy pay who spend a significant part of it on stocking up with consumer durables or on 'a good holiday'. There is enough impressionistic and hearsay evidence to allow us to conclude that there might well be considerable differences in the way individuals with the same sort of income level react to sizeable increases (or decreases) in current income, even when this is accompanied by reasonable expectations of changes in future income flows in the opposite direction. Consumer durables may be regarded as investments in wealth assets which provide a future flow of benefits equivalent to a rate of return. This, however, would require us to estimate that rate of return in the future and add it on to future income. This is clearly impracticable.

Individual behaviour may be influenced by the social security provisions. If certain benefits are unavailable to those with certain forms of wealth assets or savings above some specified amount, some people may decide to spend their additional receipts in the current period in order to qualify for benefits later. Others may not wish to apply for social security payments and so set aside their large current additional receipts to finance consumption in future periods. In other cases some redundancy payment may be in lieu of notice of termination of employment and be in effect a lump-sum payment of wages. In these cases there may be no entitlement to Unemployment Benefit.

Wealth

We have seen in Chapters 2 and 3 that the demand for money may be expressed as a function of the level of wealth rather than the level of income. These might be seen merely as alternative expressions of the same thing—wealth is seen as the discounted stream or flows of income. For most people the main source of wealth assets is their human capital which means that it is their *expected* future earnings from employment. This is a very special kind of wealth asset. Normally it cannot be converted into an immediately available lump sum, as can bonds, shares, property, or other forms of physical assets. We cannot 'sell' our future working capacity or human capital from now until retirement age to an employer for a lump sum as we can sell our house, shares, or antique furniture and paintings. Not only is there no market in which this trading can take place, but there may be laws against indentured labour and so on which prevent it. Non-human wealth assets have a lump-sum or capital value at all points in time which is the amount they can be sold for at that time. Human capital, the expected future income flows from employment, has no such lump-sum trade-in value. It is a notional figure based, not on what can be achieved today, but what the expected future sums, whatever they may be, are equivalent to today. The wealth assets of most people therefore—if we accept the Friedman approach—are notional expected, not actual, values.

As we have seen, because of imperfections in the capital market it is not easy to convert these present-value of expected future wealth assets into current income because banks are reluctant to lend against very many future years' expected income flows. They might grant some overdraft on the basis of a steady job with regular increments but they are unlikely to lend someone earning, say £10,000 a year now, who has expectations of earnings rising to, say £20,000 in ten years, which will be earned for a further thirty years, anything like the full discounted value of his future income expressed as current wealth.

It may be that for most people the next most important wealth asset is their home. This might, for many, be regarded as a fixed element in their portfolio in that they do not envisage switching between this form of asset and, say, government securities in response to interest rate changes or expected future rates of return on different types of securities.

However, the main point is that for most individuals human capital is the major wealth asset and there are two important features about human wealth assets. The current value of human wealth is notional in that it cannot actually be obtained today. It might, nevertheless, be relevant to consumption decisions if it is regarded as a flow of income in future years and not as a lump-sum wealth asset. Secondly, the future value of income flows from human wealth are uncertain. The flow of receipts from other wealth assets may also be uncertain but these can always be converted into some lump-sum cash amount. There may be uncertainty about the cash amount that will be received from their *future* sale, but there is certainty of the amount they can obtain each day. This is not so with human wealth assets. This is particularly important for the concept of human wealth as a component of total wealth if this is the main determinant of the level of current consumption. For it is not possible to form an estimate of the current value of one's human wealth without making some forecast of the probability of future employment and the levels of pay which will be received from that future employment. The levels of pay which might be forecast will depend not just upon whether one is employed, but in what occupation, with which employer, and on what conditions.

In addition to forecasting the probability of employment/unemployment it is also necessary to take account of the uncertainties regarding the level of money income receipts, or pay levels, that will be received. Professional economists do not have a very good record of forecasting future money wage levels in the UK over quite short periods. Few, if any, would hazard opinions about future wage incomes over the length of time necessary to amortize even the current stock of human capital. This would require forecasts of lifetime, or rest-of-lifetime earnings. It does not follow from this that individual employees have an equally bad, or worse, record; they could be better forecasters than the professionals, but it might be reasonable to recognize that there are a number of uncertainties surrounding the future income receipts from employment. Forecasting future income receipts in money terms is only part of the exercise. It is also necessary to forecast future prices, and the more that one follows the theoretical model of determining current and future consumption levels on the basis of the satisfaction to be obtained from future or deferred consumption, the more important are expectations of future price levels and future interest rates. The greater the emphasis placed upon *real* income and permanent *real* income, the greater the problems involved in the application of the concept. It is difficult enough for many people to form reasonably realistic estimates of their future money income, but it is much more difficult to form reasonable forecasts or estimates of future *real* incomes.

Permanent Income

Friedman's reference to the 'normal' income on which people or households base their consumption decisions is translated into the concept of 'permanent income'.

The magnitudes 'permanent incomes' and 'permanent consumption' cannot be observed directly for any individual consumer unit. The most we can do is to observe actual receipts and expenditure during some finite period supplemented by some verbal statements about expectations for the future. The theoretical constructs are *ex ante* or anticipated magnitudes while the empirical data are *ex post* or actual or realized magnitudes (1957, 20). It is not possible to measure permanent income directly in a satisfactory way. Instead, indirect estimates are made. Friedman established methods of doing this by assuming that income is composed of two elements, a permanent component (y_p) and a transitory component (y_t) so that

$$y = y_p + y_t.$$

The permanent component (y_p) should be interpreted as reflecting the effects of those factors which the unit regards as determining its capital value or wealth; it includes 'the non-human wealth it owns; the personal attributes of the earners in the unit, such as their training, ability, personality; the attributes of the economic activity of the earners, such as the occupation followed, the location of the economic activity, and so on. It is analogous to the "expected" value of a probability distribution' (Friedman 1957, 21). 'The transitory component is to be interpreted as reflecting all "other" factors that are likely to be treated by the unit affected as "accidental" or "chance" occurrences, though they may, from another point of view, be the predictable effect of specificable forces, for example cyclical fluctuations in economic activity' (21–2). A footnote to this statement says that the division is, of course, in part, arbitrary and just where to draw the line may well depend on the particular application. He concludes that the precise line to be drawn between the permanent and transitory components is best left to be determined by the data themselves, to be whatever seems to correspond to consumer behaviour.

The important point about the concept of permanent income is that it contains a necessary subjective element; it is, as Mayer puts it, a 'psychological' definition; permanent income is whatever the household thinks that it is (1972, 36). The individual consumer unit decides which part of its income is permanent and, as we have seen, this requires considerable forecasting. It also means that there can be constant readjustment of the element of permanent income. As expectations are not realized because income turns out to be either higher or lower than anticipated, some of the 'errors' in forecasting, which initially might have been seen as elements of transitory income, become absorbed into the revised assessments and forecasts of permanent income. We infer that this is what has taken place, following the Friedman view, by seeing what people do, and when working back to establish that their previous notions of permanent income must have changed, because they did not behave as we previously forecast they would. Because we cannot measure permanent income on the 'psychological' definition, it is usually measured by human plus non-human wealth times the discount rate, which we expressed earlier as $f(Z_1, r)$. There is another aspect of the subjective nature of the hypothesis of permanent income which is that the forecasting and interpretation of changes in what has actually happened can vary from individual to individual.

The sort of calculation necessary to form an assessment of one's permanent income can be expressed as:

$$y_p = [w_o^e(u_0) + w^e j_0(v_0) + w^e j_1(v_1) \ldots w^e j_n(v_n)] p^e,$$

where w_o^e is expected wage in the present job;

u_0 is the probability of becoming unemployed in the present job, either voluntarily by quitting the job, or involuntarily;

$w^e j_0$ is the expected wage in a different job with the present employer which will normally reflect one's estimate of the probability of promotion to a higher-paid job but could include downgrading in the event of reductions in staff;

v_0 is the probability of a vacancy occurring in a higher-graded job with one's present employer;

$w^e j_1$ is the expected wage in specified job with a different employer;

v_1 is the probability of obtaining that specified job;

p^e is the estimated rate of price changes in the future included so that the estimated money wage levels become real wage levels.

The larger the value of u_0 the more important are the estimates of $w^e j_1$ to $w^e j_n$ and v_1 to v_n. Unemployment with the present employer might be involuntary so that it becomes necessary for the individual to decide whether to seek employment with another employer and this will be influenced by the wage levels obtainable and the possibility of obtaining employment. It is possible, of course, for individuals to leave their present employment voluntarily either to obtain a job elsewhere or to stop working. Periods of unemployment, whether voluntary or involuntary can be fitted into the equation quite easily by regarding any unemployment benefit as a w^e with a corresponding value for u for the estimated length of the unemployment. In reality there is an extremely large number of w^e's and u's to be taken into account if we constantly seek to maximize permanent income. For many people, however, it may be sufficient to estimate the expected values of future real wages from the present job and possible promotions or upgradings with the present employer. It becomes in part a matter of individual preference and decision whether to spend time collecting information about wages and possible vacancies in many other jobs. However, if it seems that u_0 is going to increase through a larger probability of involuntary unemployment then it becomes more important to estimate expected wages and vacancy probabilities for a range of other jobs. If the general level of unemployment is rising the values of v_1 to v_n will probably be falling for most people. Thus it is the increase in u_0, the possibility of unemployment in one's present job, which may lead one to take more notice of the level of unemployment elsewhere because the general level of unemployment will have a greater effect on one's probabilities of finding other employment.

If we are considering a consumer unit which includes other members of the household then their individual permanent income calculations need to be aggregated. In this way unemployment elsewhere than the individual's place of work might become more relevant as it affects the consumer unit's permanent income. The value of the v's might be interrelated in that the probability of getting certain jobs may be influenced by the employment characteristics of other members of the consumer unit or household. For example it may not be possible for both members of a household to work on shifts if someone has to be at home to care for children, or geographical mobility may be reduced if both husband and wife wish to be employed.

The importance of the concept of permanent income, the 'normal' income referred to by Friedman, is that it focuses attention on the notion that people have expectations about their future level of income in both money and real terms. This is obviously necessary in order to forecast future income flows and thus produce a current value of wealth based on these discounted future receipts. However, this approach raises the question of estimating future income.

Future Income and Uncertainty

There is uncertainty about the level of money income from employment in future time-periods.[1] For most people there is some uncertainty as to whether they will be employed or not. It may be that at certain times many people do not believe they will lose their jobs; at other times many people may think there is a much greater risk. This will depend upon the perceptions of the general or macro-economic conditions and the more micro-conditions of the particular industry, firm, or occupation of the individual.

The key point can be put very simply. According to the Permanent Income Hypothesis, people's current consumption will be determined by what they believe their future long-term (permanent) level of income will be. This means that in order to decide how much to spend today they have to forecast their future income.

Forecasting future real income can be very difficult. There are four areas of uncertainty. First, there is the rate of change of money wages within the firm providing the employment. This will be influenced by collective bargaining as well as by economic factors affecting the industry and firm. The second is the future position of the individual within a given firm. An individual has to assess the probabilities of promotion or upgrading in his present firm and compare these with those in other firms which he might consider joining. Third, there is the development of the future rate of inflation. This will affect him no matter which firm or which job he takes and in that regard might be regarded as neutral in so far as the choice of a particular job is concerned, but if an individual wishes to have a certain standard of living in the future he might decide to seek a job in one firm rather than another, even though he dislikes the work more. If he expects his future money wages to rise faster in this firm thereby providing the desired future real wage he may change jobs. Fourth, the individual may lose his job.

Figure 4.1 plots the monthly real pay of the scale maxima for the Civil Service grades of Messenger and Principal from January 1971 to July 1984. These are simple pay rates as there are no complications from payment by results, and, because we are assuming that they represent the real pay of individuals who remained on the scale maxima over the period, there are no annual increments. It is very difficult to see how an individual could at any point in time have made good forecasts of his future real income. Additional complications which need to be added before the PIH can be applied by the two individuals assumed to be represented by these real pay movements include their assessment of the probabilities of promotion to higher-paid grades. This depends not only on the grade structure facing them, but also on the age of people in the higher grades, government measures to increase or reduce the size of the Civil Service, their individual assessment of their chances of promotion in competition with other candidates, and the future real pay levels of the grade to which they might be promoted.

It might appear reasonable, or even sensible, to postulate that current consumption is influenced if not determined by expectations about future real income but attempting to explain how people are able to implement such an approach on some sort of permanent income hypothesis is far from easy.

56 Income and Wealth

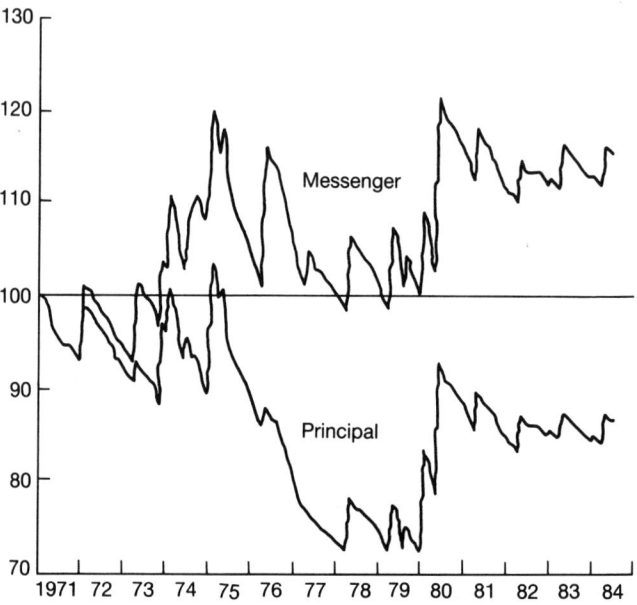

Fig. 4.1 Monthly Real Pay: Messenger and Principal Maxima

Changes in consumption will have labour market effects by influencing the level of demand for goods and services and thus employment. But if cuts in current money income are not perceived as reductions in permanent real income there will be no immediate effect on demand and so no reduction in employment or in the tightness of the labour market. Individual consumer units may interpret any reduction in real incomes resulting from a restrictionary demand-management policy as a transitory element which does not affect their assessment of their permanent income. Their level of consumption may be unaffected. The nature of the permanent income hypothesis, based on subjective interpretations and estimates of the future, means that we cannot forecast how individuals will themselves forecast their own future position and income flows in either money or real terms. We cannot therefore forecast how they will react to changes in nominal and real incomes, but at this stage it is useful to mention two important possible implications of the permanent income hypothesis.

The first has to do with labour supply. If individuals have formed views about the value of their human wealth, that is their permanent income from employment, in real terms, they may be unwilling to work at pay levels which are lower than their current views of their permanent income. The level of pay necessary to induce them to accept jobs may be much influenced by their view of their permanent income which was formed in different, in this case, for them, better economic circumstances. Of course in time they may revise their view of their permanent income downwards and accept a lower real wage, but this may take some considerable time.

The second is that they may form the view that their permanent income *should* increase through time. This view of what their permanent income is likely to be, i.e. the mean of the probabilities of future income levels, which is what Friedman refers to, may, in practice, change its nature. It may become the level of permanent income which people not only forecast but believe they are entitled to expect, and so become regarded as fair or reasonable for them to have. This is carrying the analysis or theoretical possibilities somewhat further than Friedman did, but it seems not unreasonable to suppose that individuals and trade unions may themselves translate 'anticipated permanent income' into something we may call 'entitled permanent income'. Just as the usual concept of permanent income is subject to revision and change by individuals in the light of experience and developments, so too can 'entitled' permanent income be subject to change.

Moreover, it might be useful to recognize that in the real world there can be two sets of factors leading to changes in 'entitled' permanent income. First, there are the changes in the perceptions, attitudes and expectations of individuals as a result of their experiences and perhaps changes in the pay levels of the occupation(s) in which they are engaged. These are all the things which Friedman puts forward as influencing permanent income. In addition there may be collective factors operating through, or determined by, trade unions. Trade unions can influence the rate of change of money wages and of real wages. Most Monetarists would accept this, adding that unions can do so only sometimes and at the cost of someone else's real wages or at the expense of employment.

As trade unions influence the views of their members there may be an additional element. Unions seek to increase the real income of their members. They have views about the 'proper' or fair relative wage level and they have aspirations of future wage levels. Aspirations can be seen as part of the pressures generating views about 'entitled' permanent income, or they can be regarded as additional factors. 'Entitled' permanent income can, on the latter view, be seen as the restoration of some previously experienced level, and aspirations can represent desired improvements. In a broad sense this corresponds to the distinction between defensive and offensive action by trade unions which is discussed in Chapter 9.

Assume that there is a view of a certain level of permanent real income held either by an individual or a group through a trade union. Short-term developments may lead to a reduction of current real income. Wage increases which are below both the recent rate of inflation *and* the expected rate of inflation may be accepted, albeit reluctantly. This could lead to two developments. There could be a reassessment of permanent income and an adjustment to a new lower level. Or there could be the maintenance of the same level of permanent income and the current reductions could be regarded as transitory, which might be why they were accepted. No adjustments might then be made to consumption expenditure and, perhaps more importantly for some purposes, the view could be retained that the level of permanent income, and that of 'entitled' permanent income, was the previous higher level. The individual or the trade union would then regard it as quite natural to expect to restore real wages to the level consistent with their view of permanent income, and thus would expect to receive some additional increase in the future to compensate for the temporary or transitory reduction they are currently suffering. If this is the case and if future conditions ease or the threat of unemployment is reduced or is viewed differently by the labour force or the trade union, it would be quite understandable for them to press for pay increases based on and derived from past views of permanent income or 'entitled' permanent income. This means that workers might take the view that the current wage level—in either money or real terms—is not the 'permanent income' wage level which they expect to receive for staying in a particular job. They are putting up with wages which they see as being below the fair, normal, or permanent income level, as an interim measure. On a longer-term view there will be some future roundabouts to compensate for the current swings. If they do this they may be willing to stay in the job at the lower-than-'entitled'-permanent-income wage level because they are taking a long-term view. If they believed wages would not be restored to the expected or entitled level they might leave the job. To the extent that this is so it means that the decision to stay on in a particular job is not based only on the present wage level—it is based on a longer term view. That view of expected or entitled permanent income might be mistaken in that money wages might not be increased later. But this mistake does not arise from mistaken views about the future rate of inflation; it arises from mistakes about the development of future money wages in relation to future inflation.

Expected or anticipated inflation is given a crucial role in Monetarist analysis and we are suggesting that even within the framework of analysis as developed by Friedman it is possible for pressures for pay increases to be based on other factors, although the pressures might be unsuccessful. In fact we are going somewhat further than this and suggesting that if the permanent income hypothesis is accepted it becomes centrally important to form a view as to how and when, in what circumstances, people's views of their permanent income will change, and this may be influenced by collective views and action through a trade union, and not only by the responses of the individual.

The same point can be made the other way round. If we can influence people's views about their level of permanent real income we will change not only their current consumption expenditure, but perhaps also their wage demands in both money and real terms. This is an area where politicians have had considerable trouble. They have sought to convince the electorate that their permanent real income would, on the whole, increase faster if one particular party were elected. As both main parties since the Second World War have been saying this, there has been a general expectation that we ought to be getting better off all the time. Comparisons with the performance of other countries has strengthened this view. However, when elected, political parties have found themselves faced with economic crises which have led them to seek to revise downwards people's expectations, at least in the short-run, so that the appropriate corrective action can be taken which will lead, according to the various statements of the government of the day, to better long-run performance and growth. There has thus been an attempt to reduce people's views of their permanent income and 'entitled' permanent income in the short run. The approach of the next election has tended to lead governments to emphasize the long-run growth of 'entitled' permanent income rather than the necessary short-run reductions. At the same time governments have not wanted people to behave as though they thought the reduction in real income was only transitory as this would lead them not to change their behaviour very much. They should act as though the reduction in real income was permanent by adjusting their views of permanent income and permanent consumption, even though government may be saying that in the long-run permanent income will be higher and not lower.

If people's assessment of their permanent income is not revised downwards when economic activity declines, whether the slow-down is caused by traditional demand-management policies or by a Monetarist approach of controlling the money stock, there need be no reduction in aggregate consumer demand and there may be little, if any, change in the demand for money for transactions purposes. The more uncertainty there is about future employment prospects and future real income the more uncertainty there is about what will happen to people's assessment of their permanent real income, and therefore the more uncertainty about their current consumption expenditure and their demand for money. This uncertainty might also affect their demand for money or near-money liquid assets for non-immediate consumption purposes. They may decide that it is preferable to reduce current consumption or to transfer their assets into more liquid forms, or they may decide to continue with their present level of consumption as they do not believe their permanent real income will be reduced. We simply cannot tell how they will react. Much may depend on the extent to which government is able to influence people's expectations, but governments do not operate in a vacuum. There will be other sources of influence, particularly trade unions, which might be sending out conflicting messages about future real income.

The 1979 Thatcher Government sought changes in perceptions of permanent real incomes as a result of higher unemployment which was an inevitable consequence of tighter control of the money supply. Higher unemployment can affect permanent income, i.e. people's expectations of their income in the future, in two main ways. Firstly, it can change their estimate of the real wage that is obtainable in their present employment. People may believe that they are faced with a choice between accepting a reduction in real wages and retaining their job, or maintaining, or even increasing, their real wage but increasing the probability of losing their job. They may then decide to accept a lower real wage, not as a temporary phenomenon to be made up to the present 'entitled' permanent income in the future, but as a long-term lower real wage, so that 'entitled' permanent income is reduced. If this occurs, then permanent real income is reduced as a result of decisions taken by the people concerned, either individually or collectively through trade unions. It is the fear of unemployment *affecting them* which leads to this revision rather than unemployment generally. The threat is to their own jobs, or in the case of a consumer unit, other members of the family, and not the general level of unemployment. The general level of unemployment might be indirectly considered in that it could be an indicator of the expected level of aggregate demand and so might affect the demand for the product of the individuals concerned in their present employment.

Expectations can therefore be revised, both in response to perceived changes in economic conditions and as a result of decisions taken by people, perhaps collectively through trade unions, about their own actions to influence future real wages. These expectations are not the same as expected rates of inflation which play an important part in some explanations of inflation and unemployment, but are expectations about the probabilities of obtaining future real income which are to some extent influenced by people's own actions and anticipated future actions. In particular, the higher possibility of unemployment, not in general, but affecting members of the consumer unit, may be expected to play an important role in influencing expectations of future real income. Secondly, anticipated general unemployment or unemployment elsewhere than one's current place of work may also influence expected future real income in that it can affect one's view of changing jobs to obtain higher real wages or reduce one's anticipated rate of increase of real wages from present employment.

If, therefore, people believe that their future permanent real income is lower as a result perhaps of an increase in the probability of losing their job we should expect them to cut back on current consumption. This may also lead them to accept a lower real wage in their present job. Similarly, even if current money or real income is reduced there may be little, if any, effect on current consumption expenditure if people believe this is only a temporary disturbance. Measures to reduce consumption by affecting income levels must therefore induce changes in expected real permanent income. We ought to expect, therefore, that governments trying to obtain such a change will use various opportunities to persuade people that their jobs are at risk if they do not accept some reduction in their real income and expected real income. It should be noted that according to the permanent income hypothesis it is not, strictly speaking, necessary actually to reduce current real income in order to reduce current real consumption; all that is necessary is to reduce *expected* real permanent income. In this case an important effect of rising unemployment might be not that it reduces current aggregate income of the unemployed and so leads to a lower level of current demand, but rather that it influences many other people who fear that they might become unemployed to reduce their own expectations about future real permanent income. Thus, in terms of what has become politically acceptable behaviour, governments should behave perversely. It has been widely believed that governments suffer politically as a result of rises in unemployment and they therefore take steps to prevent the figures from rising as much as they might otherwise do. Even the Thatcher Government which challenged this view by successfully fighting a general election with unemployment figures which were unprecedented in the post-war period still manipulated the figures downwards. Following a permanent income hypothesis, however, governments ought to be publicizing any increase in unemployment and even exaggerating the figures in order to induce downward revisions in people's real permanent income.

One other point about 'entitled' permanent income. A particular trade union may determine its view of the 'entitled' permanent income in the light of what happens to the income of other groups. There may be views about fair relativities or comparability which influence its wage behaviour. If this is so, then once again short-run deviations from the 'entitled' permanent income levels may be tolerated because they are seen as transitory, or it is hoped that they will be only transitory.

If the supply of money is controlled any excess demand for it can, in Monetarist approach, be brought into equilibrium only by changing permanent income. The demand for money is a function of wealth and for most people human capital is the most important wealth asset. The value of human wealth is the expected income flows from using that wealth, i.e. expected permanent income from employment. As Monetarists generally conclude that permanent income changes less quickly than current income, then in order to reduce permanent income it is necessary to do one of two things. Either the reduction in current income must be magnified so that current income is reduced by a greater amount than the desired reduction in permanent income, or some way must be found to change expectations and behaviour so that a reduction in permanent income is obtained more quickly than previously or from a lower reduction in current income than previously. If current income is a signal which takes a long time to get its message through then we can send louder signals in order to persuade people that permanent income is lower so that demand for and supply of money are brought into equilibrium as people realize that their permanent income is lower and so revise downwards their demand for money. Or, we can try to change the way in which people interpret the signals so that while previously they did not regard a given reduction in current income as heralding, or being in fact a reduction in permanent income, they now do so because of some other changes we introduce.

If governments maintain the goal of full employment, and this is understood by economic agents, it is possible that the expectation of full employment will prove to be a self-stabilizing element if incorporated into people's assessments of their permanent income. Consumption can be maintained because people do not face great uncertainties and do not revise downwards their permanent incomes. If, however, expectations of full employment are destroyed, as has happened under the Thatcher Government, there can be a destabilizing effect. People are uncertain about their future income and may alter their consumption in unpredictable ways.[2]

If people operate on some notion of permanent income and this is the main determinant of their current level of consumption it is much more difficult for government to influence consumption in the short run. It becomes necessary to introduce some sort of shock to induce people to revise downward their assessment of their permanent income, but it is unclear what sort of shock this should be or how the government should inject it. There are many things which can inject such shocks, for example a large rise in unemployment caused by increased foreign competition, but these may not be within the control of government. If this is so the economy may be much less stable than the government would like, or, perversely, could display greater stability than the government is seeking in that the level of consumption demand remains constant rather than fall in response to government's macro-economic policies. This problem becomes even more difficult if people behave according to the Rational Expectations Hypothesis discussed in Chapter 12.

Conclusions

It is because the concept of permanent income is essentially an *ex post* one depending on how people behave in the light of their expectations and subjective views and forecasts of their future income, that it does not provide a firm basis for the formulation of economic policy which requires an accurate forecast by the authorities of the demand for money. At the same time this subjective basis of the concept might provide opportunity for the government to exercise additional pressures on the demand for money if it can change people's view of their permanent income.

From the viewpoint of labour market behaviour the concept of permanent income, if we accept it as a useful device, might have three important implications:

1. If consumption is a function of permanent income, reductions in current income which are not interpreted by those affected as reductions in their permanent income will have no effect in reducing their level of consumption. The demand for goods and services, and therefore employment, will not be affected by what are regarded as 'transitory' reductions in income. It will be harder, therefore, to obtain a reduction in the level of demand in order to ease the pressures in both product and labour markets.

2. It might affect the individual's reservation wage, i.e. the wage at which he is willing to work, in that his view of his permanent income might lead him to withhold his services from the labour market until he finds a job which provides the expected income. This withdrawal from employment should not affect his level of consumption, and thus demand, if he has allowed for such a possibility of loss of income in his assessment of his long-term permanent income. On the other hand, if he has lost his job unexpectedly he might reduce his current consumption but still maintain his view of his permanent income, thereby keeping to his old reservation wage. In this case there could be some reduction in current consumption and easing in the pressure of demand in the product market. In the labour market there would be no easing of supply below the reservation wage based on the individual's view of his permanent income.

3. Trade unions and individuals may form views about their 'entitled' permanent income, which might not only be rigid or sticky downwards, but include longer-term improvements or be related to the income of other groups. This could lead to different reactions in the shorter and longer runs as unions might feel obliged to accept less than the 'entitled' permanent income for their members on a temporary basis, but seek to restore actual income to the 'entitled' level in the future.

These points emphasize the importance of attitudes about future income. Friedman, and Monetarists generally, concentrate on forecasts of probable future income flows; we are suggesting that attitudes and beliefs may influence actions to try to ensure that the original forecasts are actually realized.

Notes to Chapter 4

1. There may also be uncertainty about future income from other sources, i.e. non-employment income such as dividends or rents, but we are here concentrating on employment and employment incomes.
2. This point is discussed by Graham, in Morris (ed.) 1985.

CHAPTER FIVE

The Demand for Labour

EMPLOYERS demand labour not for its own sake but for the services it provides. Individual employers demand certain amounts of labour of *certain types*, able to provide the sort of services, or perform the tasks the employer wants performed. There is, therefore, no such thing as 'the demand for labour' in an aggregate sense of one demand curve representing the whole economy's demand for amounts of labour at different prices. Economic theory works on the view that an employer is assumed to be profit-maximizing (which includes taking cost-minimizing decisions). His decision whether or not to engage in production, and if so, the amount of different factors of production to employ, will be determined by the relative marginal productivity and cost of the factors. Each factor will be employed to the point where the value of its marginal product is equal to its marginal cost.

Marginal Analysis

The marginal cost of labour depends on a number of things. We will assume that the marginal unit of labour is an extra worker. There is firstly the wages to be paid to that worker. If the supply curve of that sort of labour (i.e. occupation) to the firm is horizontal the wage paid to the extra worker will be the same as the wage paid to the existing employees in that occupation. However, there may be other costs associated with taking on an extra employee, such as hiring and recruiting costs, screening or testing suitable applicants, and, in more complicated cases which we shall ignore for now, training costs. There may also be additional costs, such as employers' insurance and pension contributions on behalf of employees, or a payroll tax. If the supply curve of labour to the firm for this particular occupation is horizontal, i.e. if the supply of labour is perfectly elastic, if there are no hiring, screening and training costs, and if employer's insurance contributions etc. are proportional to the wage level, the marginal cost of hiring an extra worker will be the same as the marginal cost of the previous worker so the marginal cost curve to the employer will be horizontal. The marginal cost will however exceed the wage level by the amount of employer's insurance contributions, etc. We specify that in conditions of perfect competition an individual employer is faced with a horizontal supply curve of labour.

However, the supply of a particular sort of labour, or occupation, may not be perfectly elastic so that an employer cannot recruit additional workers at the prevailing wage rate. He may have to pay higher wages to recruit an additional worker. It is accepted in economic analysis that this means that the employer must also pay the higher wage to all existing employees in that occupation. This is an important assumption for it means that the marginal, or extra, wage costs to the employer of employing the extra worker is not only the higher wages that have to be paid to him, but also the higher wages that now have to be paid to all the other workers in that occupation. Individual workers do not therefore necessarily receive only the amount of wages necessary to induce them to accept employment in a particular job as a member of a specified occupation with a particular firm. They may receive higher wages if these are required to induce marginal workers to enter the firm's employ. If, therefore, a firm has to increase wages in order to recruit an additional or marginal worker, all the existing members of that occupation would receive the higher wages. This extra payment can be regarded as a quasi-rent.

The extra cost to the employer of hiring the marginal worker when faced with an upward-sloping supply curve for labour might be even greater than the extra worker's wages plus the quasi-rent payment made to other members of that occupation. It may be that the wages of other employees in different occupations in the firm have also to be increased. If trade unions, individual employees, or employers themselves have views about the 'proper' or fair relationships between the pay of different occupations the additional cost to the firm can be high.

Whether the marginal cost of employing an extra worker increases will therefore depend on the conditions existing in both the external and the internal labour market. The external market conditions will determine whether the employer faces a horizontal or upward-sloping labour supply curve. The internal labour market—the rules and procedures, customs, and practices governing behaviour and activity inside the firm—will decide whether and to what extent any increase in wages to members of one occupation are passed on to others. Of course, if it is possible for the employer to create some differentiating feature between the newly hired marginal worker and others so that the new recruit is not regarded as being in the same occupation as they are, it may be possible to avoid giving increases to the existing members of the occupation. The same simple concepts can be used to calculate the marginal cost of obtaining extra labour by working overtime rather than hiring extra workers.

The points to bear in mind at this stage are that his own wages may be only part of the additional costs of employing an extra worker. There may be other costs directly attributable to that employee. The total increase or the marginal costs of employing one extra worker include any wage increases which have to be paid to existing employees as a result of paying the new recruit higher wages than those received by existing employees. While simple economic analysis often assumes that the price of labour equals its wage which equals its marginal cost this is a very simplifying assumption which is useful only in very special and extreme circumstances.

The marginal productivity of labour in a very simple example is usually illustrated by the sort of curve as in Fig. 5.1. This shows that as additional units of labour are employed the marginal physical productivity, the addition to total output resulting from the employment of the last unit of labour, with a given amount of other factors of production, goes up, and, after a point, declines. If the marginal physical productivity curve is as shown by MPP and the marginal cost of labour measured in physical units of output produced is W_1, the number of workers employed will be L_1. For simplicity the figure assumes that the marginal cost of labour is constant and that the wage paid is the only cost of employing extra units of labour. In these special circumstances, therefore, the marginal cost of labour is constant and equal to its wage level, W_1. If an additional worker were employed so that employment rose to L_2 his marginal productivity would be less than the marginal

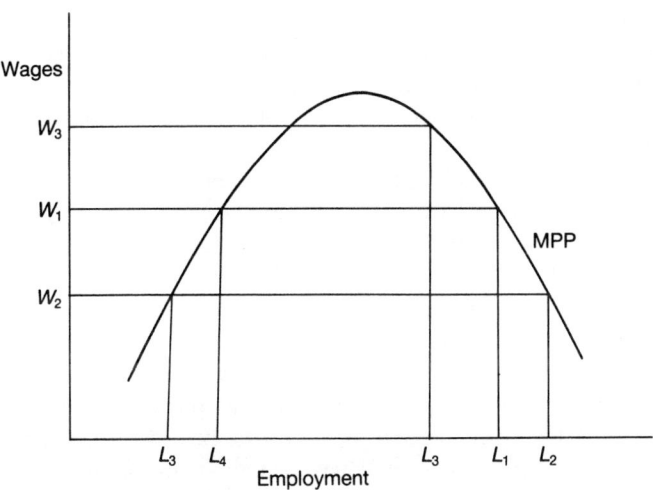

Fig. 5.1 Marginal Productivity, Wages, and Employment

costs, or wage W_1, and so it would not be profitable for the employer to hire him. We can change the units of measurement so that instead of measuring marginal *physical* productivity in terms of units produced, we multiply the units of output by the selling price of each unit, so obtaining the marginal revenue product (*MRP*). The wage level can then be shown in money wages rather than physical units produced. This is the more usual form of presentation. On very simple but rigid assumptions about the homogeneity of labour, that the amount of other factors of production—land and capital—is fixed, and that every worker employed receives the same rate of pay, we can see that for a profit-maximizing employer there is a fixed relationship between the level of wages and the number of workers he employs. If the level of wages were to rise to W_3 then only L_3 workers would be hired. For L_2 workers to be employed the wage level should be only W_2.

It should be noted that it is assumed that each worker is paid the same amount per unit of time worked and the prevailing wage level is equated to the marginal revenue product (or value of the marginal physical product) of the marginal worker. Each individual worker does not receive the value of his own marginal productivity. This simple approach assumes that each worker receives the same rate of pay because it assumes that there is only one kind of worker, that is that all units of labour are homogeneous. If there were two distinct types of labour we could draw separate figures for each of them showing the marginal productivity of each type of labour and their wages and employment levels. The two groups could receive different levels of pay according to their different marginal productivities but each worker within each group would receive the same as every other worker within that group. Alternatively, we could regard a unit of labour as composed of the appropriate amounts of each type of labour required, with the appropriate mix being determined by the technical requirements of the productive process.

The assumption that all units of homogeneous labour, for example all skilled or all unskilled workers, within the same plant are paid the same wage, and not the value of their individual marginal product, is both general in that it is almost always made in respect of employees paid by time, and important. It may not be an applicable assumption to piece-workers as those paid by some form of payment by result may receive the value of their own marginal physical productivity. This may be on an individual or group basis and the piece-work components may represent all, or only a part, of their total pay. At this stage there is no need to pursue the piece-work aspect as it is not usually part of the basic economic theory of marginal productivity employment-wage level analysis. We are left with an interesting question of why we should assume that all time-workers in a homogeneous category of labour employed in the same plant should receive the same rate of pay, rather than the value of their own individual contribution or marginal productivity.

The reason is one of fairness. It is generally accepted as fair that people doing the same work in the same place in the same conditions should receive the same rate of pay. It is an accident which worker is regarded as the first, the second, and so on, and so 'entitled' to which of the varying values of marginal productivity. With time-based payment systems it seems to be widely accepted that people should be paid for what they do or, in some cases, for what they are capable of doing. It is the 'effort-input' which determines the rate of pay, where 'effort-input' is interpreted in the widest sense of all the requirements of the job including responsibility, judgement, skill level, qualifications, and so on, as well as physical effort.

Because employers hire labour for the services it can provide or to fulfil certain tasks, different methods of payment have been designed. In some cases labour is paid on the basis of tasks completed. There is a vast variety of payment by results or bonus schemes which seek in some way or other to pay labour on the basis of its output.[1] Many other workers are paid on a time basis of so much an hour, week, or month. While the employer is hiring time-paid labour in order to obtain the output which that labour can produce, the basis of payment is the assumed or required effort-input. Each worker is employed on the basis that he can and will undertake certain tasks. We can regard these as the Job Requirements as long as we bear in mind that the job requirements may include things other than the ability to perform a certain set of current tasks satisfactorily. They may include the potential to perform different tasks in the future. In certain circumstances the job requirements may actually include features quite distinct from the ability to perform the production tasks required by the employer. If there is legislation or administrative provisions requiring that a firm employs a certain number of women or racial minorities, the job requirements for vacant jobs may include membership of the appropriate demographic group as well as the ability to perform the tasks. This additional job requirement may not apply to existing employees of the firm is required only to correct its 'imbalances' through its recruiting actions.

In many cases the Job Requirement is but vaguely expressed in the employment contract. The employer may have a fairly clear view of what he expects the worker to do in return for his pay, but this is seldom spelled out in detail with an explicit statement of exactly how much of what sort of work expressed in terms of specific tasks, the worker is required to perform. The amount and type of effort-input is often implicitly understood rather than explicitly specified and agreed.

This vagueness can have a number of implications for economic theory and analysis. There may be changes in the effort-input required by employers, or that provided by workers, which have the effect of changing the physical marginal productivity of that labour. In conceptual terms this is the same as if we introduced a different occupation to the one shown in Fig. 3.1. If the effort-input increases marginal physical productivity the MPP curve will shift upwards—and conversely if effort-input decreases. When we calculate the marginal physical productivity of any occupation and draw an MPP curve we must make some assumption about the effort-input forthcoming from the members of that occupation. If that effort-input changes for any reason we need to revise our MPP calculations.

This is well understood in real life. Employers know that output and efficiency—which we can here regard as synonymous with marginal physical productivity—can be affected in various ways and by various factors. If we change the amount or type of capital equipment we would expect physical output per man to be affected. If we use different types of labour we might expect productivity to change even though we still used the same occupational name to refer to the different sort of labour. Thus, for example, if we replace one group of fitters with another group of fitters where the second group has greater skill, or different skills and specialisms within the broad category of 'fitters', and these different skills are appropriate to the production needs or job requirements given the type of capital equipment they are to use and the sort of work to be performed, productivity might change. Of course in a strict sense we should say that we have changed the occupational requirements, perhaps from fitter type-1 to fitter type-2, but in practice we tend to blur over this. In assembly-line work effort-input might change as a result of employing younger workers. They might possess identical skills as older workers in that they are all equally capable of performing the required tasks, but one group might work faster or harder than the other, or make fewer or more mistakes.

It is also recognized in the real world that workers' attitudes and morale can affect output and marginal physical productivity. This might be the result of a decrease in the amount of physical effort given by workers or may be the result of a set of attitudes which affect the way workers respond to the work requirements and situations. For example workers may see that something is going wrong with the machine or a typist may recognize that the draft being typed contains errors. Workers may respond differently. Some, at some times, may try and put things right or inform a supervisor that a breakdown is imminent, or that there seems to be a mistake in the draft. At other time, or perhaps with some workers all the time, no corrective action may be taken or alarm sounded, with the result that marginal productivity is lower because the machine breaks down or the number of usable or correct documents typed is less. If the mistakes or breakdowns result in fewer units of output then, assuming that the price at which each unit of output can be sold remains the same, marginal revenue product will be lower. Sometimes the quality of the units produced may fall so that a lower price is obtained for each of them. In this case we might say that there is a constant, or lower, number of units a *different* physical product, but that the marginal revenue product falls because that quality of product unit has a lower selling price. What we have done in analytical terms is assume that the firm produced a different physical product with a different selling price, as happens when a pottery firm sells 'seconds' at a lower price than standard products.

The first crucial point running through this simple analysis so far is that every attempt to assess the future marginal physical product of labour, and so the marginal revenue product of labour, must necessarily include some assumption about the effort-input forthcoming from each unit of labour. In practice it is rare that the full specifications of the required effort-input are made clear when labour is hired. Moreover, the worker and the employer may have different views about the amount and nature of the effort-input to be provided in return for the specified wage. Even if they agree at the time of hiring one or both may change their views later. The effort-input sought by the employer from the worker forms part of the employer's Job Requirements when recruiting labour and influence both *MPP* and *MRP* and thus the demand for labour. It is important to recognize that effort-input is a multi-dimensional concept; it does not only mean the amount of physical effort or sweat expended by the worker.

Economic analysis often gets round the difficulties arising from the vagueness and inconstancy of effort-input in the real world by making the assumption that all labour in a specified occupation is homogeneous. Some economic models actually assume that *all* labour is homogeneous so that there is only one single occupation and every worker can do every job required by employers equally satisfactorily. This is so ludicrously unreal as not to warrant any serious attention at all. The assumption of labour homogeneity within an occupation means that the effort-input of each new recruit is exactly the same as the effort-input of each of the existing employees in that occupation. This gives us homogeneity across individual workers. It is often implicitly assumed that this effort-input remains constant so that we get a form of homogeneity through time as well. This avoids the need to keep recalculating MPP and redrawing the curve in Fig. 5.1. We shall discuss the importance of the assumption of homogeneity of labour and the complications that arise when this restrictive assumption is dropped in Chapter 6.

With payments-by-results pay systems it is output rather than effort-inputs which determine the level of pay, but the amount of bonus, or piece-work price per unit of output, is usually based on some estimate of the amount and type of effort required as an input to produce it. The distinction between effort-input and output is important in that workers may base their views, or part of their views, as to the fairness of a particular wage level by reference to the effort-input they are required to contribute. Employers may be more influenced by the output, and its value, resulting from the labour input.

There are situations where individuals employed in the same place performing the same tasks may be paid different amounts without generating unacceptable pressures of unfairness. This is usual in the case of incremental salary scales. It can be argued that those on the lower parts of the salary scale perform less work, or different quality work, as a result of their youth or inexperience. This is frequently an impossible argument to sustain, particularly in the public sector where such incremental salary scales are common yet the staffing levels are expressed in terms of absolute numbers in a particular grade, irrespective of the age or experience of the individuals employed in a particular office. There is thus no allowance made for a lower effort-input, or work output, from those in the lower parts of the salary scales when deciding how many people should be employed to perform a specified total task. It can be postulated that all workers on a given salary scale are paid the same amount over their working lives, the differences arising from age or experience merely reflecting temporary differences. If a different time scale of analysis were used—say a full working life—the differences would not appear. However, while this concept might be used for certain theoretical approaches, in practice there could well be situations where an employer regarded two individuals with the same abilities but with different ages as not being homogeneous and therefore had a distinct preference for one over the other. The employer might select the younger person because the salary cost would be lower for some significant time-period. If the employer were satisfied that the effort-input and output, or quantity and quality of labour services provided by the two applicants were the same, it would always be to his advantage to prefer the one who would be placed lower down the same incremental salary scale.

The concept of fairness with regard to pay levels is most frequently considered in relation to relative pay levels, i.e. those of different occupations, or employees in different plants. Here we are considering the special case of individuals employed on the same tasks in the same place who regard themselves, and are regarded by their employer, as homogeneous. Economic theory assumes they will be paid the same amount for the same amount of work, i.e. for working the same number of hours (ignoring any complications which might arise from the requirement to work on what is regarded as a holiday or at unsocial hours). Similarly, we would expect those who work different amounts of time to receive different amounts of pay. This concept of fairness can be seen in the parable of the labourers in the vineyard[2] where the discontent or grievance arose, not because the labourers were dissatisfied with their own rate of pay—but because someone else was paid the same as them for doing less work.

In later chapters we shall be returning to the subject of fairness and pay but at this stage it is worth emphasizing the importance of the assumption that all individuals in the homogeneous labour group or occupation employed by the same employer will receive the same rate of pay per hour, incremental salary scales apart. We cannot say that this rate of pay will be determined by the value of the marginal productivity of that labour, as it is possible that the wage could increase and, if the price of the product and so the value of the marginal productivity of labour remained the same, the level of employment would fall. Similarly, if the price of the product rose, perhaps because of a change in the level of demand, it does not follow that wages would rise; instead there might be an increase in the level of employment at the same wage level, or some combination of the two. What marginal productivity analysis tells us is that given the amount and type of capital used by an employer, and the level and type of effort-input provided by members of a homogeneous occupation, we can determine the marginal physical productivity of labour. This can be converted into the marginal revenue product of labour. If the wage level is given we can then determine the amount of labour that will be demanded by a profit-maximizing employer. We do not, of course, at this stage know how the wage level is determined; it is assumed in marginal productivity analysis that it is determined externally to the firm, which is why we say the wage level is given. With the three variables, marginal revenue product, wage level, and employment, if we know the first then either the second or the third is determined for us once we know the other. As it is usually the wage level which is known or given, we generally say that the wage level and the marginal revenue product of labour determine the level of employment in the firm.

The assumption that units of labour are homogeneous means that the changes in marginal productivity are not the result of some workers being better or worse than others. Marginal productivity first rises as the given amount of land and capital is increasingly used to its optimum capacity and then falls as too much labour is used and over-manning exists. There are economies of scale which subsequently become diseconomies of scale. In addition, the division and specialization of labour can lead to considerable improvements in productivity or output per worker. 'The division of labour, however, so far as it can be introduced, occasions in every art a proportionable increase of the productive power of labour' (Adam Smith, 9). The extent of changes in marginal productivity resulting from each of these two sources is unknown precisely, and will be much influenced by the type of capital equipment used, the sort of product manufactured, the skills required by the production processes, the internal organization of the enterprise, and so on.

The classic example of benefits to be obtained from the specialization of labour is Adam Smith's pin factory. In his example, if each worker specializes in just one of the production processes rather than each man undertaking all the operations in making pins from start to finish, productivity will increase as more pins will be produced from a given amount of capital equipment and the same number of workers. This specialization of labour raises serious problems concerning the meaning of the assumption about labour homogeneity. Without specialization all workers are homogeneous in the sense that each one is as good as every other at making pins from start to finish. With specialization each one is as good as every other in the particular process in which he specializes, but each specialist is better than each generalist in his own specialization. The specialist is better than the generalist at his specialization just because he is a specialist. He has more experience of the particular process involved and has probably acquired more skill or dexterity in the narrower range of job requirements. The specialization of labour is in fact the origin of the concept of different types of labour, or occupations or sub-occupations.

The occupational specialization may result from on-the-job training or work experience, or from specialized training or education received prior to employment. Often there may be some mixture of the two.

When an employer seeks to determine his demand curve for a particular kind of labour, in the simple example by relating the value of the marginal product of labour to the wage level, he has in mind certain tasks which he wants performed by the labour and certain levels of skill and ability which are necessary to perform those tasks to his satisfaction.

If the next unit of labour to be employed cannot perform the required job tasks then the expected change in marginal productivity may not take place. The increase in marginal productivity in Fig. 5.1 obtained by increasing employment from L_3 to L_4 rests on the assumption that the labour ($L_4 - L_3$) is just as capable of performing the tasks as labour L_3. If it is not, then marginal productivity will be below the curve MPP in Fig. 5.1. Different types of labour services will be demanded and while we can, for ease of exposition, combine these into appropriate units of combinations of different sorts of labour, it is important to remember that the particular types of labour required, with given technology and production processes, may be fixed, or outside the control of the employer. In some cases there may be the opportunity to substitute one kind of labour for another, but this may be possible only in the long-run after new and different capital equipment has been introduced, which changes the composition of the relative amounts of the types of labour services required for the capital equipment to be operated at its efficient level. Thus, the important and relevant demands for labour by employers are for certain types of labour services, which we generally refer to as occupations.

Even if we assume that all workers are homogeneous in the sense that they all have the same level of skill or training and are all capable of supplying the same level and quality of effort-input if they so choose, or can be sufficiently motivated to do so, it does not follow that all of them will do so, or will do so consistently. Some employers may therefore choose to pay above the market level of wages for that occupation, not because they necessarily hope to attract better or different workers from among the occupational labour supply, but because they wish to motivate their work-force once they have been recruited. Creating and maintaining high morale can increase MPP and MRP by minimizing stoppages to production, by increasing the co-operation of the workforce, or by encouraging them to work closer to the maximum limits of their potential effort-input. This approach may sometimes be referred to as the use of 'efficiency-wages'.

Demand for Occupations

It is rare for an employer to demand only the services of one type of labour. Usually a number of different occupations or types of labour services are demanded. The particular skills, abilities, or "effort-inputs" required by the employer will depend upon his decisions regarding the type of products or services he is to provide, the type of capital equipment and productive processes to be used, and the relative prices and efficiencies or productivities of the various factors of production. By changing the capital equipment and the productive process the employer can alter both the *amount* of labour needed to produce specified quantities of output, and the *type* of labour services, or occupations, needed. Thus we are using the term 'occupation' to refer to some sort of differentiation in the type of labour services provided by particular groups of employees.

If there were a system in which there were neatly specified occupations, each with clearly defined boundaries with formal systems of training and procedures by which we could easily and universally recognize who had the appropriate skills and abilities to perform the tasks associated with each occupation, it would be relatively simple to construct a model of the demand for various occupations. It would be determined by the value of the services to the employer, that is his forecast of the value of the output of the labour services or MRP based on his estimate of the future demand and selling prices of the completed products. We could envisage the interplay of the demand and supply curves determining the wage of each occupation.

The problem is that for many occupations there are no such natural boundaries determined by training and qualifications. In some cases there are. Craftsmen who have completed a specified apprenticeship may be regarded as members of a certain occupation. However, there are almost always some, if only a few, other individuals employed in these occupations who have not completed the apprenticeship (Robinson 1970). Other cases of recognized qualifications determining some boundaries round the occupation are architects, solicitors, accountants, nurses, and bus- or coach-drivers who require a PSV driving licence. The easy cases turn out to be traditional craft-apprenticed skills, professions, and those requiring legally specified qualifications, such as special kinds of driving licences or deputies in coalmining.

There is another group of occupations which may not have the same clear boundaries based on recognized qualifications but which possess certain generally recognized broad skill components. We might all have similar views about the general specialized skills required of a telephonist or switchboard operator, hairdresser, or bookmaker's clerk.

If there is only one employer of the occupation—a monopsonist—the occupation is defined by his Job Requirements. In other instances there may be a number of employers with almost identical requirements, as with camera crews in BBC and ITV companies. This is most clearly seen in the public sector where there are a number of employing authorities but the Job Requirements are so similar that they become regarded as identical occupations. Thus we can regard police constables as a single occupation, even though the job content varies between the Metropolitan Police and a country area. Where there are common pay scales we usually take the pay grades as the basis of some occupational definitions.

There is a group of occupations which are either very broad, such as assembly-line worker or packer, or must become quite narrow and almost specific to an individual firm. Many semi-skilled and unskilled occupations are little more than broad indicators of skills. Terms such as 'clerk' really give no more than a general indication of the experience, skill, or aspirations of individuals or a general indication of the type of work to be performed. 'Shop assistant' can cover a wide range of more specialized skills and knowledge such as might be required in an electrical appliance shop, or a ladies' fashion boutique, or be the relatively less skilled assistant found in a supermarket. A more specialized occupation in the last case might be check-out cashier.

Where a broad occupation is employed by a number of different employers it is likely that they will each have some special requirements so that the full package of Job Requirements is specific to each employer. There may be considerable overlap in the central core of skills and ability required but each employer may have his own definition of the occupation defined in terms of his own Job Requirements. This is further discussed in Chapter 6.

It is probably best to regard an occupation as a set of skills and abilities possessed by an individual, so that it is a labour market supply-side term. The demand side is better seen as the employer's Job Requirements, although these are frequently expressed as occupations. This indicates to potential employees the sort of people the employer is looking for, but because individual employers' Job Requirements often vary from each employer to employer they are not actually looking for the identical occupation when they are recruiting workers. They may recruit from a common pool but they will also be looking for specific additional qualities, or they will provide additional training once they have employed workers in order to give them the extra skills needed to satisfy the employer's Job Requirements.

Thus, while employers may recruit members of specified occupations such as craftsmen or those with professional qualifications, they are not necessarily prepared to accept every applicant who has the appropriate paper qualification. In other cases the occupational definition is so broad that it does little more than indicate a general range of skills or experiences.

We are not at all clear as to what we mean by an occupation. Sometimes it refers to the skills and abilities of workers which tells us who is a member of which occupation. More strictly it tells us who are potential members of that occupation, for they might choose to work at something else. At other times occupation refers to the type of skills that are necessary to fill a job and in these cases membership of the occupation is the minimum condition for employment. Other features of the Job

Requirement may rule out some members with the occupational skills. We shall pursue this in the next chapter.

Where there is a clear and unambiguous definition of an occupation in the sense of a recognized set of skills and abilities which is employed by more than one employer it is almost invariably because there are some organizational or institutional constraints or restrictions on entry associated with the possession of certain training or qualifications. This does not fit easily into analysis or theories based on free market forces which sees such institutional intervention as 'distortions'. Paradoxically, however, these 'distortions' may be necessary conditions for a free-market analysis which does not rest on the silly assumption that there is only one sort of homogeneous labour. Once different occupations are recognized and introduced into the analysis it is necessary to specify what the occupations are, even if this is only at the level of stating the principles by which different groups of workers are distinguished. To do this without recognizing that the institutions which confer the recognized qualifications need to specify the occupation will also generally seek to restrict entry into the occupation or profession is to be blind to reality and human nature. In those instances, therefore, where we can best define occupations we should also expect to find some restrictions on entry and these are not merely time-lags during which people are acquiring the skills or training.

What we find, in developed economies particularly, is the existence of some occupations with clearly defined boundaries, and many more where the precise labour services required by the employer are not occupations in the sense of specified skills which are employed in a number of industries or firms, but combinations of some skills used elsewhere and some skills or effort-inputs which are specific to the particular employer.

Employers in the same industry do not necessarily have the same structure of occupations, with the same definition of occupation, as Adam Smith found in his examination of pin-making factories two hundred years ago.

Different employers determine their occupational demands on the basis of their capital equipment, work organization, the expected scale of output, and their views of how much specialization would provide the most efficient method of production. Also, in the real world, custom and practice, the dead hand of history, or the recent interfering fingers of management consultants, may account for the pattern of job contents and work organization.

The Job Requirements for each employer can differ from those of all the others in terms of occupational classifications and the skills and abilities needed to perform the particular tasks at a particular plant.

The Job Requirement may also differ in another regard. A small plant may require its workers to be able to switch to other parts of the productive process on occasions.

The demand for occupations can vary among plants in the same industry as a result of different systems of work organization which may arise because of differences in the type of capital equipment used by different firms, even when they are producing identical products. Moreover, the precise meaning given to a particular occupation may vary among plants, even when the different plants are part of the same firm or organization. They and we may use the same names or occupational classifications but these may have different meanings. There is some sense in which every plant has its own set of Job Requirements and thus occupational classification.

The internal structure and composition of job tasks thus determines the content of the occupational demand of an employer, i.e. which occupations he is seeking to employ. He can, of course, change the occupational composition of his demand as his technology changes or in response to perceived difficulties of recruiting, the cost of recruiting, or the wage levels of the specific occupations he is currently employing. For example a switch to mass production methods or assembly-line production might lead him to demand fewer skilled workers and larger numbers of semi-skilled workers. The combination of skills and abilities required by the skilled workers might well change as a result of the change in production methods and technology. The semi-skilled grades might require some basic level of skill which is applicable to a large number of employers in various industries plus some additional, although perhaps relatively small, skills or abilities to perform the specific tasks in this particular employer's plant.

In one sense the semi-skilled workers might be seen as comprising a very broad occupation with many members, or potential members—all those who possess the basic skills plus the ability to acquire those relatively few additional skills specific to each employer. In another sense each grade of semi-skilled workers in each place of employment can be regarded as a separate occupation, or sub-occupation, with movement between the different sub-occupations being relatively easy in terms of skill acquisition. The most appropriate way to look at this might depend upon the purpose for which we are seeking to produce definitions, and on the practices of the individual employer. It is because the employer first determines the type of labour services he wishes to hire, although this may be constrained by institutional arrangements outside his control, that the occupational demand for labour is best seen in terms of the Job Requirements. The possession of certain specified skills, including in some cases specified qualifications, may form part of

80 *The Demand for Labour*

the Job Requirements, and may be an irreducible minimum. There may be other features in addition to these which determine the demand for particular types of labour services and the individuals regarded as suitable for providing these services.

There may be special cases where this does not occur. Arrangements may exist whereby an employer in a particular industry has to recruit his workers through a union hiring hall and is obliged to accept any recruit sent him provided only the individual is capable of and willing to perform a specified amount of work, perhaps as set out in an employer–union agreement. In addition, the agreement, or the union unilaterally, may impose a maximum amount of work that each person will perform. For example all carpenters may have to be hired through the union and each one will fix x number of roof tiles in an eight-hour working day, or each bricklayer will lay y hundred bricks each normal working day. Given the conditions set out above, this means that the employer is getting a specified amount of work per day—no more and no less—from each member of the occupation. Such rigid predetermination of the effort-input and output will arise only in extreme cases where institutional arrangements impose homogeneity on the occupation. It is only in the extreme case of institutionally imposed homogeneity of labour which deprives the employer of any opportunity to select his own work-force, that the matching of individual applicants to the particular vacancies in a firm is of no importance. But in all other cases the employer may properly wish to select from those applying to fill vacancies in his plant. This is where the concept of Job Requirement becomes more helpful.

Job Requirement

The Job Requirement, as specified by the employer, includes the ability to perform certain tasks, which may, according to the practices currently followed, mean the possession by an individual of some specific qualification. In some cases it will also include the possession of certain personal attributes or characteristics by the individual. For example it may be a necessary condition that everyone in a certain occupation possesses a specific qualification in the form of educational attainment, professional qualification, trade certificate, membership of a certain trade union or professional association, and so on. However, because not all individuals with the necessary qualification are homogeneous, the employer may wish to impose additional qualities, such as punctuality, neat appearance, willingness to adapt working hours to meet uncertain demands by the employer, or willingness to spend time away from home, perhaps overseas. In some cases the physical job tasks may be the same, or very similar, between two employers, but one may require additional characteristics because of the way the job is carried out, or the place where it is carried out. For example electricians may be doing very similar tasks but in one firm they may be performing them in people's homes repairing or installing fixtures, while in the other they are carried out on a building-site. In the former case the employer may require that the workers conform to certain standards of appearance or behaviour which may be unnecessary where work is performed on the site.

One way of dealing with this is to say that there are two separate occupations or sub-occupations. The alternative way is to say that there are different Job Requirements which have a large element in common but some differences. The second approach begins to cross the border between specifying Job Requirements in terms of the job itself and specifying the qualities to be held by an individual considered suitable to fill a particular job. This blurring of the two aspects is in practice inevitable. Employers can rarely define their Job Requirements without reference to the personal characteristics of the people who are to fill them.

These personal characteristics may well change as the job content or the range of tasks to be performed changes. For example an employer may decide that the technical job tasks of a bus-driver can be satisfied by someone holding a PSV driving-licence. This could be supplemented by additional physical personal attributes, such as tests of hearing. The employer may also impose the requirement that the individual be able to write a simple statement of an event in English in case it becomes necessary to complete an accident report. If the employer changes to one-man buses the job content of the driver changes. He now has to collect fares and issue tickets. The Job Requirements will be altered to include the ability to carry out simple arithmetical calculations involving the selling of tickets and perhaps some additional mental abilities to remember the various fare stages. In addition, the employer may impose some extra personal attributes which he requires of the one-man bus-driver. He may say that the individual must not have been convicted of any offence involving dishonesty or stealing. This might not have been a total disqualification before when the driver was not required to handle cash but it might be regarded as a necessary condition now that he is. As the driver now has direct contact with members of the public the employer might also rule out anyone who has a conviction for violence. He might add the requirement that the driver be able to communicate easily and courteously with the travelling public. These abilities and 'clean' records now become part of the Job Requirement. The occupational definition may have changed from 'bus-driver' to 'one-man bus-driver', and not all employers of 'one-man bus-drivers' may impose all the additional features to their Job Requirements.

The particular combination of characteristics and skill and effort requirements will be much influenced by the employer's organization of his productive processes and the resulting occupational structure. It will also be influenced by his practices and attitude regarding internal mobility or promotion from one occupation to another. If there is only a number of clear-cut, well-defined occupations employed by various employers with no adjustments to meet the specific requirements of each individual employer, and if it is very difficult to cross occupational boundaries, we could build up a model or system where all recruitment to fill vacancies in the well-defined occupations took place by recruitment from the external labour market. If an employer wanted more workers in a specific occupation he would recruit them from the ranks of the unemployed, or attract them from other employers. However, such simple, clear-cut compartmentalized structures of occupational organization are very rare. Normally there is some element of internal mobility within an organization, and this is particularly so in the case of white-collar employees. In these cases recruitment to some occupations takes place from those who are already employed by the organization in another occupation. Similarly, if an individual employer has special specific skill requirements he may recruit members of a particular occupation from the external market and then provide additional training to equip them to meet his special Job Requirements.

We distinguish, therefore, between the external and the internal labour market, referring to those rules, practices, and procedures which result in those already employed by the organization receiving discriminatory treatment in hiring, promotion, or the filling of certain jobs, as the internal labour market. The internal labour market is government by administrative rules. These may be determined by the employer, trade unions, collective bargaining or, in some cases, by tradition or custom and practice, the origins of which may be unknown, uncertain, or unquestioned.[3] The external labour market is more subject to the direct influence of economic pressures of competitive market forces, such as they be, and according to the extent of any constraints which have been imposed on them.

The more that the Job Requirements lead to the creation of occupations which are specific to an individual organization, the more we should expect to see the development of a well-structured internal labour market, particularly if the employer has to bear part or all of the cost of the additional specific training necessary to adapt the occupations to his particular need. Also, if the Job Requirements include aspects which are not easily quantifiable and for which no satisfactory external measure or indicator exists, or is acceptable to an employer, we should expect to see stronger internal labour market developments. For example an important part of many white-collar jobs is the exercise of judgement and the acceptance of responsibility to further the tasks of the organization as seen by those in charge. It is difficult to assess which of the unknown applicants for jobs from outside the organization possess qualities such as these. Employers or their representatives, such as senior managers, should have had the opportunity to assess the potential of their existing work-force and so may be much happier in promoting from within. They may make mistakes, of course, but they may nevertheless believe that this approach is more efficient. In some cases they may recruit from outside, believing that sufficient evidence as to suitability is available. Much may depend upon the extent to which the employer believes that the job requirement must have some element of specific skills, abilities or knowledge and experience which can be obtained best, or only, as a result of previous employment in his organization. If he thinks that the skills might be specialized but not necessarily specific to him, he may seek to recruit from outside. Thus, an employer may believe that he can recruit satisfactory people for his Finance Department from outside as, say, qualified accountants who do not have experience of his industry or product might be suitable, but be less happy about recruiting senior production engineers externally. Firms may have established the practice of not recruiting each other's personnel, particularly in the higher grades.

Developments from a Simple Theoretical Competitive Labour Market Model

Analysis based on notions of perfect competition in which each employer is faced by a completely horizontal supply curve of homogeneous labour is so unrealistic as to be useless for the greater part of labour market purposes. A simple equating of wages and the marginal revenue product of labour is also unrealistic. Labour economics has developed these concepts into ones rather more in tune with the real world. The main feature is the recognition that employers frequently have additional costs in hiring labour and often have to provide some degree of training. Labour is not homogeneous either in terms of the abilities and skills possessed by job applicants or in terms of those currently employed and those not yet employed by the firm. Once this is accepted the whole notion of a perfectly elastic supply curve of labour facing an individual employer at the prevailing market wage disintegrates.

84   The Demand for Labour

If the wage rate is given to the firm, i.e. determined completely by forces external to the firm, the firm's demand for labour is indicated by the marginal product of labour curve. In conditions of perfect competition where the firm can sell additional units of output at the prevailing market prices the marginal revenue product of labour (MRP) is equal to the value of output produced which is the physical marginal product of labour (MP_L) times the price received for each unit of output (P). Thus:

$$MRP = MP_L \cdot P.$$

Profits are maximized for the firm at the point where MRP equals the money wage (W):

$$MP_L \cdot P = W.$$

This is equivalent to:

$$MP_L = \frac{W}{P}.$$

Labour will be hired until its marginal product is equal to its wage divided by the price of product, i.e. the wage is equal to the *product real wage*.

This is sometimes stated as the point where the marginal product of labour equals its real wage but this can be a confusing formulation. Usually we refer to 'real wages' as the purchasing power of money wages, the amount of goods and services that can be bought by a given money wage. To obtain this real wage we compare money wages, or changes in money wages, with the general price level, say the Retail Price Index, as this covers the total goods and services on which wage-earners will spend their money wages. The appropriate price measure is therefore *all* consumer prices. The appropriate price for determining the amount of labour employed by a firm is the price of the product produced by that labour, its marginal revenue product. The prices of all consumer goods are not relevant. The employer is concerned with what he pays labour and what he expects to get for selling its product. It is better therefore to use different terminology for this wage—price relationship as it is confined to the prices of the product of the labour hired by a particular employer. We shall distinguish the two concepts by referring to *product real wage* when comparing the expected price of the product of labour to its wage costs, and use real wages to refer only to the purchasing power of money wages in terms of all consumer goods and services.

In the long run, the firm may change all its factor inputs and substitute capital for labour, or labour for capital. If the cost of capital is B

and the marginal product of capital is MP_K, a profit-maximizing firm will be long-run equilibrium where

$$W/MP_L = B/MP_K$$

which is equivalent to

$$W/B = MP_L/MP_K.$$

If labour costs—wages—rise faster than capital costs we should expect to see a substitution of capital for labour which, with a given level of output, will lead to less employment in that firm although employment may have increased in the capital goods sector. However, if labour was not being paid the full value of its marginal product an increase in wages may not lead to a substitution of capital. It is only when the economy and each firm is assumed to be in perfect equilibrium, and generally in a total system of theoretical perfect competition, that these effects are necessarily experienced.

This model is often used to argue that an increase in wages in relation to the product selling price or in relation to the price of capital will lead to less employment. Thus, an increase in minimum wages which is not accompanied by an equivalent increase in the product price will lower employment as the product real wage rises. If it does lead to an increase in selling price so that the product real wage remains constant, there may still be decrease in employment if prices of other products have not risen similarly. Relative price elasticities of demand for products may lead to a reduction in demand for the higher price products. If all prices and wages rise by the same proportion there may be no reduction in employment as there will be no increase in the product real wage, but there will be no improvement in real wages as all prices will have risen equally. We shall consider the results of research on the effects of increases in minimum wages on employment later, but at this stage one important point should be made. The simple model outlined here leads to the conclusion that employment will fall in relation to what would have happened if wages and product real wages had not increased and everything else had remained the same. It is a *ceteris paribus* analysis.

In the real world *ceteris* is not *paribus*. If the economy is growing it is possible that an increase in minimum wages can be associated with an increase in employment. Of course the increase in employment may not be as great as it would have been if product real wages had not risen, but it may still rise. The increase in wages could generate an increase in demand that leads to expansion in output and employment. Even within the strict formal confines of the standard neoclassical analysis therefore we cannot conclude that an increase in minimum wages or an increase in the product real wage will lead to less employment; we can only conclude that employment will not be as high as it might otherwise have been.

There are many situations when we may intervene in the workings of an economy to provide protection for workers or consumers which has the result of reducing the level of employment below that which it would have been without the intervention. Safety and health legislation which provides some minimum guarantees for workers and imposes costs on the employers may reduce output below the level it would have been in the unsafe or unhealthy conditions. Employment may be less than it would have been without the health and safety measures. Yet frequently a civilized society imposes such restrictions.

Environmental protection measures can have the same effects. As a society we may decide that while we are committed to full employment policies we do not wish to see full employment on any terms or at any cost whatsoever. We wish to see full employment with the maintenance of certain standards. We try to have minimum health and safety measures and turn to other action to create full employment. Minimum wage legislation can be seen as an *economic* health and safety measure. As a society we are saying that we are not prepared to see people work in conditions of economic risk. Provided that we can generate other economic activity to raise employment levels there is no inconsistency. The two key issues are whether or not we can generate economic activity to create and maintain full employment, and this is the essence of the Keynesian–Monetarist debate, and whether we hold a set of values which lead us to believe that intervention to provide certain minimum standards of health and safety, whether these be physical or economic, is a hallmark of a developed and civilized society.

Non-homogeneity of Labour

The simple models of the demand for labour considered above which compare the marginal revenue product of labour with its wage level is essentially static and the usual illustration of the marginal product of labour curve assumes that each unit of labour is homogeneous.

In the real world there is seldom homogeneity of labour, and certainly we should not expect to find it in a free-market situation. From the employer's viewpoint there may be homogeneity of labour-effort supplied to him in that each worker hired provides exactly the same amount of exactly equal work or effort-input, but if this occurs it will inevitably be the result of some institutional arrangement whereby the workers through their professional association or trade union, perhaps in agreement with reluctant employers, have imposed such conditions. The individual workers may be capable of supplying extra effort or different quality of effort, but they do not do so. Just as in the consumer goods market we expect to get and the producer only to supply the same amount of the same quality product for the same price as the person shopping next to us and buying the same products immediately before we do, so might workers conclude that as each of them is getting the same wage from the employer it is only right that they provide the same amount of effort-input.

Even then the employer may regard workers as not homogeneous. He may find some more pleasant to have around than others even though they only do the same amount of work.

There are two important aspects of the non-homogeneity. The first refers to differences in skills and abilities of the existing work-force. Some individuals will be better than others, more conscientious, more willing to do extra tasks, more careful, more reliable, and so on. The second distinguishes those who are already employed by the firm and potential new recruits. Frequently an employer is looking for people with certain skills or qualifications, but very often he also has to provide some additional skills or training to equip the individuals to perform the specific tasks in his factory or office. There will be some job requirements or skills and abilities that are *specific* to that particular employer. It is not to be expected that applicants for jobs will have all the specific skills required by particular employers. Employers know this and accept that in many cases they will have to provide a period of training in the specific skills they require. During this training period the marginal product of the new recruits will be less than that of those already trained and less than their own marginal product will be once they are trained. Thus, if MRP_{L1} is the value of the marginal product of a new recruit lacking the specific skills required for the efficient conduct of the employer's activities as his plant and production processes are currently organized, and MRP_{L2} is the value after training, so that $MRP_{L1} < MRP_{L2}$, then, if $MRP_{L1} = W$, so $MRP_{L2} > W$. But if $MRP_{L2} = W$ there would be an incentive for the employer to expand employment until $MRP_{L2} = W$. The workers, and their trade union, might object to receiving only wage W after they had been trained. They would recognize that they were contributing more output. It is possible to pay different wage levels to new recruits and those with the firm-specific training so that

$MRP_{L1} = W_1$ and $MRP_{L2} = W_2$ where $MRP_{L1} < MRP_{L2}$, and $W_1 < W_2$.

This often happens and is particularly the case in Britain for young people. It may not necessarily be the case that the value of marginal product of young people is less than that of older workers but the application of age-based pay scales may reflect a belief that this is so. The relationship between the age-based wage levels and the marginal productivity of young people may not be correctly reflected in the relative wage levels at different ages even when there is a general tendency for the value of marginal product to increase with age over the first few years of employment. For example the MRP of a sixteen-year-old may be only half of an adult and the pay level may be three-quarters of the adult rate. If this is so there will be a substitution of adult for young workers on the basis of the comparison of

$$W_a/MRP_a = W_j/MRP_j$$

where a refers to adult and j to juvenile or the assumed sixteen-year-old. This is the same principle as the substitution of capital for labour.

The need to provide specific training and the effect of this in raising the value of the marginal product of the worker to the firm which uses the specific training requires us to add a dynamic element to the analysis. As we have seen, one way of doing this is to provide for wage adjustments in each period in which the value of the worker's marginal product rises. However, the provision of the specific training will probably involve the employer in additional costs. Indeed, the very act of hiring an additional worker imposes some costs on an employer. He may have to advertise that he has a vacancy. This may involve considerable expense depending on the perceived catchment area for new recruits, and the ease with which they can be contracted. Except in very special circumstances (e.g. a union hiring-hall agreement) he will have costs of selection or screening the various applicants. He will have some additional overhead administrative costs in completing the hiring arrangements such as the office work in sorting out the national insurance and tax requirements. As we have seen, he may well have training costs as well. We can illustrate this by assuming that the different costs are incurred in different time periods.

If H = the hiring costs of advertising and the associated administrative work of actually putting someone on the pay-roll;

S = the screening or selection costs of sorting out the various applicants and deciding which are most suitable or meet the employer's acceptable hiring standard;

T = the cost of providing the specific training required to meet the employer's job requirements.

The cost of T may, of course, be influenced by the amount incurred for S. The more spent on screening or selection, assuming that more spent means better results, the less specific training might be necessary. If the subscripts $1 \ldots n$ refer to different time-periods we can allocate the various costs. Assuming that the new recruit commences work in period 1, the costs are[4]

$$H_1 + S_1 + T_1 + W_1.$$

The expected receipts in period 1 are MRP_1. The firm expects to obtain a higher marginal product from the trained workers so that $MRP_2 > MRP_1$. However, as this increase will not be received until the next period, its present value is $\frac{MRP_2}{1+r}$ where r is the rate of interest. The present value of the marginal product of the additional worker over the two periods, PVP, is $MP_1 + \frac{MP_2}{1+r} = PVP$. Similarly, the present value of the full marginal costs of the additional worker over the two periods, PVC, is

$$H_1 + S_1 + T_1 + W_1 + \frac{W_2}{1+r} = PVC.$$

This can be extended beyond a two-period relationship by adding

$$\frac{MP_3}{(1+r)^3} \ldots \frac{MP_n}{(1+r)^n} \text{ to } PVP \text{ and } \frac{W_3}{(1+r)^3} \ldots \frac{W_n}{(1+r)^n} \text{ to } PVC.$$

For whatever length of time one looks at the profit-maximizing employer's demand for labour will be given by $PVP = PVC$. In any situation in which $PVC_1 > PVP_1$ the firm has incurred a net cost of employment which it will seek to recoup in some subsequent period. In a two-period model, for simplicity, the surplus which the firm must recover in order that $PVC = PVP$ will be $\frac{MP_1 - W_1}{1+r}$. It is a necessary condition for the firm to be able to realize this that $W_2 < MP_2$.

Thus, in the simple example where the only labour costs incurred in employing additional labour were wages, it is possible to devise a payment system whereby wages varied precisely with the value of marginal revenue product in each period so that wages could rise as the worker became more efficient in the specific skills and tasks required by the employer. If, however, there are other costs of employment, such as hiring, screening, and training, and these, or some of these, are incurred by the employer, wages cannot equal the value of marginal revenue product in subsequent periods if the employer is to cover costs and maximize profits. An important consequence of this analysis is that wages in future periods will be less than the value of the marginal revenue products in those periods. Labour is not homogeneous through time therefore as it acquires more of the specific skills required by the current employer. The employer not only recognizes this non-homogeneity but has a vested interest in retaining the workers with specific skills in whom he has invested some hiring, screening, and training costs. These workers will be preferred to new recruits who do not possess the appropriate specific skills.

We can now see why employers may well view their existing work-force differently from the potential supply of new recruits. They may have an investment in their current work-force. If the potential recruits, or the labour which might become available to them in the future, differs from the existing work-force in that it does not possess the specific skills which the individual employer requires, the two groups of workers are not homogeneous to the employer. There are, in effect, two separate occupations. Those with the specific skills (which the employer may have paid for) and those without. The employer is therefore concerned to *retain* his current work-force until he has recouped the cost of training, etc. It is only when labour is homogeneous that the retention and recruitment of labour become merged into a single issue. When there are specific skills involved retention is important because there are no similar workers to recruit as replacements for those workers who quit the firm. There are, perhaps, potential recruits but these will incur hiring, screening, and training costs.

In some cases it is possible that the potential recruits are more attractive to the employer than his existing work-force. Improvements or changes in general education and/or training may mean that new recruits, especially perhaps if they are younger workers, may be better suited to meet the new and changed Job Requirements of the employer, than in his current work-force. It is conceivable that it is more efficient to recruit young people who are more familiar with computers, electronic calculators, and so on rather than try to retrain the existing older work-force to meet the changed job requirements following the introduction of new processes and equipment. Assembly-line production may benefit by the replacement of older workers by younger recruits who are physically more agile, strong, or capable of performing repetitive work which combines dexterity and strength.

New recruits may have attitudes and behaviour patterns which are either more, or less, attractive to the employer. They may be willing to accept monotonous work tasks, or may reject this form of work organization. They may be more or less willing to accept authoritarian systems of work management. They may expect or demand promotion opportunities in a situation where the employer does not want this. In brief, there may be occasions when the Job Requirements as currently perceived by the employer makes the retention of his existing work-force highly desirable, and so reinforce his desire to obtain a return on or recover his investment in their training, and there may be times when a replacement of the current work-force is preferred. Undue emphasis on the cost of investment in specific training ignores the advantages that may accrue from a replacement of current workers. The recouping of investment in training emphasizes the benefits to be obtained by allowing the young trees to mature into fully grown oaks. At times, however, employers prefer to get rid of dead wood.

Certainly in most cases employers are not indifferent whether their existing work-force stays or quits. They know that they are not faced by a horizontal supply curve of homogeneous labour. Put very simply, those who worked for the employer yesterday have precedence in obtaining employment with him today. Both sides of the labour market—employers and workers—see benefits in the continuity of the employment relationship. The retention of labour is therefore an important part of an employer's strategy when determining his demand for labour. He does not only want a certain number of workers; he wants particular individual workers.

Workers may realize that they are not receiving the full value of their marginal revenue product in subsequent periods but may still remain in employment with the firm. If the additional skills they have acquired is totally specific to their current employer it will add nothing to their marginal product with another employer. As long as they are receiving some premium over what they would be paid elsewhere they have an incentive to remain at this present firm. In this situation there is, strictly speaking, no reason why an employer needs to pay higher wages when the worker's MRP increases as a result of his specific training:

MRP_c is the value of his MRP when he has only general skills and is the same in firm c and all other firms.
MRP_{1d} is the value of his marginal revenue product at firm d before specific training;
MRP_{2d} is the value of his MRP to firm d after specific training,

then

$$MRP_{1c} = MRP_{1d} < MRP_{2d}.$$

The worker has no financial incentive to move provided that $W_{2d} \gtrless W_{2c}$ even though $W_{2d} < MRP_{2d}$. The worker is trapped. He has a higher MRP in firm d, but on a strict application of the theory as first presented by Oi (1962) he has no higher MRP anywhere else. Even if the employer in firm d does not pay the full increase in the worker's VMP the worker cannot obtain a higher wage elsewhere.

If the training provided and paid for by the firm is *general* so that it increases the marginal revenue productivity of the worker to all employers, then a worker who has been trained by one firm may be able to obtain higher wages by moving to another firm where his MRP_2 would be equally high, but because the second employer does not have to recoup the initial training costs, W_2 could be equal to MRP_2. There could be an incentive for some employers not to provide and pay for such general training but to recruit workers trained elsewhere. Employers who provide training always refer to this sort of recruitment as 'poaching'. If it were widespread we might expect to see a refusal of employers to provide general training, another example of a modified Gresham's Law whereby bad practices drive out good. It is also one reason why it might be undesirable to leave the provision of training to the decisions of profit-maximizing employers and was an important reason for the establishment of Industrial Training Boards. Economic theory concludes that general training will be paid for by the employees, either in the form of lower wages while employed during the training period, or by private payment for attendance at training or educational institutions. The main literature on this is American and it may describe American experience more accurately than British. Private payment for further education is much more widespread in the USA. Even so, the broad conclusions are probably still relevant. The cost of general training will tend to be passed on to the employee through lower wages while training, while the costs of specific training will tend to be carried by employers who will seek to recoup them in future employment periods.

In practice it is extremely difficult to separate training into these two categories. Almost all specific training has some value to some other employer. This may be much less than its value to the employer who provided it, but is still positive. Provided that the extra value to the employer paying for the training is sufficiently high to cover both the wage premium over what could be earned elsewhere and the recovery in future periods of the cost of training adjusted by the appropriate rate of interest, it is still in the interest of both worker and employer to participate in the type of wage–marginal revenue product relationship discussed above. Also, employers may pay for general skills which have wide applicability elsewhere.

Implicit contracts

Both workers and employers may have a shared interest in continuing the employment relationship. This can be strengthened by the employer's decisions not to adjust wages in response to short-term movements in the supply and demand for the occupations concerned. Standard economic theory following supply and demand analysis might suggest that if there are changes in either or both supply and demand, prices will respond. If wages behave like other prices this could lead to increases and decreases in money wages. Workers do not like such fluctuations in their money wage.

Reductions in money wages as a result of a lowering of the amount paid per hour or week, or with piece-work the price per unit of output, are strongly resisted. Workers do not see why they should be paid less when they are working just as hard as previously. Individual status may be seen to be associated with money wages so that a reduction in money wages even arising from a movement in the product supply and demand factors and thus in the value of the marginal product are not necessarily accepted by workers as sufficient justification to overcome their view that if they are working as hard as previously they should be paid as much. Moreover, despite what might be said about the importance of real wages rather than money wages, this conflict of fairness is seen in money wage terms. Workers might seem irrational to a theoretical economist to behave in this way if their lower money wages can purchase the same amount of lower-priced goods, but that does not alter the way in which workers and their trade unions see things and behave. Rather than have fluctuations in money wages most workers and their trade unions seem to prefer, most of the time, to have fluctuations in the level of employment. This does not mean that they are not committed to a policy of full employment but rather that at the level of the individual firm there is a preference for short-term or seasonal fluctuations in the demand for labour to be felt in variations in the level of employment rather than in the money wage level. Thus in Fig. 5.2 with the usual labour supply and demand curves S_1 and D_1, money

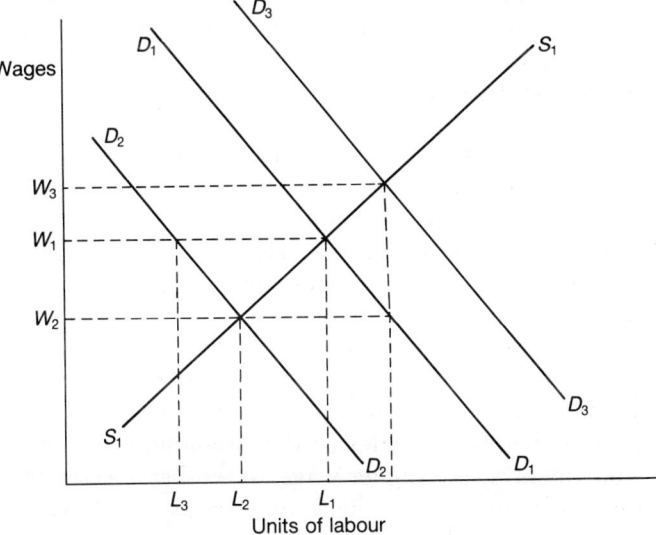

Fig. 5.2 Supply and Demand for Labour and Wages

wages would be W_1 and the level of employment L_1. The figure refers to a single occupation in one firm. There will be a series of other supply and demand curves for other occupations. If demand for this occupation falls to D_2 a purely market-based approach would suggest that money wages fall to W_2 and employment to L_2. However, if money wages are inflexible or ratchet at W_1, employment will fall to L_3. The employer will be paying higher wages than appears to be required on a market approach and less labour will be employed.

The explanation has become known as 'implicit contract' theory. There are actually two strands or explanations. The first is that workers prefer to have a regular flow of income through time rather than experience the ups and downs, rises and falls, in wages which might occur during the cycles of activity. As we can see from Fig. 5.2 if wages responded to the assumed market forces and supply remained constant, changes in demand would lead to movement of wages from W_1 to W_2 and back to W_1 or even higher to W_3 if demand improved to D_3, in the upturn of the cycle. In order to avoid such variations workers may be seen as paying an insurance premium. They may not get wages which are as high they could be at the top of the cycle when labour demand is at its peak, and in return they will not suffer reductions in money wages when demand is reduced.

The second explanation stems from the view that individual workers wish to maximize their income over some time period but are more risk averse than are employers. The income the worker seeks to maximize is his income from employment which is the product of the wage per hour or week and the probability of being employed, and the income from periods of unemployment.

This can be expressed as:

$$Y_{max} = (wh \cdot p) + (1 - p)UB$$

where w = the rate of pay per hour;
h = the number of hours worked;
p = the probability of being employed;
UB = the level of Unemployment Benefits.

If h is given—say the normal working week—the individual seeks to increase both w and p. He is unable to do this as there is some trade-off between w and p; the higher the level of wages the lower the demand for labour and therefore the lower the probability of being able to obtain employment at the higher wage. If workers decide to press for an increase in w by increasing wages, they are assumed to be accepting a reduction in p,—they have less probability of being in employment for a given h. They are in effect saying to the employer, or their trade union is on their behalf, give us the higher wages and we will accept the risk of being laid off or becoming unemployed.

American literature suggests this can be maximizing behaviour for both employers and workers. If the reduction in employment is regarded as temporary—in American terminology it is a lay-off rather than a complete termination of any employment relationship—the laid-off workers $(L_1 - L_3)$, know that they will be the first to be rehired when demand for labour recovers. The workers who are retained, L_3, know that wages could have fallen, but did not do so. They will therefore feel a greater sense of loyalty or attachment to this particular employer. The employer wishes to retain as many of his existing workers as he can, and to be able to rehire the laid-off workers when demand recovers, as he has invested in specific training for them. If the employment relationship was totally severed he might not be able to rehire the $(L_1 - L_3)$ workers and so would lose his past investment in them and have to incur additional screening and training costs in respect of any new workers hired. Moreover, the supply curve S_1 might in fact shift if the employer did reduce the money wages. Once workers have been hired and formed certain expectations about future employment, and invested part of their time and effort in receiving specific training, they may alter their supply function. They may remain with the firm only if the expectations they have built up of the way they will be treated are met. If these expectations include the maintenance of money wage levels, action by the employers to reduce these, or even inaction by them which allows labour market forces to be expressed in lower money wages, may be interpreted by the retained work-force as a breach of the understood conventions of behaviour. They may leave. As we have seen, the employer may not wish those workers in whom he has invested to leave.

We may therefore see the emergence of a pattern of behaviour, acceptable to or sought by both workers and employers, which negates the findings of standard economic theory. Money wages do not reflect all the fluctuations in demand for labour as implicit contracts develop between employers and workers.[5] There is a coincidence of interest which leads to fluctuations in the demand for labour being expressed in changes in the level of employment rather than in the level of money wages; quantities rather than prices bear the weight of the adjustment process.

Because money wages did not fall as demand for labour fell they may not rise when the labour is rehired. The labour supply curve facing the employer after the lay-off is horizontal over the length $(L_1 - L_3)$ at money wage W_1. Some of the laid-off workers may decide to accept employment elsewhere so the actual horizontal part of the labour supply curve may be somewhat less than ($L_1 - L_3$). If there is serious danger of this the firm will try to retain those in whom it has invested the greater amounts of specific training and lay off those who have received only general training.

It is possible to develop the implicit contract approach to refer to real rather than money wages. There will then be increases in money wages if prices generally are rising, even though the demand for the product of the individual firm is falling. This could lead to larger reductions in employment. It would also prevent Keynes's solution to the problem of demand-deficient unemployment from operating. This is discussed in Chapter 10. We do not have satisfactory data about movements in real wages at the level of occupations in individual firms during an economic downturn when the demand for labour is declining and so are unable to examine the extent to which real wages are rigid.

The second kind of explanation of the development of implicit contracts, that workers are more risk averse than employers and prefer to have lay-offs with rights of recall so that they are first in line for employment when demand picks up again, is much more applicable to the US than the UK. There has been very little development of lay-off and recall in Britain. If British employers wish to reduce the current work-force it is much more likely that they will declare some workers redundant, or offer voluntary redundancy terms. The legislative provisions of the Redundancy Payments Act encourages this. There are provisions whereby workers can be 'temporarily stopped'. This means that the employer has no work for them for a short period, usually up to twenty-eight days. The workers are able to claim Unemployment Benefit but are not included in the official unemployment statistics. It is understood by the employer, the workers, and the Unemployment Benefit Offices, that temporarily stopped workers will return to their employment in a short time. This is quite different from the position of laid-off workers in the US. Although they too may have expectations of recall, they are regarded as unemployed and there is less certainty that they will be recalled.

Implicit contracts can be seen, on this approach, as a form of insurance policy. Workers are not paid the full value of their marginal product in 'normal' times—the difference is their insurance premium—and in return are guaranteed protection against reductions in wages in the economic downswing. Some workers—those who run the greatest risk of being laid-off—pay the insurance premium but do not get the protection. They lose not just that part of their wages that would result from a reduction in money wages to bring the supply of labour into equilibrium with the lower demand for labour, but all their wages as they are laid off. However, because this explanation of implicit contracts is concerned with the expected swings of a business cycle so that the reduction in demand for labour is regarded as temporary and a return to the old level of demand is anticipated, the laid-off workers get a form of insurance cover by having priority in re-employment when the demand for labour picks up again. Because the reduction in demand for labour is expected to be temporary and because the lay-off procedures in the United States are based on seniority, the majority of the workers, and those who have been with the firm longest, are able to obtain considerable protection against the shortish-term fluctuations in labour demand. The newer recruits bear all the risk. This is not because they are not risk averse, or less risk averse than the more senior employees, but because they have little choice other than to accept the seniority principle if they wish to take employment with the firm. In time they will accumulate seniority and become protected against risks.

All versions of implicit contract theory recognize and seek to explain the fact that wages do not equal the value of the marginal product of labour at all times. There are occasions when workers might be paid more than their *VMP* as with the specific training type of explanation. There will then be occasions when wages are less than *VMP* as employers recover their investment in their work-force. In the risk-averse explanation workers accept less than their *VMP* most of the time in order to protect wages and jobs during temporary downturns. Employers may not seek to expand employment when wages are less than *VMP*, although basic theory might suggest that they should, because they regard the difference as insurance premia which may lead to future claims and therefore the excess of VMP over wages is not regarded as profits which can be increased by further expansion of employment. Indeed expansion of employment might increase the risk of having to pay out on the insurance policies as relatively small reductions in demand for their products could lead them to lay off some of the expanded work-force. Also, the organization of work and occupational mix required for production may be such that while there is an excess of *VMP* over wages with existing employment and production methods and levels, there would be losses if employment was increased. A chief accountant may be paid less than his *VMP* but employing a second might add very little to *VMP*. Production workers on an assembly line might be paid less than their VMP but to employ more of them might require a second production line and this might be uneconomic.

As we have seen from the discussion of specific training it might be necessary for the employer to pay workers their opportunity wage, i.e. the amount they could obtain elsewhere, but this does not mean that he must pay them their *VMP*. It is quite possible that their *VMP* is sufficiently high that the employer can pay them more than they can earn elsewhere and still make extra profit by retaining some of the difference between the opportunity wage and the *VMP* for himself. Further, a profit-maximizing employer in these circumstances may not seek to expand employment because the *VMP* from extra workers might be much less than present marginal *VMP* and less than present wages.

Some may regard these practices as distortions in a pure market system in that they prevent the economy developing in the way it would were it to behave only according to the assumptions of economic theory. However, if the distortions are widespread enough we should recognize the inappropriateness or irrelevance of economic theory which does not take them into account. Whenever the assumptions and conditions incorporated into economic theory conflict with the conditions and practices which actually exist in the real world, then if we wish to apply our analysis to actual problems and produce practical policies we should jettison the unreal theoretical assumptions.

It seems to be the case that since the Second World War downward labour market adjustments have taken place in quantities rather than prices. Employment, rather than money wages, bears the burden of bringing supply and reduced demand for labour into line. Until the current recession employers were worried that if they got rid of labour in a downturn of the economy they would be unable to get it back or recruit other workers, when the upswing came. By and large they preferred to hoard labour, particularly skilled labour during temporary recessions rather than risk a labour shortage in the near future. This can be easily fitted into the foregoing analysis if we assume that wages paid to hoarded labour are regarded as investment in the same way that training costs are, and that recruiting new labour in the future would involve not only screening and training costs but also require higher wage levels in order to compete for labour in a tightening labour market. The experience of high levels of employment, with governments of both parties committed to full employment policies, generated strong expectations that the downturns or recessions would be but short-lived. The self-interest of profit-maximizing employers operating in a context of expectations of sustained and generally high levels of demand can provide the same results as implicit contract theory in terms of the non-responsiveness of money wages downwards to perceived short-run fluctuations in the demand for labour. The difference is that quantities were adjusted rather less, particularly perhaps for skilled workers, and labour hoarding replaced lay-offs.

The main difference between the two approaches will occur when the reduction in demand for labour is perceived as long-term rather than a short-run dip which will later be corrected. American practice will be to have more lay-offs which do not result in recall. The employers may involve costs during the lay-off but these can be incorporated into the *PVC = VMP* calculations. British employers will stop hoarding labour and go for redundancies. These will result in costs of redundancy payments and a maximizing employer will compare these to the cost of hoarding labour weighted by the probability of requiring the hoarded labour in the future. If the expectations that the reduction in demand for labour is widespread and held by workers and unions as well as employers, the perceived lack of good faith in breaking the implicit contract by failing to meet the expectations of continuing employment, may not be felt. Workers may realize that the company is faced with a long-term worsening in its market position which compels it to reduce its work-force. This will be more widely felt the more that other employers are faced with similar difficulties and are taking similar action. This does not mean that workers will like what is happening, only that it may not have the deleterious effects on their attachment to the firm. Perceptions of the state of the labour market elsewhere will influence their view of the 'reasonableness' or 'acceptability' of the firm's actions in negating previously accepted norms of behaviour.

Thus, if there is general recognition that there is a fundamental change in economic circumstances and expectations of the future no longer reflect the view that full or high employment will be restored, both sides may change their behaviour. Money wages will still be very sticky but real wages may fall. There are examples of reductions in money wages in the USA in the 1980's but these are not very widespread, often relating to items of labour costs other than wages, such as fringe benefits, or referring to reductions or the scrapping of future increases which were built into a long-term contract. British experience suggests there have been very few reductions in money wages indeed, and as there is much less negotiation of fringe benefits the scope for reductions in labour costs other than money wages is accordingly limited.

Uncertainties

All economic activity takes place in conditions of uncertainty. In this context, uncertainty is a catch-all type of word; there are many dimensions to the word as there can be uncertainty about many things. It is useful for our purposes to distinguish the time-dimension. Some things are currently uncertain, and the future is always uncertain.

Economic theory seeks to limit current uncertainties by making certain assumptions. For example in conditions of perfect competition, employer's uncertainties about current labour supply and wage levels are removed by assuming that each of them faces an infinitely elastic supply of labour curve at a wage determined externally to each employer by market forces. The assumption that labour is homogeneous removes the uncertainty about the ability of new recruits to perform the job tasks. The *MPP* of existing and additional employees is therefore assumed to be known once the amount and type of capital stock is given. The employer is assumed to be faced by an infinitely elastic demand curve for his product at existing market prices. He therefore knows the *MRP* of each additional worker—it is his *MPP* multiplied by the product price. If we move to conditions of imperfect competition in the product market, the employer is still assumed to know the shape of the product demand facing him so he again knows the MRP of additional workers. In the real world of all these may be unknown.

However, even in these simplified theoretical models there is uncertainty about the future. Wages may change and the product price may alter. At any particular time the employer may know the current wage level and therefore may be able to calculate the cost of producing his output. Whether he can actually do this even in a theoretical model of perfect competition depends on the length of time it takes to produce a unit of output and the period for which it is assumed that wages are fixed as determined by market forces. If market forces determine wages each week and it takes four weeks to produce the product the employer does not know the ultimate production costs when he begins production of each unit. The period for which wages and other input costs are fixed, the time-scale of production and the volatility of product price and demand may mean that the ultimately realizable *VMP* differs from both current *VMP* and expected *VMP*.

The producer has to form some expectations, or make forecasts, about future prices in order to determine his current demand for labour. If he gets this wrong he will either make a loss, or he will make even higher profits than he anticipated but less than he might have done had he got it right.

He must also make forecasts of the future *MRP* of his work-force. Even if we assume the type and amount of capital equipment remains constant, marginal physical productivity of labour may change if workers' effort-inputs alter. This could occur if workers themselves change the effort-input as a result of change in their morale as a result of a negotiated change in the effort-bargain or as a result of the replacement of existing workers by new recruits who have different skills and abilities and lack the specific training required by the employer. An expansion of the work-force will almost always inject uncertainties into the assessment of future MRP as the extra workers will require some additional specific training and until they have been hired and some experience of their particular abilities obtained, it is unclear exactly how much training will be needed before they are able to provide a 'normal' day's input and output. The extent of the heterogeneity of new recruits in itself creates uncertainties about their future MRP and the cost of training these extra workers up to the required standards.

Even if it is possible to hire additional workers who do not require specific training there are uncertainties about future MRP. Indeed, even if the work-force remains constant so that the same people are employed over a time-period, and there is no alteration in the amount or type of capital equipment, *MRP* may change. While economic theory may assume that effort-input is constant so that workers—or more strictly their effort-input—is assumed homogeneous both among workers and through time, in the real world his assumption is unwarranted. There is considerable disagreement whether carrots, be they in the form of pay incentives, progressive or paternalistic personnel policies, pleasant working conditions, subsidized canteens used by management and manual workers alike, or generous fringe benefits, have a better effect than sticks, be they in the form of strict supervision, disciplinary procedures, downgrading, denial of promotion, or dismissal. There is much less disagreement that levels of effort-input and other aspects of worker behaviour, which affect the quality and quantity of output, can and do vary through time. The cost curves which form an important part of economic analysis do no more than show the unit costs of production *given* assumptions about the level and quality of labour inputs. The plant designer working with an accountant may be able to say that with a given amount of specified capital equipment the plant will have a certain set of cost curves so that it will produce given quantities at given costs. He can do this only by making some assumptions about the effort input of each unit of labour. What he produces are 'technically possible' cost curves. Whether these can actually be achieved depends on personnel and production management and the workers.

Thus a plant may be designed to operate at a level which achieves all the technically possible economies of scale. This may well require considerable specialization of labour and possibly assembly-line work organization. The cost curves which can be produced for this plant are those which would pertain if workers accepted the working conditions and methods, and provided the effort-inputs assumed. However, the workers may refuse to accept the working methods. They may react to the Job Requirements involving, say, a forty-five seconds' task-cycle by operating at a slower speed, by deliberately allowing faults to develop so that the assembly line comes to a halt, or by pressing through their trade union for a reduction in the speed of the line.

Workers' attitudes to the acceptance of certain job tasks may prevent the plant from achieving the efficiencies of production anticipated by the plant designer. In a number of countries there has been a rejection by workers of the enforced discipline of assembly-line production. Also there is a general tendency for industrial relations to be worse in larger plants, although it is unclear whether this is because of the size-effect, or because of the work organization and excessive specialization—which to many workers is sheer bloody boredom-effects. Technically possible economies of scale may be reduced or outweighed by social diseconomies of scale.

If there are changes in attitudes through time we should expect the *MPP* of workers to be altered. Employers, when seeking to forecast future production costs, are faced with uncertainties about the level of effort-input from existing as well as new employees.

Unless the wage level to be paid over the full length of the period covered by the employer's production plans are known there are also uncertainties about the cost of production. Thus, even if the *MPP* is known for some period ahead the cost of that production to the employer may be uncertain, and it is the cost of production in relation to the expected *VMP* which determines the employer's demand for labour.

All demand curves for labour, by a profit-maximizing employer, therefore require him to make forecasts of future demand and price of his products. How serious a problem this is depends upon the nature of the product and the probabilities that its price will fluctuate very much, and on the length of production time. If the product takes a short time to produce and is sold almost immediately as with, say, a small bakery, and if labour can be hired and fired quickly, there is relatively little risk of getting things too far wrong. If the product takes six or nine months to produce, say agricultural products or the manufacture of large complicated engineering products, he may have to stick to his production plans for some time. Even though he realizes that the price he originally forecast is not going to be obtained, he may still continue to produce in order to sell the completed product at a lower price, making a loss, as stopping production and writing off the partly made product could involve him in even greater loss. In these circumstances he would, knowingly, employ more labour than his *current* assessment of the marginal revenue product in relation to the wage level tells him. Once the production process is completed and he has sold the product to minimize his losses, he might then dismiss all his workers. Employers with costs plus pricing arrangements whereby the product purchaser agrees in advance to buy a given amount at a price to be determined by costs of production plus a profit mark-up are much less troubled by these uncertainties.

The simple model also assumes that the employer can obtain whatever amounts of homogeneous labour that he wishes at the prevailing externally determined wage level. Their effort-input will be constant. In practice neither of these assumptions may be true. If the employer cannot, or believes he will not be able to, re-recruit workers he currently lays off, he may decide to keep them on, paying them even though he does not want their current effort-input. Thus, if he expects demand for his product to increase in the future he may retain his current labour force, thereby accepting some temporary losses in order to maximize his profits in the longer run. The employer may lengthen the time-span in this way in order to keep his current employees, who are regarded by him as not homogeneous with other members of that occupation who are not currently employed by him. Or the type of work performed in his plant may be so specialized that there might be no other members of the specific occupations employed by him and if they leave his employment now they might move into other occupations with the result that he might not be able to get them back in the future, or only do so at a very high wage.

We can modify the simple analysis therefore to extend the time-scale over which the employer will seek to maximize his profits, and must recognize the element of expectations or forecasting which is inevitably involved in even this elementary approach.

The employer's demand for labour which was expressed as $PVC = PVP$ incorporates expectations about future cost levels, prices, and quantities demanded. This can be indicated by adding * to mean 'expected' or 'anticipated' so that $PVC^* = PVP^*$. Whenever PVP^* increases we should expect to see an employer to do one of two things. He can increase the price of his product, produce the same amount and take higher profits. Or he can expand production in order to take advantage of the improved expected market situation. If PVC^* has risen in line with PVP^* production plans should remain unaltered. If he is in the special case where the supply curve of labour facing him is horizontal and he has no recruiting, screening, and training costs, he will expand employment until the diminishing marginal productivity brings PVC^* into equality with PVP^*.

If the employer had been hoarding labour so that he already had spare capacity in both labour and capital equipment he would expand output first by utilizing his current work-force more fully. There could then be an expansion in output without any increase in employment. Similarly, if he can increase the effort-input per unit of time from his existing work-force, output may expand without there being any increase in employment. We can now see the importance of the assumption that all labour is fully utilized by employers so that an increase in output is regarded as equivalent to an increase in employment adjusted by any rise in productivity (output per worker).

Once we have introduced hiring, screening, and training costs whereby an employer may have made an investment in his current work-force, or people employed by him in the past, so that the labour hoarding may become good business sense and long-term profit-maximizing behaviour, we can no longer proceed from the assumption that the employer determines his demand for labour only in response to short-run considerations within an economic model based on the conditions of economic theory referred to as perfect competition. The desire to minimize PVC^* can lead the employer currently to demand labour for future or anticipated production.

The uncertainties surrounding PVP^* play an important role in the Monetarist scenario of inflation. The demand for individual products may be constantly changing. New products appear and competitors may be improving their productive processes and changing their prices. Consumer tastes are not fixed and may be altered by advertising and marketing campaigns. The economy is not in a steady state in either macro- or micro-terms. The aggregate level of demand in both money and real terms changes and so does the aggregate level of supply. International trade adds complications as both foreign demand and supply influence the expectations of the level of future demand for the output of many producers and affects the prices at which they believe they will be able to sell future output. The PVP^* for an individual producer is therefore the result of the interplay of a large number of factors.

Moreover, different individuals will respond to the amount of information generally available in different ways. Some may take a more optimistic position than others. Some may believe that even though the aggregate demand for all goods, and the demand for their class of products, is likely to fall, their own individual futures look less bleak. They may be counting on superior production or marketing skills, on the loyalty of their customers, or may just be optimistic by nature. Some may have more or less information than others, and all information about the future is uncertain. There is not the slightest reason to believe that in the real world a number of producers of similar products will take exactly the same view of the future demand and price levels for their individual products. Each individual's forecasts will be influenced by what he thinks other producers are going to do, and they in turn will be influenced by what they think he is going to do. Even if they pool their information there will be some factors outside their control or knowledge. New producers or new products may appear which affect the demand for their own output. The price of inputs such as wages, raw materials, transport, and capital equipment may change.

Government policies may affect both future demand and supply. No matter what view of the explanation of demand is adopted it must be recognized that government action is likely to have some effect on the demand for some products. If this does not occur as a result of changes in the macro-economic environment it could result from the actions of government as a purchaser of goods and services.

The demand for labour when reduced to its essentials therefore can be expressed as $PVC^* = PVP^*$ where both terms contain many unknowns and are surrounded by great uncertainties. When deciding whether to expand or curtail employment the individual producer will be attempting to forecast the future product real wage so that all items which affect the cost of labour, the physical productivity of labour, and the price and number of units of product which can be sold in the future will be relevant. Because the demand for labour means the demand for different types of labour or different occupations there are both greater uncertainties and greater room for manoeuvre. Occupational classifications are not rigid. Individuals can become members of different occupations as a result of training—on or off the job—or perhaps as a result of changes in attitudes or rules of behaviour which permit people who were not previously allowed to work in certain occupations, now to do so.

Employers can change their demand for specific occupations in response to changing production requirements and to perceived developments in the supply and demand for certain occupations. They can change the skills and abilities possessed by their work-force by spending money on training them. They have to recognize that labour is not homogeneous even with occupational classifications and devise strategies accordingly. For various reasons—their own investment in some members of their work-force, the law, trade union agreements, or the employer's perceptions of the views and attitudes of his employees and potential future employees—employers may take long-term views of their labour demand and modify their current actions. With all these qualifications, reservations, and uncertain social and institutional features of the labour market, we may nevertheless conclude that over some (unknown) time-period, which may be long and varying, employers in the private sector will tend to determine their current demand for labour on the basis of the expected real product wage of that labour so as to ensure that $PVC^* \leqslant PVP^*$. The public sector may have other criteria.

Overtime

Companies wishing to increase labour input have choices. They can recruit more labour. Whether they will choose to do so will depend on their perception of the LOS curve facing them and the relationship of this to their ALS with the costs of any adjustments such as hiring, screening, and training. They will then assess the effects of such measures on the wages of the existing workforce. (See chapter 6).

If they can alter the labour-effort input they can increase output as a result of higher productivity. This is equivalent to a shift to a different occupation, one which supplies more labour-effort per unit of time. This may increase wages. The employer has to assess the possibilities of obtaining such a change in labour effort input through some form of training, or by a productivity agreement, and the possible increase in costs.

They can use overtime. Like the second option this involves turning to the internal labour market as a source of additional labour supply, but rather than seeking to alter the type of labour supplied from the current work-force it increases the units of time of labour-effort input which the current work-force supplies. Use of either of the last two options avoids the need to have recourse to the external labour market and therefore avoids the possibility that higher wages will be imported into the firm as it moves up its ALS curve. Of course if the ALS curve is horizontal there is no such imported wage increases and the additional costs over and above the prevailing wage level are determined only by hiring, screening, and training.

Overtime increases the cost per unit of time worked to the employer as overtime premia are almost universal in the UK. Basic economic theory would hold that such premia were necessary to induce individuals to give up additional amounts of leisure. There is no substantial evidence that this is true. Overtime premia are paid because the law may require it, collective agreements require it, or both workers and employers have to come to accept it as reasonable and prevailing practice that it be paid. However, the additional cost to the employer may be less than the additional costs that would be incurred were he to hire additional units of labour from the external market. This will depend upon the shape of the supply curve facing him and the length of time for which he believes he will need the additional labour. The shorter this is and the higher the hiring, screening, and training costs of hiring new workers, the greater the possibility that overtime will be seen as a cheaper alternative. This will be the more so if new recruits are full-time employees as National Insurance contributions will be incurred by the employer for them which will be higher than any additional contributions he will be required to make as a result of overtime payments.

It may also be argued that employers will be reluctant to recruit additional workers the greater the legislative protection given to workers against dismissal or if there is a requirement to make redundancy payments. These may operate in a longer time-period assessment.

Even without these constraints, and there is not much hard evidence to support this sort of claim, employers may still be reluctant to recruit additional workers if they believe these may subsequently have to be dismissed. Employers do not like getting a reputation for dismissing workers. The need to dismiss imposes costs on employers, takes up their time, and is generally regarded as burdensome. There may, therefore, be considerable pressure within management to meet demands for additional output by introducing or expanding overtime working. This may also be attractive to the work-force.

According to the New Earnings Survey in April 1984 almost a third of all employees (30.2 per cent) received pay for working overtime and the average amount of overtime worked was 8.2 hours. More than a half of all manual males worked overtime (52.5 per cent), averaging 9.6 hours. The Department of Employment series of statistics in the *Gazette* for operatives in manufacturing industry are summarized in Table. 5.1.

Table 5.1 *Overtime Working by Operatives in Manufacturing*

	Percentage working overtime	Average hours worked by those working overtime
1970	34.2	8.7
1980	29.5	8.3
1981	26.6	8.2
1982	29.8	8.3
1983	31.5	8.5
1984	34.4	8.9

Source: *Employment Gazette*, 3 (2), Feb. 1985, Table 1.11.

It can be seen that while overtime working declined as the recession deepened there were still more than a quarter of all operatives in manufacturing working an average of 8.2 hours a week in 1981. Both the proportion and amount of overtime worked have risen since then. It is clear that overtime working is deeply entrenched in Britain. In very crude terms overtime working is equivalent to somewhere between 5 and 7 per cent of the work-force in manufacturing. Of course, this does not mean that this amount of extra jobs would be created, or could be filled if they were, by the abolition of overtime, but it is a rough indicator of the extent of overtime working even during a deep recession and suggests that there are strong reasons leading to the use of overtime even when labour markets might be exceptionally slack. It might be that the increase in the extent and amount of overtime working since 1981 reflects the uncertainty in the minds of employers of any recovery in demand for their products. They are reluctant to expand employment until they are totally convinced that the increase in demand is permanent.

If increased demand for output is met by overtime working there will be no effect on unemployment. Additional workers will not be recruited and it will not be necessary to increase wages in order to attract more labour to the firm. Indeed, it may actually be possible to maintain the existing work-force with lower rates of increase in money wages as the overtime earnings may be regarded as contributing to higher pay notwithstanding the higher hours worked and this may reduce turnover. The use of overtime to meet higher demand for output may therefore prevent increased demand from leading to pressures on the external labour market. If this is the case the expected Monetarist consequences of an increase in aggregate nominal demand which we shall discuss in Chapter 11 may not occur, or if it does, it may be only after a considerable lag in which the initial expansion of demand is not associated with an increase in employment as measured by the number of people employed. Overtime can insert a break in the assumed relationship between output and employment, and, more importantly, in conceptual terms, between changes in output and changes in unemployment.

Conclusions

Employers demand certain types of labour. These can be regarded as different occupations although we have difficulty in defining an occupation. Each individual employer may require some specific skills and abilities in addition to the general range of skills associated with a particular occupation. Each employer's own Job Requirements will determine the combinations of skills, abilities, and personal attributes he requires for each occupation although these Job Requirements can alter as a result of changing technical conditions of production and as a result of the deliberate redesign of jobs in order, perhaps, to meet difficulties in recruiting certain types of labour. In order to maximize the physical productivity of his work-force an employer may incur hiring, screening, and training costs. He does this in order to ensure that the labour employed can provide the type, quality, and quantity of effort-input required to maximize output, given the type and amount of capital equipment in the plant and the production processes in operation. If employers incur the costs of specific training they will seek to recoup this in the future by paying those workers less than their marginal revenue product. Workers may accept this because they received wages higher than their *MRP* while receiving training, or because their wage in that firm is still higher than it would be elsewhere where their specific training has less effect on their *MRP*.

Employment takes place in anticipation of the sale of the product to be produced by labour. Employers' decisions are therefore taken on the basis of expected or anticipated costs and marginal revenue products. The key question to expand or contract employment will depend on the employer's view of the expected wage and the assessment of this is surrounded by many uncertainties. Forecasted increases in future demand for the product will lead to an expansion in employment if the employer is operating under short-run optimizing conditions. If, however, the employer has anticipated the future demand he may have retained workers not actually needed to meet current production levels. Labour hoarding may occur in order that future increases in output can be met at lower costs than would be incurred if new recruits had to be hired and trained or if those with appropriate training and specific skills required higher wages to induce them to come back to the firm if they had previously been dismissed. An alternative to labour hoarding may be lay-offs with recall rights whereby those with specific training whose employment ceases when the demand for products fall are given the first choice of employment when demand revives. This allows the employer to avoid screening and training costs on new recruits. If employment rather than wages takes the brunt of adjustment to changes in demand in the product market the employer may be able to retain those workers because they will feel he is treating them fairly. The notion of implicit contracts, or with formal lay-off and recall provisions, explicit contracts, may satisfy both sides of the labour market.

The fact that labour is not homogeneous means that employers not only have initial costs in obtaining a satisfactory work-force but that they may have a strong financial interest in retaining their current work-force. Labour is not homogeneous in two important respects. Individuals at the time of applying for a job are not homogeneous, and those individuals who have been employed by a firm and acquired some of the specific skills required by that firm are not homogeneous with those who do not have the specific skills. Employers, therefore, not only demand certain occupations, they may demand certain individuals—or, to put the same point slightly differently, a period of employment with a firm in which some specific skills have been acquired transforms members of an occupation into a different occupation. The latter occupation—that with firm-specific skills—has an advantage, most of the time, over the former. Employers will continue to employ the specific skill occupation even when its current short-run costs exceed its short-run value of marginal product if the longer term position looks

110 *The Demand for Labour*

more favourable. In perfect competition this can never be so; this is one reason why the application of the apparent conclusions derived from a model of perfect competition is seldom, indeed perhaps never, directly applicable to the real world.

Notes to Chapter 5

1. In April 1984 a third of all full-time male workers aged twenty-one or over received some sort of payment by result or bonus payment, and a little under a fifth of all women. The proportion of manual male workers receiving some amount of this form of payment was 47 per cent, and 19 per cent for non-manual men. See Department of Employment, *New Earnings Survey*, 1984, Part A, Table 1 (HMSO, London).
2. St. Matt., 20: 1-16.
3. See Kerr (1954), Doeringer and Piore (1971), Robinson (1968 and 1970), and Brown (1973).
4. This assumes that the advertising and screening takes place in the same period as the employment. If they are all shown as being incurred in period 0, it complicates the discounting equation but makes no difference to the general conclusions.
5. An excellent readable fuller account of this theory with a bibliography is Okun (1981).

CHAPTER SIX

The Supply of Labour

BY labour supply we mean the willingness of individuals to provide their labour services. Individuals provide certain types of labour services to specific employers. It is therefore occupational labour supply, or the supply of labour to particular jobs which concern us. Following the discussion in Chapter 5 we can regard an occupation as the possession of certain skills or abilities related to different sorts of effort-inputs. A job is the set of skills and abilities required by a specific employer at a specific place of work. Thus we can regard each different occupation as comprising of a number of different jobs which, while they may differ in some respects, have enough common features that they can be classified in the same broader occupation. Even within an occupation which is narrowly defined there will be some differences in the Job Requirements of the various employers hiring members of that occupation.

In some cases it is fairly clear who is a member of an occupation. Some formal qualification, such as completion of an apprenticeship or the possession of a professional recognition, as in nursing or accountancy, determines who is a member of that occupation. In some cases membership of the appropriate trade union may be a necessary condition for entry into the occupation or to many jobs within it as with Equity and acting. The rules determining the qualifications necessary to enter a closed occupation may be determined by collective bargaining, convention, a unilateral decision by a union or employer, or by legislation. We can regard these as 'closed' occupations. They are closed to those who do not have the required formal qualification.

In practice there will generally be some exceptions so that even in traditional craft occupations for which an apprenticeship is considered a necessary prerequisite to entry there will be some individuals employed who have not obtained this qualification (Robinson 1970). Open occupations do not require formal qualifications. They may, of course, still require certain skills and abilities, and so are not open to everyone as some individuals cannot meet the occupational Job Requirements.

Because the Job Requirements may vary from employer to employer even though every employer requires his workers to be members of the same closed occupation it is often difficult to define precisely what we mean by an occupation in a multi-employer sense. There are different sorts of fitters, electricians, and musicians. Similarly there are different types of specialist accountants, solicitors, and teachers. Membership of the appropriate occupation may be *a necessary* condition for acceptance into a job but it is not always a *sufficient* condition. This apparent difficulty of classification could be solved if we had sufficiently precise definitions of occupations, but this would change normal usage of occupational classifications and lead us towards an individual employer-specific classification. It should be borne in mind therefore that for some jobs possession of the required qualifications for admission into a closed occupation is a necessary condition for entry, but some additional abilities or specialization might be required. In other cases individuals can seek to enter the occupation by persuading an employer that he has the required abilities. As we discussed in Chapter 5, occupation is best seen as referring to the skills and abilities possessed by individuals, and Job Requirements as the employer's specifications of the skills and abilities needed to fill a post or job. There may be considerable skills overlap of the two, but they are seldom coterminous.

The main question we wish to pursue is what determines whether an individual will offer his labour services to an employer at a given wage level? An alternative formulation might be what determines the wage level at which an individual offers his labour services to an employer?

Income–leisure trade-off

We will start by making the extreme assumption that an individual can supply labour services to only one job, i.e. there is only one job which he is capable of performing, or only one job which he in any way contemplates taking. His choice is therefore between working in this job or not working at all.

Economic theory usually approaches the question of labour supply by assuming that an individual chooses between work, which is unpleasant or has disutility but provides income and leisure. He trades-off leisure for income by accepting the disutility of work. Both income and leisure are assumed to be 'normal' goods so that as one has more of them the marginal utility or satisfaction obtained from each marginal increment is less than that received from the preceding unit. Thus each unit—say hour—of leisure given up requires an increasing amount of income to compensate the individual; and each unit, say £1, of income received, brings less satisfaction than the previous unit. An individual therefore requires an increasing hourly wage to induce him to give up successive hours of leisure. Figure 6.1 can therefore represent the hours

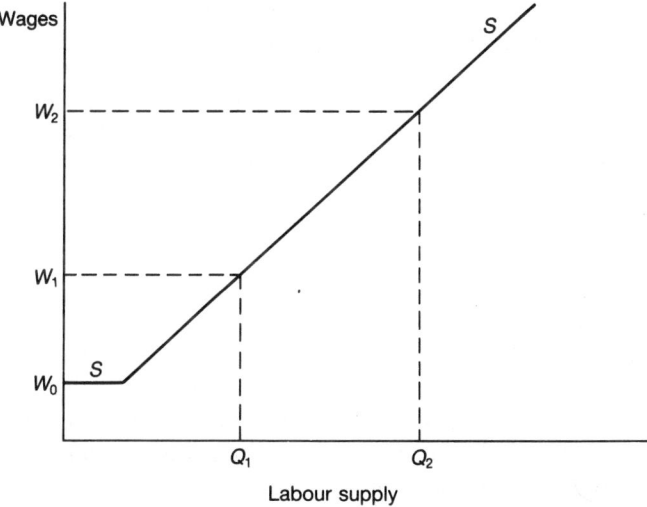

Fig. 6.1   Individual Labour Supply

of labour supply of an individual to a given occupation a, in which case the bottom axis can be regarded as showing the hours of work of an individual in occupation a and the wage level is the *hourly* rate of pay.[1]

Most people cannot choose to supply whatever number of hours of work maximizes their satisfaction. In most jobs the number of hours to be worked is either laid down by the employer or agreed by collective bargaining. The individual is therefore faced with a choice of working a given number of hours or not working in that job at all. The given number of hours may vary; in Fig. 6.1 we can suppose that Q_1 represents twenty hours a week and Q_2 a forty hour week.

The usual assumption of labour economics is that a higher rate of pay is necessary to induce people to offer more hours of work as their leisure becomes increasingly valuable to them as they give up more of it. The rate at which an individual is willing to give up additional leisure for extra work-income is his marginal rate of substitution of work-income for leisure. This may vary amongst individuals. Some may require a considerable increase in pay before they will provide forty, rather than twenty, hours a week. They may have a very strong preference for part-time work. Their family commitments may be such that they require a very large increase in pay to compensate them for full-time working.

It is possible that if the extra pay were sufficiently high they would give up the extra twenty hours. They might be able to afford to pay for their children to attend a crèche, or employ a nanny, and they might employ someone else to do their housework. Given the wage levels available to them, however, they might well decide that they will supply only a given number of hours of work. The supply curve of labour of an individual for a given occupation might therefore be discontinuous rather than a curve. There might be combinations of certain numbers of hours at certain wage levels which would be supplied. Alternatively, the individual supply curve might twist or bend its shape at various wage levels.

For most purposes it is sufficient and more realistic to confine ourselves to the labour supply price for that number of hours which are required by the employers. These are mainly determined by convention and collective bargaining and are not immutable through time. If employers are very short of labour they may well offer a different number of hours of work in order to attract some people who are not willing to supply any labour at the prevailing wage level if they have to work the prevailing number of hours. For example employers might find it difficult to obtain additional workers at wage W_2 but if they reduce working hours from forty to twenty they might attract a number of married women at the prevailing hourly wage rate (or at a lower hourly wage). To obtain more full time forty-hour workers might require a significant increase in wages for all workers.

The use of the work 'leisure' can mislead. It is used in economic analysis simply to mean 'not working', but its usual connotation is that the individual is enjoying the non-working time. We do not normally think of all our non-working times as leisure. Some of it is used in sleeping and carrying out household or family duties. Leisure is something which we normally regard as giving positive pleasure; it is when we listen to music, go to the cinema, watch TV or a football match, or indulge in whatever hobbies we may have. Most people would not regard a situation in which they had no work and no work-income as one of leisure. They might regard it as enforced idleness or unavoidable unemployment. Much might depend on whether they had other sources of income. Someone with a sizeable income from dividends might choose not to be employed and be regarded as a person of leisure, but for most people a situation in which no work was available or acceptable would probably not be regarded by them as one of a voluntary choice of full-time leisure. It is important therefore to emphasize the technical nature of the term 'leisure' in this context and we should not conclude that all those who are not working are taking a positive decision to enjoy twenty-four hours of leisure a day.

While for most purposes it is unrealistic to consider the trade-off between work-income and leisure over the full range of possible combinations of hours of work and pay levels, it may be useful when considering marginal changes to normal working hours. Overtime premium reflects the view that some additional hourly pay might be needed to persuade people to work beyond their 'normal' hours. Similarly, considerations apply to premiums for weekend or night-time working. The 'leisure forgone at these times is regarded as more valuable than leisure forgone in normal working hours and, therefore, higher hourly pay is required in order to induce people to work these 'unsocial' hours.

Reservation wage (ResW)

In Fig. 6.1 the individual provides no labour at wage W_0. That wage is insufficient to induce him to accept the disutility of work. He is regarded as choosing not to work; his unemployment is voluntary in that sense. We would say that his reservation wage is W_0.

The reservation wage plays an important part in Monetarist analysis. It is the lowest wage sufficient to induce an individual to accept a job. The reservation wage operates in the same way as a reservation price at an auction; if it is not met no trade takes place. The seller—the worker selling his labour services—withdraws from that transaction in that market. If we assume that an individual can work in only one occupation he will have a single reservation wage which will be his labour supply price, or the wage at which he is prepared to offer his services and is therefore the level of wages at which he joins the labour supply curve.

Different individuals may have different reservation wages. We can regard Fig. 6.1 as representing the labour supply of different individuals at different wage levels. The vertical axis measures wages per hour, day, or week, and the horizontal axis the number of individuals willing to work for that rate of pay. Still assuming that the individuals considered can be members only of one occupation and supply their labour to only the one job, individual Q_0 will offer to work for the firm if wages equal W_0. Individual Q_1 will not offer his services unless wages are W_1 as that is his reservation wage, and individual Q_2 requires wage W_2 to induce him to give up his leisure and accept the disutility he sees as attached to this job. If the employer wishes to increase his work-force from Q_1 to Q_2 he has to raise wages from W_1 to W_2.

Labour-force Participation Reservation Wage

If we continue with the unreal assumption that an individual can be a member of only one occupation his ResW for that occupation is also his labour force participation reservation wage (LFPResW) in that it is the wage which must be obtained if he is to accept a job rather than be unemployed. It can therefore be seen as providing the boundary between employment and unemployment. In determining this ResW we might assume that the worker asks himself/herself two questions, How badly do I need the money? What am I prepared to do to get it?

The perceived need for money will be determined by many things. The worker may act as an individual or may be part of a household or family unit which contains other income-recipients and others with needs. Different individuals will have different desired or expected standards of living. They will have different amounts of income from other sources and different amounts of savings. They will have different expectations about their future income, including their future income from future employment. They will have different abilities to borrow, and be able to borrow at different rates of interest so that their ability to trade-off future income for current income will vary. They will have different current and future commitments. Putting this another way we can say that they will have different views of their permanent income. Some will have included spells of unemployment in their assessment of their permanent income while others may not have done so. Their perceptions of the transitory nature of their unemployment will differ. Their possession of wealth assets other than human wealth incorporated in their views of their permanent income will also differ. We cannot be at all clear how workers answer this question for themselves nor can we seek to quantify their responses.

Family or household circumstances may play a large part in determining the LFPResW. If a regular wage-earner is unemployed other members of the household may reduce their LFPResW. In practice what often happens is that members of the household may take a rather different decision. They may decide to try and participate in labour market activities by offering their labour services, i.e. applying for a job or by looking for a job. Previously they may have withdrawn from labour market activities; in one sense they were unemployed but they were not actually seeking work. They had decided to spend all their time on non-employment and non-looking-for-employment activities. It is possible to say that even then they still had a reservation wage. If an employer had offered them, say, £200 a week for twenty hours' work, they would have accepted. Now, as a result of, say, her husband becoming unemployed, a wife may look for and accept a job which pays only £40 for a twenty-hour week. To say that her LFPResW had fallen from £200 to £40 is to say that those who have withdrawn from labour market activity have done so because they have a LFPResW which is so much higher than the level of actual wages paid to members of their occupation that they do not even bother looking for a vacancy which might meet their LFPResW. This is a strained and artificial way of explaining behaviour. It is preferable to distinguish between those who are not actively participating in labour market activities—they are neither working, nor with existing wage levels, family circumstances, and individual tastes and preferences, are they seeking work—they have withdrawn from labour force participation, and those who are looking for work.

Married women provide the largest group of people who are likely to enter and leave the labour force in this way. Sometimes their decision to participate is influenced by their perception of their chances of finding a job. If more jobs are provided they may decide to accept one even if the wages paid are no higher than those already paid for similar jobs. If a new factory opens in a town the recruiting personnel manager often finds that a number of married women, who are neither currently employed nor previously engaged in looking for work, apply for a job. This is a good example of demand creating its own supply. It has important consequences for some economic theory. It emphasizes the perceived availability of jobs rather than the level of wages as an explanation of withdrawal from labour market activity, or job search.

A 1980 survey showed that 60 per cent of women were working (34 per cent full time and 26 per cent part time), 5 per cent were students, and 35 per cent were not working. Of these 5 per cent were unemployed and 30 per cent economically inactive (Martin and Roberts, 1984, 10). Although unmarried women are more likely to be working than are married women—75 per cent compared with 60 per cent, if the two groups are standardized for age, and the age of the youngest child, the proportions working are exactly the same. The important factors influencing the different labour force participation rates of single and married women are therefore age, presence of children, and the age of the youngest child. 'Once these differences are allowed for, married women are just as likely to be working as non-married women. However . . . among working women married women are more likely than non-married women to be working part time' (14).

If actual or market real wages are below an individual's reservation wages for all jobs, and the individual knows this so that he is not engaged in wage or job search, we would conclude that he is economically inactive. He is not employed, nor is he unemployed, as he is not willing to accept employment on the prevailing terms and conditions. He is not therefore part of the labour supply to any occupation and this is why we would refer to him as economically inactive. However, if actual real wages rose in one or more occupation sufficiently to meet his real reservation wage for that occupation, and he knew of this, he would become part of labour supply to that occupation, although not, of course to the other occupations whose actual wage levels were still below his $ResW$ for them. Labour supply means the offer of labour at a particular point in time with the prevailing actual wage levels. There may be a 'potential' labour supply if real wages rise enough. While in some cases this 'potential' labour supply is included in the supply curve as usually drawn, so that the supply increases in Fig. 6.1 if wages rise above W_2, there may be additional supply if some people who have withdrawn from labour force activity decide to re-enter the labour market when wages so rise. Currently they may not bother to produce their schedule of occupation ResWs and labour supply, perhaps because they do not anticipate real wages rising sufficiently to induce them to re-enter the labour market. Unanticipated increases in wages might lead them to revise their views. We cannot know what the 'potential' labour supply is unless we know everyone's schedule of $RResW$ and how these might change in the future.

Unemployment and 'economically inactive' are not the same. The economically inactive are not looking for jobs at the prevailing real wage levels. The unemployed can be regarded as looking for jobs. If it is assumed that all unemployment is voluntary and that some workers withdraw from economic activity when real wages fall, as actual wages are then less than their $RResW$s, some of what appears to be an increase in unemployment would in fact be a withdrawal from labour market activity.

The decision to re-enter the labour force can be influenced by factors other than the wage level. Married women may look for work with a particular company if it provides transport, arranges hours which are convenient for getting children to and from school, or, perhaps, provides shopping facilities on the premises (Robinson 1968). All these factors can be seen as contributing to the perceived unpleasantness of work and therefore incorporated in the simple analysis which trades-off work-income against leisure. The important point for our purposes is that an increase in wages is not always necessary to induce people to offer their labour services.

In determining how badly he needs the income from employment an individual may be influenced by considerations of fairness or reasonableness. If there is a going rate for the job, determined perhaps by collective bargaining or convention, or if there is a statutory minimum wage level set by a Wages Council, he may conclude that he does not need the income so badly that he is prepared to go against the social norms by 'cutting' the rate. This point can equally well be included in consideration of what he is prepared to do to obtain an income. In this case he is not prepared to break ranks with his mates by working for less than the rate or he is not prepared to demean himself by working for less than some socially determined minimum. Other people can approve or disapprove his actions but this is no more than endorsing or rejecting his value-judgement, in the same way that we might agree someone should not kick a man when he is down. Others may believe that is the best time to kick him and avoid retaliation. Standards of morality in behaviour vary among individuals.

The question of what he has to do to obtain the wage will be determined by the Job Requirements of the openings facing him. Job Requirements will impose some unpleasant features of work on an individual, such as attendance at certain times, the necessity to perform certain tasks which might be physically or mentally demanding, in pleasant or unpleasant circumstances, and so on. They may also have some attractive features—they may provide social contacts or a feeling of satisfaction in the work. An individual can be seen as comparing all these features and deciding what wage level is sufficient to induce him to accept the package. Different individuals may require different amounts of pay to induce them to accept the same job.

One factor which Monetarists frequently mention when discussing the determinants of the ResW is the level of Unemployment Benefits (UB), which in Britain ought to be extended to include the other benefits in cash or in kind which an unemployed person may be entitled to receive. The level of Supplementary Benefits will generally be higher than UB. The argument is relatively simple. If an unemployed person receives UB, leisure, i.e. unemployment, also has an income. The attractiveness of any given wage level will therefore be less than if no UB were received. Provided the marginal rate of substitution of income for leisure remains unchanged a higher level of wages will be required to induce the individual to accept any given job than would be the case without UB. From this it seems a small step to conclude that the level of UB influences the level of ResW and therefore influences the level of unemployment.

It is argued that the relationship between income when working and income when not working—the replacement ratio (RR)—is the important variable which influences people's decisions whether to be employed, unemployed, or to withdraw from labour market participation. There is a considerable literature on this issue.[2] Much of the British research relates to the early or mid-1970s when unemployment was considerably lower than recent levels, and when, for some of the period Earnings Related Supplement increased the level of UB of some workers. Conclusions which are derived from these studies may not be applicable to the drastically changed circumstances of the 1980s. What a number of them seem to establish is that a higher RR may increase the length of unemployment, although not by a very great amount. This is relevant to job search theories which we shall discuss in Chapter 7. A great deal depends on how the levels of UB or Supplementary Benefit are calculated—whether this is on the basis of some standard or 'typical' household, and whether the actual rates of Supplementary Benefit received, or the levels to which the standard households are entitled, are used (Atkinson *et al.* 1984). The overall position is best summed up by Atkinson *et al.* 'There is, therefore, substantial scope for the conclusions drawn to be influenced by prior beliefs.'

The supply of labour at particular wage levels is less because the net increase in income from work is less. If UB were lower the net gain from employment at any given wage level would be higher and this 'ought' to be enough to induce some people who previously did not offer their labour services at that wage level, now to do so. Wage levels have to be higher than they would were UB lower in order to attract labour, and the employers' demand for labour at the higher wage is less than it would be at a lower wage. The level of employment is thereby seen as a function of the level of UB. It should come as no surprise therefore that Monetarists advocate a reduction in UB in order to lower *ResW* and lead to an increase in both the demand for and supply of labour.

The minimum flat rate benefit including any supplementary benefit 'top-up' is paid indefinitely to an unemployed man for as long as he remains unemployed; such a man will very naturally expect to be re-employed at a wage after tax and work expenses which is at least as high as this benefit, and probably somewhat higher because he may not wish to "work for nothing", whatever his personal attitude towards work. . . . Hence wages cannot effectively fall below this level for even the most unskilled worker. This level then acts as a floor under the whole wage structure . . . (Minford 1983, 2).

In fact there are many people working for wages which, after tax and working expenses, are lower than the income in cash and kind that they could obtain if unemployed.

Being unemployed, like working, has disadvantages and one of them may be the very fact that one is unable to get a job. The unemployed do not necessarily see their plight as being the result of their voluntary choice between work-income and leisure. In societies such as ours, where there is still a strong work ethic, being unemployed can carry many perceived undesirable penalties. The individual may believe that he has failed as an individual, or a husband or father, if he is unable to get a job. He may believe that this far outweighs gains from Supplementary Benefit. It is only if we assert that factors such as these do not exert any influence, or that the satisfaction derived from income is the same no matter what the source of income, that we can conclude that

Supplementary Benefit leads to higher reservation wages. If income from work provides a higher satisfaction than the same amount of income from UB individuals may work even when their net income is no higher or even less than their UB or Supplementary Benefit.

It is wrong to conclude that the $ResW$ bears some mechanistic relationship to the level of Unemployment Benefit. For some people there may be some sort of relationship, but for many more the need to work is in itself strong enough to push $ResW$s below the UB level.

The Monetarist view that a reduction in UB will lead to a lowering of $ResW$'s and thus a decrease in unemployment is therefore not necessarily the case. Indeed the effects could be just the opposite. If workers form a view of 'entitled' permanent income as discussed in Chapter 4, one consequence of a reduction in UB could be that their reservation wages increase. If the expected or entitled income over a life-term remains the same, a reduction in income while unemployed requires compensation in the form of higher income when in employment. It is possible therefore that reducing UB could, on some variants of the Friedman concept of permanent income, actually have the perverse effect of leading to higher $ResW$ and higher unemployment.

As we have seen, Fig. 6.1 can be interpreted in a different way. If we regard the number of hours to be worked as fixed at, say, forty hours a week, the vertical axis can show the weekly rate of pay for occupation a and the horizontal axis shows the number of individuals willing to provide forty hours of labour to the firm or occupation. The figure now shows the number of individuals who will offer to work in this job at different wage levels. At W_0 no one is willing to work in this occupation. At W_1, Q_1 number of people are willing to work and at W_2 an extra number $(Q_2 - Q_1)$ is forthcoming.

This is the more common form of a supply curve. If there are workers who have very strong preferences for part-time work, as well as others who prefer working the normal week, but can work on only one occupation, we can suppose that the firm has two supply curves for this occupation. One is for the forty-hour week workers and the other for the twenty-hour week workers. The number of workers forthcoming at each wage level is determined by the reservation wage of each individual.

As wages rise more labour will be provided, so that when $W_2 > W_1$, so $Q_2 > Q_1$. The elasticity of supply—the responsiveness of the supply of labour to a change in the wage level—*is* $[(Q_2 - Q_1)/Q_1]/[(W_2 - W_1)/W_1]$. On a given diagram the steeper the slope of the supply curve the more inelastic the supply of labour. If the supply curve were represented as a horizontal line this would mean that the supply of labour to the employer was perfectly elastic so that he could obtain as much of that sort of labour

122 *The Supply of Labour*

as he wished at the given wage level. It is usually assumed that the supply curve of labour slopes upward from left to right for two main reasons —the diminishing rate of substitution of leisure for income and different reservation wages amongst individual workers.

The Retention Reservation Wage

So far we have referred to the reservation as the minimum amount necessary to induce an individual, assumed to be capable of entering only one occupation or performing one job, to enter the labour market. This can be seen as the *recruitment* reservation wage; it is the lowest wage at which this individual can be recruited by the employer. This is often regarded as the same as the *retention* reservation wage, i.e. the minimum amount necessary to retain the worker in that job. There may be an important difference between the two, or more particularly, the retention *ResW* may diverge from the recruitment *ResW*.

We are still assuming that an individual can work in only one occupation. The question of changing jobs does not therefore arise. It is a general assumption of economics that all workers in the same category or occupation or job in the same place of work receive the same rate of wages. If in Fig. 6.2 the units of labour shown on the horizontal axis represent numbers of people willing to work a specified number of hours, say a forty hour week, the upward-sloping curve indicates that if

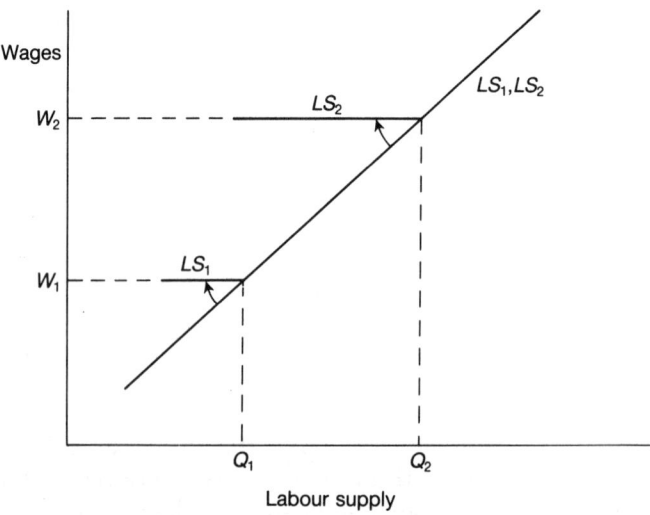

Fig. 6.2 Adjusted Labour Supply

an employer wishes to recruit additional workers to the number Q_1 he already employs, he has to raise wages from W_1. If he wishes to hire Q_2 number of workers he has to increase wages to W_2 not only for the new recruits, but also for the existing labour force Q_1 who were willing before the wage increase to work for wage W_1. This 'additional' payment $(W_2 - W_1)$ to workers Q_1 can be regarded as quasi-rent; it is a payment more than was sufficient to induce them to supply their labour. However, this conceptual approach in economic theory is based on reasoning in which each individual worker is regarded as taking decisions based only on his individual preferences or trade-off regarding work and pay divorced from considerations of fairness based on, or reflecting, inter-personal comparisons of equity or justice. Thus, if we assume Q_1 is just one worker, he is willing to work for a wage of W_1, but if he sees another worker Q_2 receiving a wage of W_2 he may decide that he is no longer willing to supply his own labour at wage W_1. His views of fairness, determined by him as an individual quite separate from any trade union organization may lead him to shift his own supply-offer of labour, i.e. raise his reservation wage, because of his own notions of fairness or equity. It might, therefore, be reasonable for economic theory to assume that the same wage has to be paid to all members of the same labour supply curve notwithstanding that this will imply that all the intra-marginal workers will receive quasi-rent as their actual wage exceeds their reservation wage. However, what it might also mean is that once they have received some quasi-rent they change their individual reservation wage, sending it upwards towards the actual wage they have been receiving, in this example, W_2. If this is so, then the labour supply curve as shown in Fig. 6.1 should be seen as a supply of labour curve which operates in the *upward* direction from any given actual wage level. It shows the amount of additional labour which will be forthcoming from the external labour market at wages *higher* than W_1 in a situation where Q_1 amount of labour is currently employed at wage W_1.

If the situation changes so that Q_2 labour is employed at wage W_2 and the reservation wage of each individual below Q_2 is revised as suggested by comparisons of fairness then the labour supply curve may alter. In Fig. 6.2 the supply curve from Fig. 6.1 is shown as LS_1 with actual wages at W_1. The revised supply curve following the payment of higher wages W_2 is shown as LS_2. It is quite possible that not all individuals revise their reservation wage in this way so that the actual labour supply curve, once wage W_2 has been paid, may be anywhere between LS_1 and LS_2.

What we are suggesting is that the *internal* labour supply—that forthcoming from existing employees—may shift as a result of changes in

124 *The Supply of Labour*

the wage level which were made in order to obtain additional labour from the external supply. The internal labour supply curve becomes horizontal (or somewhere between the horizontal and the original supply curve). If wages were then to fall back to W_1 the employer would not be able to retain Q_1 workers. In the extreme case of a shift to a horizontal supply curve at wage W_2, he would not be able to obtain any workers if wages reverted to W_1. All his existing work-force would leave and there would be no external labour supply at the lower wage of W_1.

We are not saying that this will always happen, but we are questioning the assumption that they supply curve composed of an internal and an external component always remains the same when the wage level increases. An individual's retention reservation wage may move upwards as a result of obtaining higher wages and quasi-rent. Money wages can become ratcheted, and this is not, in this example, because of trade unions, but as a result of changes in an individual's determination of his individual reservation wage.

This is illustrated in Fig. 6.3. The curve LS_1 shows the labour supply as the number of workers offering to work in this job at different wage levels. Assume the demand for labour is D_1 so that the wage is W_1 and the numbers employed is Q_1. The demand for labour shifts to curve D_2. Wages rise to W_2 and the number employed to Q_2. The demand curve

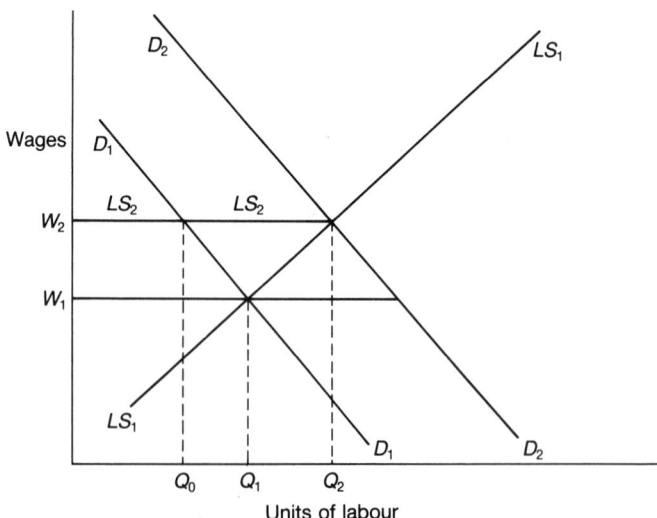

Fig. 6.3 Adjusted Retention Reservation Wage, Demand, and Employment

then shifts back to D_1. The supply shifts to become LS_2 as all the workers employed by the firm change their retention reservation wage to W_2—the wage they have been receiving following the increase in demand. If the supply curve had reverted to LS_1 the same number of workers Q_1 would have been employed at wage W_1 as originally. However, at wage W_1 no labour is forthcoming. With the restoration of demand curve D_1 the demand for labour at wage W_2 is only Q_0 but the supply is Q_2 and there is an excess supply of labour. The firm will have to dismiss $(Q_2 - Q_0)$ workers. If it tried to reduce wages below W_2 it will not be able to retain any labour. The labour market does not clear; demand does not equal supply at the prevailing wage.

Thus the *retention wage*—that necessary to induce existing employees to remain with the firm—increases as a result of workers receiving the higher wages which were necessary to recruit the additional workers. If the supply curve represents the total supply of labour to the firm so that it includes existing employees and the additional workers who might be attracted from the external labour market by higher wages, the existing workers cannot be replaced by new recruits if they leave. If members of the occupation are not homogeneous so that the existing work-force, as a result of specific training or on-the-job experience, are more productive than new recruits, the employer has added reason to retain Q_0 of his present employees, but may not be able to do so except at a wage of W_2. However, this excess supply will not lead to a fall in wages unless the existing work-force, or such members of them as the employer wishes to retain, adjust their reservation wage back to W_1. Adjustments in individual reservation wages can therefore not only change the shape of the labour supply curve to the firm, but ratchet wages with the result that the labour market for this occupation does not clear. There can be an excess supply of labour at the prevailing wage.

We do not actually know very much about what determines reservation wages. Because we assumed that an individual could work in only one occupation we could equate his reservation for that occupation with his LFPResW. This focuses attention on the employment/unemployment decision and this is the one emphasized by Monetarists. It represents the choice between work and non-work. All sorts of social, as well as economic, factors can influence an individual's determination of his LFPResW. However, as we shall now discuss the effective choice facing individuals is not whether to accept employment in a single occupation, but which occupation or different job, if any, to accept. The importance of the LFPResW as representing the crucial distinction between employment and unemployment is much diminished.

126 *The Supply of Labour*

Occupational or Job Reservation Wages

Monetarists often tend to speak of *the* reservation wage, even though they also often recognize that occupational mobility is possible, and indeed their solutions to the problems of unemployment frequently require such mobility. There may well be some wage which determines whether an individual accepts a job—any job at all—or whether he decides to be unemployed, but it is quite unrealistic, as well as contrary to the assumptions of standard economic theory, to believe that this will be the same for all jobs irrespective of the type of work involved. It is much more realistic to believe that an individual has different reservation wages for different occupations or jobs. It would not surprise me if someone refused to work on a coal-face for less than, say, £200 a week, but was perfectly willing to work as an usher in a topless theatre for much less. We will consider different reservation wages for different occupations later in this chapter.

Everyone is capable of being employed in more than one occupation or job. It is better therefore to envisage an individual as having a hierarchy of reservation wages, each one applying to a particular job or type of work. The LFPResW is the lowest of the schedule of occupational reservation wages. This is the lowest wage which the worker is willing to accept rather than remain unemployed. It will apply to a particular occupation or job and higher reservation wages will be attached to other occupations and jobs. It does not follow that the individual will remain unemployed if his lowest reservation wage is above the wage paid for *that job*. If wages for some other jobs exceed his reservation wage levels for those jobs he would be employed in one of them, assuming that he is acceptable to an employer with a vacancy.

Figure 6.4 shows an individual's reservation wages (*ResW*) for various occupations or jobs $a \ldots z$. It also shows the actual wages (*AW*) for each occupation. By wages we mean the rate of wages paid for a specified time-period which we can take as being a standard working week. It does not matter how the wage levels for each occupation or job are determined—whatever the process of pay determination, these are the wage-offers for various jobs facing the individual. The jobs or occupations are ranked by their wage level with wages rising from a to z. The individual's ranking of those occupations differs from the market wage ranking. For example he has a higher ResW for a than for e, although the market wage for e exceeds that for a. His lowest reservation wage is for g and this can be seen as his LFPResW. It does not follow that he will enter occupation g. He can choose any occupation in the ranges $d \ldots k$ or $v \ldots z$.

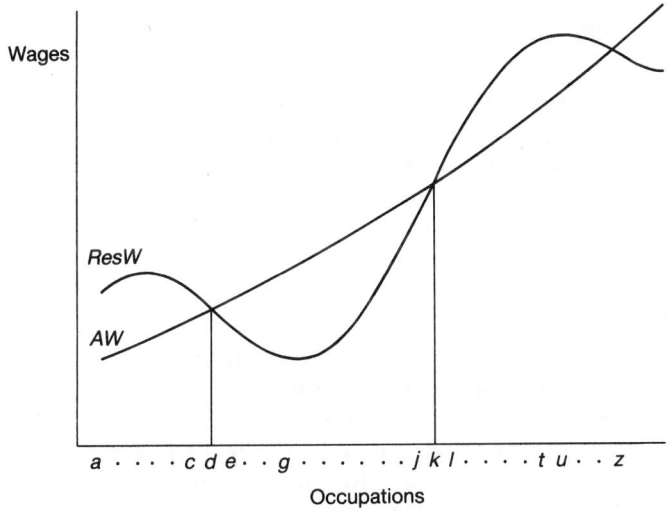

Fig. 6.4 Individual Reservation Wages for Different Occupations

There is no reason to suppose that the ranking of occupational reservation wages by any individual will be the same as the ranking of market wages for those occupations. Individuals will have different reservation wages for the same jobs so that their rankings of jobs by reservation wages will differ one from another as well as from the ranking by actual wage levels.

There will be some jobs or occupations for which the individual does not even bother to produce a reservation wage as he knows that there is no conceivable possibility that he would be accepted for them. I am not sure just what range of occupations my own schedule of reservation wages might cover—most of the time I, like many, or most, other people don't think about changing jobs—but I am sure that I have no reservation wage for certain jobs. I just cannot contemplate that I become an opera singer, professional boxer, atomic physicist, or coal-face worker no matter what wage was offered. Some jobs I can't do; and some jobs I won't do. It might be that if I concluded that unsuitable as I am for some of them, and unwilling as I am to consider doing some of the others, there was literally no other job available to me, I would produce a reservation wage for each of them. In the absence of that extremely unlikely and unanticipated event I certainly do not bother trying to work out what my reservation wage would be and I do not therefore currently have a reservation wage for them. They would not be included in my range $a \ldots z$ in Fig. 6.4.

Net Advantages

The determination of reservation wages for different jobs can be seen as a comparative process. An individual compares the total package of Job Requirements and associated work features, ranks them, and decides the minimum he would need to induce him to accept each of the jobs. Each job has some advantages and some disadvantages, including giving up leisure. The $ResW_a$ tells us how much the individual wants to induce him to accept the net disadvantages of job a, $ResW_b$ for job b and so on. When we compare the net disadvantages of a job with its pay we assume that the combined effect is to produce net *advantages*. If it does not we do not consider entering that job. Wages provide the balance of net advantages which induce us to consider working in that job. In producing a hierarchy of reservation wages we are ranking jobs or occupations by their net disadvantages excluding pay. Thus in Fig. 6.4 g has fewest disadvantages to this individual which is why it has the lowest reservation wage. He would work in that job for lower wages than in any other.

If we include the actual wages which are available for each job with the other advantages and disadvantages so obtaining net advantages we can produce a framework which might explain how individuals select the occupations or jobs for which they offer their labour services. It is only those jobs which have positive net advantages that are considered. The concept of net advantages expounded by Adam Smith in 1776 is still used as an explanation of the determinants of labour supply to specific occupations.

Each job has disadvantages: it requires the surrender of some leisure, it requires some input of physical or mental effort, the application of skills, the acceptance of responsibility, the observance of specified rules which limit one's freedom while at work, and the requirement to follow existing practices. The job content may be uninteresting so that boredom becomes a disadvantage of the occupation, or may be physically demanding.

Occupations may require a period of training or education before an individual can enter them. This is usually seen as a disadvantage in that such periods involve some loss of income. There may be an actual cost of education or training depending on the educational and related provisions in the country and industry concerned. Forgone earnings, rather than the direct costs of education and training, usually are more important in the UK.

At the same time all occupations or jobs have advantages. The most obvious of these is the level of pay. Different levels of pay exist for different occupations and presumably, all other things being equal, a higher level of pay is preferred to a lower one. Other advantages may take the form of deferred payment, such as pension, or include sickness-pay schemes, holiday pay, the length of the working week, number of holidays, or a wide variety of fringe benefits. In principle these can be converted into a cash equivalent in terms of what it costs the employer to provide them, but they can also be translated into a different cash equivalent which is the amount it would cost the individual to provide the same benefit for himself. Neither of these amounts may be the same as that placed on them by a recipient.

Other advantages may be the pleasantness of the work, the environment, the people one works with and meets, or the social status obtained from following a certain occupation. For some occupations an important advantage may be the opportunities it provides for access to other occupations or jobs. This will depend upon the prevailing practices, either informal, managerially determined or the result of collective bargaining, which in some instances will be the outcome of the rules of the internal labour market of the plant or company, and in other instances may be more widespread throughout the profession. For example the internal labour market organization of the Civil Service is such that access to the post of Permanent Secretary is limited to those already employed in the Civil Service. Part of the attractiveness or advantages of entering the Civil Service may be the possibility of promotion to Permanent Secretary or one of the other higher grades which are similarly limited in access. Other people may join the Civil Service because they believe the experience they will receive in their early years will allow them to transfer to some other occupation, for example some experience in Inland Revenue may facilitate transfer into accountancy or employment as a tax adviser.

Some occupations may offer more security of employment and generally better promotion prospects, although this might to some extent depend upon how we define occupation. For example a clerical officer in the Civil Service or in local government might have more security than a clerk doing similar work in a private company. Whether we regard this as one occupation with varying conditions between the different employers, or as three or more separate occupations each linked to a particular employer, depends upon the purpose for which we are producing the definition of an occupation.

While in one sense the Job Requirements may appear as objective in that they are the same for whoever does the job, in another sense they are essentially subjective. The assessment of the unpleasantness of the Job Requirements—the disutility of work—will vary from individual to individual. This means not just that they rank different aspects of a job differently, but that they might actually regard the same feature of a job as falling on different sides of the pleasant/unpleasant divide. A job that provides one individual with opportunity to exercise responsibility and take decisions and is therefore desirable, is seen by someone else as giving too much pressure and too many ulcers.

The individual's assessment of the net advantages of a particular job will be determined by his own set of tastes but these will be influenced by his experience and expectations. In the mining environment in which I grew up work was expected to be hard, unpleasant, dirty, and physically demanding. That's why they paid you for doing it. In the academic environment in which I now work it is none of these things. It may be intellectually demanding but most of the time we enjoy doing it—and they still pay us. Our background and experience lead us to have certain expectations about work. Some people do not expect much satisfaction or pleasure from the act of working and others expect a great deal, perhaps the bulk of their feeling of achievement comes from their work activity. It is hard to imagine someone doing a ninety-second job-cycle on an assembly line getting much satisfaction from it; it is not at all hard to imagine a social worker, a clothes designer, a draughtsman, or an architect getting considerable satisfaction from their work. Even so we must be careful. Many individuals obtain satisfaction from jobs which many of us might find to be totally devoid of interest or sense of creativity and achievement, and some of those in what are to us fascinating and interesting jobs might be bored stiff.

Our experience of work shapes our view of the net advantages of jobs. Until we *have* worked we cannot really know what sort of satisfaction or otherwise can be obtained from working. Even when we have had a job, or jobs, we still do not know what satisfaction might be obtainable from other sorts of work. Even the ninety-second job-cycle can have some attraction if previously we had a thirty-second cycle in worse conditions with a lousy boss.

Adam Smith argued that the net advantages of different occupations in a neighbourhood (or local labour market) would tend to equality, given certain conditions. The most important of these was perfect freedom. If there were marked disparities in the net advantages between occupations the forces of supply and demand in the local labour market would operate to produce equality. If some occupations had much better net advantages people would enter them, leading to an increase in supply and so a reduction in the advantages offered by employers. Similarly, if some occupation had worse net advantages people would not join that occupation and employers would find it necessary to increase the advantages in order to attract enough recruits. The time-period of adjustment might be long depending on the time necessary to obtain the skill or training and the speed with which those institutions providing the education or training responded to an increase in demand. The condition of perfect freedom was intended to exclude circumstances where there were artificial or institutional restraints on the number who could train for entry into the occupation, e.g. restrictions on the number of apprentices.

The main difficulty with the concept of net advantages is that it is essentially untestable. We cannot carry out empirical research to test its validity. The one hard piece of evidence we can find and measure is the level of pay, but just about everything else which comes into the overall assessment of net advantages is subjective and so therefore not capable of measurement. We can seek to apply the concept in a tautological way so that if people leave or are reluctant to join a particular occupation we can say that it is because the net advantages are not enough. We might be able to go further and say that they are not enough in relation to the net advantages of certain other occupations if we can find evidence that people are leaving one occupation for certain others. We might be able to say that they are not enough to induce people to work if members of an occupation leave it and stop working. We cannot say, however, that they tend to equality across different occupations.

Nor can we say what they should be in order to induce a higher supply of members of that occupation or to reduce the inflow of new entrants. This is for a very important reason. Because they are subjective, most elements in net advantages depend upon the perceptions, interpretations, tastes, and preferences of individuals. This is partly because we have different views as to what is pleasant. It is also partly because we are different physically and mentally, so that what is hard physical work for one person is not regarded as particularly hard work by another. Similarly, what is regarded as boring by one person may not be so regarded by another.

Even in the case of what might be generally regarded as advantages, such as fringe benefits, there is no reason to suppose that each individual will evaluate them equally. One person might regard the provision of a pension scheme as of considerable value which compensates for a lot of disadvantages or is worth a certain amount of money as forgone wages. Another may put a much lower valuation on the same scheme. This would be consistent with the fact that different members of the same occupation receiving the same fringe benefits choose to purchase different amounts of additional fringe benefits in the form of additional personal insurance of various sorts. Some may be more inclined to gamble on their future good health and so have a lower preference or place a lower value on the various forms of insurance cover. Others may have objectively lower probabilities of needing sick-pay schemes—they are healthier. The benefits of various insurance schemes may therefore actually be lower to them.

In the same way, people can have different evaluations of the benefit of a given amount of extra pay. While economic analysis regards higher pay as preferable, other things being equal (i.e. for the same effort in the same surroundings and with all fringe benefits, etc. the same) it does not assert that it is *equally* preferable to everyone. We can have different rates of substitution of leisure for income. This is the same as saying that it might require different amounts of pay to compensate for differences in all the non-pay elements of an occupation for different individuals. Adam Smith's approach to net advantages suggests that it is possible to make fairly strong generalizations about the uniformity of perceptions and evaluations of advantages and disadvantages as a result of values shared by, if not all members of society, then certainly clearly definable groups. Thus Smith refers to the common people and to members or potential members of the liberal profession in such a way as strongly to imply common values within each group. This view receives support from Blackburn and Mann (1979) in their study of semi-skilled workers.

It was recognized by Smith that short-term factors could interfere with the tendency for net advantages to equalize so that one of the conditions he postulates for this tendency to operate is that the trade of the occupation is in its natural state. By this he means that there are no seasonal or short-term fluctuations in demand, and that sufficient time has elapsed for supply to adjust to any underlying shifts in demand. In fact he is working on a view that the various neighbourhood occupational labour markets are in a long-run equilibrium so that there is no imbalance between supply and demand in an occupation at the prevailing pay levels. He is assuming that these particular local occupational labour markets clear. Any observed unemployment is therefore voluntary the individuals choose not to work at the prevailing level of net advantages. If they did choose to work the forces of supply and demand would operate to adjust pay levels to bring net advantages of different occupations back into equality.

Choice of Occupation or Job

We have suggested that individuals make some selection of a range of occupations when assessing their reservation wages. They only bother to form ResW for those occupations which they consider suitable or to which they believe they have some chance of entry. The determination of this range of occupations is influenced by social factors as well as the more economic ones which may be capable of testing.

Even if we postulate that all occupations are equally open to everyone regardless of social background, depending only on the education, skill, training, and qualifications of the individuals, we do not know how different individuals will evaluate the various components of the package of rewards or the job requirements. The evaluation of some components of Job Requirements, working conditions and rewards will be influenced by social and family factors which form part of a person's background and experience. Moreover, access to educational and training provisions and so to qualifications, are not open equally to all. This may be because of the nature of the provision of educational facilities, the selection procedures, or the ability of different individuals and their families to bear the costs, particularly the costs of forgone income during the training period. It may also be because different individuals, perhaps because of factors associated with social background, perceive differently the range of occupations which are open to them. They may be wrong or mistaken in their perceptions as a result of imperfect knowledge about how the labour market and employers' hiring practices actually operate, or about the real nature of the educational system and the selection procedures. Nevertheless, even if their perceptions and beliefs are mistaken they may still influence their actions and so their choice of occupation.

The level and types of skill and abilities needed to enter some occupations may effectively rule out some individuals if they believe that even though they would like to do that sort of work they are unable to acquire the necessary skills. Access to training or educational opportunities can be crucial for entry to closed occupations. In other cases there may be different reasons preventing access or which make it much easier for some to gain access than others. Family connections or relatives already employed in the occupation may make it easier for someone to enter a closed occupation by facilitating the acquisition of trade union membership or acceptance to a medical school, solicitor's or accountant's office or other professional training.

The particular local labour market in which the individual finds himself may also exert considerable influence, although this might be less important for university and college graduates and those with professional qualifications where a greater degree of geographical mobility may be found. For other groups the local labour market will be important in that this will tend to prescribe the perceived areas of choice. Educational performance may exert strong influence on the general blue-collar/white-collar choice, but within these broad areas the choice of occupation will be limited by the type of jobs locally available. In some cases the choice between blue- and white-collar employment may also be influenced. For example it may be that school-leavers in parts of the South of England enter white-collar jobs because there are relatively more of them than in parts of the North. The educational system itself may be adapted to the types of occupations available in the locality, particularly at Colleges of Further Education and Technical Colleges, so that again demand will create its own supply.

However they are determined an individual has certain preferences which lead him to evaluate jobs in a particular way which determines his assessment of their net advantages. Net advantages and comparisons of reservation wages with actual wages determine whether he regards himself as part of the labour supply for them or not.

If actual wages exceed an individual's $ResW$s for more than one occupation or job we are faced with a conceptual problem. We can say that this is a logical contradiction, and that $AW_b > ResW_b$ and $AW_c > ResW_c$ cannot both be true at the same time. For if $AW_b > ResW_b$, he will accept that job because $ResW_b$ is the amount he needs to induce him to accept it. But if $AW_c > ResW_c$ he should be also accept job c, and he cannot do both. One way round this is to argue that it is not possible for AW to exceed an individual $ResW$ for more than one occupation. This would be to impose on our interpretation of the real world a conclusion derived from the logical extension of a definition.

An alternative is to recognize that there can be a number of occupations where $AW > ResW$. The individual then either chooses to maximize in some way, or is satisfied to enter any of the occupations where his $ResW$ is met. It may be that because of imperfections or distortions in the labour market he may not be able to enter some of the occupations where $AW > ResW$. If this leaves him with only one occupation where $AW > ResW$ his problem is solved, that is the job he takes. It would be a remarkable coincidence if this were true for every individual. It is better and probably more realistic to accept that there is likely to be a combination of situations. Some jobs will not be available to him even though the AW exceeds his $ResW$. There are also likely to be a number of jobs where the $AW > ResW$. We can say that he maximizes the excess but we have no way of proving this other than to argue that he could do better for himself were he to change jobs. This might well be so and that might be the nature of things. We do not necessarily maximize other than in the tautological sense that deciding not to change is demonstration of the view that we must be happiest doing what we are doing.

Economic theory no longer places the same importance on the assumption that everyone maximizes their satisfaction or that companies maximizes profits. The notion of 'satisficing' has been introduced. The individual obtains a level which satisfies him even though this is not the absolute maximum that the should obtain. This is probably what happens in labour markets. Individuals, may not seek to maximize either their net advantages or the excess of AW over $ResW$.

Provided that the actual wages are at least equal to his reservation wage for that job an individual will consider accepting it. As there might be a number of jobs which meet this condition we cannot be sure which of them he will go for. There is an area of uncertainty or indeterminacy.

Even though some people do change jobs quite frequently for much of the time most people while in a job do not spend their time daily assessing whether they are maximizing their net advantages by remaining in that job. There is frequently an antipathy to constant change of employment. Change imposes a burden. 'Too much' changing of jobs can also make it more difficult to find another if employers think constant change is a sign of instability.

It is not contradictory to say that for any individual there may well be a number of other jobs which he would accept were he to lose his present one, but which, if his present job remains open to him, he does not try to get. His reservation wage levels for a number of jobs are below their existing actual wage levels so that he would accept them in some circumstances. If there were some change in the net advantages of his present job, as he sees them, he might decide to apply for one of these others. If, for example, a new supervisor is appointed who he finds less congenial, if they tighten up on discipline or introduce some new rules, if he loses the chance to have some 'perk' he has come to expect, or if he thinks the work is becoming too hard as he gets older, he might well begin to think of changing jobs. But most of the time most people seem satisfied to remain in their present job. This is so in some cases even though they know there are other jobs which they might be qualified to get and which they would happily accept if they lost their present one. If compelled by enforced unemployment or job-loss to make a move they could do so and maintain or even improve their net advantages. In the absence of this enforced choice they are satisfied to remain where they are.

The choice of occupation or job may therefore differ according to the employment or unemployment status of individuals. The unemployed may make more deliberate positive decisions while the employed may be more passive and require some significant change in circumstances before they contemplate moving to a different job. This change may come from reassessment of the perceived net advantages of their present job; it could arise from a perceived need to obtain higher income because of increased family commitments or an alteration in the income of other members of the household, or could come from a change in tastes and preferences of the individual. For a lot of the time though there is considerable lethargy among the employed in that they satisfice rather than maximize and so do not constantly examine the net advantages of the full range of occupations and jobs for which they might be suitable seeking to extract the last unit of net advantages. This means that the potential labour supply of their labour to other employers is less than it would were they the absolute maximizers that is sometimes supposed.

Labour-offer and Acceptable Labour Supply Curves

We have discussed some of the factors which may lead workers to offering themselves for certain jobs or occupations. They consider the perceived net advantages of a range of jobs. This range will be influenced by social and geographical factors, family background, education, and training, and these factors may be interrelated. Their perceived choice may be relatively small as with the semi-skilled workers in one town studied by Blackburn and Mann, or may be large, as with Arts graduates. Individuals may be seen as taking two decisions. The first is whether to work at all and the second is what sort of job to go for. The first decision has to be answered affirmatively before the second arises, but the type of job believed to be available and the net advantages, particularly perhaps the level of pay, believed to be attached to the various jobs which might be available, may well influence the way in which the work–unemployment decisions is taken.

To determine what is the supply of labour—that is the number of people willing to work in a particular job for a specified wage—we have to take two steps. The first is to find out how many individuals are willing to offer their labour services; the second is to decide whether or not they are regarded as part of the labour supply by the employer. Not everyone willing to work in a job at the prevailing wage should be regarded as part of the labour supply. An obvious example is professional football. There are many people who would be willing to do this job but who are not regarded as suitable.

Simple economic analysis gets round this by assuming that we know who is a member of a specified occupation. Indeed the only occasions when the employer regards the whole of the supply curve facing him as truly homogeneous and possessing all the requirements of the occupation as perceived by the employer are in situations where there is an absence of what are regarded as free market forces and instead the existence of extremely strong institutional constraints such as the union hiring hall. The more usual situation is for the employer to decide whether the various applicants seeking employment are acceptable to him. It is useful therefore to specify a labour-offer supply curve consisting of those individuals who are prepared to offer their labour in certain occupations or to perform certain job tasks at specified wages, given their perceptions of the various other employment options which they regard as open to them, or which they believe may be open to them, and the choice of unemployment. Labour-offer supply curves include those individuals who are prepared to accept the job at various rates of pay.

Not all the individuals offering themselves in this way may be acceptable to the employer. In the case of closed occupations where certain skill requirements are necessary and specified by the possession of certain formal qualifications, including, if appropriate, membership of a trade union or professional association, the employer may still wish to exercise choice based on other criteria. There may be personal attributes to do with timekeeping, motivation, or commitment to the organization as interpreted by the employer, appearance and personality according to the Job Requirements, and, perhaps, the individual's previous job record. Employers may be reluctant to employ someone who has frequently changed jobs in the past, regarding this as a sign of instability rather than a laudable attempt to maximize net advantages by getting better information about the total job content and full package of net advantages.

With more open occupations there may be two types of decision to be taken by the employer. The first relates to the same sort of personal attributes which may be relevant in the case of closed occupations. However, secondly, there will also be the need to ensure that the individual is capable of performing the task, i.e. that he possesses the necessary skills and abilities or can achieve them within the time-period regarded by the employer as appropriate for that type of labour. It may be that for many semi-skilled jobs this is not regarded as a very serious challenge as many people may be able to adapt to the particular requirements of an individual employer. The relationship between a labour-offer supply curve (LOS) and the acceptable-labour supply curve (ALS) is illustrated in Fig. 6.5.

When selecting from the labour-offer supply curve an employer is trying to find those individuals whose expected marginal revenue product (MRP^*_L) will be at least equal to the marginal cost of hiring them MC_L. In most cases the employer will have a given set of production techniques which influence the Job Requirements so that the worker has to be matched to the existing production methods in order to maximize MRP^* rather than the production methods adapted to fit the particular qualities and abilities of the new recruit. Specific training may be required in order to allow the potential MRP^* to be obtained.

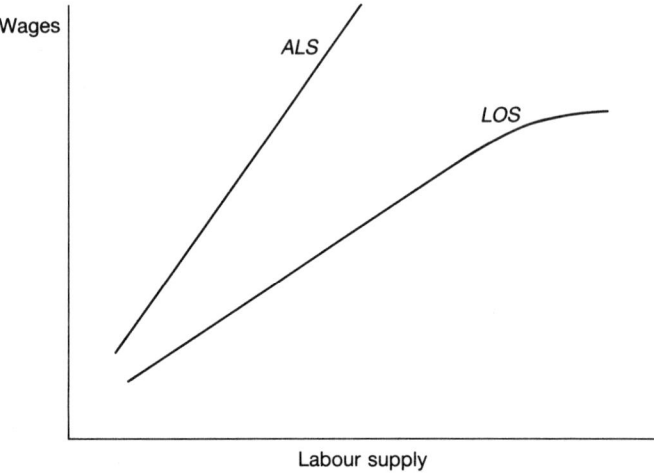

Fig. 6.5 Labour-offer and Acceptable-labour Supply Curves

The cost of this will be included in the employer's calculation of the MC_L and may vary from individual to individual in the labour-offer supply curve.

The type of internal labour market operating in an organization and the internal mobility and promotion provisions and expectations can provide additional criteria for an employer's assessment of the suitability of an applicant. If the internal labour market is compartmentalized so that there is little or no upward mobility between occupations, the selection of suitable applicants will be determined by the general ability to perform the Job Requirements of the occupation for which they are recruited. If, however, the internal labour market is structured with only a few ports of entry and considerable internal promotion and upward mobility, the selection of applicants for certain entry grade occupations will be influenced by the employer's assessment of the suitability of the applicant for upward mobility and promotion. Individuals who might be quite acceptable to perform the Job Requirements of the occupation into which they are recruited might be considered unsuitable for promotion and therefore not regarded as acceptable recruits into the entry grade. Alternatively, they might be recruited but advised that if they do not demonstrate potential ability for promotion they will be dismissed after a certain period. This will depend in part on the rules of the internal labour market which might, as a result of trade union pressure, prevent or inhibit these dismissals. Practices may vary according to the employer's perceptions of the type of labour force he wants both now and in the future.

For example banks may recruit a number of people to work as counter clerks or tellers, and see this as the first stage in a career which leads to upward mobility to assistant manager, manager, or other higher-grade posts within that bank. In Britain there is very little mobility between banks. If there is some withdrawal from the work-force, perhaps because female counter clerks leave employment after marriage or when they have a family, there will be less pressure on promotion and the career development of those who stay can progress. If, on the other hand, there is little withdrawal from the labour force there are likely to be bottle-necks on promotion and perhaps considerable frustration at the loss of anticipated promotion opportunities. While it may be possible to create two different career lines with different expectations—those who will have promotion opportunities, and those who will have far less—the fact that some are expected to provide the future higher grades means that the selection procedures and criteria will be different. Individuals who might be well suited for a non-career grade might quite properly be regarded as unsuitable for entry into the same grade which is seen as providing upward mobility.

Individuals' attempts to obtain upward occupational mobility by changing employer as well as occupation or job may increase the importance of the employer's assessment of the appropriateness of specific individuals and the evaluation of their attributes and potential capabilities. For example a salesman may apply for a job as a district sales manager with another company. The new Job Requirement will include features which were not part of the person's last job and for which there may be no direct evidence regarding his suitability. The hiring employer has to make a judgement about the applicant's capabilities. This is different from the assessment which has to be made if the salesman is applying for another post as salesman with a different company—perhaps selling a different line of product. What is happening in the first case is that the employer is deciding whether the applicant is suitable for entry, not just into a new job in the sense of a horizontal movement within an occupation—perhaps with some differences in specific job requirements—but into a new occupation. It may be that a large amount of job mobility involves a change of occupation.

With 'open' occupation and jobs, particularly in the managerial area, an employer may wish to discourage some individuals from joining the labour-offer supply curve. This can save him the cost of sifting a large number of applications. Advertisements of vacancies may include a list of qualities which applicants should possess and may refer to specific types experience. Individuals may interpret these requirements in different ways so the labour-offer supply curve may still include a number who do not meet the employer's requirements. In some cases an employer may use existing market positions as a screening device. An advertisement for a Manager for the Pay and Manpower Division of the CBI included the statement 'Salary is negotiable, but those presently earning less than £15,000 are unlikely to be strong candidates'.[3] This reflects the view that the labour market works well but that all, or the majority of employers have similar arrangements for relating the present and future pay levels of individuals, similar relationships between the provision and cost of specific training, and the amount and rate of payment of future improvements in *MRP* resulting from the acquisition of specific skills. It also accepts that those likely to be within the acceptable labour supply definition are currently employed in jobs which fully utilize their potential ability and are paid accordingly. The criteria for acceptability can be varied and sometimes not necessarily directly related to the Job Requirements or the possible skills and abilities of applicants. At the same time if the cost of sifting or testing applicants is thought to be high, the criteria may make sense to the employer.

From the employer's viewpoint he has to decide whether the various labour offers are acceptable to him. There may be a considerable labour-offer supply curve facing him in the sense that a number of people present themselves to him as applicants for a job, but the employer has to decide whether they are in his view, acceptable. If they are not, they do not form part of the labour supply curve as seen by the employer. It is both reasonable and realistic therefore to envisage two labour supply curves. There is the *labour-offer supply* curve determined by the various individuals making a choice that they wish to be employed by a particular employer, given their perceptions of the terms and conditions associated with that employment. There is the *acceptable-labour supply* curve as seen by the employer which consists only of those people from among the labour-offer supply curve who are regarded by him as acceptable.

Employers may have a preference for workers who are already in employment as opposed to those unemployed. This would not be a hard-and-fast rule but it may be that, except when there has been a redundancy situation, employers prefer to hire someone who has a job if they believe in some general sort of way that those who are unemployed are so as a result of some feature of their attitude to work or because they have demonstrated less stability in their previous employment. There is some evidence that in times of low unemployment some employers tend to regard the unemployed as 'loafers and layabouts' (Mackay *et al.* 350).

In the week before this was written I was a member of a committee to appoint someone to a vacant university post. There were seventy-seven applicants, of whom eight were interviewed. No one was appointed. The labour-offer supply was seventy-seven; we thought the acceptable-labour supply might be eight but it turned out to be nil. The committee was of the view that if the Job Requirements had been a little different —if the subjects to be covered had been changed slightly or if the balance of organization, administration, teaching, and research had been different—two of the applicants interviewed would have formed part of the acceptable-labour supply curve, although only one for each of the possible two major revisions in the Job Requirements. Until the employer's interpretation of the Job Requirements has been taken into account and the qualification or skills and abilities of the applicants considered it is not possible to say what is the labour supply as far as the employer is concerned.

A number of years ago we did some research at one plant which employed women on assembly work. The Job Requirements included strength to lift the boxes of components and finished products, height in order to reach the stacks, dexterity to fit together small and delicate components of electrical goods, and the absence of colour-blindness in order that the different coloured electric wires could be distinguished. Many applicants who satisfied some of the requirements did not meet all of them. The acceptable-labour supply curve was considerably less than the labour-offer supply. Reorganization of the work meant that less strength was required and it was no longer necessary to be tall enough to reach the top of the stacks. Men were employed to do this part of the work. (The company did not believe that men had the dexterity to fit the components together.) The acceptable-labour supply curve moved considerably closer to the labour-offer supply curve.

It is important to bear in mind that in many cases a major difficulty facing an individual seeking to obtain upward occupational mobility is that of getting acceptance by an employer. The employer's decisions as to who is, or who is not, acceptable, might very well be influenced by the state of the labour market. If unemployment is low and there is a restricted labour-offer supply curve employers may accept people who they would regard as unacceptable in other circumstances.

There may be good reasons why employers respond to a tightening labour market by reducing their recruitment standards by moving their ALS curve closer to the LOS curve. Assume that the employer is seeking to hire workers who have MRP^*_x. With the prevailing wage W_1 and other conditions of service and Job Requirements, the LOS curve provides workers with MRP^*_w where $MRP^*_w < MRP^*_x$. To obtain a worker with MRP^*_x would require wage W_2, but the marginal cost of hiring workers at W_2 would be MC_x and this is higher than W_2 because

($W_2 - W_1$) would have to be paid to every other worker in this occupation and there is a possibility that employees in other occupations would want an increase in pay in order to maintain their existing differentials. If hiring standards are lowered and the worker with MRP_w^* is hired $MC_w = W_1$ and $MC_w < MC_x$. It is true that $MRP_w^* < MC_w$ and W_1, but the employer might still decide to hire this worker. He does not necessarily follow marginal cost and revenue rules. He might believe that the extra output will be needed for only a short time and he can subsequently dismiss the new recruits but if he does not hire them to increase output (or maintain it if they are replacing other workers who have left) he will lose goodwill in the product market and some of his customers will leave him so that future sales and revenue will be less. If he believes that an increase in wages to recruit workers with MRP_x^* will have a ratchet effect on wages so that he will be stuck with a wage level of W_2 even if demand subsequently falls, and that this will spread to other occupations as differentials are maintained, a reduction in hiring standards by shifting the ALS may be seen as loss-minimizing behaviour.

It is worth while mentioning one significant difference between British and American practice. In the States it is quite common for trade union agreements to provide that if there are lay-offs (redundancies) those laid off have prior right to be recalled if the company subsequently expands employment. This right is usually exercised according to seniority or length of employment with the firm. In these cases the question of acceptability for re-entry into occupation is not usually raised. The initial entry as indicated by previous employment is regarded as providing satisfactory evidence of the suitability of the individual. In Britain this sort of arrangement is rare. If a firm is expanding employment previous employment with it may, or may not, prove an advantage. If the individual left voluntarily as opposed to as a result of a lay-off or redundancy, it might well be that the previous voluntary quitting would be regarded as a disadvantage reflecting some diminished sense of commitment. It could, in fact, indicate that after a period of wider job experience the individual realized that his net advantages were maximized at that firm.

Conclusions

Labour supply is the willingness of people to provide their labour services in certain occupations or jobs. This can be seen as the result of two decisions, although they may be interconnected. The first is whether to work at all or be unemployed. The second is the choice of which jobs or occupations the individual is prepared to enter, and the terms on which he will enter. Individuals may be assumed to have a reservation wage for each occupation. This will be influenced by their perceived need for income from work and will be influenced by family and personal factors. Each occupation or job will have certain Job Requirements which together with other features of the work situation will be assessed by the individual and the combination of advantages and disadvantages of each job will provide the net advantages of that job for that individual.

The actual wage for the job must be at least equal to the individual's reservation wage although he will not necessarily accept a job even though the actual wage exceeds his reservation wage for it. There may be a number of jobs which meet this condition and he can at any one time hold only one of them. While we could postulate that an individual maximizes the excess of the actual wage over the reservation and so chooses the job where the difference is greatest, this is probably unreal and empirically untestable in a non-tautological way. Most individuals are probably satisficers. They are content to receive at least their reservation wage and may be content to receive some excess although not the maximum that is, or is believed to be, available to them.

We know but little about how individuals formulate their reservation wages. It is often argued that the level of unemployment benefits has an important effect in raising reservation wages. This is often seen by Monetarists as an important factor determining the decision whether to work or be unemployed. In a similar way we do not know much about how people form their assessment of the net advantages of particular jobs.

The labour force participation reservation wage is the lowest money wage at which an individual will accept a job. It does not follow that he will be employed in that job even if actual wages for it exceeds his reservation wage as he might be employed elsewhere. If actual wages are below his reservation wages for all other jobs then he would accept employment in that for which he has the lowest reservation wage. For the overwhelming proportion of employment decisions the LFPResW is probably significant only if the same LFPResW covers a range of similar jobs which the unemployed individual believes form the major part of his possible job openings. What matters for occupational labour supply, or the labour offer to particular jobs is whether the actual wage level for those specific jobs equals the reservation wages for those jobs.

One important possibility is that if wages rise as a result of the employer increasing wages to recruit additional employees those employed at the higher wages may be unwilling to supply their labour at the previous wage level should the employer's demand for labour subsequently fall. Wages may become ratcheted so that the employer cannot move up and down a constant labour-supply curve. If this is so the supply of curve of labour facing him becomes horizontal at the prevailing wage level. Should his demand for labour then decrease, wages will not adjust downwards, there will be excess supply of labour at the prevailing constant wage level and the labour market will not clear.

The supply of labour should be seen in two stages. Firstly, there is the labour-offer supply curve which results from individual workers deciding to offer their labour to an employer at a given wage level. Not all of this offer will be acceptable to the employer. He will not be satisfied that some of the offers are capable of meeting his Job Requirements, or the cost of providing training so that they can ultimately meet his requirements is excessive, i.e. higher than the expected rate of return he expects to receive through the higher marginal revenue product of these workers. Acceptable-labour supply curves therefore reduce the labour-offer supply curve. It is the individual who decides whether to become part of a labour-offer supply curve. It is the employer who decides which of those in the labour-offer supply form part of the acceptable-labour supply. The standards adopted for this selection may vary, perhaps in response to labour market conditions or changing Job Requirements. There is inevitably therefore an element of uncertainty or indeterminacy about the notion of labour supply. Within limits set by the labour-offer supply curve the acceptable-labour supply is whatever the employer says it is. Employers may be able to shift their labour-offer supply by changing Job Requirements or by providing other facilities which increase the net advantages of his jobs. The provision of transport to work, alteration of working hours, or the introduction of part-time jobs may provide an increase in net advantages to some groups of potential workers so that they decide to re-enter the work-force or join this particular labour-offer supply curve. Using the concept of net advantages, the employer may change the various components in the package of rewards and Job Requirements, but it is the potential members of the LOS curve who decide whether net advantages have actually been improved. When I was a boy my grandfather taught me that it is the fish, not the fisherman, who decides what is bait. The only certain bait economic theory can provide is higher wages, and even then it cannot tell us how much higher.

Notes to Chapter 6

1. Full discussion of this approach can be found in various standard textbooks; see, for example, Sapsford (1981); Ehrenberg and Smith (1982); and Rees (1973).

2. Two good articles which refer to other studies and provide abundant references to other work are Atkinson, *et al.* (1983) and Lancaster and Nickell (1980).
3. *The Economist*, 16 June 1984.

CHAPTER SEVEN

Real Wages, Labour Supply and Unemployment, and Job Search

IN Chapter 6 we considered the supply of labour as a function of net advantages and it appeared that the level of wages was an important element in net advantages. Wages were taken to be nominal or money wages. This was a simplification used to allow us to focus on certain concepts and explanation of job choice, labour-offers, and employers' acceptable-labour criteria. We must now shift from money wages to real wages.

Real Wages

Economic theory generally, and Monetarists in particular, regard the reservation wage in real terms as being the relevant variable and not the money reservation wage. As Friedman states it 'no economic theorist has ever asserted that the demand and supply of labour were functions of the *nominal* wage rate (i.e. wage rate expressed in £'s)' (1975, 15). 'What mattered for employment, we argued, was not wages in dollars or pounds or kroner but real wages—what the wages would buy in goods and services' (1976, 13). However, as we shall discuss in Chapter 10 when considering involuntary unemployment, it is possible that at certain times on certain conditions the *supply* of labour is a function of the nominal rather than the real wage rate. Friedman's first statement may be true because he referred to both demand and supply, but it is not necessarily true for the supply side.

If reservation wages are determined in real terms and remain constant, an increase in prices requires an increase in money wages in order that the real value of wages is maintained. If this does not occur there will be a fall in real wages and if they are then below the real reservation wage some individuals are supposed to leave their jobs. In the aggregate labour supply curve analysis used by Monetarists these individuals will choose to become unemployed if the real wage obtained by them falls below their real reservation wage. More realistically they might search for a higher-paying job in a different occupation, being prepared to accept the less desirable job requirements associated with the higher pay in order to maintain a real wage income.

Figure 7.1 is an adaptation of Fig. 6.4. It uses real rather than money wage rates. An individual's real reservation wages for occupations $a \ldots z$ are shown by RRW_1 where the occupations are ranked by their real market wages $RMtW_1$. Following the discussion in Chapter 6, the individual is assumed to be willing to work in occupations d–k and u–z, but not in a–c or l–t. We will also assume that occupations u–z are closed to this individual because he does not possess the necessary qualifications.

If money wages remain constant and prices rise the actual real wages fall to $RMtW_2$. If his real reservation wages remain the same at RRW_1, the only jobs he will consider are e–j and v–z. Jobs d and k which previously had $RMtW \geqslant RRW$ no longer have so. If the person was unemployed he should concentrate his search for jobs on occupations e–j. If he was already employed in one of these he might choose to remain. If he was in d or k he would presumably look for a job in e–j or possibly u–z if he did not know that he was not part of an employer's acceptable labour supply curve for these because they were closed to him.

The marginal workers, those whose RRW lies between $RMtW_1$ and $RMtW_2$ for any job should be expected to leave when real wages fall. The usefulness of this conceptual approach to labour market analysis in

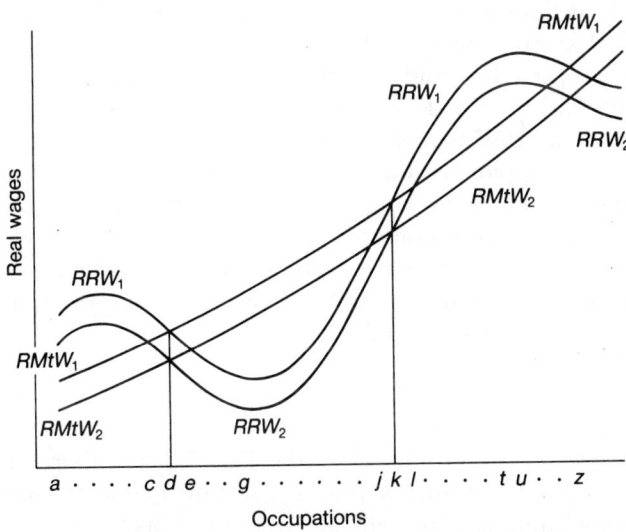

Fig. 7.1. Real Reservation Wages, Real Market Wages, and Acceptable Jobs

the real world depends upon the extent to which it is true that there are this sort of marginal workers. Remember, we are in this approach, assuming that the individual realizes that real wages have fallen as a result of inflation. He must be aware that inflation affects him no matter which job or occupation he is in. If he leaves his present job therefore it is because he thinks he can obtain entry to another job with a higher money wage and therefore a higher real wage, or else he chooses to become voluntarily unemployed.

This sort of approach which runs through the job-search literature, sees unemployment as an economic activity in which the individual is engaged in searching for a job.[1] There is often an implicit assumption that individuals have become unemployed in order to find a 'better' job. The discussion almost always interprets 'better' as higher wages. It is possible, of course, that the individual is looking for other net advantages but as long as we remember that job search or job change may be for none-wage features, we can consider this job-search concept in terms of higher wages.

Job Search

There are two main ways of looking at the job-search explanation of unemployment and labour supply. The more usual is really a *wage*-search explanation. It starts from the premiss that wages for the same sort of work in the same locality are not necessarily identical. This is realistic. (Robinson 1968 and 1970; and Mackay *et al.* 1971) A 'market determined' approach would expect wages, or net advantages, for the same sort of work in the same locality to be identical or very similar. Recognizing that this is not the case in practice, the wage-search approach sees unemployment as a voluntarily chosen productive activity in which individuals are looking for the better-paying jobs. It assumes that individuals remain members of the same occupation and look for better-paying vacancies in that occupation. The higher wage he is looking for provides his new reservation wage for that occupation and as we are assuming he remains in that occupation it is also his LFPResW.

Let us assume that the individual was employed in this occupation at a wage equal to the median (Med) wage. He believes or knows that the distribution of wages is as shown in the Fig. 7.2 and therefore leaves that job to find one with higher pay. He sets his new reservation wage at $ResW_2$ which happens to coincide with the upper quartile of jobs. One quarter of all jobs will therefore meet his new $ResW_2$ and three-quarters will fail to do so. If he does not know where the higher-paying jobs are he must search blindly among the firms employing this occu-

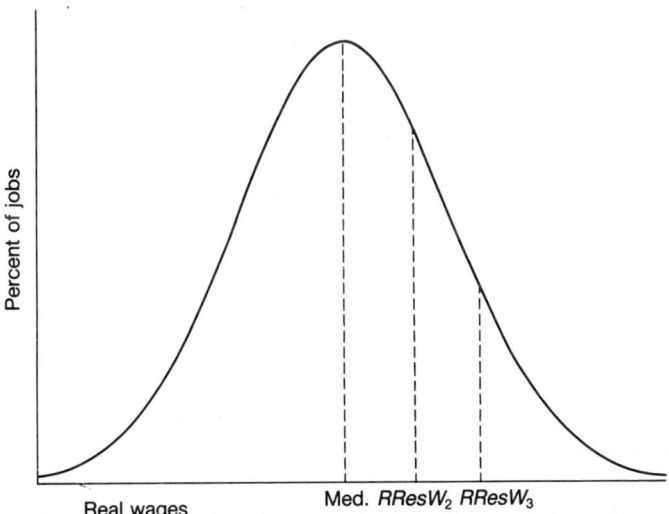

Fig. 7.2 Distribution of Wages and Probability of finding Reservation Wage Jobs

pation, so if there are vacancies he will find them in random way and will have a 25 per cent chance of success with each application. Similarly, if he had settled on $ResW_3$, which coincides with the upper decile he would have only a one-in-ten chance of finding a higher-paying job.

There is a cost to searching: in this simple model he has to give up his job in order to search. The monetary cost is the difference between his former wage and the Unemployment Benefit he receives while searching. He may decide that the cost is higher than the expected gains. This will depend on his assessment of the probability of obtaining a higher-paying job within a given time-period, i.e. at the cost of a given number of days forgone earnings compared to the amount of higher wages he expects to receive and the length of time he expects to secure them. This will be adjusted according to his preference for current versus future income. He is revising his assessment of his expected permanent income.

If he overestimated the proportion of jobs which paid more than his new reservation wage he might come to realize this and revise downward his reservation wage. For example, he may have set his new reservation wage at $ResW_3$ because he wrongly supposed that this represented the upper quartile rather than the upper decile of wages for this occupation. He therefore believed that he had a one-in-four rather than a one-in-ten chance of finding that level of pay. Experience of unsuccessful search may lead him to revise his acceptance wage to $ResW_2$ or lower.

Because we have assumed the individual remains in the same occupation we can also assume that if he finds a vacancy he will be acceptable to the employer. His search therefore is to discover which firms have vacancies and how much they pay.

When an individual starts searching for a job he has some notion of the wage which is acceptable or perhaps which is obtainable. He might be willing to accept £150 a week but think that it is possible to get £175. We will assume that any offer of at least £150 will be taken. As we discussed in Chapter 6 we do not know exactly how this acceptable or reservation wage is determined. It might be influenced by the pay received in previous employment, by what he thinks or has been told is the going or available rate, by the level of benefits received while unemployed, and by elements of comparability with perceived pay levels of other jobs.

Job-search theories emphasize one or other of two factors. They stress the importance of the level of Unemployment Benefits—the replacement ratio—in determining the reservation wage, or they emphasize the importance of the real reservation wage so that price increases which reduce real wages are seen as leading to an increase in unemployment as people voluntarily leave their jobs either to search for others with higher real wages or to become unemployed.[2] It is possible to incorporate both in an approach which makes unemployment depend on the relationship between attainable real wages and real reservation wages where the latter are themselves determined by the level of Unemployment Benefits. There are two employment/unemployment decisions to be explained. Whether to become unemployed rather than remain in an existing job, and the decision to remain unemployed searching for a desirable offer rather than accept one of the available offers. It is clear that these two types of choice are not the same and might not be influenced by the same variables, or if they are, the influence may vary between the two situations.

The second type of search explanation does not assume that people remain in one occupation. They are allowed to change occupation and therefore may be searching for a different type of job at the same or a different wage level. This is a more realistic type of job search. Frequently movement from one employment to another involves some change of occupation or Job Requirements. Some writers (Lucas and Rapping 1970) believe that job change, perhaps accompanied by geographical mobility, is the common way by which workers reduce their reservation wage. However, this may actually represent a more Keynesian interpretation. Individuals may be unable to find a vacancy at the prevailing actual wage even if their own reservation wage is below this level. For the institutional and other reasons previously discussed employers do not seek to recruit them at lower-than-prevailing wages. There are therefore simply no vacancies available to these individuals because labour markets do not clear through the mechanism of flexible wages. Rather than remain unemployed they may then accept employment in a different occupation at a lower rate of pay. Their reservation wages whether in money or real terms may not have changed at all, nor may their preference for one type of work rather than another. The 'imperfections' in the labour market create conditions in which, at prevailing rigid wages, they cannot gain entry to an employer's acceptable-labour supply curve in one occupation but can in another albeit in this example at a lower wage.

It is often suggested in academic literature that the reservation wage falls the longer the individual is unemployed. One possible explanation of this is that the more time spent searching the more accurate will be the information available to the individual about the actual levels of pay available or the pay levels of vacancies. However, there can be other explanations.

One is that the longer he remains unemployed the greater his need for the higher income he can get from working, and even though that increase might not be as high as he first wanted, before he lowered his reservation wage, it becomes more attractive to him the longer he experiences the lower income of UB. Put differently, the individual revises downwards his assessment of his permanent income by anticipating and being prepared to accept a lower wage while in employment. Another interpretation is that he revises his terms of trade-off between work-income and leisure so that the disadvantages of work are seen as less unpleasant and therefore he requires less income to compensate him for accepting them. Or, the non-monetary disadvantages of unemployment, the enforced idleness, the loss of social esteem, the failure to satisfy the perceived obligations as a bread-winner, or just the sheer boredom of having no work and a low income, become increasingly unpleasant and so require a smaller money amount to compensate for the disadvantages of work. The experience of searching for a better-paying job may add to the individual's knowledge of the actual market situation allowing him to revise his inaccurate perceptions of the availability of jobs at various wage levels.

Search theory seeks to explain both labour supply—the reservation wage determines the wage at which he offers his services—and the level of unemployment. Individuals are unemployed because they are searching for a job which meets their reservation wage and are regarded as voluntarily unemployed because they reject jobs which offer less than their reservation wage. It assumes that there are always some jobs on offer. This can be true for some workers only if employers are assumed to lower the real wage offered as labour supply increases and vacancies exceed the numbers unemployed.

In search models of unemployment the individual is assumed to maximize the expected present value of his income over some time-period which is often taken to be his full lifetime. By using the same sort of techniques as are used to estimate one's permanent income the individual is assumed to maximize the present value of his lifetime income and accept a job-offer if the wage exceeds his reservation wage which is determined by the level of unemployment benefits.

Calculations are discounted to provide a present value of the future income streams from wages and Unemployment Benefits and some rate of discount has therefore to be adopted. In making his calculations the individual is assumed to assess the probability of receiving wage offers which exceed his reservation wage and this is determined by his perception of the availability of jobs at specified wage levels. Availability means available to him, and therfore must include his assessment of the probability of becoming part of an acceptable-labour supply curve. He has also to estimate the probable future movement of wages in the various jobs and future levels of unemployment benefits. We can safely conclude that no unemployed individual is able to undertake the necessary calculation, and even if he did he would come up with a different answer from that of the economists who model the behaviour of the unemployed. There are simply too many unknowns for the individual to pursue or get right, and different individuals will make different estimates of the different probabilities. A general model will not therefore explain anyone's behaviour.

Even so it is possible that in broad terms some individuals do behave roughly in this way. Referring to their work in calculating replacement ratios Dilnot and Morris (1983) say, 'Since we have found this exercise difficult, and have used a large amount of computer time to do so, it is doubtful that the unemployed have actually performed the same calculations; but this does not mean that popular perceptions of these relationships are not substantially influenced by what they really are.'

Within the models unemployed job-searchers are assumed to continue searching for as long as the expected gains from further search exceed the costs of search, which is the difference between the expected wages and Unemployed Benefits. There is then a level of unemployment which is regarded as an equilibrium level as it reflects the optimal allocation of time of the unemployed. This becomes part of an explanation of inflation and unemployment as a result of changes in the wage probability distribution. If the actual distribution of wages is equal to the expected distribution, unemployment will remain constant, as will the level of wages and prices. Wages and so prices are assumed to be determined by the relationship between the numbers unemployed and the number of vacancies or job offers. An increase in vacancies as a result of a perceived increase in demand for products leads employers to raise wages which reduces unemployment as searchers more easily find job offers which pay wages in excess of their reservation wages. Employment rises and so do wages and prices. However when the newly employed workers subsequently discover that prices have increased they realize that the higher money wages associated with the job-offer they accepted did not provide the expected higher real wages. They are assumed to maintain their $RResW$ so that what appeared to be an acceptable money wage is now seen as unacceptable. When they do appreciate this they are assumed to quit their jobs and become unemployed in order to search for higher-paying job offers which will meet their real reservation wage.

A variation on this is put forward by Lucas and Rapping (in Phelps 1970). They conclude that non-frictional unemployment as measured in the United States consists of people 'who regard the wage rates at which they could currently be employed as temporarily low, and who therefore choose to wait cr search for improved conditions rather than to invest in moving or occupational change'. Unemployment is voluntary and reflects 'inter-temporal substitution' as workers substitute unemployment and unemployment benefits, for work and wages, over a cycle of economic activity in order to maximize their expected lifetime income and utility.

A crucial issue in this sort of explanation is whether real wages rise when employment rises. If they do there may be no failed expectations on the part of the newly employed workers. The expected excess of actual over reservation real wages may occur. (Rima 1984.) As employment expands there will be more promotion or upgrading opportunities within firms, depending on their internal labour market arrangements and this will provide an increase in real wages for some of the employed as well as opening up jobs for new entrants. If workers are on some form of payment-by-results scheme an increase in output should increase their wages. It is possible that even though real wages do rise as employment rises they do not rise *enough* so that they are still below the real reservation wages of the newly employed. We cannot test this because we have no direct measure of the real or money reservation wages of the unemployed.

A second, different, criticism is that employers may respond to an increased demand for their products and thus their own demand for more labour by adopting non-wage tactics. They may have a queue of acceptable applicants if labour markets do not clear. Or they may lower their hiring or acceptability standards, increase expenditure on training, contract out work, or buy more capital equipment. The job-search explanations do not take the actual labour market mechanisms into account and thus are unable to capture some of the factors which influence the relationship between actual, expected, and reservation wages.

There are a number of difficulties about search models. Firstly, it is not easy to imagine that in the real world a person would have accurate information about the distribution of wages without also having some idea about which firms paid higher and lower wages. Once he has some information about this his search activity is no longer random. He has some guidance where to look for his new reservation wage. The results of search activity are not therefore so strongly influenced by random probability factors.

Secondly, it is not the distribution of wages which is crucial, but the distribution of vacancies. The difference reflects a fundamental view about how labour markets operate. Remember we are assuming that individuals are members of only one occupation. If we also assume that the employer views them as homogeneous with his existing work-force, it is possible that the job-searching unemployed could replace his current work-force at a lower wage. If our unemployed person had a $ResW_2$ he could offer to work for that wage in one-quarter of the jobs and the employer ought to recruit him to replace anyone who was receiving more than $ResW_2$. Thus market forces would lead to a reduction in wages in the top quarter of jobs, and there are as many vacancies as there are employees in the top quartile. If, however, employers do not replace their current work-force with new recruits willing to work at a lower wage, then there may be no vacancies in the top quartile. It is not then the number of total jobs that matter, but the number of vacancies. It is only if employers are willing to replace the existing work-force by new recruits that vacancies equals jobs. If we drop the assumption that new recruits are seen by the employer as homogeneous with his existing work-force, the question of whether the existing jobs are effective vacancies for those with reservation wages below the prevailing wage levels for those jobs, depends on the cost of training them and the employer's views of the benefits of implicit contract arrangements with his existing employees.

For the overwhelming proportion of employees the question of replacement of existing workers by new recruits with reservation wages lower than the prevailing wages does not arise. It is the distribution of vacancies which matters for job search. Arrangements in the labour market mean that searching among vacancies is not random. Firms advertise their vacancies in various ways. Individuals can collect information about wages and certain other features of the package of net advantages provided by individual firms.

This is related to a third point. Wage job-search can be done while in employment. There may be some costs of search but they are not necessarily the cost of forgone earnings. There may be some individuals who do give up one job in order to look for another. The important question is whether the great majority of unemployed have done this. If they have not, unemployment should not be seen as voluntary job search.

The concept might still be helpful to some understanding of unemployment. It might not matter why people have become unemployed so that whether they voluntarily became unemployed in order to look for a better job, or lost their job for reasons outside their own control, is immaterial. Once they are unemployed some variant of a *job* search explanation might explain their behaviour while unemployed, the length of their employment, and the wages at which they will accept different jobs.

If we include a change of occupation as well as employer in 'job search' we add an important element of uncertainty. Assumptions about homogeneity of labour, as we have seen, avoid all the difficult questions about whether or not someone is a member of a particular occupation able to supply the sort of labour services required by the employer. Once we recognize that very few jobs with different employers are identical in their Job Requirements, and that there are few occasions in which it is clear from external objective evidence that a job applicant is able to meet the employer's Job Requirements, we have to face up to the question of the suitability of an individual for a particular job, and especially the difficulties involved when he seeks employment in a job which he has not done before.

An individual searching for a different type of job, i.e. one which involves tasks, skills, abilities, or personal qualities different from those required in his present or some previous job, is faced with uncertainties. He does not know whether an employer will accept him for that job. It may be that he knows the pay level and that vacancies exist, but the important probabilities facing him now are not those relating to the distribution of pay levels, but the probability of his being accepted for any given job vacancy. It is, by its very nature, far more difficult to obtain accurate information about this than it is about the distribution of pay levels. The information is personal to each individual. Two people with apparently similar qualifications and experiences might have different probabilities of being accepted for the same vacancies.

It should be noted that this uncertainty and probability distribution does not arise from differences in pay for the same sort of work. Indeed it arises even if there is no difference in the wage levels for members of the same occupation in different firms. A worker in a theoretically perfectly competitive labour market would have this problem if occupational mobility took place.

The uncertainty about whether an individual will become part of an acceptable-labour supply curve raises difficulties for those explanations of job search which adapt a 'queuing' analogy. (See Casson 1983.) These explanations are right to emphasize the importance of the availability of vacancies and to reject the notion that employers will reduce wages in order to absorb the increased supply of job-searching labour. However, the queues of applicants which form in response to vacancies or in anticipation of vacancies are not like bus queues in which the person at the front gets on first. At best they are queues of applicants for select clubs where the management reserves the right to refuse admission and vets applicants carefully. Being head of the queue provides no guarantee that the next vacancy will be offered, but only that one might be the first to be considered and rejected.

Again job search in the broader sense might help explain the behaviour of the unemployed, and could explain why some people become unemployed. They might be so fed up with their present job that they leave in order to find another different job—not a higher wage level for the same job. What they are searching for is a more attractive set of net advantages in a job to which they can gain admission. Gaining admission requires two things. Firstly, that there be a vacancy, and, secondly, that they are acceptable to the employer with the vacancy.

Adjustment of Real Reservation Wages

After some time spent unsuccessfully searching for a job a worker may revise his schedule of reservation wages to $RResW_2$ in Fig. 7.1. This would restore the original position and he would be willing to be employed in occupations d or k at a lower real wage. Thus the job-search approach allows for reservation wages to fall through time.

One of the problems of trying to discover how and why reservation wages change is that we do not know whether the individual is involved in wage or job search. A reduction in reservation wages may stem from revised and improved knowledge of the actual wages paid or available for specific jobs. It may also represent a recognition by an individual that he is unlikely to become part of an acceptable-labour supply curve for certain jobs which he had previously sought and is therefore an adjustment not of reservation wages but of the type of jobs for which he is now searching and willing to accept. In this case the apparent reduction in the reservation wage for those jobs which the searcher now recognizes as comprising the ones which are realistically available to him arises from his realization that certain other jobs are not open to him. He therefore revises his attitudes to those jobs which are regarded as open to him.

In the United States workers may be influenced by the lay-off and recall provisions. If laid-off workers expect to be recalled to their previous jobs when demand revives they may have higher reservation wages than if they believed they had no prospect of returning to their former employment, particularly if their former firm paid relatively high wages.

Those in employment also have real reservation wages, or *real retention wages*. The real retention wage in one's present job may be lower than the $RResW$ for a different job. People often require an increase in pay to induce them to change jobs, provided that there are no factors within the present job impelling them to the external market. Thus a change in supervisor, or action by the employer which offends workers' perceptions of fair treatment, may lead workers to leave their present jobs and accept the same or even lower pay elsewhere.

There is no a priori reason to confine the downward adjustment of reservation wages to the unemployed. Those in employment might well adjust their $RResW$ downwards as a result of inflation. An employed individual, once he is in a job, may require some premium in real wages to induce him to quit and search for another. His views of the state of the labour market, the number and type of vacancies and whether these are available to him, may lead him to reassess the attractiveness of a reduced real wage in his present job once this is supplemented by some perceived security of employment which will allow him to continue to receive the reduced real income. If he has recently been unemployed and had a period of unsuccessful job search there may be, in effect, a continuation of the downward adjustment of his $RResW$ that originated during his unsuccessful job search period. In other cases, the longer he has been employed the more unwilling he may be to face job search. His present job may have become easier for him and a new job, being more difficult, would require a relative higher real wage. Voluntary quitting to find another job involves perceptions of relative real wages and relative unattractiveness of work and the relationships may well change through time.

The probability of an individual voluntarily leaving a job when real wages fall because of inflation may be greater if the individual is deciding not between his present job and another with higher real wages, but between his present job and unemployment. Here it is not the relative real pay and relative unattractiveness of different jobs which form the basis of the choice, for inflation once it is understood, should have no effect on these. It is the relative attractiveness of unemployment compared with the unpleasantness of work for a lower real wage which provides the theoretical basis for the choice. Inflation may change this. Or it may not.

If the real income from unemployment increases in relation to real pay from employment, standard economic analysis would expect there to be a voluntary movement out of employment. Voluntary unemployment would rise. In the standard New Classical analysis there is little way round this, but in the real world things do not necessarily conform to the New Classical tenets. For many people there is a dis-utility attached to income received for not working.

The notion that there is some level of real wages expressed through the replacement ratio at which people may choose to become, and remain unemployed, while no doubt relevant and even useful on some occasions in some circumstances for some people, should not be allowed to dominate our interpretation of how labour markets actually operate in our sort of society. Precise calculations of the real wage in relation to a labour force participation real reservation wage may, for the overwhelming proportion of the work-force, be a purely academic exercise in the full pejorative sense of that term.

It is interesting though that politicians of the Right who tend to emphasize the UB–real wage relationship as a cause of voluntary unemployment seldom believe that it is applicable to themselves. There is no suggestion from them that they work as politicians as the result of the trade-off between the arduousness of their work and the income they receive. Frequently they oppose increasing the pay of politicians. They would no doubt emphasize the utility they obtain from public service and the contribution they make to the good of society. All that is needed to accept our misgivings about the general applicability of the real wage–unemployment trade-off is that the same sense of public service, or personal satisfaction from working rather than being unemployed, can be experienced by non-politicians, and in particular by those to whom politicians have preached the virtues of hard work.

It is possible that the level of unemployment benefits has some effect on the level of unemployment via a rather different route. (See Casson 1983). If there is some level of unemployment benefits provided by the state trade unions may press for higher real wages even if they suspect that this might lead to higher unemployment. The higher unemployment could result from an actual reduction in the numbers employed or because employment increases at a slower rate as a result of the higher real wages. If, as in the nineteenth century, trade unions were themselves to pay unemployment benefit to their members as part of the Friendly Society functions, they might be reluctant to push up real wages to the point where significant increases in unemployment were likely. If there is some state provision of unemployment benefits this may modify trade union behaviour. Employers too may be less averse to reducing their work-force if there is state provision of unemployment and redundancy benefits. This argument does not conclude that either unions or employers are indifferent to unemployment or that they actually seek to increase it; rather it suggests that with different provisions regarding unemployment benefits the parties to collective bargaining might behave differently. It therefore shifts the emphasis away from the reaction of individuals and their determination of real reservation wages in the light of the level of unemployment benefits, and draws attention to the attitudes and actions of others as they respond to the provision of unemployment benefits.

Real Retention Wages

The Monetarist explanation of inflation and unemployment which we shall discuss in Chapter 11 gives a central role to both recruitment and retention real wages—the level of real wages necessary to recruit and retain labour. *Recruitment real wages* might be seen as the level of real wages which are acceptable to an individual on the day he is hired. Once he has been hired the level of real wages necessary to induce him to remain in that job are the *retention real wages*, and so far as his current employer is concerned it does not matter whether the worker leaves to go to another job or to become voluntarily unemployed. It may be true that the newly recruited worker is aware that the real wage he receives on the day he is hired is unlikely to be the real wage he will get on each successive day. Money wages are adjusted periodically and prices may change daily. The potential recruit might therefore take a longish-term view of the real wages offered by an employer in that he looks at the current money wage and level of prices, and forms views about the likely developments of both money wages in that job and prices. He might also compare the likely development of money wages in other jobs in order to make comparisons of different RAW^*s in the jobs he considers entering. He has two sets of uncertainties. He does not know what will happen to prices and he does not know what will happen to money wages in the particular job he takes or in the others he might consider.

We simply do not know whether the typical, the majority, or any worker when assessing the real wages to be obtained from a particular job looks only at the level of real wages on the day he starts work, or takes a longer view.

The longer the view the greater the uncertainty, as we discussed in Chapter 4. It is almost impossible for an individual to work out precise estimates of the possible developments of his real wage income over, say, a ten-year period in the full range of job opportunities believed to

160 *Real Wages and Labour Supply*

be available to him. There are simply too many unknowns. Accurate comparisons would involve not only forecasts of the development of each firm or potential employer but also the prospects for promotion and upgrading of the individual with each possible employer. It is unlikely therefore that individuals make continuous assessments of the real wage levels expected to be obtained from a wide range of possible employers. It is more likely that individuals in employment make 'discontinuous' choices rather than constantly select from a range of continuous variables. If something happens to make one discontented in one's present job the prospects in others may be reviewed. This weakens somewhat the importance of the continuous assessment of current and expected real wages from other jobs explanation but may be more realistic. We emphasize that if individuals do make comparisons of the present and/or expected real wage in their current jobs with those in other jobs, they do so within the range of jobs which they believe they might get. They need to include some assessment of their probability of becoming part of the employer's acceptable labour supply.

Figure 7.3 charts the monthly movements in real hourly wages of craftsmen in two engineering firms in Britian, based on the wage levels at 1 January 1971. At the date the money wage levels were 75p an hour

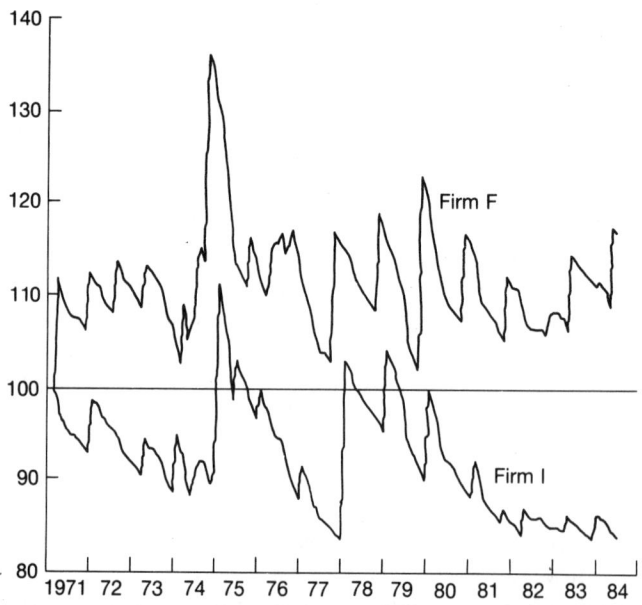

Fig. 7.3 Indices of Real Wages of Craftsmen in Two Firms
(*January 1971 = 100*)

for Firm I and 68.3p for Firm F. By June 1984 these had risen to 289p and 366p respectively. If we ignore the effects of overtime working and an attendance bonus introduced in Firm F the indices can be regarded as showing how weekly real pay varied month by month over a thirteen-and-half-year period.

While the chart would be different for different occupations in different firms, and indeed would be slightly different for other occupations in these firms, it has one feature which is common to all real wages in Britain. Periodic increases in money wages which raise real wages, are subsequently offset by month-by-month increases in retail prices which gradually reduce the real wage until the next money wage settlement. The only situations in which this would not occur would be where there were monthly cost-of-living adjustments which fully compensated for the increases in prices between general wage settlements. While some form of cost-of-living adjustments (COLAs) are not untypical in American collective agreements, they are much rarer in the UK.[4] If we take the period 1977–8 we see that each periodic wage settlement led to an increase in real wages over that prevailing at the previous settlement, in both firms. This is thought to be the normal development in a period of economic growth. Real wages rise but not of course month by month. The trend of real wages is upward but this consists of a series of upward hikes which restore the real wages lost by the intervening price rises, and provide additional real wage gains.[5]

This pattern of real wage movement in Firm I raises some interesting questions. If individuals have real reservation wages and labour markets clear so that if real wages paid are less than the $RResW$ the individuals leave the job, then we must assume one of two things. Either the labour market clears, if not instantaneously then at least very quickly, or there is some sort of averaging out over time perhaps related to expectations about future real wages, by the individual employees. If the first assumption is correct the $RResW$ of those employed in this firm in the month immediately prior to a money wage increase is no higher than the real wage received in that month or they would have left. If this is so it is unclear why real wages are increased in the general wage settlement. The relatively low real wages paid at the end of 1977 or 1978 ought to be sufficient to retain the work-force. Provided that the employer does not allow real wages to fall below that level there appears no reason to increase them in the way that occurred. If the labour market clears each day or each month in real wage terms, those employed at the end of 1977 and 1978 would be willing to stay on at the then prevailing real wage levels. All that would be required would be some system for full month by month indexing to maintain that market-clearing real wage level.

The second assumption is that such immediate or short-term adjustment is unrealistic. For various reasons we have become accustomed to a system of periodic wage adjustments and we accept the reductions in real wages between settlements. There may be some relationship between the rate of inflation and the length of time between settlements so that if inflation became very high, and real wages were falling at a much faster rate than usual, there might be very strong pressure to shorten the time between settlements. Much depends upon people's perceptions of inflation, their view of what is usual, or how far this can become unusual before it leads to pressures to change existing practices and procedures, and the ability of one of the parties to collective bargaining to persuade the other to change. Employers may not wish, or be able, to make frequent adjustments to the selling prices of their products and therefore they will resist attempts to increase their money wage costs more frequently. This is yet another area of uncertainty or indeterminacy in economics. We do not know what determines the willingness of workers to tolerate greater than usual, or greater than expected, reductions in their real wages during the periods between the wage settlements.

Of course, we can *assume* that workers expect the rate of inflation during the period following a wage settlement to be the same as that which has occurred since their last settlement. If real wages are then restored to the level of the last settlement this will maintain their future real wages at the same level. If the current settlement gives them some improvement over the last peak, they will maintain that. If inflation slows down in relation to the gains obtained in real wages in the new settlement, there will be an improvement in real wages at the trough (i.e. immediately prior to the next settlement). Thus real wages at the end of 1978 were higher than at the end of 1977, although, of course, below the 1978 settlement peak. In fact real wages for 1978 as a whole were 4.4 per cent higher than for the whole of 1977 for this occupation in Firm I. They were, however, 3.1 per cent less than real wages in the year 1976, and 4.7 per cent less than in 1975. They were actually slightly less than in 1971 and 1972 by 0.4 per cent and 0.9 per cent respectively. In 1979 the were to fall again even though they started from a higher peak so that the years 1979–81 resulted in decreases in real wages of 0.6 per cent, 3.3 per cent, and 5.3 per cent respectively calculated on a full-year-to-full-year basis. The yearly real wage for 1981 was 9.0 per cent less than for 1978.

If workers expect the rate of inflation during the life of a current wage settlement to be the same as that experienced during the previous settlement's life, they will, of course, generally be mistaken. If this mistake leads them to the conclusion that the real wages they actually receive are below their real reservation wage for that job, they should, on the basis of standard economic analysis, voluntarily leave the job. On the other hand, if they believe that the currently experienced reductions in real wages will be offset by future money wage settlements which more than compensate for the unexpected inflation during the lifetime of the current wage agreement, they may stay on. To do this requires them to change their assessments and expectations of real income from a single settlement basis to one covering a longer-time period.

In Friedman's terminology they may retain their existing permanent real income expectations in regard to total lifetime real earnings, by changing their expectations about the distribution of real income flows among the various future years. The lower-than-expected real income this year will be offset by higher-than-previously-expected real income in some future years. The problem with this is that there is nothing in Friedman's explanation of the inflationary process to give the slightest indication why any individual should so revise his expectations of the real income flows from remaining in his present job. He can revise his expectations of total lifetime income downwards by accepting that he will now have a lower real permanent income. If he does this he has revised his real reservation wage downwards, or his real reservation wage was below the real wage paid both before and after the reduction in real wages.

In Firm I annual real wages fell each year in the period 1976–83, except in 1978. There were various forms of wage-restraining incomes policies during the late seventies which may have influenced people's perceptions of the relative real wages available to them in other jobs but this should not have affected the decision whether to remain in employment or become unemployed. It is probable that the experience of this occupation is not typical of all jobs. We just do not have the information available to test this. Certainly some firms experienced different patterns of movement in annual real wage income, and for some individuals, there may have been promotion or overtime or piece-work which allowed real wages to grow year by year.

Analysis has been done for various occupations in the public sector for which data are available. The annual real wage income for the scale maxima all grades in the civil service from Messenger to Assistant Secretary fell in 1977 and 1982. So it did for scale maxima for teachers, and for the grades of university teachers and of manual workers in the NHS which have been examined. Rates of actual pay in the few private companies for which data have been obtained show the same fall in annual real wages in 1977 with, in some instances, reductions in one of the years between 1979 and 1982.

Real wages can and do fall, not only in the intervening months between money wage settlement, but over longer periods. In Firm I in Fig. 7.3 there has been a sustained downward trend in real income since 1980 and the money wage increases have done little more than provide some temporary relief against this decline followed by some sort of levelling out of real wages. This fragment of evidence does not establish that a reduction in real wages does not lead to an exodus of workers from employment into voluntary unemployment. Even the reduced real wages of 1984 might be higher than the *RResW* of individual workers if trade unions in the past had increased real wages above the RResW levels. It is also possible that the RResWs of these craftsmen were reduced as they saw the rising unemployment of the eighties and fewer other job opportunities. If, when real wages fall, only one person leaves their may be no change in the RResW of all other employees. Because their RResWs were below the existing real wage level a reduction in real wages merely reduces their quasi-rent. A reduction in real wages may therefore lead to marginal workers leaving the firm but if labour markets do not always clear in real wage terms there may well be a queue of applicants ready to fill any vacancies which result. In Monetarist terms, the greater the ability of trade unions to increase money and real wages through their monopoly power the greater the margin between individual RResWs and actual real wages in unionized firms.

The evidence from Fig. 7.3 raises an important question. If it is believed that labour markets clear in real wage terms, at what point in time do they clear? If it is immediately before a money wage settlement why does the employer increase real wages above the trough which exists immediately prior to a settlement? If it is at the peak, represented by the increase in real wages immediately following a settlement, why do workers and unions tolerate the subsequent whittling away of that real wage level? If it is some sort of averaging represented by annual real wage income, why does this vary and in some cases show not only a decline, but a trend decline over a number of years?

It is not always necessary to maintain the level of real wages. It is because people *expect* a periodic money wage adjustment that they may be willing to accept the gradual erosion of their real wage level between settlements. They are not endorsing the month-by-month reduction of real wage levels as acceptable in perpetuity, nor are they saying that the actual real wage in any one month is higher than their RResW for that job on a continuing basis. We can make the situation fit the concepts by saying that individuals have a yearly cycle of monthly real reservation wages which decline month by month during the wage settlement year, but if we do this we must look at a period longer than a year. For as the monthly RResW falls towards the settlement date it also rises at the settlement date. It is necessary therefore that we add some time dimension to our notion of the *RResW*.

The preferable way to do this is to recognize that individuals accept the month-by-month reduction in real wages between the periodic wage adjustments, whether their pay is determined by collective bargaining or market forces. The labour market does not therefore clear in real wage terms in a short run, in this case month-by-month basis. People have expectations about the future real wages which will result from the next periodic money wage adjustment. If these expectations are unfulfilled they may withdraw from the work-force or seek a higher-paying job elsewhere. Or they may extend their time-period and form a set of expectations that the real wages will rise in the next or later periodic money wage adjustments. Firm I in Fig. 7.3 was chosen to illustrate this failure of real wages to return to the levels of previous years. Just as individuals can be supposed to have a concept of permanent income so they can be supposed to have notions of long-term RResWs.

In very similar manner trade unions may regard the short-run reductions in annual real wages, i.e. allowing for the monthly decline and comparing the year or period between settlements as a whole with past periods, as temporary phenomena to be restored and compensated in future pay bargaining. If they have some view of 'entitled' permanent income, or entitled annual real wage, they may be willing to accept less than this in some years in the belief that it will be restored, or they will insist it be restored, in future years. Because neither workers nor unions are accustomed to constant steady real wages whether on a month-by-month or year-by-year basis there is no reason to believe that they base their labour market participation decisions on precise relationships between real wages and real reservation wages at specific dates. Some individuals may do this and move in and out of employment on the basis of very short-run changes in real wages, but this can hardly account for the overwhelming majority of the work-force.

The acceptance of longer time-periods also means that if real wages are falling as a result of adverse economic conditions it must not be assumed that those real wages can be maintained when things improve. There will be strong pressure on real wages not necessarily arising from a tightening labour market but as a result of trade unions and workers pressing for the restoration of the real wages to which they believe they are entitled.

In a dynamic economy we have to recognize that aspirations may lie inactive but strong for a number of years. With collective bargaining trade unions have long memories. If we have to put this in market-based economic terms then we have to accept that there will be an upward movement in collective real reservation wages leading to an increase in real wages in the future which will arise from the recollection of the 'owed' real wages from the past. Economic conditions in the future may influence the choice of time when the pressure will be exerted, but it may be that even without any economic upturn, merely with a stabilization, the pressure for restoration of the entitled real wages will emerge. Perhaps only constantly worsening economic conditions can suppress it.

We again emphasize an important point. The periodic upward adjustment of real wages followed by month-by-month reductions is not consistent with an assumption that labour markets clear in real wage terms in the short run. Yet this pattern of movement of real wages is typical in the UK. Real retention wages are not a constant.

This can be put a different way. The emphasis given to real wages typified by the quotations from Friedman at the beginning of this chapter might be misplaced. It may be that labour supply is not, over large parts of the labour-offer supply curve, for long periods of time in diverse circumstances, sensitively related to real wages. It might or might not be related to the difference perhaps expressed in real terms, between unemployment benefits and wages, but that is another matter. The supply of labour to particular jobs or employers may be much more influenced by money wages and changes in money wages, as may the supply of additional labour represented by new entrants to the work-force. If real wages generally were to fall and—to cater for the Monetarists—there was no change in the replacement ratio in real terms, we should not expect labour supply necessarily to fall. If money wages rose but prices rose faster there might well be an increase in labour supply and I personally would not expect to see any reduction in labour supply on that account. Money wages, changes in money wages and relative money wages, may exert much more influence on labour supply to particular employers and in general. (See Rima 1980 for a similar view.)

There may be some point at which real wages are so low that people decide it is simply not worth while working, but unless this is perceived as a very temporary abnormal reduction in real wages, it is difficult to see why this would lead to massive withdrawals from the work-force. People would still have to eat and pay other expenses, and in the real world, outside the shelter of economic theory assumptions, there is no well-developed capital market which would allow the majority of the work-force in the conditions which would exist when real wages fell so low, to borrow against possible future income. Indeed if real wages were driven low enough we ought to expect to see an increased supply of labour as people sought to work longer hours and other members of the household joined the work-force in an attempt to obtain some higher minimum standard of living.

While we have conducted the discussion in terms of real wages, and will continue to do so in order to treat Monetarist arguments in their own terms, we do make considerable reservations about the undue emphasis and concentration on real wages. Real wages do fall and people stay in employment.

Mobility and Labour Supply

Individuals can change occupations by acquiring the appropriate qualifications to enter a closed occupation, or by persuading an employer that they have the appropriate skills and abilities to perform the tasks which form the Job Requirements of a different occupation, or that they can acquire them. Occupational mobility provides the opportunity to increase the labour-offer supply for any occupation or job.

This mobility can be in two directions. That which is normally emphasized is upward mobility whereby the individual moves into higher-skilled occupations. It is also possible to encourage downward occupational mobility by persuading people to accept jobs which utilize less than their full range of skills and abilities, or less than that amount which they have been using. The latter is probably the better formulation for it is doubtful if anyone uses the full range of his skills and abilities in a job. There is always something else we are capable of doing which is not part of the employer's Job Requirements. An individual may be able to drive a car, type, play the flute, speak classical Greek, play darts better than ninety-nine per cent of the population, or be a very competent motor mechanic, yet none of these skills and abilities is required in his job. Many active lay trade unionists have considerable ability to organize, persuade, negotiate, marshal facts, and understand complicated arguments yet their Job Requirements may make no use of these abilities at all.

We have seen in our discussion of 'closed' occupations that possession of formal qualifications may be a precondition of entry. The acquisition of the qualification may be expensive, take a considerable length of time, and in some cases, effectively be barred to those who do not seek to enter at certain ages. It is possible to change these restricting conditions. Governments may establish training schemes which cover the cost of training and provide income in lieu of wages. It may seek to remove the restrictions on age of entry into apprenticeship schemes. It may legislate that certain job tasks are no longer to be the preserve of certain closed occupations as, for example, when it allows people other than solicitors to engage in the work of house purchase registration. Or it can open up part of the work of one closed occupation to another if it allows solicitors to appear in some courts on equal terms with barristers.

Trade unions and professional associations will often resist attempts to open up their closed occupations. Restriction of the potential labour supply is a well-established way of obtaining and maintaining higher wages. Traditional craft unions may protect their 'closed' jobs even against other craftsmen who have the necessary skills to carry out the tasks so that no 'dilution' by the introduction of non-craftsmen is involved.[6] It will never be easy to persuade organizations to surrender 'closed' occupations or jobs, and it may be additionally difficult when unemployment is high and there is fear of loss of the 'closed' jobs as a result of economic conditions. Nevertheless government can seek to change some of the institutional factors which inhibit occupational mobility. Its greatest role is in the level, type, and cost of educational and training and retraining facilities it provides or finances. An active manpower policy can make a significant difference to the possibilities for occupational change.

A dynamic economy responding to technological change will experience marked changes in its occupational labour demand. New occupations which may combine skills and training from existing occupations with new skills will develop. Training facilities may be slow to respond and the shortage of supply, expressed in the numbers acceptable to employers, may inhibit economic development and impose high costs. If wages are increased to induce new entrants the repercussions from knock-on effects on other occupations' pay may be intolerable. Individual employers may be reluctant to finance the training because they fear the skills will be valuable to other employers who will pay high wages for the trained workers thus preventing the training employer from recovering his training costs. All the institutions concerned, employers, unions, technical colleges, and universities, and the government bodies which advise or influence education and training developments, may be reluctant to move too quickly. Established sectional interests will be represented on all these bodies and there may be few voices heard advocating the needs of the dynamic challenging parts of the economy.

In a society such as ours it is irrelevant as well as irresponsible to argue that the market will take care of labour supply by offering sufficient inducements to generate an increase in both labour-offer and acceptable-labour supply. Education and training in the UK are not determined by market forces. They are institutionally based, reflecting the view that education and training are too important to leave to the vagaries, uncertainties, time-lags, and ineffectiveness of market forces. The greater the need for occupational supply adjustments, the greater the need for positive government intervention to facilitate and speed up the supply-side responses.

Geographical Mobility and Labour Supply

It is widely recognized that there are considerable constraints on geographical labour mobility in the UK. This is not to suggest that no employees are geographically mobile—obviously some are—but rather to emphasize that for most individuals their labour supply is primarily considered in terms of a local labour market related to their present or usual place of residence. There is often considerable reluctance to seek or accept work which requires a geographical move. The extent of this reluctance can be expected to vary from individual to individual, just as tastes and preferences for different sorts of consumption goods do. The increase in the number of married women in employment may decrease the geographical mobility of their husbands. It may be necessary for both of them to find a job in a different area before either of them will accept a move. It may also vary between those in different occupations as some occupations require, or have accepted, geographical mobility as one of the features necessary, perhaps, if promotion or upward occupational mobility is to be obtained. For example teachers or officials in local government may move around the country in order to obtain promotion. Managers in a multi-plant company may expect to move around in order to get more and different experience.

It is quite possible, of course, that this is just the other side of the point that some individuals have different tastes and preferences. Those who choose to enter occupations which require some degree of geographical mobility if full advantage of promotion opportunities is to be obtained, may be those who already have the tastes and preferences which do not lead them to regard geographical mobility as an unpleasant feature to be avoided. In other cases individuals may change their attitudes or tastes as they obtain more information about the way in which the upward career patterns in particular occupations operate, or as their aspirations or family circumstances alter.

In broad terms blue-collar workers are less geographically mobile than white-collar workers. This would be consistent with the view that the attitude towards geographical mobility is strongly related to the career pattern or promotion opportunities and practices of certain occupations.

Housing Policy

Monetarists emphasize the importance of housing policy and the housing market in influencing geographical mobility. The argument is that if workers are living in subsidized council houses (or, for that matter, in any accommodation where the rent is below the market level) they will require a higher real wage in order to induce them to leave it unless they are assured of similar subsidized housing in the new area. This is saying that if $RResW_a$ is the reservation real wage in the present subsidized house, where the subsidy is equivalent to S_1, the reservation real wage in another area, $RResW_b$, which involves leaving subsized accommodation, must be

$$RResW_b = RResW_a + S_1 + R_b + L, \qquad (7.1)$$

where R_b is any excess of rent in the new locality over the previous rent plus subsidy, and L is an additional wage element necessary to induce them to incur the costs and inconvenience of leaving one area and moving to another. L can be seen as a discounted rate of a lump sum which would, if given as a one-off payment, compensate the individual. Thus the individual is assumed to be willing to work for the same reservation real wage in the new location as in his present one but requires additional real wages to make up for the higher housing costs, and a payment to induce him and his family to accept the social and economic costs of leaving his present house. Many employers recognize these elements by making lump-sum payments to their employees who are required to move from one part of the country to another and, in practice, there is often a pay increase or promotion associated with the transfer as well.[7] If the cost of accommodation in the new locality is equal to the unsubsidized rent in the existing accommodation, $R_b = 0$. Because people who leave council houses in one area cannot easily obtain alternative council house accommodation and so may have to move into expensive private accommodation, R_b may be very high.

Because the housing market is not a free market but one characterized by rent controls, there is a very limited supply of private housing for renting anyway so that mobility may be hindered by the availability of privately owned accommodation.

It is the relationship between the existing real wage in the second locality RAW_b and the reservation real wage, $RResW_b$, which determines whether labour is geographically mobile or not.

If U_g is the unemployment in the economy which results from geographical mismatch between unemployment and vacancies, so that we are conceptually isolating this factor from such things as occupational change, and so on, then

$$U_g = f(RResW_b - RAW_b). \tag{7.2}$$

Proposals to reduce council house subsidies are therefore seen as leading to a reduction in unemployment presumably because a reduction in S_1 in equation (7.1) is seen as leading to a reduction in $RResW_b$ and so to a reduction in U_g. However, this should not be taken to mean that if all council house subsidies were removed tomorrow there would be an increase in geographical mobility and a reduction in unemployment.

The argument underlying the proposals seems to rest on the assumption that $RResW_a$, the real reservation wage in the present area of unemployment, is unaffected by the size of S_1. If it is not, then the removal of subsidies so that $S_1 = 0$ may merely mean that $RResW_a$ increases by the amount of the lost susbidies, in this case $RResW_{a2} = RResW_{a1} + S_1$, where 1 and 2 represent the time-periods when there is, and is not, a subsidy.

It is quite possible that following this line of analysis the removal of council house subsidies would have the perverse effect of actually increasing unemployment. If workers' real reservation wage is influenced by their living costs, a removal of subsidies would lead to an increase in the real reservation wage in their present locality. According to Monetarist argument we might expect more people to withdraw from the work-force, particularly if rent allowance is paid in addition to the flat rate benefits of social security. Unemployed heads of households would receive compensating increases in social security benefits following an increase in their rent, so it is difficult to see how this would lead to any reduction in their $RResW$. Moreover, some unemployed heads of household who did not claim social security benefits before the removal of rent subsidies might be encouraged to do so if their rents were increased and this could actually lead to an increase in their $RResW$.

The inclusion of full payment of even subsidized rent and rates in social security benefits may have some effect in raising the real reservation wage of some unemployed, as may the practice of providing rent and rate rebates for those unemployed who do not receive social security benefits, but increasing the rent paid will not lead to any increased labour mobility. Indeed, it could very well lead to a higher real reservation wage in another area. To stop including rent and rates in social security benefit entitlement would, of course, be a major issue, with implications far beyond that of trying to increase labour mobility.

There is evidence that tenants of unfurnished accommodation are more likely to be unemployed than are mortgagees (McCormick 1983). While it might be interesting to speculate why this should be, the more relevant point for present purposes is that this is the group which will have considerable difficulty in moving to another area and finding similar accommodation. The mortgagee may be able to sell his existing property, although this might be difficult if he is currently in a locality of high unemployment, and purchase in a new area. Renters have much more difficulty in finding accommodation and the rent may be considerably higher.

Recent research suggests that council house tenants are less likely to migrate to other regions than are households in other forms of tenure (McCormick 1983). This seems to be due to the reduced probability that search for alternative housing once begun will be successfully completed, or to the cost and time taken to arrange the migration. However, council house tenancy does seem to inhibit movement within regions; indeed, all tenants have a higher probability of making local moves than do owner-occupiers.

Housing—both the availability and the cost—are of importance in explaining geographical immobility. However, we should not let this barrier to mobility blind us to others. Many people may be very reluctant to move. They may not wish to leave their friends and family. They may have strong preferences or tastes for living in certain parts of the country, and with more wives working the problems of obtaining jobs for two wage-earners in a new location may be a strong disincentive.

Local Labour Markets

For a large part of the labour force, probably a sizeable majority, it is perhaps realistic to relate labour supply to some concept of a local labour market. Just what that local labour market should be is a very difficult question.[8] It depends upon such things as prevailing attitudes to the distance it is considered reasonable to travel to work, the availability and cost of transport facilities, whether shift-working or split-time working is involved, and the work arrangements of other members of the household or the age and school requirements of dependent children. The weight attached to these factors can change as a result of economic circumstances or employers' actions. If wages are relatively low in the immediate neighbourhood, or jobs scarce, people may be willing to travel further. The employer can provide transport or subsidize the cost. Hours of work can be altered to make travelling more convenient or to fit in with the preferences of employees, for example evening or twilight shifts can be introduced which may be attractive to married women. The employer can influence the labour-offer supply by non-wage action. The important element in the concept of a local labour market from the worker's viewpoint is that it does not require him/her to change home. To the extent that different individuals or different occupations have different propensities to travel to work there will be different local labour markets for people living in the same locality.

The concept of local labour market as the geographical area within which the market forces for labour might be expected to operate, or operate more sharply and clearly, is well established on economic analysis. For example Adam Smith, one of the great advocates of the desirability of free markets, and someone whom Monetarists generally regard with approval, limited his comments on the effects of competition leading to certain relationships in the pay of different occupations, to those in 'the same neighbourhood' (111). He also appears to accept that different circumstances in different neighbourhoods or localities, could lead to different supply and demand situations, and so to different relative wages for specified occupations. He says that a house carpenter will 'in most places' earn less than a mason, but 'it is not universally so' (116).

Measures to increase geographical mobility of labour can be advocated on two grounds—to decrease the level of inflation, and to decrease unemployment. If there are regional imbalances in the demand and supply of labour, and these imbalances affect the rate of change of wages in different areas, measures which reduce the imbalance by encouraging workers to move from areas of excess supply to areas where there is less excess supply, or perhaps excess demand, should reduce the general rate of increase of wages. It will depend on the relative wage elasticities of supply and demand in the different areas but, generally, we should expect the rate of wage increase in the relatively labour-shortage area to slow down by more than the rate of increase in wages in the excess supply will increase. If the processes of wage determination lead to increases obtained in the tightest labour markets pulling up wages generally the reduction of wages increases in the areas of excess demand for labour will have a greater anti-inflationary effect.

Secondly, if labour moves from areas of excess supply the level of unemployment may fall if the increase in supply in the receiving areas leads to employers demanding more labour as a result of a slowing down of the rate of increase of wages in that area. The migration of labour results in a shift in the labour-offer supply curve in the receiving area and if some of this additional labour-offer is acceptable, employers can expand employment at a lower marginal cost. The key issue then becomes whether the migrating labour is part of an acceptable-labour supply curve. The internal labour market arrangements of firms in the receiving areas will obviously affect the acceptability of external recruits.

Conclusions

Monetarists emphasize the importance of real wages in determining labour supply. Most of the time this is because they are concentrating on the work *versus* voluntary unemployment decisions and it is the real wage which is supposed to influence the individual when deciding whether to work or not. In so far as the choice is amongst different jobs or occupations, i.e. the individual has decided to work but is choosing which job to apply for or remain in, relative current money wages will be the same as relative current real wages. Inflation and the price level affect him equally no matter which job he holds. The importance of the real wage level therefore depends on how important the marginal workers are thought to be. If there are a number of them on the margin of work/voluntary unemployment, a decrease in real wages might induce them to become unemployed; if there are not many people in this category the attention given by Monetarists to real wages might be somewhat overdone.

The notion of job search has been developed to explain unemployment and the behaviour of the unemployed. Some of the models are *wage search* in that the individual is looking for higher-paying jobs with imperfect information about their location, and in some cases perhaps even about their existence. *Job search* in its broadest sense which includes the activities of individuals seeking to become part of an employer's acceptable labour supply curve in conditions where he does not know before applying for a job whether he is acceptable or not, is a more realistic interpretation of what many unemployed, and some employed, people do. Their information needs are now different and less easily satisfied.

The longer the time-period over which expected real wages are assumed to be the key variable determining the choice of employment versus unemployment, or the selection of a particular job, the more difficult it is for the individual to make the necessary calculations. Not only is the rate of inflation uncertain, so too are the changes in money wages in the various employments and the prospects for promotion or upgrading in the various jobs.

Long period assessments and calculations are difficult and probably not made by a great part of the work-force on a continuous basis.

Short-term assessments of the real wages do not seem to lead to short-term labour market clearing in real wage terms for real wages are constantly changing. They rise sharply when money wages are increased and then decline as inflation occurs. Those who believe that labour markets clear in real wage terms in the short run have an obligation to explain at which points in the development of real wages as indicated in Fig. 7.3 labour markets are clearing. They then need to explain the subsequent developments in real wages.

Real retention wages may be less than real recruitment wages. People may remain in their jobs even though real wages fall. The idea that there is short-run market-clearing in real wages terms does not accord with experience in Britain. Real wages are periodically increased by rises in money wages and then gradually reduced by rising prices. The real retention wage might only be determinate *ex post* when we see at what real wage level someone left a job. There is no reason to believe that it remains constant. In analytical terms it is not clear just which real wage level we should take as the retention real wage other than that demonstrated by a person leaving a job. If it is the level which exists immediately after a wage settlement then clearly employers ought to expect some workers to leave almost immediately as price increases whittle it away. If it is the level existing immediately prior to a wage settlement there seems no point in the employer granting a money wage rise which raises real wages. Certainly the notion that the real retention wage is determined by comparing the present money wage with some expected rate of inflation seems to have no practical basis. This notion is derived from a priori assumptions and reasoning. There is no harm in that unless the results of such a priori reasoning are believed to be valid in the real world. Monetarists tend to believe this. We ought to maintain an open mind. There is no reason to conclude that if real wages fall as a result of inflation newly recruited workers will leave their jobs. Some might, others might not. Their decisions may be influenced by the other options they perceive to face them and these options are shrouded in uncertainties and lack of information.

Occupational labour supply is influenced by occupational mobility as well as initial choice of occupation. Changes in relative wages may influence this, but so too can government policies to improve training and retraining facilities.

Geographical mobility can change the labour supply to particular jobs. Monetarists emphasize the importance of housing policy in limiting geographical mobility in the UK, and in particular the role of subsidized council house rents. This argument may be mistaken. If the ending of housing subsidies leads to an increase in the real reservation wage in the present location there is no reason to believe that real reservation wages in other locations will be lowered. This argument is especially true for the unemployed—the group most often singled out by Monetarists and the Thatcher Government as those who should be mobile, whether by getting on their bikes or succumbing to the advertising blandishments of British Rail. Those receiving Supplementary Benefits will be getting their rent and rates paid, as do some lower-paid workers. Increasing rents will merely increase the level of their SupBen. It could have no effect on their willingness to move to other areas.

Notes to Chapter 7

1. The best readable simple account of job search is Okun (1981). However Friedman (1968) and Phelps (1967) both provided early outlines of search models which are used to explain cyclical changes in unemployment. Various authors discuss the concept in Phelps *et al.* (1970).
2. See Maki and Spindler (1975), Nickell (1979), Burdett (1979), Kay *et al.* (1980), Atkinson *et al.* (1982), Minford (1983), Davies *et al.* (1982), and Dilnot and Morris (1983).
3. It is possible that an individual seeks to maximize the difference between his $RResW$ and the RAW for any occupation so that he would have chosen to be employed in occupation g in the original situation. This would in effect severely limit voluntary occupational mobility unless there were a number of occupations with identical excesses of $RResW$ over RAW. It is preferable to assme that the individual chooses any occupation where $RAW > RResW$ and this does not detract from the analysis. The labour market does not adjust as finely as the pure conceptual approach would require.
4. The Heath incomes policy permitted threshold agreements in which were widely operated in 1974 which provided average compensation for price increases above the threshold of the norm but this was an unusual occurrence which in retrospect seems to have worsened inflation.
5. For a discussion of this using industry-level wage rates during a period when the general trends were upwards, see Robinson (1963).
6. See Flanders, *The Fawley Productivity Agreements* for an excellent discussion of this.
7. See, for example, Pay Board, *London Weighting*, Advisory Report 4, Cmnd. 5660, HMSO, 1974.
8. See Robinson (1968, 1970).

CHAPTER EIGHT

Determination of Pay and Employment in a Free Market

Market forces and individual economic agents

FROM Chapters 5, 6, and 7 we can derive an explanation of wage determination in specified market conditions. If we assume that employers are profit-maximizing and that individual workers seek to maximize their utility by trading off leisure for income from work, we can hypothesize that there are labour supply and demand curves which are known and determinate. We will assume that there are a number of different occupations but that everyone knows which occupation each worker is in. We will therefore at this stage ignore the complications arising from differences between labour-offer and acceptable-labour supply curves. We will also assume that money wages are flexible in both directions. The interaction of the supply and demand curves for each occupation will therefore determine the money wage for that occupation. Each sub-market clears so that with the given structure of wage levels which emerge from the interaction of market forces each individual is either employed in the occupation and job of his choice or is voluntarily unemployed as he prefers not to work at the prevailing wage levels. Similarly, each employer is able to hire whatever amount of labour he requires at the prevailing wage levels.

There will be changes in the demand for labour by different employers as they respond to perceived changes in demand for their products. There will be shifts in the labour supply curves of the different occupations as individuals change their preferences for different types of work, achieve different skills, or respond to changes in relative wages and the perceived relative disadvantages of working in different occupations. Individuals may revise their trade-off of work and lesiure thereby altering their LFP reservation wage. If the sub-markets clear each day there will be no complication arising from the expected rate of inflation so far as workers are concerned. The money wage will last for the day and if prices rise tomorrow any real wage labour supply considerations will affect tomorrow's activity but not today's.[1] From the supply side, expectations of future prices and thus the real wage associated with any given money wage are relevant only where the labour market-clearing and wage determination processes last longer than the inflationary process as seen by workers. On the demand side expected price changes may enter the short-run considerations. If the production process lasts for longer than the labour market-clearing time-periods so that at the end of each pay determination period the employer has some work in progress he may base his current demand for labour on the expected prices and costs which will prevail over the full productive time period.

Put simply, if labour markets clear each day and money wages and prices respond each day to changing supply and demand conditions workers do not have to take into account tomorrow's prices when deciding whether the real wage today is sufficient to induce them to give up their leisure and accept the disutility of work today. If prices do rise tomorrow they can take that into consideration when making their decision tomorrow. If the production process takes a week, the employer has to estimate the course of money wages and prices over the coming week, each time he determines his daily demand for labour. Following usual cost-minimizing rules he may maximize his profits by continuing to demand labour even if the changes in money wages and the expected price for his product move out of line provided that the extra cost incurred in hiring labour to finish the work in progress is less than the expected money revenue of the finished product. If the expected marginal variable costs of labour are less than the expected product selling price he will be better off than not hiring labour and leaving the goods unfinished.

The two sides of the labour market need not take the same range of variables into account and in this extreme case of daily money wage adjustments workers need not bother about the anticipated rate of inflation when taking their decisions. This is for the overwhelming majority of workers an unreal situation. Most wages do not vary from day to day. The appropriate time-period is that for which money wages are fixed. If money wages adjust yearly it is the expected rate of inflation over the coming year which should provide the basis for the individual's expectations of the real wage of each job-offer.

Some of the changes in occupational supply and demand may result from factors external to the economic agents such as alterations in the school-leaving age or the statutory minimum age at which employment is permitted, demographic factors, or alterations in the age at which retirement pensions may be received.

Let us assume, unrealistically, but for simplicity, that the market adjustment period is sufficiently short to avoid any complications on the supply side from the expected rate of inflation. The interaction of the occupational supply and demand curves will therefore lead to changes in occupational money wage rates in each period so that each sub-market clears. For this to happen each economic agent must have sufficient information to enable him to make his maximizing decision. This does not require that his information is accurate, only that it is sufficient to enable him to assess the range of possible choices he perceives as facing him. If some of the information proves to be false he can take appropriate steps in the next period and take a different decision. The individual worker needs to have information about the rates of pay in all the occupations and jobs which he believes he is capable of doing, i.e. those jobs for which he might seek to be part of the labour-offer supply curve. He also needs information about the job requirements. The employer needs information about the acceptability of the labour supply offered and the amount that is forthcoming at each possible wage level, as well as information on which to base his expectations about future demand for his product.

There are two aspects of this process. Firstly, the gathering of information, and, secondly, the interpretation of this and the taking of decisions based upon it. The first will be influenced by the sort of institutions which exist in the labour market—such things as the ease with which information about relative wage levels and job requirements is circulated, and its accuracy. There are some aspects of circularity or indeterminacy about this. Individual workers decide whether to be part of a labour-offer supply curve at a particular wage level after considering the wage levels of all other occupations. When we draw a labour supply curve for a specific occupation as in Fig. 6.1 we assume that all other wages are given. This is, of course, while technically necessary in order to provide determinacy, unattainable, for the money wage levels of all the other occupations in a fully market-based economy will not be determined until the wages in all other occupations are known. The wage level in the occupation we are illustrating is therefore something which must be known before we can obtain the conditions that all other money wages are known and constant. But the level at which these other money wages will be fixed depends on the money wage in this occupation which is not yet fixed. The logic of the analysis provides a flexible mesh or grid in which every occupation in every firm and industry is inescapably linked to others. The mesh is assumed flexible in that relative wages can change, but they are all connected directly or indirectly. The position of none of the connecting points—the occupational wage levels—can be known until every other point, including the one we wish to look at, is known. This is an impossible position.

Walrasian Equilibrium

One approach to this insoluble issue, and one incorporated by the New Classical or neo-Austrian School, is that put forward by the Austrian economist, Walras. This says that the labour markets operate *as if* there were an invisible auctioneer. The auctioneer calls for bids from all economic agents—the employers and all possible workers—for the amount they will demand and supply at given wage levels in each occupation. If at a particular price the supply and demand for an occupation do not equate, a further wage level is announced. This *tâtonnement* process continues until there is an equality of demand and supply in every sub-market. Then, but only then, do the transactions take place. There is equilibrium in every sub-market and therefore there is general equilibrium. It is important to note one particular condition of this conceptual approach. No trade is allowed to take place until every sub-market clears. No wage settlement or employment decision is allowed to be finalized until the whole series of bids and offers match exactly.

Neither Walras nor the New Classical School actually believe that there is such an omniscient all-powerful auctioneer who conducts this *tâtonnement* process, but they may believe that markets, including labour markets, behave as though there were. It is not possible to provide evidence that will establish beyond all doubt that labour markets do, or do not, behave as if they were responding to the Great Auctioneer. We cannot, and perhaps even do not know how to, collect the appropriate data to test whether all economic agents are maximizing, and if they are, what it is they are maximizing. We can only assert that if they do not change their behaviour they must be satisfied with what they are doing and therefore they are maximizing; or, on the other side, assert that some agents are prevented from maximizing by factors outside their own control, or they maximize different things at different times in different ways.

The notion that economic agents are 'maximizing' something or other can 'explain' any actual observed behaviour, and therefore none. This does not necessarily destroy the market-clearing by maximizing agents interpretation, but says that the variables change so often that the concept is operationally useless. What is perhaps more easily acceptable is that the amount of information necessary for the agents to behave as if there were an auctioneer either does not, or cannot, exist; or if it could exist, the market institutions are incapable of providing it quickly enough or accurately enough to provide the basis for the assumed behaviour patterns.

We should emphasize the importance of the assumption that no wage bargains or employment decisions can be made until the auctioneer is satisfied that all sub-markets clear completely. This might be considered reasonable on the grounds that agents are maximizers and that one side or the other would be unwilling to conclude a bargain by making a premature settlement before the market-clearing wage was known. If demand exceeded supply on the early bids, individual workers would know that the market-clearing wage was likely to rise and they would, therefore, hold off until the higher wage was obtained. Conversely with employers if supply exceeded demand. As market-clearing requires that all agents be satisfied with the outcome of their decisions and actions in the light of their prevailing knowledge, any assumption about the rationality of economic agents appears to rule out premature bargains.

However, the outcome of the continued *tâtonnement* process could lead to less than expected increases in money wages depending on the relative wage elasticity of supply of different occupations in the totally connected interacting wage mesh. Because there are also uncertainties about each individual's possibility of becoming part of a particular employer's acceptable-labour supply curve, and these probabilities can change as a result of the decisions of other workers to offer themselves to a particular employer as relative money wages change, some workers may quite reasonably decide to make a 'premature' settlement. Similarly, some employers might settle prematurely in order to obtain an acceptable-to-them labour supply. If this occurs, any particular sub-market may not be in equilibrium. The wage may be above or below a market-clearing level but still be preferred by all parties to the employment decisions at the time it was determined. There may be other workers who are unable to make their preferred decision because, although they are willing to work for slightly less than resulting wages, the employers have already made agreements with individual workers which will last for the wage-determining period. Once that period is over all agents can revise their decisions. It is possible that some of those willing to work for a lower money wage may communicate this to the appropriate employers and become part of acceptable-labour supply curves. Employers however may be reluctant to take a chance on the acceptability of these potential recruits if this leads to a reduction in money wages which might drive away existing members of the workforce. Thus the acceptable-labour supply curve, for recruitment might be interpreted as 'acceptable as new recruits provided that this does not lead to the loss of current employees in whom the employer has invested in hiring, selection, and training'.

If either, or both, sides of the labour market prefer to reduce uncertainties by making premature wage and employment agreements the market need not clear in the understood sense of that term.

Analysis of labour markets which are regarded as consisting of atomistic individuals each pursuing his own interests and preferences can, even in theory, be supposed to arrive at the constantly market-clearing results only by the incorporation of some very extreme assumptions about the knowledge and the way knowledge is generated and interpreted, the risk aversion of individuals, and the willingness of economic agents to accept whatever fluctuations in money wages and relative money wages that emerge from the interplay of market forces. It is to the last of these that we now turn.

Wage Rigidities

There are two sorts of money wage rigidities. There may be rigidity in the absolute level of money wages so that it is very difficult to obtain a reduction in the level of money wages for a given occupation or job, and there may be rigidities in *relative* money wages, which inhibit changes in money pay relationships.

It seems to be an observable fact of life that most people resist a reduction in their money wages per unit of time worked. It may be possible though difficult, to obtain acceptance of a reduction of total money pay resulting from a cut-back in hours worked, say through the elimination of overtime but it is much more difficult to obtain acceptance of a reduction in the rate of money pay per hour, day, week, or month. Even in situations of individualistic pay determination, i.e. without trade unions and collective bargaining, people are very reluctant to accept a cut in their money wages from their current employer. If prices are constant, a cut in money wages would mean a reduction in real wages and it may be that workers are objecting to a fall in real wages because they are making some real wage trade-off in their labour supply decisions.

But when prices are falling there is the same resistance to cuts in money wages. People do not seem to object as strongly to cuts in real wages which result from their money wages rising less quickly than prices, as we illustrated in Chapter 7. The constant real wage argument seems to be flawed. Attempts can be made to save it by introducing money illusion so that the individuals are supposed not fully to appreciate the reduction in real wages that is taking place. The increase in money wages somehow misleads them into believing that their real wages are rising, constant, or not falling by the amount they actually are. There may, at some times, in some situations be greater or less money illusion, but this is not sufficient to explain the resistance to cuts in money wages. There is some deep-rooted psychological objection shared by most members of the work-force to cuts in money wages. This objection is not necessarily sufficient to say that money wages never fall, but it does seem to be strong enough to require very exceptional circumstances to obtain cuts.

The most likely explanation of this resistance is that money wage cuts are perceived to be a direct attack on the individual's status and a deeply felt challenge to his sense of fairness. If money wages fall because of changes in supply and demand, i.e. factors outside our control, we do not see why we should accept less pay. We are working just as hard, or even harder perhaps if the adverse market conditions create problems in the product market, and it offends our sense of fairness that we should receive less for the same or greater effort-input. This notion of fairness is related to our input—what we should get paid for what we do. This might be why we can, reluctantly, accept falling real wages as a result of prices elsewhere rising faster than our money wages. We believe that the other rising prices are not our fault or the fault of our employer; they are the result of decisions taken elsewhere. In the absence of collective bargaining our money wages are perceived as the result of action taken by our employer—not the result of the working of the invisible hands of competition or the painstaking *tâtonnement* process of the Great Auctioneer. It may be that when we believe this we are failing to understand the true working of an economic system, or the subtle refinements of some abstract theory, but that need not shake the basis of our belief. As we shall see in Chapter 12 the rational expectations hypothesis (REH) might lead us to conclude that if we make enough mistakes we shall learn to correct them, but that assertion is not really relevant here. We are not here discussing whether we are right or wrong in our belief that our money wages or real wages will develop in a certain way; those expectations or beliefs can be justified or not by experience. Here we are saying that we believe money wages in the absence of collective bargaining are determined by our employer and that our employer has the ability if he so chooses of deciding not to reduce money wages, even though this might lead to less employment. There is no way to prove or disprove that this is what people do believe but it seems to reflect people's attitudes.

Be that as it may, it is asserted that reductions in money wages, even in the absence of collective bargaining, are very difficult to obtain. There are rigidities or downward stickiness in money wage levels. Companies with no collective bargaining for groups of employees seldom cut money wages, even of individuals who are performing unsatisfactorily. They may withhold expected increases, or may dismiss them, but they do not often reduce their pay to the value of their marginal revenue product. It may be that piece-work payment systems do this, but lower earnings from a constant piece-work price list is not seen by the worker as a reduction in his pay unless there has been some factor outside his control which caused the lower output and earnings.

Changes in relative money wages without collective bargaining may be easier to obtain if they result from disparate rates of increase for different groups. Even in this situation though, there may be rigidities.

Individuals' sense of fairness may lead them to conclude that if others are getting pay increases they too should receive similar increases. In real life non-union situations individuals may not know what other workers are being paid, particularly among white-collar occupations. If this occurs then the conditions necessary for the theoretical analysis and the Walrasian equilibrium do not hold as they require knowledge of money wages in all occupations. Real life need not conform to the assumptions of economic theory, and it is not uncommon for individual pay levels to be kept secret.[2]

The sense of grievance which can result from some individuals receiving less increase in money wages than others can lead to them leaving the firm even though they would have been quite content to remain there in the absence of the other people's increases. This might be regarded as irrational, but if it is a possibility, and if employers do not wish to lose them, it can lead to rigidities in relative wages within the firm. The individual might realize that he is unlikely to receive a higher wage elsewhere, but still feels so aggrieved as to leave, or threaten to leave. This notion of fairness is related to *relative* treatment.

Employers themselves have views about fairness which lead them to conclude that certain pay relationships are right and proper. It is widely accepted that pay relationships should be related to the managerial and responsibility hierarchies. There is very widespread acceptance of the view that those who are senior in terms of ranking position and power in an organization should be paid more than those below them. One reason frequently put forward for increasing the pay of chairmen of nationalized industries is that this is necessary in order to provide room to increase the pay of those immediately, or fairly closely below them, in the managerial hierarchy. There is a possible related argument that the pay of chairmen is too low to attract suitable candidates, but this is a separate point. If this second argument is not simultaneously advanced, then we can conclude that chairmen are willing to continue at their present money wage level. There is no economic reason to increase their pay when that of their subordinates rises *unless* relative pay influences their perceptions of fairness and their willingness to continue working effectively in that organization. This is not the same as differences in the pay of occupations influencing an individual's choice of which occupation or job to apply for. The arguments do not say that if the pay of the chief accountant or product designer exceeded that of the chairman the chairman would transfer his occupation within the organization, as might be the case if external pay relationships changed.[3] It is the acceptance of certain notions of equity and fairness held by management as well as individual workers which imposes the constraints on internal pay relationships. The larger the firm, and perhaps the more it is influenced by modern notions of good personnel management practices, the stronger these restraints may be. This is not to say that internal pay differentials cannot widen or narrow, but rather that there are certain views about the ranking of pay of certain occupations which may restrict the ability of a firm to respond to market forces, even when there is no collective bargaining, and when no reductions in money wages are suggested.

Changes in relative money wages ought to induce labour mobility. Individuals should be expected to try to move towards the relatively higher-paying jobs. The first effect will be an increase in labour-offer supply curves to those jobs where job search and job application are accompanied by unemployment, if people search only, or best, when they are not currently employed. There will be an increase in frictional unemployment. If some of these searching individuals cannot enter an acceptable-labour supply curve there are three possible developments. They may continue to search despite their increasing experience of unsuccessful search for acceptance in the job of their choice. This will lead to a longer-term increase in frictional unemployment. Secondly, they may decide that if they cannot enter the new job of their choice they will not work at all but become voluntarily unemployed. If the change in relative wages were caused by a reduction in the money wage in their previous job we can argue whether it was the reduction in money or real wages in that job which led to the rise in voluntary unemployment. This may increase measured unemployment, but conceptually does not increase frictional but only voluntary unemployment. Thirdly, they may become part of the labour-offer supply curve of some other occupation, including their previous one, which may—will, in terms of the market-clearing model—lead to lower rates of increase, or a reduction in, money wages in the other occupations, if they become part of the acceptable-labour supply curves.

It should be accepted that relative pay and notions of fairness about relative pay, and changes in relative pay, influence labour market behaviour from both the supply and demand sides. These attitudes may inhibit the ability of labour markets to clear in the economic analysis sense because they do not necessarily operate through the expected labour market-clearing activities. Individuals may change jobs because of their perceived unfair treatment, even though they cannot obtain better material benefits elsewhere. Employers may prevent market forces from determining relative pay levels because of their fears that this would adversely affect motivation and performance, or lead to costly staff turnover, or because it would be contrary to the managerial hierarchy. As a result, internal money wage relationships may be rigid or sticky.

External money wage relationships may be more flexible. Individuals may accept that changes in money wages elsewhere lead to different external relativities. If the markets clear, workers will move in the next period and return the system to equilibrium. To forestall this employers may raise their wages, so maintaining the previous external relativities. Even if there is in fact little threat of workers' mobility employers may still maintain relativities out of a sense of fairness.

There is another reason why relative wages may be sticky. In the absence of the Great Auctioneer it is in fact extremely difficult, perhaps impossible, for an individual employer to know what the market-clearing wage level for each occupation is. All he really knows is that at the wage he is paying he is, or is not, able to recruit and maintain a work-force. He could be paying more than necessary and this might show up in longer than usual queues of job applicants, provided that they in turn have sufficient accurate information to lead them to offer their labour. Even if the queues are no bigger, they may consist of better-qualified applicants, so that even if there are no unfilled vacancies it might be possible for the employer in some situations to replace his existing employees by new recruits. In practice it does not seem that employers follow these possibilities through. They establish certain rates of pay and maintain them, and generally move broadly in line with other employers. Rather than risk falling behind in relative wages, employers tend to give money wage increases which keep them in step. This can be explained as maximizing behaviour in that the costs of misjudging the market exceed the cost of increasing money wages broadly in line with others. Management practices can lead to forms of pay comparability which are not based on the employer's acceptance of some notions of fairness but on some economic assessment of the costs and benefits of moving with others. It may be effective; it may satisfy their risk aversion but it is not market-clearing.

The existence of wage rigidities may create difficutlies for an economy subject to structural change. Labour is geographically immobile and is also often reluctant to leave one industry or type of job for another. Where there is geographical concentration of industry with dominance of local labour markets, so that there are relatively few employment opportunities in other industries in the locality there is a very marked reluctance to leave the dominating industry even when it is in a period of sustained decline. This may be especially marked if the industry's work-force has specialized skills which may have few direct applications elsewhere, as with shipbuilding or mining. A 'free market' approach based on market-clearing might require very large reductions in wages indeed before there was sufficient voluntary movement out of the industry to bring labour-offer supply and demand into equilibrium. It is much more likely that there would be a non-market-clearing situation in which wages were pegged above their market-clearing level and there was a queue of applicants for unavailable vacancies. Employers would probably maintain wages at this higher level as a result of their social judgements about a 'fair' or reasonable wage. This might be lower than the workers' views of a fair and reasonable wage but would be higher than the market-clearing level.

If there are structural changes taking place in an economy, movements in relative wages are seen as necessary for two reasons: to discourage workers in the declining industries from staying there, and to encourage them (and others) to move to the expanding sectors. Monetarists seeking to expand employment by reducing real wages may, in the real world, exert pressure on trade unions and seek to reduce their powers. However, if this is successful and results in a general reduction in real wages it will not of itself tackle the problem of relative real wages. The British economy seems to have the worst combination of features; it has structural problems, labour immobility, and a considerable degree of wage rigidities. The greater the barriers to mobility the greater must be the changes in relative wages in order to induce mobility. This is true with or without trade unions.

Pre-Keynesian economists were demoralized by the failure of policies to encourage mobility (Casson 1983). Despite attempts to encourage both mobility of labour and of new investment to create jobs in areas of high unemployment, the underlying problem seems not to have changed much in the past fifty years.

If money wages and relative money wages do not adjust in a market-clearing way the general level of prices cannot respond to bring demand and supply of products, labour, and real money balances into equilibrium. The existence of long-term contracts means that, at very least, the adjustment processes must take longer than the short-term movements in money supply. The non-synchronization of long-term contracts inhibits the emergence of a lagged equilibrium as the various sub-markets will, if they clear, be clearing at different times in response to perceived and expected changes in relative money wages and price levels. It can be seriously doubted whether even anticipated changes in the money supply can lead to a general equilibrium based on equilibrium and market-clearing in all sub-markets in such circumstances, but there can be no argument that unanticipated changes in the money supply cannot lead to the same adjustment in prices and wages with these fixed contracts in the way that might occur if there were a Great Auctioneer. The decisions on the quantities of output and employment will not be the same as in a Walrasian all-sub-market-clearing situation.

One further development of this might be to distinguish between the short- and the long-run demand for money and, following Walters (1965), conclude that the adjustment of real balances to their equilibrium level is a long-run development. This would mean that in the real world the real balance effects work through on prices only slowly. If this is so it takes a long time for changes in the money supply to work through; 'prices take years to adjust to such fluctuations' (Laidler 1982, 96). Prices cannot respond quickly enough to keep markets continuously cleared in response to fluctuations in the money supply. This has crucial implications for the New Classical School as we shall see in Chapters 12 and 13. There, when considering the role of expectations and how they are formed, the strong New Classical School concludes that the mere credible announcement of a reduction in the rate of growth of money supply will be sufficient to change both the expectations of economic agents and their behaviour, so that inflation will fall. Quite apart from the issues involved in the formation of expectations, the present argument shows that *even* if agents respond in the way suggested by the New Classical economists, prices would not move very quickly. The assumptions about rationality of agents are not enough. Other factors would prevent the quick adjustment to an all sub-market-clearing equilibrium. Laidler, as a Gradualist Monetarist, concludes that the proposition that markets always clear 'as if' there were an auctioneer, if open to an empirical test, will be likely to be found wanting. 'If this conclusion is accepted, then neo-Austrian economics must be regarded as constituting a fundamentally unsatisfactory account of the world we live in' (1982, 101).

Conclusions

One approach to labour market analysis is based on the assumed behaviour of individual workers and employers acting in an atomistic way with each economic agent 'maximizing' wages, net advantages, profits, or whatever it is that motivates him. If economic agents take their decisions based on real wages, expected prices, and real product wages, and if there are differences in the time-periods for which money wages are set, in which prices change, and over which production and employment decisions are taken, it does not follow that the market is always cleared in that supply and demand, at given wage levels with expected rates of change of wages and prices are always exactly in balance. It is extremely difficult to visualize how all the separate occupational, regional, and job labour markets can clear simultaneously. The decision by an individual worker as to which job he should apply for cannot be taken until the wages and conditions of employment of every other job which he might consider, are known. As the market-clearing wage for each job is dependent on the market-clearing wage for every other job, simultaneous market-clearing cannot take place. The assumption that markets operate as if there were a Great Auctioneer does not in fact get us off this hook. He cannot clear the market until every participant has the required interdependent sets of wage levels. Walrasian equilibrium might have some sort of intellectual appeal as a clever and sophisticated account of how well the market and each sub-market might operate in certain very particular conditions, but as an explanation of what we might expect in the real world—even one without trade unions—it is of no help. To the extent that anyone believes that it actually offers an attainable ideal, or even a criterion against which to judge the real world, actual practices, or policy proposals, it does harm. To base judgements of the real world on unreal notions and criteria is neither helpful nor rational.

Notions of fairness influence wage levels even in an atomistic market where there are no trade unions. They create rigidities in both wage levels and wage structures, i.e. relative wage levels. Individual workers may resist cuts in money wages—particularly if they believe that money wages which are paid by their employer should be related to the effort-input which they as workers are providing for that employer. They may also have notions of equity based on the treatment given to other workers in the same establishment. Notions of fairness are not confined to individual workers. Employers and managers have them too, and their notions of fairness frequently reflect an administrative or managerial hierarchy view of relative pay.

Because employers may have production time-periods longer than the employment contract it may be to their advantage to make premature wage bargains, i.e. to agree on a wage level before the market-clearing activity is finalized. Workers may prefer this if they are risk-averse and fear that a market-clearing equilibrium may leave them either without a job at certain reservation wages, or with a lower wage than they will get from a premature bargain.

Even if changes in the supply of money feed through to prices and thus wages and possibly employment, if the process takes time markets will not be cleared continuously. The neo-Austrian and New Classical versions of labour market behaviour cannot provide satisfactory explanations. Because labour is imperfectly mobile and there are wage rigidities it may be very difficult indeed for relative wages to fall sufficiently to lead to market-clearing. It is much more likely that there will be excess supply of labour with wages above their market-clearing level. An economy such as the UK subject to structural change will face severe problems. Either there will have to be very significant changes in relative wages, or there will be sustained unemployment unless it is possible to generate employment-creating activity. Monetarists believe that employment generation will result from a reduction in real wages; but that in itself will be insufficient to deal with the structural problems which require, on a Monetarist or free market view, changes in relative wages, a point emphasized by Hayek. What is unclear is how the changes in relative wages will be obtained. General attacks on trade union power cannot lead to this. While an atomistic free market model might suggest that relative wages will, or should, be determined by the decisions of the millions of labour market participants, this is unreal. Even without unions wages are interconnected. The Monetarists tend not to discuss the detailed workings of labour markets. In this they may be wise for to do so would emphasize the deficiencies of their approach. They, much more than institutionalists, need an explanation of how relative wages will respond, in the real world, to their policies. Their silence is both wise and necessary. They have no explanation and to try to offer one would expose the untenability of their reliance on a free market model.

Notes to Chapter 8

1. We are ignoring the possibility that inflation is so rapid that prices rise significantly during the day on an hour-to-hour basis. Although this could happen it is so exceptional as to be outside the bounds of normalcy for us. Alternatively we can assume that the markets clear each hour.
2. In one American university secrecy extended to the point that professors' pay-slips which were in sealed envelopes had to be delivered personally to the individual. If he was not available the envelope could not be left with the usual mail but was locked in a safe until personally claimed. I was told that this was to avoid the possibility that anyone discovered how much others were paid. There was no other reason. It would not be to prevent theft as no cheques were in the envelopes, payments being made by direct bank transfer. In another American university both pay-slips and cheques were put in my mail box without an envelope.
3. I sought to persuade the late and lamented Royal Commission on the Distribution of Income and Wealth in its study of top salaries that there was no good *economic* reason in the usual narrow sense of that word, to prevent a chief technologist or designer from being paid more than the chief executive, particularly where the chief executive did not have the ability to do the chief designer's job. British Leyland was an obvious case in point. There might be social or institutional problems but these are not an inherent part of the usual market approach Appropriate action to deal with them might enable the pay of some groups to rise without jacking up the pay of more senior executives. Not surprisingly, perhaps, I was unsuccessful.

CHAPTER NINE

Collective Wage Determination, Trade Unions, and Power

ONCE we recognize that collective bargaining takes place we are compelled to accept the inappropriateness of a model based on the atomistic behaviour of individual economic agents. If we are trying to understand the real world it is the *irrelevance* of a completely atomistic individual-based model that compels us to reject it: we are not basing this conclusion on a view of whether or not the economic model represents a *desirable* state of affairs; we are simply saying that it does not represent the world we are trying to explain.

So that the following comments can be seen in their context my own view is that collective bargaining is an inherently superior method of determining terms and conditions of employment. This is a value-judgement. The extension of notions of democracy from the political to the industrial areas of life is considered so valuable that measures to move the economy closer to the conditions assumed in the individual-based sub-market auctioneering type model are considered less desirable, no matter what the theoretical and conceptual juggling in terms of individual preferences and utility-maximization might assert. The denial of the advantages of collective action to obtain some redress of the inherent inequality of power in an individual-based model cannot, in my judgement, be compensated by whatever theoretical niceties emerge from the linguistic analysis of welfare maximization.

This judgement is based on a view that the market model of perfect competition reflects an undesirable type of economy. The assumptions that there is a very large number of small firms and employers so that no one of them can by his own actions, wittingly or unwittingly, affect the level of wages or prices in any sub-market, would in effect deny us the advantages and benefits of large-scale production and many economies of scale. 'Small' may be 'beautiful' but it can also be expensively inefficient. This is not a plea for massive impersonal organizations as the providers of employment but a recognition that perfect competition has a price-tag. In the absence of the exchange of information with strong possibilities of collusion, perfect competition may also be extremely unstable or lead to economic stagnation with less investment and growth.[1]

Not only is perfect competition by no means a desirable sort of economy in which to live, it does not exist. In the real world many individuals are in fact faced by a choice of jobs where the employer does have the power to determine, or by his own actions influence, the wage level offered. Very few if any employers are faced with a perfectly elastic supply curve of homogeneous labour at the prevailing wage rate. Wages and other terms of employment are not determined solely by market forces even when there are no trade unions. Individual workers are subject to some degree of employer discretion, not only in respect of wages, but in the hiring decision as well. Because of the assumption in the market-based models that there is homogeneity of labour, either in general or within an occupation, the theorist need not concern himself with the possibility of discrimination against individuals or groups. It is assumed that the profit-maximizing employer would not discriminate because it would be unprofitable to do so. This is not the case in the real world.

On my value-judgement, trade unions and collective bargaining are desirable, firstly, because even if perfect competition or some version of it did exist it would be undesirable, and, secondly, it does not exist anyway. This is not to say that all trade unions, and all their behaviour in collective bargaining, are always regarded as laudable. Nor are the results of collective bargaining, the joint decisions taken by both employers and unions, always desirable.

There are separate elements. There is the *processs* of collective bargaining and the institutions that are established, which provide the *system* by which wage and employment decisions are taken. Those decisions are the *results*. The results from any system, be it collective bargaining, market forces, or statutory intervention, can be assessed in terms of their effects on such things as inflation, employment, and productivity. The preference for one system rather than another may be influenced by the sort of results expected to emerge from it, but can also be based on the nature of the system itself.

This is why collective bargaining may be preferred as a *system* even if some of the results are less desirable than those which would emerge from some other system.[2] For example it is argued that collective bargaining leads to higher inflation and lower employment than would a 'market forces' system. This may be true. We may still prefer collective bargaining as a system because it allows individual workers to have some countervailing power against their employer. Others may agree in part but believe that the balance of power has swung too far so that it is desirable to shift the relative distribution of power towards employers.

Labour market and industrial relations policies may be concerned with changing either the system or the results which are likely to emerge from a particular system or combination of processes. They involve the choice and balancing of different value-judgements and preferences. At the end of the debate it is not a question of fact which can be resolved by empirical evidence but a matter of values and beliefs about the sort of society in which we wish to live and the sort of economic gains or costs we are prepared to experience in order to obtain some of our value-judgement-based conditions. Frequently it comes down to a difference of opinion between our principles and our opponents' prejudices.

The question of whether trade unions are or are not desirable rests therefore not on whether they conform to or hinder the assumed workings of some theoretical model, but whether they contribute to the sort of society we wish to see, and we may wish to preserve or establish a particular system and at the same time alter the results which emerge from it. In very broad terms Monetarists tend to want to change the system of labour market institutions and industrial relations in order to move it closer to a market-based model, so that the results which emerge—the wage and price levels and changes therein—bear a closer relationship to those which they believe would emerge from their market model. In particular they wish the labour market results to be determined by the forces of supply and demand emanating from the money supply environment.

Keynesians are more likely to support the maintenance of the existing system of collective bargaining or a modified version of it, supplemented perhaps by new institutions or changes to speed up and sharpen labour market responses to economic forces and to produce different results. British Keynesians in particular are more likely to support measures of labour market intervention which have structural effects such as active manpower and training policies and other measures to encourage occupational mobility. They may also support incomes policies which seek to influence the results which emerge from collective bargaining or the market mechanisms but which do not totally rely for their effect on changes in aggregate nominal demand. Aggregate demand and supply are not considered irrelevant but are not given the sole burden of controlling inflation.[3] A few Monetarists, the most notable one being Laidler, are not averse to measures to speed up labour market adjustment mechanisms, but would not support incomes policies.

No matter what value-judgements we hold it is necessary for us to recognize the existence of trade unions if we wish to understand the workings of our economy. Trade unions and collective bargaining make a difference to the way labour markets operate in two important respects. Firstly, a collective agreement imposes a collective reservation wage for the firm or industry which may be higher than the individual reservation wage of the marginal employees or of the best workers in the acceptable labour supply curve. Similarly this should always be the case with a statutory minimum wage. There is absolutely no point in the state setting a minimum wage, or a Wages Council wage, which is not higher than the reservation wage of acceptable workers. Secondly, a trade union may have preferences and priorities different from its individual members.

Trade Union Objectives

In one sense we cannot talk about the objectives of trade unions other than to say that unions are organizations to protect and advance the interests of their members as these are expressed through the various policy-making processes within the unions. This gives us some indication of what the objectives of unions might be, but only in the very broadest and most general way. Because there are different sorts of unions covering different types of members facing different situations in various industries and companies we ought not to expect individual unions to pursue the same specific objectives at any given time.

Unions differ in their membership coverage. There are various ways of classifying unions, such as craft, industrial, or general. Another distinction is between open and closed unions. Open unions recruit members from a wide range of industries or occupations. Closed unions may restrict their membership to specific occupations or grades, industries or localities. Open unions may be much more concerned to extend their membership to new industries, firms, or occupations and their bargaining strategies may be influenced by their recruitment policies. Internal trade union structures differ. Some are centralized while others give considerable autonomy to local branches. Some are faced by a single large employer, say a nationalized industry, and the national agreement is the major determinant of pay levels and pay changes. Others such as the T & GWU represent members in a wide variety of industries.[4]

Generalizations about trade union objectives are unlikely to be very helpful in explaining the responses and actions of trade unions in a specific bargaining situation. Nevertheless there has been considerable discussion of trade union objectives and these objectives are often incorporated in models which seek to explain wage and employment determination.

This is well illustrated in the Ross–Dunlop disagreement as to whether unions are essentially political or economic in their attitude towards any wage–employment trade-off.[5] The Ross view is that unions are political in the sense that the leadership believes that it must respond to the political pressures emanating from its membership as well as from its own internal criteria of performance. On this view unions may not see a wage–employment trade-off, or while they may recognize that one exists, may not give it much priority in their bargaining. The dominating objective is to keep up with the results of other unions which form their orbits of coercive comparison. Dunlop argued that unions are economic organizations in that they do recognize the wage–employment trade-off and that this influences the size of wage settlements they press for. This is not to deny that comparability of results plays an important part in bargaining, as is shown by Dunlop's use of the concept of customary wage contours.

Part of the Ross–Dunlop debate can be seen not as a difference of opinion about union objectives in wage bargaining but as different stages of a process. The political aspects which Ross emphasizes may describe the processes by which trade unions take their policy decisions and the importance of maintaining some degree of internal cohesion. He discusses *how* decisions are made and draws attention to the possible importance of the distinction between the leadership and the membership. Dunlop is more concerned with the end-result and believes that unions adopt wage policies which maximize their membership. It is possible to produce some reconciliation between the two approaches which might explain union behaviour at certain times. For example if a union is recruiting more lower-paid less-skilled workers it might press for a reduction in wage differentials. Ross would explain this in terms of the internal pressures within the union which influence policy-makers to give precedence to the aims of certain groups of members—the unskilled. Dunlop could provide the same sort of explanation by emphasizing that in order to increase (maximize) membership the union was adopting a particular wage approach. What is less explicit in the Dunlop approach is why some unions should seek to increase their membership by expanding the unskilled grades and others not. Ross could more easily incorporate this by analysis of specific cases which led to different policies. Neither approach could forecast that all unions would follow a particular predictable course of action. Neither should they try to because unions do not all follow such a predictable line.

To the extent that there actually are two different wage strategies open to trade unions we cannot be certain what a union will do if faced with the threat of a reduction in employment if it increases real wages. A Dunlop view might conclude that the union would contemplate the effects of the trade-off and decide accordingly. A Ross view would emphasize the importance of what had happened in the settlements of the other unions. This absence of clear determinacy is not because of something special in the nature of trade unions. Exactly the same indeterminacy can arise in the case of individuals determining their real reservation wage. One individual may base his $RResW$ on what he perceives is happening to the actual real wage of others. If he thinks their real wage is rising he may raise his $RResW$. In practice he would probably do this in terms of money wages but the result can be considered to be the same. A refusal to work for less than the perceived 'going', 'market', or 'fair' wage is not only a trade union decision. Individuals can decide this on their own. Other individuals may decide that they would rather retain their job even at a lower real wage and therefore accept a lower, or no money wage increase, in order to remain in employment. Indeterminacy and unpredictability exist at the level of the individual unless we assume them away by specifying that reservation wages are fixed.

Individual and Collective Objectives

Trade unions seek to represent the views of their members and on occasions to influence those views. It is necessary that unions try to amalgamate and reconcile the different views and objectives of their members. It would be nonsense to believe that every individual in a particular union has identical interests either in general or in specific situations. Given that there is some relationship between the level of wages and the level of employment in a firm it follows that if wages are increased beyond a certain point some jobs will be lost. It could be in the personal interests of those who retained their jobs to press for the higher wages, but in the interests of those who would lose their jobs to moderate the wage increase. A union has to reconcile these different interests. Similarly a collective agreement which specifies the criteria and procedures by which people are promoted or moved to higher-paying jobs may be to the advantage of some employees but contrary to the interests of others. Those whom management would have chosen but are prevented from doing by the agreement will be disadvantaged. This does not mean that the management decision would be better in that it would be fairer or lead to greater efficiency. Management's decision might have been based on favouritism or nepotism. Nevertheless the favourite or the foreman's nephew had an interest which is adversely affected by the union pursuing the interests of the majority.

We ought not therefore to expect that a union will or should pursue the interests of each of its members on all occasions. It cannot. The interests of some of its members will on occasions be in conflict and may be irreconcilable.

Collective Wage Determination 197

It is well understood and accepted in economic theory that it is not possible to add together the utility schedule or indifference curve maps of two or more individuals. Utility is personal. Our economic concepts do not allow us to conclude that taking away marginal income or goods from a very rich person and giving them to a very poor person will actually increase the utility of the poor person by more than it diminishes the utility of the rich person. In real life, of course, we do make just such an assumption which is the basis for progressive taxation and the redistribution of income. Economic theory cannot do this, however. This means that we cannot, strictly speaking, produce an indifference curve for a collection of individuals. International trade theory does this when it presents a country's indifference map but at very most this can only be taken as an expository device best used in special situations where there are only two goods. It cannot be extended to a trade union to demonstrate the members' collective preference for higher wages against less employment. In the terms of its own logic economic analysis cannot estalish that the utility lost by just one individual being put out of work as a result of wage increases received by a thousand of his former colleagues is less than their increase in utility. We may assume that the gains of the majority outweigh the loss of the individual but we cannot, inside the logic of accepted economic theory analysis, prove this.

Even if we could aggregate the preferences of all the individual members, the union might adopt a different set of preferences. This is not to suggest that unions ignore or fail to represent the views of their members but to recognize that in any organization the processes of decision-taking may lead to the emergence of some views which represent those of the organization as well as of the individual members. Organizations take on identities and establish preferences and objectives be they organizations of workers in trade unions, employers in their associations, or members of a church. Individuals when participating in the decision-making processes of organizations may adapt their own preferences and priorities to include what they perceive to be the interests of the organization.

A trade union is not intended merely to add up and implement the same views and objectives that its members hold or would hold if they were not union members. Some of the things which individuals might wish to have may not be obtainable as individuals acting alone. For example the establishment of procedures covering disciplinary matters or governing work rules, provide an element of due process which simply cannot be obtained by a single individual. No matter how well intentioned or paternalistic the employer is, he cannot provide the dimension of worker representation which collective bargaining can give. To trade unions the due process of joint regulation rather than unilateral determination by an employer enables workers to regain some of the dignity which is inevitably lost when they enter into a subordinate employment relationship. A simple comparison of the preferences of individuals and of those people when collectively organized in a trade union cannot therefore be made. Nevertheless we can conclude that with trade unions and collective bargaining there will be some changes in preferences and priorities. The maintenance of procedures through which collective bargaining takes place will be more important to a trade union than it would be for any individual. The insistence on not undercutting the union agreed rate will be more important, and even though the union may, exceptionally and reluctantly, agree to lower that rate it will try to insist that the reduction is agreed, and that it is not further undermined by individuals working for less. That this imposes a higher collective $RResW$ on some individuals has to be accepted. Indeed it is one of the very purposes of trade unions to redress the imbalance in the power relationships which compels individuals to accept very low reservation wages.

The fact that unions in representing the interests of their members may modify and reinterpret those interests makes them in essence neither better nor worse than other collective organizations. All joint activity requires some modification in the formulating of common policies.

In Britain the main economic objectives of trade unions has been to obtain increases in wages. There has, for most unions, been relatively little action to obtain a wide variety of fringe benefits through collective bargaining, although some unions, particularly those for white-collar workers, have obtained pension schemes and better sickness pay benefits. British tradition, unlike American, has been to obtain non-wage benefits through state provision of welfare services. Employment protection in terms of dismissal, lay-off, or redundancy has also tended to come from state provision rather than collective bargaining, although unions may seek to improve the state minimum provisions. Unions may have negotiated agreements to provide that redundancy, if it should occur, should be on a last-in first-out basis. In principle this is no different from the American use of seniority. The main difference is that British unions have not, on the whole, negotiated as many agreements as the American for temporary lay-offs or for determining the circumstances surrounding these actions.

Influences on Trade Union Wage Bargaining

Collective bargaining has mainly settled into a pattern of roughly annual wage adjustments to money wages with very little use of cost-of-living sliding-scale adjustments between the periodic settlements. Unions see themselves as having two types of wage-claim. Defensive claims maintain some past relationship, often with the Retail Price Index, so that the restoration of the real wage to the level pertaining at the time of the last settlement is seen as being no more than a defensive action to maintain living standards. Other defensive claims may be based on some pay relationship with other groups—the coercive comparisons or maintenance of wage contours. If these have been adversely affected by additional pay increases elsewhere, unions may not regard themselves as pressing for any money or real wage gain but rather as maintaining a 'fair' relationship. Of course they realize that their claim could result in a wage improvement but it is not seen as being offensive action.

Offensive claims occur when a union seeks to improve some past relationship, either in terms of real wages and the RPI, or some past wage-relationship. The orbits of coercive comparison or wage contours may be seen by any one union as providing irreducible minimum increases, but if more can be obtained a union need not feel itself constrained to limit itself to the past relationship. Defensive claims by the others are seen as being their appropriate response. The continuation of past pay-relationships does not mean that each union accepts the fairness of relativities. It may mean that no union has been able to obtain what it believes to be the fair or proper relativities, for while a union may accept the continuation of that which *is*, it is not required to accept that this is what *ought* to be. Each union in a pay contour may be seeking to move itself to a higher contour. Increases in productivity may provide the grounds for an offensive pay-claim, as may a rise in profits. Unions may believe that there should be an improvement in the real wages of their members following changes in some economic variable. As with defensive claims, these reflect views about fairness.

Given that there are various motives behind pay-claims it should not be surprising if we are unable to find a constant relationship between wage increases and other economic variables. These other variables may shift in their importance. Unions and their members may change their priorities.

While fairness and comparability are powerful forces in British pay determination they do not lead to the maintenance of rigid pay relationships which are immutable. Despite its wide usage the term 'wage round' should not lead one to conclude that wage settlements are identical in either size or timing. There are some similarities amongst some settlements at some times and these may be of great importance, but they appear to be less automatic than is sometimes supposed.[6]

In the same way while there is evidence that the 'league table' of inter-industry wages displays a considerable amount of stability over time, there are promotions and relegations. These data are different from those examined in the wage-round studies which analyses settlements on a bargaining unit basis. The inter-industry league table uses the Standard Industrial Classification groupings and each 'industry' may contain a number of bargaining units as well as forming part of a multi-sector settlement. There are also problems in interpreting the results. One study of ninety-eight Minimum List Heading industries over the period 1948–69 found that while there was a significant rank correlation coefficient suggesting that there was stability in the league table and that the null hypothesis that there was no relationship was denied, the calculation of the coefficient of alienation denied the null hypothesis that there was a perfectly stable relationship (Robinson and Mayhew 1983). The same data could be used both to show a stable relationship and to deny that the relationship was very stable.

Comparability may be used by both sides in collective bargaining. Unions and employers may believe it offers some guidance about fairness, and employers may also see it as providing a contribution to market efficiency. As we have argued, fairness may play an important part in the determination of the individual's reservation wage, and particularly occupational reservation wage-levels. The great difference with trade unions is that the individual through his union can do something extra to attain his perceived pay-relationships.

In the atomistic market any individual has certain choices facing him. Given the relative wage-levels which emerge from the market he can accept one of them or withhold his labour and be voluntarily unemployed. If we drop the assumption of a Great Auctioneer who provides full information to all economic agents, we can also allow the individual to search for a 'fairer' wage through frictional unemployment. There is no need to search if the Auctioneer does not allow anyone to strike a bargain until everyone else has done so and the sub-markets cleared. Each individual may know that if he searches or withholds his labour, there may be a tendency for wages to rise. This could lead to the desired fair wage relationships. However for this to happen other individuals must behave in the same way, and of course if they do so when they in turn respond to the 'fair' wage relationship the increase in total supply may drive wages back to the unsatisfactory level. The individual is helpless in the face of the market-clearing process; he must either accept one of the offers or be voluntarily unemployed.

Trade unions through collective bargaining can obtain and act on some of the information which a Great Auctioneer would provide. They can do more. They can change the pay relationships, or try to do so. Because unions and workers believe that wages should reflect the effort-input it is natural that they should seek to obtain the same wage level and/or increase as received by others of similar skills or who are seen as having particular effort-input relationships with the groups concerned. They may adjust their perceptions of a fair or attainable wage either upwards or downwards so that the comparison is not the only factor, and they may well seek to obtain additional wages on whatever grounds are available, but the effort-input basis of comparison is often a powerful motivating force.

Employers too have notions of fairness. Many of them do not wish to be regarded as bad employers. It may be that the growth of professional personnel managers has increased the strength of socially determined elements in management's approach to pay. Comparability may also be seen by managers as the main way by which market forces can be discovered and interpreted. Because there is no Great Auctioneer shouting out market-clearing wage levels for specified grades of labour, employers may have considerable difficulty in knowing what is happening in the labour market. The number and quality of applicants may provide some guidance, but a firm may not know whether changes in labour-offer or acceptable labour supply is special to it or general throughout the market. It may be unaware of the wage elasticity of supply of labour. If the recruitment wage is based on the supply of acceptable labour applying for jobs an increase in supply could lead to a reduction in wages or, more likely, low or zero wage increases which could result in the retention wage being too low. The firm could then lose experienced and trained labour.

The invisible hands of competition, if they exist, need to be transformed into visible form. Comparability can assist. 'One way to discern the market solution, therefore, is to use comparability, comparing like for like' (Mayhew 1983, 28). Like is not always compared with like, as in the general wage-round interpretation of events. Comparability can be crude or refined.[7] While comparability and concepts of fairness permeate British collective bargaining they do not totally determine the results. No explanation has been produced which can explain the determination of wage levels and changes at either the micro- or macro-level.

However there are two other factors that are often thought to be relevant. The first is the Ross thesis that the union needs to respond to the claims of its members. There will be changing pressures to alter differentials. Sub-groups within the union will press their particular sectional interests and the union and its leadership will respond. Similarly on a Dunlop view of maximizing membership the union may press for changes in differentials in order to increase membership amongst particular occupations.

The second is the target real wage approach (Sargan 1964, 1980). This emphasizes the importance of the real wage and goes on to postulate that unions seek to obtain a target level of increase in real wages. The difficulty in testing this hypothesis is that we cannot easily, if at all, discover what the union target real wage, or real wage increase, is, or how it is established. The general approach can be linked to the view that unions establish on behalf of their members a view of entitled permanent real income and seek to obtain this through a series of money wage settlements which will provide the flow of real income over some time-period. The annual or periodic wage-claims are influenced by past experience of changes in real income and by some view of what real wages ought to be. Just how the level of what real wages ought to be is determined is unclear. Real wages, or pressure to increase real wages, may rise either because there has been a period of growth in real wages in the past which is expected to continue, or because real wages have been falling and it is thought that enough is enough and they should now be restored to make good the past losses and even perhaps provide some additional growth. It is often argued that this occurs after a period of restrictionary economic policy by government or after an incomes policy.

Effects of Trade Unions

Unless it is thought that trade unions are totally irrelevant and have no effect on anything we need to examine what the effects are of trade union involvement in the determination of terms and conditions of employment. Although there is no complete agreement most opinion concludes that trade unions may be able to affect wages, employment, or both, in that as a result of union action the level of wages or employment, or both, may be different from those which would result from either the same market conditions as exist but were there to be no trade unions, or from the wages and employment levels which would exist in some theoretical market conditions. The latter, while often used in economic theory as the criteria against which to assess the beneficial or other effects of unions, is not very helpful. It is clear that there are many factors other than trade unions which ensure that the world in which we live does not conform to the assumptions of perfect competition. Until, for example, we specify how employers would behave in the absence of trade unions and in the absence of the rigorous but artificial constraints of perfect competition we cannot really determine what the level of either wages or employment would be in the absence of unions. We might have reason to believe that wages would be lower and employment higher, but how much higher, and in which sectors we cannot say.

Trade unions are able to influence the level of wages and employment because they are able to alter the decisions which would have been made in their absence. They are able to do this because they can change the decision-taking processes and change the location of the decision-taking. One of the fundamental objectives of trade unions is to replace unilateral managerial decision-taking by joint regulation or collective bargaining, or in some cases to substitute unilateral trade union decision-taking for unilaterial management prerogatives. By changing who the decision-takers are unions seek to alter the decisions which are taken. In order to change the processes of decision-taking and the decisions which are taken unions need to have the ability to exercise power. Trade union power can be seen as relevant to three other groups—its members, the employers, and the state or government. The power relationship can be seen as a complex two-way relationship in that unions may have power *vis-à-vis* these three parties and may also obtain power from them.

Unions and their Members

Individuals join trade unions because they believe they will personally gain by doing so. Even in the case of compulsory union membership, or the closed shop, which we will discuss below, individuals might be regarded as having decided that they benefit by accepting that job with the condition that they join the union rather than be unable to accept the job because they refused to join the union. Individuals benefit because even though, as we have discussed above, their own individual views and interests may on occasions be overriden by the union, there are other occasions when they gain. It is generally expected that wages will be higher as a result of collective bargaining although this is not universally the case. Equally or perhaps more importantly for some, unions can provide other benefits and protection which are simply not available to individuals. Modern production methods frequently involve integrated work arrangements. In these conditions the individual cannot bargain for himself. To obtain the benefits of economies of scale the employer has to impose collective conditions. An assembly line in a car plant cannot operate efficiently if individuals fix their own working times or work speeds. Large production units need standard conditions and management frequently prefers uniform provisions for its employees and uniform procedures. One individual alone cannot exercise sufficient countervailing power against an employer in order to obtain change, and it is simply not feasible to try and arrange terms and conditions on an individual basis.

Although economic analysis often concentrates on the wage effects of trade unions when looking at the results of bargaining, unions also exercise considerable influence over the effort-input. The effort-bargain is no less important than the wage-bargain and to some workers at some times it is far more important. There is no objective definition or quantification of what is a 'fair' day's work. It is something which is established by tradition, custom and practice and bargaining, or is imposed by one party. One of the significant contributions of trade unions has been their success in reducing the amount of physical effort required in some jobs. The evil of 'sweated labour' did not refer only to the miserable wages that were paid; it also included the excessive demands on effort-input. Employers are well aware of the union impact on the effort-bargain and the consequences this may have for both productivity and costs.

However it is not necessarily the case that changing the processes or organization of bargaining at plant level alters the relative power of management and unions. The formalization of plant bargaining may have no effect on managerial power or on unions' control of the effort-bargain (Batstone 1984).

If trade unions obtain wage increases this may lead the employer to seek to increase efficiency. High wages may lead to high productivity rather than be the result of it as employers seek to extract some efficiency return for the higher pay.

We have previously suggested that the establishment of due process in the form of disciplinary or promotion procedures require some collective voice. So too does pressure to improve health and safety at the work-place.

Membership of a trade union offers protection against the arbitrary or unreasonable actions of management. Not only can the union procedures and the collective strength of the union be brought to bear in support of individual grievances but the union may provide expert advice and assistance. Shop stewards, branch officials, full-time officers, and perhaps legal advisers retained by the union are available to help individuals.

People may make deliberate decisions to join a union based on assessment of the benefits compared to the subscriptions and the possible restraints on individual action involved in membership of a group. Others may join out of habit or principle or because most other people at that place of work are in the union. In some cases people may join in order to obtain access to some services provided by the union for its members such as admission to a training-course which will help promotion at work.

A consequence of joining a union is that the members are required to accept some constraints on their behaviour. They should not undercut a union wage or agreement. They may be required to strike, or not cross picket lines. The union's ability to ensure that its members observe union policy rests ultimately upon the moral persuasion it can bring to bear on them.

The 'Closed Shop'[8]

This term is commonly used to refer to a situation in which membership of a specified union or unions is a condition of employment. Membership may be pre-entry or post-entry. In the former case only existing members of the union may be hired. In the latter, individuals are required to join the specified union on employment. There are few issues in industrial relations which raise such emotive responses as the closed shop. Minister of State for Employment John Gummer told a CBI conference: 'I take a clear moral view of closed shops. I am opposed to them, and this Government is opposed to them.'[9] He also said that the latest estimate of the number covered by closed shops was 'less than 4½ million'.

To unions the closed shop serves two purposes. It provides an additional power over some, and presumably a minority of its members, and it prevents employees from enjoying the benefits of union bargaining without paying membership subscriptions. Many union gains are available to all employees in the appropriate occupations in that place of employment. Members and non-members alike benefit from a union agreement which reduces the pace of work or the speed of an assembly line. Wage increases are received by members and non-members. These improvements which are enjoyed by those who paid for them and those who did not are referred to in economics as 'public goods'. Many trade union gains are 'public goods' to non-members in the establishments covered by the agreements.

Pre-entry closed shops give the union some control over the supply of labour. If only those already members of the union can be employed it is possible for the union to restrict the labour-offer supply curve. Post-entry closed shops do not provide this control device, but, it is argued by critics, allow the union to impose rigid discipline over its members. Fear of expulsion from the union, which would mean loss of that job, is said to allow unions to impose policies which the members do not really support. This is the same criticism that is levelled at statutory closed shops such as the legal profession, accountancy, or the medical and nursing professions, where membership of an appropriate body is a legal requirement for the exercise of one's profession, not merely at a particular place of work, but anywhere in the country. Individuals may be expelled or struck off for various reasons over which the law has no control.

We do not know whether or to what extent the closed shop gives the unions significantly extra power or allows them to impose policies on a reluctant or antagonistic membership, and, in the latter case, if it does, whether unions actually utilize that opportunity.

In order to exercise power *vis-à-vis* employers unions need to be able to influence the actions of their members, or they need to be able to collate the views of their members and organize collective responses. The most obvious and perhaps effective power that unions have is to influence the supply of labour to employers. There are two aspects to this. Firstly, they can influence the internal supply of labour, i.e. the current employees. They can bring their members out on strike, or impose a work-to-rule or overtime ban. By co-ordinating the actions of the work-force they are able to prevent the internal supply of labour from presenting itself for employment. This is an additional reason why unions prefer to have complete membership. They do not wish to see their actions to deprive employers of internal labour supply jeopardized by the continued attendance at work of significant numbers of non-members.

Secondly, they can influence the external labour supply. By picketing they may be able to prevent the employer from hiring replacement labour during a strike. In many cases in Britain this is not a major feature of picketing. There is, in most strikes, relatively little attempt by employers to recruit replacement labour. It may happen in some cases, but generally the employer wishes to have the strikers back at work. He can seldom find homogeneous replacements and attempts to hire 'scab' or 'blackleg' workers are likely to prolong and intensify the dispute. Most picketing is to stop the movement of goods and products rather than prevent the entrance of scab labour.

Unions generally have the ability to prevent the replacement of their members by recruits from the external labour supply who might be willing to work for lower wages, or accept higher effort-input requirements. They may have less power to prevent employers from substituting contracted-out activities or the buying-in of components which were or could be produced in-plant. Thus there can be a form of replacement of high-paid union workers by others who may or may not be trade unionists. Also firms may relocate in other areas. This is a well-known phenomenon in the US where companies have moved from the unionized North-East to the non-union South or the sun-belt states. There may be some similar tendencies in Britain as companies close down plants in certain areas and open new ones or expand elsewhere. These may be non-union or may be unionized, but considered more 'reasonable'. Also the relocation may allow the company to introduce new equipment which drastically changes the capital–labour ratio. One of the ways in which unions have sought to protect jobs is by resisting the introduction of new equipment and technology, or demanding certain manning-scales and requirements which the employers regard as uneconomic.

While unions may be able to influence or control the labour supply in certain situations, there may be limits on this and the employer may have other responses which are outside the union's control.

In a broader context unions may be able to influence the external labour supply by restricting the numbers trained in the skill or occupation. The restrictions may be unilaterally imposed by, say, a craft union limiting the number of apprentices in relation to the number of craftsmen in an establishment, or jointly agreed by union and management. The influence of this on the wages of a particular bargaining unit may be small and indirect. It will be influenced by the relative importance of the bargaining unit to the total supply of the skill.

To make a simplified distinction. Union action to restrict the external supply of labour is an attempt to use market forces by changing them. Control of the internal labour supply is a rejection of market forces; it seeks to prevent the market from working by imposing a collective prohibition or restriction on labour supply for a period. It is intended to be only a short-term measure. The strike is seen as a means of exerting pressure on the employer but once it is settled the union intends to restore the internal labour supply by the same people.

It is the union's ability to co-ordinate and influence the supply of labour of its members that provides it with its major bargaining weapon against employers. There will always be arguments about whether the members actually do support a strike and a number of employers, and probably all Conservative governments, believe that trade union leadership does not reflect the 'true' views of the members. The question of the genuine representativeness of leadership, or whether leaders should be representatives or delegates, is one that bedevils political theory and all organizations.

At the end of the day the union's side of the power relationship in collective bargaining, within such legal framework as has been provided, depends upon its ability to restrict or stop the supply of labour to employers. Its ability to do this may be influenced by closed shop or compulsory membership arrangements, but even then will depend on the internal decision-taking processes of the union and the extent to which the membership avail themselves of their rights to participate. Closed shop arrangements cover something between a fifth and a quarter of the total employed labour force. The majority of trade unionists are probably not in closed shops. Trade unions must be able to carry their members with them. The main reason they can do this is that the decision-taking processes and union leadership generally ensure that industrial action is not sought unless there is membership support for it and for the objectives it is seeking to secure. In turn members recognize that they obtain benefits from union membership and so may be willing to support industrial action. The ultimate source of union power or influence *vis-à-vis* members is the members' consent. The miners' dispute of 1984–5 illustrates both aspects of this.

Right-wing critics of unions often accuse them of having intolerably excessive powers over their members. For the most part this is quite misconceived. Most trade unions have but little power over their members if by trade unions we mean the national leadership. In the vast majority of cases such power as is vested in the union is located at regional or local level, often in the plant, and is exercised not by the union operating through its formal structure of the branch but by shop stewards operating in a twilight world or no man's land. British national trade union leadership is relatively weak, certainly in comparison with American unions. The powerful Fleet Street unions, for example, are effectively immune from national control. Union rule books, often with their basic framework laid down in the nineteenth century, may provide for very considerable local or district autonomy or discretion. Twentieth-century developments, and particularly the rise of shop stewards, have seen an extension of power outside the rule books. There may be agreements with local management, which may be written or unwritten, or there may have been a haphazard development based on custom and practice, but much of the power of work groups in the private sector is exercised through shop stewards who have established and consolidated their power base by extending the agenda of collective bargaining at plant level. By obtaining improvements in wages and conditions shop stewards have attracted the support of their members. Because there is often a multiplicity of unions in a plant, and co-ordinated action is desirable, stewards frequently operate outside the confines and remits of their union rule books, establishing joint arrangements in their place of work with stewards from other unions. Any one national union may be unable to exercise control or power over them even if it wished.

Certainly when members or stewards break agreements, or are accused of doing so, unions are requested to exercise *more* power over them. To this unions frequently respond that they are unable to do so. Either they do not have the formal authority or they do not have the effective authority. Thus there is a body of opinion which holds that far from British trade unions being too strong, they are too weak. The national unions do not have effective control over their members or stewards or the means to implement control.

Against this it has been argued that unions do have the power but are unwilling to use it. It is argued that there are sanctions available to unions to ensure that their members keep to agreements but that unions, while willing to discipline members who break some union rules are unwilling to discipline those who break agreements with employers. This is one reason why some advocate legislative change whereby unions would be liable for damages or fines if their members broke agreements. It is thought that this would force unions to exercise control and authority over their members. This criticism seems not to be willing recognize that there are occasions when a work group is so aggrieved that it insists on taking industrial action no matter what its union representatives and leaders say.

Trade Unions and Employers

The ability of trade unions to influence the labour supply to employers provides the basis for the frequent references, particularly by Monetarists, to trade union monopoly powers. The true monopolist can restrict supply, immune from the fear of new entrants, and with a given demand curve reap the benefits of a higher price. Whether he will do so will depend on his cost curves. A producer in perfect competition can restrict his supply but this will have no effect on the price he receives. He has therefore no incentive to do so other than the fact that with given cost curves he should not produce more than the level of output where marginal costs equal marginal revenue which is the same as the price. If he restricts output below this point he is failing to maximize his profits. The monopolist can determine either the price he will charge or the amount he will sell, but not both.

We must assume that once he has taken his decisions regarding profitability a monopolist has no inherent interest in the number of units he sells; if he adopts marginal cost and revenue analysis and if this leads to a very small number being sold at a very high price, so be it. Political considerations may lead him to modify his behaviour if he does not wish to run the risk of government ending his monopoly, but the economic considerations are clear enough.

A trade union does not behave in this way. It must take some account of the employment effects of its decisions—the number of units of labour sold is important both to it as a union, and to its members who will be affected by the pricing-employment decisions. While there may be some desired pejorative connotations in referring to unions as 'monopoly suppliers', in most cases the term is inaccurate as very few unions have an absolute monopoly control over supply, and in all cases it is misleading because unions do care about the number of jobs that will result from their wage policies. Of course unions may differentiate between the employment effects on their current members, and the possible effects on those who are not yet members but would be if employment expanded. The latter may receive less priority. In just the same way, employers do not pay much regard to the expansion of employment of those not currently employed by them when they take their decisions. In this case we say that it would be unprofitable to expand employment and somehow conclude that this is reasonable. In the case of unions there is a tendency to believe that it is selfishness which leads them to insist upon receiving a 'fair' wage even if this denies employment opportunities to others. This is merely to indulge in the use of value-judgements, but often cloaked in economic jargon about 'normal profits' or market-determined rates of return.

The problem is that monopolists can be assumed to be maximizing a single variable—profits. More recent, complicated, and realistic analysis recognizes that monopolists may not be simple profit maximizers; they may pursue other objectives and so their price and output decisions become indeterminate. With trade unions there is no single variable that we can reasonably assume they are trying to maximize. Various writers have assumed that unions maximize a particular thing. Some specify this as the total wage bill; others the extra wages obtained by union membership compared to competitive conditions; others that it is the expected utility of the median-aged union member.[10] Generally economists assume that unions try to maximize utility by combining wages and employment. There is no satisfactory model which includes determinate variables which unions seek to maximize. 'What is clear is that unions have many aims other than obtaining wage increases, and that sometimes those aims conflict with, or at least put constraints on, the achievement of wage increases' (Mayhew 1983, 24).

We often find that the employer is not faced by the conditions assumed in perfect competition. He frequently has some element of monopsonistic power. He may be the sole or a large 'buyer' of certain sorts of labour in that locality and is thus able to influence the wage level by his own demand and actions. The combination of a monopoly element on the union side and a monopsonistic element on the employer's side result in what is referred to as bilateral monopoly. Neither side of the labour market operates according to the assumptions of perfect competition.[11] In this situation economic theory provides no determinate wage and employment level. We cannot say what the wage level will be and therefore it is not possible for us to assess the effects of trade unions or the monopsonistic power of the employer. What would be generally agreed, however, is that wages will be higher than if there were no trade union and the labour supply side of the market operated under conditions of perfect employment.

Trade Union Effect on Wages

Monetarists seem agreed that unions can have no continuing effect on the rate of money wage changes. According to Friedman a strong trade union can create social conflict, drive people out of work, and create unemployment, 'But it cannot create *continuing* inflation' (1975, 31, emphasis in original). Trade unions

> play a very important role in the structure of the labour force and the structure of *relative* wages. But, despite appearance to the contrary, a *given* amount of trade union power does not play any role in exacerbating inflation. It is true that if relatively weak unions become strong, *in the process of going from weak to strong* they may exert an *interim* inflationary influence. They will in the process drive up the real wages of their members. This will reduce the level of employment in their sector (30, emphasis in original).

This is either a tautology or unfounded. If the 'process of going from weak to strong' means that real wages rise as a result of inflationary wage settlements then it is tautological. It need not follow that inflationary increases in money wages lead to increases in real wages; this depends on what happens in other sectors of the economy. If all unions in Britain obtained wage increases of 50 per cent it would not follow that their real wages would increase; that would depend on what happened to other incomes and prices. Moreover it does not follow that higher money or real wages will lead to unemployment only, or even, in that sector, this will depend on what happens elsewhere. As the then Employment Secretary Norman Tebbit said, 'The point is simple. But worth emphasizing. Pay increases for any one group of workers affect job prospects not only for that group but also for other groups.'[12] If the price elasticities are right there may be no employment effect in the industry receiving the inflationary pay rise. This is quite crucial of course for it means that retribution is not inevitable. It also means that unemployment may result in an industry as a result of wage and price increases elsewhere, no matter how non-inflationary its own pay settlements.

It may be that unions collectively can have different effects than a union singly. If the force of coercive comparisons leads unions to match the offensive pay increases of those unions which are 'going from weak to strong' the inflationary process will be intensified and could be perpetuated. It requires recourse to the Quantity Theory of Money to argue that inflation could only be perpetuated if the money supply continued to rise. But if there are sufficient rigidities in relative wages and other unions press defensive pay-claims there is no reason why inflation could not continue with adverse consequences on employment. To avoid this it is necessary for unions to accept that some defensive pay-claims cannot be met. This they may well do as the reduction in real disposable income in 1981–2 demonstrates.[13]

There is much Monetarist support for the view that unions cannot cause continuing inflation.[14] Acceptance of the view that inflation always and everywhere is a monetary phenomenon might exclude trade unions from any role in the macro-level economic process. If only changes in the quantity of money cause inflation unions have no part to play unless they can influence changes in the quantity of money. Other Monetarists are less sure that unions cannot cause inflation, 'whilst a reduction in the power of unions might slow down inflation we can have no confidence in such a prediction' (Parkin 1972). Griffiths seems unsure. 'At a time of inflation, all trade unions are able to raise nominal (money) wages' (IEA Readings 17, 1978, 106). We cannot disentangle cause and effect from this.

In principle it ought to be possible to test whether unions have any effect on wages and the inflationary process by comparing the rate of change of money wages with unions and collective bargaining and the rate of change without trade unions but everything else remaining constant. Such tests are not possible. One way round this difficulty has been to compare union wage levels with non-union wages in similar occupations and industries, or sectors of the same industry. Much of the early work was American following the impressive pioneering study by Lewis (1963). The research results differ in the size of the union effect ranging from hardly any to 15–20 per cent.[15]

British research based on analysis of those covered by collective agreements has suggested figures of a union wage differential of something in the region of 20–5 per cent.[16] Metcalf suggested that 'a figure of 20 per cent may not be dreadfully in error' (1977). Layard *et al.* found an average union differential for manual workers of 25 per cent for workers covered by a collective agreement but 'We stress, however, the very approximate nature of the finding' (1976). 'Among non-manual workers we find no reliable evidence of an effect of collective bargaining on relative wages' (ibid.). Mulvey and Abowd (1980) conclude that statistical bias in the analyses could lead to errors of half the found differential. The general findings were consistent with the views that the union differential increases as unemployment increases, lower skilled occupations may obtain larger gains from union membership, and that the gains of non-manual workers were smaller or non-existent

An earlier analysis produced estimates between zero and 10 per cent (Burkitt and Bowers 1976). Blanchflower (1984) provides an excellent summary of the results. His own detailed analysis concludes that the union effect for semi-skilled manual workers, excluding agriculture and coal, is about 10 per cent, and 14 per cent in the non-manufacturing sector.

One of the major difficulties in estimating the union differential is that of producing a reliable estimate of the earnings function and ensuring that comparisons are made among workers of similar skill, ability, and quality. Addison believes the effect might be only '3 to 4 per cent when you allow for the fact that high wages might be a cause of unionism as much as unions causing high wages. One would expect an employer who faces high union wages to seek to improve the quality of his labour, so that union labour is of a higher quality' (IEA Readings 20, 1979, 74.) Stewart sought to allow for the individual characteristics of workers and estimated an average union effect of 7.7 per cent.

Plant-level, rather than industry-level, bargaining gives rise to higher union effects. An important difference between British and American union effects is that in Britain there are probably relatively more non-union members *directly* affected by the outcome of collective bargaining. Union membership is only an indirect indicator of the coverage of collective bargaining. The appropriate comparison is between wages determined by collective bargaining and those determined by 'market forces'. In many industries in Britain it is not possible to find a satisfactory basis of comparison as there are insufficient non-union 'market force' wages. Even when there are, the existence or absence of a union differential does not really establish whether unions are able to increase money wages or not. If non-union employers follow collectively bargained wage increases no 'union effect' or no change in the 'union effect' will be observed. Non-unionized employers may choose to do this in order to keep out unions or because changes in the union rate have become accepted as the going or market rate. As we have suggested earlier in the absence of the Great Auctioneer, employers have to discover what the market rate is, and if they make mistakes the consequences could be costly.

The conclusion 'Trade Unions, then, do not have much effect on raising *money* wages—apparently less in Britain than in the USA' (Clark 1981) is misleading. He is referring to the relative money wages obtained by unions in collective bargaining, and non-unionists. This does not allow for the union-threat effect which leads employers to increase money wages in order to avoid having to recognize and bargain with unions. The existence of a zero union wage effect is perfectly consistent with the possibility that trade unions can raise average money wages of their members and non-members. It is only the acceptance of a priori positions which, following the Quantity Theory, leads to a conclusion that aggregate money wages cannot rise faster than the rate of increase of the money supply, that leads to the conclusion that if trade unions increase money wages those of some other groups must rise by less than the rate of money growth; but these other groups may not be non-union firms in the same industry as the union members. They may be in a quite different industry. No union effect would be picked up by comparing organized and unorganized firms in the same industry.

Monetarists differ in their views of the ability of unions to raise wages and generate inflation. Friedman does not really blame them for this. With a given strength unions, to him, merely respond to anticipated inflation by increasing money wages to maintain real wages. Minford believes that unions seek a constant mark-up over non-union wages but does not specify what the union real wage target is, how it is formed, or why it varies from sector to sector even when trade union membership proportions are about the same.

However, the perceived inability of unions to continue to raise the money wages of their members does not lead all Monetarists to conclude that the union effect is unimportant. Because they can on occasions raise money and real wages above their market level, it is argued that unions drive down real wages elsewhere. The above-equilibrium wage levels in the union sector lead to less employment in that sector, and this increases the labour supply to the non-union sector with the effect of driving down wages there (Minford 1982). However, if there are obstacles limiting the downward movement in non-union wages those wages will not fall enought to absorb the increased supply of labour to the non-union sector. The main obstacle seen by most Monetarists is the level of Unemployment Benefits which by raising the individual reservation wages reduces the effective supply of labour to the non-union sector. Thus some sort of equilibrium is found in both sectors. In the union sector the union-imposed higher wages leads to a cut-back in the demand for labour. In the non-union sector the level of Unemployment Benefits leads to a cut-back in the supply of labour as individuals choose to be voluntarily unemployed and live off their unemployment benefits.[17]

There is a problem with the sort of union versus non-union wage differentials as expounded by Minford. 'In the non-union sector, wages clear the market. Naturally, because of the union mark-up, all workers in the industry would prefer to work in the union sector. Therefore labour supply to the non-union sector is equal to total labour supply minus the demand for labour in the union sector' (1981, 11). This gives the impression that the unionized sector is somehow determined by exogenous forces. But if some workers are denied employment opportunities in the existing union sector, and if, as Minford states, all workers would prefer to work in the union sector because of the higher wages, it is unclear why they do not take their unionization with them and why the non-union sector does not become organized. One reason may be that it is not possible for unions to develop and apply the monopolistic-type practices Minford ascribes to unionism because of some product or labour-supply features. This is not actually advanced as the reason but could perhaps be put forward. However, this would require some explanation of the economic or market determinants of unionization and this is not forthcoming.

Part of the trouble is that commitment to classical economics and the yearning for a situation in which individuals behave in an atomistic way, leads to self-imprisonment in a framework in which the individual worker has to choose from the various options he perceives to be facing him and these options consist only of job-offers and voluntary unemployment. The option of changing the job-offers through union membership which leads to changes in the terms of employment tends to be ignored because this would be seen as an additional distortion moving further away from the conceptual purity of the 'free market' paradigm. Workers however need not accept self-imprisonment. They can seek to unionize hitherto non-union sectors. Of course if this happens, in the Minford model, it will lead to higher unemployment, but even if that is true it does not mean that it will not occur. Those who retained jobs in the newly unionized sector would have higher wages. It would also, in the Minford model, lead to relatively larger reductions in non-union real wages, to the extent that Unemployment Benefits do not provide a floor. This would still be voluntary unemployment in this model because the individuals were choosing to be unemployed because the replacement ratio was so high.

In addition to influencing the supply of labour, unions may be able to influence its demands by changing the effort-input element of the Job Requirement or by insisting upon certain manning-scales. They can influence the type of labour to be employed as well as the amount. Such action may lead to less employment but this may not actually mean unemployment for some of the existing work-force. If changes in the effort-input leads to higher labour costs and so higher product prices the effect may be to slow down the rate of growth of demand, output, and employment rather than to create unemployment. In periods when the economy as a whole is expanding this may be the more common form. There is then no fall in employment but rather a reduction in the rate of growth of employment. This is not directly observable nor will its impact on trade unions be the same. Their members currently employed are not threatened. Non-members who might have found jobs may be adversely affected and some union members who might otherwise have transferred to these jobs may be unable to do so, but these opportunity costs of improvements in terms and conditions are different from directly experienced costs expressed in unemployment of currently employed members.

Conversely, if the balance of power shifts significantly towards employers there may be changes in the effort-input requirements and a reduction in manning-scales. It is often argued that there is considerable overmanning in Britain in comparison with other industrialized countries. 'Moreover, it is important to recognize that, in the UK, a very significant part of the increase in unemployment over the past five years is simply the emergence into the open of the unsustainable disguised unemployment of the second half of the seventies, when overmanning—in manufacturing in particular—was rife' (Nigel Lawson 1984). He went on to say that the potential for catching up with the productivity levels in manufacturing in the rest of Europe is now being realized. 'In the short term this represents a very painful adjustment. But in the longer term it will mean not only higher living standards, but higher levels of employment too.'

Overmanning is equated to disguised unemployment, but of course what is overmanning and what is a difference of opinion about the amount of effort-input that should form part of particular Job Requirements rests upon value-judgements. There is no unambiguous definition of the 'proper' effort-input for a job. There may be cases where it is apparent to all observers that some workers are unnecessary in order to obtain a given amount of production. In the large majority of cases there is unlikely to be such consensus. One person's overmanning is another person's fair day's work.

One astute commentator on the British scene believes that British unions and their members have taken a conscious decision to enjoy some of their rewards from work in the form of lower effort-input rather than higher earnings (Nossiter 1978). He suggests this may be an indication of a more civilized society. It is not necessary to endorse the view that there has been a conscious decision to substitute less effort for less pay, it could result from a desire to reduce excessive work-speeds or work-loads without a full appreciation of the terms of the wages trade-off. Whether one accepts the argument or not it underlines the point that the level of effort-input required by jobs, or which should be required by jobs, is not given by technology, objective market forces, or act of God. It emerges from the decision-taking processes within industry and is the result of the relative distribution of power, social conventions, prevailing standards of reasonableness, and history. That there may be a trade-off between effort-input, wages, and employment does not lead to the conclusion that any particular trade-off it natural, pre-ordained, or the best.

What is important for present purposes however is not the debate about how hard other people should work, but the point that if trade union power is reduced sufficiently and employers increase the effort-input requirements and replace workers by capital equipment, far from employment rising, it may fall. Mr Lawson believes this to be short-run painful adjustment. He believes that in the long run a weakened trade union movement in an economy which is subject to stronger free market pressures will be unable to resist a reduction in real wages somewhere in the economy. This will be necessary if the demand for labour is to rise, and it is by an increase in demand following a reduction in the product real wage that his expected growth in employment will occur. On his analysis the expected growth in employment will actually depend on the interplay of two opposing forces. One will increase demand for labour by reducing product real wages as trade unions are weaker, and the other will reduce the demand for labour as employers become relatively stronger and cut their work-forces by getting rid of 'overmanning'—that is by increasing the effort-input of the remaining work-force and by substituting capital for labour. There is no a priori reason to believe that the increase in demand will be sufficient to overcome the forces leading to a reduction in demand. It could go either way depending on the shift in relative strength and the reactions of employers.

We could see the emergence of perverse effects whereby a reduction in union strength led to a reduction in employment and a long-term reduction at that. The sectors and firms which survived might be 'leaner and fitter' and imbued with the competitive spirit sought by the government, but they might employ fewer people. While, as Mr Lawson foresees, living standards might rise, this improvement might be confined to the smaller number of employment.

Trade Union Strength

As we have seen Friedman believes that increases in union strength allow them to increase the real wages of their members although at a cost of higher unemployment for them. Either this is a tautological relationship in that higher real wages mean that unions have increased their strength or we must be able to measure union strength in some way and then demonstrate that changes in it lead to changes in real wages. There is the same tautological theme in Griffiths's view. 'Such an increase in real wages is a once-for-all increase as a result of labour exploiting its monopoly power. Once its power has been fully exploited it will be unable to increase real wages in this way' (IEA Readings 17, 1978, 107). A union can apparently increase real wages as long as it has unexploited monopoly powers at its disposal and we ascertain that it has exploited all its monopoly power when it stops increasing real wages. It is not clear how we should regard an increase in real wages resulting from changes in productivity or shifts in real demand for the product and labour.

We cannot measure trade union strength directly. We can measure membership, and membership density—the proportion of a work-force that is unionized—but this is not necessarily an indication of changes in union power vis-à-vis an employer. It might be thought that we should measure union strength by the extent to which unions are able to achieve their objectives, but as we cannot quantify trade union objectives this approach would merely involve us in a tautological trap of equating power with the apparent results of power. Merely assuming that wage increases are objectives of unions does not allow us to conclude that if wages, or real wages, rose unions must have more power, and that real wages have risen because unions have more power. However, if trade union power is regarded as the ability to widen the union–non-union wage differential this is not a tautology. It might not be the appropriate test of power but it is capable, in principle, of measurement, although as we have discussed, interpretation of the results of such comparisons is far from easy.

The measurement of trade union membership density—membership as a propotion of total work-force—has serious deficiencies. We might expect different effects from a given increase in union density depending on what accounts for it. The recruitment of additional members in existing bargaining units might add little to a union's bargaining power. A 5 per cent gain in membership when, say, 90 per cent of the bargaining unit is already organized may have much less effect than an increase of 5 per cent when only 55 per cent of the unit is organized. In other cases the increase in membership in a highly organized unit might reflect some deep-rooted discontent among the work-force, and this could lead to higher demands and more pressure to attain them.

Employment changes in existing bargaining units or union-organized firms or industries can affect density measures. Some industries such as the public sector in Britain are highly organized. If the public sector grows the number of trade union members will rise. If parts of it, such as coalmining decline, the number of trade unionists as a whole might fall. The percentage union membership within an industry might remain much the same as the industry grows or declines, but the change in the relative size of industries can affect the overall or national trade union membership density percentage. Changes in the composition of the work-force can affect total union membership density as different groups seem to have different propensities to join trade unions. By and large a relative growth in female employment, particularly part-time, is expected to reduce the union membership density ratio.

An increase in union density obtained from an *extension* of membership by recruiting workers in areas not previously organized could well have different effects from the *deepening* of membership in existing units. Extension could lead to the establishment of collective bargaining in new bargaining units. This could have a greater effect on wages than an equivalent increase in density obtained by *deepening*. It is probably the case that changes in union density in the United States more generally mean extension of bargaining, or a growth in the size of existing bargaining units, than the deepening of union membership to workers already covered by bargaining units.

Until recently we had very poor data on union membership by individual industry. Price and Bain (1983) have now provided estimates by SIC Order but useful as this is, the SIC Orders do not correspond well with bargaining units so that changes in wages may result from a great variety of factors other than a change in trade union membership. Further, if density changes because of structural shifts in the economy as some industries grow and others decline, the observed changes in wages may owe much more to the underlying forces causing the structural shifts than to union membership density. To all intents and purposes we can regard the manual workers in the coalmining industry in Britain employed by the NCB as fully organized. Over the last twenty or thirty years there will have been no significant changes in union membership density.

Even if we could sort out these complications there is a further problem. It is not clear whether an increase in union membership causes increases in pay or whether high wages cause, or lead to, an increase in union membership.

Leaving this aside it does not follow that union strength as measured by membership-density figures provides a satisfactory index of union strength in bargaining. In addition to membership indicators there is something we can refer to as union militancy, or the propensity to use, and perhaps even create additional sources of power.[18] No union ever knows what its strength is at any time. In part its strength may be influenced not only by market conditions in both product and labour markets, but by the perception of these conditions by it, its members, and the employers. Union strength is relative; it needs to be weighed against the strength of employers and on occasions the government.

Economic theory is fond of supposing that strikes are the result of misunderstandings between the two sides about the other's objectives and willingness to sustain costs, and each party's own changing willingness to bear the costs of a dispute. Standard analysis is to draw an employers-offer curve and a union concession curve which have some point of intersection. Each side is assumed to modify its position through time so that the curves converge.[19] If the two sides had accurate information as to the other's curve and its own did not change as a result of the information, strikes could presumably be avoided. However, because it is assumed that it is only the experience of the costs of a strike that induces either party to shift its curve, it may be that the strike has to be experienced before an agreed compromise settlement can be achieved.

In the real world strikes are seldom so rational, although the perceived costs and gains do enter into the decisions. Strikes may take place or be encouraged by employers in order to change the attitudes of the other side even though this will not impose any serious cost. It may be necessary to establish credibility for a strike threat, or for the employer to demonstrate that he will take a strike rather than concede. While this can be forced into an analysis of rational maximizing behaviour it is really imposing too much order and rationality into strike situations to do so. To many observers strikes may be regarded as evidence of irrationality in that some form of arbitration or exchange of information could theoretically arrive at the same result. Strikes may become virility symbols. They can also be learning processes in which one side or the other discovers just how much power it really has and the extent to which this may have changed. This may not be known before the strike as neither side can know what the other will do during the dispute. Power can be not only found, but created, as new ways of exerting or avoiding pressure are discovered and developed. The responses of other unions and employers, public opinion, and the government may be crucial and unknowable before the event.

Legal provisions affect the relative strength of the sides by permitting or prohibiting certain actions, assuming of course that they are, or can be, implemented. Any consideration of the strength of British trade unions since 1964 which ignores the see-sawing legislation of Labour and Conservative governments must be deficient. Similarly any assessment which ignores militancy, uncertain though the factors which influence this might be, will also fail to take into account shifts in the relative bargaining positions. While influenced by perceived economic conditions militancy is not totally determined by them.

In fact we have no satisfactory predictive explanation of militancy. One reason is that we have no satisfactory indicator of it. The rate of change of real wages is unsatisfactory as a measure. This could result from 'market' forces, and we have no reliable basis of comparison to show what would have happened without the militancy. Strike incidence is not necessarily a good guide to either power or militancy. A really powerful union may not need to strike and indeed a strike with an interruption to production and sales could actually lead to a weakening of both the union and the employer. In one sense both strikes and picketing are signs of weakness; the most powerful groups need actually to do neither. On some occasions, however, strike activity may indicate that unions are using their power to a greater extent, or testing how much power they have. There need be no consistency in human behaviour through time or across groups. As with so much of economics it is the assumption that everyone is always maximizing that causes the difficulties. Just as firms are not always, or perhaps hardly ever, actually on their production-possibility frontier obtaining the highest possible output from the combination of given amounts of factors of production, so too trade unions need not be on their equivalent production-possibility frontier—the optimum combination of wages and all other terms and conditions of employment including the effort-input requirement, and employment. A great deal of economic activity consists in moving closer towards the production-possibility frontiers.

Moreover industrial relations are not conducted by coldly calculating economic agents responding only to pure economic laws or predetermined patterns like computer programmes. Both sides may be calculating, but they are responding to organizational and social pressures as well as 'economic' maximizing forces. Unions and union members may regard some feature of a collective agreement or work rule, or the procedural content of bargaining, as so important that they will participate in strike activity even though they know that the expected monetary losses through forgone wages will not be recouped for a very long time-period. A 'principle' becomes at stake or honour or virility seems to be challenged. Because workers and their unions wish to shift the balance of power in industrial and employment relations and, in workers' eyes, obtain a greater degree of dignity in their employment situation, they may be willing to take industrial action which is not based on some precise economic calculation of monetary costs and gains.

Whether we accept the distinction between power and militancy, or whether we simply refer to trade union power, there seems widespread agreement that until the onset of the present recession towards the end of the seventies there had been a marked increase in union power (and militancy) since the thirties.

The recession of the eighties has shifted the balance of power. Unions have less power or behave as if they have. There is no satisfactory explanation of the precise reasons why they have less power and how much less power they have. The best that can be said is that the fear of unemployment affects the willingness of trade union members to press for wage increases which might threaten their jobs. The fear is of losing one's own job. If there are possible effects on other people's jobs this will have much less restraining influence on the members or work group, although if they are in the same union it might exert more influence on union officials. Such an approach is not unreasonable. It is also what economics leads us to expect. Some groups will be able to obtain improvements, perhaps sizeable improvements, in real wages. Others may accept reductions. Unions will try to protect jobs but individuals might prefer to accept redundancy if this is accompanied by redundancy payments in excess of the statutory amounts.

While it might be thought that we cannot satisfactorily estimate the effect of the rise in union power by simply taking union membership density ratios as an indicator, Minford, using the Liverpool University model, has in fact done so. 'The unionization rate in 1963 was 43 per cent; by 1979 it had risen to 56 per cent. Our estimates indicate this would have raised total real wages, once fully worked through, by 13 per cent compared with what they would have been' (1982, 75). Non-union real wages would have been depressed by about 13 per cent. Apart from the objection that union membership is a defective indicator of union power he also assumes a high union wage mark-up of 25 per cent. He concludes that *'the substantial rise in union power since the early 1960s has raised unemployment by about one million'* (73, emphasis in original). His conclusion is that 'Only changes in laws and institutions which take away union power will remove its effects on unemployment, output and the interests of non-unionized workers' (75). These conclusions result from the assumptions fed into the model.

Trade Unions and Government

Most British Monetarists believe that, at least until the advent of the Thatcher administration, trade unions had the power to force government to ensure a high level of demand, or increase the money supply, in order to try to maintain an excessively high level of employment. The adoption of what Hicks called the Labour Standard whereby the level of employment, rather than the price of gold under a Gold Standard, dictated the rest of economic policy was seen as a major cause of inflation resulting directly from the power of trade unions to coerce governments. The broad bipartisan acceptance of full employment was seen by Monetarists as the root cause. They believed that full employment meant in effect over-full employment, that is employment levels higher than that determined by the natural rate of unemployment. To placate the unions, it was argued, governments pumped in excess money supply.[20]

The power of unions was seen as coming from two main sources. First, was their ability to influence their members in political elections. A party which appeared to challenge the high employment levels would, it was believed, incur dire political consequences, in part inspired by trade unions. Even Hayek belived this.

I do not believe that any democratic government can stay the course of a slow reduction of inflation over years—at least not in a highly industrialized country. Even 20 per cent unemployment would probably be borne for six months if there existed confidence that it would be over at the end of such a period. But I doubt whether any government could persist for two or three years in a policy that meant 10 per cent unemployment for most of that period' (1984).

Unemployment in the UK reached 10 per cent in June 1981 and did not fall below that level for the next four years. It was perhaps appropriate that the second edition of Hayek's monograph should appear exactly three years after unemployment hit the 10 per cent level.

Chancellor of the Exchequer Nigel Lawson made the same point in his Mais Lecture when referring to the post-war trends towards 'ever more *ad hoc* interference with free markets' by saying that those who did this, including governments from both parties, 'did so because they had reached the conclusion that political and electoral pressures in a democracy gave them no option'. The policies of the Thatcher Government which he described as the British Experiment 'is a political experiment. It is the demonstration that trade union power *can* be curbed within a free society, and that inflation *can* be eradicated within a democracy' (Lawson 1984, emphases in original).

Second, was the ability of unions to use industrial strength to obtain changes in policies. In addition it was widely believed that British trade unions would be able to ensure that a Labour Government maintained high employment because of the special links between unions and the Labour Party. Experience of the 1974–9 Labour Government challenged this view and the unions' angry response to rising unemployment and wage restraint under the Social Contract played a major part in Labour's defeat in 1979.

That Thatcher Government not only questioned the power of trade unions to insist that government maintain high employment through monetary and other policies, it actually questioned whether the unions had much power at all. The post-war traditional tripartite approach whereby unions through the TUC were consulted on almost all aspects of economic and social policies was ended. Consultation took place only when and if the government wished it to, and this was seldom. It was as though the government suddenly decided that the TUC had no clothes. In the early years it looked as though neither it nor many of its affiliated unions had. 1984 saw rather more challenges.

It is clear that unions may on occasions be able to influence government action in order to change the level of employment. It can no longer be taken for granted that governments will respond to union pressure.

The government can also influence the strength of unions through its legislation. As we shall discuss in Chapter 16 industrial relations legislation can seek to change the balance of power between employers and unions. The legal immunities of trade unions can be changed as in the 1980, 1982, and 1984 legislation. This can affect the circumstances in which industrial action can take place, by whom, and what methods may be used to further that action. It does not necessarily follow that employers will use their legal rights, but governments can alter the context in which bargaining takes place and power exists or can lawfully be used. Pat Lowry, Chairman of ACAS, told a CBI conference: 'The fundamental question was whether employers individually would use the laws that collectively employers' organizations had been demanding so strongly on their behalf.'[21] In one sense this question raises exactly the same issues as those views which allege that unions do not represent their members.

Changes in the law regarding the closed shop or union elections may be seen as shifting the power of trade unions *vis-à-vis* their members and employers. Unions may seek to prevent the enforcement of restrictive legislation, and employers may be unwilling to incur the hostility of unions by using their legal rights. They may be more prepared to do so against employees of other companies, say with secondary picketing.

Government in their role of employer may send signals to other employers which may change the results of wage bargaining. The Thatcher Government's reluctance to go to arbitration may encourage other employers to do the same and this may result in lower wage settlements.

Trade union power in relation both to their members and to employers may be affected by government policies and the ability of government to introduce such policies may be affected by its perception of public opinion. The eighties have witnessed, so far, a decline in the public support or good opinion of trade unions generally.

Conclusions

The existence of trade unions participating in collective bargaining means that economic analysis based on individual atomistic models is irrelevant. Unions do not behave the same as the amalgamation of individuals in a theoretically perfect market. They cannot and should not. They cannot because there is no way an organization can take collective action that is exactly the same as the sum of all the individual decisions. It should not because unions were formed in order to change the processes and results that exist in their absence.

We cannot specify in any precise, consistent, and determinate way the objectives of trade unions. Some unions will give greater priority to wages and others to employment at certain times. At other times they may reverse this. There is no reason to expect all unions to have the same priorities and objectives any more than we expect all individuals to have the same utility functions and expenditure patterns. What we should expect is that unions will resist money wage cuts when times are bad and reluctantly accept some reduction in employment. When times are good they will probably go for both wage improvements and employment expansion.

Unions have the power to increase wages over the level that would pertain without unions. This generally means that employment in those firms or sectors is less than it would be at the lower wage level but the effect on increasing employment by reducing real wages might be relatively small as we shall consider in the next chapter. Many Monetarists believe that unions cannot continually increase money wages in the absence of an increase in the money supply. There is no evidence to support this assertion. Monetarists recognize that unions can increase money and real wages when they become stronger but we are unable to define or quantify trade union strength. We should certainly not do this on the basis of changes in wages; this would be tautological and equate cause to effect.

We can discuss some of the factors which might influence trade union strength, and correspondingly employers' weakness, but we do not know much about what causes shifts in these. More importantly we do not know what induces unions to use their strength or exercise militancy. There seems no reason to believe that unions use all their strength all the time.

The sources of union strength lie in its ability to influence the supply of labour, although it might also be able to influence demand. It can withhold the internal labour supply through strike action if it is able to persuade its members to support it. In modern circumstances there is in Britain relatively little attempt by employers to substitute external labour supply for the internal one during a strike. Unions influence the external labour supply by restricting access to the skill or training provisions and in a minority of cases by obtaining a pre-entry closed shop.

To equate trade unions to monopolists is wrong. A monopolist has no interest in the number of units sold as such. Trade unions are concerned about the number of their members in employment.

Established practices buttressed by trade union strength ensure that in the overwhelming majority of cases employers do not seek to replace the internal unionized labour supply by external supply. Replacement workers are not hired and high-wage union workers dismissed if unions force up wages and obtain favourable effort-bargains. Firms may achieve some similar effect by buying in services rather than employing their own labour or by relocating in an area where wages are lower or unions regarded as more reasonable.

Unions in the post-war period until the late seventies appeared to have the power to ensure that governments followed economic policies designed to maintain a high level of employment. Such power as they had in this regard seems to have been reduced by the advent of the Thatcher Government. In addition the Thatcher Government is seeking to reduce trade union power by industrial relations legislation. The intention is to obtain different results from bargaining by changing the processes by which decisions are taken, the sanctions available to unions in disputes with employers, and the ability of unions to influence the internal labour supply.

Notes to Chapter 9

1. These conclusions are derived from Richardson (1960) which provides a powerful indictment of the uncertainties and inadequacies of perfect competition.
2. This is well illustrated in Flanders (1964) in his analysis and advocacy of productivity bargaining.
3. This is set out at more length in Robinson (1979) and Robinson and Mayhew (1983), ch. 8.
4. Good descriptions and analyses of trade unions and industrial relations can be found in Clegg (1979) and Bain (1983).
5. See Ross (1948) and Dunlop (1950). The debate has changed its format and to some extent its terminology in recent years but the essential issues still provoke disagreements.
6. Wage rounds are examined in Knowles and Robinson (1962) and Elliott (1976). For a concise discussion of wage rounds, see Mayhew (1983).
7. See Kessler, in Robinson and Mayhew (1983).

8. The pioneering work on this subject in the UK is McCarthy (1964). See also Dunn and Gennard (1984).
9. Speaking at a CBI conference reported in *Personnel Management* Aug. 1984, 9.
10. See, for example, Dunlop (1950); Hieser (1970); Johnston (1972); Rosen (1970); De Menil (1971); Calvo (1978); Farber (1978); McDonald and Solow (1981); and Dreze and Modligliani (1981). There is a good summary in Mayhew (1983).
11. For further discussion see, for example, Sapsford (1981). There is a good illustration of this case in Hunter, in Robinson and Mayhew (1983).
12. Department of Employment, *Employment News*, 100, Aug. 1982.
13. In the twelve months to Mar. 1982 real disposable income fell by about 3 per cent (Sir Geoffrey Howe to the Treasury and Civil Service Committee, 1981-2, HC 270, Mar. 1982, Q. 171).
14. See, for example, Hayek, letter to *The Times* 8 June 1980, and Hobart Paper 87 (1984); Walters (1978); Clark (1981); Burton (1980). Friedman has made the point often (1970, 1974, 1975).
15. Clark (1981) provides a very concise summary of the main research findings. Parsley (1980) provides a more extensive survey.
16. See Pencavel (1974); Mulvey (1976); Mulvey and Foster (1976); and Nickell (1977).
17. The simplest and clearest summary of this view is in Minford (1982), but he provides a fuller more theoretical version in Working Paper No. 8103 (1981).
18. See Robinson (1980) and Ulman (1982).
19. See, for example, Hicks (1963). There is a good discussion of the way economists look at strikes in Mayhew (1979).
20. See IEA Readings 17 (1978) and especially Jay (1976).
21. Reported in *Personnel Management*, Aug. 1984, 9.

CHAPTER TEN

Unemployment

PEOPLE are unemployed when they are capable of work, willing to work, but not in a job. Each of these three aspects requires expansion but they are intended to exclude those who are not capable of work because of illness or disability and those who do not wish to work. Some might not wish to work for various reasons, such as married women who have for family reasons opted out of the labour force. Others may have other sources of income, including perhaps state-provided benefits, and prefer not working to working. In the terms in which we considered labour supply in Chapter 6 we exclude those whose preference for leisure over employment leads them not to present themselves for any occupational labour-offer supply curve. We also exclude those who are not capable of work, i.e. those generally agreed not to possess the minimum requirements necessary to become part of any employer's acceptable labour supply curve.

The labour-offer supply curves tell us how many people are prepared to work in particular occupations at specified wage levels given their perceptions of alternative employment opportunities, other sources of income, and preferences for leisure versus work and income. Some of these offers will not be accepted by any employer so that the individuals are not able to find jobs which are acceptable to them given their current labour-offer supply prices.

They may not be able to find a job for one of two main reasons. No employer may be willing to accept them as part of an acceptable supply curve because they do not possess the qualities or abilities and skills which employers are specifying as necessary for acceptance in those occupations given the employers' current requirements. Or, they may be acceptable to employers in terms of skills and abilities, but the employers have no vacancies on existing terms of employment. Put simply, this means that some employer may be willing to hire them in the specified occupation, but not at the prevailing rate of pay given the other applicants for employment, including his present work-force. If the employers' demands for labour were higher, perhaps because pay was lower, they might be offered jobs. They might not be prepared to accept them at a lower pay level.

Some might be unemployed because of imperfect knowledge of the labour market. Individuals may be unaware of some job-offers and some employers may have unfilled vacancies because they do not know that there are suitable people looking for work. Others may be unemployed because their normal employment is seasonal and, either it has become traditional to have periods of unemployment between the regular seasonal work, or there are no suitable offsetting seasonal jobs available. Employers may be reluctant to hire people from seasonal occupations in the off-period because they believe they will lose them later.

In 1942 Keynes wrote a Memorandum in the Treasury estimating the numbers in the different categories of unemployment.[1] His categories were:

(*a*) the hard-core unemployables;
(*b*) seasonal;
(*c*) frictional, moving between jobs;
(*d*) occupational or geographical mismatch due to lack of mobility;
(*e*) demand deficient due to a deficiency in the aggregate effective demand in the economy.

There are other ways of classifying unemployment but for the moment we will consider this set of categories which seek to distinguish on the basis of the causes of unemployment.

(a) Unemployable

We can regard these as those individuals who are not likely to become part of any employer's acceptable-labour supply curve at any realistically expected wage level. This might be because of their physical or mental disabilities, or it could be that it includes some who do not satisfy the condition that they really do wish to work. In practice it is sometimes difficult to apply the latter criterion. With the former, some of them could conceivably become employable if the wages fell low enough, but the level to which they would have to fall before an employer would regard it as worth while to employ them is so far below prevailing and expected levels that the possibility can be ignored.

b) Seasonal unemployment

In some trades or industries employment varies seasonally. Holiday resorts are an obvious example. In some cases such as the construction industry it may be possible as a result of technological developments to reduce seasonality. Workers may accept that there will be periods of unemployment although they might also be willing or eager to work in other jobs in the off-season intending to return to their 'normal' seasonal employment in due course. Figures of unemployment can be adjusted by removing the seasonal factor based on past trends.[2]

(c) Frictional unemployment

At any particular time there will be some people not actually in employment because they are in the process of moving from one job to another. The labour market does not work perfectly smoothly and some unemployment is the result of these frictions in the operation of the market mechanisms. A simple example is where someone arranges to go into a new job but has a period of time between leaving the first job and taking up the other. This can be seen as *ex ante* frictional unemployment; the individuals know they have other jobs to go to and are in a transitional stage.

In other cases people may leave one job without actually having arranged to take up another. They may have left their previous job because they did not like it and believed that they would find a preferable one quite quickly, or they may have lost their job because of redundancy or because their employer thought they were unsuitable. In many cases the employer cannot really decide whether someone in the labour-offer supply curve is properly part of his acceptable-labour supply curve until he has actually employed the person and assessed his abilities and performance. There may well be some mistakes and recruits dismissed. In other cases the employee decides to withdraw from that particular employer-specific occupational labour supply curve after he has gained experience of what the job actually entails and what the job requirements really are. There is then a search by the individual for another job and perhaps a search by the employer for another recruit. This can be seen as *ex post* frictional unemployment if the individual finds another job reasonably quickly. We do not know what 'reasonably quickly' means exactly and it is a matter of judgement as to how long a time we select. *Ex post* frictional unemployment, which may be by far the most common type of frictional unemployment, rests upon the individual moving into employment within some specified time-period. He may have high expectations of finding another job quickly but may be wrong, in which case he is no longer frictionally unemployed but will move into one of the other categories. It may be possible to make reasonably reliable estimates of the proportion of people becoming unemployed in a period who will find jobs within, say, four weeks, but this is only an estimate based on past trends and could be wrong, and it does not tell us which individuals will move into jobs and which will remain unemployed for longer than the frictional period.

Part of this frictional unemployment which on more modern explanations is referred to as job search can be seen as the process of gaining knowledge about actual working conditions which influence the individual's choice of which occupational labour-offer supply curves to join. It might, therefore, be expected to be particularly prevalent among new entrants to the work-force. Frictional unemployment is an important element in the concept of the 'natural rate of unemployment' (NRU) which is part of the analysis of many Monetarists.

(d) Mismatch and structural unemployment

Even if the economy is operating at some stable level of activity, say at full employment level, or is growing at some steady rate, there will be changes in the structural composition of output and employment. Some firms will grow and some decline. New products will appear and old ones go. New methods of production resulting from technological change will alter the demand for particular occupations, and some industries will decline or disappear as a result of technological change, new inventions, or the emergence of foreign competitors. As the demand for products alters, so will industries and firms grow and decline.

In the 1980s there is a bitter disagreement about the extent of structural change that is occurring, or should be allowed to take place in the fuel sector. In this case one group of workers represented by the National Union of Mineworkers is seeking to limit the change in the structure of British fuel-supplying industries. Structural change can be the outcome of market forces responding to technological change or it can be induced, and perhaps deferred or prevented, by government. Where market forces determine the changes it is not always immediately clear whether rising unemployment in a particular industry is the beginning of structural change and so should be regarded as structural unemployment, or whether it is a temporary phenomenon resulting from the cyclical down-swing in demand. Various statistical measures can be devised to try and separate the structural components from general cyclical elements but there is often some uncertainty whether the initial increase in unemployment in a sector is structural, cyclical, or demand-deficient.

Unemployment can exist alongside vacancies for the same occupations because of imperfect information or because of a mismatch between the location of the unemployed and of the vacancies. Occupational mismatch can occur when there are imbalances between the jobs sought by the unemployed and the jobs offered by employers.

One approach to quantifying occupational mismatch is the 'U-minus-V' method, which subtracts the number of occupational vacancies from the number of those in the occupation who are unemployed. However, this lays great emphasis on the idea of a 'permanent' occupation. In practice people change their occupation and some people regard themselves as having an occupation only in a very general sense of being, say, a process factory worker or an assembly-line worker. The occupational mismatch is a concept better used in those cases where individuals have specified skills which they intend to continue using in future jobs. Some occupations have practically no unemployed members from which employers can recruit. For example very few recruits into the police service have previously worked as policemen, and very few unemployed policemen are seeking re-employment as policemen. Occupational mismatch may result from the growth and decline of different industries which require different sorts of skills and different types of labour.

The 'U-minus-V' method assumes that there is little occupational mobility, that we have accurate counts of the unemployed by occupation, and a reliable measure of the true number of vacancies by occupation. As the notification of vacancies in the UK is a voluntary act by employers the number notified is far less than the number of true vacancies. Official estimates suggest that only one-third of vacancies are notified. The notification ratio varies between occupations (Rosewell and Robinson 1980). The reported occupational composition of the unemployed provides ambiguous information. Some are classified according to their last job, some according to their normal occupation or trade, and some according to the type of job they are seeking. Changes in the number of vacancies notified to Job Centres are poor indications of changes in labour market pressures.

There is a regional or geographical element in the mismatch. There may be unemployed people in particular occupations in one locality and vacancies which they would be capable of filling in another part of the country. Because labour is not perfectly mobile, and there are often powerful social and domestic reasons for this, regional imbalances can persist for long periods. Labour might be more mobile if higher rates of pay were offered or if other factors which inhibit mobility were changed. As we shall see later, Monetarists frequently refer to these 'imperfections' in the labour market.

Structural unemployment results from changes in the types of activity undertaken in an economy. These result from changes in product demand which feed through into changes in demand for labour in both quantitative and qualitative terms, and from changes in production processes which alter the amount and type of labour needed to produce a constant level of output. In a dynamic economy we should expect that the amount of labour needed to produce a given level of output, or to meet a given level of aggregate real demand, will decline through time as a result of technological change and improvements in efficiency. At any point in time therefore there will be observed mismatches in the supply and demand for particular types of labour as the labour market is in the process of adjusting to the structural changes as well as experiencing such unemployment as may result from technological improvements or substitution of capital for labour and increases in the efficiency of labour utilization. Some mismatches, other than those arising from frictional factors affecting the speed of labour market adjustments, might therefore be regarded as snapshots or stills taken from the continuing moving picture of structural adaptation. It is therefore extremely difficult to separate mismatch and underlying structural unemployment from current frictional unemployment, and indeed it is difficult to assess how far current mismatches will correct themselves through market mechanisms or can be corrected or reduced as a result of government intervention. What seems currently to be a mismatch in supply and demand may well be the symptoms of a fundamental shift in the structure of employment and production.

If there are structural changes taking place in an economy, reducing real wages may have little effect on the demand for labour in that sector. If unemployment has risen because firms have introduced more and improved machinery, thereby replacing labour with capital, it is unlikely that a fall in real wages will have much effect on employment except perhaps in the long run. Firms have already installed the new equipment. The relative costs of labour and capital might affect their subsequent investment decisions but that might take a considerable time. Reductions in real wages before the new equipment was bought might have influenced the decision so that there might have been less labour substitution, but once the change in the production methods has taken place reductions in real wages are very unlikely indeed to result in an expansion of employment, and indeed might cause even more unemployment if aggregate demand is reduced as we shall discuss in the next section.

Structural unemployment might arise because real wages, or product real wages, are considered too high, but cutting them might not cure this sort of unemployment. It does not follow that the reversal of the perceived cause of unemployment provides a solution. The level of real wages may be important in causing both frictional and structural (and therefore some mismatch) unemployment but reducing real wages may not reduce unemployment arising from these causes. Any cuts in real wages, or slowing down in their rate of growth, may limit or prevent further increases in unemployment, but that is not the same as reducing the current level.

Where the structural changes result from new inventions or developments which lead to new products the level of real wages is unlikely to be a major factor in determining structural unemployment. Teamsters and farriers would have experienced structural unemployment as a result of the motor vehicle almost irrespective of their real wage level, and the makers of gas mantles could not avoid structural unemployment after the development of electric lighting no matter how meagre the subsistence wages at which they were prepared to work.

Some recent research (Layard and Nickell 1985) concludes that there is no evidence that structural unemployment measured by changes in relative unemployment and vacancies by sector of industry has increased. This conclusion like others based on the published official statistics, assumes that the notification ratio of vacancies remains constant and that the classification of the unemployed by sector refers to the job which they last held and not to the sector in which they are looking for work.

(e) Demand-deficient unemployment

For many policy purposes this category of unemployment is the most important. Certainly this was the part that most concerned Keynes and the question of whether unemployment can be reduced by raising the level of aggregate demand lies at the heart of the Monetarist controversy. We have already looked at this in the discussion of the Quantity Theory in Chapter 2. Essentially the debate is about whether an increase in aggregate money demand will lead to an increase in employment and output, or only to an increase in money wages and prices. Keynes argued that some unemployment was the result of insufficient demand in the economy in that if the level of aggregate demand was increased employers would respond by increasing output and employment and could do so without increasing real wage levels. The crux of the argument is that labour markets do not clear in real wage terms, i.e. that at certain times there are people unemployed who would be willing to work at existing real wage levels if jobs were available.

In fact Keynes said that in a demand-deficient situation there would be people willing to work at slightly *lower* real wages if these were lowered by increasing prices rather than lowering money wages (1936, 15). This recognized the practical difficulties in actually reducing money wage levels. It also allowed for the possibility that there is some element of money illusion so that constant money wages with higher prices will not result in a reduction in labour supply as people may not appreciate real wages have fallen.

This argument need not rely on there being money *illusion* in that people may be fully aware that real wages have fallen. Instead it may be a reflection of motivation and behaviour in that people object to an actual cut in money wages which is regarded as demeaning, or believe that their friends and workmates will regard them as undercutting if they take a lower money wage. While money wages may sometimes fall, there is a widespread and pervasive opposition to cuts in money wages which seems to reflect some deep-rooted perception of fairness and reasonableness. No matter what economic theorists may say about rational behaviour, maximization of long-term real income or any other explanation, it has to be recognized that in the real world, in most countries, at most times, there is tremendous resistance to cuts in money wages, and that such cuts do not often take place. Whether they should, and whether there would be gains to all or most of the economic participants if they did, are in large part irrelevant questions if there are powerful forces preventing them. It should be accepted as a fact of life that money wages are very sticky or rigid, downwards. Incidentally, this should not be seen as something caused by trade unions although trade unions can be expected to resist attempts to reduce money wages. The stickiness exists where there are no trade unions, and union organizers recognize that attempts to cut money wages provide good occasions for recruiting members.

While unemployed people may not be willing to accept a job-offer if the money wage in that job has been reduced, they may be willing to do so if the real wage has been reduced as a result of higher prices. Increases in money wages to maintain the real wage level may not be required, and if this is so, there can be only one of two possible explanations. Either the labour market does not clear in real wage terms, i.e. that before real wages fell as prices rose, the labour market was not in equilibrium as some workers were then willing to work for lower real wages, as they are now prepared to do. Or, there has been a shift in the real-wage labour-offer supply curve so that some people, who were not willing to work for the lower real wage before, are now prepared to do so. This could result from their reassessment of the probabilities of obtaining jobs at higher real wages and so be a change in their assessment of their permanent income. If real wages in all jobs are reduced (other than just the real wage in the one job) they may accept the lower real wage in that job. Real-wage labour-offer supply curves may be short-term and therefore unstable.

On the demand side the lower real wage is seen as the reason why employers offer more jobs. They may not have been prepared to do so on previous real wage levels but will do so when real wages fall thereby reducing product real wages. Keynes believed that this was necessary if profit-making employers were to increase employment. As it was assumed that marginal productivity would fall if output and employment increased there would be a fall in product real wages unless prices rose faster than money wages. As the employer cannot reduce the product real wage by cutting money wages his demand for labour will rise to absorb (some of) the excess labour supply only if the price of his product rises. If many employers increase their price the resulting increase in all (or many) prices with constant money wages will reduce the product real wage, demand for labour will rise and there will be additional labour supply forthcoming at the lower real wage level.

If money wages were flexible in both directions so that the reduction in the product real wage could be obtained through lower money wages demand-deficient unemployment might still arise. It is possible that, as money wages fall and labour costs are reduced, prices are also cut, maintaining the product real wage. If some producers use the reduction in money wages and labour costs to reduce prices in order to try to obtain a large share of the market other producers may be obliged to follow suit. In these circumstances a reduction in real wages cannot be engineered through cuts in money wages even if these were acceptable to workers and unions. Constant money wages and rising prices are the only effective way of increasing the demand for labour. The pricing assumption made in Monetarist models of the economy discussed in Chapter 11 assume that prices move with wages. If money wages fall so do prices and so there is no reduction in the product real wage.

A crucial question is whether it is actually necessary to obtain a reduction in real wages and so product real wages in order to increase employment when aggregate demand increases. If it is, it may prove very difficult, if not impossible, to reduce demand-deficient unemployment. Trade unions will not readily accept a reduction in real wages, especially at a time when employment is increasing. If, however, marginal physical productivity is not falling as employment rises there may be no need to reduce real wages in order to reduce product real wages. Increased output with prevailing money wages and prevailing prices will not, in these circumstances, lead to a fall in the product real wage. An increase in aggregate nominal demand may then lead to an increase in real output and employment. Moreover, if imported raw material prices are falling, an increase in aggregate nominal demand with constant money wages and prices will actually lead to an increase in the product real wages, as seems to have occurred in the 1930s. Conversely, if prices of imports are rising, as they do with the worsening exchange rate, tolerated if not induced by the Thatcher Government, there will be a rise in product real wages unless selling prices rise faster than money wages.

If the increase in aggregate demand leads to an expansion of output from new factories which use modern equipment incorporating recent technological improvements, total employment may rise and product real wages may fall. The increase in employment may not be as great as it would have been with the old production methods but there will still be an increase.

It may not therefore be necessary for real wages to fall in order to reduce demand-deficient unemployment. It is only if it is believed that the labour market is always in equilibrium and that marginal physical productivity is declining that a reduction in real wages is necessary in order that the product real wages can fall to provide the necessary incentive to employers to increase output. Recognition that many plants may be organized so as to have a level of production with constant marginal physical productivity and costs, and acceptance of the observable fact that unemployed workers are willing to accept jobs without an increase in real wages, are sufficient to allow us to conclude that an expansion of aggregate demand may lead to an increase in output and employment.

Demand-deficient unemployment may arise as a result of technological change. If, as technology improves, a smaller number of workers is needed to produce a given level of output unemployment may rise. This might appear as structural unemployment, especially if the technological changes are associated with shifts in product demand. However, it is also demand-deficient unemployment in that an increase in aggregate demand is necessary in order to raise the demand for products to a level which meets the available labour supply.

The concept of demand-deficient unemployment as developed by Keynes stems from the view that labour markets do not always clear in real wage terms. There are occasions when the demand for labour is less than the supply at prevailing, or even lower, real wages. Money wages do not fall for institutional and psychological reasons. They may even rise. Inflation is the way in which demand can be increased to take up the available labour supply. This distinction between the demand and supply sides is important to the discussion of whether unemployment is voluntary or involuntary.

Voluntary and Involuntary Unemployment

We can regard unemployment as *voluntary* if people are not prepared to accept jobs which they are capable of performing on existing terms and conditions. Involuntary unemployment exists when people who would form part of the acceptable-labour supply curve of one of the employers within their range of desirable or sought-for jobs, if a vacancy existed, are prepared to accept jobs at existing pay levels (i.e. with current terms and conditions) but are unable to find employment.

Any concept of involuntary unemployment must include some criteria for determining the range of vacancies for which the unemployed person is suitable. We have expressed this in terms of his acceptability to an employer given the existing terms and conditions of employment which include the Job Requirements, and we should add, the state of the product market, production costs, and product real wage level. If there were a vacancy the unemployed person would be recruited but is not hired because no vacancy exists and employers do not replace their existing work-force by new recruits even if the new potential recruits are prepared to work for a lower wage. We cannot quantify the precise level of involuntary unemployment on this definition at a particular point in time. Individual employers may have some idea of the number of people who have applied to them for jobs and how many of these would be acceptable. Even if we could collect all these figures we could not simply aggregate them as some individuals may have applied to, and be found acceptable by, a number of employers.

Determining whether someone is voluntarily unemployed is no less difficult, unless it is asserted that all unemployment is voluntary because an individual can always offer to work for less than the prevailing wage level and the observed fact that he does not reduce his reservation wage and supply price to an employer to get a job is taken as conclusive proof that he is choosing to remain voluntarily unemployed. This would be to ignore basic facts of life. Employers do not on the whole behave in this way. They do not seek to replace their existing work-force by new recruits at lower wages, although they may replace some of their work-force if their Job Requirements change and the existing workers do not have the appropriate abilities or are considered less suitable for training than new recruits.

Any concept of 'involuntary' unemployment involves some criterion for determining the range of vacancies for which the unemployed person is suitable. It is clear that some individuals are not suited for some jobs—they do not on any objective or subjective tests possess the skills, abilities, or aptitudes to perform those jobs.

There are limits on the extent of occupational change which we regard as 'reasonable' and it is only within these limits that refusal to accept a vacancy is regarded as voluntary unemployment. If occupations are regarded as a hierarchy of skills the upper limit is set by the skill component in the Job Requirements of the vacancy related to the skills possessed by the individual. This limit may be raised if the employer with the vacancy provides training which transforms the existing skills of the unemployed so that the Job Requirements can be met. The lower limit which determines the downward movement in the occupational hierarchy depends on what is regarded as 'reasonable'.

We might say that a physicist was voluntarily unemployed if he refused a job-offer as a mathematics teacher but not if he refused a vacancy on the assembly line in a car plant. Yet we might say that a bus-driver who refused the assembly-line job was voluntarily unemployed. These are subjective judgements and unless we specify certain conditions about the extent of occupational change that is part of our definition of 'voluntary' or 'involuntary' unemployment there is no way of avoiding this overtly subjective element. Any such specification would, of course, itself be subjective.

What we are left with is a view that at certain times there are people unemployed who would be willing to accept employment on existing terms, or at slightly lower real wages if jobs were available. This does not mean that their own real wage might not fall considerably. Individuals might be prepared to accept a much lower real wage if they lose their previous job; the existing or slightly lower real wage refers to the levels existing in the jobs where the vacancies appear.

There are other judgements to be made before we can decide whether someone is voluntarily or involuntarily unemployed. The geographical location of the vacancy might be taken into account. A vacancy in the same occupation at the same rate of pay might be considered 'reasonable' if it is within a certain distance of the unemployed person's home, but unreasonable if it is farther away.

We might also wish to impose some condition regarding the rate of pay. Consider the example of a craftsman, say a printer, who becomes unemployed for reasons which most people would accept as outside his control. His firm closes down and he is made redundant. If he is offered a job as a labourer in the same town we might regard him as involuntarily unemployed if he refused it. The downward occupational mobility might be regarded as unreasonable. If he were offered a vacancy as a printer so that he was carrying out his previous occupation we might regard any such refusal as voluntary unemployment, or we might say that if the job-offer was at a wage very much lower than his previous one, or below the recognized rate, or the trade union rate for printers in that locality, it would be reasonable for him to refuse and therefore he would be involuntarily unemployed. This not only incorporates an element of 'reasonableness' into the definition of voluntary and involuntary unemployment; it does so with regard to the wage level.

Any system of unemployment insurance has to deal with the question of 'reasonable' or 'unreasonable', or voluntary and involuntary, unemployment. Refusal to accept a 'reasonable' job offer usually leads to some sanction. However, the administrative rules defining reasonableness and voluntary unemployment are not necessarily those which economists adopt.

The concept of involuntary unemployment can be relevant at both the micro- and the macro-level. With the former we examine the position of an individual and decide whether he is voluntarily or involuntarily unemployed on the basis of his skills, abilities, qualification, and past employment record in relation to the job vacancies which face him. This inevitably involves the use of certain subjective criteria relating to the extent of occupational change which is considered reasonable, the terms on which a vacancy should be accepted, and perhaps the geographical location of the vacancy. This is the sort of judgement people make when they refer to the unemployed as 'workshy'. If we say that someone is involuntarily unemployed we are saying that in our opinion it is reasonable that he is unemployed as there are no suitable jobs available. What is regarded as suitable is influenced by social, political, and economic factors as well as our personal set of moral values, which may coincide or not with the set of criteria used in the administration of social security schemes.

The macro-level concept of involuntary unemployment is derived from the notion of demand-deficient unemployment. There is an excess supply of labour at prevailing money and real wage levels. Aggregate employment will rise if aggregate demand is increased by government measures even though this may result in some inflation. Indeed, it has to result in some inflation if a fall in product real wages is what generates the increased demand for labour, although it may not actually be necessary to cut real wages when aggregate demand increases.

Monetarist and Voluntary Unemployment

Not all economists, including some non-Monetarists, would accept that there is a concept of involuntary unemployment. 'The essence of modern theories of unemployment is that unemployment is a *productive* activity and the result of *choice*. (Even the laid-off worker can be assumed implicitly to have been offered an option to continue work at lower wages.)' (Addison 1981, 89, emphasis in original).

Let us clear the laid-off worker point up first. An assertion that he has been offered and refused the option to continue working at a lower money wage is simply just not warranted. To assume that he has means flying in the face of evidence. There are some circumstances when even an offer to work for nothing would be refused. The other costs of production would not justify employment and production in the face of perceived market conditions.

The first sentence in the Addison quote might be better if it read: '*Some* modern theories see *some* unemployment as productive activity and the result of choice.' As we have seen, the permanent income hypothesis allows for the possibility that some individuals anticipate periods of unemployment when estimating their permanent income. This does not mean that they have chosen to be unemployed; it means they correctly anticipated the unemployment. Theories of job search may regard some unemployment as a productive activity but it does not follow that all the unemployed decided to become or remain unemployed in order to search for a better job. Some may have left their previous job to search for another. Some may have lost their job and then looked for another. This might be productive activity, but it is not necessarily the result of choice.

Despite Addison's statement, even the most cold-blooded of modern economic theorists do not regard *all* unemployment as voluntary. They might place great importance on the unwillingness of individuals to accept the reduction in wages necessary to induce some employer to hire them and refer to this as voluntary unemployment, but they still leave room for some involuntary unemployment. The cause of it is not the unwillingness of individual workers to appreciate their 'true' market worth and adjust their acceptable wage level, or reservation wage, accordingly. It is the perceived harmful effects of state interference. To these modern theorists, if the state, in a 'misguided' attempt to improve the conditions of lower-paid workers, should impose minimum wage levels it may create involuntary unemployment.

For example assume that some individuals have low marginal revenue products, i.e. the wage they are able to obtain from an employer based on the value of their contribution to the employer's productive process, is low, but they also have a low reservation wage so that they are willing to work for that low wage. If legislative provisions impose a higher wage than the value of the marginal product and the reservation wage, these individuals will be unemployed—not because they are unwilling to work for a wage equal to the value of their marginal product, but because the law prevents them from doing so. By imposing a minimum wage in excess of the assumed market-clearing wage—that which is acceptable to both employer and worker—the individuals are involuntarily unemployed. The voluntary labour market transaction that might take place between him and the employer is legally prevented. This person is truly involuntarily unemployed.

Yet while many of the new breed of economists might accept this, they are also extremely reluctant actually to call it involuntary unemployment, perhaps because of its Keynesian connotations. Or it may be that once it is conceded that there can be one sort of involuntary unemployment the doors of reason are opened to there being others. The extreme member of the new extreme school of thought might seek to argue that it is still voluntary unemployment as the individual could choose to obtain higher skills and training, perhaps by investing time and/or money in education or training programmes, thereby increasing his marginal productivity and so his value to an employer, who would then hire him at a wage above the statutory minimum. This would be not only to stretch the linguistic analysis implication of the meaning of 'voluntary' past breaking-point, but also to ignore the simple fact that there may well be individuals who do not have access to training to give them skills and abilities sufficient to provide a value of marginal product equal to the statutory wage. This is why advocates of minimum wage intervention also frequently support education and training programmes to improve the skills of the lower paid.

Minford regards all unemployment as voluntary. According to him trade union monopoly power raises wages in the union sector above the market-clearing levels. There is, therefore, excess supply of labour to the union sector. Unable to obtain employment in that sector this labour is diverted to the non-union sector. 'These additional supplies of labour force wages down there, until supply is equal to demand' (1983, 62). However, the supply of labour to the non-union sector is diminished as a result of the social security system which creates a floor to wages, i.e. the reservation wage is determined by the replacement ratio. 'Consequently wages cannot fall enough to create much additional demand' (63). Unemployment is regarded as voluntary because the supply of labour is lower than it might be as a result of workers choosing not to accept wages below some 'floor' created by the social security system. Presumably, on this argument, if they chose—were prepared—to work for lower money wages it is assumed that demand would expand sufficiently to absorb them all, although, of course, wages might have to fall very considerably before demand increased sufficiently. 'It is a technical convention in economics to call the decisions of these people "voluntary", because they are doing their best even in poor circumstances, but they could just as well be described as involuntarily forced out of the union sector' (63).

If the 'technical convention' means that 'voluntary', when used to refer to unemployment, does not have the same meaning as in everyday usage—and there are a number of economic terms where this is so—it also means that none of the moral judgements normally associated with 'voluntary' action should be made about the unemployed. We should not, for example, assume that it is the fault of the unemployed that they are in that condition. We should not assume that they are themselves responsible for their unemployment, and we should not allow notions of self-inflicted hardship to influence our decisions about how society should treat the unemployed in regard to social security payments. We should regard 'voluntary unemployment' as neutral in the sense of whether it is reasonable or unreasonable for those individuals to be unemployed. Such schizophrenia is not likely to be found amongst politicians or public opinion generally. 'Voluntary' unemployment has, and will continue to have, the connotation that it is the individual's own decision which causes his unemployment.

The association of moral responsibility with the term 'voluntary' unemployment—which, if 'voluntary' was but a technical convention, would not exist—is present in Minford's analysis and proposed remedies. He says: 'In principle, the state should only provide benefits where the unemployed can get *no* job, however unpleasant or low paid' (1983, 46, emphasis in original). This is no technical convention; it is a straightforward assertion of a value-judgement taking advantage of the linguistic ploy that 'I have principles—you have prejudices'. It deals with the question of the boundaries of 'reasonableness' when deciding whether someone is voluntarily or involuntarily unemployed by appearing to abolish the concept of reasonableness altogether.

He proposes new rules for payment of unemployment benefit. He suggests that there be a pool of jobs called 'workfare' consisting of all vacancies notified to Job Centres plus any specially designed community work schemes. After six months' unemployment, three months for those below twenty-five years of age, benefits would be denied anyone refusing a 'workfare' job. For the first six months in such a job the previously unemployed person would receive his entitled unemployment (and related?) benefits if these are greater than the market wage rate for the job plus in-work benefits. After six months his benefits would fall to the market rate plus in-work benefits. A private firm would refund the state at the market rate for the job. This would, it is claimed, lead to an increase in the number of private sector low-wage vacancies 'as firms got to hear of people filling them, more would come on to the market. At present it is a pointless expense to advertise jobs at low wages which are marginally competitive with benefits' (46).

The explanation given for the low notification rate of low-wage vacancies is rather odd. If they are notified to Job Centres there is no expense in advertising. The use of 'market rate' is confusing. The wage currently offered by the firm cannot be taken as the 'market rate' for, almost by definition, that wage is too low to attract people into the job. What we can reasonably infer from this is that the *market* rate—if this means market clearing rate, at which supply equals demand—is higher than the currently offered wage rate.

However, it seems likely that 'market rate', as used by Minford, means the wage rate offered by the employer. The proposal is really to subsidize employers for the first six months of a new recruit's employment by making up the difference between what the employer pays and what the worker would get in benefits were he unemployed. It is Speenhamland with a vengeance. It positively encourages employers to reduce the wage rate offered. They know there will be a bountiful supply of unemployed people fearful of the denial of *all* benefits if they reject the job-offer—no matter how low the wage. Moreover, the unemployed would be unable to protest about the unsuitability or unreasonableness of the job. 'Workfare' jobs are 'a pool of jobs which *must* be accepted as a condition of benefit' (46, emphasis in original).

The description of unemployment as 'voluntary' when such Draconian proposals are presented is no mere technical convention. It reflects deeply held moral views that all unemployment is the result of deliberate voluntary choices by individuals.

This is to stretch the meaning of the word 'voluntary' to the breaking point of denying the relevance of any substantive content to the terms on which 'free' choices are made. All criminal laws, for example, contain some provisions which allow the circumstances in which the act took place to be taken into account in determining the responsibility of the individual charged with the offence. It is recognized that in some circumstances conditions are such that the individual cannot be held to have freely or voluntarily chosen to undertake or perform the action in question. The notion that all unemployment is voluntary therefore denies all considerations of minimum human standards or any concept of the basic dignity of labour or civilized behaviour, and seeks to inject into labour economics a complete disregard for social, humane, and psychological considerations that is totally rejected in all other aspects of human behaviour. There just is no room whatsoever for any mitigating circumstances. If the individual does not seek to reduce his acceptable wage level to whatever is necessary to induce some employer to employ him, it is because he has decided to be voluntarily unemployed in that he will only trade off his leisure for somewhat higher wage levels than necessary to induce some employer to offer him a job.

Measuring Unemployment

The two main methods of collecting statistics of the numbers unemployed are by using statistics gathered as a result of some administrative actions or by carrying out surveys based on questionnaires which ask people about their employment position and their employment intentions. The administrative series come from five main sources: (i) the Employment Offices of the Manpower Services Commission or the Careers Service which deals with most of the unemployed aged under 18 years; (ii) Unemployment Benefit Offices at which claims for unemployment benefits are made; (iii) National Insurance records; (iv) DHSS local offices in regard to unemployed people claiming supplementary allowances; and (v) the National Unemployment Benefit Systems computers. Survey data are collected through the population census and through interviews. In addition, there is the biennial European Communities (EC) Labour Force Survey from 1973 onwards, covering about 85,000 households and, from 1971, the continuing General Household Survey, covering about 12,000 households. The Family Expenditure Survey covers about 10,000 households a year.

Surveys allow much more information to be collected about the individuals on such things as employment history, reason for unemployment, and whether those who are seeking work are registered as unemployed. The main disadvantage is 'that they rely on the quality and relevance of the replies by individuals who show varying degrees of realism and appreciation of the kind of jobs they would expect to get and the related pay and conditions of work' (*Employment Gazette*, May 1980, 501). In the language we have been using this means that people may regard themselves as part of certain labour-offer supply curves when an objective or realistic assessment would conclude that they have very little, if any, chance of becoming part of those employers' acceptable-labour supply curve. Nevertheless, the official view is that it is possible to reconcile the data from the population censuses and household surveys with that from administrative sources 'to provide broad estimates of the unregistered unemployed'.

Official Statistics of Unemployment

While some countries use the survey method, the main source of official statistics on unemployment in the UK was the series of the number of registered unemployed produced by the Department of Employment. Until October 1982 the statistics showed the number of people registered as unemployed at Employment and Benefit Offices who were capable of, available for, and seeking work.[3] The figures were therefore based on administrative decisions regarding registration. Registration was mainly, but not totally, in order to receive unemployment or social security benefits. Some people, mainly married women who may not have been entitled to benefits in their own right, may not have registered even though they were capable of, available for, and seeking, work. Some others may have done so. It is thought that the spread of Job Centres to replace the old-style employment exchanges may have encouraged more people not entitled to benefits to register (*Employment Gazette*, May 1980, 500). Some who registered as unemployed were not included in the count. These included adult students aged eighteen or over seeking vacation work, non-claimants to benefit seeking part-time work only, those temporarily stopped who have been suspended or laid off by their employer for short-periods and expect to return to their previous employment, and so are not unemployed in the sense of having lost their jobs, but were available for work on the days in question, the disabled requiring sheltered employment, and the out-of-work sick. From November 1982 it was no longer a requirement of claiming unemployment and related social security benefits that the individual be registered as unemployed at an Employment Office or Job Centre. Registration became a voluntary act and some non-claimants may have continued to register. Since November 1982 statistics of claimants are obtained from the Unemployment Benefit Offices.[4] This is a significant change in the basis of the regular Department of Employment series of unemployment and the two systems were run in parallel for part of 1982 to see if it were possible to provide a basis for linking them. Apart from any change in the continuity of the overall series of unemployment figures there was a serious loss of information about the occupational composition of the unemployed. The switch to collection of statistics by UBOs means that the quarterly series giving details of the occupations of the unemployed is no longer provided. It is understood that such an analysis was regarded as too expensive to introduce into the computerised UBO system. The Employment Services Division will continue to produce half-yearly analyses of the occupational composition of the voluntary registrations, but it is very doubtful if this will be as useful a series as the quarterly one based on *all* registered unemployed.

The 1982 change in the basis of the official monthly count of the numbers unemployed was very important. 'The change in the basis of the unemployment count is an inevitable consequence of the introduction of voluntary registration on October 18.'[5] Because registration is now voluntary, many unemployed people may not register; registration may involve extra expenses in attending a Job Centre as well as additional time. Only unemployed claimants for benefit are now included. 'The term "claimants" in the unemployment count is used to include those unemployed people who claim unemployment benefit, supplementary benefits, and national insurance credits.'[6] Strictly speaking, the definition should be those who *successfully* claim UB, Supplementary Benefit, or insurance credits. Claimants who are refused all three on the grounds of ineligibility will not be counted and it is not necessary for an individual to claim all three in order to be included.

Basing the official count of unemployment on benefit claimants obtained from the computerized records of the Unemployment Benefit

Offices also means that those unemployed who find a job or move off the claimants' register for some other reason will be traced more quickly. The previous manual count led to some delay in movers-out of unemployment being reflected in the unemployment figures. To this extent the previous series of registered unemployed always overstated the number unemployed on any particular date. The new method includes some people who would not have been counted previously, as the severely disabled unemployed are now included. The combined effect of these three factors was to reduce the official count of unemployed in October 1982, when figures on both methods were produced, by some 246,000.

Exclusion of non-claimants	− 161,000
Reduction in time-lag for removing those who have moved out of unemployment	− 108,000
Inclusion of severely disabled unemployed	+ 23,000
Net effect	− 246,000

While Prime Minister Heath was not able to reduce inflation at the stroke of a pen, Prime Minister Thatcher was able to reduce the official count of unemployment by a quarter of a million at the push of a computer switch. The changes in methods reduced the percentage rate of unemployment in October 1982 seasonably unadjusted and including school-leavers from 13.8 per cent to 13.1 per cent, and from 12.8 per cent to 12.4 per cent seasonally adjusted, excluding school-leavers.

Further statistical refinements and improvements to correct discovered defects in official series may lead to a further reduction in the official series of the percentage rate of unemployment. Recent work by the Department of Employment suggests that the series of estimates of the provisional employment and working population series for periods after mid-1981 are too low.[7] This has led to revised estimates. 'Any understatement in the employment figures also has some effect on the calculation of the unemployment rate. Use of the adjusted figures would reduce the rate, but the effect would be negligible and accordingly the adjustment will be held over for incorporation on the occasion of the next revision' (*Employment Gazette*, June 1983, 244). What is considered 'negligible' is a matter of judgement but the effect could be to reduce yet further the official unemployment percentage rate by 0.1 or 0.2 percentage points. If their policies are driving up unemployment, government might welcome even negligible contributions to reductions in the official figures.

It is interesting that the first statement by the Department of Employment about the effects of the change in methods estimated that the effect would be to reduce the unemployment figures by 'very broadly some 50,000' (*Employment Gazette*, April 1981, 202). That article did not give details showing how the 50,000 was arrived at, but a subsequent 1982 article stated that they had expected there to be a reduction of some 120,000 as a result of excluding non-claimants, an increase of 20,000 from including the severely disabled, and a further *increase* of 50,000 as a result of switching to a computer-based, rather than a manual, count, making a net drop of 50,000.[8] The 1982 article went on to say that they now expected the switch to a computer-based count to lead to a reduction rather than a rise in the number counted as unemployed, and that the manual count was probably still overstating the actual numbers unemployed as a result of industrial action taken by civil servants in their 1981 dispute and the current high levels of unemployment. (This is presumably their way of cautiously saying that with the increase in the work-load arising from higher unemployment, staff at Job Centres and Careers were unable to make good any deficiencies arising from the 1981 dispute because of work pressure or shortage of staff.) However, somewhat surprisingly, the article did not put forward any estimate of the likely reduction in the unemployment count likely to result from the switch to computers. They said that their latest assessments suggested little or no difference to the effects of excluding non-claimants, including the severely disabled, but were silent on the expected effects of the computers. Some public indication had been given that the change would lead to a reduction in the official count, but the only figure on record was the 50,000 drop. This was now reckoned to be too low, but we did not know by how much. In the event it was around 200,000 too low.

The reason for introducing the change was to abolish the requirement that the unemployed had to register. Secretary of State for Employment, Norman Tebbit, said: 'Our reason for introducing it is that it saves £10 million a year and enabies us to use some 1350 less Civil Servants in conducting the count' (reported in the *Daily Telegraph*, 3 December 1982). One cannot help but ponder the question posed in a *Daily Telegraph* editorial of the same day. 'Would Mr Tebbit have been so keen to switch to the cost-saving computer if his officials had warned him that the unemployment total would have risen by 250,000?' There is also the question of when he was advised it would lead to a reduction of 250,000 rather than 50,000, and why the rest of us weren't told?

The 'adjustments' to the official count continue. In the 1983 Budget the Chancellor made two provisions 'to help older workers'.[9] From April 1983 men aged sixty and over no longer have to sign on at an unemployment benefit office to secure national insurance credits. Occupational pensioners below the normal retirement age can therefore obtain credits towards their state retirement pension without signing on. By 12 May 1983, 93,600 men no longer had to sign on. Under the second provision, men aged sixty and over can, from June 1983, qualify for the higher long-term rate of supplementary benefit as soon as they come on to Supplementary Benefit. After the June 1983 increases in benefit rates this meant the difference between the long-term weekly rate for a couple of £54–5 rather than the ordinary rate of £43–55. The long-term unemployed are normally denied the higher long-term SupBen rates. This provision therefore provides a strong incentive to older men to switch to the long-term Supplementary Benefit levels of benefits rather than remain signing on as unemployed. It was estimated that this will reduce the number signing on by some 40,000 (Department of Employment press release, 3 June, 1983).

Both these provisions can be justified on grounds other than reducing the number of the official unemployment count. Many occupational pensioners may have effectively retired and withdrawn from the labour force and so ought not perhaps to be included in the unemployment figures. There also seems no good reason to deny the long-term unemployed the long-term Supplementary Benefit levels; if these minimum income standards are considered appropriate for those receiving Supplementary Benefits for long periods they should be received irrespective of the source of the misfortune leading to the need for supplementary benefits. The decision to deny long-term benefit levels must rest on the view that they would act as a disincentive by raising the replacement ratio and so the reservation wage. However laudable the objectives might be, it is the case that both will have the effect of reducing the official count of unemployment, even though they were slipped in as Budget changes rather than declared steps to reduce the official count.

There is now a plethora of special employment and training measures introduced by governments of both parties, initially to deal with what were seen as short-term temporary special problems of unemployment in certain areas or among certain groups, but which have become increasingly recognized as much longer problems. In December 1984 an estimated total of 661,523 people were covered by the various measures (see Table 10.1).

In the absence of these schemes not all 662,000 would have appeared in the official count even before the October 1982 changes. Some of those in the Young Workers' Scheme might have been employed perhaps by the same employers in the absence of the special schemes. While there may be administrative action to prevent the more extreme cases of substitution of trainees for previously employed posts there is undoubtedly some substitution or displacement effect. Some of the

Table 10.1 *Special Employment and Training Measures: Numbers covered December 1984*

Community Industry	8,000
Community Programme	130,000
Enterprise Allowance Scheme	39,000
Job Release Schemes	79,000
Job Splitting Scheme	1,023
Training in Industry	1,500
Young Workers' Scheme	63,000
Youth Training Scheme	340,000
Total	661,523

Source: Department of Employment press release, 31 Jan. 1985.

young people on these schemes would have been employed in the absence of the schemes but others would have become part of the unemployed. The official estimate is that the direct effect of the special measures in December 1984 was to reduce the number of people claiming unemployment benefit by about 475,000. However, as the press release goes on to say, this estimate 'depends on a number of uncertain assumptions and is the Department's best estimate of the direct effects only'.

The combined effect of the change in the official count, the requirements regarding occupational pensioners and men over sixty years of age and the special measures, might be to reduce the officially recorded unemployment figures by something in the region of 750,000. There are also other unemployed people who appear in neither the new or the old official count of registered unemployed. The survey method of estimating unemployment can pick up these individuals. The Labour Force Survey in 1981 estimated that there may have been some 400,000 unregistered unemployed. Of these some 130,000 were men and over a half of the 270,000 women were looking for part-time work.[10] On the basis of this additional information the conclusion has been drawn that the new official statistics of unemployment understate the 'true' figure by something like one million. It is interesting to note that the Manpower Services Commission estimated that for mid-1981 the omission of the unregistered unemployed and those on special measures came to about three-quarters of a million people.[11] This was before the October 1982 change removed an additional quarter of a million.

Against this it can be, and has been, countered, that the official measure even on the new basis includes a number of people who ought not to be regarded as unemployed as they are either unemployable or not actually looking for work. The Labour Force Survey 1981 estimated the number of registered unemployed who were not regarded as unemployed by the survey because they were not looking for paid work in the week before they were interviewed for the survey, as 400,000. This total is the same as the number of unregistered unemployed found by the survey.

According to the view one takes about the meaning of unemployment and particularly the requirement to be looking for or seeking work, one can come up with quite different estimates of the numbers unemployed. As the *Employment Gazette* says, neither the count from administrative records nor the results of a particular survey

> should be regarded as providing a unique indication of the level of unemployment as each has some special features. For a number of reasons, some people who are seeking work do not register for employment or claim benefit, and therefore do not appear in the monthly count. On the other hand, some people included in the monthly count, who may register for a number of valid reasons, are not actively seeking work and so would not be counted as unemployed by a survey (June 1983, 265).

There is an argument about the number of 'truly' unemployed which is more than mere number quibbling. If there are fewer unemployed than we are led to believe, then perhaps the economy is doing better than we think; or if some of those appearing in the statistics as unemployed are not really looking for work, then there might be less pressure or concern to take action to stimulate the economy and create more jobs. Conversely, if there are significantly more unemployed than the official count suggests, then the economy is in even worse shape than we are led to believe, and this might provide grounds for taking stronger measures to deal with the situation. We will, therefore, consider some of the arguments which suggest that the official statistics of unemployment overstate the 'true' level of unemployment, a view favoured by some Monetarists.

(a) Capable of work

We have seen that the severely disabled requiring sheltered employment were excluded but are now counted. In December 1979 there were a further 120,000 disabled people included in the total of 1,355,000 who might have had difficulty in finding jobs in open employment. In addition, there are some people who say they are looking for work and are available for it, but given the existing condition on the labour market are 'unemployable or virtually so', but there 'is, however, no firm evidence on which to make even a broad estimate of the number who may be considered unemployable whether through lack of capacity or of application' (*Employment Gazette*, May 1980, 501–2). In effect what the Department of Employment is saying is 'We are fairly sure there are some but we do not know how to count them accurately'. The Department carried out exercises in 1973 and 1976 to try and estimate the number of unemployed whose employment prospects were poor. These estimates inevitably rest on subjective assessments made by the staff of local employment offices of people's employment prospects and are, understandably, influenced by perceptions of local labour market conditions. An individual who is regarded as having poor employment prospects in one locality might have better ones elsewhere. Both surveys showed about 135,000 adult males with poor prospects even though unemployment for adult males had increased from 453,000 to 888,000. Some disabled people were included in the 135,000. In so far as those with 'poor employment prospects' equate to the unemployables or those not really capable of work, these two surveys suggest that the number does not fluctuate directly with the general level of unemployment of adult males. Also, it turned out that some 15 per cent of those classified as having poor employment prospects actually found some employment for some period in the six months following the survey. The official Department of Employment conclusion is that 'Experience suggests that while some individuals are very difficult to employ, it is not possible to draw a clear line in terms of a set of subjective characteristics which would be operationally practicable in subdividing the registered unemployed on the basis of those who are employable and those who are not' (*Employment Gazette*, May 1980, 502).

(b) Available for work

This is essentially an administrative requirement needed to satisfy the Unemployment Benefit tests. An individual cannot obtain Unemployment Benefit if he lays down conditions such that he is not in fact available for work. This provision may impinge particularly on married women with children who wish to work between certain times, on certain days, or with other conditions. Some registered unemployed are seeking only part-time work. It becomes a matter of judgement how far they should be regarded as part of the available labour supply, according to the definition of labour supply that we are using. These individuals might also exert different sorts of economic pressures on the labour market and so have a different effect on changes in money wages in so far as these respond to supply and demand factors. If employers demand more part-time workers, as they seem to be doing, the question of who should, or should not, be included in the unemployment figures, if these are to provide a satisfactory indicator of labour supply, because more important.

(c) Seeking work

There are differences between the number of people counted as seeking work according to whether we measure them by counting the registered unemployed or gather the information by survey methods where individuals are asked whether they are actively looking for, or seeking, work and may be questioned about the steps they have taken in their active search. Some writers have argued that there are significant numbers of the registered unemployed who are not looking for work. Miller and Wood (1982) interpret the General Household Survey data to conclude that some 13 per cent of the registered unemployed were not looking and 'this lack of urgency' remains fairly constant at about 12 per cent of registered unemployed as the numbers of registered unemployed fluctuates. A survey by Daniel (1974, and also see 1981) showed 12 per cent who did not intend to find a job because of age, health, or domestic and family circumstances; the figure falls to 10 per cent if confined to males.

Occupational pensioners registering as unemployed or claiming national insurance credits towards their state pension may have been in this category although the 1983 Budget changes will have reduced their number. Others may conclude that, given their state of health and the general condition in the labour market, they are so unlikely to find a job that they no longer believe it is worth while looking. Repeated failure to obtain a job, and the feelings of personal rejection that may go with this, lead them to withdraw from labour market search. This 'discouraged worker effect' may be much more marked amongst those on the fringes of labour market activity, those marginal workers who are at a disadvantage in job competition and whose employment prospects are disproportionately adversely affected as the general level of unemployment rises. They are, in effect, concluding that they have the highest propensity to be excluded from the employer's acceptable-labour supply curve when there is a strengthening of competition when more workers offer themselves for job vacancies. The official view is that 'the number of "discouraged workers" in the UK is believed to be small . . .' (*Employment Gazette*, May 1980, 501).

If workers believe that they are very unlikely to be hired in existing economic circumstances, perhaps because they recognize that no matter what some economic theory might say, money wages are sticky downwards and real wages may be above some theoretically optimum level, then not only is it odd to regard them as voluntarily unemployed, it is also very odd to expect them to continue searching. The better the information they have and the more accurate their assessment that they are unlikely to be hired, the more rational it should be for them to stop wasting their time in fruitless search. To expect someone to keep on looking for something which he does not expect to find is not only to impart irrationality to him, it also requires irrationality or illogicality on the part of the commentator. Not searching does not mean not wanting to work.

It can be rational and sensible to want to work while recognizing that in existing circumstances there is no possibility of obtaining a job. Of course it can be argued that if they *really* wanted to work they would reduce their labour supply price or their preferred job choice or both, but this is both circular and unrealistic. Some individuals cannot lower their expected job choice very much; they are already at the bottom of the skills and ability hierarchies. Others appreciate that in the world in which they live individuals cannot in many situations bargain down their wage by offering to work for less pay than those already in employment. These might be regarded as 'sociological' factors and not part of an 'economic' analysis or explanation, but this is not a satisfactory distinction if we wish to explain the real world in which we live. If these factors influence behaviour which economists wish to study they need to be taken into account.[12]

We are unable to measure very precisely either those who are not looking for work or those who are voluntarily unemployed. In the first case we have to have some criterion of 'looking'. There must be some minimum activity which qualifies and, although different surveys adopt criteria, none is totally satisfactory. In the second case we should know something about the person's attitudes and motives and frequently these cannot really be known but only inferred from behaviour and we might well get them wrong. Moreover, even if someone was not looking for work if offered a job he would take it. This is not necessarily voluntary unemployment.

The October 1982 change will have adverse effects on the reliability of the occupational classification of the unemployed. The benefits claims offices (UBOs) do not have experience of occupational classification, and this will lead to some problems about producing accurate figures of the categories of the unemployed. From the viewpoint of estimating where labour market pressures might arise, the sort of labour that is available, and the appropriate training provisions to ease re-employment this could have most regrettable consequences. As we shall see, it can make estimates of the natural rate of unemployment more difficult and it will, of course, increase the difficulties involved in trying to use a 'U-minus-V' approach to the quantification of mismatch unemployment. But the crucial issue is whether or not we should regard all unemployment as voluntary or whether we believe that in reality there are, at certain times at least, some people who are involuntarily unemployed. As we have discussed, this is a complex issue and rests, ultimately, on views one holds about how the labour market actually operates, rather than how it might, or should, in some theoretical situation, and upon whether one accepts certain limitations on what is regarded as the effective range of choice within which one is held to choose freely. If we believe that there are some jobs which it is reasonable to expect an unemployed person not to accept without this leading to the conclusion that he is then voluntarily unemployed we reject the totally voluntary interpretation of unemployment. We may not be able to specify precisely what the range of reasonableness for an unemployed individual is, and in practice this might not coincide with his own range of perceived job openings which form part of his own family of labour-offer supply curves. This family of curves may change as a result of experiences in the labour market and changes in perceptions of the possibilities of gaining admission into an employer's acceptable-labour supply curve. The concepts are therefore imprecise and in some ways indeterminate, but that does not mean that they are of no value in explaining labour market behaviour and in influencing the way we perceive and analyse labour markets, merely that we cannot quantify precisely.

It is said that there is another group of registered unemployed who are not looking for work because they choose to receive unemployment and related social security benefits instead of accepting one of the job-offers which they believe face them as the replacement ratio is too high.

An official view is

there is a very small proportion of the unemployed who would receive less in work than they receive from social benefits and support—most of these are men with two or more dependent children to suport who would be among the lower paid when in work. A greater number would have only a small margin extra when in work than when out of work, but the effect on their willingness to work is negligible. Certainly, there are many who prefer to work even if they receive only a relatively small amount, if anything, above that which they could claim in social benefits (*Employment Gazette*, May 1980, 502).

As we have seen from the discussion of replacement ratios in Chapters 6 and 7 it is very difficult to produce firm evidence to support the case that high replacement ratios arising from unduly generous unemployment benefits have much deterrent effect on the willingness to work of most people. As Atkinson (1981) says: 'there is no strong evidence that there is a large proportion of volunteers among the unemployed watching the monetarist experiments of the early 1980s. It does indeed appear to be a "conscript" army.'

However, it is also recognized that the evidence regarding unemployment benefit and unemployment duration in Britain is far from robust. 'There is, therefore, substantial scope for the conclusions drawn to be influenced by prior beliefs' (Atkinson et al. 1984). There are also complications in that some of the research tried to assess the effect of unemployment benefits on the length of unemployment, that is the decision whether to remain unemployed or to accept a job; while other work seeks to test whether the replacement ratio influences the decision to remain employed or become unemployed.

While there seems little evidence to support the view that there are large numbers of unemployed as a result of a voluntary choice not to work resulting from the relationship of unemployment and social security benefits to earnings, it can still be argued that if benefits were even lower there would be a greater incentive to find work. This cannot be denied, but neither can it be proved that the people adversely affected would be able to find work. If job openings are limited and real wages do not adjust downward in a situation where employers' demand for labour, of the type that can be provided by the unemployed, increases, reducing benefits will not lead to a reduction in unemployment. This may not prevent critics of the present arrangements continuing to press for reductions in the replacement ratio but it should be understood that such economic evidence as we have does not lend support to their view or the expected effects on unemployment. It may be that such views are immune to influence by evidence and reflect some preconceived notions about how people 'ought' to react or how they would do so in some abstract and theoretically perfect economic system. Moreover, even if real wages did adjust downwards there would be numbers of unemployed who would still find it difficult to obtain work.

Conclusions

Firstly, if we accept that some unemployment is involuntary we have to recognize that we might not be able to measure this component of unemployment. Things that rest on people's attitudes and motivations cannot be measured precisely. The permanent income hypothesis which incorporates the notion of anticipated, and therefore apparently in some ways 'acceptable', or even desired, unemployment recognizes that the individual can change his assessments and seek to reduce the periods of unemployment or increase anticipated income, even when his previous anticipations have proved to be correct. Secondly, if we accept that there can be involuntary unemployment it follows that at certain times there are unemployed people available and willing to accept jobs at the prevailing wage levels. We are agreeing with the Keynesian view that there is a category of unemployment which is involuntary, and the result of demand-deficiency. However, we go further than this and suggest that a reduction in real wages might not be a necessary condition for the ending of demand-deficient unemployment. It may be possible to increase aggregate nominal demand and see an increase in both employment and real output with no fall in the product real wage. If labour markets do not clear in real wage terms and employers are not faced with declining marginal productivity, an increase in aggregate demand can lead to a reduction in unemployment as both the supply and demand sides of the labour market respond to the higher demand. If trade unions are successful in their pressure to increase real wages during this process the attempt to increase employment may be frustrated.

It is not possible accurately to measure the amount of involuntary unemployment. Indeed, we go further and conclude that it is impossible in practice to separate the figures of unemployment into their frictional, structural, demand-deficient, and voluntary components. This classification might be useful for purposes of analysis and for suggesting possible remedies, but it cannot be applied.

Thirdly, the real-wage labour-supply curve can shift. This means that the unemployed may, as a result of their experience of unemployment and perception of changing economic circumstances, reduce the amount of pay they require in order to accept a job and they may withdraw from labour market participation even if real wage levels do not fall because they conclude that they have no chance of getting a job in the current economic circumstances. Similarly, those in employment may change their real-wage labour-supply curve, that is, their labour-offer supply curve to their present employer, as a result of changes in their perception of economic conditions. This can affect not only the wage which is expected in present employment but also that which is acceptable. If real-wage labour-offer supply curves do shift fairly quickly or frequently there are areas of indeterminancy in our analysis unless we can quickly pick up the fact and nature of the shift. This is perfectly reconcilable with classical economics. The supply and demand curves hold only as long as tastes and preferences remain the same. The realization that they may change significantly alters the confidence we can have in the forecasts of future responses to changes in the demand for labour or movements in real or money wages.

The official count of the number unemployed is the result of an administrative decision which may not be totally immune from

258 *Unemployment*

political consideration and which can provide opportunity for an unscrupulous administration to manipulate the method of compiling the official statistics. There is no unique measurement of the 'true' level of unemployment. The various concepts used in economic theory are probably all incapable of being translated into hard official statistics as they all involve some element of subjective judgement. This applies to the concept of the Natural Rate of Unemployment which is so important to the Monetarist view of inflation. We do not know how to relate the official statistics accurately to the concept. Even if we did, there is little reason to suppose the relationship would remain consistent. One consequence of this is that, no matter what the available evidence might suggest, the committed Monetarist can remain secure in his beliefs isolated from factual evidence by the conceptual definition of the NRU and the truism it represents. At the same time, we must recognize that the official statistics of unemployment may not indicate whether we are moving closer or away from the NRU, or whether the NRU itself (if there is such a thing) is changing.

Finally, a note of caution. Beware of 'official' forecasts, at least from the Thatcher Administration, of the result of 'technical' changes in official statistics. Their initial forecast of the reduction in the number recorded as unemployed resulting from the change in the system in October 1982—50,000—turned out to be wrong by a factor of five.

Notes to Chapter 10

1. See Kahn in Worswick (1976) and Armstrong and Taylor in Creedy (1981).
2. *Employment Gazette*, Aug. 1979, 780.
3. See 'A review of unemployment and vacancy statistics', *Employment Gazette*, May 1980, 497–508; *Unemployment Statistics: Report of an Interdepartmental Working Party*, Cmnd. 5157, HMSO, London, 1972; Lord in Creedy (1981); Thatcher in Worswick (1976). The most comprehensive discussion of the development of the official series of unemployment statistics in the UK is Garside (1980). The changes in Nov. 1982 are described in 'Compilation of the Unemployment Statistics', *Employment Gazette*, Sept. 1982, 389–93.
4. See *Employment Gazette*, Apr. 1981, 201–3.
5. Department of Employment press release 'Unemployment—Change in the Count', 18 Nov. 1982.
6. Ibid.
7. 'Employment and the Working Population', *Employment Gazette*, June 1983, 242–4.
8. 'Compilation of the Unemployment Statistics', *Employment Gazette* Sept. 1981, 201–3, was the first article. The details of the estimated total of

50,000 were given in 'Compilation of the Unemployment Statistics', *Employment Gazette*, Sept. 1982, 389-93.
9. Department of Employment press release, 'Unemployment and Vacancies: May 1983 Summary', 3 June 1983.
10. For a good summary of the results and a discussion of the different ways of counting unemployment see 'The Unemployed: Survey Estimates compared with the Monthly Count', *Employment Gazette*, June 1983, 265-7.
11. Manpower Services Commission, *Corporate Plan 1982-86*, London 1982.
12. See, for example, Wood (1972) and (1975); Miller and Wood (1982); and Miller (1980).

CHAPTER ELEVEN

The Macro-economic View of Inflation and Unemployment

The Phillips Curve

IN 1958 Professor Phillips published an article which had great influence on many people's thinking.[1] His work suggested that there appeared to be a connection between the level of unemployment and the subsequent percentage increase in money wage rates as shown in Fig. 11.1. This was based on data for the UK covering the period 1861 to 1957. Phillips caught the imagination and it became fashionable to believe that the argument could be carried through to the conclusion that there was a simple and stable inverse relationship between unemployment and the rate of wage change and inflation.[2] It was then only a relatively short step to the conclusion that the way to reduce and control inflation was by manipulating the level of unemployment, although the original article by Phillips did not justify this conclusion, he did not himself seek to draw it, and his methodology and use of data did not permit this sort of policy decision. Alternatively, unemployment could be reduced if an increase in inflation were accepted. Changes in unemployment preceded, and might therefore cause changes in money wage rates.

There were criticisms of Phillips's methodology and, in particular, his use of a rather unusual averaging technique which was necessary to obtain the smooth and apparently neat-fitting curve that holds so much attraction. The disaggregated figures show that there had been all kinds of wage rate increases for a given level of unemployment except, perhaps, that there was little evidence that very high rates of increase in wage rates had been obtained with very high levels of unemployment, (Knowles and Winsten, 1959).

The data used by Phillips meant that there were some serious questions about the direct relevance of his analysis to actual economic problems in Britain. He used the Index of Wage Rates (and Minimum Entitlements) and this did not refer to the same groupings over the full ninety-seven-year period and measured only some of the elements in pay. The unemployment statistics did not have the same coverage over the full period and were derived from different sources (Garside 1980). All in all the Phillips curve was the outcome of some special statistical

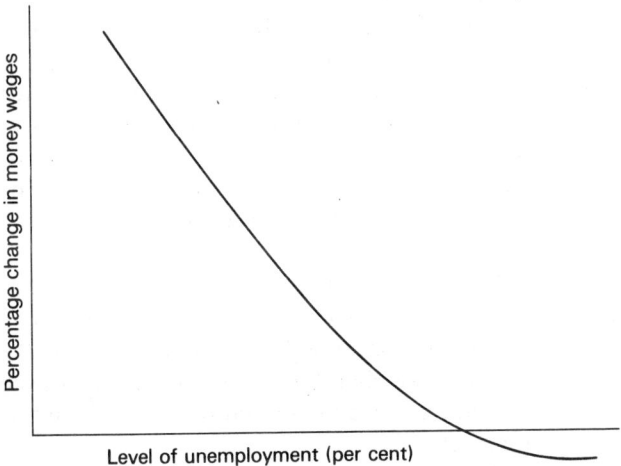

Fig. 11.1 The Phillips Curve

techniques based on dubious data which drastically reduced its relevance to real world problems and policy-making.

Inflation and Unemployment

However, notwithstanding these weaknesses the Phillips Curve caught on. The next stage was to relate price changes to unemployment as Fisher had done earlier, although Phillips himself did not do this. Translating wage-rate change into price changes raises problems. The first is that factors other than the rate of change of wages might influence price changes; the movement of import prices is particularly important in a country as dependent on foreign trade as Britain. Secondly, prices can change as a result of variations in indirect taxation such as VAT. Thirdly, even if a more reliable wage indicator than the Wage Rate Index is used, it is necessary to take account of changes in productivity before any simple inference about the effect of changes in wages on prices can be drawn. Fourthly, the wage–price mark-up may change as employers alter their profit margins. Thus, if we wish to establish some connection between the level of unemployment and inflation we need, at the very least, to establish that there is some connection between unemployment, changes in wages, changes in unit labour costs, and prices.

The possible economic explanations which could be advanced to underpin the apparent Phillips curve relationships were relatively simple. If inflation and unemployment were related this could be because inflation was the result of demand-pull. Low levels of unemployment meant that there were high levels of employment and demand. Competition in the product market could lead to rising prices and this could feed through into higher wages in order to maintain real wages. Competition for labour could then explain why wages and prices rose. Alternatively, it could be a cost-push phenomenon. When unemployment was low trade unions had more strength and were able to drive up wages.

On one explanation increases in wages were a function of unemployment where unemployment was a function of the level of demand. On the other, wage increases were a function of trade union power and behaviour where trade union power was a function of the level of demand. The Phillips curve therefore, while possibly describing what had happened, did not provide an explanation or establish the causality of the 'facts' it described.

That there could be, and indeed probably were, some sort of interrelationships was known prior to the Phillips curve. We have already referred to Fisher. In another interesting explanation of the way in which economic variables might behave at different levels of employment MacDougall had said 'the higher the level of employment the faster will prices tend to rise *both* because the bargaining power of trade unions will be stronger and that of employers weaker *and* because productivity will be growing more slowly' (1957, 596-7). This hypothesis was not the result of detailed econometric analysis but reflected a general body of accepted understanding of the way in which the economy might operate as it moved towards high, and very high, levels of employment. This view which takes account of changes in the strength, and relative strength of trade unions and employers, could be consistent with a sort of Phillips curve approach.

Changes in money wage rates could be converted into changes in labour costs to employers, by including, for example, such items as employers' contributions to national insurance, or other forms of fringe benefit provisions such as sickness payment or pension schemes, with changes in productivity taken into account. Various assumptions about the rate of change of import prices and the relationship between production costs and selling prices, perhaps by assuming some sort of constant mark-up percentage might be necessary if the analysis were to have predictive powers. The combined effect of these additional factors and the particular assumptions adopted would change the shape of the curve from that originally obtained from the data used by Phillips.

The general conclusion that came out of the various analyses which used prices rather than wages was much the same, at least for a time.[3] There was some sort of trade-off between inflation and unemployment.

Prices rose faster when unemployment was lower. Some analyses emphasized the importance of the rate of change of unemployment rather than the level of unemployment as such.[4] This could affect the terms of the trade-off; at certain levels of unemployment, if unemployment were falling there could be a different rate of inflation than if that level of unemployment existed in a situation where unemployment was rising. (Phillips had found that when he examined the disaggregated data there were 'loops' suggesting that the rate of change of wage rates was influenced by the direction in which unemployment was moving as well as the level of unemployment itself.)

The notion that there was some sort of trade-off between inflation and unemployment was widely accepted by many economists, government advisers, and decision-takers. It fitted in with a general Keynesian approach and was acceptable to advocates of demand management as the main tool of economic control. In the UK demand management policies often involve both monetary and fiscal policies. Thus, an increase in money supply might well be accompanied by reductions in taxation. In these circumstances there may be effects from both the monetary and the fiscal changes so that the results observed are not necessarily caused by the monetary expansion. It was believed that by influencing the general level of demand it was possible to influence the level of employment. If an expansionary policy were followed, unemployment would fall and inflation rise. It was up to the government to decide whether that price was worth paying.

The generally prevailing attitude amongst economists and policy-makers in the post-war period was that priority should be given to maintaining high levels of employment, and there was widespread self-confidence that this objective could be achieved by judicious manipulation of the level of demand using both fiscal and monetary policies, supplemented where necessary, and according to the political ideology of the government of the day, by more direct government intervention to impinge on specific industries or areas. There may have been some disagreement about the precise degree to which the economy would, or could, respond to fine-tuning, but relatively little disagreement about the ability to influence the broader bands of economic policy. No matter what the differences of detail, or the more sustained divergences between the main political parties, the maintenance of a high level of employment was accepted by all. On occasions it might be necessary to undergo a reduction in employment, or a rise in unemployment, usually because of constraints imposed by a balance of payments deficit under a regime of fixed exchange rates, but these were regarded as temporary disturbances or the fluctuations around the high or full employment level which were in practice unavoidable.

The acceptance by both electorate and government that high employment was possible as well as desirable had a tremendous impact on the psychology of economic policy-making and on the claims made by different groups in society. Further, experience of sustained periods of high employment influenced the economic behaviour of idividuals operating in the labour market, as well as their group behaviour through trade unions, work groups, or, on the other side, employers' associations. The view developed that the *political* necessity to maintain a high level of employment might override the economic assessment of the consequences of adopting the Labour Standard approach. An even stronger interpretation was that it was not possible, politically, to permit, far less induce, such levels of unemployment as might be necessary to prevent inflation, or to hold it to acceptable levels.

In the sixties the Phillips curve originally appeared to offer considerable scope for policy choice. Demand management could be assisted by other measures to reduce the inflationary impact of high employment levels through various forms of wages or incomes policies, or controls on prices. Structural change could be introduced to make the economy work in a less inflationary way by reducing bottlenecks or speeding up market responses to economic forces on the labour side by an active manpower policy covering such things as improved training facilities, inducements to labour mobility, and so on. As time went on confidence began to wane. The economic fluctuations increased. Each cycle experienced higher levels of unemployment and the stop–go approach to policy appeared to require bigger and bigger squeezes to obtain apparently less successful results. If there were an inflation–unemployment trade-off, it looked as though the terms of the trade-off were changing.

Economic literature referred to the possibility of moving to a new, different Phillips curve as well as moving along one particular inflation–unemployment curve which was fixed through time. Econometric equations which had appeared to provide statistically satisfactory explanations of the past relationship of key economic variables failed to predict future movements in prices.

Both Monetarists and non-Monetarists criticized the Phillips-type inflation–unemployment model although not necessarily for the same reasons. Some who might be called Institutionalists, Structuralists, or adherents of the Sociological approach drew attention to the role of institutions operating in the labour market, such as trade unions and employers' associations, or to the existing and changing methods and processes of pay determination. The institution of collective bargaining and the changes that were taking place were seen as relevant to the development of inflation and therefore by implication to any inflation–unemploymet trade-off. The extension of collective bargaining or trade

Inflation and Unemployment 265

union membership in Britain was thought to influence pay developments. Changes in payment systems, particularly forms of payments by results, were considered relevant. Attitudes towards trade unions as well as managerial authority, the use of coercive comparisons in wage determination, and a strong feeling that fairness, covering both the relationship of pay in different occupations and industries and the 'low-paid' worker, should affect pay increases, may all have shifted the previous inflation–unemployment relationships. The mere fact of a sustained period of high employment combined with steady, albeit relatively slow, economic growth in the post-war period may have affected the way in which individuals and organizations behaved in pay and price determination. Political parties had fostered expectations of continued growth and improvements in living standards. Further, there may have been important changes in perceptions of power as a result of the adoption of Labour Standard types of policies, and as the stop-go cycle developed some sort of learning process and changed sets of anticipations may have developed which led to changes in behaviour. For these sorts of reasons non-Monetarists can come to the conclusion that if there were an inflation–unemployment trade-off either it had altered, or that there may once have been such a trade-off but there was no longer. Those who believed that there never was any stable and predictable trade-off would use the same set of factors to justify their original scepticism.

Monetarists reject a stable Phillips curve or its usual translation into an inflation–unemployment trade-off. They argue that money wages (and it might not matter for this point which definition of wages we take, money wage rates or standard weekly earnings) are in themselves of little relevance. It is *real* wages which matter and we can infer nothing about real wages from a statement about money wages. It is clear therefore that *if* the relationship suggested in the original Phillips curve is interpreted as a causal relationship about the effects of unemployment on wage changes, and this could be used to 'explain' wage movements, it would not tell us whether workers were becoming better or worse off. It would imply that the increase in wages would be the same, for a stated level of unemployment, whether prices were rising, rising quickly, were fairly stable, or even falling. Non-monetarists also recognize the relevance of *real* wages rather than just nominal money wages, for example, Hicks in his article referring to the Labour Standard.

While rejecting a stable Phillips curve Monetarists nevertheless believe that there might well be some short-run trade-off between inflation and unemployment. The Phillips curve, and all that was associated with it, need not therefore be abandoned. 'There is no need to assume a stable Phillips curve in order to explain the apparent tendency for an acceleration of inflation to reduce unemployment. That can be explained by the impact of *unanticipated* changes in nominal demand on markets characterized by (implicit or explicit) long-term commitments with respect to both labour and capital' (Friedman 1977, 12). The new and crucial element is that of anticipations or, put more starkly, 'only surprises matter'.

While this retains some of the inflation–unemployment trade-off, in some circumstances, it reverses the direction of causation. Instead of changes in the level of unemployment feeding through to changes in the rate of change of money wages, the Friedman version has changes (acceleration) in inflation leading to a reduction in unemployment.

The Expectations-augmented Phillips Curve

The demise of the Phillips curve in the face of overwhelming evidence that it could no longer be used for policy purposes led to the emergence of the expectations-augmented Phillips curve. This has become an almost universally accepted part, not only of the Monetarist's armoury, but of that of many other economists also. It is derived from one basic proposition which is then developed by theoretical analysis and reasoning. The essential starting-point is the assertion that it is *real* wages rather than money wages which determine the supply of labour. We have considered this in Chapter 7. Then, given the assumption that wages are determined by market forces of supply and demand, and that the level of unemployment can be taken to represent the relationship between supply and demand for labour, it is fairly straightforward to develop a model which relates the rate of changes to the level of unemployment.[5] Changes in unemployment are taken to be the inverse of changes in employment so that movements in one are assumed exactly equal to opposite movements in the other.

Figure 11.2 shows the usual supply and demand curves for labour. As is usual in this type of analysis they are aggregate supply and demand curves and although we have argued in Chapters 5 and 6 that aggregate demand and supply curves are meaningless we will follow the usual practice in this case in order to explain the concept in the terms used by its proponents. If wages are at W_2 market forces will raise them to W_0. At all wage levels below W_0 there is excess demand for labour $(D - S)$ indicated by the difference between the demand and supply curves at each wage level. It might be assumed that wages will rise faster the greater is the excess demand so that if wages were at W_2 they would increase more quickly than if they were at W_1. This will depend upon the conditions existing in the labour market, and the

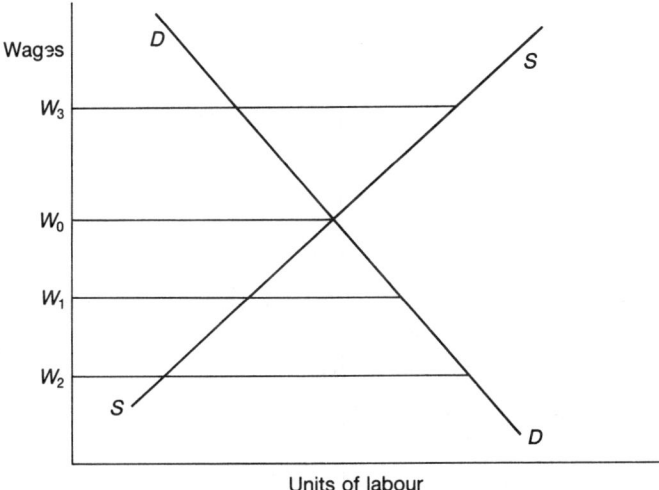

Fig. 11.2 Labour Demand and Supply

responsiveness of wages to excess demand. If we were considering occupational labour markets the ease, cost and time taken to switch occupations, or for new entrants to be trained in the particular occupation would be relevant. The simplest assumption, but not necessarily the most realistic, is that the percentage rate of change of wages is proportional to the percentage excess demand for labour. The rate of change of wages in this purely market-determined model is therefore

$$w = a[(D-S)a[(D-S)/S]S]. \quad (11.1)$$

The faster that wages adjust to disequilibrium between supply and demand the larger will be a. As the figure suggests, the model assumes that if there is excess supply so that $(D-S)$ is negative as with wage W_3, wages will fall to W_0. If we assume that wages adjust equally easily and quickly in each direction the same equation holds whether there is excess demand or excess supply. If we believe that wages are more sticky downwards, we can change the relationship so that

$$w = b[(D-S)/S] \text{ where } S>D. \quad (11.2)$$

We can then show the relationship between the rate of changes and excess demand as in Fig. 11.3. Excess demand for labour is shown on the right-hand side of the vertical line and the larger the excess demand the higher the wage increase. As we are showing the *increase* in wages necessary to obtain equilibrium, w_2 is above w_1 as a larger wage increase is necessary to bring the wage *level* W_2 in Fig. 11.2 to the

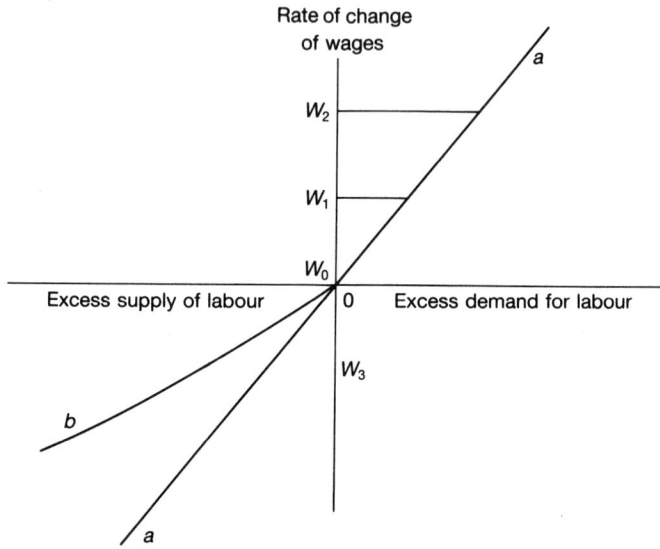

Fig. 11.3 Excess Demand for Labour and Rate of Change of Wages

equilibrium level of W_0 than is needed to bring wage level W_1 to the equilibrium level. Conditions of excess supply where $(D-S)$ is negative, are shown to the left of the vertical line. The position illustrated by wage level W_3 in Fig. 11.2 is shown here as requiring a wage reduction in order to restore equilibrium. If the downward flexibility of wages is as easily obtained as upward flexibility, i.e. if a expresses the adjustment process in both excess demand and excess supply situations the stright line *as* shows the relationship between excess supply and the rate of fall in wages. If, however, wages are sticky downwards so that coefficient b applies, the relationship is shown by the line *aob*. If the equilibrium wage of W_0 is to be reached this requires a higher level of excess supply, i.e. more unemployment.

We cannot actually see or measure the excess demand for, or excess supply of labour, although we may get some indications by job vacancy statistics, advertisement, actually seeing people out of work, and so on. We therefore try to relate the excess demand for labour to unemployment or the Unemployment Rate as measured by whatever statistics we use. Figure 11.4 shows the relationship between excess demand and unemployment. Even when there is no excess demand or supply there will be some unemployment. As we discussed in Chapter 10, there will always be some frictional unemployment and there may be others appearing in the unemployment statistics for various reasons who are

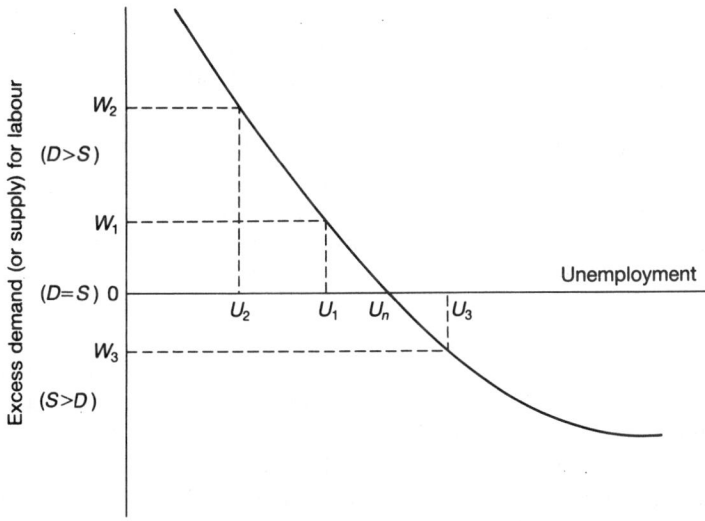

Fig. 11.4   Excess Demand for Labour and the Rate of Unemployment

not part of any employer's acceptable labour supply even though they are seeking work and are included in the official unemployment statistics. This level of unemployment shown as U_n is sometimes referred to as the natural rate of unemployment (NRU) and will be considered in detail in Chapter 14. As excess demand increases it may be possible to reduce the usual level of frictional unemployment as jobs are easier to find and are filled more quickly. If there is excess supply of labour, unemployment may move at the same rate as the increase in excess supply. The curve in Fig. 11.3 is therefore not linear. This assumes, if not honesty, then at least consistency in the way in which unemployment is measured. If the government changes the rules so that the Unemployment Rate statistics exclude some people usually included then the slope as well as the location of the curve in Fig. 11.3 will change.

From Figs. 11.2 and 11.3 we can obtain the wage change–unemployment trade-off. From Fig. 11.2 we know that where there is no excess demand for labour the rate of change of wages is zero, and from Fig. 11.3 we know that this is at a level of unemployment U_n. Similarly, if there is excess demand for labour $(D>S)$ as at W_1 which leads to an increase in wage of w_1, this is associated with a level of unemployment in Fig. 11.3 of U_1. If there is excess supply of labour $(S>D)$ as with W_3 this is associated with a decrease of wages w_3 and with an Unemployment Rate U_3. If we plot the various possible combinations of excess demand or supply positions as represented by the wage changes resulting from those disequilibria positions against the Unemployment Rates associated with each excess demand or supply positions, we obtain the curve shown in Fig. 11.5.

What we have at this stage might seem no more than the original Phillips curve that shows a relationship between the rate of change of wages and unemployment. There are, however, two crucial differences. First, *real* and not money wages are the crucial pay variable. Second, this version has been obtained, not by some form of examination of data—however suspect the data may be—but obtained solely by economic theory from the assumption that wages change in response to and only in response to changes in excess demand and supply of labour. There is really no more good reason to call it a Phillips curve than there is to call it a Fisher or a MacDougall curve. They had both used the same idea earlier than Phillips. The bad reason for keeping the name Phillips is probably that it had become part of the common currency of economics and the new developers wanted to benefit from some aspects of an existing trade name.

Monetarists, building on the concepts used to produce the wage change–unemployment trade-off, tended to add the further assumption that changes in wages after, perhaps, some appropriate offset for productivity changes, could be translated into changes in prices. It is a common assumption in Monetarist analysis that prices reflect a percentage mark-up on costs. For most purposes this is taken to be the

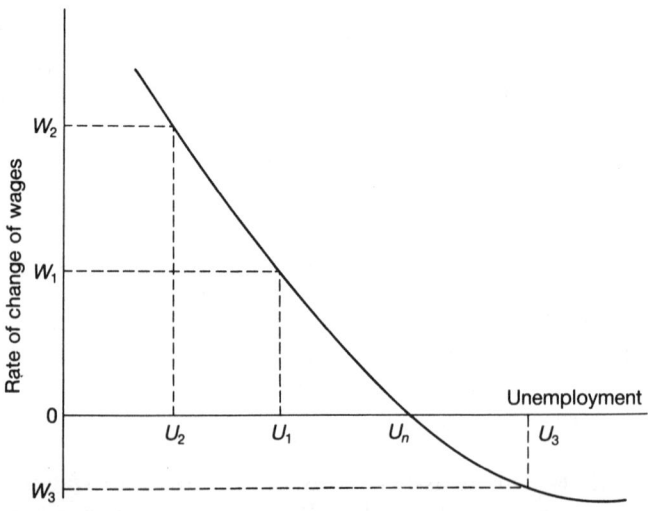

Fig. 11.5   Rate of Change of Wages and the Level of Unemployment

same as assuming that prices change in proportion to wage changes. Thus the wage change–unemployment trade-off becomes an inflation–unemployment trade-off. If we now make the assumption that it is real wages which matter for labour supply and the relationship between expected selling prices of his products in relation to expected money wage and productivity of his employees—the product real wage—which matter to an employer, we can move from money to real wages.

If there is no inflation then Figs. 11.2–5 can refer to either money or real wages. If, however, there is inflation, the advocates of the expectations-augmented Phillips curve argue that it is the *expected* real wage during the period of employment which determines the supply curve of labour, and the *expected* costs of his inputs and the expected selling price of his products the expected real product wage which determines the employer's demand for labour.

If this is so it should be noted that the expected future prices, or inflation rate, which the two sides of the labour market take into account, need not be the same. Workers, when deciding whether to become part of a labour supply curve presumably base their decisions on the expected money wages and the expected prices of those goods and services on which they will spend their income. For simplicity we may assume that this can be represented by the Retail Price Index or some other general Consumer Price Index, although it does not follow that any general price index reflects at all accurately the price changes of that package of commodities actually purchased by any individual worker or household unit. The employer, in determining his demand for labour, is concerned with a narrower range of expected prices, viz. those of his factor inputs and the prices of the commodities he plans to produce and sell. He may be interested in general price movements only to the extent that they influence the expected real value of his profits or dividends for his (or his shareholders') general consumption expenditure.

We will assume that labour markets clear, or act as though they do, and that the demand for labour is a function of the expected product real wage and the supply of labour is a function of expected real wages. Figure 11.6 shows the demand for labour by an employer given his expectations of the future price of his products with existing money wages. We use money wages here as the employer is assumed to determine his future demand for labour from a position of equilibrium in real terms. With existing money wages his demand for labour will depend on the prices he expects to receive for his products. Curve DP_0^* represents his demand for labour when he expects no change in the price of his products. Similarly, the supply curve of labour SP_0^* represents the supply of labour to him when workers expect prices to remain

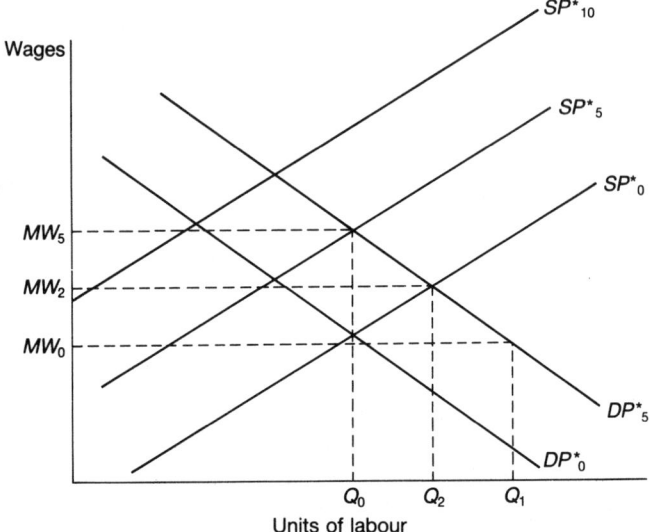

Fig. 11.6 Labour Demand and Supply at Expected Rates of Inflation

constant. The market-clearing wage is MW_0 and the level of employment is Q_0.

If the employer believes the price of his product will rise by 5 per cent while wages remain constant, his demand for labour shifts to curve DP_5^*. An increase in the price of his product and no change in money wages represents a fall in the product real wage and at money wage MW_0 he will demand Q_1 labour. If workers continue to expect no inflation the labour supply curve remains at SP_0^*. At money wage MW_0 only Q_0 labour is supplied so the employer is unable to obtain Q_1 workers. The equilibrium position with DP_5^* and SP_0^* is Q_2 level of employment at a higher money wage of MW_2. The employer is willing to pay MW_2 because the anticipated increase in the selling price of his product lowers his product real wage by more than $(MW_2 - MW_0)$.

If workers anticipate an increase in inflation of 5 per cent they will move to SP_5^*. The new equilibrium with DP_5^* and SP_5^* results in a money wage level of MW_5 and employment at Q_0. If workers and employers anticipate the same rate of change of prices and act according to the assumptions of this model equilibrium will always be at a level of employment Q_0 which is equivalent to the natural rate of unemployment (NRU).

If the workers and employers anticipate the same rate of change of prices—the first looking at all prices or those which enter into their consumption expenditure, and the second those which apply to the products they purchase as raw materials and the selling prices they receive for their products to obtain the product real wage, changes in the anticipated rate of price change will have no effect on the level of employment. They may affect only the level of money wages. If workers anticipate lower rates of price change than employers there may be increases in both money wages and employment for as long as those differences in expectations persist. If workers anticipate larger price changes than employers as where SP^*_{10} intersects with DP^*_5, money and real wages rise and employment falls.

The employer's demand for labour at any given money wage level will vary according to his estimate of the future selling price of his product. Different employers may, correctly, expect that the future increase in the prices of their product will differ from that of the average rate of price increase. There is no reason to believe that each and every price rises at exactly the same rate as the general rate of inflation. In micro-analysis of different sectors or firms the two sets of expected future prices considered by workers and employers could lead to different expectations and so a current equilibrium position in either money or real terms, could become a disequilibrium position. Aggregate analysis, particularly if it follows the lines of the Quantity Theory, can overcome this difficulty by assuming that as some prices rise by more than the average, others will rise by less and the set of expectations will adjust to the movements in relative prices.

Leaving aside any complications arising from the adjustments which take place if the two sides have different expectations or if they have the same expectations but because they are looking at different collections of prices come to different conclusions about the effect of expected price changes, we can conclude that for a given set of money wage levels there will be a family of labour supply curves, each one representing a different amount of labour offered at a particular expected rate of inflation. Similarly employers will have different demand curves for different levels of future prices.

In Figure 11.7 we bring together the conclusions from Figs. 11.5 and 11.6. The vertical axis can show both the rate of change of wages or inflation—the rate of change of prices—by taking the additional step of assuming that there is some given relationship between wage changes and prices changes. The general practice is to show price changes on this axis so that the curve represents an inflation–unemployment trade-off. We follow this practice, but to underline the point that the theoretical analysis from which the curve is derived is essentially to do with labour market behaviour we also show it as measuring the rate of change of wages with price changes shown to be a function of the rate of

274 Inflation and Unemployment

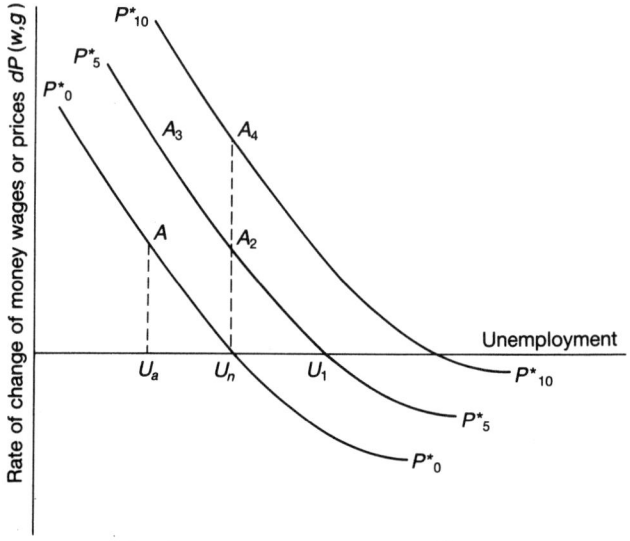

Fig. 11.7 Expectations-augmented Phillips Curve

of change of wages and productivity. Friedman (1975) uses the rate of change of money wages while Friedman (1977) uses the rate of inflation. The curve p^0 shows the relationship when no inflation is expected. It is the same as the curve in Fig. 11.5 and is regarded by Monetarists as the real wage labour supply curve. The curves p^5 and p^{10} show the relationships if the expected rate of inflation is 5 per cent and 10 per cent respectively Thus, with no inflation the labour market is in equilibrium at U_n. This is the same as the employment level of Q_o on Fig. 11.6. If, however, everyone expects 5 per cent inflation, then, because it is assumed the supply price of labour is determined in real terms and not just in money wages, if money wages did not rise, unemployment would increase to U_1. The change in the expected rate of inflation from zero to 5 per cent would mean that employers and workers were now on curve p^5 and with no change in money wages the horizontal axis marked 0 change in money wages intersects curve p^5 at a level of unemployment U_1. This would be entirely a supply-side effect. With expected inflation of five per cent and no increase in money wages it is assumed that some workers would withdraw from the work-force.

Once we label the vertical axis to show the rate of change of money wages and not just the rate of inflation this becomes clear. It is also very important because it underlines the fact that each of the trade-off curves is actually no more than a real wage labour supply curve.[6] With expected inflation of 5 per cent and no change in money wages the demand for labour ought, of course, to rise as employers would foresee greater profits. Some of the expected inflation even with constant money wages could lead to increases in each producer's costs but there would still be an increase in his expected profits from the fall in the ratio of money wages to expected selling price.

However, even though the demand for labour would rise, employment is shown as falling as unemployment increases from U_n to U_1. This can only be because the expected 5 per cent reduction in real wages leads some workers to withdraw from employment. They are no longer prepared to work when real wages are expected to fall. Employers would obviously wish to hire more workers at the prevailing money wage levels but they cannot get them. U_1 is not an equilibrium position. Money wages should rise in response to the excess demand for labour. If we assume that the increase in money wages leads to a change in the expected rate of inflation the economy would move to curve p^5 where unemployment fell to its previous level U_n as the combination of inflation and the expectation of inflation, and the increase in money wages, leaves the original real wages and real wage labour supply curves unaffected. In the simple example illustrated in Fig. 11.7 we show this by the intersection of the curve p^5 and the line through W_n being at 5 per cent on the vertical axis showing the rate of change of money wages.

The Short-run Trade-off between Inflation and Unemployment

We can now use this analysis to provide the Monetarist explanation of the inflationary process as developed by Friedman. This analysis always starts from some assumed stable position. For simplicity we will assume that this is represented by the zero expected inflation curve in Fig. 11.7. It would not make any fundamental difference if we had started from a curve of any positive rate of inflation: it is expositionally easier to start from a position of price stability but this should not be taken to suggest we ever reach such an equilibrium.

The economy is therefore in a position represented by U_n with a rate of increase of money wages equal to the rate of productivity growth and no change in prices.

Now, assume that there is an increase in aggregate nominal demand caused by an unexpected increase in the money supply.

This will come to each producer as an unexpectedly favourable demand for his product. In an environment in which changes are always occuring in the relative demand for different goods, he will not know whether this change is special to him or pervasive. It will be rational for him to interpret it as at least partly special and to react to it by seeking to produce more to sell at what he now perceives to be a higher than expected market price for future output. He will be willing to pay higher nominal wages than he had been willing to pay before in order to attract additional workers (Friedman 1977, 13).

Responding to the perceived increase in demand for his product the employer, according to Friedman, decides to do two things. He increases output in order to sell more goods and he raises prices. He could of course have chosen to do only one of these. All the expected increase in demand could have been met by allowing prices to rise, or he could have tried to hold prices constant and met all the expected increase in demand by producing more. This second possibility would be ruled out by Monetarists on the grounds that the employer could not produce more at existing prices as he would be unable to recruit more workers at prevailing real wage levels. This is clear from the last sentence in the Friedman quote. Higher nominal wages are necessary *in order to attract* additional workers.

If this is so it explains why all the expected increase in demand is not met by increasing output and selling at prevailing prices. The employer cannot recruit additional labour at prevailing wage levels. If higher wages are necessary, labour costs are expected to rise because it is assumed that the employer is facing decreasing returns. Higher labour costs mean higher prices because it is assumed that prices bear a constant percentage relation to labour costs, i.e. as wages rise selling prices rise equally. To increase output, the argument runs, it is necessary to increase money wages and so the prices of the employer's products will rise. He believes he is able to increase prices when he anticipates an increase in nominal demand because he believes that some of this increase is special to him. If he thought that demand everywhere were rising at the same rate as he believes demand for his product is rising, he might conclude that nothing would change in real terms. It might be necessary to increase prices to cover higher costs of inputs, including labour, but there would be no increase in the *real* demand for his products and therefore no point in increasing output. The belief that there has been a shift in *real* demand towards his product is therefore necessary to induce the employer to increase output.

The assumption that the labour market has cleared so that no additional workers can be recruited at current money wages—given the expected rates of inflation, in this case zero, this also means at current real wages—leads to the conclusion that it is necessary to increase money wages in order to expand output. The firm is assumed to be working at full capacity so that output cannot be increased without more workers. In the Friedman version, followed by Monetarists generally, the employer is both *willing* and *compelled* to increase money wages in order to attract more workers. If he were not compelled by labour market conditions there seems no reason why he would raise wages. His perception of an increase in real demand for his product leads him to conclude that he can afford to increase wages but it is the conditions assumed to exist in the labour market which lead him to do so. We emphasize this point because it is absolutely central to the Monetarist explanation of the nature of any trade-off there might be between inflation and unemployment.

Movement up the Phillips curve from U_n on p^0 is therefore movement along a real-wage labour-supply curve. The amount of increase in money wages necessary to induce more workers to accept employment is shown by movement along the curve. In Fig. 11.7 in order to induce $(U_n - U_a)$ workers to accept employment an increase of 5 per cent in money wages, with an expected rate of inflation of zero, is required. Similarly, if money wages fell by 5 per cent, employment would fall and unemployment rise to U_1 as the reduction in real wages led to some workers withdrawing from employment.

We should note that the expectations-augmented Phillips curve showing the relationship between inflation and unemployment is, in the Friedman version, essentially a curve for a single employer. The rate of change of prices shown on the vertical axis is the rate of change of the prices of that employer. Thus there is no necessary contradiction in an employer believing that he can move from a position of zero change in his prices in a situation when he expects zero inflation (represented by U_n on curve p^0) to point A on curve p^0. Here he is expecting prices generally to remain constant so there is zero inflation but the price of his products to rise by 5 per cent. The effect of an increase in the price of his product on the general level of prices could be negligible. It would, of course, be very odd were he to expect all prices to rise by 5 per cent but still remain on the p^0 curve which represents his expected rate of inflation as being zero.

The particular slope and location of each individual employer's curve may well vary according to the nature of the real-wage labour-supply curve facing him for those occupations which he wishes to recruit: we will assume that when aggregated they correspond to the macro-economy curve. The employer is assumed to increase money wages and expand employment. This is illustrated in Fig. 11.7 with a move along curve p^0 from U_n and no inflation, to U_a where *his* prices rise by 5 per cent but he still expects zero inflation generally.

Money wages have risen and workers and potential workers, like the employer, have not yet appreciated that the increase in aggregate nominal demand may cause all prices to rise. They, like the employer, are still operating on curve p^0, and interpret the rise in money wages as a rise in real wages.

Both employers and workers are underestimating the future rise in prices; both interpret the course of events thus far as representing an increase in workers' real wages, i.e. in their real purchasing power. The employer is also interpreting the events as an improvement or no change in his product real wage, i.e. the ratio of money wages to expected future selling prices of his products. Employment has increased and there has therefore been an inflation–unemployment trade-off.

However, both employers and workers will realize through experience that their original expectations of zero inflation have been proved wrong. For, just as this individual employer has increased his prices, so, too, have other employers. This has led to a greater increase in prices than first expected and also to individual employers revising their estimate of their own future selling prices or levels of demand, as some of their input prices will have risen. As inflation is experienced expectations of future inflation will be revised.

But this situation is temporary, let the higher rate of growth of aggregate nominal demand and prices continue, and perceptions will adjust to reality. When they do, the initial effects will disappear, and then even be reversed for a time as workers and employers find themselves locked into inappropriate contracts. Ultimately, employment will be back at the level which prevailed before the assumed unanticipated acceleration in aggregate nominal demand. (Friedman 1977, 14).

If prices generally rise by 5 per cent employers and workers will change their expectations about future inflation. It is assumed that they therefore both move to curve p^5 on Fig. 11.7. With this rate of anticipated inflation and the money and product price rise of 5 per cent that has taken place, equilibrium will be restored at a level of unemployment of U_n. The employer will not wish to employ the additional workers once he realizes that the increase in aggregate nominal demand did not lead to any increase in the real demand for his product and the newly employed workers will not be willing to work at the prevailing money wage levels. The increase of 5 per cent in money wages is now seen as not being an increase in real wages as prices generally have risen by an equivalent percentage. As the real wage is no higher than it was in the original equilibrium position of U_n without the increase in money wages, the newly recruited workers, assumed to have the same real reservation wages as they had initially, are not prepared to work for the same real wage. This is the other side of the coin that assumed an increase in money wages was necessary in order to induce the additional workers to accept employment when the expected rate of inflation was zero.

The new equilibrium position is therefore A_2. If aggregate nominal demand is again increased it might be assumed that employers will respond in the same way, anticipate some increase in real demand and move along curve p^5 to A_3. Employment will rise and unemployment fall as workers again perceive this to be an increase in real wages. As both employers and workers come to realize that prices generally are rising by, say, 10 per cent, they will revise their expectations about inflation and move to curve p^{10} with a new equilibrium position at A_4.

According to this, attempts to lower the level of unemployment by increasing the money supply can therefore have only short-run effects and in the process of obtaining this short-run reduction in unemployment there will be an increase in the rate of inflation. This bedrock of modern Monetarism is, as Friedman himself admits, oversimplified:

But it does highlight the key points: what matters is not inflation *per se*, but unanticipated inflation; there is no stable trade-off between inflation and unemployment but there is a 'natural rate of unemployment' (U_n), which is consistent with the real forces and with accurate perceptions; unemployment can be kept below that only by accelerating inflation; or above it, only by accelerating deflation' (Friedman 1977, 15).

On this analysis while there is a short-run trade-off between inflation and unemployment, there is a no long-run trade-off. The long-run Phillips curve is vertical as shown by the line U_n in Fig. 11.7. U_n is the 'natural rate of unemployment' (NRU). This is the level of unemployment at which the economy is in stable equilibrium.

If we put this in terms of the Quantity Theory it is the same as saying that in the short-run an increase in M may affect Y because both producers and workers misunderstand the consequences of the increase in demand resulting from the increase in M. Once they understand this all the effects of an increase in M are felt on P. Y remains at a constant equilibrium level, perhaps growing at some trend rate determined by productivity growth. Because Y is thus fixed in a long-run equilibrium, so is E. W changes with M. The long-run stable equilibrium level of E is the counterpart of the NRU.

It is interesting to note one feature of this model. It does not require, or even suggest, that money wages are reduced. Real wages rise and then fall because of the increase in money wages and the subsequent increase in prices. Equilibrium is *not* restored because money wages are cut, but because money wages stay at the higher level and prices rise.

There is a further argument that in fact the long-run Phillips curve might be positively sloped so that higher inflation is associated with higher, not lower, unemployment. We will not pursue this here. This argument differs from the vertical long-run Phillips curve in that it is not derived from the same set of economic assumptions and concepts. It draws its main support from empirical observations which show that in many countries higher inflation has been associated with higher unemployment. However, while some of this may be the result of certain aspects of the way in which faster rates of inflation affect expectations of future inflation, and the responses of employers to these higher expected rates, it is much more likely that the explanation lies in trade union behaviour and the factors which determine the natural rate of unemployment. What we have experienced, therefore, is much more likely to be a move in the level of the natural rate of unemployment which explains the apparent breakdown of any long-term stable vertical Phillips curve. The natural rate of unemployment is discussed in detail in Chapter 14.

Weaknesses in the Expectations-augmented Phillips Curve Approach

At this stage it is useful to mention some of the important assumptions underlying the long-run vertical Phillips curve analysis so far. The labour market is assumed to clear or, at least, to behave as though it cleared. This means that with a given real wage level (or a perceived real wage level which might be different from that which actually obtains) the labour market clears in that when employment rises employers must increase real wages (or perceived real wages). Whether employers do this is the second stage of the process, but the first stage is clear. Employment cannot be increased without an increase in (perceived) real wages. Conversely, reductions in real wages lead to a rise in unemployment because workers voluntarily leave employment.

Secondly, the real-wage labour-supply function operates in a very short time period once perceptions of the existing real wage have been adjusted. It may take time before workers appreciate that there is higher inflation, but once they have done so they respond in their real wage supply function very quickly. Once they understand that their real wages have fallen below their real reservation wage they leave employment. This follows the explanation of Friedman that it is *expected* inflation that determines the labour supply. This means that workers require protection or maintenance of their currently perceived real wage. Thus, from the supply side at least, the labour market is assumed to clear as quickly as workers' perceptions of their real wages change. For those who remain in employment rather than choose to become unemploymed because the real wage no longer meets their reservation real wage, the past is forgotten. All that matters is maintaining that real wage in the future by obtaining increases in money wages which meet the rate of inflation. It is emphasized that it is the supply side which is alleged to generate the inflationary process. Moreover, it is also assumed that the real reservation wage does not fall. If it does, then of course, even when workers appreciate that inflation is higher than they originally expected, they may continue in employment at the perceived lower real wage.

If the demand for labour decreases as employers realize that their original expectations were misfounded, a sufficiently large reduction in real reservation wage could cause a revival of demand and maintain the employment level at U_a. Friedman and others generally assume that reservation real wages are fairly rigid, given the various institutional arrangements of an economy. The main exception is that an individual's reservation wage may fall the longer he is unemployed, but that is not relevant to the possibility raised here. We are suggesting that the reservation real wage of those in employment might fall during periods of inflation. Alternatively, they might rise. What we are rejecting is the notion that they should be assumed to be stable for longish periods of time.

It is because he believes they are stable that Friedman resorts to a borrowed homily to explain why the short-run reduction in unemployment does not last. Accept that workers believe the increase in money wages means higher real wages. They then discover that this is not so as inflation is higher than expected. Quoting Lincoln, Friedman says: '. . . but you can't fool all the people all of the time' (1975, 21). They realize real wages are not higher and the newly recruited workers voluntarily return to unemployment. He, and other Monetarists, are fond of using expressions like fooling or tricking people to account for the effects of unanticipated price increases. But, of course, it does not follow that it is necessary to try and fool all the people all the time. I may know full well that prices are rising faster than my money income, and faster than I expected, but I may still remain employed; and so may many others. It depends upon my view of the alternative. Continuing in employment at lower real wages may now seem preferable to unemployment. I may have changed my real reservation wage. It is only because it is assumed, or asserted, that the expectations-augmented Phillips curve slopes downwards from left to right—that it is a labour supply curve—and that it is fixed or stable for fairly long periods that a reduction in real wages in relation to expected real wages leads necessarily to a fall in employment and an increase in unemployment back to the natural rate.

It is the belief that the labour market was in equilibrium in real wage terms so that in order to recruit more workers the employer *had* to increase real wages, and that those workers will choose to revert to unemployment when they discover that real wages have not in fact risen, that leads Monetarists to say that the workers were fooled. Moreover, by using Lincoln's quote, Friedman suggests someone deliberately tried to fool them. But this is not so. The employer thought real wages *were* rising. He did not anticipate the general increase in prices. If he had, he would not in Friedman's analysis have wanted to hire the extra workers to increase production. It is the belief that once employed the workers will retain the same real reservation wage and require the same real wage to induce them to remain in employment as they needed to induce them to accept employment that leads to the conclusion that they will leave when they realize that there has been no lasting increase in real wages.

This assumption that the labour market always clears or behaves as if it does, is not a reasonable explanation of large parts of the labour market at many times. It is simply not the case that employers always have to increase real wages in order to hire more employees. Many firms can increase employment without raising wages. The extent to which they can do this will depend on the conditions in their local labour market, or for some firms for some occupations, the conditions in a wider labour market if geographical labour mobility is a feature of the occupations concerned.

Monetarists ought to be aware of this. They frequently refer to the ability of trade unions to raise wages above their market level. This leads to an excess supply of labour to the unionized sector, as 'all workers would like to have a union job . . .' (Minford 1983, 11). If this is true it should be quite obvious that unionized firms ought to be able to attract more workers without increasing wages. It does seem odd that Monetarists who emphasize the distorting effects of trade unions in forcing up wages above their market-clearing level should also assert that these employers have to increase real wages in order to recruit more workers.

In other cases firms may be able to recruit more workers by non-wage strategies, such as changing working hours, offering part-time employment, or providing transport facilities (Robinson 1968). These may be particularly effective in the recruitment of married women. Some of the measures may increase total labour costs but this is a demand-side argument, not a supply-side one relating to an upward-sloping labour supply curve. Alternatively, it can be seen as action to shift the labour supply curve to the right so that while the curve still slopes upward from left to right more labour is available at given wage levels. No matter what particular form of conceptual expression we adopt, the conclusion is the same; in the real world it is just not correct to work on the assumption that firms have to increase real wages in order to attract more labour and increase the numbers employed. If the non-wage measures increase costs the demand for labour may not increase. It is possible that firms could decide that the non-wage measures were as expensive as increasing wages and that therefore they were not worth introducing.

If there are unemployed individuals who would be willing to accept employment on the existing terms and conditions then, if labour market institutions can be made to operate more efficiently by bringing these workers into contact with those employers wishing to recruit additional workers, there can be an increase in employment without any increases in wages. If Keynesian involuntary unemployment exists and the individuals concerned are, or can become, part of an employer's acceptable labour supply, no increase in wages is necessary in order to expand employment. If the unemployed possess the appropriate characteristics and aptitudes to match the employer's job requirements, they are part of his acceptable labour supply as soon as they apply for a job. If they do not the employer may decide to alter his requirements.

A rational employer will decide according to the relative costs of the two approaches. Lowering recruitment standards may mean that the marginal productivity of labour falls and so the value of marginal revenue product falls. However, as we are considering how employers react to a perceived increase in demand for their product, this reduction in marginal revenue product may still lead to an increased demand for labour. Alternatively, employers may lower their recruiting standards but bear the cost of additional training to bring the new recruits up to the former acceptable recruitment standards. Again, the perceived increase in demand for his products may make this a viable policy for a rational profit-maximizing employer if he believes he can afford a higher product real wage in the light of his expectation of an increase in demand for his products.

Both the possibility of involuntary unemployment and the options open to employers to change the relationship between labour-offer supply curves and acceptable-labour supply curves, provide opportunities for an increase in employment, accompanied by a reduction in unemployment as recorded in the official count, without an increase in wages. The second option could increase labour costs (including training) or reduce the value of the marginal product, but these are demand-side considerations. The importance of this is that they do not require that workers believe their real wages are rising so that there are no erroneous expectations on the supply side which, when they are seen to be wrongly based, lead to a voluntary withdrawal from employment.

If the employer's expectations turn out to be wrong because inflation is general so there is not the growth in demand for his product that he anticipated, he may reduce the demand for labour. The question then becomes whether those currently employed, including the new recruits, will seek to maintain the previous level of real wages. This is not the expected *higher* real wages of the Friedman account, but the level of real wages existing in the original equilibrium situation. If the labour market does not always clear in real wage terms so higher wages are not necessary in order to expand employment, prices will not rise as they do in Friedman's model. If inflation is less, some of the employer's anticipated increase in real demand for his product will occur. His demand for labour will remain higher and a lasting increase in employment will have been achieved.

It should not be too difficult to accept that some firms can attract additional labour without increasing wages or they can adjust their acceptability standards and, while accepting some increase in labour costs or reductions in marginal revenue, this may still justify expanding employment when they perceive an increase in demand. The more important issue is whether these firms can do so only by passing on the problems to other firms. It may be that the extra labour they hire comes from other firms. These secondary firms can be expected to seek to recruit replacements and might also wish to expand employment and output if they too perceive an increase in demand for their products.

If may be that this leads to a reduction in the product real wage for some employers as they recruit less suitable workers. This may lead them to increase their prices but this could well be by less than they would have to do if they maintained hiring standards and increased wages. The key relationship is that between the real wage elasticity of supply of labour and the reduction in the MRP of those workers recruited when hiring standards are lowered. The price increase resulting from a lowering of hiring standards could well be less than that which would follow an increase in real wages. If this is so then it could well be possible to increase employment following an increase in aggregate nominal demand as not all of that increase would be passed through in higher prices. It would not be the case, therefore, that unemployment would return to the previous NRU. An expansion of employment could be possible.

However, if one believes that even in the non-union sector the labour market does not always clear in real wage terms it could be possible to expand employment without increasing real wages. It is only the assertion that non-union labour markets always clear that leads to the conclusion that in this part of the economy an increase in real wages is necessary in order to induce unemployed workers to accept a job.

While there may be some vacancies in some places which cannot be filled at prevailing real wage levels, it is hardly likely that in 1985 the great majority of the 3 million officially recorded unemployed are voluntarily unemployed because the level of real wages offered is below their reservation wage. Were demand to increase it seems extremely probable that many unemployed would be willing to accept a job on existing terms and conditions.

The assumption in the expectations-augmented Phillips curve that an increase in real wages is necessary in order to induce unemployed workers to accept a job, is not warranted. The assertion that a perceived increase in real wages will prove to be unfounded as prices rise generally in response to the widespread increase in money wages is equally unwarranted. The conclusion that if this occurs the newly employed workers will choose to return to voluntary unemployment as their expectations of higher real wages are not met may also be wrong. The general thesis that the long-run Phillips curve is vertical so that there is no trade-off between unemployment and inflation is by no means necessarily valid. If labour markets are not in equilibrium an expansion of employment can take place without inflation. In other situations there may be some inflation resulting from an increase in aggregate nominal demand but it may be less than the initial increase in aggregate demand. There may be some inflation and some reduction in unemployment.

This should not be taken to suggest that the original Phillips curve idea as set out by Phillips still holds, as there may be no *constant* relationship. There may be pressures to increase real wages which are quite separate from changes in the aggregate level of demand. Rather than there being a Phillips curve which provides the terms of a trade-off we might envisage a range of possibilities. Sometimes we might be able to expand employment with little or no inflation. At other times there may be inflationary pressures without there being any change in aggregate nominal demand. They key question is, what is happening to real wages? These are not fixed and stable, nor do they necessarily change at a constant trend rate. If they fall, and workers and the unemployed accept this so that their real reservation wages are also reduced, employment may expand. We shall discuss this in Chapter 14 when we consider the natural rate of unemployment.

The expectations-augmented Phillips curve is an odd mixture of static and dynamic elements. It seeks to incorporate expectations of future price movements so that decisions are taken on the basis of expected real wages and expected product real wages. It is dynamic in that producers and workers are assumed to respond dynamically to changes in expectations. It is static in that it supposes that real reservation wages and real-wage labour-offer supply curves are static, in a market-clearing situation. Versions which do not rest on market-clearing (referred to in Chapter 14) nevertheless assume that real wages behave as though there was market-clearing as employers increase real wages when they increase their demand for labour. In the real world real reservation wages and real-wage labour-offer supply curves are not static. Trade unions and their members may adopt a target real wage approach. They also have aspirations which they seek to translate into real wage improvements. At other times they accept reductions in real wages, no doubt expecting them to be temporary perhaps as part of a permanent income hypothesis approach.

Conclusions

The original Phillips curve plotted a relationship between the rate of change of money wage rates and the level of unemployment. The notion that there was a causal relationship between the level of unemployment and the subsequent rate of change of pay—measured in different ways—attracted considerable attention. It appeared to offer policy makers a range of choice. They could adopt certain demand-management policies to influence the level of unemployment if they were prepared to accept the inflationary consequences, or they could decide to reduce the rate of inflation if they were prepared to pay the price of higher unemployment. Almost as soon as the idea had received widespread, but not universal, acceptance, the methods which had initially seemed to establish it, destroyed it. The old or expected relationships no longer held.

Monetarists, led by Friedman, presented the expectations-augmented Phillips curve. This had two important differences from the original. It did not claim to be based on empirical observation or analysis of what had actually happened to inflation and unemployment. It was derived solely by economic reasoning from a priori premises. Secondly, the chain of causation was reversed. Short-term reductions in unemployment now followed increases in aggregate nominal demand resulting from variations in the money stock. This worked through the expectations of employers and workers, both of whom misunderstood the consequences of perceived increases in demand resulting from an increase in the money stock.

The analysis led to an emphasis on the natural rate of unemployment. Increases in the money stock, it was argued, could lead to a temporary reduction in the level of unemployment. This would lead to higher inflation which when properly appreciated and incorporated into people's expectations would cause the economy to move back to the NRU. There is no possibility of a lasting decrease in unemployment from monetary policy. Long-term equilibrium is always at the NRU. The only effect increasing the money stock has is to generate unanticipated inflation which leads to the temporary increase in employment. Anticipated inflation has no effect on employment.

The analysis rests very heavily on the assumption that labour markets clear in real wage terms. It is assumed that employment can be increased *only* if employers raise money wages and workers believe this means that real wages are rising. The expectations-augmented Phillips curve is essentially a real-wage labour-supply curve. If labour markets do not always clear in real wage terms the analysis has no explanatory value for policy-makers. If an increase in demand leads to an expansion of employment at prevailing money wages, the reduction in unemployment may be more than temporary.

There are a number of reasons to believe that many employers may be faced by an excess supply of labour at prevailing real wages. Monetarists assert that this is so because of the ability of trade unions to raise wages above their market-clearing level. The important question might then shift to whether the non-union sector is faced with an excess supply of labour at prevailing real wages? If it is thought that it is, or it is at some times, the inflationary consequences of increasing employment via an increase in the money stock need not occur. If some employers have to increase money wages in order to attract additional workers, there may be some inflation following an expansion of aggregate demand, but this may be less than the rate of growth of money stock or aggregate demand. In this case there may be both a rise in employment (fall in unemployment) and some inflation, but the decrease in employment may be sustainable.

The conclusion that the long-run Phillips curve is vertical is derived exclusively from economic theory and not from applied research. Its premises seem unwarranted as representations of the situation in the UK in the 1980s. The argument that the curve is vertical should be rejected. A great deal of what Monetarism appears to have to offer to policy-makers goes with it, and should also be rejected.

Notes to Chapter 11

1. Phillips (1958).
2. It is worth noting that the underlying argument itself was not new; for example as early as 1926 Professor Irving Fisher had published an article which had the same general theme of the connection between unemployment and inflation. Irving Fisher: 'A Statistical Relation between Unemployment and Price Changes', *International Labour Review*, June 1926, reprinted in *Journal of Political Economy*, Mar./Apr. 1973.

3. See M. Bronfenbrenner and F. D. Holzman, 'A Survey of Inflation Theory', *American Economic Review*, 53(4), 1965.
4. See R. G. Lipsey (1960); Parkin and Sumner (1972); Trevithick and Mulvey (1975).
5. One of the best fairly simply explanations of this in an undergraduate textbook is in Ehrenburg and Smith (1982), ch. 16. Their account draws heavily on Lipsey (1960).
6. Laidler (1982) draws the same conclusion but not perhaps quite as strongly.

CHAPTER TWELVE

Expectations

'What we anticipate seldom occurs; what we least expected generally happens.'
Benjamin Disraeli, *Henrietta Temple* (1837), bk. ii, ch. 4

EXPECTATIONS of the future price level lie at the heart of the Monetarist explanation of the relationship between unemployment and inflation. It is argued that when an unanticipated increase in the money stock occurs employers misinterpret the increase in aggregate nominal demand as, in part at least, an increase in real demand. They expect some increase in the real demand for their product as they do not expect all the perceived increase in nominal demand to become only price rises. They therefore form mistaken expectations about the future rate of inflation. Because of this they believe that the price they can charge for their product will rise in relation to prices generally so that they can increase money wages without increasing the product real wage.

Similarly workers and unemployed workers form expectations of the future inflation rate which prove to be too low. Because they do not fully anticipate the amount of inflation that would occur they believe that the increase in money wage is and will remain an increase in real wages, and it is in response to this expectation of an increase in real wages that some of the unemployed are induced to accept employment and provide the additional labour input assumed necessary to increase output. The combined results of similar actions by many employers and workers lead, in the long run, only to an increase in prices and money wages with no additional employment. Because the product real wage does not fall employers do not want more labour and because real wages have not risen the additional workers are assumed to prefer to go back to voluntary unemployment. Real output and employment revert back to the NRU. The short-run benefits from the inflation–unemployment trade-off occur only because there are misperceptions about the level of inflation that is to occur.

If expectations had been correct there would have been one of two possible developments. If the original expectations had been fulfilled the short-run increases in employment would have continued. However, as we have shown Monetarists believe this cannot occur. In their view, the increase in the money supply which caused the misplaced expectations of an increase in demand for products in real terms *inevitably* becomes an increase only in money terms. To them the short-run trade-off must give way to a movement back to the NRU and the only interesting question for employment policy is how long will the short-run benefits last? The first possibility—that the short-run expectations prove correct in the long run—is therefore ruled out by Monetarists, but allowed as a possibility in some circumstances by Keynesians.

The second possibility is that the original expectations fully took into account the higher rate of inflation that the Monetarists are confident will occur. There is therefore no misperception about the future rate of inflation and no mistaken belief that the increase in aggregate nominal demand includes some increase in real demand. In this case there is no short-run trade-off. Employers correctly interpret the increase in money supply as heralding only additional inflationary pressure which will increase wages and prices generally and therefore do not seek to attract any additional workers. Similarly workers correctly conclude that inflation will increase. Those already employed on the basis of the real wage compared to their real reservation wage will need higher money wages to induce them to remain in employment now that they have revised upwards their expectations about future inflation. Employers will be willing to grant these money wage increases because as a result of *their* revised inflation expectations they believe they can increase the prices of their products and thus keep the same product real wage with higher money wage levels. Output and employment remain at the NRU level with no short-run deviations. This is the position of the New Classical School and the only interesting question left for them is the extent to which the official unemployment statistics accurately measure unemployment as they define it, i.e. some definition of frictional unemployment which excludes the voluntarily unemployed and particularly those who while receiving Unemployment Benefit are not really looking for or willing to accept work.

If the expectations-augmented Phillips curve with its central tenet that in the long-run employment will always return to the NRU is to be of value to policy-makers there are two important questions which need to be answered. First, is the question of how expectations of the future rate of inflation are formed? Second, is whether expectations of future price levels are the only expectations that matter?

Expected Rate of Inflation

Within the broad Monetarist school there is considerable division about the determinants of changes in expectations of future inflation. The Gradualists, typified by Laidler, believe that expectations are based on previous experience of inflation—they assume adaptive expectations. The New Classical School typified by Minford believe that economic agents will revise their expectations, not simply by comparing their recent actual rate of inflation with their previous expectations, but by noting the intention of the monetary authorities to change the money stock they assume rational expectations.

Milton Friedman in his exposition of the expectations-augmented Phillips curve assumed adaptive expectations.

This difference of opinion can have considerable importance for Monetarist policies. The first approach might be seen as requiring changes in the money stock which feed through into different rates of inflation as a necessary precondition for the revision of currently held expectations of inflation. The second argues that expectations can be changed irrespective of the recent rate of inflation provided the announcement of intention by monetary authorities is believed. In this version expectations will be revised as soon as the credible announcement is made. It is not actually necessary for the change in the money stock to have been introduced and its effects felt; the mere announcement of credible monetary targets is sufficient.

If private economic agents are assumed to take their decisions on the basis of real wages and future prices, and decisions are taken at discrete intervals of time, it is necessary for them to take into account the rate of inflation expected to occur during the period covered by their decisions. We need therefore to make some assumption about how they form their expectations about the future rate of inflation.

The simplest, but not necessarily most warranted, assumption would be that the expected rate of inflation in the coming period is the same as the rate actually experienced in the current one so that,

$$p_2^* = p_1, \qquad (12.1)$$

where p^* is the expected rate of price change,

p is the actual rate of price change,

and subscripts $1, 2 \ldots n$ are different time-periods.

This would mean that employers and workers are assumed to project into the next period the rate of inflation experienced in the current one. It would require short time-horizons in that only the inflation in the current period influenced expectations about inflation in the next. It would also mean that no matter what relationship held between expectations and actual inflation in the current period, current expectations were forgotten and only the actual rate of inflation influenced expectations about the next period. We can include the effects of expectations in the past period by amending (12.1) to

$$p_2^* = bp_1 + (1-b)p_1^* \text{ where } 0 < b > 1. \qquad (12.2)$$

The time-periods for which expectations are formed might be long, as in, say, an annual wage agreement, and therefore price expectations in any one period might be affected by actual price developments in that period rather than only in prior periods as assumed in (12.1) and (12.2).

In this case we can assume

$$p_2^* = bp_2 + (1-b)p_1^*. \tag{12.3}$$

As p_1^* was determined in the same way so that

$$p_1^* = bp_1 + (1-b)p_0^*.\tag{12.4}$$

We can reformulate (12.3) so that

$$p_2^* = b \sum_{j=0}^{\infty} (1-b)^j p_{2-j}.$$

The larger is b the less important are past periods in influencing our current expectations.

However large or small b is, this form of equation is one of adaptive expectations. Economic agents base their expectations of inflation on past experience although exactly which past experience—how far back they go and how important each past period is—depends on the size of the coefficient b that is adopted. For practical purposes, if the expectations-augmented Phillips curve actually operates b determines the short run. It effectively tells us the period of time in which expectations of inflation have not fully caught up with the actual rate of inflation and therefore both sides of the labour market are taking their decisions based on faulty expectations.

If the product market is in equilibrium

$$Y_2 = Y_n + \alpha(p_2 - p_2^*) + e_2 \qquad \alpha > 0, \tag{12.5}$$

where Y_2 is the level of real output in period 2;
Y_n is the level of the natural rate of output in period 2;
e_2 is a random disturbance of output from its natural or equilibrium level with a mean value of zero.

The variables are often expressed in logarithms and equation (12.5) is sometimes referred to as the Lucas–Sargent (1978) aggregate supply equation. This states that actual output will equal the natural rate when all expectations are fulfilled and as we are assuming that equilibrium in the output market means there will be equilibrium in the labour market equation (12.5) can be converted into an employment equation.

$$U_2 = U_n - \beta(p_2 - p_2^*) + e_2 \qquad \beta > 0. \tag{12.6}$$

The α in (12.5) becomes β in (12.6) because the quantitative relationship of a given difference between actual and expected prices might be different in the output and labour markets. The sign before the second expression in the right-hand side of the equations changes because the effects of a difference between actual and expected prices are thought to be different in the two types of market. If actual prices exceed expected prices as in (12.5) output will be increased following the usual expectations-augmented approach as employers perceive an increase in real demand, and so output exceeds its natural or equilibrium level. This leads to an increase in employment so unemployment falls. In addition the fall in real wages, or expected real wages as a result of higher than expected price increases, may lead some individuals to withdraw from labour force participation. The actual level of unemployment will fall below the NRU due to pressures from both the demand and supply sides of the labour market.

Two things are clear from this sort of explanation. First, the economy will deviate from its natural level of output or unemployment as a result of differences between actual and expected prices,—this is the expectations-augmented Phillips curve again—or because of a non-systematic random disturbance—e—which, because it has a mean value of zero, is over some period of time cancelled out by offsetting disturbances in the other direction. Second, the determination of price expectations is crucial. This follows from the view that $p_2 = p_2^* + e_2$.

The rate of inflation is expressed in its simplest form as:

$$p = ay + \beta(p_2^* - p_1), \qquad (12.7)$$

where y is some measure of the deviation of output from its 'full employment' level. If the full employment output is the NRU and the economy is actually operating at the NRU then ay is zero and all inflation is a function of the change in expected inflation, there will be no change in the *actual* level of inflation. This is the same as:

$$\begin{aligned} p &= au + bp^*e \\ p_2 &= bu + \alpha(p_2^* - p_1), \end{aligned} \qquad (12.7a)$$

where u, the level of unemployment, is a function of the deviation of the economy from its 'full employment' or NRU level, i.e. $(U_n - U_2)$. If the expected rate of inflation is a function of actual inflation in the previous period, and the economy is at the NRU, expectations will not change.

If the economy is at the NRU and there is no change in the money supply, actual inflation will be the same as expected inflation, and expectations will not change. Because expectations do not change and the money supply is constant, actual inflation will not change. Expectations will be fulfilled and so everyone is assumed to continue as before. Employment and output remain at the NRU level and the circular causation of stability remains undisturbed—because actual inflation remains constant the expected level of inflation remains unchanged so that actual inflation remains constant.

We can make this more realistic by adding another variable Z which is a vector of all other influences which influence inflation.[1]

$$p_2 = ay + \beta(p_2^* - p_1) + Z. \tag{12.8}$$

This is both helpful and unhelpful for some purposes. It helps because it means we are no longer constrained by the very rigid assumptions that all expectations are fully met or that all wage increases which fully incorporate fulfilled expectations of future price increases lead to fully matched price increases giving different values to the parameters a and b. It also allows us to introduce any other variables in the vector which reflect institutional, political, or sociological factors. In addition all price changes can be determined by exogenous factors in the Z if we assume that a and b are zero.

The sizes of the a and b coefficients are obviously crucial. If a is positive, then for a given set of expectations of price inflation, prices would rise more in an economy operating above its 'full employment' level, and rise less than expected in a depressed economy. To a Monetarist coefficient b would be expected to be equal to unity. Keynesians might assign a value less than unity to coefficient b but equally might emphasize some positive variables in Z which could lead to faster or slower inflation than concentration on y and p^* alone would do. British and American Keynesians might well disagree about the size of coefficient b and the relative strength and durability of elements in Z.[2]

Equation (12.7) is an expression of the aggregate supply function. The variable ay measures departure from the full employment level in a situation where the changes in output and employment, y, represent voluntary decisions by economic agents operating in markets which clear. This is yet again the point that in order to increase employment it is necessary to offer higher real wages, or what are perceived to be higher real wages, in order to induce individuals to leave their voluntary unemployment and accept work. Equation (12.7) is derived from

$$y = \frac{1}{a}(p - p^*) \tag{12.9}$$

combined with equation (12.4).

This gives a rather different explanation of unemployment. The cause is not in the failure of markets to bring together all willing buyers and sellers in *ex ante* mutually satisfactory trades, but rather in a failure of markets (and other social institutions as well, perhaps) to convey sufficient information to enable the expectations upon which those trades are based to be formed accurately in an economy subject to stochastic shocks (Laidler 1982, 17).

If there were some way to provide sufficient information to enable individuals to form accurate expectations there would be no variations in output and employment from its 'full employment' or NRU level. 'Thus the manner in which expectations are formed must play a vital role in the analysis of fluctuations in output and employment about their natural rates.'

Adaptive Expectations

The first approach to the formulation of an explanation of how expectations develop was the adaptive expectations one. Assume that p has been constant for some time so that

$$p_2^* = p_1^* = p_1.$$

If $p_2 > p_2^*$ assume there will be a revision of expectations of inflation in period 3 so that $p_3^* > p_2^*$. The question is, by how much will p_3^* rise? We can express the relationship as;

$$p_3^* - p_2^* = (1-b)(p_2 - p_2^*). \qquad (12.10)$$

In the special case where j is zero this means that the actual rate of inflation in the current period is assumed to be repeated in the next. This is the assumption in equation (12.1). It is both very simple and perhaps unrealistic. It requires that economic agents take no notice of all the previous periods of constant inflation which are represented in equation (12.4) and become totally converted to a new set of expectations based on their experience in just the one period where $p_2 > p_2^*$. It was thought therefore that $0 < j < 1$ might be a more appropriate assumption. If $j = 0.5$ this would mean that we carry forward to the next period half of the unexpected inflation in the current period. As long as inflation was rising we would of course continue to underestimate the actual rate of inflation which we were to experience. This would allow some short-run (which might, however, be very long) trade-off of inflation and unemployment. Indeed if there were no factors other than those in equation (12.4) so that the vector Z in (12.8) was zero it could be possible for the short run to develop into a very long run provided that j remained constant at 0.5. This would mean, of course, that there would be an increasing gap between experienced and expected inflation which would result in a continual reduction in real wages. This continual reduction in real wages is assumed to be unrealistic or unattainable because the determination of money wages is regarded as a function of the 'expected' real wage. Thus

$$w_2 = f(U_2) + p_2^*. \qquad (12.11)$$

This is the usual statement that U or Y represents the demand for labour and there is an upward-sloping real-wage labour supply curve. If unemployment falls real wages will rise as a condition for obtaining the reduction in unemployment; voluntarily unemployed workers require an increase in expected real wages to induce them to accept a job. Given their expectations of inflation the money wage rate will have to rise. Given the usual assumption that prices respond to money wages so that,

$$p_2 = w_2, \qquad (12.12)$$

the increase in money wages feeds through into equivalent price increases. (We have earlier considered the possibility of adjusting this relationship to take account of changes in productivity.)

Equation (12.11) would require a coefficient of less than unity for the p^* variable to allow the short run to be extended to a very long time-period, and the real-wage labour supply assumption says this could happen only if workers failed to appreciate what was happening to their real wages, or, although this is seldom mentioned, if they reduced their real wage labour supply price. Adaptive expectations with a p^* coefficient of less than unity seem therefore to require that workers continually fail to appreciate the speeding up of inflation or accept continuing reductions in their real wages.

These possibilities are rejected on the grounds that it is just unreasonable or unrealistic to expect workers to react like this.

The adaptive expectations version requires that people continue to make the same mistake in the formulation of their expectations. More precisely in its aggregate form it requires that the weighted average of expected inflation is consistently less than the actual rate of inflation which occurs. This does not actually require that we all keep repeating our mistakes. It does require that enough, but possibly different, people make the same sort of mistake in each period so that the combined effect of their errors, when added to those who correctly anticipated inflation, or even overestimate future inflation, leads to the aggregate wage and price decisions based on our various expectations, being wrong by a consistent underestimation.

Rational Expectations

The Rational Expectations Hypothesis (REH) emerged to deal with the weaknesses of an adaptive expectations explanation.[4] Its starting-point is relatively simple. Economic agents who base their actions on expectations which turn out to be systematically wrong suffer a loss of utility and fail to maximize whatever it is that motivates their actions. They have, therefore, an incentive to obtain more and better information so that their future actions will not be subject to these errors. In economic terminology they should obtain better information, and incur costs in doing so, to the point where the marginal benefits of the improved information equal the marginal costs incurred in obtaining it. The economic decisions of agents are not necessarily always based on completely accurate information but their errors will not be systematic. They will not continue to make the same mistake.

In the course of correcting past and current mistakes we may overshoot so that our response is greater than it would be if we had perfectly accurate information on which to base our expectations, but it is supposed that these errors of underestimation and any compensating overreaction will cancel out so that we tend, on average, to get it right. The errors we make in any one period or in respect of any one decision, will therefore be randomly distributed in an assumed normal distribution, around the 'correct' expectations and decisions. Thus it is not absolutely essential to the REH that all economic agents have an accurate model of the economy which provides completely reliable information, although sometimes this might be what some REH advocates are saying. The hypothesis can stand as long as the errors are not systematic and this means that if they are turning out to be consistently wrong in one direction—say continually underestimating the rate of inflation—the agent will take steps to correct his expectation and revise his behaviour.

There are three important issues arising from the REH for labour market analysis. First, if labour markets always clear, and if individuals make only random errors, how is it that we get deviations from the NRU? If the random errors of individuals cancel out we might expect that as labour markets clear the level of output and employment would always be at the level of the NRU. Different individuals might be in or out of employment at any particular time depending on whether their individual random error led to them under- or overestimating the expected rate of inflation, but the labour market as a whole ought to be in equilibrium. U would be constant but the individual composition of the U would vary.

Only reply is to argue that the economy always *is* at the NRU but that the NRU itself increases or decreases in response to the distribution of the random errors, because of changes in the variance of the distribution of random errors for each individual, or in the distribution of errors between individuals. Thus, if the errors in anticipating the 'true' inflation rate became larger in both directions, while remaining normally distributed, so that on average everyone still got it right, the larger swings in the size of the errors might lead people to spend more time looking for a job. This would increase frictional or job-search unemployment and thus the NRU. It would then appear that the economy was not operating at the NRU level, but that would be because we had not appreciated that the NRU had changed. This still leaves us unclear why there should have been a pattern of fairly regular business cycles which seems to suggest that deviations from 'full employment' or the NRU do take place regularly. Or it requires an explanation of why the distribution of the random errors and individuals' responses varied in an apparently regular cyclical manner.

Second, there is the question of the economic model on which the expectations of each individual economic agent are based. We can accept that for anyone to form expectations it is necessary they have some view of the factors which influence developments. This is all we need mean by the term 'economic model'. It may be a sophisticated and massive econometric model or a very crude set of simple factors. But if it is correct to assume that it is *expected* real wages, and not currently perceived real wages, which determine the labour market decisions, there has to be something on which to base expectations, and this something is an economic model. In passing it might be worth mentioning that no creator of a sophisticated econometric model that I have met has ever had recourse to his computer when asked what he thought was going to happen to his own real wages. In every case they have included some variables which were not in their model. It may be of course that I have not asked enough or the right econometricians. It is much more likely that there is a more important explanation. The econometric models tend to be aggregate or macro-economic models as does the economic theorizing underlying the Monetarist position. Even if the theories and models are correct at the macro-level, individuals seem to realize that their own real wages and expected future real wages, are influenced by a number of micro-economic factors. The distinction between macro-theory and the crucial micro-explanations and analysis on which labour market participation and the real-wage-from-employment versus voluntary unemployment choices are based, might be quite different, or even incapable of being handled by the macro-model.

The REH incorporates the belief that individuals will learn to avoid systematic errors in the formulation of their expectations. It is the failure of economic agents to 'properly' appreciate and include in their decisions the effects of an increase in the money supply which leads to the short-run real effects. What if the economic model on which the agents are acting does not follow a Monetarist path so that in the model used by economic agents increases in the money supply lead to increases in real output and employment? The REH advocate would argue that experience will, in time, teach them that their model is wrong and that the resulting systematic errors will lead to a loss of utility through the failure to attain expected real incomes. Except in theoretically perfect models where an increase in the money supply is *asserted* to lead to an equal change in all prices and money wages, there is no reason to conclude that the massively large number of adjustments in employment, output, and pricing decisions which will follow an increase in aggregate monetary demand, will lead to such an exactly proportionate effect on all sectors and all firms. It is much more likely that some sectors will obtain benefits in real terms. This might be the result of 'distortions' or market imperfections which would not occur in the theoretically perfect model, but in the real world of actual decisions, a rational person should base his actions on the results he expects to see, and not upon what some theoretically perfect economic model tells him would happen if a whole lot of unreal conditions existed. It would be contrary to the experience of many economic agents to act on the assumption that changes in the money supply affect only money wages and all prices in such a way as to leave real wages unaffected and to have no effect on real variables, particularly at the micro-level.

Many economic agents may give little if any direct attention to changes in the money supply in their economic model. If, however, there are other variables which are systematically linked to the money supply which do feature and to which they always react as if they were responding to changes in the money supply the results will be the same. Strong adherents of the REH conclude that the assumption that agents do not make systematic errors is sufficient to permit the economist analysing their behaviour to postulate that they act 'as if' they understood the operation of the economy of which they form a part (Laidler 1982, 84). The particular model from which they derive their expectations is regarded as irrelevant. The condition that errors are not systematic will drive them to accept the link between money supply and price and money wage effects *because that is what will happen in practice*. If, as we have suggested, that is not what happens in practice to some economic agents, then, of course, the logical necessity of accepting this conclusion disappears.

This version of REH seems at first sight to be strengthening a Monetarist position by concluding that even if all economic agents do not have a complete Monetarist economic model in front of them grinding out the analysis from which their expectations are derived and on which their actions are based, they will nevertheless act as if they swallowed the full paraphernalia of Monetarism. Not to do so would lead them to make systematic errors, and these have been ruled out by definition. (If they have not gone by definition, they have done so on the ground that it is contrary to the attainment of an economic agent's objectives to consistently act in a way which fails to meet those objectives.) However, this is really no more than a series of logical propositions superimposed on a particular set of economic concepts—Monetarism. Once the proposition that changes in the money supply will have only price effects is questioned the whole superstructure of logical extension from the initial premises collapses.

Third, there is the question of how people learn they are making systematic mistakes and how they then take action to correct this. As we have suggested, not all agents will be making mistakes in the sense that they do experience no increase in their real wages other than in some short-run period. Some groups, employers, and employees in some firms or sectors, may experience long-run increases in their real income following an increase in the money supply. These may not be as large as they anticipated but they may still be positive. Presumably people learn they have made a mistake when they realize that their current real wage is below the level of their real reservation wage.

They then try to find out why their real wages are less than expected. They work out that it is because of the increase in money supply which generated the increase in aggregate nominal demand.

Many people are unlikely to follow this line of reasoning. Moreover, even if they do, it does not follow that the perceived reductions in real wages will lead them to withdraw from the work-force to become voluntarily unemployed. They might decide to change their real reservation wage.

It is difficult to obtain accurate up-to-date information about the development of one's own real wage. We may form some general impression by comparing changes in our money wages with the Retail Price Index, but this is only a general impression. The composition and weighting of the different items in our individual package of consumption goods will not be the same as that for the RPI. While we may get some idea from the Press, or other media, about general price movements this is not really enough to provide the sort of information necessary for the proper application of the REH.

Some items are bought only infrequently. Changes in the price of durable consumer goods may therefore be of relevance to an individual only at certain times. This is used by some advocates of the REH to explain why the economy can move away from its NRU even though markets are continuing to clear.[5] Because some workers have not been affected by the higher prices their real wages have not yet fallen, or are not seen to have fallen. The markets can clear because these workers are still enjoying the higher real wages, but once the higher prices enter their consumption activities there will be, or they will perceive that there is, a reduction in their real wages and the level of activity will revert to the NRU level.

On this approach a worker is assumed to misunderstand what is happening to his real wages because he has not, during the period of the increase in prices, made one of his periodic purchases. Assume he buys a consumer durable once a year. He is regarded as setting aside one-fifty-secondth of the cost of a new washing-machine out of his weekly pay. He calculates the amount needed to buy the machine at the end of the year on the basis of the price at the start of the year. After fifty-two weeks he will find that he has not set aside enough. Inflation has taken place which he did not appreciate because he was not actually buying a machine until the end of the year. He is now assumed to withdraw from employment because his real wages have not risen—he cannot buy the new washing-machine in fifty-two weeks. His behaviour might conceivably be as ludicruous as this. It is much more likely that he will try and increase his money wages or get his trade union to do it. It is also possible that he will remain in employment at his current wage. If he does he may be able to get the washing-machine in another four or five weeks. If he decides to become unemployed he has probably to abandon all hope of getting the new machine. True, his real wage might be less than he expected but this could well be more attractive to him than the even lower real income when unemployed.

If he or his trade union can increase money wages to obtain the expected real wage, the employer's demand for labour might be reduced as the real product wage may have risen. This might lead to higher unemployment, but not because the worker has chosen to return to voluntary unemployment, but because the employer's demand has been reduced. There will then be imbalance between demand and supply in the labour market—the worker will be willing to be employed at the lower real wage even though he pressed for a restoration of real wages, but there is insufficient demand to provide him with employment. There will be demand-deficient unemployment. Employment might be stable at this new level but it is not a labour market-clearing natural rate of unemployment.

Information about price levels and changes is not provided free nor is it comprehensive. Maximizing individuals may conclude that the cost of obtaining more accurate information outweighs the benefit and they will therefore act on the basis of inadequate or out-of-date information. The REH assumes that at some stage the losses resulting from so acting will become apparent to economic agents and they will then devote more resources to obtaining better information as they realize the benefits from so doing. The costs of obtaining information are not necessarily financial. They might be the opportunity cost of foregone leisure activities involved in collecting information about movements in the prices of all the items entering the consumption package. We know that many people do not spend time collecting information about all the prices of all the goods currently part of their consumption package. Very few shoppers know the different prices charged for such things as tea, sugar, butter, baked beans, and meat in the various shops in their customary shopping locality. How much less precise is their knowledge of the actual rate of change of all these various prices over time. What is much more likely is that individuals have some broad idea of the movement of some prices and perhaps some vague idea of what has happened to the RPI over some particular period. Their view of what has actually happened to their real wages may very well be heavily influenced by what has happened to certain prices.

Individuals are not 'desiccated calculating machines'. I doubt if even professional economists sit down and work out the movement in prices of all items entering their consumption packages and form expectations about their future levels. They may do this for a few items. Individuals generally may base their views of what is happening to their real wages on the basis of certain prices. This may not fit in with the suppositions of economic theory—so much the less realistic is economic theory.

It is very likely that housing costs influence individuals' assessments of their real wages to a much greater degree than a collection of other items which represents an equivalent proportion of their expenditure pattern. An increase in housing costs of 20 per cent if housing represents, say, a quarter of total expenditure, is likely to be perceived much more acutely than an increase in prices of consumer goods which leads to the same 5 per cent rise in the cost of living. Politicians are aware of this even if economic theorists are not. They are reluctant to let interest rates rise too high, fearing the backlash from the mortgaged electorate. There is an interesting political economy paradox here. The more that right-wing Monetarist governments encourage house-ownership, which for many, means, most of the time, house-purchasing, the less scope might there be for the implementation of Monetarist policies which require interest rates to rise as the money supply growth is reduced.

If economic agents respond to certain prices more than others they might still act as though they were following an REH but they would actually be making mistakes. If they did not realize this then the economy could shift away from the NRU for long periods of time. If they subsequently learned of their errors they are presumably assumed to rectify the situation by moving to a maximizing position which would maintain the NRU.

Changes in the Money Stock or Monetary Targets?

There is debate even within the Monetarists camp as to whether it is necessary for economic agents actually to experience changes in the rate of inflation before they revise their expectations of the future inflation rate. There is often asymmetry in the discussion of the expectations-augmented Phillips curve and Monetarist proposals to reduce inflation. The no-long-run unemployment–inflation trade-off analysis is usually based on what happens when the money stock is increased and there is an unanticipated *increase* in aggregate nominal demand. Proposals to reduce the rate of inflation are concerned with the reverse direction—how, if at all, does a reduction in the rate of growth of the money stock lead to a reduction in the rate of inflation.?

Even if the case for the expectations-augmented Phillips curve could be established as showing the inevitable consequences of an increase in aggregate nominal demand—and we have sought to demonstrate that it cannot—it does not follow that a reduction in the rate of growth of money supply will have equal but opposite effects. Economic behaviour does not necessarily provide mirror images. For example we have suggested in Chapter 6 that the supply of labour may not respond in equal but opposite ways to increases and decreases in money wages. Expectations may not respond in asymmetrical fashion. However, we will follow the usual practice and assume that we can accept reverse causation.

To reduce inflation, therefore, Monetarists argue it is necessary either to reduce the money supply or to persuade economic agents that the money supply is going to be reduced. The first approach—from adaptive expectations—requires an actual reduction to be implemented and its effects experienced. Reduction in money supply in this context means a reduction in relation to the money supply which is assumed to be forthcoming and which provided the basis for the formulation of economic agents' expectations of the future rate of inflation. Because the money supply is then lower than anticipated it will not be possible for all producers to sell all their planned output at anticipated prices. Using the Quantity Theory approach $M_2^* > M_2$ so $(P_2 Y_2)$ must be $< (P_2^* Y_2^*)$. If Y is constant, say because the economy always operates at its NRU, or (on some particular definition) its full employment level, this means that $P_2 < P_2^*$ and $Y_2 = Y_2^*$. A reduction in the anticipated rate of growth of the money supply will, on this basis, lead to a reduction in the actual rate of inflation, compared to anticipated inflation.

Prices will rise by less than money wages. The employer will not increase money wages by as much as anticipated because he will find that he cannot increase his product prices by the anticipated amount, and to increase money wages to the extent anticipated with $P_2^* > P_2$ will lead to an increase in his real product wage. Workers will accept a lower than expected increase in money wages because prices generally are rising less than anticipated so their real wages and expected real wages can be maintained with a smaller rise in money wages.

It may not be quite as simple as this even with basic Quantity Theory approach which assumes that V—the velocity of circulation— is constant. We can assume, within the Monetarist model, that $P_2^* > P_1$ and $M_2^* > M_1$. On the basis of these expectations employers may have agreed to increase money wages so that $W_2 > W_1$ as $P_2^* > P_1$. If the increase in money stock is less than anticipated so that $m = (M_2 - M_1) < (M_2^* - M_1)$, the increase in prices that is possible with a constant output is less than expected. $P_2 < P_2^*$. However, if money wages have been increased on the basis of P_2^* the employer will have to accept an increase in his real product wage if he increases his price by only P_2 rather than by P_2^*. With the higher real product wage he will demand less labour. Unemployment should therefore rise in the next period. This will depend on the subsequent rate of increase in money wages in relation to anticipated inflation. Workers may be willing to accept an increase in money wages which is less than the anticipated increase in prices in period 3 as their real wages in period 2 were unexpectedly higher as $(W_2 - W_1) = (P_2^* - P_1) > (P_2 - P_1)$.

Alternatively in period 2 the employer might be unwilling to see an increase in his real product wage. He would then maintain P_2^* for his product even though this was above the general rate of increase in prices. This might be expected to lead to a fall in demand for his product so his $Y_2 <$ his Y_2^*. In this case there would be a deviation from the NRU. Employment and output would fall and not all of the effects of the change in the money stock would be on prices. There could also be an increase in labour supply as real wages are higher than expected, or than usual. This could lure real wages down, or lead to involuntary unemployment. It might be argued that this is but the opposite effect of the short-term increase in employment and output that follows the increase in aggregate nominal demand in the usual formulation of the expectations-augmented Phillips curve.

In this sort of explanation the experience of changes in the money stock leads employers to revise their anticipations of future price and output levels and this feeds through into wage determination. The increases in money wages are based on the expected price and output levels that can be accommodated by the anticipated rate of inflation. The anticipated rate of inflation on this approach is based upon previous experience and so is a form of adaptive expectations.

The New Classical School, as we have stated earlier, see a short-cut in this process. On the basis of the REH expectations can be altered merely by the monetary authorities making a credible announcement of their intention to change the money stock. Once again the REH and the New Classical School are taking us into the realms of linguistic analysis. Everything depends on what is meant by 'credible'. Presumably the New Classical School would say that it was a credible announcement if economic agents revised downward their expectations of future inflation and this expressed itself in lower rates of increase in money wages and prices. If they did not reduce not only their expectations of future inflation rates, but also their anticipated rates of increase in money wages and prices it might be concluded that they did not believe the authorities' announcement was credible. It is a marvellous betting system. If people do what the dogma asserts they will do, it is because the conditions of the theory have been met. If they do not reduce the rates of money wage and price increases, it is not because the theory is wrong, but because, by definition, a necessary condition has not been met—the announcement was not regarded as credible. The New Classical School tipster cannot lose. He not only makes the bets, he makes the rules.

Even though one might believe that the perpetuation of systematic errors involved in claiming any realism for such a model ought to lead the REH advocate rationally to conclude that the 'mere announcement' strategy flies in the face of all British experience, the intellectual isolation that is provided by the logically necessary conditions and reservations implicit in the strong REH, allow its advocates to continue to maintain the logical consistency of their position, albeit at the expense of reality. It is, perhaps unfortunately, a fact of life that those who base their policy recommendations on a tautology are immune from the otherwise devastating attacks from evidence. It makes no difference whether the policy advocates are of the Right or the Left; as long as the conceptual position from which the policy proposals are derived contains some necessary condition which can only be established *ex post* by the achievement of the objectives sought in the policy proposals, there is no reason to believe that the advocates will reject their tautological base in the face of contrary evidence.

There is an extra degree of protection in the model. The reduction is in anticipated rates of increase in money wages and prices. We do not actually know what they are. It is only if the economy is in a complete New Classical School equilibrium that we can infer the anticipated rates of change of money wages and prices. If there has been some regular rate of growth of money stock we should expect to see reductions in the actual rate of growth of money wages and prices. It is emphasized that we are assuming that monetary policy affects only the rate of growth of the money stock and therefore the rate of growth of money wages and prices. We would not expect to see the average *level* of money wages and prices actually fall unless there was an actual decrease in the money stock rather than a slowing down of its rate of increase.

The New Classical School see a two-stage learning process. Actually some of them do not seem to envisage a learning process; they appear to believe the world already operates according to their tenets of how rational economic agents are postulated to behave. The first stage is that economic agents recognize that monetary targets (the announcements of the monetary authorities) do influence or determine the money stock. Secondly, that changes in the money stock do affect the rate of change of prices and if the required changes in prices are not immediately forthcoming there will be some adverse effect on unemployment when the rate of growth of the money stock is less than anticipated. Gradualists accept the second of these but not necessarily the first.

If economic agents operated on a model which incorporated a full understanding of the Monetarist position and all sub-markets cleared the mere announcement or belief that the monetary authorities intended to reduce the rate of growth of money supply would be sufficient to lead them to behave in such a way that there were only monetary and no real effects. Because everyone included the price effects in their expectations there would be no confusion about any change in real demand. If, however, they did not incorporate all the Monetarist assumptions or did not understand how the economy operates, 'they would have to learn about the changed regime by making systematic errors, recognizing them as such, and eliminating them by some unspecified trial and error method' (Laidler 1982, 85). Full knowledge and acceptance of a Monetarist position will therefore lead to instantaneous and correct interpretation of an announced change in the money supply, assuming, of course, that economic agents believe that the announced change, and only the announced change, will be implemented, and implemented fully. In these circumstances inflation could be reduced not by a stroke of the pen but by the mere announcement of a credible intention to change the money supply.

Government evidence given to the Treasury and Civil Service Committee during its study of monetary policy did not support the New Classical School. The then Chancellor of the Exchequer, Sir Geoffrey

Howe, did not believe that unions or employers perhaps, were much influenced by monetary targets. He told the Committee, 'and it may be that most pay bargainers spend more time having regard to the prospects for their firm and their place of employment and the availability of cash than they do minutely studying monetary targets' (HC 161-II, 2822). This view was shared by the then Governor of the Bank of England, 'I am not suggesting that every pay bargainer has it in mind that those targets are there. I wish they had' (Q. 955).

Sir Geoffrey was quite clear that the mere announcement of monetary targets did not lead public sector pay bargainers to take the appropriate decision—and this is the area where he as Chancellor could be expected to be able to exert much more direct influence over the outcome, at least on the employer or management side of the bargaining table. 'Merely by saying that is my monetary target does not achieve the right degree of contraction in public sector pay bargaining. You have also to accompany that by taking decisions in relation to them' (Q. 829). Part of those decisions was the implementation of cash limits for the public sector. 'They are all part of a piece' (Q. 829).

Mr (now Sir Peter) P. E. Middleton, the Deputy Secretary, now Permanent Secretary to the Treasury told the Committee 'I think that monetary policy affects expectations and monetary targets affect expectations'. That is, apparently, both what the monetary authorities do, and what they say they are going to do, affect expectations. However this is rejected in his next sentence. 'What I do not think is the mere fact that you announce a monetary target causes everybody to spring into action and operate as though there has been an immediate change.' He went on to say that the important thing was *meeting* the set targets 'which is a thing with which the credibility of the policies grows. So, I think the more the Government stick to their policies, the more they can convince people they are going to stick to them, the more you would expect them to affect expectations, but I do not think the mere fact that Government announces things affects anything at all very much' (Q. 236).

He believed that changes in the money supply affected inflation through expectations but that the changes took different lengths of time in different sorts of markets. 'I think they (expectations) adjust quite quickly in the financial markets, and not surprisingly take much longer in other markets, particularly the labour market . . .' (Q. 238). Sir Geoffrey Howe made a similar comment. 'Of course, as a matter of analysis, the response of financial markets to monetary policies . . . is likely to be quicker than the response of the labour market . . .' (Q. 652).

Mr Richardson the then Governor of the Bank of England shared the scepticism. 'I certainly have not abandoned any hopes that monetary policy will also make itself felt through expectations which will affect wages: I accept that that is coming more slowly. It does seem to me that in certain areas of the economy it is coming' (Q. 434).

It would be the height of irrationality for any economic agent to give much credence to the announcements of the British monetary authorities. There is no evidence to lend credence to the view that they do actually control the money supply to the announced changes. There is considerable evidence that they do not, and perhaps even cannot. This is true even when the monetary growth target is a range rather than a single figure for a single definition of money. If it is a range, any precise and determinate guidance to economic agents disappears although the range of uncertainty facing them may be reduced.

The announcement of monetary targets is not enough. The REH advocates would agree; they refer to credible announcements. However as we have seen this is a tautology. Expectations might be affected by experienced changes in the money supply if economic agents ascribe their experiences to the changes in money supply rather than to something else. However even committed government supporters of Monetarist policies do not believe that the learning process from experience of reductions in the money supply will necessarily be quick. Sir Geoffrey Howe acknowledged this to the Commons Committee. 'Of course, all the evidence you have received acknowledges that the conquest of inflation involves a short-run loss of output and a short-run loss of employment. No one can be sure how short or long the short run is. Certainly the conquest of inflation involves both those things and we said so in the medium-term financial strategy' (Q. 652).

These comments about the longer time it takes for the labour market to adjust and Sir Geoffrey Howe's recognition that there will be a reduction in output and an increase in unemployment as a result of a reduction in the rate of growth of the money stock mean that the economy does not currently operate in the way that it should. The second stage of the learning process is not completed. It is necessary therefore to change the way in which people behave.

Changes in Behaviour, Expectations, and Monetary policy

Recognition that it is necessary to change the way in which people behave if monetary policies are to have their desired or claimed effects, is a major shift in the attractiveness of Monetarism as a basis for policy. It no longer offers any presumed relatively smooth transition from high to low inflation. It no longer even necessarily offers much certainty that inflation will be reduced. If people's behaviour has to be changed we must ask two questions. Why is it expected that their behaviour will change? What happens if it does not?

The need to change behaviour was emphasized by Treasury and government spokesmen to the Treasury and Civil Service Committee. 'When you set out with a set of policies which are basically designed to try and change the way people behave—to try and get them to behave according to a different set of macro-economic considerations (which is basically what you are doing with a monetary target)—I think you must expect the effects to build up over time (Mr Middleton, Q. 237). Not only is this a rejection of the New Classical School and an endorsement of the Gradualists, it is also a clear statement that those responsible for determining wages did not respond to monetary targets. The assertion that people *do* respond to monetary targets is plainly not an accurate statement of behaviour. Part of the government's policies consisted of trying to persuade people to do just this. If they were already doing it there would be no need to change their behaviour.

The question he had been asked referred to 'actually achieved reduction, in the growth of broad money supply' not to monetary targets. When reminded of this in the next question he said that the speed with which changes in the money supply affect changes in the inflation rate does depend on how quickly expectations adjust. He could be arguing that monetary targets do not have the desired effect because pay bargainers do not believe government will actually achieve them. The more likely explanation is that pay bargainers do not respond to changes in the money supply in the way Monetarist policies wish. This is why their behaviour has to be changed. As he said in reply to a later question, 'What I was seeking to say there was that I do not think you can expect any model to incorporate the structural changes in behaviour which the Government are trying to bring about' (Q. 286).

The structural changes are the changes in behaviour. Monetary policy therefore is not merely working on existing arrangements, responses, and behaviour, obtaining the desired price and output effects simply by changing the level of stimuli injected into the economy. Government is seeking to, and in Britain, at least so far as the practical advocates and implementors of Monetarism are concerned, must, obtain changes in the way in which people respond to any level of stimuli as represented by changes in the money stock.

This was stated quite dramatically even if inaccurately by Sir Geoffrey Howe. 'Nobody has ever suggested that the setting of a target *or the achievement of one* would govern the out-turn of pay bargaining' (Q. 825, emphasis added). On the contrary, a great deal, if not the whole, of the Monetarist case rests on the assertion which he denied. The achievement of a monetary target which led to a reduction in the money supply *must* govern the out-turn of pay bargaining if control of the money supply is to have the effect of reducing inflation. It may not do so in the short run—as we have seen output and unemployment might be affected—but if it does not do so in the long run Monetarism has no contribution whatsoever to make to reducing the rate of inflation. Its very *raison d'être* has gone.

If Sir Geoffrey is right it means that there is a curious and stark asymmetry contained in Monetarism. Increases in the rate of growth of the money stock inevitably generate inflation because achieving a *higher* monetary target does govern the out-turn of pay bargaining and so prices, but achieving a *lower* money target does not govern the out-turn of pay bargaining. Some Keynesians who hold strong institutionalist views of labour market behaviour might accept the second part of this statement as holding over certain lengths of time in some circumstances. I would have no problems with it. But I would expect some degree of contraction in aggregate nominal demand at some point to have some effect on the out-turn of pay bargaining. The achievement of a monetary target might not *govern* the out-turn but it could influence it. Surely if Sir Geoffrey's statement is accepted it must mean that the effects on pay bargaining of an increase in the supply of money are also uncertain. If this is so the whole of the expectations-augmented Phillips curve analysis should be abandoned.

Monetarists would not accept Sir Geoffrey's disclaimer. They might qualify it by substituting 'influence' for 'govern' but this would weaken the certainty with which they assert that the long-run Phillips curve is vertical. Or they might insert 'in the short run' thereby allowing the same transitional effect on output and employment following a downward change in the money supply as they include the short-run effects of an unexpected increase. The problem with this attempt to rescue Sir Geoffrey is that in his statement the change in the money supply is not necessarily unexpected. According to him the reduction of money resulted from the setting and achievement of a monetary target. The change in money supply should have been expected and therefore if the Monetarist model works ought to have determined the outcome of pay bargaining. The other possible explanation is that pay bargainers did not believe that the target would be achieved. Based on their experience this would have been a justified belief.

The changes in behaviour are assumed to occur as a result of increasing unemployment and loss of output. The growth in aggregate nominal demand is assumed to be lower than previously and this necessitates revisions of output and pricing plans by employers. The first effects are likely to be on output as expectations of the increase in money wages are, in the UK, much more influenced by past rates of inflation than expected rates. It is this structural or behavioural relationship that a Monetarist government must seek to change. If in addition money wages have been rising for other reasons, say productivity, profitability, or comparability, the Monetarists must also try and squeeze these out of the system by inducing a change in behaviour. Exhortation, cash limits, speeches attempting to persuade bargainers or their members that 'excessive' wage increases will lead to unemployment, for them or for others, and anything else which might affect the level of pay increases such as trade union power are, in Sir Geoffrey's words, 'part of a piece'.

This was foreseen by Sir Keith Joseph the political pioneer of the rebirth of Monetarism in Britain. His 1976 Stockton Lecture was titled 'Monetarism is not enough', and in his February 1979 talk to the Bow Group he said 'Most people now see monetary discipline as a necessary but not sufficient condition for economic growth and efficiency' (2). His 1976 theme was that monetary policy cannot be expected to work in the public sector as it does in the private. 'If the whole economy were private, then all firms would be subject to the resulting constriction—and only the unsound would need to go. But the whole economy is not private. Nearly two-thirds is statist, and insensitive in itself to contraction of the money supply' (2). One of the implications of his Stockton Lecture was that the government should cease diverting resources to the public sector. 'Monetary contraction in a mixed economy strangles the private sector unless the state sector contracts with it and reduces its take from the national income' (7). 'We shall need to explain that subsidized employment is not really saving jobs because the subsidies have to be paid for and the paying for them loses more jobs than are saved' (7).

In his 1976 talk, entitled 'Solving the Union Problem is the Key to Britain's Recovery', he asks 'Why won't the unions bargain responsibly?' (3). His answer points to the legal as well as the monetary framework within which they operate.

The national good can be secured only by changing the framework, the rules of the game and then ensuring that everyone plays fairly by them. . . . No, the unions cannot bargain responsibly so long as government provides a framework—monetary, fiscal, and legislative—which discourages effort and encourages irresponsibility, and so long as unions have the power to respond to inflation in a way which makes it more difficult to end it (3).

The agenda for change is therefore considerable. Not only must monetary policy change, so too must fiscal policy, the legal provisions, and union power. It is not only the rules of the game which have to be changed but the way in which people play. They have to change and play 'fairly' by the new rules. Instead of the inevitable responses induced by changes in money supply and the expectations of future price and real output levels, a change in attitudes whereby responsibility and fairness influence behaviour is seen as necessary. Sir Keith recognizes the force of coercive comparisons. If all other unions are going for high wage increases no single union can do otherwise. 'We cannot expect a union leader to choose unilateral disarmament on behalf of his members' (4). He suggested various legislative changes to correct the 'imbalance' in union power. The implication of his remarks was that trade unions in Britain had the ability to drive up money wages in excess of the increases in money supply. A Conservative Government would reduce that ability. He had less to say about how unions might be induced to change the way in which they respond to given situations in which the rules and framework have been changed.

This is the missing link in the political economy of Monetarist policy-making. The automatic or quasi-automatic feed-through from money stock to wage and price changes to expectations to actual changes, is recognized as unrealistic, save perhaps in a situation where massive unemployment prevents unions from influencing money wages and employers respond to price changes, actual or anticipated, solely on the basis of their product real wage and workers' real reservation wages. In other circumstances the multiplicity of objectives involved in collective bargaining and particularly the force of coercive comparisons lead inevitably to the conclusion that we do not know how, in the real world, pay bargainers will react to a reduction in the rate of growth of the money stock. It is necessary therefore for Monetarism to be supported by other measures to change the expectations and behaviour of bargainers. These need to change the rules and the spirit in which the game is played. Not only is Monetarism not enough; fear may not be enough. The fear of unemployment resulting from increases in money wages in excess of increases in the money stock cannot be relied on to create the 'responsibility' that Monetarist policies need. At some sufficiently high enough level of unemployment, impotence, within a framework which has substantially shifted the balance of power between unions and employers, may, on Sir Keith's argument, be enough, but whether that union impotence can be achieved is uncertain.

The debate between the Gradualists and the New Classical School is much concerned with this question of how best to influence expectations, attitudes, and behaviour. However, it must be emphasized that if this debate is only about how to influence expectations of future rates of inflation it is unlikely to deal satisfactorily with inflation. Important items will be excluded from the agenda. We will consider these in the next chapter when we discuss trade unions and expectations.

Conclusions

Expectations of future price increase lie at the heart of the Monetarist explanation of inflation and unemployment. Inflation occurs because employers and workers wrongly estimate the future rate of inflation and so get their real product wage and real wage estimates wrong. If they did but properly understand the relationship between changes in the money stock and changes in prices they would not make these mistakes; inflation would be limited to the rate of change of the money stock adjusted as appropriate for productivity changes, and unemployment would be at the NRU.

The New Classical School, incorporating the REH into their analysis, argue that economic agents ought in their own interests and to maximize their own profit or utility functions, to base their decisions on the credible announcements of the monetary authorities. This means that the monetary authorities should announce their monetary targets and achieve them. If this happens people will adjust their behaviour as soon as the next credible announcement of monetary targets has been made. There will be some uncertainties if the target is a range rather than a precise figure and if targets for more than one definition of money are used but, it can be argued, this will still be better than a situation where no one believes the announcements of the authorities and people do not expect the targets to be implemented. If the monetary authorities make their announcements and the smooth and painless transition to lower inflation without adverse real effects does not take place, the strong REH advocates may continue to cling to their belief that economic agents do in fact have a proper understanding of the way in which the economy operates, but suggest that the authorities' announcement was not believed. The intellectual cocoon surrounding the REH can remain intact by concluding that one of the logically necessary conditions has not been met, and the beauty of this is that whether the necessary conditions have been met is determined *ex post*. Thus if inflation does not respond to the mere announcement it is not because the concept is wrong or silly, but because the necessary conditions do not, by definition, exist.

There is little if any basis on which rational observers of British experience would come to the conclusion that the announcements of the monetary authorities should be believed. They have not earned credibility and even if they did it does not follow that inflation and unemployment respond to changes in achieved monetary targets in the way postulated by Monetarists.

The Thatcher Government does not believe that the mere announcement of monetary targets is sufficient to bring down inflation. They do not believe that actually achieved reductions in the rate of growth of the money stock will bring down the rate of inflation without there first being some adverse effects on output and employment. They believe that just as there is a short-run trade-off between inflation and unemployment when the money stock increases unexpectedly, so is there a trade-off when it decreases. It appears that they believe this to be true even when the slow-down in the rate of growth of money is expected as well as achieved.

Sir Geoffrey Howe has told us that setting monetary targets is not enough. Sir Keith Joseph has told us that Monetarism is not enough. The one may not lead to the desired change in expectations of future price levels. The other may not lead to the desired change in behaviour not least because there are other expectations and attitudes which influence pay bargaining. Changes in the behaviour of pay bargainers must also be obtained. This should lead us to recognize that this is because expectations of future inflation are not the only set of expectations that influence pay determination. Once this is accepted the inadequacies of the expectations-augmented Phillips Curve are apparent. More than control of the money stock is needed; or using only control of the money stock will impose very high costs in terms of unemployment and lost output before inflation is brought down to the desired levels.

Debates about whether price expectations are adaptive or formed on an REH model, while perhaps having some contribution to make, are in themselves insufficient to explain the processes and results of pay bargaining. It is interesting to note that the first revivalist wave of Monetarist explanations using the expectations-augmented Phillips curve included adaptive expectations. The switch to a REH is a more recent attempt to salvage the basic position. Either version suffers from a major omission. Other expectations, and in particular the expectations and aspirations of trade unions and their members, need to be taken into account.

When considering the REH we should ask three questions. First, is this a sensible view of how expectations are actually formed? That this is not so is apparent. Second, if it is the way expectations are formed, is this enough to generate the conclusions that advocates of the REH draw? The answer to this is also 'No', because the REH also needs market-clearing in order to reach the conclusions of its advocates. At the same time demand-management policies may also work if they change people's behaviour. Supply-side policies which alter incentives through a lowering of marginal tax rates are intended to affect people's behaviour. Third, can we generate the same effects without a REH? This is possible as some models using Keynesian approaches incorporate a fixed amount of real labour supply so that there is equilibrium in real terms irrespective of the level of prices. A vertical aggregate supply curve in real terms means that shifts in aggregate demand in money terms merely lead to different prices.

Notes to Chapter 12

1. This is the same form as used by Laidler (1982, 13).
2. See Laidler 1982, ch. 1.
3. No evidence is presented to establish that you can't fool all the people all the time, but it may not be logically possible. If only one person demonstrated that everyone else had been fooled all of the time the statement would be valid. If no one person did this we still wouldn't know whether everyone had been fooled or not.
4. Important developments of the REH can be found in Sargent and Wallace (1975) and (1976); Lucas (1972); Phelps (1967); and Barro (1976). Various papers on the subject are brought together in Fischer (ed.) (1980).
5. See Lucas (1975).

CHAPTER THIRTEEN

Expectations and Trade Unions

THE Monetarist explanations of inflation and unemployment, as we have seen, assume that economic agents, employers, and workers alike, respond to a single variable—the expected rate of inflation. However, once some economic agents have more than the single objective of maintaining the real wage level, the expected rate of inflation is not the only factor which should be considered when seeking to understand, explain, and forecast their behaviour.

As we discussed in Chapter 9 trade unions do not act merely as aggregations of the individual preferences and objectives of all their individual members. They have to translate individual preferences into a set of collective priorities, and a trade union can have additional objectives of its own. Because a trade union has a number of objectives it is influenced by more than a single variable.

Trade unions do not, generally speaking, make explicit reference to the expected rate of inflation, and so the maintenance of the real wage current at the time of the pay settlement, in their pay bargaining. It is much more likely that trade unions pay more attention to the correction of past developments—compensation for past prices or the restoration of some established relationship with some other group—or to the establishment of some new relationship to 'correct' some perceived injustice or attain some additional objective.

Expectations and Aspirations

The REH approach rests on the view that because the economy is assumed to be in some sort of equilibrium in real terms all that is necessary to maintain that equilibrium position is the maintenance of real values. Thus, if all prices and all money wages fall by 50 per cent it is assumed that real activity will be unaffected. Similarly, if it is expected that prices will rise by 50 per cent an increase in money wages and other money incomes of 50 per cent will maintain the equilibrium. This general approach is totally unsuited to a model which includes trade unions, and is totally inapplicable to a world where trade unions exist and bargain about wages. This is because trade unions have aspirations as well as expectations.

Expectations in the REH approach apply to prices, and through prices future demand for products and thus of labour. Aspirations refer to features which reject the assumed stability of the existing situation and therefore reject the notion that the existing situation is a stable equilibrium. Trade unions always seek to improve the terms and conditions of their members. Generally this means that they seek to obtain higher wages, lower hours, reduced effort-input, or obtain some additional fringe benefits or other net advantages. In some cases improvement may mean betterment over the conditions which would otherwise exist rather than an actual betterment over existing conditions. Thus in a declining industry subject to structural change a trade union may have aspirations to prevent a worsening of conditions as its first priority but will probably also seek to obtain some improvements as well.

Almost by definition trade unions can be said to reject the assumption that the existing situation—no matter what that situation may be—is an equilibrium one in the sense that the preservation of the existing real wages and effort-input or job requirements is regarded as the totality of its objectives. Even if unions were influenced by the sort of factors assumed in the REH approach and based their wage settlements on expected changes in prices, it would be but one part of their activities. The expectations element would still be supplemented by their aspirations which would lead them to press for further improvements.

It is possible to assimilate this into the REH approach by broadening the range of factors included in expectations. Instead of the preponderant weight being given to expectations about future price levels, it would be necessary to include expectations about future real wage levels, and, importantly, future relative wage levels.

In all countries free trade unions are competitive. It may be that the structure of British trade unions with a multiplicity of unions in an industry or even at the same place of work may add to the intensity of inter-union competition, but even in countries with different union structures inter-union rivalry and competition exist. Members judge their leadership, and the leadership judges itself, by making comparison with the collective bargaining results obtained by other unions. In some cases the law may actually encourage this. Legislative provision for periodic ballots to decide whether a work-force wishes to be represented by a trade union, and if so, which particular union, may lead to greater competition which expresses itself in pressure for higher wage settlements and better working conditions. Advocates of competitive markets or opponents of the closed shop do not always seem to understand that trade union competition may generate greater pressure on wage levels. Or, they actually want atomistic individual competition where there are no, or only very weak, trade unions.

While we do not believe it is relevant to a situation in which the majority of workers have their pay determined by collective bargaining or minimum wage provisions, it might be useful to consider the implications of a REH model.

Fluctuations in the supply of money, whose effects on prices are not anticipated, can have real effects on the economy. Even the strongest of the New Classical School apply their tautologies only to anticipated and fully understood changes in the money supply. Unexpected changes will affect output and employment decisions even in a model which assumes perfect market clearing.

Trade unions might be expected to be surprised less often or less easily than individual workers. They have research departments which monitor economic developments. True, these research departments may be using different definitions of money and different statistical series, but the REH 'explains' that if they continue to use the wrong ones they will realize the cost of their mistakes and ultimately correct them. In practice it might not work like this. Unions could conclude that a fall in employment was the result of other factors. Cognitive dissonance could influence them. Much more importantly, if the unemployment is experienced by other groups there is no mistake by unions who push up their own wages and there are no costs which the existing members are required to bear.

If trade unions get their expectations of future inflation right it does not follow that their actions will be, or in the best interests of their own members *ought* to be, based solely on future inflation. If any unemployment effects are felt by others, it needs to be established why an individual union should modify its actions. In exactly the same way an employer may increase the price of his products in the full knowledge that if aggregate nominal demand is fixed the contraction in real demand may be felt by other producers. There is nothing in Monetarist morality which criticizes him for this. It is the free working of market forces.

Trade Unions and a Walrasian Auctioneer

There is another set of expectations which is relevant to trade unions. If economic agents are to accept the full implications of a Monetarist model, and particularly a New Classical School model with its reliance on market clearing and totally flexible money prices and wages, they must have views about how every other economic agent is going to respond.

If the money supply were to be reduced the 'proper' New Classical School result is that prices and wages would fall proportionately with no reductions in real wages. If some agents believe that other agents will not react in this way then their 'rational' response depends, not upon what the model and REH tells them *should* happen *if* everyone responded in a particular way, but rather on what they estimate will be the result of some agents not conforming to the assumptions. The more realistic trade union reaction to a reduction in the money supply or its rate of growth is to anticipate that the responses of economic agents will vary from sector to sector, sub-labour market to sub-labour market, and firm to firm.

Even though there may be strong institutional forces, custom, and practice which establish wage contours and orbits of coercieve comparison among wage levels, or rates of change of wages, particularly in the trade union organized collective bargaining, Wages Councils, and arbitration areas of the economy, these are not so rigid as to impose absolute uniformity. They prescribe the areas of decision-taking rather than impose completely predictable outcomes. The relative bargaining strength and militancy of trade unions vary from sector to sector. Employers' perceptions of the future demand for their product and their expected product real wages vary. These factors could well lead to different responses even when the change in money supply is anticipated; they are almost certainly likely to do so when that change is unanticipated. Yet in these circumstances the New Classical School still persists in believing that the labour markets will clear. In the face of uncertainies and lack of knowledge about how the relative structure of wages and prices is changing, somehow or other each wage settlement is consistent with an aggregate set of wage and price decisions which equates supply and demand in all markets. Yet the theory provides no guidance as to how wage and price decision-takers faced with this uncertainty and lack of information about how the others are behaving, and will behave in the future when their next wage settlement falls due, manage to incorporate these various and different responses into their own decision-taking, and do so in such a way that leads to market clearing.

This leads to two specific criticisms of the New Classical School. The first is that economic agents do not actually behave in this way. They do not seek to take into account *all* the decisions of *all* the other economic agents and feed these back into a general equilibrium model in order to decide what they should do. Study of the arguments advanced in bargaining does not necessarily enlighten us about the real underlying motives of the parties or their real objectives. Anyone who has ever arbitrated a wage claim is only too aware of this. It may be that sometimes we can reasonably infer some conclusions about what the parties want and what they are doing, but this is not easy and cannot always be done. It is the hallmark of the great arbitrators that they do it better than most. The second is that even if they sought to do this they do not have the ability quickly to perceive the range of options open to them. Real-world markets do not provide sufficient information and incentives always to harmonize the actions of economic agents.

While employers may take a broader macro-economic view, neither unions nor managements try to operate a Walrasian-auctioneer-type market-clearing wage adjustment process; they look at some sub-markets more closely than others. No collective bargaining takes place on the assumption that the real wage level existing immediately prior to a periodic money wage settlement is market-clearing in the sense that sellers are willing as a normal part of their behaviour to continue to accept that real wage in the future so that they require only sufficient increases in money wages to compensate for expected inflation. Moreover employers, the demanders of labour, do not believe, and do not act as though they believed, that it is sufficient for periodic money wage settlements only to provide cover for expected inflation. Even the government, which if it is of a Monetarist persuasion, might be expected to base its wage policy for public employees on the doctrines to which it subscribes and to which it seeks to convert others, recognizes that the expected rate of inflation alone does not provide sufficient increase in money wages to maintain equilibrium at the NRU. When the government offers different wage guide-lines to different parts of the public sector, be these through cash limits or direct intervention, it is not saying that there will be different rates of inflation for the various groups of workers. It is offering and seeking to obtain different rates of change of real wages, in some cases perhaps because it believes that the wage levels in the past were in excess of market-clearing. In other cases it is because the government recognizes that it is not feasible to try to reduce the real wages below some level which is related to past real wages or some view of entitled real wages.

The existence of trade unions prevents a Great Auctioneer type of model from operating. Unions do not allow their members to make individual bids which undercut the collective wage offer. Their members generally do not wish to. The institutional developments and practices which emerge from collective bargaining, as well as the preferences of large employers, also inhibit the making of individual wage bids by non-union employees. Union members always wish to prevent this undercutting. It is an integral part of trade union objectives and behaviour to prevent the auctioneer-type system from working. They will not accept the downward adjustment in money wages which is a necessary feature of a Walrasian system, nor will they accept the displacement of existing unionized employees by lower wage-bidding individuals. A union may in exceptional circumstances agree to a reduction in money wages but this has to be a collective reduction emerging from the process of collective bargaining under pressure. It cannot tolerate a reduction in money wages resulting from the inflow of cheaper (lower wage bidding) labour replacement.

Trade unions must be seen as having expectations about a wide range of factors. These go beyond such 'neutral' variables such as the rate of price change and include the 'right' or 'proper' distribution of income between pay and profits, relative pay levels and movements, and changing rather than merely maintaining present terms and conditions of employment. These are normative issues involving value-judgements. Some of them can be regarded as aspirations in that they are things the union may not yet have achieved rather than expectations, which in the narrower technical sense of the REH seems to refer to the maintenance of equilibrium positions and relationships.

We can illustrate this fairly simply. Statistics seem to suggest that there has been a trend increase in real wages. A Monetarist explanation which emphasizes the importance of expectations only in the 'expectations of future inflation' sense, will find this very difficult to explain. Once trade union aspirations are introduced it is much easier to account for actual developments. Trade unions seek to improve, and not merely maintain, the real wages of their members. They therefore take into the bargaining-room a variety of expectations and aspirations. We do not know just how these influence actual pay outcomes but that is no reason to ignore them.

The very existence of collective bargaining with periodic adjustment of money wages injects uncertainties and rigidities into the process of wage determination. In Britain we do not have the added complications of multi-year contracts, but even a system where by and large money time-rates of wages are adjusted annually with settlements in different industries falling due at different times, is enough to cause some delays or distortions to a theoretical model. Instead of day-to-day adjustments in money wages to reflect different supply and demand positions we might suppose that there would be once-a-year adjustments. If different sectors are settling at different times it is extremely difficult to see how each sub-market settlement can fully take into account the decisions of all other sectors over the life of their contract. However, the key analytical difficulty for the New Classical School here lies not so much in the annual bargaining, or longer for the United States, but from the fact that settlements do not take place at the same moment of time. If the Walrasian auctioneer were to hold daily auctions but held them for different sub-labour markets at different times of the day, not even the most dedicated New Classical analyst could pretend that a general equilibrium would result.

The length of the wage agreement or contract may influence the length of time during which some sub-markets are out of equilibrium and thus the speed with which the economy reverts to its NRU level, but they do not themselves prevent the attainment of the general equilibrium at the time of settlement. The fact that different sectors settle at different times does that.

This might appear to lend weight to arguments in favour of the synchronization of wage settlements.[1] However, synchronization in the real world with trade unions runs into a major problem once it is recognized that trade union wage settlements are not independent of each other.

Because trade unions are competitive organizations and because the notion of fairness which exerts such an important influence on British pay determination is essentially a comparative notion, there is an all-important element of interconnectedness in wage settlements. We may be unsure about the exact extent of this—the connections will vary from bargaining unit to bargaining unit and may change through time, but we do know that wage settlements are not regarded as separate from other settlements. This means more than the interconnectedness arising from labour market factors related to occupational mobility or the cross elasticity of labour supply. It refers to connections established by institutional pressures or tradition which may have but little labour market justification in a strict economic sense.[2] Different groups will base their view of what is an acceptable wage settlement, in part if not in full, on the basis of what certain other groups have obtained.

Relative pay levels and changes in pay levels affect people's view of the fairness of their own pay and they affect trade unions' acceptance of the resulting pay relativities. This is not some mere bargaining tactic by trade unions. As the Pay Board stated: 'The main consequence of the pervasive notion of fairness is that no pay increase stands alone' (Cmnd. 5535, para. 13). The notion of fairness is pervasive, even though different groups may have different views as to what is fair. Their views, influenced by the past, create expectations of relative pay relationships which are projected into the future. They are independent of the rate of inflation or the expected rate of inflation. They may be capable of change and may change as a result of developments within the group concerned—say alterations in Job Requirements or recruiting levels—or as a result of pay developments of other groups. To ignore these views is to fail to understand a powerful factor in pay determination.

The same thing may arise with individuals in an assumed Walrasian auction as an individual may change his supply-price as he discovers the wages offered to other types of labour. With a trade union acting collectively for a group of workers there is greater opportunity to influence the wage settlement than exists for any individual worker. Trade union views of acceptable wage settlements may therefore exert greater influence on actual outcomes and unions' views of what is acceptable will be determined not only on the basis of their expectations of inflation but on their aspirations.

Trade unions may base their acceptable-wage level on what is happening to pay of non-unionized personnel in the firm or industry as well as on what is happening to other unionized sectors. If non-union pay levels are not determined in the synchronized negotiations unions cannot do this. If non-union pay is determined simultaneously with collective bargaining units, management has lost its discretion. This might be discretion to give higher pay in order to prevent unionization or discretion to react to market forces as they are perceived. Either way it may be a price management is unwilling to pay. If they do agree to total synchronization it should lead to the unionization of management anyway. If their pay is determined in a single all-embracing discussion, they have obvious benefits from being represented. The strongest argument for synchronization, or the widening of bargaining units, is that only those groups covered by a bargaining unit can, with any certainty, have their relative pay levels determined by that bargaining unit. It may not be possible to produce enduring or mutually acceptable pay relationships between two separate bargaining units (Robinson 1973). If the pay of people outside a bargaining unit, even a massive synchronization of all those covered by collective bargaining, is regarded as pertinent to the decisions about the acceptable level of pay and relative pay of those within the bargaining unit, no lasting decisions may be possible, and indeed it may not even be possible to produce a short-run agreement. This is obviously relevant to policy action to change bargaining structure. It is however also clearly relevant to the REH. Without knowledge of what is going to happen to the non-union employees, the parties to collective bargaining, but particularly the trade unions, cannot form the sort of views which the REH requires them to form if a general equilibrium position is to emerge.

While unions wish to obtain relative improvements in the pay and conditions of their members, in both time and in relation to some other groups, they are first concerned to maintain terms and conditions wherever possible. Defensive claims by unions provide the base on which they seek to build improvements. However, as we have sought to demonstrate, the real wage defensive action is not as rigorously 'rational' as Monetarists and New Classical economists would have us believe. Given the institutional arrangements for periodic wage adjustment it cannot be. Only completely price-indexed pay settlements could do that, and neither side in Britain has sought to establish these. When they enter pay bargaining, therefore, trade unions, and their members, have a set of expectations that some pay relationships will be maintained, and this includes the restoration of money wages to compensate for price changes since the last settlement. In this regard, trade unionism unions are backward-looking.

At the same time they are sideways-looking. They are concerned about what other unions are currently doing. The expectations of one particular trade union about the level of pay settlement which is both reasonable and attainable is influenced by what some other group has obtained. In 1984 it was widely believed that the government delayed making and announcing its decision on the Review Body Report on Nurses because it hoped that the teachers would first settle.[3] They were mistaken but this does not alter the view that they believed one public sector settlement would influence the outcome of others. The Association of University Teachers, which is occasionally stirred to gird its flab, frequently waits until other groups have settled, in the hope that it will be able to ride on their coat-tails and get a higher settlement than they would have done if they had settled at their due date before someone else had set some sort of pace.

Sometimes then unions look forward to other settlements which they think will be helpful to them by setting a higher level. Sometimes they look forward and anticipate government action. If a wage freeze, or some other form of wage restraint or income policy is expected, unions may settle early or quickly in order to avoid the expected restraints. It is a sort of disintermediation which is well established in banking and financial circles when similar restraints are imposed or anticipated.

It is possible that if inflation increased very substantially, going well above the rates which have been experienced, pay bargainers might change their attitudes and give more attention to the expected rate of inflation.

Estimates of future real demand for the employer's product may influence trade union bargainers. They may take the consequences of increases in money wages and so product prices into account. If the fear of job loss through higher wages and product prices influences unions, or employers, the perceived relevant prices and price changes are much more likely to be those for a narrower range of competitive products than the general level of prices. It is quite possible that the expected rate of change of some prices—and these might be those of foreign competitors—influence pay bargaining, but this is not the same as the general level of inflation. The future general price level is seen, in Monetarist theory, as influencing the supply side of the labour market through the expected real wage level, and as we have argued, this may be of much less importance and relevance than Monetarists suppose.

Employers may give more attention to the expected general price level when making their assessment of the scope for increases in their own product prices. Employers may therefore be more forward-looking than trade unions (Mayhew 1979). However, this does not mean that their expectations will necessarily feed through and influence trade unions or the pay settlement. If trade unions decide that a reduction in employment is preferable to a lower increase in money wages, or are prepared to gamble that the employer's assessment of the output and employment effects of an increase in money wages will turn out to be wrong, it is quite possible that pay increases will be in excess of the anticipated general rate of inflation. This outcome might be acceptable to employers. It could be preferable to them in comparison with the cost of a strike. It might not be their first preference position, but it could be their chosen position given their assessment of the range of realistic options available to them.

It might be argued that comparability leads to the same behaviour as would consideration of the expected rate of inflation. If each union bases its wage claims and settlements on what others have achieved, or are expected to achieve, this might lead to the same sort of results as the inflationary expectations motivation would if future price changes bear some steady relationship to changes in money wages. Unions might, therefore, be regarded as behaving 'as if' they followed the expectations-augmented Phillips curve approach. However, this does not imply that the initiating movement in a comparability-based set of wage increases is determined by expectations of future inflation derived from expectations about future money supply. The initiating wage settlement could have been determined by a trade union obtaining improvements as a result of pursuing some of its aspirations. Moreover, comparability is stronger amongst groups of bargaining units so that there are series of overlapping orbits of coercive comparisons rather than a single monolithic comparability relationship.

Until we can establish the causes of the initiating movements which generate the comparability-based settlements it would be misguided to assume that these are based on expectations of future price changes, either in general or in the initiating industries or firms.

Multiplicity of Expectations and Aspirations

If the only expectations which mattered were those of future inflation, it would be necessary that trade unions operated with the same economic model as the Government. Suppose that inflation has been running at, say, 10 per cent a year. If the Government wishes to end inflation it would annouce a money supply growth rate equal to the expected rate of productivity on the assumption that productivity did not lead to lower prices. Trade unions would have to accept that if the increase in money supply were 2 per cent, there would be a reduction of some 8 per cent in their real wages since the time of the last settlement. True, the real wages immediately before the current settlement would be maintained, but this reduction in real wages would not be acceptable, as a long-term situation. If it had to be tolerated for a short run it would merely lead to very strong pressures to restore the losses in the succeeding settlements. Of course these attempts might be only partly successful, but if it is accepted that there would be such attempts which would be at least partially successful, the quick-fix solution fails. A once-for-all adjustment of the rate of growth of money supply does not squeeze all the inflation out of the system.

Even if the considerable reduction in previous real wages was obtained there would be a series of future repercussions in which unions and workers would seek to get their 'fair' or 'entitled' wage increases. The greater the rate of inflation the larger would be the loss of real wages since the time of the last settlement. It is only if one believes that the market clears at each moment in time that one can so ignore the past.

Workers and their unions must be seen as having no memory—only expectations. And these expectations are of nothing more than maintaining the real wage levels at the time of each wage settlement, with perhaps something extra for productivity growth. *In addition to having no memory, trade unions must have no aspirations.* Even if individual workers can be assumed to behave in this way, and it would be an heroic assumption, trade unions cannot be assumed to have no memory of past real wage levels. To require this would be suicidally heroic.

As Sir Keith Joseph has said, there are rules of the game and these may be observed by employers as well as trade unions. Established practices and conventions influence not only the range of factors which are regarded as appropriate to pay determination, they also influence the expectations and aspirations of the two sides to collective bargaining.

This was well illustrated by the Governor of the Bank of England, Gordon Richardson, when commenting to the Treasury and Civil Service Committee on the pay negotiations then underway, but deadlocked, with the staff of the Bank of England. In justifying an offer of 17 per cent, he referred to the cash limit of 14 per cent, the union's view of 'what has happened in comparable situations and in that respect the analogues do play a part', the need to restore the decompression of internal pay differentials that had resulted from previous incomes policies, and the fact that the settlement was part of the previous pay round. When asked about the force of comparability in pay determination he said 'Yes, that is certainly a strong force to overcome' (Q. 453). The monetary targets of 7–11 per cent which were to run until the following April, were seen at that time (July 1980) as relevant to the next pay settlement.

There is in fact nothing in his evidence or in the comments by the Chancellor or Treasury spokesmen to indicate that the expected rate of inflation played any part in the determination of the pay of their employees. This could be for the reason Sir Keith Joseph gave in his 1976 speech that the public sector is not subject to the same disciplinary pressures flowing from monetary policy as in the private sector. But there was no evidence presented by them to establish that expectation of future price changes determined the pay of any other group of employees. They argued that it ought to do so, and unemployment would descend on those who ignored this rule, but that is not the same as saying that this is how people have behaved, do behave, or will behave.

If unions are unable to obtain a wage increase high enough to meet either past or anticipated inflation, this does not mean that they or their members will necessarily regard this as a mistake in their expectations. They may regard it as something to be made good later. They may have obtained some concession elsewhere in bargaining, and they may have obtained more than the employer first offered. They may still believe that the union has achieved more than the individuals would have got on their own. The union-determined and union-enforced collective reservation wage may still exceed the individual reservation wages, and so even a reduction in the real wage can leave all individual employees with real wages which exceed their own individual reservation wage.

If trade unions did base their forecasts of inflation on changes in monetary targets or the money stock, they may not react in the way Monetarists suppose. They could accept lower real wages. If the money stock is reduced they could go for higher real wages and accept some reduction in employment. This is equivalent to a rise in the NRU resulting from a shift in real wage labour supply curves.

Even if we suppose that unions and other economic agents have an economic model on which they base their actions this is not, in the UK, a model in which the quanity of money plays much part. Trade unions believe that the level of employment is capable of influence by government action. In this they are traditional Keynesians. Government may refuse to take the appropriate action, but that is another matter. So far as the unions are concerned, the economy can be, and should be, on a labour—rather than a gold or money supply—standard. This contrasts with the attitude of German trade unions. For the whole post-war period they have accepted a form of the Quantity Theory so that the pronouncements of the Bundesbank regarding the future rate of change of the money supply exert considerable influence on pay bargaining and settlements.

An essential precondition for the success of a stabilization policy guided by monetary growth targets (apart from the determination on the part of the monetary authorities) is a basic public consensus ensuring a wide measure of support for the central bank's aims and actions. For this reason the Bundesbank has always emphasized that, besides government budget policy, the voluntary co-operation of management and labour is indispensable if inflation is to be brought under effective durable control without lasting underemployment.[4]

There is no such consensus in Britain. A reading of the minutes of the oral evidence of the Treasury and Civil Service Committee on Monetary Policy makes it clear that the Government yearned, and yearned deeply, for one. The Government references to structural changes and changes in behaviour accepting the spirit of the changed rules and so on, are all pleas for the creation of a consensus. The desired consensus, of course, is a Monetarist consensus which espouses Keynesian demand-deficient unemployment and requires acceptance of real wages at, on the most favourable interpretation, their current level irrespective of the stage in the bargaining process or beliefs about fair relativities. Most government spokesmen would probably prefer a reduction in real wages below their present level in order to increase international competitiveness.

The independence of the central bank from direct overt government intervention in Germany means that the union response of urging Government to relax the monetary squeeze is not regarded as tenable. Rather than seeking to avoid or counteract the restrictive monetary policies therefore German unions have followed the practice of containing their wage settlements within a macro-economic framework which imposes a money-wage–employment trade-off. They have generally moderated their money wage settlements; although there have been occasions of dispute, these have usually been over relatively small extra increases.

Trade Unions and Real Wages

Although Keynes believed that a willingness to accept a reduction in real wages was necessary to reduce demand-deficient unemployment it does not follow that such a reduction need take place. If there are constant returns to scale employers may be willing to expand output and employment at existing real wages if this allows them to maintain their product real wage. A decrease in product real wage might not be necessary. If an increase in aggregate demand leads to an increase in demand for products employers may increase output and employment with existing real wages and existing product real wages. If unions and employers believe that an increase in aggregate demand can be made into an increase in real demand by expanding output and employment at prevailing wages and prices there need be no expectation of higher inflation. The product real wage can remain constant because there is excess supply of labour at the prevailing real (and money) wage level. If there are unused economies of scale available to the employer the product real wage may fall. Employers may not have sought to utilize their spare capacity by cutting prices to stimulate demand if they believed that other producers would also reduce their prices so that there would be relatively little increase in demand but a fall in revenue.

If unions will accept constant real wages then it is clear that both output and employment can expand following an increase in aggregate nominal demand. Monetarists would accept the conclusion but do not expect it because of their view that it is necessary to increase real wages in order to expand employment.

If we make two assumptions, the expected Monetarist development may not occur. First is that if the real wage supply curve is horizontal, more labour is forthcoming at prevailing real wage levels. Second, the employer is not faced by diminishing returns. Both of these may be realistic assumptions, if not always in all firms at least sometimes in a number of firms, and particularly if output and employment have been falling. If aggregate nominal demand then increases there are no labour market reasons why expected real wages have to rise in order to induce an addition to labour supply. Or on the demand side to fall in order to obtain a reduction in the product real wage.

If real wages do increase when aggregate nominal demand increases it will be either because of misunderstandings about the shape of the real wage labour supply facing the firm, or because of trade union pressure. The first should not arise. Firms have information about the real wage labour supply facing them. They have applications for jobs and the higher the current level of unemployment the greater the number of applications might be. In any case, the Monetarist argument that trade unions raise wages above their market-clearing levels concedes that unionized firms can increase employment without increasing wages. It is the second cause which is the more important. Trade unions will expect to raise real wages as employment in the firm of industry expands. This is the sort of development their long-term past experience leads them to expect. They may also be seeking to recoup any losses or slowing down in the rate of growth of real wages that occurred as unemployment rose. It is trade union expectations of increases in real wages, not of higher future inflation, that generate the inflationary pressure and prevent the expansion of employment.

Monetarists might respond that even if this is an acceptable account of what happens in the union sector it will be necessary to increase real wages in the non-union sector if firms there are to increase their workforce, or even perhaps maintain the same level of employment as some of their workers will move to the union sector when additional employment opportunities at existing real wages arise. This argument depends on the assertion that non-union labour markets always clear, and there is no evidence that this is so.

If unions press for, and obtain, higher real wages when demand increases it might be thought that even if labour markets do not clear, they act *as if* they did, because an increase in demand for labour in the union sector leads to an increase in both money and, for a time, real wages. This is true only in a general sense that there will be pressure to increase wages. It is untrue in that the rate of increase in real wages in a market-clearing model is determined by the real wage elasticity of supply of the unemployed workers. The rate of change as a result of trade union pressure may lead to faster or slower rate of change of money wages than would the 'market force' of labour supply responding to its occupational and labour force participation reservation wage levels. The pressure from trade unions will depend on their expectations of what is both reasonable or fair and attainable. It is, therefore, a function of a collection of expectations about a range of factors other than the expected rate of inflation.

Unions and their members have come to expect regular increases in real wages in excess of the productivity growth of their firm or sector. This does not mean that they will always obtain such increases but they will not easily forgo them. The most powerful restraints that can be placed on union action to secure these increases in a free bargaining situation come from the fear of unemployment. This unemployment, if it is to have the restraining effect, is unemployment amongst those pressing for the real wage increase. Unemployment elsewhere, say other members of the same union, may have some effect, but it will not be so strong or direct as fear of unemployment among the group itself. It may be that sufficient monetary squeeze exercised for long enough will generate such fear among large numbers of trade unions and affect many bargaining groups. But this could take a very long time or need very large increases in unemployment elsewhere before each bargaining group starts to believe that its own employment prospects are threatened. The Monetarist's short run, during which there is trade-off between unemployment and inflation, this time working to increase unemployment, could be a long short-run. Moreover, it could be that it never stops. If the only effective pressure is fear of loss of one's own job it may need rising unemployment to create and fuel that fear. Once unemployment levels out there will be less pressure.

A trade union might still seek to maintain or increase real wages, even if there is fear of unemployment. Its members might choose that. It may be believed that the threat of unemployment can be removed as a result of government policy to provide special assistance to the industry. The terms of voluntary acceptance of redundancy might make unemployment a less feared result although unionized manual workers never obtain the lavish generosity of the golden handshakes given to some top executives.

It is realistic to expect trade unions to seek to increase the real wages of their members. It is also realistic to recognize that no trade union can increase the real wages of its members faster than the rate of their productivity growth unless someone else's real income rises at a slower rate or falls. The someone else may be employers or shareholders, consumers or other workers. It may be the taxpayer if it is the public sector which gains. The fact that such redistribution will take place will not of itself discourage trade unions from seeking increases in real wages in excess of productivity gains, any more than an employer's attempts to increase his real profits by more than the rate of growth of productivity, which involves the same sort of transfer of real income from some other group, prevents him from so doing.

To argue that such considerations *should* influence either trade union or employer behaviour is to invoke a value-judgement regarding fairness or equity. Monetarist critics of trade unions ought not to do this for they base one of their criticisms of trade union behaviour on the unions' attempts to replace the 'objective' allocative efficiency of the market by subjective value-judgements and notions of fairness. With trade unions 'Wages are no longer to be determined by demand and supply but by alleged considerations of justice . . . The market is thereby deprived of the function of guiding labour to where it can be sold' (Hayek 1984, 18). What the Monetarist can do is to seek to reduce the ability of trade unions or pay setters to redistribute in certain ways but cannot, or, if they are to maintain logical consistency should not, preach against income redistribution as such. It is the nature and extent of income distribution under the existing system of collective bargaining to which they object.

We are back to the problems raised in the previous chapter. The enunciation of a monetary target is not enough. Actual control of the money supply is not enough. Changes in the fiscal and legislative framework in which pay bargainers operate may not be enough. A change of attitudes and thus of expectations and aspirations is also required. To put the practical Monetarist case bluntly, something has to be done to stop trade unions and their members seeking higher increases in wages than are justified by increases in their productivity or marginal revenue product in a non-general inflation situation. To stop them trying to increase their wages in this way, one of two things is necessary. Either they must be taught that they cannot hope to achieve them, or they must be 're-educated' so that they do not seek to obtain increases in excess of productivity (or MRP) growth because it is immoral or antisocial to do so.

There are a number of different ways in which trade union expectations might be changed. In the last resort they all consist of one or other, or a combination, of two elements—compulsion or persuasion.

The first approach probably requires considerable structural changes to be introduced in Britain. Monetarists, ranging from the extreme views of Hayek (1904) and Minford (1983) through more moderate versions (IEA Readings 14, 1974; 20, 1979; 24, 1980) (not all contributors are Monetarists) and Brittan (1982), to Sir Geoffrey Howe, Sir Keith Joseph, and Nigel Lawson, as practising Monetarist politicians, have emphasized the need to introduce structural changes. The need to reduce the power of trade unions is a common theme. Many of the other structural changes may have more effect on the Natural Rate of Unemployment than on the rate of inflation, as we shall discuss in Chapters 14 and 15. In the strongest version the policy prescriptions are based on the crude view that it might be possible to ignore the expectations and aspirations of trade unions. It might not matter what unions and their members expect; if they are sufficiently weak they can do nothing about their expectations. This is the *impotence* approach.

There have been proposals from the Conservative Party to reduce the power of trade unions for many years.[5] The Heath Government tried with the 1971 Industrial Relations Act which attempted to legitimise and formalize trade union power and collective bargaining processes. It was an attempt to provide a framework within which 'responsible' collective bargaining could take place, and trade unions and employees were given some new legally based rights. Convential wisdom and such research as we have suggests that it failed.[6] The Thatcher Government adopted a step-by-step approach with the 1980, 1982, and 1984 Acts, which, as we shall discuss in Chapter 16, were a more direct attack on trade union power and provided them with no additional rights.

Peter Jay believed that it might not be politically possible to enact legislation which restricted union power, and if it were the legislation might not be enforceable.

Trade unions can mobilise a political resistance to such legislative action which conventional monopolies could never muster; and, even if their political support fails, their industrial power is something which conventional monopolies, which depended heavily on the rule of law for the exploitation of their advantages, could never have deployed. So a simple direct attack on trade union power offers no harmonious solution within the constraints of our present political economy, even if it is supposed that the advantages of curtailing collective bargaining would outweigh the other real social costs of seeking to deprive a sophisticated public of the other benefits which it believes it gets from trade union membership (Jay 1976, 27).

Since 1976 it has proved possible to enact such legislation. The political power of unions proved in both 1979 and 1983 to be less than anticipated. It remains to be seen whether their industrial power has also withered away.

Statutory incomes policies imposed on unwilling trade unions might be as seen as one variant of the impotence approach. The power of trade unions to increase money wages might be restrained by making it unlawful to raise wages by more than some specified amount. Monetarists condemn incomes policies which are seen as undue distortions with market mechanisms which lead to subsequent pay explosions when the statutory restraints have inevitably to be removed. It is none the less clear that incomes policies are intended to influence the expectations of workers and unions, and they seek to influence both expectations of future price rises and expectations of obtainable increases in money wages.

Other versions emphasize the *ignorance* approach. Unions, or perhaps their members, are not properly informed so that they do not fully appreciate the consequences of their actions. Or their expectations are mutually inconsistent in that they want both higher real wages and no loss of employment. They do not realize that they cannot have both. The two main problems with this are, first, that for many years governments have been telling them that they can have both, not necessarily as much of each as they would like, but some of each. Experience until the late seventies suggested governments were right. Second, even if the views based on general post-war experience are wrong some groups of workers in some trade unions can have more of both. If they form expectations of continually rising real wages in excess of their productivity growth without loss of employment, they will be able to fulfill their expectations. Someone else may pay the price but the expectations of the first groups can be achieved. They are not forming their expectations on the basis of ignorance. As we have previously pointed out, Conservative Government spokesmen changed their message and switched from emphasizing the unemployment effects on the groups receiving the 'large' pay increases, and instead pointed out that 'one man's pay rise is another man's jobs loss'.

This leads to the *responsibility* approach. This emphasizes the macro or social consequences for others of pay rises in excess of productivity improvements. The weakness of this approach is that it does not fit easily into a general philosophy which emphasizes the advantages of a free market system in which every one in the pursuit of their own interests contributes to the general good. It is difficult for workers in a manufacuring plant to see how, in a free market competitive system which is based on Monetarism, their wage restraint will protect the job of someone else.

Peter Jay advocated a *conversion* approach, 'which will not involve a crude frontal onslaught on the industrial rights and powers of working people. *They need somehow to be "disalienated" enough to become infected with the entrepreneurial realities which confront their present employers, so that they will accept a non-inflationary market-determined environment as setting the level of rewards that can be afforded*' (Jay 1976, 27, emphasis in original). Even though the actual level of profitability might be low inflationary wage settlements will continue

if all working people believe that at the margin any restraint shown by them disappears into the bottomless pit of shareholders' dividends. But might it not perhaps be different if those working people themselves were the entrepreneurs of the firm, in the sense that it formally belonged to them, that its broad policy was decided by them and that it hired and fired the professional management and decided the terms on which it wished to reward itself, its managers and those who supplied it with capital? (28).

If workers could be converted into owners as well as employees, it is argued, they would exercise wage restraint and trade unions would 'wither away because a different and better way has been found of securing not only the direct financial interests of their members but also a much wider range of advantages—such as a direct say and involvement in the conduct of the enterprise to which you belong—as well' (29).

A marriage of Monetarism and Syndicalism if it could be arranged —either by agreement or shotgun—is seen as the only effective way of combining high employment with low inflation. There is, however, little evidence that worker-owners would behave in the restrained manner suggested or that they would not continue to press governments to maintain a high level of demand which permitted them, or some of them, to increase real income through higher prices.

The *consensus* approach seeks to persuade trade unions of the inescapable relationships between changes in aggregate real output and aggregate real income. It must also include some distributional element. Even if unions agree that there is some relationship at the aggregate level it does not follow that they accept that the aggregate relationship imposes some specific relationship on sectors or companies. Workers and unions in firms where the rate of productivity growth exceeds the national average might well claim that they should have pay increases in excess of the national average. Those with below average productivity gains, or conceivably with reductions in productivity, might argue that they are working no less hard then the growth sector and so are entitled to similar increases. Other groups might press for above-average increases to remedy some past wrong or restore some previous relationship. Consensus is required at all levels of pay determination.

Because trade unions do not operate with the same economic models as Monetarists there is no obvious reason why consensus about inflation and unemployment policy should emerge. Indeed we have just suggested that there may be little consensus within the trade union movement about the desirable or acceptable development of wages amongst different groups and unions. Proposals have been made from time to time to alter the structure of bargaining in order to facilitate agreement amongst different unions and employers but there is little evidence that much progress is likely to be made in the near future under a Thatcher Administration.

The *social contract* approach seeks to obtain consensus by extending the area of union participation in economic and social policy-making in exchange for their acceptance of some degree of wage restraint. The experience of the Labour Government's attempt in 1974-9 is widely interpreted as establishing the futility of this approach, although it is not always clear whether in the critic's view that attempt failed because of factors specific to it, such as the failure adequately to control the money supply, or because of inherent defects in any policy which relies on voluntary agreements with competing and decentralized trade unions.

There is a wide range of options apparently available to those who believe that structural or institutional changes are a necessary condition for the attainment of high employment with low inflation. That there is disagreement within the broad Monetarist school is not surprising. There is similar disagreement amongst non-Monetarists. Friedman appears to believe that trade unions do not possess the power continually to increase wages. They can do so only in the process of increasing their strength, but he provides no criteria by which we can ascertain when unions are increasing their strength. Others believe that they can continually increase wages only if they are able to pressure or persuade governments continually to increase the money supply. Others, following Hayek, believe that the legislative provisions—and in Britain the enactment of trade union immunities is emphasized—give unions the power to generate inflationary pressures and result in the level of unemployment being higher than it need be, or would be in a 'freer' market situation.

Keynesians are much more likely to accept the notion of trade union power and their ability to increase money and real wages. Whether they can increase all real wages is a much more contentious issue, but the notion of cost-push inflation where unions force up money wages is generally accepted. It may be that unions can do this only within certain limits which might be influenced by institutional, legal, social, political, and economic conditions, and their attempt to do so may be influenced by factors internal to the union as well as these external ones. If these constraints vary through time, as does the willingness of unions to use such strength as they believe they possess, we are left with considerable indeterminacy. Strong generalizations about the ability of unions to do particular things, or about the specific expectations which influence them, may be neither helpful nor even possible.

In this case, and it is the most realistic interpretation, we have to recognize that the expectations which influence unions are not only expectations of future price changes. They include expectations of government policies and reactions in a wide area; they include the results of other people's pay bargaining, and the results of labour market forces which may be increasing the pay of certain groups both union and non-union. They include changes in profits, productivity, working arrangements, and perceptions of fairness. Perceived opportunities to change or restore some past pay relationship may influence the expectations of achieving some of their aspirations. In addition, the constantly changing patterns of product demand will be exerting market pressures on pay levels quite distinct from any anticipated change in the general level of prices. Perhaps more important is the fact that increases in real wages in excess of productivity growth in particular sectors or firms do not lead automatically or necessarily to decreased employment in those sectors or firms. They may lead to lower-than-otherwise growth in employment, but that is quite a different matter.

There may be no objective reason whatsoever why unions in some sectors should exercise restraint in the rate of increase of their members' money wages because their employment prospects may not be threatened. The difference in the Monetarist position between those who argue that unemployment retribution will afflict those who increase their money wages by more than the increase in the money supply and those who argue that the penalities may fall on others is a crucial one. The latter have no built-in corrective automatically working to revise the expectations and behaviour of trade unions. They are compelled to turn to a responsibility approach of some sort, and urge unions to accept a particular set of moral judgements. They may incorporate coercion in their attempts at persuasion, but they cannot rely on the ultimate self-interest argument.

Changing trade union expectations is a much more complex task than that assumed in a model based on individual worker decisions. Once trade unions are introduced into the analysis the ridiculousness of assuming that the maintenance of existing real wages is the only motive and that therefore the only expectations which matter are those relating to the future rate of inflation is self-evident. Because unions have expectations about a number of factors and also have aspirations to improve the conditions of their members, concentration only on expectations about future price levels is inadequate. First, it diverts attention away from many other important factors which influence pay bargaining, and, second, the expected rate of inflation rarely exercises much direct influence on British collective bargaining.

The maintenance of an equilibrium position in real terms is not what collective bargaining is about. Neither the adaptive expectations, nor the REH explanation, can provide a satisfactory account of pay determination, and indeed they each provide a misleading account because they focus on a largely irrelevant variable. Trade union expectations and aspirations will influence pay bargaining and employment, but these will be a range of expectations which will vary in focus and in the selection of priorities from time to time and from union to union. Indeterminacy will be widespread. As we have said before, this is difficult, and perhaps even unacceptable to large parts of economic theory, but so much the worse for economic theory or those who continue to subscribe to this version of it. The real world is much more complex and it is frequently uncertain and indeterminate. We might not like this, but it is the world in which we live.

Summary

The Monetarist assertion that expectations of future inflation rates determine wage and employment decisions on both sides of the labour market is seriously mistaken once the existence of trade unions is recognized. The analysis may be seriously defective when applied to an atomistic individual labour market but is clearly irrelevant to labour markets which include trade unions and collective bargaining. Trade unions and their members have a number of expectations about different things which might include the future rate of inflation, but there is very little evidence to suggest that the anticipated rate of change in the general price level plays much part in British collective bargaining.

Trade unions give much attention to what is happening to the wages of other groups. Employers often believe that the expectations of their work-force which include some form of comparability are legitimate. Neither a REH nor a market-clearing Walrasian-auctioneer approach can satisfactorily incorporate trade unions with their variety of objectives and expectations. Once a simple single objective—the maintenance of expected real wages—is seen as inappropriate, we are led to the conclusion that there is, and will be, a considerable area of indeterminacy about trade union objectives which emerges from their multiplicity of expectations about different things. We cannot conclude that any single economic variable will influence trade union behaviour in a predictable or consistent way.

Trade unions have accepted at least part of the Keynesian analysis. They believe there is involuntary demand-deficient unemployment which can be reduced by appropriate action by Government. What is less clear is whether they ever accepted, or if they did, whether they still accept, the Keynesian qualification that the reduction of demand-deficient unemployment requires a reduction in real wages. However, given the imperfections in the labour market and the fact that it does not always (ever?) clear in real wage terms, an actual reduction in real wages might not be necessary. Employment can expand if real wages are held constant or rise by no more than the rate of productivity growth. If employers are faced by horizontal returns to scale an expansion in aggregate nominal demand with involuntary unemployment can lead to an expansion in output and unemployment.

The crucial question then becomes, not whether unions will accept a reduction in real wages, but whether they will accept sufficient degree of restraint in the growth of real wages. Practising Monetarists, such as Sir Keith Joseph and Sir Geoffrey Howe, recognize that it is necessary to change trade union attitudes and behaviour. Monetary targets, or even achieved changes in money supply, will not do this. Legislative and structural change are necessary, as is some change in attitudes. There are various ways of seeking to change union attitudes and behaviour involving various combinations of coercion and persuasion. The Thatcher Administration has tried a variety, as we shall discuss in Chapter 16. They do not yet appear to have come up with the right mixture.

What is clear is that outside the sophisticated superstructure of economic theory there is no justification for the view that changing monetary targets or the quantity of money will induce the desired behaviour.

In the real world there is no reason to believe that changing people's views about anticipated inflation will lead to a return to the previous level of real activity, i.e. the former NRU. Other considerations will affect wage changes. Some groups can obtain increases in money wages in excess of their productivity growth and not experience a reduction in their employment. To a Monetarist it should be 'rational' for them to do so.

The most that might emerge from a Monetarist position is that fear of losing one's own job might induce changed behaviour. In the British context this might well mean that rising unemployment is a necessary condition for the reduction of inflation. There is then no Natural Rate of Unemployment but there might be a rate of change of unemployment which will create less inflation. We shall pursue this further in Chapters 14 and 15.

When policy proposals to moderate inflation without high levels of unemployment are being considered it is vital to bear in mind that unions have a number of different objectives and therefore will have expectations that certain other objectives as well as inflation and the general level of unemployment will be dealt with. Relative wages are very important to unions, and it is of little attraction to any trade union to advise it that the best interests of its members would be served by it advising them to change jobs in response to changing labour market pressures and changing pay differentials. Also, unions believe that social considerations are relevant to pay determination. As long as they have some expectations that the pay bargaining processes can, or should, lead to bargaining results which reflect these social value-judgements, such as equity and fairness, their behaviour will be different than if they were concerned only to maintain the real value of their existing wage levels. It is very doubtful indeed if sufficient pressure can be exerted on trade unions to lead them to abandon their social objectives and consideration of equity and fairness. The Pay Board in its Relativities Report concluded that social factors were too deeply ingrained into the British system of collective bargaining to be ignored and so could be relevant considerations for their proposed Relativities Board (Cmnd. 5535, 1974). Unless it is believed that such factors can be expunged from pay determination it has to be recognized that they will form part of the expectations of trade unions and of employers, as well as of individual members of unions.

Notes to Chapter 13

1. These types of proposals are discussed by Brown, in Robinson and Mayhew (1983). Also see Blackaby (1980).

2. See Pay Board Reports, *Anomalies*, Cmnd. 5429, and *Relativities*, Cmnd. 5535.
3. Review Body for Nursing Staff, Midwives, Health Visitors and Professions Allied to Medicine. *First Report on Nursing Staff, Midwives and Health Visitors 1984*, Cmnd. 9258, HMSO, London, June 1984.
4. See Memorandum by the Deutsche Bundesbank to the Treasury and Civil Service Committee on Monetary Policy, II and oral evidence of Dr Dudler, HC 163-11 (1980-1).
5. See, for example, Inns of Court Conservative and Unionist Society, *A Giant's Strength*, London, 1958; Conservative Political Centre, *Fair Deal at Work*, London, 1968; Stephen Abbott, *Industrial Relations: Conservative Policy*, Conservative Political Centre, London, 1966.
6. The most detailed study of the 1971 Act is Weekes *et al.*, (1975). Some observers of the industrial relations scene believe that had the 1971 Act operated for a longer time it might have had some effect in changing behaviour.

CHAPTER FOURTEEN

The Natural Rate of Unemployment

WE have seen that the expectations-augmented Phillips curve analysis leads to the conclusion that if the actual level of unemployment is below the 'natural' rate there must be accelerating inflation, and if the actual rate is higher than the NRU there will be falling prices. The NRU is therefore the only level of unemployment which is consistent with a constant rate of inflation. Inflation need not be zero.

At the NRU the rate of inflation could be any positive or negative rate provided that it remains constant. At this level of unemployment people's expectations about the future rate of inflation will be borne out. If there is an NRU, it 'would be that which rules when aggregate demand and supply in the economy were in balance, so that there was neither upward nor downward pressure upon the rate of inflation'.

Using the expectations-augmented Phillips curve, it is concluded that

$$w - p = f(U), \quad (14.1)$$

where w = the rate of change of money wages,
p = the rate of change of prices,
U = the percentage rate of unemployment.[1]

On the assumption that it is expected prices which determine the outcome of wage determination and that all expectations are met,

$$p = p^*, \quad (14.2)$$

where p^* = the expected rate of change of prices. There is unlikely to be zero unemployment, and in any case zero unemployment and equilibrium in the labour market are not the same. We can regard $f(U)$ as

$$F(U) = a - b(U). \quad (14.3)$$

We can then rewrite equation (14.1) as

$$w = a - b(U) + p^*, \quad (14.4)$$

which is an algebraic statement of the expectations-augmented Phillips curve.

If, following a rational expectations approach, wage increases equal expected price increases, the NRU associated with a constant rate of inflation is

$$NRU = \frac{a}{b}. \quad (14.5)$$

Increases in real wages in long-run equilibrium are equal to the rate of growth of labour productivity, g, so

$$g = w - p = f(U) \quad (14.6)$$

and

$$NRU = \frac{a-g}{b}. \quad (14.7)$$

What this means is that the NRU is the rate of unemployment at which all expectations will be fulfilled. Expectations here means expectations of future price levels. It is assumed that there is a unique level of unemployment at which all expectations will be realized. If the level of unemployment is lower than this prices will rise more than anticipated, and conversely. However if the NRU consists of the two components of unemployment—a and b, it is important to know how each component is determined.

If a is a constant it means that there is some pressure on real wages even in a static equilibrium economy, so there may be pressure on real wages irrespective of changes in the level of unemployment. If we assume that a is positive it means that if b remains constant so that total unemployment does not change there will still be pressure to increase wages. To maintain a constant level of inflation would therefore require a constantly rising level of unemployment to offset the effect of the a component adjusted for any productivity growth. Thus if there is any pressure for real wages to rise irrespective of the level of unemployment the NRU will not be a constant figure. Friedman would have no problems with this because he assumes that real wages rise only as a result of excess demand for labour after allowing for improvements in productivity. It is crucial to note the importance of this assumption. If real wages rise faster than productivity growth when there is no excess demand for labour the NRU will increase. The belief that the NRU is stable relies on the validity of the assumption that real wages rise only as a result of productivity growth and excess or deficient demand in the labour market. We can now see the importance of the Monetarist assertion that trade unions cannot cause continuing wage and price inflation. If this assumption does not hold it has to be recognized that the NRU is indeterminate until we have discovered just what has happened to real wages. This indeterminacy would then prevent Monetarists from asserting that the economy will always revert to the NRU. It may move to a new NRU but if the location of the new NRU is unknown they cannot claim that there is no long-run trade-off between inflation and unemployment.

The a component may be a general expectation that real wages will rise and may be shared by trade unions, workers, and employers. At other times a could be negative so that reductions in real wages were accepted, for either a short or longish time. We have suggested at various points that there are forces other than the productivity of the work group concerned, or excess or deficient labour demand which influence the level of and changes in acceptable and expected real wages. Attempts by trade unions to translate some of their aspirations into improved real wages, or the successful application of offensive wage claims, could lead to increases in real wages which are not simply a function of productivity or excess demand for labour.

To the extent that New Classical economics has a concept of full employment equilibrium in which there would be some frictional and possibly structural unemployment, the NRU is the same as the full employment equilibrium unemployment rate.

Friedman used the term 'natural rate of unemployment' following an earlier use by Wicksell of the term the 'natural rate of interest'. He regards it as the rate of unemployment which would be 'ground out by the Walrasian system of general equilibrium' (Friedman 1968). Friedman uses it in a context of theoretical analysis in which markets clear, so that it is the rate which would emerge in a market-clearing system if the market decisions have embodied in them the actual structural characteristics of the labour and commodity markets, including market imperfections, the cost of gathering information about job vacancies, and labour availabilities, the cost of mobility, and so on. 'But the label (NRU) is unfortunate since it suggests that the unemployment rate in question is normal or unavoidable.' (Brittan 1982, 54). The NRU is, of course, neither normal nor unavoidable; in fact, there is nothing natural about it at all. It is merely the rate at which inflation is constant because all expectations of future inflation are constant.

Non-accelerating Inflation Rate of Unemployment (NAIRU)

The use of the term 'natural rate of unemployment' has become associated with a Monetarist interpretation of inflation and unemployment, in two important respects. There is an assumption underlying the concept that labour markets clear in real wage, or more importantly, expected real wage terms, and, secondly, there is the assumption that the economy will settle down and operate at the NRU level. Unemployment might be shifted away from the NRU as a result of unexpected shocks but once these have been absorbed and understood economic activity will revert to the level associated with the NRU, although, of course, the actual level of the NRU may have changed.

Some economists, while accepting perhaps a general Monetarist position, need not believe that labour markets clear. Others—non-Monetarists—might wish to dissociate themselves from both of the implications of the NRU as advocated by Friedman, and believe that markets do not clear, so that while there may, at a specific point in time, be a unique rate of unemployment which would be associated with a constant rate of inflation, they are agnostics or even atheists on the question of whether the economy has a built-in tendency to operate at that level, or even whether it ever operates at that level. It might be thought that with given processes of pay determination, certain attitudes of unions and employers regarding the relationship between pay, price increases and productivity, legal provisions regarding collective bargaining and the powers of trade unions, the provision of wages councils, and making appropriate assumptions about the prices of imports, there is some level of economic activity represented by a given rate of unemployment (as measured in the official statistics?) at which inflation will remain constant. This would be the non-accelerating inflation rate of unemployment (NAIRU).

Acceptance of this view does not necessarily lead to acceptance of the concept of an expectations-augmented Phillips curve for that implies some relatively stable rate of trade-off between inflation and unemployment. We could believe that there is a NAIRU, that labour markets do not clear, that there is demand-deficient unemployment, but that there is no stability in either the trade-off between unemployment and inflation or in the NAIRU itself. If, at a given time, there is some level of unemployment, output, and aggregate demand which is consistent with stable inflation, it might be considerably influenced by changes in import prices as trade unions respond to past increases in prices by pressing for increases in money wages. However, this rate of unemployment might be unstable in that the maintenance of economic activity at the same level of unemployment might not result in constant inflation. The NRU can change and be changed by deliberate policy of government. Thus the NRU associated with any given rate of inflation can change. Equally the NAIRU associated with any given rate of inflation can change. In like manner the rate of inflation associated with any given level of unemployment can change. The important point which we shall develop in this and the next chapter is that neither the NRU nor NAIRU should be expected to remain constant and fixed.

Equilibrium or Disequilibrium?

The NRU rests on equilibrium in the labour markets. NAIRU may not require this assumption. Much depends on which version of the NAIRU we accept. Phelps *et al.* (1970) has a number of early versions of a natural rate, NAIRU, or equilibrium level of unemployment. Some of these are equilibrium models in that supply and demand for labour are assumed equal at the prevailing wage level. Others are disequilibrium models in that there may be excess supply of labour but the level of unemployment may be stable. Imperfections or other arrangements in the labour market may prevent supply and demand from coming into equality. In this case some workers are off their supply curves in that they are willing to supply labour at the prevailing wage but are unable to do so because of job rationing. There is involuntary unemployment in a Keynesian sense, although this may be represented as voluntary—unemployment arising from the effects of unemployment benefits on reservation wages. They tend to emphasize the importance of job search as an explanation of unemployment.

Post-Keynesian writers may use the concept of a NAIRU without emphasizing job search. For example Rowthorn (1977) emphasizes the importance of collective bargaining and the attempts by both sides to increase their real income—a variant of the target real wage approach. The attempt by both unions and employers to obtain some of their aspirations can lead to additional inflationary pressures. Real income may include the effect of tax changes so providing a net real income target wage. The level of aggregate demand may exert influence on both sides in collective bargaining. Union power may be less if demand falls and unemployment rises, and employers may feel less able to press for and obtain higher real profit incomes if demand is depressed and competition more intense. In this collective bargaining version of NAIRU the stable inflation rate of unemployment is that which creates conditions in which neither side seeks to increase its share of real disposable income. The NAIRU is therefore the level of unemployment which stabilizes the relative power of unions and employers so that each accepts the maintenance of existing real incomes plus any improvements resulting from an increase in productivity offset by the net effects of changes in taxation. Existing real incomes here do not mean the level pertaining immediately prior to the wage settlement. As discussed in Chapter 7, compensation for inflation since the last wage settlement is normally an important element in wage bargaining. Equilibrium is determined by industrial relations variables rather than labour market factors in a Walrasian market-clearing model.

Constant inflation requires compatibility between the sum of union, employer, and, through the taxation effects, government's claims on real resources, and total real output. There may be redistribution within the aggregate amount of real resources available as some firms obtain increases in relative wages and/or profits and others lose.

This version of NAIRU introduces many of the features of collective bargaining and union and employer aspirations. It is more realistic but less determinate in that we may not be able to know in advance what the real income claims of the various parties will be, or precisely what factors will influence them or to what extent. It is clear that the level of NAIRU could be very high. It can also be very variable.

Rejection of the market-clearing connotations of the NRU means that we are no longer constrained by the associated concepts that wages rise only in response to anticipated price increases or productivity growth. We are now able to introduce the idea that money wages may rise as trade unions seek to increase the real incomes of their members, or as employers try to increase profit margins. If, as we believe, trade unions tend to generate pressure for increases in real wages above the rate of productivity growth, we might well expect the NAIRU to have a tendency to rise. Increases in unemployment may exert some temporary restraining effects but there seems no reason to believe that a constant rate of unemployment will. Thus trade union pressure to increase the real income of their members can be seen as a shift in the real wage supply curve or an increase in collective reservation wages. If this happens the NAIRU will increase. The NRU would increase if individual workers increased their individual reservation wages but any unemployment then resulting would be regarded by Monetarists as voluntary.

We can group the various explanations into four main types. A traditional Keynesian view might be that labour markets do not clear in real wage terms as exemplified by demand-deficient unemployment. The assumption that real wages can, and indeed need, to fall to reduce demand-deficient unemployment is regarded as sufficient to conclude that the economy is not at its NRU. True, removing this demand-deficient unemployment involves some inflation according to the original Keynesian explanation but once that has worked its way through the economy could be at its NRU. Acceptance of the existence of demand-deficient unemployment means that it is not believed that the economy always operates at the NRU, although moving to it might involve additional inflation.

Post-Keynesians might modify this. They need not accept that a reduction in product real wages caused by rising prices is a necessary condition for the removal of demand-deficient unemployment. They can more readily accept that the economy can operate for long periods below the NRU and that an increase in aggregate nominal demand can push the economy nearer to the NRU. The addition of a target real wage or collective bargaining element means that the NAIRU is not determined only by the supply of labour responding to employers' demands and the resulting wage level. The bargaining process and the resultant wage determine employers' demands which then determine how much of the labour supply offered is employed. Supply may exceed demand and employment is determined by the relationship between the employers' demand for labour resulting from his perceptions of the state of the product market and the wage which emerges from the pay-determination process. Thus, rather than supply and demand for labour interacting to determine wages, demand and some process of wage determination interact to settle how many of the labour-offer supplies are accepted and thus the level of unemployment. Some unemployed workers may then not be on their supply curve; there is an excess supply of labour. The actual level of unemployment may, or may not, coincide with that which would be consistent with constant inflation.

Monetarists also tend to belong to one of two main groups. The extreme New Classical School believes that markets clear on the basis of rational expectations. If this is so the economy is always at the NRU for there is not even a short-run trade-off between inflation and unemployment if the REH leads to expectations and behaviour responding immediately and 'correctly' to changes in, or announcement of, intention to change money supply. They may also adopt a Lucas–Rapping intertemporal substitution of labour hypothesis to labour market-clearing (although in the original explanation Lucas and Rapping assumed adaptive expectations).

Thus, when we are below the NRU in a boom, wages are higher than usual or than expected on some version of a permanent or expected income hypothesis, so workers increase their supply of labour. When we are above the NRU in a slump the reverse holds. Experience of employment in the boom when wages are higher than usual leads to unemployment in the recession when wages are less than usual. Thus, without rational expectations the economy may be away from the NRU over the course of a trade cycle but will tend to revert to it as employers adjust their wages and labour demand in response to their perceptions of unemployment and vacancies, and workers adjust their labour supply decisions in response to the relationship between actual wages and expected, normal, or average wages over a time-period.

Other Monetarists may reject the intertemporal substitution of labour. They may also prefer some form of adaptive expectations but still tend to emphasize the role of expectations. This is not the same as an explanation which emphasizes that trade unions respond to past increases in inflation seeking to restore the real level of pay at the last settlement plus some improvement factor on a real wage target approach. The latter does not require that unions respond to expected inflation. Seeking to obtain compensation for past price increases does not imply that the same rate of increase is expected in the future. It is only necessary to try to force this sort of explanation into a model if it is believed that labour markets always clear in real wage terms. If they do not, future real wages can fall without an increase in voluntary unemployment.

Like Friedman, job search theorists (Phelps et al. 1970) see labour supply as a function of the real wage or the replacement ratio. While it may be the case that if real wages were extremely low workers might decide that they did not compensate for the disutility of work, there is very little evidence to support this. Emphasis on the importance of the replacement ratio recognizes that the level of real wages obtainable from work is compared with the level of real income obtainable from unemployment, but emphasis merely on real wages does not adequately deal with the question of how workers and their families are to survive when unemployed. Attempts to introduce consideration of permanent or normal wage levels and income (Lucas and Rapping) are one way round this, for this implies that workers have, or expect to have, some income from some sources in the future.

Recent attempts to test various hypotheses have not provided much supporting evidence for the NRU or the job search based NAIRU explanations. The intertemporal substitution explanation of Lucas and Rapping (1970) is rejected or not substantiated by Ashenfelter and Card, Altonji, Clark and Summers, and Andrews and Nickell (all writing in Greenhalgh et al. 1981). The view that real wages adjust to provide equilibrium is not supported by either Bruno and Sachs or Grubb et al. The first find that following an increase in import prices real wages adjust downward only after unemployment has risen, whereas if employment were to remain constant they should adjust *as* import prices rise. Unions and workers can be seen as responding to past inflation. The second, Grubb et al., find that the NAIRU has increased in OECD countries. This explanation says that the feasible rate of increase in real wages consistent with a given employment level has fallen as a result of increases in the price of imports and a slowing down in productivity growth. However, the target real wage has not been reduced accordingly. To obtain lower growth in real wages it has been necessary to have an increase in unemployment, or in inflation, as there is nominal inertia in the system so that money wage increases do not adjust as much as they 'should' and higher inflation is the mechanism whereby the 'excessive' increase in money wages is prevented from becoming overly excessive increase in real wages. Put in our terms this means that trade unions and workers have not adjusted their aspirations in line with the changes in the feasible improvements in real wages which are determined by import prices and productivity. They have been able to obtain larger increases in money wages and this is probably because they have been strongly influenced in their bargaining by their view that they should receive compensation for inflation since their last wage settlement. This is a form of adaptive expectations in that past inflation influences current action, but need not imply that it is the *future* rate of inflation (derived from experience of past inflation on an adaptive expectations interpretation) which determines wage movements. 'In our approach the prime source of difficulty is that people are *trying* to achieve too high real wages' (Grubb et al., 29). This can be seen therefore as a form of the collective bargaining version of NAIRU.

While the NRU, as explained by Friedman, can differ in some very important regards from some versions of the NAIRU so that moving from the NRU to the NAIRU may be much more than the choice of preferable terminology, we shall in this and the next two chapters refer to the natural rate of unemployment. Much of what we say is equally relevant to various interpretations of the NAIRU. However, if a collective bargaining version of the NAIRU is adopted greater emphasis needs to be given to those factors which determine both the trade unions wage claims, and the forces such as union militancy and the wage determination processes which translate those claims into wage settlements. We shall use the term natural rate of unemployment because it has become and remained part of economic jargon, but it is emphasized that this rate of unemployment is in no way natural, unavoidable, desirable, constant, or perhaps even knowable and measurable. Nevertheless the concept might be important and policymakers concerned about inflation and unemployment might take account of the underlying forces connected with it.

At the NRU 'Unemployment is zero—which is to say, as measured, equal to "frictional" or "transitional" unemployment, or to use the terminology I adopted some years ago from Wicksell, at its natural level' (Friedman 1977, 14). Thus at the NRU the "true or correct' unemployment statistics *should* reflect only those in the course of changing jobs or searching for jobs. Unemployment will be positive but should not include the voluntary unemployed, i.e those who are not actually looking for work or willing to accept work on the perceived prevailing terms and conditions. 'The term the "natural rate" has been misunderstood. It does not refer to some *irreducible minimum* of unemployment. It refers rather to that rate of employment which is consistent with the *existing real conditions* in the labour market. It can be raised by introducing additional obstacles' (Friedman 1975, 24, emphasis in original). It can presumably also be lowered by removing 'obstacles'. The switch by Friedman, so that the natural rate of *unemployment* is translated into the rate of *employment*, is not just another example of verbal slipperiness and suggestiveness; it reflects two important complications. The first, the assumption that when we talk about changes in unemployment we are at the same time talking about equal, but opposite, changes in employment, is true only as long as the aggregate of employment and unemployment remains constant, i.e. as long as $E + U = 1$. Second, because unemployment to Friedman and other Monetarists, for conceptual purposes, means frictional or transitional unemployment, the actual series of unemployment statistics used may not accurately represent and measure unemployment as they use the term. By switching to employment Friedman does not have to express the NRU in quantitative terms. By focusing on employment he shifts the emphasis to the labour market activities which result in supply and demand for labour being equal and the only true unemployment in that situation consists of those moving between jobs. As we have discussed in Chapter 10, official and other series of unemployment statistics can measure different things and may include people who do not satisfy the definitional requirements of the concept of unemployment which is being used, and may exclude some who do. As Friedman recognizes: 'The determinants of the natural rate of unemployment deserve much fuller analysis for both the United States and other countries. So also do the meaning of the recorded unemployment figures and the relation between the recorded figures and the natural rate. These issues are all of the utmost importance for public policy' (1977, 15).

The Determinants of the NRU

In his 1968 paper Friedman referred to legal minimum wage rates, the legislative provisions of the American Walsh-Healy and Davies-Bacon Acts requiring certain minimum wage rates to be paid to government contractors, the strength of trade unions, the provision of employment exchanges, and information about job vacancies and labour supply, 'and so on'. In answering questions following his 1975 lecture he said 'Trade unions play a very important role in determining the position of the natural level of unemployment' (30.) In his Nobel Lecture he mentioned the effectiveness of the labour market, the extent of competition or monopoly, the barriers or encouragements to working in various occupations, 'and so on'. He also referred to two American developments. The composition of the work-force has altered. Women, teenagers, and part-time workers enter and leave the labour market and change jobs more frequently than others. As they form a larger proportion of the work-force, we should expect to see higher frictional unemployment. Also he said that unemployment and related benefits have become more widely available and more generous in duration and amount so that the unemployed will wait longer in the hope, generally fulfilled, of being recalled to their former job, and can be more selective in the jobs they consider. The improved unemployment benefits will induce more people to enter the labour force. (1977, 15.) There is little in common in his various illustrations apart from the ending 'and so on'.

This is perhaps not surprising for as Friedman puts it, 'the natural rate of unemployment' . . . is not a numerical constant but depends on "real" as opposed to monetary factors'. Or, in Laidler's terms,

it would be a 'natural' unemployment rate in the sense that its value was determined by the structure of the 'real' side of the economy—the institutions of the labour market, etc.—and not in the sense that it was unvarying. It would however, be *independent* of the inflation rate, and thus would not be susceptible to being altered by orthodox Keynesian macro-economic demand-management policies, (1975, 45, emphasis in original).

If we feel compelled to follow the modern trend and express economic analytical statements in the form of equations we would say that the NRU was determined by a vector of real factors such that

$$\text{NRU} = f(Xs), \text{ where } Xs = \infty - 1.$$

To Friedman, 1 is the money supply, and to Laidler it is orthodox Keynesian macro-economic demand-management policies. Everything but the money supply or orthodox Keynesian macro-economic demand-management policies can affect the natural rate of unemployment. It is not surprising therefore that a comprehensive list of its determinants is not forthcoming. Laidler does however add some other factors: the geographical distribution and skill mix of job vacancies and unemployment, which affect the rapidity by which supply and demand adjust in the labour market, the age distribution of the unemployed and their educational characteristics, barriers or subsidies to geographical mobility of labour and jobs such as trade union restrictions and council house subsidies, and barriers or subsidies to the acquisition of new skills. The NRU 'would not be a variable which could be expected to remain constant' (Laidler 1975, 44–5).

Laidler differs from Friedman and many other Monetarists in some important respects. He does not oppose government intervention *per se* nor does he believe that it is a necessary part of the Monetarist position to do so. He does not rule out the use of fiscal demand-management policies in all situations. If the economy is operating above the NRU it may then, but perhaps only then 'be appropriate to use traditional demand management tools to increase employment'. This is a very important special case, for it recognizes that the economy may not always be operating at the level of the NRU and may as a result of, say, large structural changes in the economy, or the existence of greater than usual frictions, be running for some time above the NRU. Demand-management policy in this situation is not being used to reduce the NRU but to enable the economy to move to the NRU. As he goes on to say

> We must, therefore, be able to measure the natural unemployment rate with some confidence if we are ever to be in a position to deploy fiscal weapons to influence employment and output in a useful fashion. The amount of disagreement there has been in recent years about just what is the value of the natural unemployment rate . . . suggests that in the current state of knowledge we are in no position to estimate that rate with any degree of confidence of all (1982, 173).

Friedman too, while not suggesting that there might be this role for demand-management policies, draws attention to the difficulties of actually quantifying the NRU.

The NRU can be determined by a fantastically wide range of factor and is expected to change through time. Yet in Monetarist analysis it is perhaps the key policy factor for a government wishing to avoid inflation and maintain employment at as high a level as possible. 'One problem is that we cannot know what the "natural" rate is. Unfortunately we have as yet devised no method to estimate accurately and readily the natural rate of either interest or unemployment. And the "natural" rate will itself change from time to time' (Friedman 1968, 10.) The first sentence might rule out the possibility of ever knowing the NRU. The second suggests that it may be the current state of ignorance, perhaps arising from defective techniques or inadequate statistics. The third raises the possibility that even if we ever did measure it by the time we had done so the information would be out of date, having a high rate of obsolescence and a short useful life-span.

It is therefore difficult for a government to avoid inflation while maintaining employment as high as possible. It can know after the event whether the economy was operating above or below the NRU by seeing whether inflation rose or fell, but of course if it then took appropriate corrective action on the money supply it might be compounding an error if the NRU had in the meantime changed. It is hard enough to hit a moving target but if the only clue you have is whether or not the shot would have hit the target if it had not moved it is not very easy to know where to re-aim.

Despite the difficulties some estimates of the NRU for the UK have been made and these are set out in Table 14.1.

Interestingly Beenstock states that although the NRU in 1983 is approximately 6 per cent 'provided that the labour market does not experience any adverse shocks like another oil price hike, it will take several years before unemployment comes down to that level'. If this is right it really does bring out the total uselessness of the concept of the NRU as a policy-operational device. I doubt if anyone, including Professor Beenstock, believes that *if* the NRU is above 6 per cent in 1983, it will remain so for the next several years. If unemployment falls to 6 per cent over the next several years it might then be as far removed from the then current NRU as it was at the time he wrote his article. There is great danger of our becoming the uncritical in pursuit of the unquantifiable.

Both Keynesians and Monetarists agree that there will be some frictional unemployment. Some of this will be *ex ante* frictional, and some might be *ex poste* expected-frictional in that the individuals left their previous jobs believing that they would find another one quite quickly. There will almost certainly be some structural unemployment as a result of changing employers' demand for different skills or

Table 14.1 *Estimates of the NRU for the United Kingdom*

Author	Period	Estimate NRU per cent	
1 Parkin, Sumner, and Ward	1956–71	1.7	
2 Sumner	1968–78	3.2	
3 Liverpool Research Group	1981 on	(8–8.5) 2 million	
	late 1970s	6.0	
	late 1960s	2.5	
	early 1960s	1.5	
4 City University Business School	1983	6.0 approx.	
		Model 1	Model 2
5 Layard and Nickell	1955–66	1.96	1.96
	1967–74	4.12	4.03
	1975–9	7.80	8.61
	1980–3	10.72	11.20

Sources: (1) Parkin, Sumner, and Ward (1976); (2) Sumner (1978) (3) Liverpool Occasional Paper 1, *Economic Outlook*; (4) Quoted by Professor Beenstock of the City University Business School in, 'There are more than Two Ways of compiling Unemployment Figures', the *Guardian*, 27 July 1983, 17; (5) *NIE Review*, Feb. 1985

changes in the geographical location of job offers as a result of structural change in the economy. There may be some individuals who are deliberately choosing between work, leisure, and income in an intertemporal sense of deciding to have periods of unemployment interspersed with periods of employment. Even though we might not be able to measure accurately just how many people are unemployed in this equilibrium state, for the reasons discussed in Chapter 10, we can see that there might well be some conceptual level of unemployment we can envisage as consistent with stable inflation.

However, even if we cannot adequately measure the NRU it may be possible for us to take action to change its relative position. Following the various authors who have mentioned specific factors which influence the NRU we might be able to consider measures which will raise or lower it. Then even if we do not know whether the economy is actually operating at the NRU level or away from it, we might be able to reduce the level of the NRU and so the actual level of unemployment in the economy without generating any additional inflationary pressures.

If we start from Friedman's definition of the NRU 'Unemployment is zero—which is to say, as measured, equal to "frictional" or "transitional" unemployment' (Friedman 1975), 14) we can express frictional unemployment (FrU) as determined by,

$$FrU = f(QR, LO, UB(PI), AW/IRW, OcD_i/OcS_i(a \ldots n), \\ LFC, LFPR, UB(Inst.), HP, LMI, OM), \qquad (14.8)$$

where

QR = Quit rate which may be influenced by LMI;
LO = Lay-offs including dismissals and redundancies which may be influenced by legislation;
UB(PI) = Unemployment Benefit including all welfare payments to unemployed, which may be adapted to a permanent income view of combining wages and UB over some time-period;
AW = Actual wage levels whether by 'market' forces, collective bargaining, or law;
IRW = Individual reservation wages;
OcD_i = Demand for labour in occupation i;
OsS_i = Supply of labour in occupation i;
(a . . . n) = geographical or local labour markets;
LFC = Labour force composition; demographic features—age, sex, etc.;
LFPR = Labour Force participation rate
UB(Inst.) = Institutional features of the UB provisions, rules, etc.

HP = Hiring practices and policies, e.g. internal labour markets, legislation
LMI = Labour market information; availability, cost and access to labour market information on wages and vacancies, including the accuracy of the individual's assessment of the probability of admission to the acceptable-labour supply curve of those jobs within his area of search. LMI may be influenced by the provision of Job-Centres and the amount of quality of services they provide;
OM = Occupational mobility, restrictions on entry to occupations, training provisions time and cost.

The level of 'frictional' unemployment will be determined by two main factors: the numbers looking for jobs and the amount of time it takes to find jobs. This will be determined by quit rates and lay-offs and dismissals which explain the movement into unemployment of those previously employed, and changes in the labour force participation rate which can influence the number of people not previously employed immediately prior to their unemployment who enter the labour market to look for work. Similarly, withdrawals from labour force participation can reduce the number who would otherwise be frictionally unemployed looking for jobs. The level of unemployment and related benefits might influence both the decision to join the work-force and the length of search for a job once unemployed. The imbalances in demand and supply for various occupations in different regions may influence both the occurrence and the duration of unemployment, and the demographic composition of the work-force can affect the level of frictional unemployment if some groups have a higher propensity to change jobs with periods of unemployment between jobs. The level of Unemployment Benefit, perhaps expressed as a proportion of earnings from employment—the Replacement Ratio—might influence the length of spells of unemployment, and the administrative provisions or institutional rules setting out the conditions in which unemployment and related benefits can be received might also have some effect. The hiring practices of firms, for example whether recruitment for all grades is from external sources, or whether there are internal labour markets which restrict the number of occupations or levels at which outside applicants are hired, may affect the number and types of vacancies and so the length of unemployment for those seeking certain sorts of jobs. The amount of labour market information, the ease with which it can be obtained, and its accuracy may influence both the incidence and length of frictional or job search unemployment. If workers believe that there are more higher-paying vacancies than actually exist, or if they have misguided views about their own probabilities of becoming part of an employer's acceptable-labour supply curve for certain jobs, they may become frictionally unemployed in order to get one of the expected higher-paying jobs, and remain unemployed searching for one for a longer time. The ease and cost with which individuals can change jobs and enter new occupations as a result of the acquisition of additional skills may affect the length of frictional unemployment, as may obstacles to entry into new occupations.

Individual reservation wages are determined by the labour force participation reservation wage for the lowest-paid occupation the individual will enter plus a premium to compensate for the additional disutility of working in any other occupation. The minimum reservation wage (LFP(IRW)min) is determined by the value of leisure, the unpleasantness of work in the lowest-paid acceptable job, household or family arrangements regarding income-sharing and expenditure and the level and administrative rules relating to Unemployment Benefit and other social security benefits including any disutility effects of the source of income is regarded as affecting the utility derived from it.

$$\text{LFP(IRW)}_{\min} = (\text{VL, Unwork, HY, UB}) \qquad (14.9)$$

VL = Value of leisure
Unwork = Unpleasantness of work in lowest paid acceptable job
HY = Household or family unit income and income-sharing and expenditure arrangements
UB = Unemployment Benefit including all welfare payments and provisions to unemployed individual. The effect of UB may be negative if the *source* of income affects the utility derived from it.

The reservation for a particular occupation, i, (IRW_i) is therefore:

$$\text{IRW}_i = (\text{LFP(IRW)}_{\min} + f(i)) \qquad (14.10)$$

where

$f(i)$ = the additional wage necessary to induce acceptance of work in occupation i, with appropriate adjustments if geographical mobility is required.

Equation (14.11) explains further the relationship between actual wages and individual reservation wages (AW/IRW) as a cause of 'frictional' unemployment in the assessment of the NRU. The market wage in equation (14.11) is assumed to be determined in a Walrasian system so that there is equilibrium in every occupational labour market, at the prevailing wage as everyone is employed who wishes to be and employers have no unsatisfied demand for labour at that wage.

$$\text{MtkW} = f(\text{D}_{Li}, \text{IRW}_i), \qquad (14.11)$$

where
>   MktW = the market wage for occupation i, and
> D_{Li} = the employers' demand for labour in occupation i which is determined by expected product real wage, the expected marginal productivity of labour in occupation i, and the future product selling price.

Actual wages (AW) may exceed the MktW which would emerge from a Walrasian system as a result of the impact of minimum wage legislation, collective bargaining, or other institutional or legal factors which result in decision-taking processes which create results which differ from those in a Walrasian market situation. Legislation may raise wages without imposing a statutory minimum. This occurs if there is equal pay requirements or legislation which prevents discrimination in employment. In the absence of the legislation wages of the protected groups would probably be lower. Employers may unilaterally raise wages above the MktW level if they use comparability or employer wage surveys to determine the level of pay of their own employees. Trade unions might be given special attention if it is thought that they have the ability to exercise some sort of monopoly power over labour supply which they exercise on behalf of their members. In particular, trade unions might establish a collect reservation wage which is higher than the individual reservation of their members, or of some of them, which they impose through their ability to take collective industrial action. Or the mere existence of a union may lead individuals to raise their individual reservation wages as they have more confidence that they will not be undercut by others with lower individual reservation wages. While this may be seen as part of the CB effects it is distinguished here as some proposals by some economists and governments seek to operate on the excess of AW over MktW by directly affecting the ability of trade unions to impose a higher collective reservation wage or to reduce the amount of that excess. So,

$$AW = f(\text{MktW, Leg, CB, TU}). \qquad (14.12)$$

Leg = Legislative provisions which directly raise actual wages above their 'market' level, e.g. minimum wage laws, wages councils, Fair Wages Resolution, Walsh-Healy, Davies-Bacon

CB = Collective bargaining or other legal and institutional arrangements, e.g. statutory arbitration provisions, industrial relations legislation on recognition, bargaining rights, strikes and picketing, enforceability of agreements or contracts. Voluntary CB arrangements, arbitration, use of comparability

TU = Effects of trade unions. Essentially an assumption that trade unions can increase wages of bargaining units by imposing or enabling a collective reservation wage (CRW) to be set which is higher than the IRW. CRW > IRW through CB or Leg, or as a result of TU decision-taking processes or 'unrepresentativeness' of TU leadership and decisions or their 'power' over their members.

Occupational mismatch (OcD_i/OcS_i) is, at a given point in time, determined by employers' demand for that particular occupation D_{Li}, and the existing number of people in that occupation, i.e. those with the appropriate skills and abilities to form part of the employers' acceptable labour supply curves. Some of this total number of workers will not form part of the LOS curves to employers given the existing structure of relative wages and perceived Job Requirements and effort-inputs in different jobs. Some people will be working in other occupations. Thus equation (14.4) encapsulates not only the market wage explanation but also the decisions of those who could be part of occupation i, whether, with the existing structure of wages and Job Requirements, to be members of it. Those whose IRW_is exceed $MktW_i$ are not part of the LOS curves. In the real world the important comparison for an individual is between AWi and IRW_i. This will determine whether he will offer himself for a job with the employer but if there is, with existing actual wages, no vacancy, the individual cannot obtain a job by offering to work for less than AWi.

It may be that the supply of acceptable labour to occupation i is insufficient to meet the demand. There may be possibilities for some individuals to move into the occupation by retraining or which adapts their existing skills, or by training new entrants. Thus at any given level of wages the NRU would be lower if, in cases where there is occupational mismatch, an increase in supply of the appropriate kind of labour, or occupation, occurred. Removing difficulties to occupational mobility may lower the NRU. The number of people who could form part of the occupational supply to occupation i can change through time as more individuals acquire the necessary skills and abilities. The net addition to possible labour supply will be the difference between those who leave because of retirement or occupational change and those who enter as a result of switching from some other occupation by acquiring the appropriate skills or returning to this occupation. This can be referred to as $(i)t$ where t indicates there will be some time-lag before the supply change is effective.

$i(t)$ = (Unwork*/Unwork*$_{min}$), HK_i cost, HK_i type, HK_i stock, Trg_i, AW_i/AW_{a-n}

HK_i cost = Cost of obtaining appropriate human capital to be acceptable in occupation i;

Unwork*$_i$ = the expected unpleasantness of work in occupation i;

Unwork*$_{min}$ = the expected unpleasantness of work in the least unpleasant job in the case of new entrants to the labour market, or of the unpleasantness of other jobs which have been experienced in the case of job-changers;
HKI type = the nature of the human capital to be acquired in occupation.
HK stock = the existing stock of human capital, experience, and ability of the individual.
Trg$_i$ = The ease or difficulty of obtaining access to training for occupation i. Restrictions or time-lag on access to training affects IRW by enabling individuals to determine a higher IRW as supply is restricted. Legislative, collective bargaining, or unilaterally imposed TU restrictions may influence Trg$_i$.

Geographical imbalances between occupational labour supply and demand for members of a given occupation may raise the NRU

$$IRW_{ia} = (IRW_{il}/P_1)(P_a^*/P_1) + \text{Mob}. \qquad (14.13)$$

Individual reservation wage in locality a compared to IRW in locality 1
P1, P$_a^*$ = prices in locality 1 and anticipated prices in locality a respectively. Housing costs may be particularly important, including in UK access to subsidized local authority rented housing. Availability, or non-availability of privately owned rented housing may be an important factor in P$_a^*$.
Mob = Amount to compensate for inconvenience and cost of geographical mobility.

It is generally believed that a person's IRW is higher for a job in a different area which requires geographical mobility than it is for the same Job Requirements which do not require geographical mobility.

There can be two factors influencing this. One reflects the expected differences in prices and costs in the two locations. This adjustment, which can be either upward or downward, is necessary in order to maintain the assumption that reservation wages are formed in real wage terms. The weaker or less realistic this assumption the less important is this component. Secondly, there may be some additional payment required to compensate for the inconvenience and cost of moving. If other members of the household are currently employed at the existing location the cost of mobility may include some element to reflect the expected probability of them obtaining jobs in the new location at certain specified wage levels. British writers emphasize the importance of housing costs in impeding geographical mobility and therefore in raising frictional unemployment and the NRU. In particular the great domination of local authority housing in the rented housing sector and the practice of subsidizing local authority rents are seen as exercising an especially pernicious effect on potential labour mobility.

There are obviously many other factors which contribute to the determination of the NRU. For example changes in the school-leaving age or the number of places available in higher education will affect the number of young people in the labour market looking for jobs, and might also affect the demand for labour and the acceptability of young people to employers. Reductions in the provisions of public transport can reduce the distance people can travel to work and thereby increase unemployment. Closing nurseries and crèches or the introduction of legislation restricting child-minding activities can reduce the number of mothers in the work-force.

The factors shown in the equations above are those most frequently mentioned by Monetarists.

It is clear that there is no reason whatsoever to justify an assumption that the NRU is likely to remain constant through time, and a host of reasons why it should not. Changes in any of a multitude of factors will lead to a rise or fall in the NRU.

The NRU and the Level of Aggregate Demand

As we have seen Friedman and other Monetarists believe that the NRU is independent of the level of aggregate nominal demand. It cannot, therefore, be influenced by changes in the money supply and is impervious to demand-management policies. This view rests on the correctness of the assumption that in long-run equilibrium where all price increases are fully anticipated real wage increases are determined only by changes in productivity. If this is not the case so that there are some other factors which influence changes in real wages, any changes in these will change the NRU. If unions or individual workers increase their real reservation wages so raising real wages we might expect employment to fall. It may not necessarily do so; this may depend on the way in which the government responds. On a Monetarist analysis there would be a fall in employment which might be ascribed to an increase in trade union power allowing them to raise real wages. Conversely if unions or workers lower their real reservation wage and are willing to accept reductions in real wages there could be a fall in the NRU.

It is possible that when unemployment is high employers may feel unable to maintain their customary wage–price mark-up. Unions, while possibly weaker as a result of the recession, may still be able to increase money wages by a larger percentage than employers believe they can increase their product prices. Indeed this may be the

Monetarists' expected pattern of movement out of a recession. Nigel Lawson drew attention to the 'initial decline in profit margins' as the Thatcher Government reduced inflation (1984, 18). It is possible therefore that when we try to measure the NRU by using published statistics of unemployment we are picking up some factors other than pure changes in the NRU. If profit margins vary over the course of the business cycle and they affect the level of unemployment and the NRU as measured at the time, it is no longer obvious that the NRU cannot be influenced by demand-management policies, for these may affect the business cycle.[3]

Many of the factors included in the equations above may be affected by the level of aggregate demand. We know that job changes vary with the level of economic activity. Workers will be less inclined to leave a job to look for another when the level of unemployment is high and the number of vacancies low. Marginal workers may be discouraged from re-entering the labour force. Employers may tighten their standards of acceptability in a recession, and, as there is less pressure of demand for products, may be prepared to leave vacancies unfilled for a longer period while they undertake more rigorous screening of job applicants.

Equilibrium

To Friedman whose concept of the NRU reflects a Walrasian system, market-clearing means that there is equilibrium in both labour and product markets. Those who adopt a NAIRU approach may have an equilibrium or a disequilibrium model of the labour market. Job-search models which include strong supply-side effects as labour withdraws from employment into voluntary unemployment (e.g. Lucas and Rapping 1970) are generally equilibrium models although some version of job search may incorporate disequilibrium in labour markets by adopting a job rationing or queueing element. This has the same effect as involuntary unemployment in Keynesian terms. At existing wages supply exceeds demand and some workers are unable to supply the labour they are willing to offer, not because they do not meet employers' acceptable-labour standards, but because there are no vacancies. Some element of wage stickiness is necessary to explain why this excess supply of labour does not lead the employer to replace the existing work-force at lower wages. The collective bargaining version of the NAIRU uses a different sort of equilibrium. This is equilibrium in a power and bargaining sense and there is no reason to suppose that equilibrium here means that labour supply and demand are equal, and indeed collective bargaining equilibrium will almost certainly be associated with an excess supply of labour and so with labour market disequilibrium.

However, whether one accepts either a NRU or a NAIRU approach there is the possibility that the level of unemployment and, therefore, equilibrium in labour markets, may not be consistent with equilibrium in the output and demand for products markets. If the output market is clearing so that the demand for, and the supply of, goods and services is in equilibrium, does this mean that the labour market is also in equilibrium? It may be that this would be the case in a completely pure Walrasian system with perfect competition in every sub-market. But not even extreme New Classical School adherents believe that this represents the real world. As we have seen, Friedman believes that the NRU is determined by 'real' factors which include what he would regard as distortions to a perfect competition or Walrasian model.

It is possible to conceive a situation in which there is equality of demand and supply in the output market but disequilibrium in the labour market. In the Friedman NRU model this is assumed to correct itself by adjustments in labour demand and supply responding to corrected expectations of real wages and product real wages. If an expansion in output and employment is later cancelled out when both employers and workers appreciate that the increase in money wages and prices did not represent a reduction in product real wages or a rise in workers' real wages, labour market equilibrium is assumed to be restored as workers voluntarily choose to be unemployed. If, however, as we have suggested, they adjust downwards their real reservation wages and are content to remain employed even when they appreciate that inflation has occurred, there will be no automatic move back to the former labour market equilibrium position. Instead, there will be demand-deficient unemployment as these workers would be willing to work at the prevailing real wage levels but employers no longer demand their services as they do not wish to produce the extra output.

Let us assume that the economy has been running below the NRU level and that inflation has been rising. A reversal of government policy, perhaps resulting from the election of a new government less committed to the maintenance of low unemployment, results in the economy being operated at the NRU level and inflation stabilizes at a steady rate. After a time the government concludes for whatever reasons that this steady rate of inflation is too high and therefore seeks deliberately to run the economy with unemployment above the NRU level. This means that the increase in aggregate nominal demand is less than anticipated. Prices will be rising less quickly than expected. Real wages might rise if money wages have, following Friedman, been adjusted to reflect expected inflation. Employers will cut back on output and employment. They will be able to increase prices by less than expected and some price increases which have taken place should be annulled. It may not be easy to obtain this downward flexibility in prices.

Monetarist explanations seem to assume that producers have no control over their prices. Prices are seen as being determined by market forces (Friedman, 1974, 1975, 1977 and Lucas and Rapping 1970). Thus, employers increase production when they perceive an increase in the price of their product. If there is an increase in all prices and employers correctly perceive this to be an increase in all prices they do not change their output; it is only when some of the general price increases are mistakenly interpreted as increases in demand for their own products that employers are assumed to increase output. This is a very peculiar view of employers. It sees them as having no control over their prices but passively responding to the market, and raising prices by adopting a constant price-wage mark-up, as wages rise in order to recruit more labour. Many employers do not behave in this automatic unthinking way.

Employers may adjust either output or prices, or both, in response to perceived changes in demand for their product. The choice they make will influence their demand for labour. It need not follow that equilibrium in the product markets is matched by equilibrium in the labour markets. When there is a reduction in demand and output it is more likely that there will be disequilibrium in labour markets as both money and real wages and their rate of change either adjust very slowly or do not adjust at all. There will then be an excess supply of labour.

If there is a long-term tendency for the labour–capital ratio to decline as a result of technological improvements less labour will be needed to produce a given output. The reduction in employment could feed back through lower incomes into imbalances in demand and supply in the output markets. There is no inherent reason why the subsequent adjustments should lead to equilibrium in both markets.

With a collective-bargaining-based NAIRU there is no a priori reason to suppose that the NAIRU is associated with equilibrium in product markets. It does not follow that equality of bargaining power is a function of the supply and demand position in the product market. Fear of unemployment by the existing work-force may be a powerful deterrent to trade union attempts to increase real wages, but even with a tight monetary policy real demand will be increasing in some sectors, and so real wages could well rise. Unless it is assumed that these will be offset by reductions in real wages in other sectors there is no reason to assume that inflation or the NAIRU will remain constant, or that the actual level of unemployment will be the NAIRU level.

Reductions in the labour–capital ratio resulting from technological change and improved efficiency mean that a given output can be produced by less labour. If this occurs the NAIRU will change. However, trade unions may seek to prevent it from occurring. They may press for job maintenance, and the mixture of real wage improvements and job maintenance provisions that emerge from collective bargaining will influence not only the NAIRU but the actual level of unemployment as well. In a situation in which labour markets do not clear there is no reason whatever to assume that output market equilibrium will be associated with labour market equilibrium in either an unemployment–vacancies relationship or in a constant rate of inflation sense.

Measuring the NRU

All attempts to relate the concept of the NRU to the available statistics of unemployment have difficulties. The Friedmanite version of the NRU as 'true' frictional or transitional does not form the basis of official statistics. As we have seen in Chapter 10 the current official UK series of unemployment reflects administrative decisions and is based on entitlement to Unemployment Benefit. To try to discover the NRU it is therefore necessary to adjust the figures of measured unemployment.

$$\text{Measured } U = Fr(U) + \text{NonE } U + \text{SETM} + \text{Vol } U \pm SR. \qquad (14.14)$$

Friction unemployment is 'frictional' in the Friedman sense of the NRU.

NonE U = Non-employable unemployed who may appear in the unemployment statistics, e.g. the 1982 changes included 23,000 severely disabled persons previously excluded. It may be argued that in addition there are some who are virtually unemployable even though they are not regarded/registered as severely disabled—'the hard-core unemployables'.

SETM = Special employment and training measures, schemes introduced by government specifically to alleviate unemployment, but are not employment.

In December 1984 there were some 662,000 covered by SETM. The Department of Employment estimated that this reduced the number who would otherwise have claimed Unemployment Benefit and therefore have been included in the measured unemployment figures by 475,000. The assumption, used in the concepts relating to the NRU, that $E + U = 1$ does not correspond to reality.

VolU = Voluntary employed who may be included despite the UB rules.

SR = Rules and conventions adopted in compiling the Measured Unemployment statistics. For example the change of rules in October 1982 reduced Measured U by 246,000, and the 1983 Budget changes removed a further 130,000. (see Chapter 10).

It is doubtful if the NRU can ever be measured accurately. The concept rests on an assessment of the motivation or attitudes of the unemployed—whether they are truly frictionally or structurally unemployed, or whether they are voluntarily unemployed, and we have no satisfactory way of classifying the unemployed by these criteria. Further, even if we could adjust the official statistics there would still be some involuntary unemployed included if there were some individuals who were unemployed because the actual wage levels resulting from legislation or collective bargaining were higher than their individual reservation wages and the value of their marginal productivity to employers. These can only be regarded as frictional if it is accepted that they will remain permanently searching unless the value of their marginal productivity to an employer increases. This Flying Dutchman component of 'frictional' unemployment can be removed only if the statutory or collective bargaining provisions are abolished. Even then there could be some individuals whose expected marginal revenue product was so low as to make it virtually inconceivable that they would be employed.

The various attempts to quantify the NRU which we showed earlier in this chapter might be welcomed as valiant attempts to shed light on a particularly difficult concept. As indicators of the level of unemployment which the government should aim at in order to ensure stable inflation they are of little use. This is not because these individual estimates are erroneous but because the very nature of the concept as well as the basis on which official statistics are compiled prevent any reliable quantification from being made to form the basis of policy-making, or indeed be relevant to actual policies in the real world at all. The best that can be claimed is that the NRU should be regarded as a somewhat indeterminate range of unemployment figures, and a range which is constantly shifting.

If the NRU is unknowable, in practice if not in principle, the centre-piece of the Monetarists contribution to employment–inflation policy has gone. If the government cannot know what the NRU is, it cannot form a rational or correct view about what it should be doing to the money supply. Policies based on other economic approaches are not affected so adversely by the impossibility of knowing the NRU. Keynesian-based demand management policies, possibly supplemented by other structural policies or incomes policies, do not rest their approach on the two variables of the NRU and the quantity of money. They are more concerned to change the rates of inflation and unemployment rather than to move to a particular specified equilibrium position.

One point should be emphasized. The level of real wages is crucial to the determination of the NRU. If, as we believe, the level of acceptable real wages is not constant but subject to change as a result of various social and political, as well as economic factors, there is both an element of uncertainty in all attempts to quantify the NRU and a margin of opportunity for governments. If it is possible to obtain acceptance of lower real wages the NRU will fall, provided that the reduction in real wages does not lead to such a reduction in anticipated demand for products that employers will reduce rather than increase their planned output. Conversely, if real wages rise output and employment may fall as employers anticipate lower real demand for their product even after taking a reduction in the profits and reducing the wage–price mark-up.

Real wages do vary, they rise and fall, in the short-to-medium run. There is no reason to believe that individual real reservation wages do not also rise and fall through time. Changes in acceptable real wages, whether this be seen as changes in individual or collective real reservation wages, may, even within the confines of a Monetarist analysis, be of more importance in changing the NRU than many of the factors listed by Monetarists.

Conclusions

The NRU is obviously of vital importance to an economy run on Monetarist policies. It is the level of output and employment at which the economy will operate in the long run. Short-run deviations may occur but the economy will adjust back to the NRU. According to Friedman it is determined by 'real' factors which presumably includes everything but the quantity of money. We have indicated (equations 14.8 and after) some of the variables which can influence the NRU. These show the considerable scope available to a government to influence the level of unemployment and output. But they also show the folly of assuming that the NRU is likely to remain constant. There is a vast array of factors which can, do, and will shift the NRU.

It has been argued above that the more important of these may be those factors which influence the individual, and perhaps more particularly, the collective, reservation wages of different workers. The central role of industrial relations and the legal, economic, and political contexts which influence the processes and especially the results of collective bargaining, have been emphasized. In particular, it has been argued that the real wage labour supply price or reservation wage is not constant, and should not be expected to be. Indeed there is likely to be a long-term tendency for trade unions to raise it.

The concept of the NAIRU has been developed to escape the market-clearing equilibrium connotations of the NRU. With NAIRU there may be equilibrium only in the sense that at that level of unemployment inflation will be constant and presumably all price expectations will be met. In some versions there may be the notion of the balance of collective bargaining power rather than the balance of supply and demand in the labour markets. However, this could lead to a constantly rising NAIRU if trade unions are able to increase real wages faster than the rate of productivity growth. A target real wage level at which the economy will operate at any time may not be known or known in advance. Acceptable real wages may be lower than the target real wage or the perceived fair or 'entitled' real wage as trade unions accept what are seen as temporarily low real wages which are subsequently to be restored to their 'proper or fair' level. The NAIRU will then be unstable.

NAIRU explanations emphasize either the labour market adjustment factors such as LMI, LFPR, and HP, or may concentrate on the industrial relations factors in equation (14.12).

Even if there is some advantage in the concept of the NRU for theoretical purposes it is of little, if any, practical use. We cannot measure it, and if we could, by the time we had done so and interpreted the effects of our policy measures, it would almost certainly have changed. Some of the proposals for lowering it might actually have the perverse effect of raising it by leading to an increase in real reservation wages.

The NRU or NAIRU should be seen, at best, as providing broad guidance as to the sort of policies which governments should introduce if they wish to increase employment. To Monetarists they provide the only ways of increasing employment in the long run. Keynesians will add the possibility that an increase in aggregate demand might do so, and do so more quickly than the micro- or structural policies associated with attempts to shift the NRU.

Finally, we should remember that to refer to the NRU or NAIRU at all may indicate a prior political judgement. It is just as meaningful to refer to the NRI—the Natural Rate of Inflation—as being that rate which is consistent with a constant level of unemployment.

Notes to Chapter 14

1. This account follows that used by Thirlwall (1983).
2. For further discussion see Thirlwall (1983) and Brown in Thirlwall (1982).
3. For a more detailed and more technical discussion see Thirlwall (1983).

CHAPTER FIFTEEN

Changing the Natural Rate of Unemployment

WE have sought to demonstrate in Chapter 14 that the NRU or NAIRU cannot be known as a quantified rate of unemployment, and that even as a concept it is of little assistance to policy-makers because, determined by a multitude of factors, it is likely to be subject to constant change. There might therefore seem little point in continuing to use the concept. We will do so for two reasons. First, it is not only an accepted, but a central, part of the Monetarists' approach to the labour market and as we are considering Monetarism we shall continue to use their terminology. Second, governments which reject Monetarism have nevertheless to deal with the problems of inflation and unemployment, and while the NRU is of little assistance because the implied precision of the level of unemployment associated with constant inflation is misleading, the notion that there are features of the 'real' economy which may influence the level of unemployment associated with constant, or with higher or lower, inflation, is useful. Thus without accepting the concept of the NRU, we can discuss, in terms associated with the NRU, factors which might raise or lower the level of unemployment associated at a particular time with any given level of inflation, or conversely, the rate of inflation associated with any given level of unemployment without accepting that there is any stable or known rate of trade-off between the two. It is not necessary to accept that there is either a Phillips curve or an expectations-augmented Phillips curve to believe that some features of the economy may reduce unemployment without increasing inflation.

As Monetarists deny any role for governments to influence inflation or unemployment in the long term through demand management or monetary policy, action to change the NRU is the only area open to them if they wish to influence the level of unemployment. The only significant exception to this is the point made by Laidler that demand-management policies may enable an economy operating above its NRU to move more quickly towards it in some circumstances. Different policy areas which may be available to governments will be grouped under broad headings to indicate their interrelatedness. This will follow general Monetarist lines but it does not follow that the measures will necessarily have the results expected by Monetarists. We will indicate the variables from Chapter 14 which are relevant to the different policy measures.

Changing the Employment/Unemployment Decisions of Individuals (UB, QR, LO, LFC, LFPR, IRW)

Unemployment and related benefits

The level of unemployment benefits and other payments to the unemployed is regarded by most Monetarists as an important factor in determining individual reservation wages, the incidence and length of periods of unemployment. Put simply, this argument rests on the view that people may choose to become or remain unemployed because the net gain in disposable income which they would receive from working is insufficient to induce them to accept the unpleasantness of working. If the replacement ratio (RR) were lower, it is argued, there would be a greater incentive to find work, or the reservation wage would be lower. Thus, at any given level of wages, the lower the RR the greater the incentive to find and accept a job, the lower the reservation wage and the lower the NRU.

A variation is based on absolute levels rather than some ratio between unemployment income and reservation wages so that a reduction in the *absolute* real level of UB could increase the incentive to work without there necessarily being any reduction in the RR. The social security system is seen as providing a floor below which wages will not fall (Minford 1982). If the floor were lowered real wages could, and presumably would, fall and the demand for labour would presumably rise. The acceptable RR could be the same before and after the cuts in benefits, but real wages would be lower. Indeed, on this interpretation the RR could actually rise if Unemployment Benefits were cut and there could still be a reduction in real wages and unemployment. On this view it is the level of Unemployment Benefits which hold up real wages and not the replacement *ratio*. This is particularly important in Minford's explanation, where the trade unions may have the power to prevent wages falling in the organized sector and the level of Unemployment Benefit floor limits the extent to which the surplus labour to the unorganized sector can drive down real wages. This 'involuntary' unemployment thus raises the NRU.

Unemployment Benefit may also increase the NRU in another way if 'the availability of unemployment insurance makes it more attractive to enter the labour force in the first place' (Friedman 1977, 15). The increased participation rate in itself may increase the NRU and, if the additional participants have higher than average propensities to be unemployed more frequently or for longer periods, this too may raise the NRU.

The replacement ratio is not an unambiguous concept nor is it easily measured. General practice is to measure it as the ratio of income when out of work to income from the last or normal job. This is the historical or backward-looking RR. Of more relevance to the notion of incentive or disincentive to accept a job if unemployed is the future or forward-looking RR. This is the ratio of unemployment income to expected income from the *next* job, and it is this which links up with the concept of the individual reservation wage for the unemployed, by indicating, perhaps, the amount of wage-income necessary to induce the unemployed individual to accept a job. The historical RR might be relevant to the decision to leave a job voluntarily and become unemployed, but the decision to remain unemployed ought, within the framework of the economic analysis which emphasizes this approach, to be determined by the future RR. There may obviously be connections between the two. Expected future earnings may be based on experienced past earnings, at least initially, although, as the job-search literature suggests, expectations of future earnings may change as a result of the experience of unemployment and job search.

There have been a number of studies attempting to assess the effect of RRs on unemployment.[1] They all face certain problems. It is extremely difficult to calculate the RR of an individual as it depends very much on the specific family circumstances of the individual concerned. Estimates of average RRs for individuals with 'typical' family responsibilities, e.g. married with a non-working wife and three dependent children, have been made in some studies but even if some degree of accuracy is obtained in the calculation of the entitlement to various benefits there is a major problem relating to the estimate of the income when in work. Average earnings for various occupations can be used but there is considerable spread of earnings around the average so that the lower-paid individuals will have higher RRs than the average. Even the calculation of typical benefits encounters problems as an allowance for rent is included in Supplementary Benefits and this will vary from individual to individual. The studies seem to agree that the ratio of benefit to net income for the assumed typical married man with two children rose fairly steadily through the 1960s, with a sharp jump in 1966, following the introduction of the Earnings Related Supplement to Unemployment Benefit.

The DHSS undertook a cohort study of just over 2000 men who registered as unemployed in autumn 1978, and remained unemployed for at least three months, so the analysis is not typical of all unemployed males, but is perhaps representative of about 40 per cent of them.[2]

The ratios calculated by the DHSS do not take account of such things as tax rebates, redundancy payments, or fringe benefits from employers when in work, such as free or subsidized meals. For 46 per cent of the sample the benefit–earnings ratio was less than 50 per cent, and only 16 per cent had a ratio above 80 per cent. Six per cent received benefits larger than their net earnings. Family income replacement ratios were generally higher. Slightly more than one-third had a ratio of less than 50 per cent: 'These men were predominantly young and single' (240). One-quarter of the sample had ratios of 80 per cent or more. Something like a third of these would have had lower income replacement ratios if they had claimed the full range of benefits to which they were entitled when at work. More than a half of married men with one or more dependent children did not claim means-tested benefits, such as reduced local authority rents, free school meals, or Family Income Supplement, while working.

Two of the factors which influence the relationship of income in work to income out of work are family responsibilities and housing costs. In general, the greater a man's family responsibility the smaller the difference between his income in and out of work. Social security assistance with housing costs can cause high income replacement ratios. If rents were increased and Supplementary Benefit continued to include a full rent allowance, the effect would be, of course, to increase the ratios. About 40 per cent of men received Supplementary Benefit. For just over one-tenth of the men the DHSS survey was unable to establish any record of payment during the nine weeks over which benefit income was averaged. These men at least can be totally cleared of the charge of being voluntarily unemployed because their unemployment-related benefits are too high; they were not receiving any.

Other characteristics of those with family income replacement ratios of more than 80 per cent are related to family and individual circumstances. Men with dependent wives were more likely to have high ratios than men with working wives. Men with occupational pensions accounted for almost a quarter of the group and were nearly all over the age fifty. None received Supplementary Benefit.

Estimates by Kay and Morris, taking account of the ending of ERS and the taxing of benefits, suggest that some 2 per cent of the working population might be better off not working, while 36 per cent of the short-term unemployed, and 43 per cent of the long-term unemployed, would lose half their income. The average short-term RR would fall from 74 per cent in 1978 to 58 per cent and the average long-term RR from 60 per cent to 55 per cent. 'Our calculations show that almost half the population would lose more than half their income if they were to be unemployed for any substantial period' (Kay and Morris 1982,

268). These estimates assume that individuals take up their full entitlements to Supplementary Benefits, rent and rate rebates, etc. and to the extent that they do not do so the calculations overstate the RRs.

Short-term RRs have had 'a very dramatic fall' (268) as a result of the ending of ERS and the taxation of Unemployment Benefit[3]. It is the support of Supplementary Benefit which has prevented them from falling even further—particularly the provision of a payment of rent in Supplementary Benefits.

It is simply not possible to establish by statistical analysis the extent to which, or even whether, high RRs have an effect in encouraging people to become unemployed or to remain unemployed. However, it should be noted that the rules governing payment of Unemployment Benefit provide for the suspension of benefit for up to six weeks if the individual left his last job of his own free will without 'just cause'. Any disincentive effect will be determined by the individual concerned, as will his reservation wage. An RR in excess of 100 per cent might provide no disincentive to work to individuals who believe that work is an expected and desired part of life in our society, or who feel stigma or loss of status if unemployed. Others might find an RR of 70 or 80 per cent sufficient to weaken their resolve earnestly to seek work. Further, as we discussed in Chapter 10, individuals might receive great disincentive to look for work from the prevailing economic circumstances and their perception of their relative attractiveness to potential employers. Any attempt to manipulate the levels of Unemployment and Supplementary Benefit in order to try to influence incentives must therefore rest on value-judgements and opinions about the way people behave, and what it is that motivates them.

The DHSS cohort study asked participants about their expected earnings if they found a job and the minimum they would accept. 'From the answers given it seems that many arrived at a minimum acceptable wage by simply deducting a few pounds from what they considered it reasonable to expect from the sort of work they were seeking' (*Employment Gazette*, January 1981, 31). A preliminary conclusion before detailed study of the effects of inflation on the expected and acceptable earnings figures, was that 'in real terms few of the unemployed expected an increase in their net pay and even fewer required an increase. By contrast, probably at least one-half were willing to accept a drop in their real pay' (32). 'In real terms at least one-third of those who had returned to work appeared to have taken a cut in their earnings' (31).

If this is a reasonable representation of the position of unemployed men there seems no need deliberately to reduce the real level of benefit in order to induce the unemployed to accept lower real wages. Their failure to take into account the effects of inflation in reducing the real value of their previous earnings already does this. It depends on how large a cut in real wages is being sought, perhaps for other reasons.

Reductions in reservation wages of some groups may lead them to apply for jobs which they previously ignored, but if the number of jobs offered does not increase this means only that there will be more people applying for the same number of jobs. Some of those now voluntarily unemployed, perhaps because their replacement ratio is high, may get some of the future vacancies if their RR is reduced. They will be offset by an equivalent increase in the number of involuntary unemployed who are unable to find vacancies at the prevailing wage levels, no matter what their replacement ratios might be.

If one believes that wages, perhaps only real wages, are flexible downwards as a result of supply-and-demand factors, then reductions in RRs may have some effect in reducing unemployment if the lower ratios lead to lower reservation wages. If there is a shift in real wage labour-offer supply curves, employment will rise and the NRU will fall. The key variable is then the wage elasticity of demand for labour.

It is important to emphasize the key role of the assumption that wages adjust to supply and demand in this way. An extreme version of this view is incorporated in the Liverpool economic model. 'Unemployment, for example, is voluntary. If a man loses his job owing to a surprise shift in demand against his firm, he then chooses to work elsewhere—probably at a lower net-of-tax wage (and with the cost of moving) or to take social security benefits. Wages go to a level at which demand for labour equals supply, given these benefits' (Minford and Peel 1981, 4.) Labour supply is influenced by benefit levels and supply and demand for labour determine wages.

This Liverpool model suggests that 'a 10 per cent real cut in all social security benefits to the unemployed' has the result that 'real wages fall by 10 per cent and competitiveness increases by 18 per cent, permanently'. 'Unemployment falls as more people choose to work rather than take benefits' (5). A reduction of real benefits in its full impact 'reduces the real wages of those *in* employment as well as the unemployed and therefore spreads employment to the unemployed' (16). To a Monetarist there is further attraction in reducing the real benefit levels. It would reduce the PSBR or allow reductions in taxation. Minford and Peel estimate that every 10 per cent reduction in real benefits would save directly about £2bn per year in 1981–2 prices. It might be objected that such a cut in real benefits would impose socially undesirable hardship on a section of society which is already deprived as a result of unemployment; the deprivation can be in terms of real income or the social effects of being unemployed in a society in which the cultural values place high importance on the status associated with employment. Minford and Peel's reply would be: 'Those who remain unemployed will be worse off, but their decision to remain unemployed will be a voluntary one; the question society must ask is whether the subsidization of the unemployment decision is worth the cost in output and employment' (16).

It is no doubt morally easier to adopt a Pontius Pilate attitude to the moral issues surrounding the question of how society should deal with the unemployed if one believes that unemployment is voluntary and asserts that supply and demand do, rather than perhaps should, determine wages. It is more difficult to wash one's hands of responsibility if one does not accept the definitional tautology that all unemployment is voluntary. However, it is important to note that Minford and Peel's argument does not rest upon a reduction in the replacement *ratio*. In their model it appears that both real benefits and real wages decline by 10 per cent so that the average RR might be unaffected. Indeed, if the unemployed seek work in certain parts of the labour market, perhaps that sector where wages are more flexible downwards, which might be the non-union sector, real wages there could fall by more than the 10 per cent reduction in average real wages, so that the RR could actually rise. It is the reduction in real benefit *levels* which pull down real wages which is assumed to lead to more employment and a reduction in the NRU.

If even high RRs, say those over 80 per cent, do not have any strong disincentive effects, the argument in favour of reducing benefits must rest on a belief that there is a strong positive incentive effect to find work from low RRs, say about 50 per cent. Those with high RRs tend to have large families or be low wage-earners already. In the great majority of these cases it is likely that reducing their RRs will have little significant effect on the labour market; it will not drive down real wages in the non-union sector very far, if at all, and is unlikely to have any noticeable effect on the Natural Rate of Unemployment. There may be substitution as some unemployed take jobs, passing on their employment to others. The NRU will then decrease only to the extent that these new unemployed have a greater tendency to withdraw from the labour market than have the present unemployed. This would be reducing the NRU in a statistical sense. For the rest, the NRU will fall only if the real wage labour-supply curve shifts as the unemployed reduce their real reservation wage and this leads to an expansion of employment opportunities through an increase in demand for labour.

As Kay *et al.* (1980) point out, it is a political question how society should treat its unemployed, and no doubt this will be influenced by the extent to which one believes that the unemployed are to some extent responsible for their own position. It is difficult to arrive at the conclusion that in 1985 large numbers of the unemployed are voluntarily so, and this might lead us to question whether reducing the RR is really intended to provide an incentive to people who are not disposed on present RRs to look for work, to start actively seeking it, whether on bicycles, through Job Centres, or by other means, or whether the real intent is to obtain the reduction in real wages of those *in employment*, not by effectively reducing the RR but, as Minford and Peel advocate, by so cutting real living standards of the unemployed that they are driven to obtain work at lower real wages than currently exist.

It is not the replacement ratio which generates the pressure, but the depressed absolute living standards of the unemployed who seek to obtain some minimum standard of living by somehow driving down real wages because their out-of-work real incomes are intolerable. It is a remarkable alliance of the Monetarists' and Marx's reserve army of the unemployed coerced by a less than socially acceptable minimum subsistence level of Unemployment Benefits.

The administrative rules and the way in which they are implemented might also affect the NRU. The rules of the UB scheme are intended to prevent voluntary unemployment and individuals receiving Unemployment Benefit are required to be available for and to accept suitable employment openings. Clearly there is considerable room for interpretation of these requirements. It is also sometimes claimed that a considerable number of the officially counted unemployed actually have some paid employment through 'moonlighting' or some other form of participation in the grey economy. Folklore is plentiful but hard evidence, understandably, hard to come by. It would no doubt be possible to reduce the numbers appearing in the official statistics as a result of administrative action but this might merely be a euphemism for a return to the hardness of the Means Test of the thirties. The key area is that which determines whether an unemployed person has refused a 'reasonable' job-offer. This requires that a view be taken on the amount of occupational and perhaps geographical mobility it is regarded as reasonable to require an individual to accept if benefits are to be denied, and also on the wage level which is thought reasonable. No administrative system of unemployment or related social benefit can avoid these questions. We are unable to distinguish voluntary from involuntary or socially reasonable unemployment unless we provide such criteria.

If *any* vacancy within a specified locality which was within the range of abilities of an unemployed person was regarded as 'reasonable' and all unemployment and social security benefits denied unless the job-offer was accepted (as proposed by Minford and Peel), then it might well be the case that wages in the lower-paying jobs would be filled at even lower real wages than currently exist. It is also possible that this would lead to an increase in demand for labour in that sector and that unemployment and the NRU would fall. This would occur on the assumption that the individual's real reservation wage for these jobs would be reduced if all Unemployment Benefits were denied him. This would be taking the social security benefits wage-floor argument to its extreme. It is doubtful if such an extremity would be politically tolerable even in the present climate of hardening attitudes, and it would certainly be repugnant to anyone with concern for the plight of the unemployed. It could be defended only on the view that all unemployment is truly voluntary. Its employment effect would come through a changing of the range of occupations which unemployed individuals were compelled to consider. For example an unemployed fitter, draughtsman, or public sector professional made redundant by the government's cut-backs could presumably perform the job requirements for a vacancy as a canteen assistant and they could be denied benefits unless they accepted a job-offer as such. Sheer economic necessity might lead them to do so under a different UB regime. However, unless the demand for such jobs had a high wage elasticity of demand it is likely that the end result would be the displacement of existing workers, or those with less skills, merely transferring the burden of unemployment to other members of society. The employers, of course, might be reluctant to hire these enforced applicants, believing that they would move on as soon as a better opening became available, or that they were 'overqualified', which is sometimes a euphemism meaning that they would be unlikely to tolerate the working conditions and might try and organize a union.

Measures to crack down on 'moonlighting' and similar activities might have the effect of exerting stronger pressure on some individuals to look for a job, but whether this actually increases employment and reduces the NRU depends on the extent to which real wages would become flexible downwards *and* employment expands as a result of such a reduction in real wages. In the Keynesian explanation of involuntary unemployment a reduction in real wages alone was not sufficient to expand employment; there also had to be an increase in demand so that employers wanted to hire more labour.

In the last resort the opportunity for such measures to reduce the NRU will depend on political factors which determine attitudes to, and treatment of, the unemployed. As long as unemployment, or a significant part of it, is regarded as something outside the control of most people there will continue to be some element of compassion and caring in our treatment of the unemployed which should protect them from the worse ravages of the extreme voluntary unemployment advocates.

Research by Layard and Nickell (1985) concludes that the Replacement Ratio effect has influenced unemployment by around 0.4 percentage points since the 1950s, but that the level of UB was only one factor to be considered. The easing or hardening of the application of the UB and Supplementary Benefit rules could have had an effect, as could changes in people's attitudes to receiving UB and their attachment to the work-ethic.

Quit rate (QR)

The quit rate, or voluntary leaving of jobs, may be influenced by changes in the administration of Unemployment Benefits of individuals expecting to have a period of unemployment before the next job. Concentration on the NRU should not lead us necessarily to conclude that reductions in the QR and so in frictional unemployment is always desirable. The most efficient allocation of resources is a trial-and-error process, particularly in labour markets. Individuals do not know whether they will like, or be good at, a particular job until they have experience of it. Employers cannot really tell which members of their labour-offer supply are really acceptable until they have tried them out. People's preferences for certain types of jobs change and their abilities develop as a result of experience. Undue inhibition on voluntary mobility or QR, could lead to an inefficient allocation of labour with people stuck in jobs they neither like nor perform well. The first of these could lead to poor morale and low productivity and the second can obviously reduce efficiency if there are other people elsewhere who can perform the job better but are themselves inhibited from moving. What we should be looking for is a system in which there is perhaps quite considerable mobility as people test out different sorts of jobs and match the job requirements against their abilities and preferences, yet which, by the provision of better labour market institutions, reduces frictional unemployment in both incidence and duration. This could be done by improved facilities for job change while still employed so that frictional unemployment becomes minimized and is no longer needed as part of job search. Certainly the greater part of white-collar professional job mobility seems to be the result of on-the-job search without frictional unemployment.

Lay-offs, dismissals, and redundancies (LO)

Employers' decision to shed labour will be influenced by the level of demand and expected demand for their products, changes in the capital–labour mix which may be influenced by technological advances, the existing relationship between manning scales or capital–labour mix and the optimum or attainable mix, decisions regarding the location of production, and trade unions' willingness to accept reductions in employment. The latter may be affected by the financial provisions made available to the redundant employees and the individual workers may have different views and preferences from trade unions. Individuals may accept redundancy if the financial provisions are considered satisfactory and this was an important reason for introducing the Redundancy Payments Act. Trade unions, taking a broader and longer-term view, may seek to preserve employment opportunities for other members and future members of the work-force. Legislative provisions may facilitate the acceptance of redundancy, for example by allowing workers to receive the equivalent of a state retirement benefit before normal retirement age on conditions that they withdraw from the work-force, i.e. they do not claim Unemployment Benefit.

Lay-offs and/or redundancy need not lead to an increase in the NRU if the redundant workers are able to obtain other jobs without any intervening period of unemployment. Provisions to help redundant workers find other jobs before their redundancy date can therefore allow job changes without any frictional unemployment. In cases of large-scale redundancies Job Centres may open special offices on the employers' premises to help those under notice of redundancy to find other jobs. This is one reason why employers may be required to give prior notice of redundancies in order to qualify for the full contribution to redundancy payments from the Redundancy Payments Fund. Such advance notice will reduce the NRU only to the extent that there are suitable jobs available for the redundant workers. If there are insufficient jobs available the assistance to workers under notice of redundancy may only lead to a shift in the incidence of unemployment as they get jobs which might otherwise have gone to other unemployed people.

Labour force composition (LFC)

The composition of the labour force is a function of the demographic features of the population, the labour force participation rate decisions, and the administrative rules adopted regarding the definition of the unemployed. A change in the minimum and maximum ages which provide the normal boundaries of unemployment will alter the definition and coverage of what is meant by the labour force. As those undergoing full-time education are not counted as unemployed a change in government policy regarding the encouragement or provision of educational facilities beyond the normal or minimum school-leaving age will have the effect of reducing the number of younger members of the work-force. To the extent that this group tends to have a higher rate of job change with intervening periods of unemployment, the NRU and recorded level of unemployment will fall.

Improved information about work and different sorts of jobs, and more and better counselling of young people about job opportunities, might lead to a better match-up between young workers and employers' job requirements. We ought to expect new and recent entrants to the work-force to have higher job turnover as they gather experience about the range of jobs available to them, the actual nature of work and job requirements, and their own aptitudes.

Considerable involvement with various MSC programmes for young workers and school-leavers under the Youth Opportunity Programme and various special schemes, and discussions with employers, leads me to the conclusion that schools do not equip many young people with appropriate information with which they can make realistic choices of jobs. It may be that some young people have expectations of job content, job satisfaction, or pay levels which are unrealistic and that their high turnover is part of their search for their high expectation levels, so that their early years of employment consist of a process of downward adjustment of their expectations and aspirations to a more attainable level. If this is so, improved information flows during the last years at school might help them form more realistic expectations. It may also be that the education system is not providing them with the skills and abilities to perform the sort of jobs which they are encouraged, or independently come to believe, they might get. The Careers Service could provide this sort of guidance if it had more resources, but often this is too late a stage.

There is, and will remain, a debate about the purpose of the educational system and the extent to which it should prepare people for the sort of work experience and range of employment opportunities they are likely to face rather than assist them to develop as full human beings. Without seeking to adopt a position of urging that the educational system become only a preparation ground for the workers of the future with no intellectually broadening content, it does seem to be the case that if the products of the educational system are regarded by employers as not possessing the skills, aptitudes, and attitudes which match the job requirements there is a danger that unemployment will remain high. Employers may not be willing to change their job requirements or incur the cost of providing the additional training necessary to take the young people up to the employer's perceived acceptable standards. If we are concerned about the level of unemployment, and particularly the high incidence among young workers and school-leavers, we may perhaps have to consider whether some action might not be necessary to ensure that the educational system does better to ensure that its products are closer to the requirements of employers. Unemployment is too serious a problem and its consequences for both the individual and society too painful and costly, for us to ignore possible methods of dealing with a main contributory factor.

The number of married women in the labour force may also increase the NRU if they have a higher propensity to change jobs, although this will now have less effect on the NRU as measured by published official statistics of unemployment as the new system of counting excludes some of them. However, over a number of years this effect will diminish as an increasing number of married women in full-time employment contribute fully to the National Insurance scheme and become entitled to claim Unemployment Benefits.

Labour force participation rate (LFPR)

LFPR varies mainly as a result of the decisions of married women to enter or leave the work-force. Males not undergoing full-time education have high participation rate with the exception of special groups such as occupational pensioners—those who have retired from their 'normal' job with a pension from the employer but have not yet qualified for the state retirement pension.

Married women's participation rate may be influenced by the age and size of their family as a result of the social convention that normally it is wives who stay at home to care for children. The perceived opportunity to obtain employment may influence their decision, so that demand creates its own supply as more married women become available for work the greater the number of jobs open to them. The earnings or employment position of husbands or other members of the household may also influence the participation decision. Taxation policy regarding the joint or separate taxation of husband and wife's earnings which can affect the net disposable income from a given gross wage may also exert some influence, as may the willingness of employers to adapt working hours to meet the family needs of married women (Robinson 1968). The provision of crèches or nurseries may encourage married women to enter the labour force and their abolition discourage participation. These factors may also influence the decisions of single-parent heads of households.

There is room for manoeuvre for government to influence the LFPR decision which will have an impact on the NRU, both in terms of total labour supply and in terms of the extent and incidence of frictional unemployment if some groups have higher propensities to change jobs. To the extent that these groups do not appear in the official unemployment figures there may not be any obviously noticeable effect on the

NRU, but this is the consequence of the relationship between the NRU and the official count as indicated in equation (14.14).

Individual reservation wage (IRW)

To the Monetarist believer, the individual reservation wage lies at the heart of the determinants of the NRU for this, in the absence of 'distortions' from trade unions or legislation on minimum wages, establishes the supply of labour. The employers' demand for labour, interacting on the real wage labour supply curve, determines the location of the expectations-augmented Phillips curve and thus the level of the NRU. If the labour supply curve does not slope upwards, however, as we have discussed in Chapter 14, the NRU is not a single point but a range of different levels of unemployment and there is then scope for demand-management policies to expand employment without inflation. The importance of the individual reservation wage, or allowing for 'distortions', the collective reservation wage, to a Monetarist explanation of the NRU cannot be over-emphasized.

We have previously discussed views about the relationship between the IRW and the level of Unemployment Benefits. The position is clearly put by Hermione Parker (1982). Labour is not immune from the laws of supply and demand. In the absence of social security the wage-floor which might result from the interplay of supply and demand is the 'minimum living wage' (24). Because of competition from single people this could be lower than the minimum living wage for a family with only one wage-earner. If government introduces income maintenance for the unemployed the floor is set by social security plus an allowance for the disutility of work and Parker concludes: 'A net reward of £10 for a full week's work is taken as the absolute minimum necessary to offset what economists call the disutilities (disadvantages) of work. A few people might be satisfied with less; but most would expect more' (43). In fact there are many people receiving less than £10 a week to cover the disutility of work and they continue working. Whether the particular sum advanced by Parker is right, or even whether it is necessary to offer any premium in a society in which the work-ethic is so strongly imbued—or at least was until perhaps the ravages of unavoidable unemployment led people to reject old standards and attitudes in the face of perceived helplessness to influence their own fate and find work—the principle is asserted by Monetarists that the IRW is a function of UB.

In the absence of social security provisions for the unemployed there is still some minimum wage level or some floor to the IRW. To Parker this is the 'minimum living wage'—a notion which is in fact devoid of quantification. It could mean the minimum level of wage income on which it is possible for an individual to survive physically and still be in good enough physical condition to remain in employment, but we do not actually know what this level is. It is likely that there is some socially determined content to the minimum living wage so that it is not a bare physical subsistence level. Moreover, the social elements can come in the Parker approach. Single people may be willing to accept a wage on which they cannot physically survive if their parents are willing to subsidize them. If this happened, then the wage-floor would vary with the willingness of parents to subsidize their working children, which could be influenced by social factors, and the number of young people wanting to enter the particular occupations.

Central though the concept of the IRW is, there is in fact no basis on which we can calculate or specify in quantifiable terms what are its determinants. We can list various factors but we can then do no more than hope to influence the direction of change. A government determined to lower the IRW and which accepted the importance of the link with the level of UB, would be led to the inevitable conclusion that only a reduction in the real level of benefits paid to the unemployed *while they were unemployed* would have significant effect on their IRWs. This would of course run into direct conflict with any concern on social policy grounds for the welfare of the unemployed as it would require a reduction in their already low standard of living.

According to traditional economic theory if jobs could be made less unpleasant there ought to be a reduction in the reservation wages for them as there would be less disutility to overcome. Against this is the observation that most of the really pleasant and interesting jobs seem to be better paid than the hard unpleasant ones and that therefore there does not appear to be the inverse relationship between unpleasantness and pay which might be inferred from Adam Smith, but instead a Millsian relationship where pleasantness and pay often go together. Certainly there is little evidence of Monetarists advocating job enrichment as a way of reducing wages.

The area in which it might be possible to exert influence over IRW is that of expectations or attitudes as to what is a fair wage for a given job. This is a social as well as perhaps an economic question. In this regard Marx's notion of a socially necessary minimum wage is a better guide than the concept of a subsistence wage with its Malthusian connotations of bare physical survival. Wages are a social matter as well as an economic variable. People do have views about the lowest wage which it is proper or fair to accept, and while this may be influenced by social security provisions and other sources of income or support, it is not a rigid or automatic function of these factors. Moreover, no matter what some economists may say about the inevitability of economic forces or the dire consequences of preventing them from operating, society has advanced to the stage where it is not prepared to tolerate certain wage levels, even if the individuals are prepared, or compelled by lack of any other means of support, to accept them. But in many cases before that society-determined minimum is reached there may be pressures from the greater part of the work-force not to accept what are seen as exploitation or sub-acceptable levels. The socially determined minimum living wage may well exceed that based on economic forces.

Nevertheless, there may well be some scope for government to influence socially accepted standards. A sustained campaign of education, or indoctrination, according to your own value-judgements, might lead people to lower their IRW by persuading them either that they will not get a job at that wage level and they should therefore discontinue what will otherwise be a perpetually fruitless search for an impossibly high wage level, or that it is unreasonable or unfair to expect such a wage level in the present conditions. These both have the same effect but follow different lines of reasoning or persuasion. There are some who already adopt this strategy with young workers seeking to convince them that they are being priced out of jobs by high wage demands. This is discussed in Chapter 16.

The Operation of the Labour Market (LMI, HP, OcDi/OcSi, OM)

Labour market information and functioning (LMI)

The ways in which the unemployed job-seekers link up with employers with vacancies and become part of their acceptable-labour supply curves can obviously exert a considerable influence on the size of the NRU. The more quickly that job-seekers can be matched with vacancies for which they are acceptable the shorter the period of unemployment. There are two aspects to this. The sorting out of the various options, and the bringing together of suitable supplies and demands. The first involves, on the worker's side, a process of selection or decision-taking regarding the labour-offer supply curves he decides to join. On the employer's side it involves the assessment of the suitability of the individual job applicant in relation to those of other members, actual or potential, of the labour-offer supply curve, and the arrangements in the internal labour market which determine the jobs which are filled by recruitment from the external labour market.

On both sides of the labour market there are areas of uncertainty. The market institutions and arrangements can be seen as consisting of provisions which reduce both the uncertainty about the external conditions—those factors which are external to the parties to a particular employment offer or acceptance, and the personal factors which relate to the suitability of the particular individual for the specific vacancy in question. The external factors will include such things as the range of jobs available and the wages or conditions and job requirements attached to them. In some ways these might be regarded as objective features of the various local and occupational labour markets. The internal factors are more subjective in that they involve the individual applicant's assessment of the range of vacancies and the wages, etc. associated with them, but also include his suitability or acceptability for them. The external labour market information is general and impersonal in that it is the same for everyone. If there are vacancies in four firms for thirteen fitters this will be true no matter which individual collects the information. The personal labour market information is specific to each individual; some will be acceptable to some employers and not to others, and some may be acceptable or unacceptable to all.

Imbalances or mismatches in occupational supply and demand in the external labour market sense may require measures to shift the occupational demands and supplies. Imbalances due to personal factors may require action to change the aspiration of some job-searching individuals or the attitudes of employers as to the acceptability of some members of their labour-offer supply curves. Such a clear, neat division may be easier to make in principle than in practice but it is nevertheless an important and useful distinction in that it emphasizes that some of the frictional job-search unemployment may be due to different causes. In particular, job-search unemployment which arises from the continued attempt to enter an employer's acceptable-labour supply curve for which all employers believe the individual is unsuitable stems not from misperceptions about the number of vacancies and the wages etc. attached to them, but from misperceptions about one's own abilities or, perhaps, from misperceptions due to inexperience and ignorance of the general relationship between rewards and job requirements. Young people may have special problems in this regard.

Governments can seek to improve the workings of the labour market by enlarging the role of the employment service, but even an enlarged employment service is unlikely to provide all the information for which job-seekers may be looking. Some of the features of a job which influence its attractiveness or 'net advantages' may include such things as what sort of foreman they will be working under, the tightness or 'reasonableness' of the firm's disciplinary procedures, the willingness of the employer to respond favourably to personal requests for occasional time off, or changes in working time, or swapping duties, the opportunities for perks or 'fiddles', and so on. These might well be pieces of information which neither employment exchanges nor employers themselves are able or willing to provide. Informal contacts through friends and relatives might therefore be a much more effective source of information for some workers but may not be generally available. The information about wages from the official sources might not be very helpful either. Job-searchers might be interested in bonuses or overtime earnings available to them, rather than in averages or 'standard' hourly or weekly rate of pay. Information about the actual working conditions, job content, and job requirements from the worker's viewpoint might be very difficult to obtain without actual experience of the particular job in question. Even when this is obtained by experience it is impossible for the worker individual to make a full choice from all the jobs for which he could become part of an employer's acceptable-labour supply curve as no person can accumulate the knowledge of these job conditions and requirements in respect of jobs he has not actually done. This information is necessarily imperfect. This might not matter if the individual believes that the job in question is as good as he is likely to get, or is satisfactory in the light of past experience.

It is possible, of course, for government to take the view that such information is best provided by the market itself and that institutions and arrangements will develop to correct any deficiencies and defects in the availability of information. Private employment agencies and the activities of individuals and employers seeking to maximize their own utility or profit functions might be expected to develop satisfactory arrangements, and if they choose not to do so it might be because they calculate that the cost of doing so outweighs the expected advantages to them. If this is the case it is unclear why the state should provide any information about vacancies or become involved at all in the hiring process, except in so far as information about vacancies is necessary in order to apply the administrative requirements of the Unemployment Benefit schemes and test whether the claimants have made reasonable efforts to find or accept a job. Without some information of the availability of jobs it is difficult to see how any benefit scheme which includes some obligation on the individual to accept reasonable job offers as a condition of receiving benefit can be implemented.

The Thatcher Administration supports the concept of private employment agencies and is sympathetic to their claims that the Job Centres and Professional and Executive Register scheme might somehow constitute unfair competition to their private profit-making activities, but not to the point of abolishing all the Job Centre placement activities. This recognition that there is a proper role for a state employment service should be taken to its obvious conclusion that if we wish to reduce the NRU by cutting down on the frictional job-search as well as wage-search activities we should consider enlarging the Job Centre system rather than cutting it down.

There is inevitably some element of conflict among the various objectives of an employment service which operates, from the employer's side at least, on a voluntary basis. The notification of vacancies and the request for assistance in filling them is a voluntary act by employers. There is no statutory requirement that they notify vacancies and except in time of war it is doubtful if there is wide demand for compulsory notification. It rings too much of a totalitarian regime. If employers are to notify on a voluntary basis they need to be satisfied that it is in their interests to do so. This places constraints on the Job Centres, who may wish to give special priority to the placement of long-term unemployed but who must bear in mind the individual employer's criteria for acceptable-labour supply. If Job Centres continually submit candidates regarded as unsuitable by the employer the obvious response of the employer will be to complain or to stop using the Job Centres as a source of recruitment. The latter step will further limit the ability of the employment services to place the unemployed. If employers believe that the long-term unemployed are unlikely to be acceptable, perhaps simply because they have been unemployed long term, Job Centres may be under considerable pressures to give priority in submission, not to those considered most deserving or necessarily best suited on other criteria, but those who meet the employer's requirement that they have not been unemployed for a long period. It may be that in some cases the mere experience of long-term unemployment reduces the individual's suitability for a job. His skills may be rusty or out of date, and there may have been some deterioration in morale and incentive. However, a long period of unsuccessful job search may have increased commitment and incentive.

'We have placed considerable emphasis on the issue of screening in examining employers' attitudes to the Job Centre (and in particular on the requirement that the Job Centre screen out "unsuitable" applicants).'[4] The end result is that submissions for vacancies are affected by age and length of time unemployed, and the short-term unemployed—less than four weeks—are more likely to be hired.[5]

There may, perhaps in times of rather lower unemployment, be opportunity for the public employment service to seek to change employers' attitudes so that they modify some of their generalizations regarding stereotypes among the unemployed. However, these factors may not exert much direct influence on the NRU in that they influence which individuals obtain jobs and which remain unemployed, but if there is any firm relationship between actual ability to meet requirements and length of unemployment, resulting from either a loss of skills or motivation, the perpetuation of long periods of unemployment among some groups of the unemployed could lead to a long-term rise in the NRU. In terms of the basic concept used previously, the prolonged unemployment could lead to some individual's value of marginal product falling below the even lower market wage that might result from the application of Monetarist policies, thereby leading to a permanent increase in the NRU.

The type of information that is available and the framework of attitudes and expectations within which it is interpreted, as well as the market mechanisms for bringing together buyers and sellers of labour, can exert considerable influence on the ease and speed with which the unemployed find jobs. In the artificial world of the Walrasian auctioneer this process is easily taken care of; during the *tâtonnement* process everyone (except perhaps the auctioneer) is unemployed, and then everyone who wants to work is immediately in employment. During the auctions those not employed are voluntarily unemployed because they have not found an offer that is acceptable to them. The buyers of labour are able to determine who is acceptable to them merely from the wage bids, perhaps because everyone is a member of a particular occupation and is known by the employer to be so and is therefore acceptable to the employers. As we have seen in the real world, the absence, in the main, of the conditions arising from the assumption of labour homogeneity means that the frictional unemployment, which results as *both* sides of the labour market need to find out about what the other is really offering, is an expected feature of even a full-employment economy, compounded by institutional frictions which often lead to gaps between leaving one job and starting another.

Skills Mismatch, Training, and Retraining (OcDi/OcSi, HKi, HK type, HK stock, Trgi, OM)

The NRU would be influenced by 'the way in which the skill mix required to fill vacancies was matched by that among the unemployed: that is, by the rapidity of adjustment of supply to demand in the labour market' (Laidler 1975, 44).

The adjustment need not necessarily be on the supply side. It is quite possible that the demand for particular skills or occupations changes in response to perceived supply positions. Employers may reorganize work by changing the job requirements just as they alter recruitment standards in response to their view of the type and quality of labour available to them. They may change their capital equipment so that they are able to reduce their demand for skills in short supply. Some adjustments may take time but others can be made fairly quickly.

It may be thought that a large part of labour market adjustment, particularly if unemployment is higher than usual, takes place on the supply side. The more that unemployed individuals desire jobs in their current occupation, and the greater the extent to which workers are in occupations which fully utilize their skills, the larger will be the impact on the NRU of mismatches in the skill content of U and V. Two sorts of skill mismatches can occur. In the first, the skills required to fill the vacancies are higher than those possessed by the unemployed. In the second, the unemployed have higher skills than are required to fill the vacancies.

A comparison of the occupational statistics of vacancies and unemployment for the UK, formerly published quarterly in the Department of Employment *Gazette*, shows that the first is the typical situation.[6] Even though there were problems with such comparisons, as the majority of vacancies are not reported, and the reported occupations of the unemployed may refer to their last job, the job they say they are seeking, or officially the sort of work for which the Job Centre thinks they are most suited or most likely to be hired, the statistics, nevertheless, provided some indication of the skill mismatches. There are always higher U/V ratios for unskilled and lesser skilled jobs with any given level of demand. The NRU will be higher than it would be were it possible either to change the composition of occupational demand by reorganizing job requirements so that more less-skilled labour was demanded, or to increase the skills possessed by the unemployed. An improvement in the mismatch would affect the NRU in two ways. The direct effect would be that some of the existing vacancies would be filled by the unemployed, thereby reducing the level of unemployment. The indirect effect would be that because the supply of higher-skilled occupations was increased there might be less labour market pressure on their wages which might not increase as quickly or by as much and this could reduce the rate of increase of wages in other occupations which maintained customary different tasks. As this would reduce the rate of increase of labour costs, and so prices, it would be possible to have a constant rate of inflation with a lower level of unemployment.

Measures to encourage changes in the skills of the unemployed are therefore obvious ways of reducing the NRU. Skill acquisition involves costs, either to pay for training or education, or as income forgone as a result of training rather than working. The training costs can be borne by the individual, as might be more common in the United States than in the UK, by the employer, or by the state. 'A broad estimate is that total resources currently going into vocational education and training amount to about £4bn a year. Very roughly, half of this comes from the taxpayer through government and half direct from industry, although proportions vary considerably between occupations, levels of qualification and areas.'[7] The total cost is about 2.5 per cent of GDP.

The main cost to employers is the wages, and there are also the salaries of training staff or course fees. Employers may also absorb the costs of providing on-the-job training (OJT) when workers are paid wages in excess of the costs of their current output while receiving informal training or are gaining the experience needed to fulfil the job requirements.

There may be some skill mismatch of the second type. Some unemployed may have skills for which there is no demand and the vacancies would not require their abilities. If there is unwillingness to move down the skill hierarchy the NRU will be higher as the skilled workers remain unemployed. If they are willing to accept lesser-skilled jobs, the NRU might fall or might not. It could fall if the increased labour-offer supply curve leads to a fall in wages in the lesser-skilled jobs which in turn leads to an expansion of employment. If, however, it does not lead to a reduction in wages, but merely to a shift in the employer's acceptable-labour supply curves, there will be a displacement effect. The higher-skilled will take jobs which would otherwise have gone to those who had only the previously acceptable level of skills, and the lesser-skilled will become unemployed. A crucial issue therefore is the determinants of wage levels. If wages are determined by market forces there might be a reduction in wages or an increase in productivity as a result of employing the higher-skilled workers at the same rate of pay, either of which could lead to a fall in the NRU.

Professionals and craftsmen in particular are reluctant to abandon their skills and trades after spending many years and incurring considerable costs in acquiring them. There will always be resistance to enforced downward occupational mobility. The UK has too few, rather than too many, skilled workers. What is needed to enable skilled workers more easily to adapt to changing requirements are measures to encourage people to change and improve their skills rather than work in less-skilled jobs.

The provision and cost of training and retraining obviously influence the supply of occupational skills. There has been a serious decline in the number of draft and technician apprentices in the engineering industry. The number of apprentices recruited by the industry halved between 1979 and 1982—the first four years of the Thatcher Government.[8]

The MSC's New Training Initiative sought to work towards a 1985 target whereby 'training should be to standards of competence without regard to age and that this should be accepted and implemented in both national and local practice by that date'.[9] It is doubtful whether the target will be achieved by 1985. There is deep-rooted reluctance by trade unions to accept adult trainees as fully qualified craftsmen. The

Manpower Services Commission has worked hard throughout its existence to obtain easier access to retraining facilities, but while the length and content of apprenticeship training for those entering as young people have undergone considerable change there has been less advance in regard to adults.

Monetarists have frequently criticized restrictions on entry into occupations, whether these be by trade unions or professional associations. Indeed, on occasions Friedman seems to suggest that even the licensing of medical practitioners is a harmful practice (Friedman and Friedman 1980). However, as long as employers, or the public, value the possession of some qualification as an indication of at least some minimum competence in certain fields or skills it is difficult to see how we can avoid some form of limitation over entry. It may be that if the examining body was external to the trade or profession there might be less tendency for the examining function to be converted into a restriction of numbers. The absence of external tests or qualifications would involve employers in higher selection and screening costs and this increase in labour costs could lead to less employment and so a higher NRU.

While it may sound attractive to assert that there should be no barriers to occupational mobility, what this frequently boils down to is the argument that there should be no improper barriers which merely or mainly operate to restrict supply to the advantage of the present members of those occupations. There are always some barriers—the abilities of individuals. There will always be some recourse to the use of qualifications as a screening device. There will no doubt always be reluctance on the part of the present members of an occupation or profession to train and admit large numbers of new entrants where this is seen as leading to a worsening of the terms and conditions of the present members. Measures to facilitate occupational mobility will therefore be a mixture of what might be economically desirable from the viewpoint of the general public, or the wider economic interest, and what is attainable given the interests of the existing members of an occupation. There will be, and perhaps can be, no absolute or perfect situation, but rather a series of changes, each of which might represent some compromise between the various interests.

An active labour market policy based on positive intervention to speed up the labour market's responses to skill shortages and mismatches can have a considerable part to play in reducing the NRU. Even if the Hayek argument that 'Full employment cannot be maintained by preserving a conventional, outmoded wage structure, but only by adjusting wages in each sector to changing demands, raising some wages and lowering others' (1980, 56) is accepted in its entirety there is still a valuable contribution from positive action in manpower policies. The market response may be slow and costly. The MSC are fully aware of the dangers in leaving it to market forces. Employers may be reluctant to invest in training when they have no guarantee that they will be able to retain the trained workers and recoup their training costs. Individuals may have insufficient funds to finance themselves. Hayek implies that the desired changes are only in relative wages, but these are desired only to facilitate the movement of labour from sector to sector. The wage mechanism alone is not the most sensitive or effective instrument for reallocating labour. An economy such as the UK which needs to adapt to changes in technology in order to compete requires an adaptable work-force able and willing to acquire new skills. Without government finance and intervention such changes are likely to be sluggish, insufficient, and inflationary. They will also lead to higher unemployment than need be. This is a great area of contradiction for Monetarists. As they are generally non-interventionists and advocates of market forces, they are reluctant to espouse increased government expenditure and intervention in training and manpower policies, yet these are the essential requirements for lowering the NRU in a technologically changing society.

SETM

As was shown in Chapters 10 and 14 SETM cover a substantial number of people. While they may have intended to provide the unemployed with additional training the better to equip them to find a job, they also have the effect of reducing the level of unemployment as officially measured. Between 1975 and August 1982 British governments introduced eighteen different measures.[10] Some were intended to operate on the demand side of the labour market by offering various forms of employment subsidies to prevent redundancies or short-time working, or to encourage employment expansion, either in general or for specific groups, or in certain locations or types of activity. These include the Temporary Employment Subsidy (see Deakin and Pratten 1982 for an excellent description and analysis of the effects of this scheme). There have been various Community Enterprise Schemes, Youth Opportunity Programmes, and the Youth Training Scheme, which include provisions to increase the demand for labour by offering employers wage subsidies and the opportunity to use trainees on productive work.

Some schemes offer job protection subsidies, perhaps to meet what are seen as temporary difficulties, while others encourage the creation of new jobs through some form of wage subsidy or a reduction in payroll taxes. EEC regulations may limit the type of scheme if it is thought it leads to unfair competition. Schemes may be more or less cost-effective. There is often a 'dead-weight' effect where employment would have been maintained even without the payment under the scheme. There may be a 'substitution' effect where employment is protected in the sectors receiving the support but falls elsewhere. The gross cost of the scheme may be much reduced by the saving on Unemployment Benefit and additional tax receipts on income from the maintained employment. Deakin and Pratten estimate that the TES had a net cost of only 30 per cent of the gross cost and each job saved added about five times its own gross cost to total output.

The Young Workers' Scheme introduced in January 1982 works directly on demand through the wage level. It provides a subsidy of £15 a week to the employer for each sixteen- or seventeen-year-old employed in their first year of employment, provided that the wage paid is less than £50 a week.

The Enterprise Allowance Scheme pays unemployed people who wish to start up their own business a flat-rate taxable payment of £40 a week for a maximum of fifty-two weeks. Applicants must have been in receipt of Unemployment or Supplementary Benefit for at least thirteen weeks and have at least £1000 to invest in their business.

Various special measures can be designed to encourage some individuals to withdraw from the labour force.[11] They reduce LFPR and may include a provision that participants must be drawn from those currently included in the official count of the unemployed. Some of the special measures not only have a direct obvious effect in reducing the numbers counted as unemployed but they are designed to do so. Others have the more laudable aim of helping firms or industries over what are expected to be temporary problems. Others seek to improve the skills and work experience of the unemployed, particularly the young unemployed. It is the last two types which should be encouraged. The manipulation of the recorded unemployment figures reduces the NRU only in the sense of creating a statistical facade. Measures to enable the unemployed to move into productive employment are the desired way of reducing both the recorded number of unemployed and the NRU. What is unfortunately unclear is the extent to which the vast amounts of public money spent on SETM and particularly the Youth Training Scheme does actually lead to any marked improvement in the skills, abilities, and employability of the young unemployed.

In July 1984 the various schemes were 'helping around 550,000 unemployed people and another 140,000 in jobs at a cost of some £2¼ billion a year'.[12]

Geographical Mismatch between Vacancies and Unemployment

At any moment of time there will be a number of unemployed and a number of vacancies. Some of these will be for the same skills but in different locations. It is recognized by all writers that labour is imperfectly mobile so that it is much more difficult to fill vacancies by hiring unemployed the further away those vacancies are from the homes of the unemployed. The greater the disparity between the geographical locations of vacancies and unemployment the higher the NRU.

Special measures could be introduced to encourage firms to expand employment in areas of high unemployment, but generally speaking Monetarists do not support increased government intervention through subsidies and similar measures to influence the location of industry, preferring to rely on market forces with as little government interference as possible. This leads them to turn their attention to those factors which are thought to hinder labour mobility, particularly if these can be ascribed to government intervention. The blame for a too high NRU can thereby be placed at the door of government, and the solution of increased reliance on free market forces reinforces their general position of reduced government involvement in economic affairs.

There are two aspects of the geographical mobility of labour. The first refers to the physical area of job search undertaken by an individual given the present place of residence; this covers the geographical area in which the individual regards it as reasonable to travel to work. The precise boundaries will, of course, vary from person to person. It might also be affected by the activities of other members of the household. Husbands and wives may take joint decisions regarding travelling to work together, or regarding the hours which either, or both, are prepared to spend away from home; this might be influenced by such things as the size of their family. The availability and cost of public transport can be relevant; the increase in private car ownership leads to an expansion of the geographical area of job search and increases in the cost of private motoring might reduce it. Policies regarding the subsidization of public transport can affect an individual's decisions regarding the distance he is prepared to travel, given the existing wage levels.

The second aspect is the ease with which individuals change their places of residence and, more particularly, the ease or difficulty with which unemployed workers respond to labour market conditions by moving to areas where there are vacancies. Again, we are currently assuming that wage levels are given for it is possible to argue that unemployed workers will move large distances to fill vacancies if only wages rise *enough*. We do not, of course, know just how much is enough, but for present purposes of examining the NRU and its determinants we assume existing real wages are fixed. The provision of grants and assistance to workers prepared to move to areas of labour shortage is one way of increasing geographical mobility. Some allowances are currently available but they are not very high and are insufficient to induce large geographical movement.

Some 2 per cent of the population migrates to another region each year, but movement out of depressed local labour markets is lower than from other areas (DTI 1984).

Mobility (MoB)

Housing policy

British Monetarists emphasize the importance of housing policy and the housing market in influencing the NRU.[13] One factor is the effect that the subsidization of council house rents has on increasing the NRU. The argument is that if workers are living in subsidized council houses (or, for that matter, in any accommodation where the rent is below the market level) they will require a higher real wage to induce them to leave it, unless they are assured of similar subsidized housing in the new area. This is saying that if RRW_a is the reservation real wage in the present subsidized house, where the subsidy is equivalent to S_1, then the reservation real wage in another area, RRW_b, which involves leaving subsidized accommodation, must be

$$RRW_b = RRW_a + S_1 + R_b + Mob \qquad (15.1)$$

where R_b is the excess of the rent in the new locality over the previous rent plus subsidy, and *Mob* is an additional wage element necessary to induce them to incur the costs and inconvenience of leaving one area and moving to another. *Mob* can be seen as a discounted rate of a lump sum which would, if given as a one-off payment, compensate the individual. Thus the individual is assumed to be willing to work for the same reservation real wage in the new location as in his present one but requires additional real wages to make up for the higher housing costs, and a payment to induce him and his family to accept the social and economic costs of leaving his present house. Many employers recognize these elements by making lump-sum payments to their employees who are required to move from one part of the country to another and, in practice, there is often a pay increase or promotion associated with the transfer as well. If the cost of accommodation in the new locality is equal to the unsubsidized rent in the existing accommodation, $R_b = 0$. Because people who leave council houses in one area cannot easily obtain alternative council house accommodation and so may have to move into expensive private accommodation, R_b may be very high. Because the housing market is not a free market but one characterized by rent controls, there is a very limited supply of private housing for renting so that mobility may be hindered by the availability of privately owned accommodation.

It is the relationship between the existing real wage in the second locality RW_b and the reservation real wage, RRW_b, which determines whether labour is geographically mobile or not.

If U_g is the unemployment in the economy which results from geographical mismatch between unemployment and vacancies, so that we are conceptually isolating this factor from such things as occupation change, then

$$U_g = f(RRW_b - RW_b) \qquad (15.2)$$

Proposals to reduce council house subsidies are seen as leading to a reduction in the NRU presumably because a reduction in S_1 in equation (15.1) is seen as leading to a reduction in RRW_b and so to a reduction in U_g. However this should not be taken to mean that if all council house subsidies were removed tomorrow there would be an increase in geographical mobility and a reduction in the NRU.

The arguments underlying the proposal to reduce council house subsidies in order to encourage labour mobility rests on the assumption that if S_1 is lower the real reservation wage in the present location will be lower and so the RRW in another area will be less. This does not fit in at all easily with the Monetarist arguments about the impact of Unemployment Benefits of the RRW. In the UK unemployed workers, excluding wives living with their husbands, may qualify for social security benefits as well as unemployment benefit. Householders are entitled to payment of their housing rent and rates and/or rent rebates. Reducing council house subsidies might have no effect on the real income of unemployed householders as the higher rents would be offset by higher social security payments. Their unemployment income will not therefore be affected and so there need be no effect on their RRW in their present location. There may be some effects on the distribution of resources between central and local government but that is another issue.

If RRW_a does not fall as a result of ending council house subsidies it is difficult to see how there can be any effect on RRW_b. Indeed the perverse effect which should be expected by those holding strong Monetarist views about the necessity to provide a financial incentive to the unemployed to induce them to accept the disutility of work is that the real reservation wage in both the present and other localities should rise. If the increase in rents leads to higher money income from benefits to the unemployed merely to maintain the same level of real net disposable income, then, if there is some relationship between unemployment real income and the real reservation wage, a higher money reservation wage is necessary in order to maintain the same real net disposable income reservation wage. The more reliable is the Monetarist version of worker motivation and the role of the replacement ratio in real terms the more should we expect to see the ending of rent subsidies lead to an increase in the NRU. Moreover, some unemployed heads of household who did not claim social security benefits before the removal of rent subsidies might be encouraged to do so if their rents were increased and this could actually lead to an increase in their RRW, and a further rise in the NRU.

Recent research by McCormick (1983) concludes that, relative to mortgages, tenants of unfurnished accommodation—both council and private—are more likely to be unemployed. So too are outright owners of their homes. After allowing for various contributory factors the higher probability of being unemployed is about 70 per cent for both groups. After further allowing for the higher rates of unemployment in those regions where council housing is concentrated the higher unemployment of renters in relation to mortgagees is in the 35–63 per cent range. McCormick suggests that both owners and renters may have higher 'natural rates' of unemployment than mortgagees. For owners, it may be due to their wealth and lack of short-term liquidity to meet mortgage payments. There is no evidence from this research that social security provision is patently generous and so the higher unemployment amongst tenants reflects a combination of locational and demographic characteristics together with a public policy towards unemployment incentives which is reasonably neutral between workers entering the rental or owner-occupier sector (304).

To cease including rent and rates in social security benefit entitlement would, of course, be a major issue, with implications far beyond that of trying to increase labour mobility and reducing the NRU.

There seems to be a misunderstanding of the relationship between labour mobility and the NRU. Thus Wood (1975) states that 'politicians help to raise the "natural" rate of unemployment more permanently by obstructing the mobility of labour through, for example, policies to perpetuate the housing shortage (rent control, planning restrictions, protected tenancies) . . .' (51). In a later work Miller and Wood said that 'Council housing and rent restriction are a major obstacle to the movement of housing to where it is most productive. Rent controls should be abolished to allow landlords to put their property on the market for letting and the purchase of council houses by tenants should be made even more attractive' (1982, 69). They go on to argue that statistically there has been an excess of housing over households for a decade, and this might now be approaching 1 million. 'The abolition of rent control could thus lead to a decline in rents and substantially improve mobility of labour' (70).

It is very difficult to understand why rent controls lead to higher rents. If there is an excess of housing we should expect landlords to charge less than the permitted maximum under the rent restrictions. However, even if this apparent misunderstanding of the way in which markets might work is removed, it certainly does not follow that the excess of housing is in areas which are experiencing a relative shortage of workers, i.e. those into which geographical mobility would take place. The crucial issue is whether rents in those areas would be higher than rents paid by the unemployed in their present location taking into account the provisions of social security benefits. Unless 'freeing' rents led to a reduction of rents in the new areas in relation to rents currently paid in the current location, increased labour mobility could be expected only at higher money wages than currently prevail. But at higher money wages employers may demand *less* labour.

Increased geographical mobility does not in itself lower the NRU. If the migrants more easily become part of employers' acceptable supply curves in the receiving areas there may be no more than a substitution effect as they take jobs which otherwise would have gone to residents in those areas. This might have some effect in preventing a fall in employers' expected VMPs, but this is not likely to have a very significant effect on the NRU. Much may depend on the terms on which the mobility takes place. If rents or housing costs rise either money wages must rise or real wages fall. Reductions in real wages can, of course, lower the NRU, providing that employers' expectations of future demand is not adversely affected as a result of a reduction in aggregate demand. It is difficult to avoid the conclusion that what many advocates of 'freer' housing markets are after is a reduction in real incomes through higher housing costs, which, by cutting the replacement ratios, force the unemployed to migrate in order to accept jobs which, while having lower real wages than previously, still ofter more than the real level of unemployment benefits.

Regional Policies

The general Monetarist view of regional policies is neatly summed up in the Thatcher Government's White Paper on Regional Industrial Development (Cmnd. 9111). 'Imbalances between areas in employment opportunities should in principle be corrected by the natural adjustment of labour markets. In the first place this should be through lower wages and unit costs than comparable work commands elsewhere' (para. 9). The problems faced by this approach are spelled out in the next paragraph. 'There is, however, little evidence that regional wage rates respond readily to variations in regional unemployment. Indeed, regional differentials in wage rates have tended to narrow over the last twenty years.'

Labour mobility, of which there 'has already been a great deal of adjustment' cannot be relied upon to provide a satisfactory solution to regional inequities in employment (para. 11). 'The government therefore conclude that wage adjustments and labour mobility cannot be relied upon to correct regional imbalances in employment opportunities' (para. 12).

Mobility may help, or may merely transfer the burden of unemployment within the receiving areas. Wage flexibility would help but is difficult if not impossible to achieve, or has been to date even with massively high unemployment. Traditional regional policies may have had an impact earlier, but this now seems to be much less (Fothergill and Gudgin 1982). We seem to be left with the conclusion that a more even spread of employment opportunities resulting in a more even distribution of unemployment could lower the NRU. It might reduce the rate of increase of money and real wages by preventing bottle-necks of labour shortages in some areas. This can be seen as providing more wage-elastic ALS curves in those areas which generate the inflationary wage pressures. However, while the concept seems reasonable enough, governments have been unable to provide policies which have sufficient success in relocating employment opportunities on a large enough scale. They may have prevented the situation from becoming seriously worse, but that is not sufficient. Policies which encourage migration can have a longer-term perverse effect if they lead to a situation where the remaining work-force is considered unsuitable by employers thereby detracting them from locating in areas of higher unemployment.

Government Measures (Leg. CB)

Government action may affect the NRU both directly and indirectly. Direct measures include minimum wage provisions and other intervention which provide a floor which is higher than the 'market' level[14] and result in actual wages exceeding the market wages which would result from the interplay of demand and supply where the latter are determined by individual reservation wages. Government may expect indirect effects by creating conditions in which it is possible for groups, particularly trade unions, to increase actual wages above the market levels. Both types of intervention have the effect of raising actual wages above the individual reservation wages. There is, in effect, the substitution of higher collective reservation wages for the individual reservation wages.

The most obvious legislative intervention which directly increases actual wages over the IRW is the provision of statutory minimum wages. In some countries, such as the United States, minimum wage provisions may be general, and in others, such as the UK, specific industries may have statutory minima implemented through Wages Councils or the Agricultural Wages Board.[15] It seems fairly obvious that the minimum wages should be higher than those which would result from market forces. While Wages Councils minima are legally enforceable 'Evasion of wage-council orders is extensive' (Metcalf 1981, 70). There is little doubt that even in times of low unemployment there are people willing to work in Wage Council industries for less than the minimum rates. At the same time it is possible that the abolition of Wages Councils could lead, over a period of time, to relatively higher rates of pay. Trade unions might extend membership and collective bargaining and obtain higher wages. In some covered industries 'a majority—perhaps a large majority—already have their terms and conditions negotiated by local collective bargaining' (Sharp 1978, 1262).

It is believed that minimum wage provisions impinge most severely on the employment opportunities of 'persons with low skills' and particularly 'a poorly educated teenager' whose services to an employer are worth less than the minimum wage. 'We regard the minimum wage rate as one of the most, if not the most, anti-black laws on the statute books' (Friedman and Friedman, 1980, 237 and 238).

Similar views have been expressed about the UK. 'The minimum wage stops young unskilled workers from obtaining on-the-job training which they could "buy" through accepting a low wage. It becomes unprofitable for an employer to hire unskilled workers—young, female, immigrant or disadvantaged—if he can employ a skilled person for the same wage' (Miller and Wood, 41). They then go on to estimate that if the abolition of Wages Councils increased employment by 25 per cent of the 3.5 million people covered and led to a reduction in pay of 20 per cent 'employers could take on a million extra people for the same outlay (and without any fall in aggregate demand)' (71). This is, of course, a tautology based on the wage-fund theory. It calculates a million extra jobs on the grounds that total outlay, i.e. total wages, remains unaltered. The percentage increase in employment is then *by definition* determined by the assumed percentage decrease in wages. Whether there would in the real world be this result is unknown, but such arithmetical manipulation does nothing to further our analysis. They go on to say that abolishing Supplementary Benefit for teenagers would dramatically reduce youth unemployment. Young people just entering the labour market are not entitled to Unemployment Benefit as they have not made sufficient contributions; abolishing Supplementary Benefit would therefore mean they had no benefit income at all. Presumably they would therefore accept jobs at very low wages. 'Employers would be in a position to create such jobs with the knowledge that there would be enthusiastic young workers keen to take them.' From a research viewpoint, but not from that of the long-term consequences, it would be interesting to see just what 'enthusiastic' and 'keen' meant in these circumstances.

Almost all the empirical work, and indeed the theoretical studies, of the impact of minimum wages on employment has been done in the United States.[16] For the UK the 'only thorough examination appears to relate to the establishment of the trade boards in 1909, when quite large pay increases did not reduce employment' (Metcalf 1981, 67). American empirical research has most frequently studied teenagers. 'Time studies typically find a 10 per cent increase in the minimum wage reduces teenage employment by one to three per cent . . . We believe that the lower half of that range is to be preferred' (Brown et al, 1982, 524). The effect on young adults (20–4 years) is negative and smaller than that for teenagers, and the direction of the effect on adult employment is uncertain in the empirical work as it is in the theory. Some adults may be employed at minimum wages in preference to teenagers who would receive guaranteed wage levels but be less skilled or less adjusted to employment conditions. Part of the disadvantage to young people may arise from their relative uncompetitiveness with adults if they both receive the same pay. It should be borne in mind that American provisions for the minimum wage, with the exception of students under a special programme, does not include differentiated lower minima for teenagers, unlike British Wages Council rates which are age-related for a few years. Three Canadian Provinces have no sub-adult minima for young people. This difference in provision might be expected to lead to different effects on the employment or non-employment of young people.

Abolition of the minimum wage level would presumably lead to a reduction in the pay offered to the less qualified or to slower and lower rates of increase in money wages. Advocates of abolition ought also to be advocating reductions in Unemployment Benefits in order to ensure that the lower wage offered is sufficiently attractive to the unemployed to lead them into employment. This is the problem discussed previously. If society decides that its citizens are entitled to a certain minimum standard of living it may run into problems if the wages obtained from uninteresting, unsatisfying and frequently unpleasant work are very close to the minimum guaranteed level. Many workers in Wages Council industries are women, and married women may not be eligible for Unemployment Benefits and Supplementary Benefits. The level of benefits might therefore be less important than is sometimes supposed.

The view that the abolition of minimum wages would generate employment opportunities which, albeit at low pay, would help the unemployed by allowing them to enter the work-force, obtain skills, and then move onwards and upwards to better-paid and more highly skilled jobs is supported by references to the United States in the nineteenth century and Hong Kong in the twentieth century (Friedman and Friedman 1980). Both these economies, however, are characterized by large inflows of immigrant labour from very depressed and oppressed societies. They are not typical of modern industrial societies and are certainly not models which modern societies would choose to follow.

We simply do not know whether the existence of Wages Councils has had any effect in reducing the level of employment in the industries concerned. A priori reasoning may suggest that it should have had, but a priori reasoning does not always describe or explain what happens in the real world. Wages Council minima are not high. Abolishing councils might have no sizeable impact on employment; certainly we should ignore the arithmetical tautologies of Miller and Wood. American evidence does not suggest that the minimum wage had a marked effect on the overall level of employment. It is more likely that its effects have been on the composition of the unemployed with adverse consequences on the young, unskilled, and ethnic minority groups and corresponding benefits for older, more experienced whites. The same effect may occur if wages for young inexperienced workers are set too high in relation to the rates for experienced adult workers. It is necessary to choose between socially desired policies and what are considered to be economically necessary ones. This is why many critics of proposals to abolish minimum wage provisions also advocate better education and training *facilities* so that school-leavers are better equipped to enter the labour market and possess skills and abilities which increase the value of their services to employers.

A Parliamentary Question to Norman Tebbit, the then Secretary of State for Employment, asking if he would commission a survey to discover whether, and to what extent, employers were inhibited from recruiting new employees as a result of Wages Council awards received an unencouraging answer. 'It is self-evident that wages are ultimately limited by the ability of employers to pay . . . There is little doubt that the higher the level at which councils set minimum wages the fewer people will be employed, but I am doubtful that a survey could readily quantify this' (*Hansard*, 6 July 1982). The effects of minimum wages on the NRU are established by a priori reasoning but the quantification is apparently too difficult. However, as we shall see in Chapter 16, John Gummer, Minister for Employment, does not share Mr Tebbit's scepticism.

Legislation requiring public contractors to observe certain minimum wages or conditions of employment can also have the effect of raising actual wages above their 'market' level whether the market level be determined by individual reservation wages and employers' demand curves, or on some other basis. The Fair Wages Resolution of the House of Commons or the Bacon-Davis and Walsh-Healey Acts in the USA may have this effect.

Proposals to shift the balance of power away from trade unions are commonplace among Monetarists. While this may be expressed as a desire to remove or reduce the 'monopoly' power of unions by permitting the economy to move closer towards the conditions which are assumed to exist in a free market economy, such proposals, in the conditions which actually face us, are, of course, the same as shifting the balance of power towards employers. The question of the appropriate or 'right' balance of power among different groups in a pluralist society is one for constant discussion and reassessment, and the particular views one adopts will reflect one's value-judgements. The Confederation of British Industry has expressed concern that the balance of power has shifted too far in favour of organized labour with adverse economic consequences on the whole economy, and ought in the national interest to be moved back to some more moderate equilibrium.[17]

Legislation governing trade union immunities and rights in the event of industrial disputes, primarily strikes but also lock-outs, may be thought to lie at the heart of the trade unions' ability to increase wages and restrict the effective labour supply. Legislation may seek to control the circumstances in which a strike can be called, the process of that decision-taking, the employer against whom strike action and picketing may take place, the time at which striking is protected, and whether certain groups have the right to strike at all. In Britain it is sometimes argued that a central element in trade union power is the fact that unlike the United States the collective agreement is not a legally enforceable contract between the union and employer, although its terms may become part of the contract between the employer and each individual employee. This means that the union may be able to break a procedural agreement and take strike action even though it has agreed not to do so, without fear of legal proceedings with the risk of damages.

Legislative action to change the rights of trade unions, the relationship between union leaders and rank-and-file membership, the processes of decision-taking, particularly with regard to industrial action, the system of ratifying or accepting employers' offers or concluding agreements, provision for the compulsory recognition of trade unions for purposes of collective bargaining in appropriate circumstances, and other measures which influence the establishment of collective bargaining, the rights and legal immunities of the parties to bargaining, the methods and type of sanctions which can be used in particular circumstances, provisions requiring the election of trade union officers or officials, and administrative rules regarding such things as the payment of tax rebates during a strike may all affect the balance of power and thus the ability of trade unions to raise actual wages above some assumed theoretical market level.

The government may also seek to exert influence through its role as employer. Public sector employment accounts for some 30 per cent of total employment in the UK.[18] The degree of direct involvement of government through Ministers or Civil Servant representatives varies from effectively complete control of the 'management side' of the negotiations in the Civil Services and NHS, to more indirect pressure combined with possible threats regarding future financial provisions in local government and the nationalized industries. There is widespread belief that the government should always set an example with public sector pay, although this is usually interpreted to mean that the government should take the lead in exercising wage restraint and moderating wage increases. If it is thought that public sector pay increases set some sort of pattern or influence the development of pay in the private sector there may be strong pressure on government to hold down public sector increases even to the point of breaking established agreements or denying trade unions their right to go to arbitration (see Chapter 16).

Governments influenced by Monetarist doctrines are particularly likely to be opposed to the use of comparability as a system for determining the pay of public sector employees. Both the Thatcher and Reagan Administrations have strongly attacked comparability for Civil Servants, even though this was the established system of pay determination. The stronger the belief in the desirability of subjecting the economy to market forces the greater the rejection of the use of administrative concepts which might be seen as incorporating social factors such as equity. In the same way arbitration on substantive issues or interests, which leads to the establishment of the terms of an agreement rather than the interpretation of an existing agreement, may be discouraged, both for public sector employees and for the private sector. Governments may have an area of discretion whether to interfere in a dispute in the private sector by establishing special courts of inquiry etc. which act as a sort of advisory arbitration panel. By not setting up such inquiries and by letting it be known that government will be generally unresponsive to such action they may generate a climate in which unions settle for less than they believe they would have obtained from a 'fair or independent' tribunal.

The introduction of additional or new financial controls on public bodies may be intended to limit their ability to offer wage increases above some predetermined amount. Cash limits for the Civil Service and other parts of the public sector may be seen as having such an intent. While it is possible to argue that cash limits do not totally inhibit collective bargaining over pay increases[19] they do, or are intended to have, a restrictive effect. While it may be possible to argue that there is no total pre-emption of collective bargaining, there is at very least a significant reduction in the area of bargaining, and in many cases an effective constraint on the size of the wage increase which is obtainable.

The possibility of conflict between the government's role as an employer with obligations to bargain with unions representing its employees, and its role as government with the ultimate responsibility for managing the nation's finances is ever present in a democratic society. Generally a pluralistic democratic society evolves some form of compromise which permits government to satisfy both of its responsibilities, but an administration which gives overriding priority to the reduction of the level of wages or wage increases may so change the processes and systems that a proper balance of responsibilities seems to be abandoned. Monetarists are especially likely to follow this road. They have an almost built-in antipathy to public sector activity, even though this is not a necessary component of the modern versions of the Quantity Theory. In addition, reduction in public sector wages has the added attraction that they permit lower taxes or lower government borrowing. The first is also associated with the package of political beliefs of many Monetarists and the second is probably an element in all the macro-economic versions of Monetarism. The public sector is doubly exposed to attack therefore. Governments will seek to obtain the demonstration effect to encourage private sector employers to hold down wages and the predisposition to reduce taxes and public borrowing will lead to action to reduce the public sector pay-bill.

Governments may recognize the great difficulty of obtaining reductions in money wages and seek to cut real wages. This could decrease the NRU if public sector employment expands even though real wages fell, which could happen if labour markets do not clear in real wage terms and the unemployed preferred to work for even lower real wages in the public sector rather than remain unemployed. If public sector employment does not expand the lower real wages could lead to lower taxes or interest rates as the PSBR falls, and this could lead to an increased demand for labour elsewhere, thereby lowering the NRU.

It is possible that the success of the government in reducing real wages in the public sector could actually lead to an increase in the NRU. If labour markets clear, it might be argued, following a Minford line, that all unemployment is voluntary. Any reduction in the real wage level might then lead to an increase in unemployment if marginal workers decide that the reduced real wages no longer meet their real reservation wages. This will be influenced by what has happened to the real level of Unemployment Benefits and the stability or otherwise of the marginal workers' real reservation wage levels. The New Classical Monetarist could, however, just as easily conclude that the NRU would rise in these circumstances as fall. To ensure that it fell he would advocate a reduction in real Unemployment Benefit levels at least equal to the reduction in real wages and presumably, even greater, to encourage some of the unemployed to accept a job voluntarily.

Those who reject the extremity of the New Classical School might conclude that a reduction in the NRU was likely to follow a reduction in public sector real wages for as long as that reduction could be maintained. The irony of this is that those who believe the measures might be effective, though not necessarily desirable, do so because they emphasize the social element in pay determination, in particular the force of comparability and its powerful effect in influencing prevailing notions of what is either fair or attainable. It is the very rejection of the social or institutional elements in pay determination as undesirable and inhibitive of the working of market forces which leads Monetarist governments to reject established pay systems which incorporate comparability, either directly or indirectly. The more successful government is in breaking the use and force of comparability and other social and institutional elements in pay determination the less will be the effects of reductions in public sector real wages on the private sector, and therefore the less the effect in reducing the NRU.

Other legislation may have an effect on the NRU even though it may not have been designed to do so. For example the Redundancy Payments Act 1965 and the Unfair Dismissal provisions of the 1971 IRA (as subsequently amended) have had two effects. Firstly, they have made employers more careful in their selection of new recruits. This may have lengthened the time taken to fill vacancies if changed screening processes lead to longer delays in recruitment, thereby increasing frictional unemployment. Secondly, the provision of redundancy payments which increase with length of employment with the employer, has led to an increase in 'voluntary' redundancy by older workers so that the traditional practice of 'last-in-first-out' has been modified as long-service employees perceived the opportunity to obtain lump-sum payments on redundancy. Thus, instead of facilitating labour mobility and encouraging movement within the labour market, the RPA may have had a greater effect in encouraging movement out of the labour market as older workers opted for a form of early retirement with a lump-sum payment perhaps instead of an occupational pension.[20] This will increase the measured level of unemployment to the extent that these redundant workers are included in the official statistics.

Shifting the Expectations-augmented Phillips Curve

The expectations-augmented Phillips curve analysis as used to demonstrate the effect of increasing the money supply, rests on an assumption about the stability of the curve. It is assumed that the demand and supply decisions for labour, once taken, will change in money terms only as a result of changes in the expected rate of inflation. In real terms they are stable, and this is why it is necessary for labour to believe, mistakenly, that there is an increase in real wages if unemployment is to be reduced. If, however, there is a change in the real wage labour decisions the curve will shift. If workers decide that they will give up 'leisure' and accept the disutility of work only in return for a higher wage then employment will fall, and the NRU will rise. Similarly, if workers are prepared to accept a lower real wage, employment will rise and the NRU fall, provided only that as a result of the lower real wage there is no reduction in employers' perceptions of the level of real demand for their products. This is, of course, an important proviso. If money wages fell and all prices fell proportionately there would be no change in real terms, and this is an assumption frequently made by Monetarists in consequence of their belief that money and prices are but numeraires responding to changes in the money supply and not affected by real activities. However, a reduction in real wages requires that money wages fall (do not rise as fast) in relation to prices generally.

In Fig. 15.1 the curve $P_a^* W_a^*$ is the initial expectations-augmented Phillips curve. It is assumed to be a stable equilibrium position in that prices and wages are each expected to rise by a per cent a year and these expectations have been met. It is also assumed following the usual Monetarist explanation that prices are a fixed percentage mark-up on wages so that both prices and wages rise by a per cent. The

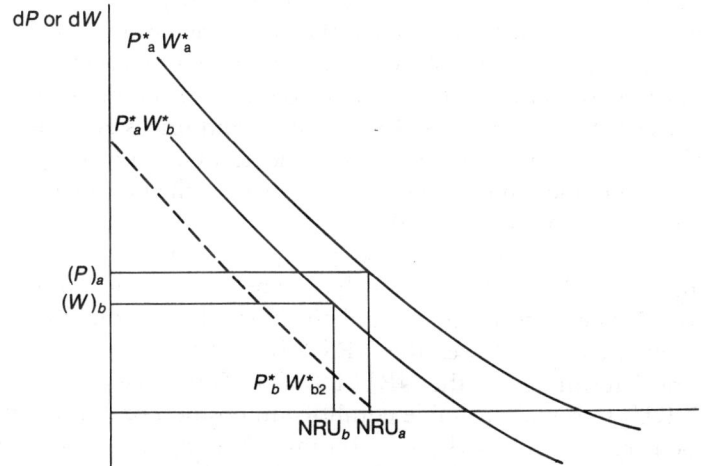

Fig. 15.1 Expectations-augmented Phillips Curve and Revised Reservation Wages

equilibrium position is indicated by a rate of price increase of a per cent on the vertical axis and the NRU is given by NRU_a. It is now assumed that workers adjust their real reservation wages downwards, perhaps as a result of the various measures introduced by government to achieve this end. With an expected rate of inflation of P_a^* workers are now willing to supply the same amount of labour for a rise in money wages of only b per cent where $b<a$. Employers recognize there has been a willingness to accept lower real wages and therefore the previous fixed mark-up relationship between wages and prices is seen as no longer relevant. Employers may well accept that this is the long-awaited sense of realism they have advocated which allows profits to be increased so that investment may take place and future employment be safeguarded. Workers may see it as a desperate unfair sacrifice necessary to preserve their jobs. That there are different attitudes or even different degrees of fundamental commitment or acceptance does not at this stage matter. The effect is to lower the curve $P_a^*W_a^*$ to $P_a^*W_b^*$. Prices are expected by both sides of the labour market to rise at the same rate but wages by a smaller percentage. Unless employers believe that the demand for their product in real terms, i.e. the physical quantity demanded, will fall the result is to shift the NRU to NRU^b. At that point the employer-producers' expectations of a rise in prices of a per cent are proved correct, and workers' expectations of an increase in wages of b per cent with an inflation rate of a per cent, i.e. a fall in real wages, are also proved correct.

At each lower real wage, $P_a^*W_b^*$, the same quantity of labour is forthcoming as was previously supplied at the higher real wage $P_a^*W_a^*$. At the lower product real wage employers will demand more labour so we are assuming that the employer expects to be able to maintain the same ratio between the future price of his product and prices generally as in the initial curve. As more labour is demanded, and more is supplied as a result of the reduction in real reservation wages, the new expectations-augmented curve lies below $P_a^*W_a^*$.

We are here ignoring the view that wage increases are often much more influenced by past inflation than expected inflation in order to follow the Monetarist approach and to show why a reduction in real reservation wages will lower the NRU. In fact this may be the most important determinant of the NRU to most Monetarists.

For NRU_b to remain a stable equilibrium position on this analysis it would be necessary for workers to continue to accept reductions in real wages. It would not be enough for them to accept a once-for-all cut. However, this would imply that real profits continued to rise and that employers continued to believe that they could go on selling the same physical amount of products, even though real incomes were falling. This is very unlikely although companies which export all their product might not see any reduction in their real demand. What is much more likely is that after some period of falling real wages employer-producers will recognize that prices cannot continue to keep rising faster than money wages without some effect on real demand, i.e. physical quantities demanded, and, just as in the orthodox Monetarist account of the effects of an increase in aggregate demand, they will seek to have some of the expected change in aggregate demand for their products influence quantities and not merely prices. They will therefore revise downwards their expectations of price inflation on the basis of their perceptions of what is happening to real demand for their own products. As they appreciate that in order to maintain real demand and output they cannot continue to raise prices by more than money wages, and so revise downward the P^* of their own products, so will they adjust downward their expectations of P_a^*.

However, this is not the same as a movement to a lower expectations-augmented curve in the usual analysis. For example curve $P_a^*W_b^*$ can be envisaged as equal to a curve $P_b^*W_b^*$ in a usual map of curves. Then if expectations of the inflation rate fell from a to b the NRU would, possibly after some adjustment, revert to NRU_a, which would be the typical long-run NRU position. Curve $P_a^*W_b^*$ is different as we have seen. It changed the real product-wage by leading to a change in the ratio of money wages and product prices of an individual producer and the economy generally. Even uniform expectations of a future inflation rate of $P_b^*W_b^*$ will not therefore lead to the same equilibrium position as it would have done on the initial map of expectations-augmented Phillips curves. There will have been an increase in demand for labour as a result of the fall in the real product-wage which, with the lower real reservation wages, will have shifted the NRU downwards. Those marginal members of the work-force who in the usual account are willing to enter employment only if they believe real wages are rising, and who voluntarily leave to become unemployed once they discover that real wages are not higher, no longer quit, and the employer no longer wishes to get rid of them. The fall in real wages can therefore lead to a reduction in the NRU even when all participants in the labour market adjust their price and wage expectations to b per cent. The acceptance of a once-for-all cut in real wages can lead to a reduction in the NRU to NRU_b because it leads to a new set of expectations-augmented Phillips curves.

We illustrate the new expectations-augmented curve for $P_b^*W_{b2}^*$ by the dotted curve in Fig. 15.1. Each of the initial curves for a given rate of expected inflation can be redrawn on the initial map by a dotted curve which will be below its previous level for the same expected rate of inflation, and differentiated by the subscript 2 to indicate the revised position after the change in real wages.

It is obvious that if real reservation wages subsequently increase there will be a reverse tendency. It becomes crucial therefore whether the reduction in real wages illustrated here is accepted in the long run, or is but a temporary accommodation to extreme economic conditions. The other important question is whether employers will continue to maintain and increase their demand for labour when the product real wage falls. If they do not, because the lower real wages leads to a fall in real demand, the sacrifice of real wages will have been for naught. Monetarists have great difficulty facing this because it could involve them in accepting the validity of Keynesian demand-deficient unemployment and that would seriously threaten their macro-economic analysis and prescription.

Real Wages and Employment

It is widely believed that lower real wages will lead to an increase in employment, 'market economists, who have never doubted that, other things being equal, higher real pay means fewer jobs . . .' (Brittan, *Financial Times*, 6 February 1985). The quotation implies a symmetrical relationship; it refers to higher real wages meaning fewer jobs, and the converse is held to be equally valid. 'Other things being equal' might be an important qualification. If aggregate real demand falls as a result of the lower real wages, employment might not rise, and could even fall. The Treasury (1985) produced a Review of the empirical evidence of the relationship between employment and wages. Their conclusions were both suitably circumspect, in that they concluded that the evidence and the econometric models only 'suggest' certain conclusions rather than firmly establish them, and somewhat optimistic. If real wages were 1 per cent lower they thought employment might be one-half to 1 per cent higher.

However, there are other ways of stimulating employment which do not require a reduction in real wages.[21] For example Sargent's analysis concludes that the fall in employment cannot be explained in terms of the fall in the reduction of the real product wage alone and that the lack of effective demand must also have been a factor. The product real wage, or cost of labour to the employer in relation to the selling price of the product, is influenced, not only by the wage costs, but also by National Insurance contributions, etc. These non-wage costs may have added nearly 2 percentage points to the level of unemployment since the early 1960s and 3 percentage points to the NRU (Layard and Nickell 1985).

Most models assume that cuts in real wages result from lower rates of increase of money wages in relation to prices. The effect on aggregate demand is then crucial. However, any reductions in real wages can be offset, or even more than offset, by increases in non-wage labour costs which could lead to a reduction in employment. Even the Treasury model cannot provide a firm basis on which to forecast the effects of a reduction in real wages as it is unable to specify the combined effects of, say, a reduction in real wages and a reduction in taxes. If a tax reduction does not lead to lower wage settlements there will be less employment growth than if it does. However, there seems to be wide agreement amongst economists from different points in the Keynesian–Monetarist spectrum that tax cuts are a much less effective way of increasing employment than an increase in public expenditure or a reduction in National Insurance contributions.[22]

The argument that real wages 'ought' to be cut to expand employment, and that the refusal of trade unions to accept such cuts is an important cause of unemployment, is by no means established. Nor is it the case that a reduction in workers' real wages would necessarily lead to an expansion of employment, or a fall in the NRU.

Conclusions

The NRU is determined by all the 'real', i.e. non-monetary, factors in an economy. Any attempts to lower the rate of unemployment without generating additional inflation in the long run must be directed towards reducing the NRU. There are basically three ways of doing this. The first is to obtain a lowering of reservation wages. Individual reservation wages may be lowered if unemployment income is reduced. This is based on the standard economic approach that some premium is necessary to induce people to give up leisure and accept the disutility of work. If that premium remains the same a reduction in the base of unemployment income will lead to a lower reservation wage. Individuals will then accept employment at lower wages than previously, in the moderate version in real wage terms, and in the strong version in money wage terms also. Essentially the purpose is to change the employment–unemployment trade-off decision of individuals and is heavily dependent on the belief that all or most unemployment is voluntary. Where trade unions exist collective reservation wages may be established which are higher than individual reservation wages. Measures to reduce the ability of unions to establish, and in some versions to enforce on their reluctant membership, excessive reservation wages may also decrease unemployment. Secondly, actual wages resulting from the processes of collective bargaining, legislative intervention, government policies regarding public sector pay, systems of pay determination, and the use of institutional practices which incorporate social considerations into pay determination, may exceed the levels which would result from a more market-oriented system. Measures to reduce trade union power will affect both of these general approaches, and the call for less government involvement in economic activity generally accompanies the political and ideological positions of Monetarists. Thirdly, steps may be taken to improve the functioning of the labour market so that there is less genuine frictional unemployment as employers and job-seeking workers are brought together more quickly. If occupational imbalances in the demand and supply of labour exist measures may be taken to extend and improve training and retraining facilities and perhaps to reduce the cost of these to both worker and employer. Geographical imbalances may be tackled by removing what are seen as distortions in the housing market, or by the encouragement of mobility through grants and allowances. All measures seem to require more and better labour market information about job openings, the type of labour unemployed and looking for work, the terms and conditions prevailing in various jobs, and the job requirements and probabilities of becoming part of an acceptable-labour supply curve on various terms in prevailing conditions.

All three approaches may require some reduction in the real wages sought by the unemployed, but the first two rely heavily if not completely on this. The conflict between the economic and social aspects of government policy is inevitably emphasized by the first two approaches. As yet we but imperfectly understand the nature of the process of determination of individual or collective reservation wages. Similarly, we have little knowledge of the possibilities for obtaining enduring reductions in real wages, particularly if these are brought about by enforced changes in collective bargaining arrangements and practices. It may be that trade unions will accept reductions in their power and influence in the long run, and, in the pursuit of collective bargaining gains or more broad political objectives, they may accept a changed role in an industrialized society. Or, they may take part in a strategic withdrawal to regroup their forces and prepare for the future when they hope to redress the enforced shifts in the balance of power. Very large increases in the level of unemployment may lead to discontinuities in the trade-off of relative power and bargaining strength and in the acceptability of real wage reductions by unions, their members, and the electorate generally. If it is the rate of change of unemployment, rather than the actual level, which exerts the greater influence, then even a stabilization of unemployment at a historically high level may provide the circumstances for a restoration of previously held views about the 'fair' or acceptable real wages by the work-force. If the traditional British approach to wage bargaining—that past decreases in real wages due to price rises should be made good in future settlements—persists, then the time-scale may be lengthened so that an ending of the increase in unemployment leads to strong bargaining pressure for pay rises to raise real wages. If this happens, the apparent gains in reducing the NRU at such a tremendous social cost in terms of unemployment, social conflict, and lost output, will have been for no more than a temporary easement with a legacy of great bitterness. If, however, it leads to genuine shifts in attitudes, perhaps influenced by recollections of the hardship of large-scale unemployment, there may be a moderation of the real wage objectives of unions and workers which allows a longer-term reduction in the NRU.

Notes to Chapter 15

1. See, for example, Maki and Spindler (1975); Atkinson and Flemming (1978); Kay, Morris, and Warren (1980). Dilnot and Morris (1983) has a useful bibliography.
2. See Sue Moylan and Bob Davies, 'The Disadvantages of the Unemployed', *Employment Gazette*, Aug. 1980, 830–2; Sue Moylan and Bob Davies, 'The Flexibility of the Unemployed', *Employment Gazette*, Jan. 1981, 29–33; R. Davies, L. Hamill, S. Moylan, and C. H. Smee, 'Incomes in and out of Work', *Employment Gazette*, June 1982, 237–43; Sue Moylan, Jane Millar,

and Bob Davies: 'Unemployment—the Year After', *Employment Gazette*, Aug. 1982, 334-40.
3. The assumption is made that the effective burden of taxation of benefits falls on the income received when unemployed. This is so only for tax-rebates which are not now given to the unemployed. The effect of the tax is felt on return to work.
4. 'How Employers see the Public Employment Service', *Employment Gazette*, Nov. 1982, 472. Also see M. MacKay *et al.* (1971) and Rosewell and Robinson (1980).
5. See A. McGregor (1978) and *Employment Gazette*, March 1974.
6. The October 1982 change in the basis of the official unemployment figures means that this occupational breakdown of the unemployed is no longer available.
7. Norman Tebbit, speech to the British Association for Commercial and Industrial Education, 12 Oct. 1981, Department of Employment Press Release.
8. See Fidgett (1983).
9. *MSC Annual Report 1983-4*, Manpower Services Commission 1984, 20.
10. Articles on special employment measures have appeared in the Department of *Employment Gazette*. The Nov. 1979 issue examined the development of schemes from Apr. 1978 to June 1979, and the Nov. 1982 issue extended this period to Mar. 1982. See also Metcalf (1982).
11. Some of these are discussed in Chapter 10.
12. 'Tom King Annouces Extension of Employment and Training Measures', Department of Employment press notice, 30 July, 1984.
13. See, for example, Wood (1975); Millar and Wood (1982); Brittan (1982); and Laidler (1975).
14. The debate on the desirability of Wages Councils or a statutory minimum wage can be obtained from Forrest, IEA Hobart Paper 101; and various publications by the Low Pay Unit, such as Low Pay Pamphlet 24, 1983, and those by Pond and Wingard (1983) and Neuburger (1984).
15. The standard works on the development of Wages Councils are Guillebaud (1958) and Bayliss (1962). There are currently some 3 million workers covered by Wages Councils and the Agricultural Wages Board. For a recent analysis and discussion of the effects of Wages Councils see Craig *et al.* (1982).
16. The most comprehensive source is the Report of the Minimum Wage Study Commission, US Government Printing Office, May 1981. Vol. I contains the Report and Vols. II-VII, the research studies undertaken by the Commission's staff. Vol. V on Employment and Unemployment is the most relevant of these for present purposes; Vol. VI on Inflation also has a bearing on the matters considered here. The findings of Vol. V are summarized and more easily accessible in Charles Brown, Curtis Gilroy, and Andrew Kohen (1982). This source will generally be used here for convenience. There is a good review of North American literature in 'The Impact of Minimum Wages on Youth Unemployment', *OECD Observer*, 117, July 1982, OECD, Paris.

17. See Confederation of British Industry (1980).
18. See S. Briscoe (1981).
19. See speech by Barney Hayhoe MP to the Institute of Personnel Management, Harrogate, Oct. 1981.
20. See Hepple, in Bain (1982).
21. See Bank of England Panel of Academic Consultants, *Employment, Real Wages and Unemployment in the United Kingdom*, Panel Paper 24, Bank of England, Oct. 1984.
22. Reported in *The Times*, 13 Mar. 1985.

CHAPTER SIXTEEN

Policies of the Thatcher Government

THE Thatcher Government of 1979 came into office committed to Monetarist doctrine and policies. The adoption of Monetarism marked not only a rejection of the broadly based Keynesian views of economics which had been a feature of all post-war governments, it also reflected a very significant shift in political attitudes within the ascendant group of the Conservative Party.[1] As Nigel Lawson MP said:

> But during the 25 years that followed Churchill it was a very different outlook that gained the ascendancy: the philosophy of social democracy, with its profound faith in the efficacy of government action, particularly in the economic sphere, and its deep commitment to the notion of 'equality'. To a greater or lesser extent the Conservative party embraced both these delusions. (1980, 2.)

Parties differed in their preferences for different techniques, their willingness to experiment, the relative attractiveness of different economic and social priorities, and their attitudes towards trade unions, but not on the fundamental issue of what sort of techniques should be adopted to deal with inflation. Both parties rejected incomes policies when out of office and both introduced them when in office. There were significant differences in social policies but both were committed to full employment and there was not very much difference between them as to what constituted full employment. Perhaps ironically, it may be that both governments spent more time in holding back employment to prevent over-full employment and very high inflation (for the times) than in actually generating additional demand to increase employment, but they were committed to full employment.[2]

The results of the 1979 election endorsed the end of consensus between the parties, and the passing of power within the Conservative Party to those who rejected that past consensus. Like all good conservatives Lawson sought to establish that this policy was no more than 'the reversion to an older tradition'. 'To the extent that new Conservatives turn to new sages—such as Hayek and Friedman—'this is because they are reinterpreting old sages such as Hume, Burke, and Adam Smith and because 'economics now occupies a more central place in politics than in the golden age of Disraeli and Gladstone' (2–3). 'The economic policy of the new Conservatism has two basic strands. At the macro-economic level, our approach is what has come to be known as monetarism . . . At the micro-economic level, our emphasis is on the free market, in contradistinction to state intervention and central planning' (3). But, to describe the new Conservatism 'purely in terms of an approach to economic policy would be manifestly inadequate—it goes a good deal wider than that . . .'.

The battle for control of the soul and organization of the Conservative Party had been led on the intellectual front by Sir Keith Joseph, and his Centre for Policy Studies. Outside the political ranks the Institute of Economic Affairs had produced and encouraged much research advocating free market and generally Monetarist positions. Much as the Fabian Society had generated thought and policy proposals in the pre-war and early post-war periods, so the IEA, although not politically linked to a party, stimulated ideas and policies which were attractive to the new Conservatives. Indeed, the IEA was probably the most effective source of ideas and policy proposals for any group of policy-makers in any party during the decade prior to the election of the Thatcher Government.

The struggle within the Conservative Party, while resulting in a massive victory for the new troops, was not total. A minority continue to press for their version of Conservatism, which while sharing some of the older consensus views and remaining deeply sceptical of Monetarism, often stresses *its* links with the traditional Toryism of the Conservative Party. Social responsibility for the less fortunate members of society and the duties and obligations which go with rights and privileges are emphasized. Whether this be social democracy or not it results in deep and bitter disagreements within the Conservative ranks. Probably the most pungent and certainly the most literate and best-written attack on the new Conservatism has come from Sir Ian Gilmour, Conservative MP. 'Hence an economic policy does not stand by itself. It cannot be separated from its political and moral context. This is, of course, a reassertion of the Tory tradition and a rejection of the notion that economics is a combination of iron laws and mathematical formulae, the former beyond human control, the latter beyond human understanding' (Gilmour 1983, 2). The Conservative success in 1979 was described by another Conservative critic 'as not so much an advance to a new Monetarism as a return to old values' as far as the electorate was concerned (Norman St John-Stevas 1982).

The policies of the Thatcher Government are Monetarist, and they are Monetarist in the broad political sense as well as in the stricter economic meaning of seeking to control the rate of inflation through the money supply. The rejection of 'social democracy' and the return to 'the mainstream' of Conservative policies and beliefs means that the government embraces much of the free market and right-wing ideology that frequently but not necessarily accompanies acceptance of Monetarism. Control of the money supply is therefore one plank, but only one, in a platform of policies. It provides the basis for the macro-economic policy but is supported by various other measures.

Control of the Money Supply

The basic economic policy of the new Government was set out by the then Chancellor Sir Geoffrey Howe in his 1979 Budget Statement. 'We are committed to the progressive reduction of the rate of growth of the money supply.'[3] The reasoning behind this is discussed in Chapters 2 and 3. The selected monetary aggregate was £M3 for which an annual target growth range of 7–11 per cent was set until the end of financial year 1979–80. The target was a range which allowed the authorities flexibility to respond to the prevailing and expected economic circumstances. £M3 was selected because it was thought to provide the best indication of the supply of money for policy purposes.

The following year saw the introduction of the Medium Term Financial Strategy (MTFS) 'the corner-stone of the government's economic policy' (Lawson 1984, 11). This innovation set out the government's projections for both the money supply and the PSBR over a four-year period from 1980–1 to 1983–4. By announcing the government's medium-term intentions it was presumably hoped that individuals would form their expectations on the basis of more reliable and credible information than had previously been available. (See Chapter 12 for the theory behind this.) In this way their actions, it was hoped, would be modified in the light of the expected price movements which would result from the announced money supply growth figures. The rate of increase of £M3 was to decline from a range of 7–11 per cent to 4–8 per cent at the end of the period. The PSBR was to decline from 4.75 per cent of the GDP in 1979–80 to 3.75 in 1980–1 and then by 0.75 per cent each year to only 1.5 per cent of GDP in 1983–4.[4] The PSBR projections, unlike those for £M3, were not targets, in that it was recognized that they might depart from the desired path because of the effects of the economic cycle or recession. Even so it was expected that the PSBR at the end of the period would be below the 1978–9 and 1979–80 levels. Government expenditure was projected to fall from £71 billion in 1979–80 to £67½ billion in 1983–4 in constant 1979 survey prices. Thus there was to be a cut in real government expenditure of 5 per cent.

While it might prove necessary for the government to change policies in a number of ways not reflected in the projections, they were quite firm on one point. 'But there would be no question of departing from the money supply policy, which is essential to the success of any anti-inflationary strategy' (FSBR 1980-1, 19). The Chancellor announced the ending of the 'corset' and indeed hoped that the anticipated increase in £M3 which would come from the disintermediation effects might be contained within the announced target figures.

By November 1980 £M3 was growing at more than 20 per cent p.a. but the Chancellor said he would keep the existing targets until the April 1981 Budget.

The MTFS began by concentrating on £M3. As Mr Lawson told the Zurich Society of Economics, 'for the 4-year path set out in the medium-term financial strategy—we have (like our predecessors, but unlike most other countries, incidentally) chosen broad money as the most useful guide. I believe we were and remain right to do so. Narrow money has the advantage of being easier to control, but it suffers from being almost too easy to control' (1981, 11). (See Chapter 3 for a discussion of the different definitions and measurements of money.)

By 1982 the government had changed its mind. They had not had much success with their favourite £M3 so decided to back three horses. They now concluded

No single measure of money can fully describe monetary conditions. They have to be assessed in light of all the available evidence. Sterling (£M3) has risen faster than the target range set for it last March . . . To make more explicit the way in which a range of indicators is monitored, the target ranges for monetary growth will now apply both to the two broad measures of money— £M3 together with PSL2 and to the narrower measure, M1 (Treasury, Economic Progress Report 143, March 1982, 2).

The target range for the three measures for 1982-3 was raised a little to 8-12 per cent. Despite the Zurich claim of Nigel Lawson the government did not find narrow money M1 'almost too easy to control'—it rose by some 14 per cent on a March-to-March basis in 1982-3.

The 1982-3 Budget set target ranges for three monetary indicators—£M3, PSL2, and M1 a measure of 'narrow' money. They were all to be kept to a range of 8-12 per cent. The targets for 1983-4 were reduced slightly to 7-11 per cent.

The target ranges and actual out-turns for the years 1980-1 to 1983-4 are shown in Table 16.1.

It can be seen that the government had little success in its early years. However, it introduced new monetary indicators and by 1983-4 had most of them within its ranges. In October 1983 Nigel Lawson, now promoted to Chancellor of the Exchequer, told the Lord Mayor's banquet 'M0 could have a more important part to play as a key in-

Table 16.1 *Target Ranges for Monetary Indicators and Actual Out-turns*

	Target		Growth of monetary aggregates, Feb.–Feb.							
	£M3	PSL2	M1	M0	Non-interest-bearing M1	M1	M2	£M3	PSL1	PSL2
1980–1	7–11	–	–	–	–	9	–	20	17	15
1981–2	6–10	–	–	3½	4	8½	–	14½	13½	12
1982–3	8–12	8–12	8–12	3½	–	11	6½	10	8½	9
1983–4	7–11	7–11	7–11	6¼	–	11	9	9¾	9¼	12¼

Note: – indicates that no figure was given in the *FSBR*.
Source: Financial Statement and Budget Reports 1980–1 to 1984–5.

dicator of the growth of narrow money' (EPR 162, 2). M1 was scratched almost as soon as it left the starting-line. Even as M0 was introduced another starter was being prepared. 'M2 was specifically designed as a measure of transactions balances. But it is still relatively new . . . I think and hope it will come to play an important part in policy decisions. But its time has not yet come.'

The *Financial Statement and Budget Report 1984–5* dutifully produced six monetary measures:

Table 16.2 *Six Monetary Measures*

	Per cent change during year					
	M0	M1	M2	£M3	PSL1	PSL2
Feb. 1983–Feb. 1984	6¼	11	9	9¾	9¼	12¼

Source: HC 304 (1984), Table 2.1.

The target ranges for £M3, M1, and PSL2 had been 7–11 per cent. Over the period shown all but PSL2 had remained below the target maximum, and M0 had risen by less than the lower end of the target range. On this showing the attraction of M0 is fairly obvious. For 1984–5 the government has cut back to two targets. Narrow money —M0—should be in the range 4–8 per cent, and broad money—£M3 —within the range 6–10 per cent. However as we have seen the government is grooming M2. On past form it is quite likely that by the time M2 is fit to run the government will fancy M-something else.

The government has showed considerable inventiveness and agility in specifying and respecifying its monetary targets. First, it has worked in ranges rather than more precise rates of growth. This may have some effect on changing expectations if the announcements become credible, but on any sort of precise expectations theory the use of targets must leave something to be desired. Ranges do not permit the formation of precise expectations about future levels of demand in either nominal or real terms. They may indicate that future nominal demand will grow at a lower rate but not indicate how much lower. There is quite a lot of difference between 7 per cent and 11 per cent growth in aggregate nominal demand. Second, while one may agree with Mr Lawson 'None of the Ms is a perfect guide to the underlying concept they seek to reflect' it is a little more difficult to accept his statement 'But there never was a time when it was thought that one monetary indicator said all that there was to be said about monetary conditions' (EPR 162, 2). They may not have thought it said *all* there was to say but the Government gave the impression in its early days that £M3 said all that anybody needed to hear in order to conform to the 'proper' Monetarist model and formulate the right expectations.

Their very adroitness in discovering, devising, and backing different monetary measures had detracted from the apparently simple and straightforward message and prescription of Monetarism. There are so many indicators, each to be kept within some fairly broad range, that economic agents cannot be expected to respond to the same, yet alone the appropriate, monetary indicator. Given the six indicators produced in the 1984 *Financial Statement* quoted above, and assuming that correct rational Monetarist decisions can be taken on the basis of an indication of future movement of 1 per cent, the range of 7–11 per cent provides thirty different possible key indicators. Restricting ourselves to the 1984 favoured two, M0 and £M3, and again working in 1 per cent steps, there are still ten different individual indicators on which economic agents could form their expectations and twenty-five combinations of possible pairs of the two indicators.

Committed Monetarist theorists might argue that notwithstanding formal declarations and speeches, the Thatcher Government is not really Monetarist in its actions. They can point to the failure to control the money supply to the declared targets even when these were ranges rather than a precise figure. They can argue that the adoption of more than one monetary variable prevents economic agents from forming expectations properly as they are not sure which of the variables the Government will seek to control. Just as any religious extremist can accuse members of any religion of not really practising what is preached, so can the Thatcher Government be accused of not really being true Monetarists in practice.

There is, of course, some justification for this. The rate of growth of the various monetary variables has exceeded the targets. The Government has changed its monetary variables. It would be wrong however to conclude that this necessarily means they are hypocritical in their public advocacy of Monetarism. The hard-line true believers' objections can be valid only if it is in fact possible to do the things the Thatcher Government is criticized for not doing. If it is not possible actually to control a given monetary variable with the means available, it is unreasonable to deny the intent or sincerity of those who may be trying to do the best they can. If people themselves act in such a way as to reduce the importance of a chosen monetary variable, far from criticizing the Government for shifting ground and changing its key control variable, this ought to be recognized as evidence of commitment to the cause. Failure to achieve an objective is not necessarily evidence that strenuous efforts are not being made to achieve it. It might be evidence of this; but it might also be evidence that the objective is unattainable. We might conclude that people are misguided, even daft, for trying to achieve what is known to be unattainable, but this does not mean that they are not sincere in their search for the unachievable or dedicated and resolute in their intentions.

Before the Thatcher Government is condemned for faint-heartedness, far less duplicity, in its avowed intent to pursue Monetarist' policies it is first necessary to establish that the foundation-stone of that policy—the control of the rate of change of quantity of money precisely defined—can actually, in the real world, be achieved. This the Monetarist theorists have not done. Their criticisms of the Thatcher Government are therefore based on a priori reasoning and assertions about what ought to happen rather than on realistic assessments of what could have happened in practice.

While there may be less certainty about the ability to do this effectively and there have been changes in the view of the most significant measure of money, the commitment to control the money supply seems no less firm than when the Government took office. The PSBR is clearly much higher than the Government would like even perhaps after allowing for the cyclical effects of the recession. Any confidence they had about the existence of a known or consistent time-lag relationship between changes in the supply of money and inflation has, or should have, gone.

In some ways the grounds of the debate have shifted. It is no longer a simple question of whether Monetarism works or not; instead there are quasi-technical debates about the most relevant definition and measurement of a monetary aggregate. The rate of growth of the real money supply and the real PSBR have received more attention. The original believers can retain their faith by shifting the precise variable they use. The sceptics don't particularly care which precise variable is used; they are convinced that there is no consistent relationship.

Public Expenditure

PSBR

The government seems to have increased the importance it gives to the PSBR. Its early attempts to control the money supply were not successful. Emphasizing the central role of the PSBR allowed it to continue with its aim of controlling the money supply through the PSBR and also obtain the benefits it believes will occur by reducing the public borrowing. There will be less 'crowding out', although this should really be seen as 'pricing out' resulting from any depressing effects on private activity which comes from higher interest rates. Given the massive spare capacity in the British economy the notion of 'crowding out' due to a lack of resources available to the private sector as a result of increased activity by the public sector is ludicrous. To a Keynesian emphasizing the importance of the level of aggregate demand and the crucial part played in this by government expenditure, the decline in private sector activity resulting from decreased demand might well be much greater than any 'pricing-out' effects.

Further the goal of reducing the PSBR gives added impetus to pressures to increase privatization. Right-wing Conservatives have long held the public sector to be anathema. Selling off the profitable parts will provide cash flows which reduce the need to borrow. In another sense they can be seen as part of the PSBR; they provide physical assets rather than undated Consuls to the private sector in return for a sale or cash which never has to be returned as the assets are irredeemable. Also by removing the profitable part of the public sector they allow political attacks on public ownership. If only the less profitable parts are left it is easier to make the political point, misleading though it might be, that public ownership is always unprofitable and therefore undesirable.

Quite apart from their view that there is a strong connection between the PSBR and the money supply the Thatcher Government has raised the objective of controlling the PSBR to a policy goal in itself.

Control of and reductions in public expenditure are an essential feature of Thatcher Monetarism. Not only does this reduce the PSBR: it also allows tax reductions to provide 'the reinvigoration of the supply side of the economy' (Lawson 1981, 21). The policy-induced recession actually caused government expenditure and the PSBR to rise. As part of their response the government strengthened the use of cash limits as a form of control on central government and associated measures to influence the nationalized industries and local government.

Measures to shift the NRU

As we discussed in Chapter 15 a government may seek to lower the NRU or NAIRU. The Thatcher Government has taken various steps to do this.

Cash Limits

Cash limits as now operated are essentially a means of limiting expenditure by specifying the government allocation of funds to a department for the forthcoming financial year in cash amounts rather than providing an amount in current (i.e. prior to the year in which expenditure will take place) prices which are subsequently raised by whatever is necessary to provide the same *real* level of activity in the forthcoming year.[5] For example prior to a financial year the Government has to allocate and provide funds for a department. In the past it would announce next year's allocation in this year's prices and at this year's costs. Any increases in costs and prices that arose between this year's announcement of next year's figures and the time, next year, when they were actually spent, would be made good by government increasing the financial allocation. Current practice, following the Chancellor's Budget statement of 10 March 1981, is for the next year's allocation to be expressed as a percentage change on this year's actual figures, with different percentage increases for pay and other items. Thus the 1982 allocation for additional cash in 1983–4 was 'to provide for average increases in wages and salaries bills by 3½ per cent from due settlement dates' (EPR 150, October 1982, 3.)

The Treasury statement goes on to say 'It is not a pay norm.' The argument that it is not a pay norm can be based on three grounds. First, it is possible for the department to switch some funds from non-pay to pay expenditure thereby permitting an average wage increase of more than 3½ per cent. This obviously means that the non-pay items are not essential and suggests that there might have been reprehensible laxity in the formulation of budget and appropriations. Second, there is some 'slippage' in the pay bill as some employees leave and are not immediately replaced, or the age distribution with a incremental salary scale system changes, so that the total wage bill for a given number of employees falls, thereby permitting an average increase of more than 3½ per cent. Third, there is a reduction in the number employed so that in effect the 'slippage' becomes formalized and permanent. The first two possibilities may have carry-forward effects requiring 'additional' expenditure in the next year, which could be undesirable and undesired even by those who might utilize them in any one year in order to have a higher wage increase. The third implies that there will be a reduction in the level of services provided by the given wage bill plus cash limit increase, unless there is an offsetting increase in productivity, or that manning scales are currently excessive and manpower reduction can occur with no effect on the level of services provided. If this is the case it is surely better to sort this out directly rather than indirectly by having a trade-off of jobs for above-cash limit wage increases.

With all three possibilities it is a wage kitty and a form of pay norm. The main difference is a linguistic one—it is not a precisely predetermined pay norm, but pay restriction it certainly is. Moreover it is designed to be just that. The intention is to stiffen the backs of official-side negotiators, to change trade union attitudes by emphasizing the limited amount of cash available to finance a pay rise, and to press upon unions and their members that wage increases above a certain level will threaten their jobs.

The Treasury tries to reconcile the apparent contradiction that cash limits are not pay norms by shifting ground. 'Cash limits do not in themselves constitute a public sector pay policy. They are a mechanism of public expenditure control which can be used to give effect to whatever policy the government of the day may decide is appropriate for the pay of each public service group.'[6] The reference is to policy rather than a pay norm, but what they are actually saying is that cash limits is a public sector pay policy, but one which allows different pay norms to be applied to different parts of the public service if the government so choose.

Nationalized industries are subject to a similar sort of pressure by government control of their external financing limits (EFL). 'The external financing limits of nationalized industries are also treated as a form of cash limit'.[7] The EFL's are the amount of funds which the government permits them to raise from external non-governmental sources through borrowing. If these are constrained the ability of nationalized industries to grant wage increases is limited by their ability to raise prices and maintain sales, or reduce costs. Local authorities are subject to similar pressure by control of the rate support grant which can be regarded as the central government's contribution to local authority financing and control of their capital expenditure. Both local authorities and nationalized industries 'will be constrained' (EPR 150, 3.)

Government has had considerable problems in controlling local authority expenditure as there is an element of discretion provided by the ability of LAs to increase rates. This permits higher spending, higher employment levels, and larger wage increases. Moreover, it does not follow, as the government once thought, that such increases in rates would lead to political retribution as local electorates replaced profligate councillors, in the way that consumers are supposed to move away from higher-priced products. Cash limits can be really effective only if the organization has no other source of income or finance. If it has, the 'kitty' is subject to constraint, not control.

The government's response was to introduce an additional element of control and penalties. In 1984 legislation was finally enacted after a series of Conservative as well as Labour protests in both Houses of Parliament. Central government provides grants to local authorities on the basis of grant-related expenditure assessment (GRE), a complicated formula by which the Department of the Environment determines how much of the central rate support grant should be allocated to each authority. The GREs are also regarded by the government as the amount which responsible and efficient authorities *should* spend on providing services. 'Spending very substantially above GRE can be explained only by very high levels of provision or considerable inefficiencies or a combination of both' (Cmnd. 9008, para. 1.25). This means that some authorities spent more than the central government believed they ought, their rates increased and political retribution did not take place. The attempt to create a political substitute for market forces which would keep down the rate of growth of rates had failed.

To replace the countervailing pressure of the electorate the government—perhaps rather perversely for one committed to a free-the-people and a free market approach—imposed administrative controls.[6] There are two elements of control. First, an authority which exceeds its expenditure target will lose part of the central government grant it would otherwise have received. In 1985 the loss will be the yield of a 7p rate for the first 1 per cent of overspend, 8p for the next 1 per cent, and 9p for each 1 per cent thereafter. Second, certain local authorities named as high overspenders will be rate-capped. The amount of rate they will be allowed to levy will be fixed by the government. Any rates levied to meet spending above government ceilings will be illegal. Mr Patrick Jenkins, Secretary of State for the Environment, named eighteen rate-capped local authorities on 24 July 1984. All but two were Labour-controlled.

In 1982 the then Secretary of State for the Environment, Michael Heseltine, set up a new audit commission to oversee the local government auditors. Its 1984 report was strongly critical of the government's methods of seeking to control local authorities' expenditure; it 'rubbishes the government's system . . . of funding and controlling local-authority spending'.[9] The GREs were found to be based on out-of-date or misleading expenditure. 'The system of targets and penalties is counter-productive.' Authorities could have higher targets in one year if they had spent large amounts in the previous one—the penicillin-bacteria syndrome.

Conservative no less than Labour members of local authorities protested against the government's imposition of controls, arguing that the independence of local government, its responsibility and accountability to local electorates, and the proper balance between central and local powers were being threatened. The protests were to no avail. The government was more concerned to try to impose control over public expenditure and borrowing and prevent some local authorities increasing expenditure financed by increases in rates rather than central government finance than they were to maintain the established extent of local government authority. An additional element of influence over pay rises for local authority employees has been established, but the main labour market impact was intended to be on the level of employment in local authorities. This would increase umemployment.

The importance of cash limits as a means of influencing pay developments in the Civil Service, National Health Service, and to a lesser extent in nationalized industries and local authorities should not be down-played by linguistic points concerning the precise definition of a pay norm. The effect on pay determination could be far-reaching. If the cash limit system prevails it means in effect that the main component of pay bargaining is determined in the House of Commons and not at the bargaining table. The cash limit figure is the crucial decision. All that is left for the bargainers are the questions affecting the distribution of the cash limit increase and any marginal effects of slippage or jobs trade-off.

This is recognized by the Treasury.

> There is therefore a potential difficulty in reconciling the operational requirements of the cash limits and Parliamentary Estimates systems with the desire for meaningful pay negotiations . . . In practice, what appears as an administrative problem is fundamentally a policy problem of the relationship between meaningful pay negotiations and judgement by the government of what can be afforded.[10]

This problem was shelved rather than solved in the 1982 Civil Service pay negotiations. Following the 1981 Civil Service strike resulting from the government's unilateral abandonment of the agreed system for determining Civil Service pay, the Government informed the Civil Service unions 'naturally the costs of the settlement will be a factor in next year's negotiations. But I repeat my assurance that the government will be prepared to enter into the negotiations without a predetermined cash limit. There will be room for genuine negotiations.'[11] This concession serves to underline the point that if cash limits are determined before bargaining takes place there is unlikely to be room for genuine negotiations.

The government later confirmed that if the 1982 negotiations failed to reach agreement the Government 'will accept recourse to the Civil Service arbitration tribunal but on the understanding that the government reserves the right, if necessary, to ask the House of Commons to approve setting aside the tribunal's award on grounds of overriding national policy'.[12]

There are two significant features of this. First, the Government indicated willingness to accept recourse to arbitration, which it was previously committed to do, but which it had refused in 1981. The reluctance to accept the intervention of a third party in public service pay determination was eroding a little. Second, the government stated its right to ask the House of Commons to set aside the findings of the Civil Service arbitration tribunal. Acceptance of arbitration was therefore only partial. The government was accepting arbitration but not as a method of determining pay. It reserved the right to reject the arbitrators' findings if it did not like them.

This is a particularly dangerous precedent. Arbitration in the UK rests on the voluntary principle. The two parties agree to go and they agree to accept the findings or awards. In some cases—the public sector provides various examples—as a result of a standing agreement either party may refer an unresolved issue to arbitration. Thus one party may not actually wish to have arbitration on a particular case, but its desire to have arbitration as a *process* for settling unresolved issues leads it to accept the *principle* of unilateral reference to arbitration even on those occasions when it would prefer not to go. The Thatcher Government broke such an agreement with the Civil Service unions in 1981 and pressed other public sector industries to withdraw their agreement to unilateral access to arbitration. After years of government encouragement of peaceful resolution of disputes, the Thatcher Government has reversed policy and seeks to minimize if not abandon the use of arbitration in the public sector. It may hope to obtain temporary advantage from the shift in the balance of power, but unless it foresees a permanently depressed economy it cannot hope that the rejection of arbitration will do other than lead to more industrial conflict. It is possible, of course, that it might try to prevent this by withdrawing the right to strike in parts of the public sector, or by obtaining no-strike agreements with unions in essential services. The Government's record of breaking agreements with the Civil Service unions will not encourage unions to trust them in no-strike agreements.

The threat to have the House of Commons reject an arbitration award raises serious issues. Under such a threat the arbitrators must do one of two things. They can ignore it and produce the best award they can. If this is rejected, the process of arbitration runs the risk of falling into disrepute. This may be the Government's intention, but if so, ought to be stated openly and recourse to arbitration refused the unions. The issue of arbitration could then be dealt with in its own right. Alternatively, the arbitrators, concerned to ensure the viability of even a humiliated arbitration process, may modify their award in light of the maximum they think the government will accept without asking the House of Commons to reject. Instead of deciding the case on its merits within the terms of reference, which is the traditional role of British arbitrators, they become contaminated by the political manoeuverings of government policy-makers. While arbitrators may properly take into account the acceptability of their findings and the effect this may have on the continued role of arbitration, this should be done within the context of the fairness and equality of their findings within the terms of reference, and not on the basis of a prior threat issued by one party that they will reject the award unless they get their own way. The government threat, if it is an indication of things to come, may well provide a direct challenge to the integrity of arbitrators and the arbitration process. It is an action totally to be deplored.

The use of cash limits with its effective exclusion of the major issue from pay bargaining might be intended to focus attention on the jobs–pay trade-off. Increases above the cash limit can be obtained if the number of employees is reduced. The Bank of England justified a pay increase of 17 per cent with a 14 per cent cash limit on these grounds.[13] If the level of services required from the agency is reduced the cash limit should be correspondingly reduced. Any additional pay increases ought to arise from the application of productivity bargaining.

Given high unemployment levels it would be totally unrealistic to expect a trade union to pursue jobs trade-off very far or very seriously. If the cash limit figure becomes the effective determinant of the pay increase we should expect trade unions to turn to the source of its origin. Increased politicization of public sector unions is a natural development of the cash limit system.

A precondition for the enforcement of a strict cash limit policy for the Civil Service is the abolition of comparability as the method of determining the pay levels of Civil Servants. Clearly it would be intolerably inconsistent to have a system which said that pay levels should be determined by the level of pay for comparable work elsewhere but the money to grant those pay levels were not forthcoming. The abolition of the comparability pay system was therefore a logical, even though not necessarily a defensible, decision of the Thatcher Government once it adopted a cash limit approach to pay. To abolish comparability necessitated the unilateral breaking of agreements honourably entered into by previous governments. The Thatcher Government had no scruples about breaking these agreements although there seems no doubt there would have been howls of outrage from the Conservative benches had the unions behaved in so dishonourable a way.

The scrapping of the Pay Research Unit and comparability system was also in accord with general Monetarist views. In so far as there is an explicit labour market element in Monetarism one strand seems to be an associated belief that pay ought to be set by market forces and that comparability has no constructive part to play in pay determination. As we have seen, this is contrary to practice in large parts of the private sector, but this seems not to diminish the conviction of this Government that comparability, particularly for the public sector, results in only harmful effects on the economy. The only time, it seems, that comparability might have a place is during election periods. During the 1979 campaign the Conservatives pledged themselves to accept the outcome of the Clegg Commission which was investigating various groups of non-Civil Service public employees on a comparability basis. 'That phase, however, is now over: the Clegg Commission has been abolished, the Civil Service pay system has been set aside, and a firm control of public service pay costs has been reimposed.' (Lawson 1981, 18.)

In its evidence to the Megaw Committee, set up to advise on a new system for determining Civil Service pay, the government, through the Treasury, argued strongly for 'supply and demand' to be the main determinants. They did not, however, go into much useful detail on how supply and demand should, or can, be used to determine recruitment policies for occupations which are seen as long-term career appointments. Mistakes in the quality of new recruits may not be apparent for a number of years by which time it will be too late to take corrective action without drastically changing the whole career pattern and expectations of the work-force.

There is an inevitable area of conflict in public sector pay with collective bargaining. Free collective bargaining runs the risk that the financial outcome might be burdensome or unacceptable to government. Measures to limit the financial burdens of bargaining and to retain the ultimate control of government expenditure to the legislature may lead to measures such as cash limits which effectively remove the heart from free collective bargaining. Various systems have been tried to minimize the conflict and ensure that public employees remain entitled to the same rights as other employees—the right to participate in collective bargaining. Comparability was such a system. From the Government's viewpoint this has the disadvantage that the amount of revenue to be found to finance the pay claims is outside the hands of government unless it adjusts the level of services it provides. The present imposed solution cannot be expected to endure, but the basic problem will. For our purposes the important point is that cash limits, the abrogation of an agreement freely entered into and which provided constitutional (in a collective bargaining sense) ways for determining pay but which was nevertheless destroyed at the stroke of a pen, and the refusal to go to arbitration in 1981, which provoked a not unexpected Civil Service strike, should not be regarded as accidental accompaniments of Monetarism. They or similar actions are necessary for a government committed to a Monetarist policy which seeks firm control of the PSBR and government expenditure. It is perhaps the case that the Thatcher Government gave the impression of actually enjoying doing all these things and that its anti-public sector actions do reflect a strong ideological position. This too ought to be expected in practice from Monetarist governments even though it may not be formally a part of the revised Quantity Theory of Money.

Trade Unions

Trade unions are disliked by Monetarists because of their effects in preventing wages and relative wages from responding to labour market forces. They impose rigidities in both the level and structure of wages. In addition they may create obstacles to entry into occupations in the same sort of way that lawyers restrict entry into their profession and impose demarcation rules and manning requirements, such as the use of and level of payment of juniors when QCs are hired. Among Monetarist theorists the main impact of trade unions is seen in their influence on the natural rate of unemployment. As we have seen in Chapter 9 there is disagreement among Monetarists as to whether trade unions can continually raise wages or can do so only when unions are growing in strength, although when we examine this proposition it turns out to be little more than a tautology. Governments and policymakers seem to accept that unions may have the ability to raise wages above their market-clearing levels and do so for sustained periods of time.

It is not surprising therefore that the Thatcher Government should have sought to reduce trade union power. This is in one way a continuation of the policy adopted by Edward Heath in the Industrial Relations Act of 1971. In another sense it incorporates not only political or ideological opposition to trade unions and the shift in the balance of power in industry and the economy which accompanies a strong trade union movement, but also the extension of the criticism of unions derived from a Monetarist analysis. The Thatcher Government may therefore be seen as having the natural responses of right-wing Conservatism, buttressed by recourse to an apparently value-free economic theory. This permits even blatant discriminatory action against unions to be cloaked in a veil of intellectual respectability rather than be exposed as deliberate action on sectional interest grounds. While particular measures may owe more to partisan political prejudice than to the application of straight Monetarist teachings the two are intertwined and mutually reinforcing so that it is reasonable to regard the various interventions in labour market and trade union areas as the political interpretation and extension of Monetarism even though they may not be necessary components in a package of 'pure' economic theory.

In listing the achievements of the government in its first year or so Nigel Lawson referred to the considerable progress made in microeconomic level policies in rolling back the frontiers of the state and improving the functioning of the market economy. He included the 1980 Employment Act, 'which will improve the working of the labour market by providing redress against a limited number of the worst abuses of trade union power' (1980, 6).

The main legislative actions against unions by the Thatcher Government are the 1980 and 1982 Employment Acts and the 1984 Trade Union Act. The 1980 Act removed such legislative support for the development of collective bargaining as we had in the UK. The legislative measures to seek to enforce compulsory recognition of trade unions for purposes of collective bargaining which could be ordered by ACAS in appropriate circumstances under the 1970 Employment Protection Act were repealed. Unions did not object very strongly to this as the courts had effectively emasculated such rights as were once thought to have been provided. Relatively few cases of compulsory recognition had occurred and this encouraged the view that compulsion might not mean all that much. What is unknown is the effect that the back-stop remedy of possible compulsory recognition had on the granting of recognition voluntarily.

Schedule 11 of the 1975 EPA, following provisions dating back to the Second World War, allowed the provisions of collective agreements or the generally prevailing terms and conditions to be applied to employers in the same trade or industry which did not take part in collective bargaining if the terms and conditions in those firms were less favourable than the bargained or generally prevailing ones. The Central Arbitration Committee which decided these issues believed that this protection was necessary for the protection of some unorganized workers who might otherwise be exploited.[14] Many employers had not opposed but even welcomed this provision. It ensured that unorganized competitors were required to observe some minimum terms and conditions thereby protecting the organized employers from the abuses of undercutting from unfair competition. The history of collective bargaining is replete with examples of employers seeking to obtain protection against 'unfair competition' from unorganized employers.[15]

Many governments had appreciated the logic and reasonableness of this desire and accepted it as a small price to pay for the general benefits to be obtained from the encouragement of collective bargaining. The Thatcher Government apparently does not believe that there is 'unfair' competition, at least in the labour market. All labour market competition is seen as fair and desirable, and to the extent that it reduces the powers of trade unions by undercutting terms and conditions imposed by exercise of their 'monopoly' powers, is actually regarded as laudable. Schedule 11 allowed trade unions in the pursuit of the interests of their own members and their employers, to afford some protection to the unorganized. The abolition of Schedule 11, by definition, means that the protection which was given to the weaker sections of society has been taken away. Conditions in the product market will determine whether this leads to any reduction in trade union strength. If the unorganized low-paying firms can provide sufficient competitive threat to the organized sector in terms of both price and quantity of product, the resulting pressure of product market economic forces may lead to unions becoming relatively weaker. This will not necessarily make their employers relatively stronger as they will be faced by more intense competition; it will be a shifting of relative power and viability from the organized to the unorganized sector and so, if it is successful, will be so by threatening the organized employers no less than the unions.

Reducing protection to the weak and unorganized is an essential part of the mainstream Monetarist labour market policy. Friedman frequently extols the virtues of Hong Kong and nineteenth-century United States where large inflows of immigrants flock into low-paid work.[16] Driving down wages is the Monetarist way of reducing unemployment, and while we may condemn and abhor the Thatcher Government attacks on the unorganized, we should not be surprised by them.

The 1980 Act changed the law regarding peaceful picketing during an industrial dispute. Picketing is now lawful only by those who attend at or near their own place of work (or head office if there is no fixed place of work) or by trade union officials at the place where their members work. This is intended to stop the 'flying pickets, and the

'Rent-a-picket'. The Act appears to limit immunities against liability for interfering with a commercial contract where there is secondary action to one supplier or customer either side of the employer with whom the dispute exists, and where the action 'is likely' to achieve the purpose of obtaining the objectives of the dispute. This brings the courts in to assess the likely effects of industrial action. Much disagreement is likely to occur over this. The 1982 Act narrows the definition of 'trade dispute' to which immunities are granted. A dispute must now be 'wholly or mainly' related to a list of subjects given in s. 29 rather than just be 'connected' with them. Again the courts will have considerable discretion to determine how much or little is 'wholly or mainly'.

Clearly the restrictions on lawful picketing and secondary action are intended to shift the balance of power in industrial disputes. Their effectiveness will be influenced by the willingness of those whose interests are adversely affected by actions now excluded from legal immunities to initiate legal proceedings. Previous experience has shown a general unwillingness of most employers to initiate legal action against their own employees or their trade unions. The employment relationship is seen as a long-term one which would be damaged by legal action. Such consideration is unlikely to deter action against non-employees in the case of secondary action of some picketing and we should expect to see an increase in the role of the courts. As the legislation gives the courts considerable freedom to evaluate the likely outcome of action and the main or whole content of the action, there will undoubtedly be continuing conflict over the role of the judiciary in industrial relations. While the removal of legal immunities from purely political strikes may be widely regarded as unexceptional, the restriction of immunities to disputes which are wholly or mainly related to the list of approved items in s. 29 of the 1982 Act may turn out to be more restrictive than this. The courts may deny immunities to trade union actions which are not purely political but which cannot, in the courts' views, satisfy the 'wholly or mainly' test as the courts interpret it. Additional restrictions on the definition of a trade dispute which can attract immunities were the removal of disputes between workers and workers in the 1980 Act and the limitation to disputes between workers and *their* employers in the 1982 Act.

Unions are now liable for damages for actions once protected by immunities although the amount of damages is limited by a sliding scale according to the size of the union. None the less for a union with 100,000 members it is as high as £250,000. More important, perhaps, is the possibility that court orders will be issued against unions, which, if they are disobeyed, could lead to fines for contempt, and these fines are both determined by the courts and unlimited. It may be argued that this is as it should be. Unions should obey court orders. However, it is widely recognized that there are situations where a trade union is simply unable to ensure that its members obeys either its own instructions or a court order. In a free society this may be unavoidable, and is not something confined to supporters of Solidarity against the official trade unions in Poland. While in the latter case it may be hailed as a worthy expression of freedom, which it is, it may be no less unavoidable with democratic trade unions. The legislation recognizes this by providing for unions not to be liable in certain situations if they can establish that they did not authorize or endorse the unlawful actions. It remains to be seen whether the British judicial system proves capable of properly understanding the complex and delicate nature of the chain of command and responsibility that runs through many trade unions.

Legal immunities are a necessity for British trade unions if they are to be allowed to function in the way that unions are allowed to do in any free society. Either unions must be given positive rights to take strike or other industrial action in specified circumstances or they must be given legal immunities for certain actions in appropriate circumstances. The application of common law reflecting a total commitment to free trade, the non-interference with trade, and unreal assumption that economies do and should work on the basis of individual atomistic decisions and actions so that collective action becomes a conspiracy, ensure that anything a trade union does effectively to pursue the interests of its members would leave them exposed to criminal and civil actions. The question is not therefore whether in the absence of a declaration of positive union rights, unions should receive immunities, but rather how much immunity for what sort of action in what circumstances should be given to whom? The Thatcher Government has restricted the immunities and this is at least as much for the expected economic effects in terms of collective bargaining results as for any moral principle. By changing the *processes* of collective bargaining, and in particular the types of sanctions that can be used by unions in certain situations, it is intended to alter the *results* of collective bargaining.

The two Acts attempt to reduce the incidence of the closed shop by declaring that dismissal for non-membership is unfair if the reason for non-membership is one of conscience or other deeply held personal conviction, the person was not a member of a union when the Union Membership Agreement (UMA) was signed or is a non-member where the UMA was signed after 14 August 1980 without the approval of 80 per cent of those entitled to vote as being covered by the UMA. Thus, irrespective of a 'deeply held personal conviction', a new recruit to a firm which had signed a UMA after 14 August 1980, is legally regarded as unfairly dismissed if the reason for dismissal was his refusal to join a union under a UMA which had not been approved in a secret ballot of 80 per cent of those entitled to vote. This is a very high electoral participation requirement. In the 1983 general election in only nine constituencies did the turnout reach 80 per cent or more (Butler and Kavanagh 1984, 328).

The 1982 Act applied even tighter restrictions. Dismissal for nonunion membership is now automatically unfair unless there is a UMA providing for employees to be a union member, and the UMA must have been approved in a secret ballot within the preceding five years before dismissal. Any new ballot on a UMA must have been approved by either 80 per cent of those entitled to vote, or 85 per cent of those who voted. In 1983 no MP received 85 per cent of the votes cast; the highest was 70 per cent.

The amount of compensation for unfair dismissal for non-membership is much higher than for other forms of unfair dismissal, it could exceed £30,000, and under the new legislation the individual so dismissed can enjoin the union to the action thereby making the union liable to pay part of the damages. Under the 1971 IRA the employer could enjoin the union, but in practice did not do so. Employers believed their long-term interests would be adversely affected by enjoining the union. An aggrieved dismissed member will feel no such compunction and has no similar long-term continuing relationships to inhibit him. We should expect to see unions enjoined in these unfair dismissal cases and this will engender bitterness. Moreover the 1982 Act introduces retrospectivity, so that individuals who were dismissed between September 1974 and the 1980 Act can claim unfair dismissal for nonunion membership as though the 1980 Act had been in operation. Compensation will be paid by the Department of Employment.

The then Secretary of State for Employment, Norman Tebbit, believed that the closed shop provides great power to unions. 'They benefit from the widespread practices of the closed shop which gives them authority over a vast number of conscripts who are press-ganged into the union army.'[17] However, he does not seek to ban the closed shop because 'I do not believe it would work.'[18] But he believes the new provisions will mean that 'Closed shops might continue in name only but in practice they would cease to have any real effect if employers refused to sack non-union members.'

The question of the 'number of unwilling recruits press-ganged into the union army' becomes important when considering the possible economic effects of ending the closed shop. Usually a UMA is established when the overwhelming majority of employees are union members. Employers frequently prefer a UMA in order to avoid the difficulties over a few individuals, often individuals who have once been members of the union but left over some personal difference. Put most sharply the criticism takes the form that a closed shop allows an unrepresentative union leadership to impose its will on all employees compelling them to support strikes or other industrial action against their wishes. This action leads to higher wages or less efficiency than would otherwise result and therefore steps to weaken the power of the trade union leadership is apparently supported on both ideological and economic grounds. If it were a case that only a few individuals would ignore the strike decision and seek to continue working there would be little effect on the outcome. Employers might actually prefer that a few individuals do not try and turn up for work, they could not continue production and it would exacerbate ill will. The key issue might well be the representativeness of trade union decisions.

The 1984 Trade Union Act included the three main changes.[19] Part I requires that the voting members of a principal executive committee union be elected by secret ballot of the members at least every five years. Some General Secretaries or Presidents who have a vote or a casting vote on the executive committee may have been appointed rather than elected or elected on a once-for-all basis. If they are to retain their voting rights on the executive committee they will be required to submit to periodic election. Ballots are to be postal or in appropriate circumstances at the work-place.

Part II removes immunity from legal action in cases where trade unions do not hold a ballot before authorizing or endorsing a call for a strike or any other industrial action which breaks or interferes with the contract of employment of those called upon to take part. It also makes it a condition of immunity that a majority of those voting vote in favour of the action, that the ballot is held no more than four weeks before the industrial action begins, and that the ballot satisfies the requirements of 5.11. This section says that entitlement to vote must be given to those and only those whom it is reasonable for the union to believe will be called upon to take or to continue to take strike or other action. Immunity will be lost if any member is called upon to strike after being denied entitlement to vote.

Part III deals with trade union political funds. It is now necessary for unions to ballot their members every ten years if they wish to continue to have a political fund financed by the political levy. This part became effective from 31 March 1985 and unions wishing to continue their political fund had to hold a successful ballot before 31 March 1986.

Part II may lead to great problems. It will be left to the courts to decide the circumstances in which a union is held to have authorized or endorsed a strike or other industrial action. There may be many unofficial and unconstitutional actions at shop-floor level about which the union may have had no knowledge prior to the event. These provisions became effective on 26 September 1984 and according to the Department of Employment apply to any industrial action 'which is initiated by a trade union after that date'.[20]

Critics of trade union frequently assert that the leadership is unrepresentative, and that members are dragooned into decisions with which they do not agree. It is not a question of whether every member agrees with every decision; in a democracy dissent and disagreement are the expected features of any large organization. The weight of the criticism is that on some important issues, primarily those affecting collective bargaining decisions on the size of the pay increase which is acceptable and the use of industrial action to obtain the settlement sought, trade union representatives adopt a more militant position than would their members. The evidence for this is scanty. American experience of compulsory ballots under emergency provisions shows that union members back their unions rather than accept the employers' last offer (Cmnd. 8778). In Britain there have been a few occasions when unions were overruled by their membership. They do not seem to be at all typical and the situations in which they occur, for example at British Leyland, are by no means typical of the whole trade union scene. Members of Parliament in both main parties are required to subject their own preferences and wishes to those of the parliamentary leadership much more frequently than is a trade union member compelled to obey a strike or bargaining decision against his will. The MP may be in much the position painted by critics of the closed shop. If he or she rejects the leadership's decision, the withdrawal of the Whip is as likely to result in their future loss of job as MP as it is with the UMA.

The whole of the Thatcher approach to union members participation and union decision-taking rests on the belief that the membership is more moderate than the leadership. From such research that we have at shop steward level the opposite is much more likely to be the case.[21] At certain times the balance of emphasis might shift but on the whole it could be a very serious mistake to conclude that union members will consistently settle for lower wage increases and decide on fewer strikes than do trade union leaders and the existing decision-taking systems inside the various trade unions. Indeed Mr Tebbit appears to recognize this on occasions as when in his anti-union speech he commented favourably on Mr Joe Wade the General Secretary of the National Graphical Association.[22] The problems, if problems they be, with industrial relations in newspapers is not a militant leadership buttressed by closed shop provisions insisting on the continuation of past manning scales and high wages in the face of a reluctant press-ganged membership.

It is that the members themselves refuse to make the concessions demanded by management and also seek to increase their wages.

While the 1984 legislation on union elections and strike ballots is intended to have considerable economic effects, its impact will depend upon the political soundness of the underlying analysis of the nature of trade union decision-taking. It should not be surprising if a requirement to hold more trade union elections more frequently leads to competitive electioneering by potential office-holders. That this seems not to be appreciated by professional politicians is worrying. The Conservative Party accepted the Clegg Commission's forthcoming reports on public sector in the 1979 general election campaign even though it subsequently regarded this as unwise.

General Pay Increases

Special measures have been introduced to affect public sector pay, and the Civil Service in particular has seen the abolition of its established agreed processes for pay determination and the scrapping of the comparability system and threats to the use of arbitration. In the absence of a formally declared incomes policy it is less easy for government to exert direct influence on pay in the private sector. However there were some legislative and administrative supports which impinged directly on private sector pay and the Thatcher Government has sought to dismantle these. As we have seen Schedule 11 of the EPA has been repealed.

Since the nineteenth century successive British governments have followed a policy of requiring public contractors—those firms in the private sector working on government contracts—to pay fair wages to their employees. This was last expressed in the Fair Wages Resolution of 1946. Generally speaking fair wages means the rates laid down in trade union agreements for the same sort of labour. The provisions ensured that the public did not benefit from wages which were below those considered reasonable on the basis of collective bargaining. In addition to ensuring that public work is not performed by exploited workers, they also ensure that those employers who bargain with trade unions are not placed at a competitive disadvantage in public contracting by being undercut by cheap-labour firms. As with Schedule 11 it is a widespread attempt to ensure fair and not excessive or exploitive competition. Many countries including the UK have accepted International Labour Convention No. 94 which is a statement of the acceptance of the principle of the Fair Wages resolution.

Conventions of the ILO have no legal backing. Each member country is free to accept each Convention as it chooses. The Conventions do, however, express the general principles of good industrial relations as determined by the ILO, and reflect the judgements of governments, employers and trade union organizations which make up the ILO delegations. Collectively the ILO Conventions are the nearest thing we have to an international code of good industrial relations and accepted standards of decency and fairness in employment relationships. The Thatcher Government announced in July 1982 that in addition to rescinding the Fair Wages resolution it also intended to denounce the ILO Convention No. 94. This was necessary if the Fair Wages Resolution was to be rescinded. On 16 December 1982 the House of Commons agreed 'That the Resolution of this House of 14 October 1946 relating to Fair Wages Clauses in government contracts be rescinded from 21 September 1983' (*IDS Report* 392, 1).

There is therefore now no requirement that public contractors observe any minimum wage conditions other than such as may exist under an appropriate Wages Council. The provision of fairness conditions are seen by the government as the same as the use of comparability—they are institutional devices which give trade unions unnecessary protection, provide a ratchet effect on wages, and prevent the workings of the forces of free market competition in wage determination. The notion of unfair competition is rejected and so far as labour is concerned, any and all competition which results in the lowering of wages is desirable. As with Schedule 11 it will be the weaker sections of the work-force which will be adversely affected.

There has been considerable pressure by Conservative MPs to abolish Wage Councils which currently fix statutory minimum wage levels for about three million workers. The government sought views about the future of Wages Councils in 1984. Because of commitment to an ILO Convention these councils could not be abolished immediately even if the government so wished. However, after June 1985 the government can give twelve months' notice of its intention to denounce the ILO Convention and Wage Councils could then be scrapped.

Responding to the government's request for its views the CBI supported the retention of Wages Councils if five reforms were introduced.

1. Restriction of the power of Councils to fix only a single adult rate and related youth rates rather than a collection of rates for different occupations.

2. Exemption from Wage Council Orders on application for companies with established collective bargaining procedures.

3. The wage rates for youths were considered to be too high. Freezing them while periodically increasing adult rates as necessary would correct this.

4. A full review by the government of the case for the continued existence of each individual council.

5. Improvements in the '*modus operandi*' of the Councils which affect the part played by the independent members, the written information provided by the parties, and the organization of meetings.

These reforms were regarded as absolute necessities. 'However they (members of the CBI) would prefer a substantial package of reforms to the complete abolition of the whole Wage Council system. But if the suggested package is not adopted in its entirety and the performance of Wages Councils does not improve then they would back outright abolition.'[23]

Mr John Gummer, then Minister of State for Employment, indicated that he, and perhaps the Government, were doubtful of the need to retain them.

We will look with a most searching eye into the operation of wages councils and examine fairly . . . whether their existence and operation increase unemployment. If that turns out to be true it would be a dereliction of duty were the government to continue the system merely because we have always had it and merely because Winston Churchill proposed it in 1909.[24]

Always apparently means since 1909!

In 1985 the then Secretary of State for Employment, Tom King, announced the government's intentions on policy changes regarding Wages Councils. Legislation is to be introduced which will remove all protection for young people aged less than twenty-one. The Councils will be empowered only to set a single minimum hourly rate and a single overtime rate for adults. It will also be easier to modify or abolish individual Councils. The government is giving twelve months' notice to the ILO of its intention to renounce the Convention.

Existing employees will retain protection under s. 15 of the 1979 Wages Councils Act which incorporates the provisions of Wages Council orders into contracts of employment. Thus, unless the government amends this provision, those workers will retain the enforceable Wages Council provisions which exist at the time the new changes are introduced. In this case the changes will affect only new recruits. Those under the age of twenty-one will receive no protection. This is a remarkably regressive step. It removes protection from young people, one of the groups which have always been thought in need of legislative cover. On the present government proposals, employers will be able to pay young people as little as they can get away with, make no premium payment for overtime, and indeed insist on whatever hours of work they wish. Given the massive imbalance between unemployment and vacancies for young people there is no doubt that many unscrupulous employers will impose terms and conditions of employment which have no place in the twentieth century.

The second change will have two important effects. It will abolish any statutory wage differentials in these sectors and will remove the need to pay premium for work done on Sunday or public holidays. There will be only a minimum overtime premium. If the government also changes the law regarding Sunday trading and permits many more shops to trade on Sundays, employees can be required to work on Sunday at the same rate as in normal non-overtime hours. This will affect many adults, and particularly the part-time workers who will probably be recruited as a result of Sunday opening. Unless it is believed that the extension of shops opening to Sundays will lead to an increase in the amount of aggregate sales, an expansion of part-time employment on Sunday will be accompanied by a reduction in the numbers employed on other days. Total employment measured in hours worked might not rise by very much but there could be a substantial shift from full-time to part-time employment.

It might be expected that any examination of Wages Councils would show that they had some deleterious effect on employment. Their very purpose is to raise the wages of some of the covered workers above the levels that would exist without the Councils, and it is a common assumption of economics that higher wages (or prices) leads to lower demand. That assumption depends, of course, on *ceteris paribus* conditions and on the assumption that markets are in equilibrium with profit-maximizing employers. In reality not only are these assumptions unlikely to be strictly met but it is no longer apparently self-evident that higher wages will lead to lower employment. Craig *et al.* (1982), in an excellent detailed study of six Wages Councils concluded that in some circumstances they could have a stabilizing effect by concentrating demand on more efficient firms with long-term benefits for efficiency and employment. 'Minimum wage protection which raised pay for low-paid occupations is unlikely to have a significant employment effect' (137).

The Thatcher Government is the first one since 1909 to believe that instead of providing a minimum of protection for the weak and unorganized sections of the work-force the Government should actively pursue a policy of exposing them to harsher and unconstrained market forces even if these be the result of monopsony of the employers' side of the labour market. They are seeking deliberately to lower wages rather than provide a minimum living standard in the hope this will lead to greater expansion of employment. It is the first government in seventy-five years to deny that there is such a thing as a low-pay problem. Indeed it is trying to establish that even the lowest-paid groups are actually a high-wage problem in that the only way to expand employment is to drive down even further their low wages. The point is well expressed in the title of monograph attacking statutory intervention to protect the weak, *Low Pay or No Pay?* by David Forrest (1984).

The argument was well put by Winston Churchill in the House of Commons in 1909.

> It is a serious national evil that any class of His Majesty's subjects should receive less than a living wage in return for the utmost exertions. It was formerly supposed that the working of the laws of supply and demand would naturally regulate or eliminate the evil. But where you have . . . no organization, no parity of bargaining, the good employer is undercut by the bad and the bad employer is undercut by the worst . . .[25]

We are being forced back to reliance on the laws of supply and demand, but with no reason to believe that there will in fact be all that much increase in demand although there might well be a worsening of conditions as employers in some sectors are dragged down by the worst.

The Young Workers' Scheme introduced in January 1982 is another measure to reduce wages, or as the Department of Employment put it in their monthly press releases giving the unemployment figures, 'designed to encourage employers to take on more young people at realistic wage rates'. From April 1984 young people who 'left school at sixteen and who have been out of school for a year' and those leaving at seventeen immediately on leaving education, qualify for the scheme. Employers are able to claim a subsidy of £15 a week in respect of eligible youngsters earning £50 or less a week in their first year of employment.

It has been reported that a Department of Employment study of the effects of the Young Workers' Scheme shows 'that only one subsidy in thirteen represents a new job created'.[26] This suggests that the Government 'is paying over £6,000 a year for every job (after accounting for savings in unemployment benefit and gains in tax).' The conflict between different objectives is highlighted in Pond's comments about Wages Councils. The wage ceiling under the YWS is lower than the minimum rates set by some Wages Councils but 'the government has refused to check applications under the YWS to ensure that firms are not receiving the government subsidy for paying illegal low wages'.

On this evidence it would seem, either, that the level of pay for young workers is not a major inhibiting factor in the expansion of employment, or, that these wages would have to fall much more significantly before any sizeable employment effects were felt. It may be that in the absence of the YWS subsidy the twelve out of thirteen existing jobs receiving support would disappear. If this is so the YWS is really an employment-maintenance rather than an employment-generating scheme.

Unemployment is severe among young people. One explanation of this is that youth wages are too high in relation to the skills and abilities of young people when compared with adult wages, skills, and abilities. Just as employers may choose between different factors of production on the basis of their relative productivity–cost ratios, so may they choose between different types of labour, and in this case, different age-experience-skill types of labour, to the disadvantage of young people.

While there is no clear evidence establishing their relative wage levels as the cause of youth unemployment, some research results, although hedged with reservations about the data limitations, are consistent with this view. Concentrating on the period 1969–81 a Department of Employment study concluded 'the employment of young people under 18 years of age appears to have been reduced by increases in their average earnings relative to the average earnings of adults (this is especially apparent for males)' (Wells 1983, 1). However, two other findings should be noted. The average earnings of young people relative to adults do not appear to have risen since the mid-1970s. Avaricious youth hardly seems the explanation for the growth in youth unemployment since the mid-seventies. Also, 'Changes in youth employment are strongly associated with changes in the general level of employment, but are generally more rapid.' As the economy goes, so goes youth, only more so. Conservative Ministers seem agreed on the effect of relative wage–skill ratios but seem less clear on who causes the relatively high wages of young people. In February 1982 Norman Tebbit apparently told the House of Commons Select Committee on Employment that the youngsters themselves were responsible. 'It is not always easy these days for a youngster of sixteen . . . to earn from his employer the sort of wages which are currently very often being asked' *The Times* (25 February 1982) also reported him as saying that young workers should bargain with employers saying that if the employer paid a wage of £25 the youngster could get another £15 under the Scheme. (At that time the £15 subsidy was conditional on a wage of not more than £40.) In March 1982 Tebbit said 'Unemployment among young people is not high because of their own actions but because they have been priced out of jobs by other people's greed'.[27] In April he supported his general position on the relationship between youth unemployment and their wage levels by quoting from Sir Terence Beckett, Director of the CBI, to which he urged possible critics 'should listen carefully'. 'Given the choice between a youngster with little experience, and a trained man who has been "through the mill", *at the same wage* everybody knows which the employer would prefer'[28] (emphasis added). The condition that they be paid the same wage is not, of course, the same point as that about their relative wages. David Waddington MP, Parliamentary Under-Secretary of State for Employment echoed the view that trade union leaders were responsible by asking them to show pay restraint in order to show their concern for the unemployed.[29]

While there may be some confusion about who causes the high wages for young workers there seems none about the effects. They lead to higher unemployment. The Young Workers' Scheme is therefore designed to increase employment of young people by holding down their wages and by separating through the subsidy the level of wages paid, from the wage cost to the employer. It is an obvious attempt to change existing wage differentials. What is not obvious or discussed by Ministers are the effects that the success of the Scheme might have on unemployment of older or adult workers. If the Scheme leads only to an expansion of employment there might be none, and indeed, a Keynesian (not therefore a Thatcher Minister at the Department of Employment) might expect that if the employment of young people expanded sufficiently there could be some secondary expansion of demand leading to reduced unemployment among adult workers. However, if, following the substitution of types of labour argument, the Scheme merely means that young people are employed *instead* of adults all that will have been obtained will be a switching of the incidence of unemployment towards older members of the work-force. This could well increase the PSBR as they are likely to be entitled to higher levels of UB and SupBen than youngsters and their forgone tax payments from higher incomes could be greater. However, the YWS has attracted pitifully few takers. Employers have not responded by increasing their demand for young workers even though the cost to them has been greatly reduced.

The perceived need to blame trade unions and their leaders for youth unemployment leads to even more confusion, and an important rejection of some of Friedmanite Monetarism. In his speech to businessmen in London in March 1982 Tebbit said, 'Although excessive wage increases do not affect existing workers adversely they do affect potential recruits.'[30] This was evidently considered sufficiently important to be spread to a wider audience than that reached even by a Department of Employment press release and was quoted on the front page of the Department's *Employment News*.[31] It can hardly have been a mistake or misprint therefore. It is one of the most remarkable statements ever made by any politician. It says that workers can get whatever wage increases they like without adversely affecting their jobs. Fortunately trade unionists do not believe this. They do recognize that some level of wages could jeopardize their own interests. The Tebbit doctrine is a rejection of the expectations-augmented Phillips curve and Monetarism. It means that even if expectations about inflation are wrong and wages rise too much there will be no reduction in the demand for labour or in their real wages. A fall in either would obviously affect their interests adversely and so would be ruled out.

Tebbit opened his speech by saying that there are seven deadly delusions which Britain must destroy if more jobs are to be created. The combined weight of the seven is totally insignificant in comparison to the delusion that wage increases cannot adversely affect existing workers. While marvelling at the audacity of the man in developing this argument—he was trying to establish that the excessive wage increases caused the misery of unemployment among the young and that therefore trade unions were the really guilty ones for the tragedy of the enforced idleness of so many of our school-leavers—and while trembling at the thought that the holder of the view that workers cannot jeopardize their own interests by excessive wage increases could hold high office in a British government and be responsible for employment questions, we will reject his statement as a responsible statement of Conservative views or policy. Clearly the rest of the Conservative Party does not believe it, and neither, I suspect, does Mr Tebbit. Existing jobs can be adversely affected by excessive wage increases. Trade unions believe this although they may hold different views as to what constitutes 'excessive'.

The Thatcher Government holds the view that excessive wage increases can cause unemployment among those already employed. It is not clear why a Monetarist should hold this view. If money and prices are but symbols which cannot and do not affect the level of real activity, it ought not to matter what happens to inflation. With a floating exchange rate and a Government which has no exchange rate policy as such but leaves it to the market, high inflation should be taken care of by movements in the exchange rate. For a real or pure Monetarist it is only if the excessive wage increases lead to a rise in real wages that unemployment should occur. This is equivalent to a raising of the expectations-augmented Phillips curve for each anticipated rate of inflation and therefore a rise in the Natural Rate of Unemployment.

Different measures are attempts to lower the collective reservation wage, either by shifting the balance of power away from trade unions, or by reducing or ending the legislative underpinning which enforces a collective reservation wage which is higher than the assumed reservation wages of the individuals or employees' acceptable-labour supply curves.

Training

In 1980 and 1981 the then Chairman of the MSC submitted papers to the National Economic Development Council warning that economic development would be held up unless more people were trained in skills which were in high demand. Unemployment and the NRU would then be higher than they need be. The Director-General of the NEDC took the same line in a paper he submitted in December 1980. 'Future skill supplies, and, therefore, our ability to respond to an economic upturn, may be curtailed as a result of the present recession.'[32] The 'number of apprentices and other long-term trainees taken on by firms fell from around 100,000 a year in the late 1970s to 90,000 in 1980-1 with another sharp fall expected in the current year, despite larger numbers in the relevant age-groups (Cmnd. 8455, para. 56). Companies are short of funds and are pressed to confine expenditure to short-term essential needs. Training to meet possible demands from an upturn may have a very low priority when companies are struggling to survive.

The MSC's Review Body stressed the need for training to meet the requirements of the 1980s. In particular, from the viewpoint of our interest in the NRU, they referred to the changing pattern of occupational demand which would lead to an increase in the proportion of the work-force employed technicians and technologists, and a decrease in the proportion employed in jobs requiring little skill. The structural and technological change expected during the decade was expected to lead to the emergence of new occupations and the decline of old with radical changes in many jobs. They forecast a potential mismatch between the supply and demand for skills.[33] Following their consultative document, 'A New Training Initiative', the MSC published their proposals for a national strategy to achieve a fundamental reform of training, in 'A New Training Initiative: An Agenda for Action' (December 1981). The Government's response drew substantially on the recommendations.[34] Much emphasis was placed on the Youth Training Scheme to guarantee from September 1983 a full year's foundation training for all those leaving school at the minimum age without jobs, with improved incentives for employers to provide training. An important element was to provide training which would allow youngsters to change jobs and skills more easily.

The inadequacies of training and retraining for adults was bluntly admitted. 'We have until now assumed that the training given in a person's first job is all he will need for the rest of his working life' (Cmnd. 8455, para. 8). That would be bad enough were the work-force to receive reasonable training in their first job. '*Yet in 1979 nearly 40 per* cent of the 700,000 school-leavers who found jobs received no training at all. About another 20 per cent were receiving training for only eight weeks or less' (para. 18, emphasis in original). If the Department of Employment is right in its statement of assumption about the satisfactoriness of training in the first job, it is almost beyond understanding why we do not have much greater skill mismatch than seems to be the case. The changing job requirements and structural changes that have occurred must have necessitated additional training. This has probably taken the form of on-the-job training.

The debate about the most effective way of financing training and ensuring that the right amount of appropriate training and retraining is undertaken will continue and is beyond the scope of this study. Two main points should be noted. The Youth Training Scheme will reduce the NRU. To the extent that school-leavers who would otherwise be unemployed, are on some form of training or work experience course, the numbers registered as unemployed, and therefore the NRU as conventionally measured, will be lowered. It might not be lowered as much as supporters of the scheme might wish. Employers may substitute trainees for young people they would otherwise have employed so that their increased unemployment is transferred from sixteen- to seventeen-year-olds. If the adult training and retraining proposals and the new apprenticeship and professional arrangements are introduced there should be an increased supply of more highly skilled workers which could reduce the rate of increase of money wages and so the NRU. However, as the MSC conclude: 'market forces alone will not produce training of the quality or quantity required' (December 1981, para. 14). Large though government expenditure is it is probably insufficient and the abolition of a majority of Industrial Training Boards, with a move to the voluntary financing of training seems almost designed to inhibit future expansion of employment.

The Unemployed

Belief that most if not all unemployment is voluntary, and that the unemployed consist primarily of scroungers and the work-shy content to live off overly generous social security payments, leads a Monetarist government to look closely at the level of benefits. Reductions in the level of unemployment benefits are doubly welcome to the Thatcher Government. By lowering the Replacement Ratio they should lead to lower reservation wages and thus a reduction in wages or their rate of increase. They also lead to a fall in the PSBR. A government in Britain faces difficulties in mounting a direct assault on the level of UB and other benefits to the unemployed. Unemployment and Sickness

Benefits are generally lower than the amount of Supplementary Benefit entitlement for married men who have no other sources of income. To reduce UB would therefore merely result in offsetting payments of Supplementary Benefit and the same amount of total receipts. To provide lower levels of Supplementary Benefit for the unemployed might be regarded as unduly discriminatory if the level of Supplementary Benefit is regarded as the minimum necessary for the maintenance of the socially determined basic standard of living, although the denial of the long-term benefit rates to the unemployed does just this.

The scope for direct reductions in the level of UB is therefore somewhat limited. The Thatcher Government approached the issue indirectly. The government announced in 1980 that it intended to tax UB, or Supplementary Benefit to the standard rate of UB where Supplementary Benefit rather than UB was received by the unemployed, plus, where appropriate, a wife's standard UB payment. As the introduction of the necessary administrative arrangements would take time the government said that in the meanwhile it would not raise UB standard rates by the full amount of the increase in the RPI. This broke the conditions of the Rooker-Wise amendment which required the indexing of social security benefits. UB was raised by five per cent less than the RPI increase. However, when the taxation of UB was introduced in July 1982 the 5 per cent cut in the real value of UB was not restored. This led to Conservative back-bench revolts by MPs who believed that the government had not only failed to honour an understood commitment, but that such discriminatory action against the unemployed was a betrayal of fundamental Tory principles. It was seen as a rejection of the duties and obligations necessarily incumbent upon those more fortunate members of society which counterbalanced their rights and privileges. Increasing the hardship endured by the unemployed, particularly at a time when unemployment was rising and, it was thought, for reasons outside the control of the unemployed, was a clear breach of Disraelian principles. The last revolt resulted in eighteen Conservatives voting against the government and a further six abstaining, reducing the normal government majority of thirty-nine to eight.[35] To forestall further internal opposition the Government subsequently announced that it intended to restore the 5 per cent cut although not immediately. Not all Conservative MPs believe that unemployment is voluntary or that the unemployed are undeserving of the real level of benefits received in 1980.

The taxation of UB differs from that of earnings. No adjustment is made to tax payments or refunds until the end of the tax year or the return to work of the unemployed individual. UB will not therefore be reduced during unemployment. Even if tax were levied during the receipt of UB this would not normally result in a reduction in the amount of benefit received as the weekly equivalent of the annual standard personal allowance for a married couple exceeds the standard taxable rate of UB. No tax liability actually occurs on the UB received. Rather, the effect is to increase the amount of tax which will be paid on any earnings received subsequent to receipt of UB as a result of obtaining work later in that tax year.[36]

Prior to July 1983 UB was not taxed and the weekly personal tax allowance of an unemployed worker could be 'saved' and carried forward to offset tax liability against earnings later in the tax year, or, if the unemployed taxpayer had been employed prior to unemployment in that tax year, be offset against past tax liabilities and so lead to a refund of tax already paid that year. This was held to be inequitable. If individual A received, say, £4250 as a result of working half the year and receiving UB during the other half he would pay tax only on his earnings. Individual B who earned £4250 as a result of working for a lower rate of pay for 52 weeks in the tax year would pay tax on the full amount of his earnings. On a simple example of a married man in tax year 1982–3 the difference in net after-tax income of the two individuals would have been about £350.

However, while one view of equity might lead to support of the change one consequence of it could be to provide a distinctive to return to work during the tax year, in relation to the previous rules. Prior to July 1983 each week of unemployment allowed the full amount of the weekly equivalent of the tax-free personal allowance to be carried forward. Now only the difference between this and the lower rate of UB, for a single or married couple as appropriate, can be carried forward. In 1983–4 with a tax rate of 30 per cent this means that an unemployed married man could actually lose £13.12½ a week for each week of unemployment on return to work. In order to obtain the same net income from employment as he would have done under the old rules this man would need to find a job that paid £18.75 a week gross more for each week of unemployment than he would prior to July 1983.

If an unemployed individual has developed some sort of permanent income hypothesis as developed by Friedman and combines his annual net income from employment and unemployment as some of the voluntary unemployment explanations would have us believe, the result of the Thatcher Government's July 1983 measures could be to increase reservation wages. Thus if he had been unemployed for ten weeks and there are only ten weeks left in the current tax year he would need an extra £18.75 gross in his new job. If there were only five weeks left in the tax year he would need a higher wage of £37.50 a week and £9.37½ if there are twenty weeks left before the end of the tax year. If he takes a longer view than the current tax year he will require smaller increases in gross pay to maintain his expected net income, but his reservation wage will still be higher than before the July 1983 changes were introduced.

It is not claimed that all unemployed workers behave in this way, but then it is not claimed here that the permanent income hypothesis associated with the voluntary choice of employment and unemployment determines the incidence or length of unemployment for the greater part of the work-force. Some Monetarists, however, ought to expect the sort of response we have outlined.

Against this it can be argued that the withholding of tax rebates to the unemployed, and incidentally to strikers, will have a reverse effect. Prior to the 1983 changes both the unemployed and strikers were entitled to tax rebates if they had paid tax during the current tax year. In 1983 this could have been equivalent to £16.12½ a week until all the tax paid during that tax year had been refunded. The Government's new rules withholds money from the unemployed. As we have seen, because the weekly tax-free personal allowance for a married couple is higher than the level of UB, there is during each week of unemployment some unused tax-free allowance. If tax has been paid earlier in the tax year this unused allowance is reducing the accrued tax liability of the individual because he could offset it against the tax he has already paid. He is therefore on the usual application of the PAYE tax system, entitled to a rebate until he has received back all the tax previously paid that year. The Government's denial of this rebate was, on 1983 figures, an improper withholding of £3 a week from a married man who had paid enough tax earlier that year. (The difference between the weekly tax-free personal allowance and weekly UB was £10 and the standard rate of tax 30 per cent.)

Withholding this tax refund can result in a larger reduction of the net income received by the unemployed than occurred as a result of the initial refusal of the Thatcher Government to raise UB by the increase in the RPI which sparked off the Conservative MPs back-bench revolt. The greater and longer-lasting injustice was accepted.

This may be because it is believed that reducing the income of the unemployed in this way will encourage them to accept a job. If this is on some sort of permanent income hypothesis it requires the unemployed to have rather short time horizons. In order to obtain their tax refunds before the end of the current tax year they are assumed to lower their reservation wage and accept a job. But that lower wage which is assumed to be now acceptable might be expected to persist in future tax years and so result in a lower long-term income. Either the unemployed are assumed to accept this because they want their tax refund quickly, or they might quit the low-paying job as soon as they have received their tax refund. It is difficult to see a consistent view of labour market behaviour running through the Thatcher Government's actions here, but this may be because the only consistent element is the desire to reduce the net income of the unemployed.

If reservation wages are not affected by the taxation of UB there will be no labour market effects. Paradoxically, if the unemployed behave in a broad Monetarist way and act on expected permanent income hypothesis tenets it is quite likely that there could be a perverse labour market effect and reservation wages could rise. To minimize that effect would require that UB be reduced at the time of its receipt but that may not be politically possible even if it could be held to be socially desirable. If one believes that much unemployment exists because of a shortage of aggregate demand and is involuntary, placing additional hardship on the unemployed is not only socially and morally indefensible it is economically perverse. The Thatcher Government apparently believes that unemployment is voluntary and that reservation wages can be lowered by taxing UB and that this will lead to greater job search for lower wages with corresponding effects in reducing the natural rate of unemployment.

The withholding of tax rebates to those on strike, or unable to work because of a strike in which they are held to have a direct interest, is naked discrimination. These individuals are clearly and legally entitled to a tax rebate under normal tax regulations in exactly the same way as anyone else whose income falls or stops. They are doing nothing illegal. If under new or future legislation a particular strike is held to be illegal special regulations might apply, but as long as individuals are taking part in lawful industrial action there seems no justifiable reason to withhold tax rebates from them. I happen to believe that the activities of some currency speculators are immoral and harmful to the economy. In many cases the effects may be more harmful than a strike. Yet if employees of speculators are laid off they are entitled to tax rebates. If we decide who is and who is not entitled to tax rebates on moral grounds we enter a murky and dangerous area of insoluble difficulties.

Withholding tax rebates to strikers can deny them the full rebate of £16.12½ a week. They will receive the accumulated rebates on return to work but it may be that the government hopes that the denial of this during the course of the strike may shorten strikes. The provisions will not, on past experience, apply to many strikes, as most strikers would not receive a rebate until they had been out for two weeks and very few strikes last that long. However, in some cases there will be an effect and it will impose hardship on strikers and their families.

Housing and Mobility

The Thatcher Government sees subsidized local authority rents as inhibiting labour mobility, increasing the NRU and/or inflation, and causing higher taxes or rates. In addition to attacking subsidies in order to remove perceived obstacles to the freer working of the labour market and increased geographical mobility of labour there were other economic and social reasons for their action to generate pressure to raise council house rents.

The Housing Act 1981 has created 'very strong incentives for authorities to raise rents and so do away with the need for subsidy. On present trends, all such central government subsidy will disappear in two or three years' time, except perhaps in some London boroughs' (*Public Money*, 2(1), June 1982). Local authority subsidies are also expected to be withdrawn.

Commentators seem to agree that in a free market situation rents would rise. This could lead to a fall in demand and perhaps an increased supply of housing for rent, and it is this factor, the provision of houses available for rent in those areas where there is at present an insufficient supply of labour at prevailing real wage levels, or where there would be an increased supply of labour perhaps at lower real wage levels, which would increase geographical labour mobility and thereby lead to a reduction in the NRU. A reduction in the NRU occurs only if workers accept a cut in real living standards. If they do not there could be higher rents for all, not just those in subsidized council houses. If workers do not accept lower living standards then removing rent subsidies and controls has the perverse effect of increasing the NRU.

It is widely believed amongst those involved in collective bargaining that some elements in the cost of living have a greater impact than do equivalent increases in other items. Thus, increases in rents might lead to stronger pressure for compensating money wage increases than a general increase in prices. What is important in this regard is not whether people are rational, irrational, fooled, misguided, or subject to some sort of illusion similar to the money illusion which might affect all economic agents in times of rising inflation. The important point is that if people respond to certain price increases more strongly than to other equivalent price increases by pressing for compensating money wage increases then removing rent controls would have the perverse effect on the NRU, unless the pressure for higher money wages can be resisted.

Another aspect of housing and geographical labour mobility is that of owner-occupiers. There are tax reliefs on mortgage interest, and option mortgages, whereby those who by virtue of low income would not obtain the benefits of tax relief, obtain mortgages at lower interest rates with the government compensating building societies. In 1981–2 mortgage interest tax relief was £2030 million, cash subsidies to local authority tenants were £1277 million, and option mortgages cost £240 million. In 1982–3 subsidies to local authority tenants were due to fall to £917 million, and the cost of option mortgages to rise to £300 million (*Public Money*, 2(1), 64). Brittan believes that the tax relief on interest makes 'it politically difficult to phase out the subsidization of the rents for council dwellings and rent controls', but as we have seen, the Thatcher Government seems not to regard it as so politically difficult. Brittan goes on to criticize the tax reliefs as 'they also encourage over-investment in a single residence relative to other assets, which can hardly be good for mobility' (1982, 126).

Established rules which limit the size of mortgage according to repayments based on a proportion of income related to the number of working years before retirement can impose limitations on the range of houses effectively open to a potential migrant. The higher the rate of interest, allowing for any tax or similar reliefs, the smaller the additional capital sum mortgage which will be granted, and so the smaller the range of houses open to the migrant. Restrictive monetary policies are associated with higher interest rates.

Reducing the Public Sector

The government is committed to reducing the size of the public sector on ideological grounds and because it is hoped this will result in a lower PSBR and/or taxes. One estimate concludes that between 1979 and mid-1984 when 'proceeds of council house sales (6¾ billion since 1979) are included, PSBR targets have been eased cumulatively by well over £8 billion' (Buckland and Davies 1984, 32). It is the intention to sell off parts of British Airways and British Telecom among others.

Government has pressed local authorities and the NHS to contract out services where possible by calling for tenders from the private sector firms to provide certain services. Some authorities responded enthusiastically, seeking private tenders for refuse collection, and school cleaning. A DHSS circular in September 1983 told the ninety-three district health authorities to invite tenders from private contractors and the existing NHS work-force, and accept the lowest. The main areas to be affected were cleaning, laundry, and catering. There are indications that reducing costs may not be the sole or even relevant criterion. It was reported that the Minister of Health 'insisted that the Cornwall health authority must hire a private firm . . . to handle laundry from ten Cornish hospitals even though the authority calculates that the NHS will lose more than £47,000 on the deal'.[37]

In some cases contractors have changed the terms of service of the former NHS employees taken over when services have been contracted out. This may take the form of less hours of work each week, or a reduction in the holdiay pay provisions or other fringe benefits. But government hopes that pay levels might fall as a result of the use of private contractors appears to have suffered a set-back. In May 1984 the Contract Cleaning and Maintenance Association agreed to pay NHS wage rates by writing this into a code of conduct for its health-care section.[38] Of course, not all members may follow the code and some firms may not be members of the Association. However, this decision, taken to reduce opposition from members of authorities concerned that private contractors would tender on the basis of reduced wages, cannot have been welcome to the Government. It reduced the possibility of low wages leading to more jobs, meant that private firms could compete only on the basis of greater efficiency rather than cheap labour, and effectively restored to the NHS cleaning contracts the protection of the abandoned Schedule 11 of the 1971 Employment Protection Act. More importantly it effectively restored the protection of the Fair Wages Resolution.

In June 1984 NUPE claimed that private contractors were obtaining about 60 per cent of ancillary service contracts put out to tender by district health authorities.[39] It is not clear how many of these were obtained before the commitment to pay NHS pay levels. Private contractors appear much more successful than in-house tenders in cleaning and slightly more so in laundry tenders. They have little success in catering. This is probably due to the nature of catering in hospitals—special diets and fluctuating daily numbers of patients and meals. NUPE also claimed that a number of contracts had proved unsatisfactory as contractors had not provided the expected level of service. This complaint has also been made about local authority subcontracting.

Trade unions naturally oppose private contractors replacing local authority and NHS employees. Strikes have taken place over the proposed introduction of private contractors. When Birmingham City Council announced its determination to submit refuse collection to private tenders, the unions initially resisted but then the city's own refuse collection staff submitted a tender, which would cost £3.5 million less than the current cost of providing the service and have 300 fewer people. 'Its concessions on manpower and productivity represent the determination of the manual workers to protect some jobs rather than risk losing all if a private firm wins the contract.'[40]

Policies of the Thatcher Government

The total number of public sector employees fell from 7.4 million in 1979 to 7.0 million in 1982. However, because employment in the private sector fell at a faster rate, public sector employment as a percentage of the total in employment rose over the period from 29.2 per cent to 29.8 per cent.[41]

In the year mid-1981 to mid-1982 private sector employment fell by 2.9 per cent and public sector by 2.2 per cent. The largest fall in the public sector was in the public corporations with a reduction of 108,000, of which 28,000 jobs were transferred to the private sector. The process of cutting back the squeezing jobs in the public sector and the policies of privatization and subcontracting will continue. The indications are that this will result in fewer but lower-paid jobs. There is no evidence from the experience of local and health authorities to suggest that there is a lower-pay–more jobs trade-off; in fact it is the reverse; low pay and less jobs are compliments not substitutes.

Conclusions

There are clearly discernible themes running through the Thatcher Government's labour market policies. First, is the attempt to increase the effectiveness of market forces. The rejection of practices and institutions of collective bargaining which moderate the harsher forces of competition, particularly as these affect the weaker or unorganized sections of the work-force, means that wages in those sectors are likely to rise at a reduced rate. Thus the ending of Schedule 11 and the Fair Wages Resolution are intended to subject the wages of some groups of workers to greater pressure by removing institutional and legal protection. The desire to end the use of comparability in the public sector reflects the view that comparability somehow produces results which are different from those which would result from the interplay of market forces, and not only different, but higher. Cash limits can be seen as an administrative device to create effects which are thought to be similar to those of a certain type of market forces. The cash limit is seen as acting as a specific demand for labour curve, one with unitary price (wage) elasticity of demand.

Second, the perceived power of trade unions to increase money wages, or to prevent them falling, is challenged by the industrial relations legislation. The ending of the compulsory recognition procedures can be seen as an attempt to discourage the extension of trade union membership and collective bargaining and the Employment Acts of 1980 and 1982 will have a reinforcing effect in that the use of secondary industrial action and mass picketing tactics are no longer lawful. These tactics might be especially helpful to a trade union seeking recognition where it does not at that time have sufficient strength to bargain collectively. Limitations of their use might therefore slow down trade union growth. This would prevent the organized sector growing and therefore mean that a larger proportion of the economy was more subject to market forces and freer from institutional constraints or 'distortions'.

Further the legislative changes may make it more difficult for unions which are recognized to exert as much bargaining strength. The withholding of tax rebates to those on strike, i.e. who are considered to have a direct interest in the outcome of the strike which might include some unable to work but who do not regard themselves as being on strike but rather as unable to work because of the strike—is a particularly discriminatory action. Unlike those receiving UB there is no tax liability accruing and therefore no administrative reason to withhold payment. Indeed, it cannot be claimed that payment of rebates to strikers would be administratively impossible because it was happening prior to 1983. The motive is purely and simply to deny to strikers benefits under the tax provisions which are available to all other taxpayers. In this regard strikers may be treated more harshly than convicted criminals. Without in any way condoning any particular strike and without denying that some strikes can do immense harm to other parts of society, it is necessary to recognize that measures to prevent the exercise of the right to strike by the creation of deliberately discriminatory administrative rules raise some profound questions about the nature of a free and democratic society.

Third, the approach to UB and related benefits reflects the Monetarist view that wages are ratcheted by the level of benefits and that some reductions in the Replacement Ratio is desirable in order to lower reservation wages. If reservation wages can be lowered there will be an increased supply of labour as some of those who are now regarded as voluntarily unemployed will begin to look for work. Money wages may then fall on a Minford view, or rise less quickly, or not at all on a modified institutional view.

All three can be seen as attempts to influence reservation wages. The first two seek to act on collective reservation wages, those determined by trade unions or institutional substitutes for collective bargaining. The third turns to the individual's reservation wages. Measures to increase geographical mobility, including the ending of subsidies on local authority rented property, can be seen as attempts to lower reservation wages and keep down the level or rate of increase of wages. They are all designed to lower the natural rate of unemployment by obtaining reductions in real wages below the levels which would otherwise exist. While there are ways of lowering the NRU by active manpower policies and effective retraining programmes which seek to ensure that the labour force is better equipped to meet expected future requirements these do not play any significant part in the Thatcher Government's policies. The programme for young people and particularly the unemployed school-leavers cannot be seen as being devised in order to tackle future manpower requirements in a constructive way. They are measures to give the unemployed something to do, to try and mitigate the worst effects of the present recession, and to lower the statistical measure of unemployment. Much effort and much money has gone into action to lower the published figures of unemployment but relatively little to increase employment other than the reliance on the general beliefs of Monetarism. The lowering of the real wage and thus the standard of living, has been given priority. Within the self-imposed Monetarist framework there is little else the government could have done. If demand-management policies are discounted all that remains is to manipulate the NRU and the Government has chosen to do this by direct attacks on the real wage thus effectively lowering the expectations-augmented Phillips curve for each expected level of inflation so that a new equilibrium is reached which incorporates a rate of increase of money wages which is less than the expected rate of inflation.

Drastic increases in the level of unemployment appear to have provided temporary success. It is far from clear that this success can be maintained in the face of stability and far less of growth in employment.

If we look at the range of policies introduced by the Thatcher Administration we cannot but be impressed by the way in which they support and co-ordinate each other. The labour market policies ranging from trade union (or anti-trade union) legislation to the harsh treatment of the unemployed can be seen as consistent and mutually reinforcing. They are all directed to changing the economy and its institutions in the way required by Monetarist theory. It may be that the outsider assessing the different individual pieces of legislation in this way imparts a sense of coherence and long-term planning by the government which does not in fact exist. No one outside the policy-making circles can know. Nevertheless the various policies of the Thatcher Government—whether intended or not—provide a greater degree of consistency and coherence than has been provided by any other government since the war.

Notes to Chapter 16

1. See Keegan (1984) for a very good and readable account.
2. See Matthews (1968), Scott (1978), and Brittan (1964).
3. Hansard, 12 June 1979, 968, col. 242.
4. See *Financial Statement and Budget Report, 1980-1*.

5. Cash limits were first introduced in 1974–5 and greatly extended in 1976–7 but were essentially in the form of constant prices rather than prospective cash expenditures. The best short account of cash limits is 'Cash Limits and the Public Expenditure Process', Note by HM Treasury, Jan. 1982. Evidence submitted to the Inquiry Into Civil Service Pay, chairman Sir John Megaw.
6. HM Treasury, Note to Megaw Committee Jan. 1984, para. 19.
7. Ibid., para. 3.
8. The approach and analysis are discussed in *Rates: Proposals for rate limitation and reform of the Rating system*, Department of the Environment and the Welsh Office, Cmnd. 9008, HMSO, 1983.
9. *The Economist*, 11 Aug. 1984, and Cliff Davis-Colman in *Municipal Journal*, 3 Aug. 1984.
10. HM Treasury, Note to Megaw Committee, paras. 22 and 23.
11. Letter from the Lord President of the Council to the Secretary General of the Council of Civil Service Unions, 6 May 1981, quoted in HM Treasury, Note on Cash Limits to Megaw Committee, para. 34. The full text of this is published in the *Bulletin of the Council of Civil Service Unions*, (5), June 1981, 74.
12. Letter from the Civil Service Department 'with the authority of ministers' to the Secretary-General of the Council of Civil Service Unions, 17 July 1981, quoted in HM Treasury, Note to the Megaw Commission, para. 34. The full text is in the *Bulletin of the Council of Civil Service Unions*, 1 (7), Aug. 1981, 106–7.
13. See evidence of Mr Gordon Richardson, Governor of the Bank of England to the Treasury and Civil Service Committee on Monetary Policy, 21 July 1980, HC (163-II), Q. 453.
14. See Central Arbitration Committee, *Annual Report 1979*, London.
15. See Sidney and Beatrice Webb (eds.), *Industrial Democracy*, 1920.
16. See Friedman and Friedman (1980).
17. Norman Tebbit, speech to the American Chamber of Commerce, 13 July 1982; see Department of Employment press release and *The Times* report 14 July 1982.
18. Norman Tebbit, speech to the Essex Branch of the Freedom Association, 22 Oct. 1982, Department of Employment press release.
19. A short account of the content of the Act is provided in the Department of Employment press release 'Trade Union Act 1984', 27 July 1984.
20. Ibid. There seems no provision in the Act which limits its application to action initiated after 26 Sept. 1984 so it could apply to action started before that date which continued after it.
21. See McCarthy (1966); McCarthy and Parker (1968); Goodman and Whittingham (1973); Boraston *et al.* (1975); Batstone *et al.* (1977, 1978); Taylor (1980); and Hyman in Bain (1983).
22. Speech to American Chamber of Commerce, 13 July 1982, see report in *The Times*, 14 July 1982 where John Lloyd comments that 'Mr Wade, who is unused to such praise from Tory ministers or employers, will no doubt be embarrassed by it'.

23. Covering letter from Sir Terence Beckett CBE, Director-General CBI to Tom King, Secretary of State for Employment, enclosing the CBI comments, 22 June 1984.
24. Hansard, 15 Feb. 1984, col. 285.
25. House of Commons *Hansard*, 28 Apr. 1909, 4, col. 388.
26. Chris Pond, 'profligate schemes', *New Society*, 12 Aug. 1982, 261–2.
27. Department of Employment press release, Norman Tebbit, MP, 'The True Economics of Employment', 31 Mar. 1982.
28. Department of Employment press release, Youth Wages do Affect Unemployment says Tebbit', extract from a speech at Bournemouth to the National Association of Pension Funds, 23 Apr. 1982.
29. Department of Employment press release, 'Pay Restraint is Action to Help the Unemployed says Employment Minister', speech to Coventry Chamber of Commerce and Industry annual dinner, 7 May 1982.
30. Department of Employment press release, 'The True Economics of Employment', 31 Mar. 1982.
31. *Employment News*, 96, Apr. 1982.
32. See *The Times*, 8 Dec. 1980 and 5 May 1981, and MSC, *A New Training Initiative: A Consultative Document*, May 1981.
33. MSC, *Outlook on Training: Review of the Employment and Training Act 1973*.
34. See *Department of Employment, A New Training Initiative: A Programme for Action*, Cmnd. 8455, Dec. 1981.
35. See *Daily Telegraph*, 19 Nov. 1982.
36. See Inland Revenue Leaflets IR 41 'Income Tax and the Unemployed', March 1982; IR 42 'Income Tax—Lay-offs and Short-time Work', March 1982; and IR 43 'Income Tax and Strikes', March 1982. Also 'Taxation of Benefits', *Employment News*, 98, June 1982, Dept. of Employment.
37. The *Guardian*, 27 Mar. 1984.
38. *The Economist*, 26 May 1984.
39. *Financial Times*, 27 July 1984.
40. *The Times*, 15 Nov. 1982.
41. CSO, *Social Trends*, 14, 1984 edn.

CHAPTER SEVENTEEN

Counter-Inflationary Policies

MONETARISM is a counter-inflationary policy. To Quantity Theorists inflation results from changes in the quantity of money. An increase (decrease) in the money stock leads to higher (lower) prices. Control of the money supply will therefore create the desired rate of change of prices and, for the convinced Monetarist, this rate of change can be in either direction so that the general level of prices can fall if there is sufficient contraction of the money supply. As a theory Monetarism can be neither proven nor disproven. It is accepted or rejected on theoretical grounds according to individual decisions about the relevance and reasonableness of the assumptions contained in the theory. The existence of a long and variable time-lag between changes in the money supply and inflation means that it may never be possible to shake the confidence of the committed believer; any apparently contradictory evidence can be disregarded on the grounds that there has been a change in the relationships or the time-lag. In itself this is not sufficient to lead to the rejection of Monetarism. There is no reason at all to believe that any real world economic relationship is, or should be, consistent. Institutional and structural changes as well as shifts in attitudes and behaviour resulting from economic developments and experience, including government policies (dis-intermediation perhaps) can alter the measurable relationships between two or more economic variables. This is as true for a Keynesian as a Monetarist explanation and analysis.

The inability to provide consistent forecasts of real world developments is not therefore the basis on which one should reject Monetarism or any other theory. Despite the frequent claims of theorists of various persuasions that predictability is a necessary condition for the acceptance of a theory the strict application of such a rule would leave us devoid of any theoretical content worth having. There are just too many changes in too many variables and influencing factors for us (yet?) to be able to establish analytical relationships which provide the predictability which the acceptance of a theory ought to require. Economics is not the same as the hard or real sciences; in fact, it is not really a science at all. We cannot repeat experiments in the real world and we cannot obtain the strict and controlled testability of theses which is possible in chemistry or physics. If we reject Monetarism it should be because we conclude, on the basis of such evidence as is available, interpreted as best we can, combined with our judgements about the validity of the assumptions, that the theory does not explain economic behaviour satisfactorily. Thus, for example, the assumption that labour markets clear in either money or real wage terms seems not to be warranted as a reasonable assertion about the way in which the UK labour market operates. Much may depend on just what is meant by 'clear', but it does not seem possible to find a situation in which *all* employers could obtain all the labour they demanded or would use, at the prevailing wage, and everyone who was able and willing to work on the existing terms and conditions was able to find a job, or was voluntarily unemployed. There may be developments which are regarded as tendencies towards market-clearing, but this is not the same as asserting that markets do clear. We do not know how far the tendency would go or whether it would ever actually lead to clearing.

The labour market may never get to a position of equilibrium; it may oscillate to lesser or greater extent around some assumed equilibrium position, but the extent of the oscillations and the movement in the assumed equilibrium position may be due to a wide range of factors which currently are but imperfectly understood and not amenable to quantification. A Monetarist can accept all this. It may, to him, be no more than saying that the Natural Rate of Unemployment may change quickly and in an unexplained or unexpected way, and that if it does, the rate of inflation and/or unemployment will change in an unexpected way. Thus the rate of inflation may not be as easy to control as advocates of Monetarism sometimes appear to suggest. If the NRU increases significantly, but this is not appreciated for some time, the imposition of what appears to be a tight control of the money supply might actually lead to an increase in inflation. It is only if the NRU is constant that inflation can be effectively limited to a predetermined rate of the control of the money supply.

The main premises and conclusions of Monetarism rest on untestable assertions or prove to be truisms dependent for their apparent usefulness on some special definition or on the observance of strong *ceteris paribus* assumptions. This is especially so for the labour market content of Monetarism although, as we have discussed, Monetarists tend to give little direct attention to labour market issues even though they are central to the determination of prices and inflation even in their own analysis.

Yet despite the various objections raised in previous chapters it might appear that Monetarist policies are working. In both Britain and the USA governments apparently committed to Monetarist views and espousing control of the money supply do appear to have reduced the rate of inflation, and in the UK's case, very significantly. However, as we have seen, there is very considerable disagreement as to whether the Thatcher Government did actually control the money supply all that tightly, and the Commons Treasury and Civil Service Committee was not convinced. One explanation may be that expectations were strongly affected, not by the rate of change of the money supply—either as announced or experienced—but by other statements of government. The widespread and apparently justified belief that the Thatcher Administration would 'do something about the unions' may have affected the rate of change of wages much more than any rational expectations-based views about the quantity of money. The economy may have been pushed to a level of activity far below its NRU level of activity and there may have been significant reductions in the real reservation wages of many groups of workers in the face of severe increases in the level of unemployment. Trade unions may have altered their attitudes; there may have been a shift in power between them and employers merely because many people expect this to occur when unemployment rises significantly, for power cannot be measured except by its results.

That all these factors can be incorporated into a Monetarist explanation by referring to the NRU and so on is not really enough to justify acceptance of the Monetarist doctrines. It merely confirms that Monetarism as a theoretical explanation, when it includes all the possible implications and interpretations of its assumptions, can be used to justify or explain anything and everything *ex post*.

By its emphasis of the central role of the money supply Monetarism inevitably draws attention away from these other factors, and it does so not just because of crude simplification by critics but as a result of the emphasis given to the central role of the quantity of money by its own advocates.

A government adopting Monetarism as the basis of its policies must either accept the long-term non-inflationary level of unemployment as given by the NRU and outside its control and so seek to influence only the rate of inflation, or it must seek to change the NRU as well as control inflation through the money supply. Moreover, because expectations are not determined in the way supposed by the New Classical School, it is probably necessary that the Government take additional measures to influence the expectations of those responsible for pay and price determination. The very use of the phrase 'those responsible for pay and price determination' is a denial of the premises of the extreme New Classical School for it rejects the notion that pay and prices are determined by the pure market forces of supply and demand and recognizes that there is actually a process of determination applied by individuals or groups which leads to pay and price decisions which are different from those which would result from the application of pure supply and demand. If we really believed that the human agencies involved in pay and price determination did no more than transmit the inevitable outcome of the market forces it would be as silly to refer to them as responsible for pay and price determination as it would be to say that a telephone wire is responsible for the content of the message that is sent along it.

Whether one is a Monetarist or not one cannot avoid the conclusion that no government has seen fit to rely on the views of the rational expectations school. It has not been accepted that all that needs to be done is to announce the future rate of change of the money supply and make those announcements credible. Additional messages and announcements of intentions have been made and additional measures to influence those responsible for pay, if not price determination, have been made. Governments, even those sympathetic to a Monetarist position, recognize that there are other expectations and other factors, including aspirations, which influence pay changes and inflation.

It is here perhaps that the Monetarist explanation of labour market behaviour seems most inappropriate. Because they start from, and constantly hark back to, a view of how the labour market would behave in conditions of competition in the absence of trade unions, Monetarists seem unable to formulate views about how trade unions might influence behaviour and wages. We should add that non-Monetarists do not have the answers but they do seem more aware of some of the effects, and try to incorporate unions and collective behaviour into their analysis in a rather more sophisticated way than just reference to the monopoly power of unions. Governments seem much more aware of the role that unions might play in influencing a large range of expectations, not just of inflation but of unemployment, training and retraining facilities, possibilities for occupational mobility, and the various broader social and economic objectives unions may support. Moreover, British governments, no matter what their political persuasion, seem to recognize that expectations of future inflation are by no means the sole, or even perhaps the major, factor in wage bargaining, or in pay determination where there is no collective bargaining. Compensation for past price rises is seen as a major element in pay determination and it is the need to break that backward link that dominates all government-thinking when producing counter-inflationary policies. Monetarism appears to offer a way out by concentrating on future inflation and the Thatcher Administration has certainly emphasized their belief that future inflation rates should be lower than those of the past if people will be sensible.

Their very emphasis of the importance of future inflation rates suggests that pay bargainers and others do not normally give this first priority, for if they did there would be no need to keep telling them to do so. Moreover, employers are fully aware of the importance of the pay claim based on past movements in prices. Thus, it is not the case that a Monetarist counter-inflationary policy is merely the application of control of the money supply to established methods of pay determination. It is far from that. It requires the introduction and maintenance of new bases for determining pay. It seeks to change the pay determination processes so that they behave as they would *if* the rational expectations hypothesis were true. Instead of the REH being true because that is how people behave, it is necessary to make people behave as though the REH were true.

Thus, if all labour sub-markets were in equilibrium in real wage terms and there was real wage flexibility in both directions, it may be that the expected rate of inflation would be the only factor that influenced labour supply, and if expectations were correct, we might believe we would be able to maintain the equilibrium position. This means that everyone accepted the prevailing sets of relative wages as satisfactory, or if they did not, they sought to change them, not by increasing pay in their present job, but by moving to employment in those jobs which they thought had relatively too high pay levels. If they were unable to obtain employment there because they did not become part of any employer's acceptable-labour supply curve we must assume that they withdraw from the labour force into voluntary unemployment, which might have some effects on the general equilibrium position, or, more likely, on a REH view, they recognize the realities of the situation and their own previous exaggerated view of their own abilities, modify their views, and return to work at their old job, content with the previous relative wages in the light of their reassessment of their own acceptability, or undergo a period of training to become part of an acceptable-labour supply curve. Such acceptance of the implications of external labour mobility in response to perceived inequities in relative wages is unrealistic and always has been for many parts of the labour force. Some individuals may have behaved in the way outlined, but the more general response is to seek to obtain better terms and conditions in the present place of employment. The REH, and to some extent the general Monetarist position, requires that individuals and trade unions accept that external mobility or occupational mobility are the only ways of obtaining redress for perceived inequities in relative pay. This is a necessary condition for future wage movements to be determined only by the expected rate of inflation after making allowance for any increase in labour productivity or in productivity generally which is not passed on in the form of lower prices.

Governments seem to be more realistic than these economists. Sir Geoffrey Howe, giving evidence to the Treasury and Civil Service Committee, when asked about the three different monetary aggregates used by government and their impact on pay developments, said: 'I think it may have been unduly optimistic to imagine that a study of one or other or all three of these ranges was likely to be in the forefront of the minds of actual pay bargainers . . . I think the number of technicians who study these matters with the assiduity that you display is, and always will be, relatively small. Nevertheless, the impact on pay bargainers of the actual success on inflation is quite important.'[1]

It is success in reducing past inflation, and not expected inflation, that may have an impact, and while this could support an adaptive expectations view, it surely reflects more than that. The earlier part of the quotation indicates that not much effect on pay is expected merely from the announcements of targets for monetary aggregates. It is the actual development of inflation that might have an effect, and this is because compensation to restore real wages is important.

In any case the important expectations may not be those concerning the future inflation rate. They may have much more to do with protection of employment, what is happening to wages in other parts of the economy or other firms, whether a choice has to be made between wages and other conditions of employment, and, for 30 per cent of the UK labour force, government policy for the public sector. It may be countered that concern for employment is merely a reflection of the expected rate of inflation in relation to increases in wages and labour costs. To the extent that there is some element of validity in this it should be emphasized that the important point is that the general rate of inflation merely serves as a sort of proxy for future demand for the product of the workers concerned. The implication is that if they increase their wages and labour costs faster than the general rate of inflation their employer will suffer competitive disadvantage *vis-à-vis* other producers generally and the price elasticities of demand will lead to a reduction in demand for their products and so to unemployment for them.

Two points should be noted about this interpretation. First, it does not depend upon real wage equilibrium in the labour market, and indeed takes as given that some reduction in real wages can be made without a loss of employment, i.e. there need be no increase in voluntary unemployment as people leave when real wages fall. There is no failure of expectations as a result of higher than expected inflation; instead it is an argument that requires workers to take a lower money wage increase, and thus a reduction in real wages in order to protect their jobs. Second, the demand-for-products argument can be influenced by many factors other than the general rate of inflation, and could, in some cases, lead to higher money wages if the elasticities of demand were favourable.

The recognition that it is not merely the expected rate of inflation that influences wage claims and settlements is crucial. Once we accept this it becomes obvious not only that Monetarism may be a deficient policy approach because of its obsessive concentration on a single variable, but that the quantity of money may not even be the most important factor which government can manipulate in order to influence the set of expectations and attitudes which affect pay determination. Once we liberate the important expectations from the confines only of the future rate of inflation and include the wide spectrum of factors which can influence pay developments, it becomes clear that the important set of expectations is that which determines what is an acceptable wage increase to labour—trade unions and individuals. We are seeking to influence not only what people expect to happen, but what they will accept or tolerate without undesirable economic, industrial, or political consequential responses. Thus, for example, acceptance of a reduction in real wages can be part of expectations in the same way that there can be a lowering of the individual or collective reservation wages in the Monetarist analysis with the expectations-augmented Phillips curve.

The crucial expectations in pay determination are therefore expectations about what is *attainable* in the perceived conditions. These expectations may be influenced by considerations of the perceived effects of particular wage increases on current and future employment, and interpretations of what is attainable may be influenced by beliefs about what is fair or equitable. These may be influenced by what is happening or thought to be happening elsewhere. What is attainable may be affected by the actual or perceived states of both product and labour markets, and by views of the actions and responses of the other side of the pay bargaining table. The expected rate of inflation may be an influence, but it is but one, and by no means necessarily the most important one. The important considerations are in some ways more narrow than this. If there is a severe increase in foreign competition in the particular product market the expected *general* rate of inflation may be of little importance. If there are traditional strong imitative wage behaviour patterns the first settlement may be much more important for the followers than their views on the general rate of inflation. The point must be repeated; it is only if it is believed that all labour sub-markets clear constantly in real wage terms, and, apart from 'true' frictional job-changing unemployment, that all unemployment is voluntary, that the expected rate of inflation can have the vital role that is given to it in a Monetarist explanation. Once this rigid and unreal assumption is rejected it is necessary to seek to discover just what factors do influence pay changes, and if we seek to express these in terms of expectations we can do no more than put it in terms of expectations of attainability with all the unanswered questions regarding the determination of what is considered attainable that are necessarily invoked. While this may sit ill with economic theory which prefers to have apparent determinacy, even if this involves the use of precise sounding words to cover up very imprecise situations such as with the Natural Rate of Unemployment, it is nevertheless much more helpful to an understanding of what actually goes on.

Choosing a Counter-inflation Policy

Governments are required to adopt some policy towards inflation. They may also weigh the importance of reducing and controlling inflation against other policy objectives, such as high employment, economic growth, interest rates, and so on. The particular balance amongst the various objectives is a matter of political choice and while some governments may give preponderant importance to reducing inflation, we would normally expect governments in democratic pluralist societies to seek some more balanced set of policy objectives. While the main discussion will concentrate on the counter-inflation objective it is stressed that this ought not to be regarded as the only, or necessarily the most important, of the aims of government. If this is so, then it follows that Monetarism is unlikely to commend itself to most governments pursuing a balance of objectives, for Monetarism concentrates almost exclusively on the rate of inflation. Some Monetarists, such as Laidler (1982), however, point out that other policies might be introduced to deal with unemployment.

Essentially, governments can choose among three main types of policies to tackle inflation. These are macro-economic policies, structural policies, and prices and incomes policies (Robinson 1979).

Macro-economic policies in an earlier day would have been described as demand-management policies. Essentially they seek to influence the pay and price decisions which emerge in an economy by controlling the economic pressures which determine or affect those decisions. Thus, orthodox Keynesian demand-management policies were widely adopted as a means of influencing pay and price developments as well as the level of employment. This sort of policy can be illustrated as an attempt to moderate the economic pressures so that the decisions which emerge as a result of the established processes and institutions of decision-taking alter to reflect the government's objectives. To slow down the rate of increase of prices it is considered necessary to reduce the level of economic pressure by reducing the level of economic activity.

Some increase in unemployment and reduction in output are therefore accepted as part of the process of control although this may be regarded as only a short-run requirement. It is as though we were to regulate the gas flame in order to change the temperature of the water in the kettle.

Structural policies seek to alter the processes and institutions through which the economic pressures exert themselves, thereby changing the pay and price decisions which will emerge from any given level of demand. Active manpower policies which speed up the adaptation of the labour markets to changes in supply and demand, housing policies which encourage labour mobility, regional policies which affect the type and location of investment, restrictive trade practices and monopoly policies, and industrial relations legislation which seeks to alter the balance of power in collective bargaining are all forms of structural policies. The intention is that with a given set of economic pressures the pay and price decisions will be different as a result of changes in the processes and institutions through which those decisions are made and expressed. The purpose is to obtain different decisions without the necessity to alter the general economic conditions thereby avoiding the need to lower the level of economic activity and thus the level of output and employment. This is the same as changing the container in which the water is being heated so that it becomes a better (or worse) conductor of heat.

Prices and incomes policies are intended to induce those responsible for taking pay and price decisions to take decisions which differ from those they would have taken, given their institutions, in the same economic conditions, but in the absence of the policy. The policy seeks to induce or coerce decision-takers to change their behaviour and deliberately take decisions which are not those they would have taken had they been left to operate in their usual way. Incomes policies are intended to allow the economy to run at a higher level of activity with a lower rate of inflation. In terms of the old Phillips curve they seek to move the curve downwards. They act as a filter between the flame and kettle. If successful for a given inflation rate they allow the level of output and employment to be at a higher level than would otherwise be possible, or conversely, result in a lower rate of inflation for any given level of economic activity.

We use the term macro-economic policies rather than demand-management policies to take account of the revival of Monetarism. As Monetarists decry the full range of demand-management policies, relying instead solely on monetary policy as the control mechanism of inflation, although fiscal policy may be relevant to other things such as the PSBR and interest rates, it is necessary to use a new term which embraces both demand-management policies and Monetarism. It is not suggested that governments must choose only one of the three policies. Demand-management supporters also recommend structural policies, and, some of them at least, also support incomes policies. Structuralist policies are seldom regarded as sufficient to control inflation, but rather they are seen as making important contributions to help the other main policy approaches. As we have seen, Monetarists advocate structuralist policies, although in their analysis they do so not to affect the rate of inflation as such but to change the natural rate of unemployment.

Nigel Lawson (1984) is aware of the distinction. He says that the Thatcher Government, unlike its Keynesian predecessors from both parties, will use macro-economic policy (control of the money supply) to deal with inflation. Unemployment, he argues, cannot be dealt with by macro-economic policies. Instead, micro-policies are needed. By this he means that structural policies affect the Natural Rate of Unemployment. In practice his Government's policies seek to lower the NRU by reducing real wages. Inevitably their approach requires that there be first an increase in unemployment. It is by no means clear that there actually will be a second stage in which both actual unemployment and the NRU decline. Incomes policies seek to moderate inflation without increasing unemployment. It is therefore biasing the case against incomes policies to compare merely their effects on inflation with the effects of Monetarism on inflation. The effects on unemployment are no less important to incomes policy advocates.

This bias is also reflected in the emphasis given to the natural or non-accelerating inflation rate of unemployment. Policy-makers could equally well speak of the Natural Rate of Inflation—that rate at which unemployment would be constant.

Incomes policy supporters do not claim that incomes policies can succeed irrespective of the level of economic pressure and they recognize that there are some limits on the extent of change in behaviour that can be induced. The general economic policies, whether these be seen as demand-management or the money supply, are therefore regarded as relevant and important by incomes policy advocates, who would conclude that the type of macro-economic policies adopted, and the resulting pressure of economic forces, can impose limits on what might be expected from an incomes policy. Few supporters of incomes policies would regard the money supply as the only, or even perhaps the most important of the economic variables to be used in macro-economic policy. On occasions it might be important, but at other times Keynesian views of the possibility of obtaining an expansion in output and employment by increasing aggregate demand through an increase in the money supply would dominate the policies of income policy supporters.

Real Wages and Counter-inflation Policy

Any government seeking to introduce a counter-inflation policy should start by recognizing that it will require, at least in the short run, a reduction in expected real wages. This will be difficult to achieve. We have come to expect economic growth and rising real income as normal. Given the established bargaining practice that the first objective of a wage agreement is to make good the ravages of past inflation so that real wages at the time of the new settlement catch up to the level attained in the previous settlement, it is clear that the increase in money wages can be lower than the rate of inflation since the last settlement only if there are no increases in money wages because of productivity increases with the benefits of productivity growth passed on in the form of lower prices, and the increase in productivity is sufficient to cover the difference between the past rate of inflation and the future rate of inflation sought by the government.

The Monetarist is unconcerned by this. It is future real wages in relation to the expectations of those employed, and particularly those marginal workers who entered employment as a result of a perceived increase in real wages, which determine policies. Supporters of incomes policies have to face up to the difficulties which will arise as a result of the policies' attempts to prevent real wages returning to their previous level, or to do so until the rate of inflation has been brought down. When advocating their policies there is a marked reluctance to emphasize, not only that a temporary reduction in real wages extending beyond the reduction which normally occurs between wage settlements, is not only an expected, but a necessary feature for the success of the policies.

The application of a counter-inflation policy requires either that the reduction in the rate of inflation—the amount by which the norm or permitted aggregate increase in money wages can exceed the immediate (previous settlement period) rate of inflation—be no higher than the rate of productivity growth, or that there be a reduction in real income since the time of the past settlement on which 'expected' or 'fair' real income is based. As long as unions and/or their members and employers involved in collective bargaining or other methods of pay determination accept that some real wage level of the past, typically that resulting from the previous settlement, was fair, and that maintenance of that real wage level is reasonable, a counter-inflation policy is constrained by the rate of productivity growth. Moreover, pay increases arising from productivity increases mean that there is no 'equivalent' amount available for price reductions.

Despite their public claims to do otherwise, counter-inflation policies do not operate on the basis that increases in money wages will be sufficient to ensure that real wages are maintained by allowing all the forms of productivity growth to be passed on in form of lower prices. To do this would require a zero norm. Even then, real wages would be maintained only if productivity growth, and so price reductions, were sufficient to make good the inflation, or price increases, since the last settlement. While we have had periods of zero norms and pay-freezes in the UK, the associated conditions have been neither present nor expected. We ought therefore to recognize that counter-inflation policies as implemented through incomes policies are based upon some period of reduction in real wages.

Monetarism and Incomes Policies compared

In this very important regard, that a reduction in some past level of real wages is required, there is no difference between an incomes policy and the Monetarist approach when considering the essential nature of their counter-inflationary impact and their requirements as successful policy measures. They both need to change established behaviour, and it is behaviour established not only by and in collective bargaining, but also in other sectors where compensation for past price increases is regarded as a fair and reasonable basis for pay adjustments. To this extent there is a basic similarity between Monetarism and the views of incomes policy advocates (Robinson 1979 and Ulman 1979). There are, of course, far more fundamental differences between the two schools than this similarity. Both are saying that it is necessary to obtain some reduction in real wages from past, although not necessarily current, levels, and they are both saying that it is necessary to influence expectations in order to achieve this. The Monetarists are unconcerned about the reduction in real wages from some past level because it is current and expected future real wages which determine the important labour market decisions for them. Influencing expectations of future prices is therefore the key as that will ensure that the pay, price, and labour market decisions are based on accurate information and correct perceptions, and, if the quantity of money is controlled, real wages will rise from any given point in time, only as a result of correctly interpreted views of future real demand and future real wages.

Incomes policy advocates tend to recognize the importance of the past real wage level. This may be expressed in different ways so that some may refer to institutional pressures arising from the nature of trade union behaviour or political processes or competition within and between unions. Others may use the notion of a target wage in which past real pay levels play an important part. They all believe that in order to obtain lower inflation it is necessary to obtain lower increases in money wages (or additional increases in productivity not accompanied by additional increases in money wages as a result of the productivity growth), and that this will lead to a reduction in real wages. It is because it leads to a reduction in real wages in comparison with some point in the past and not only to a reduction in real wages in comparison to the level prevailing at the time of the next wage settlement, that incomes policy advocates are so aware of the many difficulties involved in implementing a policy.

If all that mattered was ensuring that future real wages did not fall, the task, while difficult, would be considerably easier. It is because the expectations which matter are not merely those of expected price movements, but of attainable wage increases, and the difficulty of reconciling what is perceived to be attainable with prevailing notions of equity, that income policy advocates recognize the complexity of their task. They are seeking to persuade, or induce by various combinations of persuasion and coercion, those responsible for pay and price decisions to take decisions which require the rejection of established practices. They are seeking to change behaviour and to change expectations of what is attainable and fair. They seek to do so without placing all the weight, and indeed no weight or as little as seems possible, on a rise in unemployment as the main cause of changes in expectations and behaviour. As Sir Geoffrey Howe told the Treasury and Civil Service Committee he was trying to change the rules of the game, so are incomes policy advocates.

Both groups are wanting to change expectations, but different expectations. Even though the future rate of inflation may be part of the set of expectations and attitudes relevant to an incomes policy advocate it is but one of a set and may not be the most important one. Neither group gives much publicity to the requirement that real wages will and need to be lower that than they were at some time in the past. The Monetarist does not do so because he does not think it relevant. To him labour market participants base their decisions on current real wage levels and their expected future value. The incomes policy advocate does not do so because he seems to believe that to admit that real wages will be lower, and perhaps lower for some time, will prevent the acceptance of his policy. Further, the more that income redistribution forms part of an incomes policy, the lower, or the longer will be the delay before there is a restoration of real wages of those not benefiting from the redistribution. If there are powerful groups able to defeat or inflict damage on the policy, the more may the advocate feel it unwise or impolitic to emphasize this essential policy requirement.

Such coyness or deception may prove more harmful to the policy than an open statement of both the policy requirements and its goals. The intention is that in the longer-run real incomes will be higher as a result of the reduction in the rate of inflation. The alternative to incomes policy requires higher unemployment and a lower total level of output and income. Incomes policy seeks a different distribution of a higher level of output and real income. This means that prices do matter, and real decisions are affected by money and prices. A lower rate of inflation will allow both real incomes and employment to be higher. If these are goals worth struggling for, then it may be worth giving a full and honest explanation to those who will be affected by the policies. An incomes policy which seeks to deal with inflation will involve a reduction in real incomes in comparison with some previous level and in comparison with expected or 'considered-fair' income, and probably for some time. It will require a reduction in the expected rate of increase of money and real wages. It will require, if not the abandonment, then the temporary setting aside, of customary pay determination practices. It will require changes in pay relationships and in the time-periods over which individuals and unions regard the restoration of real wages as normal, fair, or necessary. To obtain these changes in behaviour it is surely preferable to explain as fully as possible just what is required.

Even if the rate of inflation is reduced as a result of other factors or by other policies the need for an incomes policy will be no less if the extravagant wastes of unemployment are to be avoided and remedied. An expansionary economic policy will carry the danger of great inflationary pressure as unions seek to obtain what they perceive as their entitlement to fair redress. There is little to suggest in either the UK or the USA that the present recession has caused any *fundamental* change in trade union attitudes or that a recovery will lead to drastically different wage behaviour. Comparability, pattern-bargaining, wage leadership, and institutional pressures for 'fairness' or to maintain past relationships may play less part in pay determination when unemployment is rising and jobs are seen to be at stake, but it should not be assumed this will survive a recovery. Employers may tend to think it will; trade unionists differ.[2] Accumulated 'lost' real wages will be pressed for and there will be strong pressure to obtain even greater protection from a repetition of the present hardships. The drastic reduction in the training of skilled workers could lead to acute shortages and bottle-necks with the expected labour market inflationary consequences. There is a very real danger that a sustained economic recovery and expansion would be dissipated by the ravages of inflation. The need for an incomes policy arises not only from the experience of current inflation but from the fears of future inflation.

While there is an important similarity between Monetarism and incomes policies there are more important differences. The change in attitudes and behaviour required by Monetarism is obtained by the pressure of rising unemployment leading to a revision of both expectations of future inflation and expected real income. Some acceptance of lower real wages is necessary and it is obtained by coercion. The coercion of rising unemployment is buttressed by associated measures to enforce reductions in individual and collective reservation wages. Reductions in the real level of unemployment benefits or the real replacement ratios and the weakening of trade union bargaining strength are important factors in the Monetarist adjustment process. The fatal weakness of the longer-term Monetarist position is the assumption that such enforced changes will survive the ending of the adverse and worsening economic conditions which allowed them to be enforced. It is much more probable that unions will press for restoration of lost ground when circumstances improve. Moreover, by deliberately using the political process to obtain some of the conditions appropriate for the Monetarist solution there will be a natural response by those adversely affected to use the political process to obtain redress.

Incomes policies seek to obtain the changes in attitudes and behaviour by persuasion, although if this proves insufficient coercion may also be used. A significant difference is that any legislative restrictions are seen to be temporary and do not in themselves change the fundamental balance of power permanently.

Instead of deliberately reducing the real living standards of the unemployed, an incomes policy often seeks to include elements of social justice in its policy objectives. This may require a greater or longer-lasting temporary reduction in real wages and so encounter trade union opposition. To the extent that it does so, it challenges the sincerity of trade union commitment to income distribution and seeks to test whether unions are in fact prepared to redistribute towards the less fortunate members of society or whether such claims are but empty rhetoric, or claims on which to build yet higher real incomes for certain sections of the organized labour force.

Incomes Policy as an Alternative

It is now commonplace and fashionable to decry incomes policies as doing no more than at best providing a temporary delay in the rate of inflation. At the time, however, such delay was avidly sought by policy-makers. Experience might have taught us to improve incomes policies. Perhaps more important, experience of Monetarist policies might have taught us that incomes policies and their perceived interference with the processes of free collective bargaining may be a preferred alternative. The experience of Monetarism may well be seen by many as far worse than incomes policy. While there will be search for third options, at the end of the day there seems little choice other than one between the use of economic pressures, whether these be control of the money supply alone or a combination of demand-management policies which exert their influence on pay through the pressure of economic forces as interpreted through the prevailing institutions, or an incomes policy of one form or another. Structural policies can be put forward to change the way in which economic forces express themselves in pay and price decisions, but these cannot provide a continuing solution. When the structural changes have been made, the choice will still lie between controlling inflation through economic measures alone or using an incomes policy.

An incomes policy cannot prevent inflation and maintain employment irrespective of the economic policies pursued. Nor can macroeconomic policy. Monetarism has been unable to reduce inflation without a massive increase in unemployment and it has been tried for a much longer period than has an incomes policy in the UK. There are limits to the contribution either policy can make.

Monetarism may reduce inflation at an exorbitant cost in unemployment. As we have seen, this is not coincidental. The rise in unemployment is necessary to ensure that there is a downward revision in expected or acceptable real wages obtained through a lowering of individual and collective reservation wages. It is not the reduction in the expected rate of price change which reduces current inflation: it is the fear of unemployment, and this is generated by experience of actual increases in unemployment. Less extreme schools of political economy reject this excessive preoccupation with the one variable—inflation, and seek to maintain some balance between controlling both inflation and unemployment. Even then it is far from clear that Monetarism can maintain its control over inflation if the fear of imminent unemployment is reduced. The assumptions about labour market behaviour implicit as well as explicit in the theory are just not realistic enough to lead us to conclude that some equilibrium position in which real wage increases, and money wage bargaining to obtain real wages, will stabilize around a position where the only objective in money wage bargaining at the aggregate level will be to provide protection against expected price increases. Even those willing to accept the continuation of the present high levels of unemployment should be wary of concluding that this price will buy them continued low rates of inflation. To obtain this even without significant economic expansion might well require changes in behaviour and attitudes for which there are no grounds for believing have occurred or will do so.

Such changes are much more likely to be achieved by discussion and reason than by coercion. An incomes policy therefore offers some hope while Monetarism seems to offer us no long-term hope for dealing with *both* inflation and unemployment. If there is one good thing to be salvaged from the destruction created by the Monetarist experiment, it is the possibility that having faced the alternative those involved in pay determination might reassess their opinions and recognize that an incomes policy might at least offer the possibility of reconciling the objectives of lower inflation and lower unemployment.

The experience of being subjected to the hardships of enforced experiments in Monetarism has also left us a further legacy. The changes which have been enforced have built up a tremendous amount of resentment and determination to obtain redress when circumstances permit. Even relatively modest improvements in economic conditions might therefore be accompanied by much stronger inflationary pressures than would be expected on the basis of past behaviour. Unless it is believed that the 'battle for the hearts and minds' has been won, and that there have been fundamental shifts in attitudes of individuals in their labour market behaviour which will be carried forward when employment increases, and that trade unions have abandoned their traditional bargaining attitudes and criteria, then it must be expected that economic improvement will be accompanied by considerable upward pressure on wages. The Monetarist, isolated in his self-spun cocoon of belief in labour markets clearing in real wage terms, need worry only about some autonomous rise in real reservation wages, and even this will lead him to conclude that unemployment will increase but not inflation. Others may conclude that attempts to obtain some past-based level of real wages and relative wages will exert greater influence in pay determination when employment rises. On this view the upward movement in real reservation wages, whether these be individual or collective, is not autonomous but is contained within the system. It is a time-lagged, rather than an autonomous, response. It results from the present successes of the Monetarist policies imposed on a labour force, and it is a total failure to comprehend the nature of trade unions, industrial relations, and collective bargaining to regard any subsequent upward revision of real reservation wages as autonomous and not to expect it.

The very success of the brutality of the Thatcher translation of the broader version of Monetarism into a package of measures affecting the labour market therefore has the apparently paradoxical result of making an incomes policy more necessary, not less. If unions have learned the right lessons from their bitter experience, it may be they will give a better reception to incomes policy proposals. There will still be their instinctive response that incomes policies interfere with free collective bargaining which is an inalienable right of all members of a democratic society. Yet, while there is much in this claim, and certainly totalitarian societies of Right or Left make sure that free and independent trade unions are destroyed, the claim to free collective bargaining unhindered by any legal constraints has not really been accepted since the heyday of *laissez-faire* when unionism was weak or non-existent. Certainly free collective bargaining unshackled by state intervention is not a pure principle for which a trade union can go to the stake today. They have accepted, and to some extent endorsed, legislative constraint on their freedom to bargain whatever results they choose or could obtain from employers, by their acceptance of legislation on equal pay, equal opportunity, and laws which prevent discrimination in hiring based on sex or race. These laws do not affect only the unorganized sectors. Nor can it be claimed that the actions which are now legally proscribed never occurred under collective bargaining.

It is accepted that the law can interfere with the *results* of collective bargaining, and that is what the debate over free collective bargaining is, essentially, about. At times the debate spreads to interference with the *processes* of bargaining, but the fundamental objection to an incomes policy is that it limits the rights of unions and employers to determine the content or results of bargaining. This objection is of course valid. Incomes policy is intended to alter the results. But it is not unique in doing so as the range of legislative intervention on the content of bargaining demonstrates. The real argument therefore is not one of pure principle—in industrial relations it seldom is—but rather one of balance. Does an incomes policy lead to too much government intervention in the content of bargaining so that there is no longer a sense in which the trade unions can be regarded as free, but are instead, but puppets of the state?

One's position will depend on one's values. There seems little in British experience to suggest that incomes policies have so tilted the balance that the essential rights and freedoms have been suppressed. Much depends on the content of the policy, the way in which it is implemented, and how the policy is determined. The greater the participation of unions in the policy formulation, the less is the denial of total collective bargaining rights. Instead there is a transfer of bargaining rights, upwards, away from bargaining with individual employers or an industry association towards bargaining with government about the whole range of economic and social policies (Robinson 1966). Appropriate policies can therefore preserve free collective bargaining by adapting to changed requirements. The recognition that macro-economic developments are an inevitable concern of both government and trade unions should lead to a change in the location of bargaining. Just as collective bargaining at the level of the plant or firm requires constraints and restrictions on the behaviour of individuals, so does bargaining about macro-economic policies require restrictions and constraints on bargaining at industry or plant level. This is no more a necessary denial of free collective bargaining than was the acceptance of the Equal Pay Act which prevented unions from freely negotiating lower rates of pay for women doing the same work as men in the same place. Nor is it essentially any different from the emergence of industry-wide or company-wide collective bargaining. Whether it is considered too high a price to pay depends on how one values the possible benefits and how one evaluates the alternative.

If incomes policies are eschewed there seems little option left to governments but to rely on macro-economic policies, and in current circumstances these seem more likely to be of a Monetarist than a Keynesian variety. We just do not know how to combine free and unhindered collective bargaining and price determination with high, far less full, employment. If choosing free collective bargaining requires the acceptance of high and continuing unemployment, slow rates of growth, constant downward pressure on real unemployment benefits, and other restrictionary actions to control public expenditure and the PSBR, this may be too high a price for society to pay.

If a choice has to be made, and there seems no way of avoiding one, an incomes policy, with all its defects and difficulties, offers more hope of obtaining control over inflation without the disastrous consequences in terms of unemployment than do economic-control policies, and certainly far more than does Monetarism. If, however, the evils of enforced unemployment are considered unavoidable, or even good for the souls (of others), probably because one feels secure in one's own employment and future real income position, then incomes policy may seem not worth the effort. But a society which claims to be concerned about the plight of all its members, a society which seeks to have even a modicum of compassion as well as efficiency, ought to worry about unemployment and reductions in real living standards of the less fortunate members. The purpose of economic growth and efficiency ought to be to provide decent living standards for *all* citizens, and not merely those fortunate enough to have access to education, training, and employment. Too frequently these attributes owe more to ancestry than equity or ability. That this view represents a particular set of value-judgements is of course correct. So too does Monetarism, although it demonstrates an unbecoming coyness about spelling out the underlying value-judgements and often seeks to hide behind a veil of 'inescapable' economic logic.

Economic policy is based on political economy and economic theory is but an intellectual technique to apply specific assumptions to stated problems. The essential elements in policies relate to value-judgements. We must choose what sort of society we wish to live in and then adopt policies which try to create that society. If we want a society in which unemployment is not regarded as voluntary and determined by the unemployed themselves, if we wish for a society in which unemployment is lower and in which disadvantaged members are treated with compassion and understanding, then we reject Monetarism, not only because its theoretical tenets are unsound and its assumptions unwarranted, but because as a policy it will not provide the sort of society we want. It will create and perpetuate high unemployment, depress real living standards, generate constant pressure on the real income of both the employed and the unemployed, restrict public expenditure, and, whilst doing this, claim absolution or even freedom from guilt and responsibility in the name of inevitable market forces.

To move towards a society in which equity can be associated with efficiency and in which unemployment is regarded as an evil no less than excessive inflation, it is necessary for us to intervene in economic matters. We must exert control over the economic environment and influence attitudes and behaviour by reason and not by brute force and fear. An incomes policy offers some hope. It will involve many painful adjustments but these, though shared by all, will be less painful than the adjustments of unemployment imposed by Monetarism which are shared by a minority, although a growing minority. This is, in one regard, the basic nature of the choice we have to make. In the pursuit of control over inflation should we seek to obtain our goal by imposing a very heavy burden of unemployment on a minority, or should we seek to spread the burden amongst us all? Indeed, should we go further and seek to ensure that some sections bear no burden but gain additional benefits by the redistributionary content of an incomes policy? At the end of the day perhaps it is the way we answer this question which will determine whether we stand on the side of Monetarism or incomes policy. Robert Lekachman (1982) expressed it in the title of his biting and witty attack on Reaganomics: 'Greed Is Not Enough'. Compassion, concern for others, and the pursuit of social as well as economic objectives should be the distinguishing feature of a democratic society. Monetarism certainly cannot provide these features, does not claim to do so, and indeed would probably argue either that they have no part of economic theory and policy or that private charity and goodwill should provide. An incomes policy associated with appropriate macro-economic and structural policies offers the possibility of attainment even though the achievement of success may prove long and difficult.

We might not succeed, but we should try.

Notes to Chapter 17

1. House of Commons, Fourth Report from the Treasury and Civil Service Committee, Session 1980–1, *The 1982 Budget*, HC 270 (March 1982), Q. 171.
2. There is a good debate on whether the recession in the US has led to permanent changes or temporary adjustment in collective bargaining in New York University *Conference on Labor* (1983). See, in particular, the papers by Friedman, Miller, and Schlossberg. The title of Miller's paper sums up the issue: 'Bargaining 1982: Trends or Aberrations'.

Bibliography

Addison, John T., 'What Price Unemployment?' *Economic Affairs*, 1(2), 1981.
Atkinson, A. B., 'Unemployment Benefits and Incentives', in J. Creedy (ed.), *The Economics of Unemployment in Britain*, Butterworths, London, 1981.
—— and Flemming, J. S., 'Unemployment, Social Security and Incentives', *Midland Bank Review*, Autumn 1978.
—— Gomulka, J., and Micklewright, J., 'Unemployment Benefit, Duration and Incentives in Britain', *Journal of Public Economics*, 23, 1984.
Bain, A. D., *The Control of the Money Supply*, 3rd edn., Penguin Books, Harmondsworth, 1980.
Bain, G. S. (ed.), *Industrial Relations in Britain*, Blackwell, Oxford, 1983.
Barro, R. J., 'Rational Expectations and the Role of Monetary Policy', *Journal of Monetary Economics*, 2, 1976.
Batstone, Eric, Boraston, Ian, and Frenkel, Stephen, *Shop Stewards in Action: The Organisation of Workplace Conflict and Accommodation*, Blackwell, Oxford, 1977.
—— *The Social Organisation of Strikes*, Blackwell, Oxford, 1978.
—— *Working Order*, Blackwell, Oxford, 1984.
Bayliss, F. J., *British Wages Councils*, Blackwell, Oxford, 1962.
Beveridge, W. H., *Full Employment in a Free Society*, Allen & Unwin, London, 1944.
Blackaby, Frank (ed.), *The Future of Pay Bargaining*, Heinemann, London, 1980.
Blackburn, R. M., and Mann, Michael, *The Working Class in the Labour Market*, Macmillan, London, 1979.
Blanchflower, D., 'Union Relative Wage Effects: A Cross-section Analysis using Establishment Data', *BJIR*. 22(3), Nov. 1984.
Boraston, Ian, Clegg, Hugh, and Rimmer, Malcolm, *Workplace and Union*, Heinemann Educational Books, London, 1975.
Briscoe, S., 'Employment in the Public and Private Sectors 1951 to 1981', *Economic Trends*, 338, Dec. 1981.
Brittan, Samuel, 'Full Employment Policy: a Reappraisal', in G. D. N. Worswick *The Concept and Measurement of Involuntary Unemployment*, 1976.
—— *How to End the 'Monetarist' Controversy*, 2nd edn., Hobart Paper 90, Institute of Economic Affairs, London, 1982.
Brown, C., Kilrow, G., and Kohen, A., 'The Effects of the Minimum Wage on Employment and Unemployment', *Journal of Economic Literature*, 20(2), 1982.
Brown, R. N., Enoch, C. A., and Mortimer-Lee, P. D., 'The Interrelationship between Cost and Prices in the United Kingdom,' Bank of England Discussion Paper 8, 1980.

Brown, William, *Piecework Bargaining*, Heinemann, London, 1973.
Buckland, Roger and Davis, E. W., 'Privatisation: Let the Market Decide', *Economic Affairs*, 4(4), July-Sept. 1984.
Buiter, W. H., 'The Macroeconomics of Dr Pangloss: A Critical Survey of the New Classical Macroeconomics', *Economic Journal*, 90(357), Mar. 1980.
Burdett, K., 'Search, Leisure and Individual Labour Supply', in S. A. Lippman and J. J. McCall, *Studies in the Economics of Search*, 1979.
Burkitt, B. and Bowers, D., 'Wage Inflation and Union Power in the United Kingdom: 1949-1967', *Applied Economics*, 8, 1976.
Burton, John, 'Trade Unions' Role in the British Disease: An Interest in Inflation' (and discussion), in *Is Monetarism Enough?*, IEA Readings 24, Institute of Economic Affairs, London, 1980.
Butler, David and Kavanagh, Dennis, *The British General Election of 1983*, Macmillan, London, 1984.
Calvo, G., 'Urban Unemployment and Wage Determination in LDCs: Trade Unions in the Harris-Torado model', *International Economic Review*, 19, 1978.
Casson, Mark, *Economics of Unemployment*, Martin Robertson, Oxford, 1983.
Chater, Robin E. J., Dean, Andrew, and Elliott, Robert F., *Incomes Policy*, Oxford University Press, Oxford, 1981.
Clark, Colin, 'Do Trade Unions Raise Wages?' *Journal of Economic Affairs*, 1(4), July 1981.
Clegg, H. A., *The Changing System of Industrial Relations in Great Britain*, Blackwell, Oxford, 1979.
Cmnd. 7858, *Monetary Control*, HMSO, London, 1980.
Confederation of British Industry, *Trade Unions in a Changing World: the Challenge for Management*, London, 1980.
Craig, Christine, Rubery, Jill, Tarling, Roger, and Wilkinson, Frank, *Abolition and After: the Paper Box Wages Council*, Department of Employment Research Paper 12, London, 1980.
—— Rubery, Tarling, Roger, and Wilkinson, Frank, *Labour Market Structure, Industrial Organisation and Low Pay*, Cambridge University Press, Cambridge, 1982.
Creedy, John (ed.), *The Economics of Unemployment in Britain*, Butterworths, London, 1981.
Daniel, W. W., *A National Survey of the Unemployed*, The Social Science Institute, Vol. XL, Broadsheet 546, London, 1974.
—— *The Nature of Current Unemployment*, British-North American Research Association Occasional Paper 6, London, 1981.
Davies, R., Hamill, L., Moylan, S., and Smee, C. H., 'Incomes in and out of Work', *Employment Gazette*, 90(6), June 1982.
Deakin, B. M. and Pratten, C. F., *Effects of the Temporary Employment Subsidy*, Cambridge University Press, Cambridge, 1982.
De Menil, G., *Bargaining: Monopoly Power versus Union Power*, MIT Press, Cambridge, Mass., 1971.
Desai, Meghnad, *Testing Monetarism*, Frances Pinter, London, 1981.

Dilnot, A. W., and Morris, C. N., 'Private Costs and Benefits of Unemployment: Measuring Replacement Rates', *Oxford Economic Papers* 35 (Supplement), Nov. 1983.
Doeringer, Peter B. and Piore, Michael J., *Internal Labor Markets and Manpower Analysis*, D. C. Heath & Co., Lexington, Mass., 1971.
Dreze, J. H., and Modigliani, F., 'The Trade-off between Real Wages and Employment in an Open Economy (Belgium)', *European Economic Review*, 15, 1981.
Dunlop, J. T., *Wage Determination Under Trade Unions*. Kelley, New York, 1950.
Dunn, S. and Gennard, J., *The Closed Shop in British Industry*, Macmillan, London, 1984.
Economic Journal, 91, Mar. 1981.
Ehrenberg, Ronald G. and Smith, Robert S., *Modern Labor Economics: Theory and Public Policy*, Scott, Foresman & Co., 1982.
Farber, H. S., 'Individual Preferences and Union Wage Determination: the Case of the United Mine Workers', *Journal of Political Economy*, 86, 1978.
Fidgett, Tony, *The Engineering Industry: its Manpower and Training*, EITB Reference Paper RP/2/83, Engineering Industry Training Board, London, 1983.
Fischer, Stanley (ed.), *Rational Expectations and Economic Policy*, University of Chicago Press, Chicago, Ill., 1980.
Fisher, I., *The Purchasing Power of Money*, Macmillan, New York, 1911.
—— 'A Statistical Relation between Unemployment and Price Changes', *International Labour Review*, June, 1926.
Forrest, David and Dennison, S. R., *Low Pay or No Pay?* Hobart Paper 101, Industry Economic Affairs, London, 1984.
Fothergill, S. and Gudgin, G., *Unequal Growth*, Heinemann, London, 1982.
Friedman, Milton, 'The Quantity Theory of Money: a Restatement', in M. Friedman (ed.), *Studies in the Quantity Theory of Money*, University of Chicago Press, Chicago, Ill., 1956.
—— *A Theory of the Consumption Function*, Princeton University Press, Princeton, 1957.
—— 'The Role of Monetary Policy', *AER Papers and Proceedings*, 58(1), 1968.
—— *Monetary Correction*, IEA Occasional Paper 41, Institute of Economic Affairs, London, 1974.
—— *Unemployment versus Inflation*, Institute of Economic Affairs, London, 1975.
—— 'A Theoretical Framework for Monetary Analysis', *Journal of Political Economy*, 78, 1970.
—— *Inflation and Unemployment: The New Dimension of Politics*, IEA Occasional Paper 51, Institute of Economic Affairs, London, 1977.
—— and Friedman, Rose, *Free to Choose*, Secker & Warburg, London, 1980.
—— and Schwartz, A. J., *Monetary Trends in the United Kingdom: their Relationship to Income, Prices and Interest Rates, 1867–1975*, University of Chicago Press, Chicago, Ill., 1982.
Garside, W. R., *The Measurement of Unemployment: Methods and Sources in Great Britain 1850–1979*, Blackwell, Oxford, 1980.

Gilmour, Ian, *Britain Can Work*, Martin Robertson, Oxford, 1983.

Goodman, J. F. B. and Whittingham, T. G., *Shop Stewards*, 2nd edn., Pan Management Series, Pan Books, London, 1973.

Gordon, Robert J. (ed.), *Milton Friedman's Monetary Framework*, University of Chicago Press, Chicago, Ill., 1970.

—— 'Output Fluctuations and Gradual Price Adjustment', *Journal of Economic Literature*, 19(2), 1981.

Greenhalgh, C. A., Layard, P. R. G., and Oswald, A. J. (eds.), *The Causes of Unemployment*, Clarendon Press, Oxford, 1983.

Griffiths, Brian, 'The Economics of Labour Power: Can Trade Unions Raise Real Wages?', in *Trade Unions: Public Goods or Public Bads?*, IEA Readings 17, Institute of Economic Affairs, London, 1978.

—— and Wood, Geoffrey, E., *Monetary Targets*, Macmillan, London, 1981.

Grubb, D., Jackman, R., and Layard, R., 'Causes of the Current Stagflation', in C. A. Greenhalgh *et al.* (eds.), 1983.

Guillebaud, C. W., *The Wages Councils System in Great Britain*, Nisbet, London, 1958.

Hayek, F. A., 'Full Employment at Any Price?', IEA Occasional Paper 45, Institute of Economic Affairs, London, 1975.

—— '1980s' Unemployment and the Unions', Hobart Paper 87, Institute of Economic Affairs, London, 1980.

—— 1900s Unemployment and the Unions, Hobart Paper 87, 2nd edn., Institute of Economic Affairs, London, 1984.

Hendry, D. F. and Ericsson, N. R., 'Assertion without Empirical Basis: An Econometric Appraisal of Friedman and Schwartz's "Monetary Trends in . . . the United Kingdom" ', Bank of England Panel of Academic Consultants, Panel Paper 22, Oct. 1983.

Hicks, J. R., 'Economic Foundations of Wage Policy', *Economic Journal*, 65(259), 1955.

—— *The Theory of Wages*, Macmillan, London, 1983.

Hieser, R., 'Wage Determination with Bilateral Monopoly in the Labour Market: a Theoretical Treatment', *Economic Record*, 46, 1970.

House of Commons, Ninth Report from the Expenditure Committee, *Public Expenditure, Inflation and the Balance of Payments*, HC 328, HMSO, London, 1974.

Hyman, Richard, 'Trade Unions: Structure, Policies and Politics', in G. S. Bain (ed.), 1983.

Institute of Economic Affairs, *Inflation: Causes and Cures*, IEA Readings 14, London, 1974.

—— *Job 'Creation'—or Destruction?*, IEA Readings 20, 1979.

—— *Is Monetarism Enough?*, IEA Readings 24, 1980.

Jackman, Richard, Mulvey, Charles, and Trevithick, James, *The Economics of Inflation*, 2nd edn., Martin Robertson, Oxford, 1981.

Jay, Peter, *Employment, Inflation and Politics*, Occasional Paper 46, Institute of Economic Affairs, London, 1976.

Johnson, Christopher, *The Failure of Monetarism*, Manchester Statistical Society, Manchester, 1982.

Johnson, Harry G., 'The Keynesian Revolution and the Monetarist Counter-Revolution', *AER Papers & Proceedings*, 61, 1971.
Johnston, J., 'A Model of Wage Determination under Bilateral Monopoly', *Economic Journal*, LXXXII, 1972.
Joseph, Sir Keith, *Reversing the Trend—a Critical Reappraisal of Conservative Economic and Social Policies*, Rose, Chichester and London, 1975.
—— *Money and the Monetary System*, Stockton Lectures, London Business School, London, 1976.
—— *Solving the Union Problem is the Key to Britain's Recovery*, Centre for Policy Studies, London, 1979.
Kantor, Brian, 'Rational Expectations and Economic Thought', *Journal of Economic Literature*, 17(4), Dec. 1979.
Kay, John and Morris, Nick, 'No Longer Rich on the Dole?' *New Society*, 18 Feb. 1982.
Kay, J. A., Morris, C. N., and Warren, N. A., 'Tax Benefits and the Incentive to Seek Work', *Fiscal Studies*, 1(4), 1980.
Kerr, Clark, *'The Balkanization of Labor Markets'*, in E. Wight Bakke *et al.*, *Labor Mobility and Economic Opportunity*, Technology Press of MIT, Cambridge, Mass., 1954.
Knowles, K. G. J. C. and Robinson, D., 'Wage Rounds and Wage Policy', *Bulletin of the Oxford University Institute of Statistics*, 24, 162.
—— and Winsten, C. B., 'Can the Level of Unemployment Explain Changes in Wages?', *Bulletin of the Oxford University Institute of Statistics*, 21, 1959.
Laidler, David, 'The Influence of Money on Economic Activity: a Survey of Some Current Problems', in G. Clayton, J. C. Gilbert, and R. Sedgwick (eds.), *Monetary Theory and Policy in the 1970s*, Oxford University Press, Oxford, 1971.
—— 'The Crisis—When and Why did it Start?' in *Inflation: Causes, Consequences and Cures*, IEA Readings 14, Institute of Economic Research, London, 1974.
—— *Essays on Money and Inflation*, Manchester University Press, Manchester, 1975.
—— 'Monetarism: An Interpretation and an Assessment', *Economic Journal*, 91, 1981.
—— *Monetarist Perspectives*, Philip Allan, Oxford, 1982.
Lancaster, T. and Nickell, S., 'The Analysis of Re-employment Probabilities for the Unemployed', *Journal of the Royal Statistical Society*, 143(2), 1980.
Lawson, Nigel, 'The New Conservatism' (A talk given to the Bow Group, 4 Aug. 1980), Centre for Policy Studies, London, 1980.
—— *Thatcherism in Practice: A Progress Report*, Speech given to the Zurich Society of Economics, HM Treasury press release, London, 14 Jan. 1981.
—— *The British Experiment*, The Fifth Mais Lecture, text provided in HM Treasury press release, London, 18 June 1984.
Layard, R., Metcalf, D., and Nickell, S., *The Union Coverage–Non-Union Coverage Wage Differential*, Centre for the Economics of Education, London School of Economics (mimeo), London, 1976.

Layard, R., and Nickell, S., 'The Causes of British Unemployment', *National Institute Economic Review*, 111, 1985.
Lewis, H. G., *Unionism and Relative Wages in the United States*, University of Chicago Press, Chicago, Ill., 1963.
Lipsey, R. G., 'The Relation between Unemployment and the Rate of Change of Money Wage Rates in the United Kingdom, 1862-1957', *Economica*, 27, 1960.
Low Pay Unit, Who Needs Wages Councils? Pamphlet 24, London, 1983.
Lucas, R. E. jun., 'Expectations and the Neutrality of Money', *Journal of Economic Theory*, 4, 1972.
—— 'An Equilibrium Model of the Business Cycle', *Journal of Political Economy*, 83, 1976.
—— 'Tobin and Monetarism: A Review Article', *Journal of Economic Literature*, 19(2), 1981.
—— and Rapping, L. A., 'Real Wages, Employment and Inflation', in E. S. Phelps, *et al.*, 1970.
McCarthy, W. E. J., *The Closed Shop in Britain*, Blackwell, Oxford, 1964.
—— *The Role of Shop Stewards in British Industrial Relations*, Royal Commission on Trade Unions and Employers' Associations, Research Paper 1, HMSO, 1966.
—— and Parker, S. R., *Shop Stewards and Workshop Relations*, Royal Commission on Trade Unions and Employers' Associations, Research Paper 10, HMSO, 1968.
McCormick, Harry, 'Housing and Unemployment in the UK', *Oxford Economic Papers*, 35 (Supplement), Nov. 1983.
McDonald, I. M., and Solow, R. M., 'Wage Bargaining and Employment', *American Economic Review*, 1981.
MacDougall, Donald, *The World Dollar Problem*, Macmillan, London, 1957.
McGregor, A., 'The Placement Activity of the Employment Service Agency', *BJIR*. 16, 1978.
MacKay, D. I., Boddy, D., Brack, J., Diack, J. A., and Jones, N., *Labour Markets under Different Employment Conditions*, Allen & Unwin, London, 1971.
Maki, Dennis and Spindler, Z. A., 'The Effects of Unemployment Compensation on the Rate of Unemployment in Great Britain', *OEP*. 27, 1975.
Martin, Jean and Roberts, Ceridwen, *Women and Employment: A Lifetime Perspective*, Department of Employment, Office of Population Census and Surveys, HMSO, London, 1984.
Mayer, Thomas, *Permanent Income, Wealth and Consumption*, University of California Press, Berkeley, Calif., 1972.
Mayhew, Ken, 'Economists and Strikes', *Oxford University Bulletin of the Institute of Economics and Statistics*, 41(1), Feb. 1979.
—— *Trade Unions and the Labour Market*, Martin Robertson, Oxford, 1983.
Meltzer, Allan, 'Monetarist, Keynesian and Quantity Theories', in T. Mayer: *The Structure of Monetarism*, W. W. Norton & Co., New York, 1978.
Metcalf, David, 'Unions, Incomes Policy and Relative Wages in Great Britain', *BJIR*. 15(2), 1977.

—— *Low Pay, Occupational Mobility and Minimum-Wage Policy in Britain*, American Institute for Public Policy Research, Washington, DC, 1981.
—— 'Unions and the Distribution of Earnings', *BJIR*. 20, 1982.
Middleton, P. E., Mowl, C. J., Odling-Smee, J. C., and Riley, C. J., 'Monetary Targets and the Public Sector Borrowing Requirement', in B. Griffiths and G. Wood (eds.), *Monetary Targets*, 1981.
Miller, Robert, 'Who are the unemployed?—the Irrelevant 1930s', *Journal of Economic Affairs*, 1, 1980.
—— and Wood, John B., *What Price Unemployment? An Alternative Approach*, Hobart Paper 92, Institute of Economic Affairs, London, 1982.
Minford, A. P. L., 'A Rational Expectations Model of the UK under Fixed and Floating Exchange Rates', *Carnegie Rochester Conference Series on Public Policy* 12 (The State of Macroeconomics), 1980.
—— *The Problem of Unemployment*, Selsdon Group Policy Series, 5, London, 1981.
—— 'Trade Unions Destroy a Million Jobs', *Journal of Economic Affairs*, 2(2), 1982.
—— *Unemployment: Cause and Cure*, Blackwell, Oxford, 1983.
—— Minford, Patrick and Peel, David. 'Is the Government's Economic Strategy on Course?' *Lloyd's Bank Review*, 140, Apr. 1981.
Morgan, Brian, *Monetarists and Keynesians: their Contribution to Monetary Theory*, Macmillan, London, 1978.
Morris, Derek (ed.), *The Economic System in the UK*, 3rd edn., Oxford University Press, Oxford, 1985.
Mulvey, C., 'Collective Agreements and Relative Earnings in UK Manufacturing Industry in 1973', *Economica*, Nov. 1976.
—— and Abowd, John M., 'Estimating the Union/Non-union Wage Differential, a Statistical Issue', *Economica*, Feb. 1980.
—— and Foster, J., 'Occupational Earnings in the UK and the Effects of Collective Agreements', *Manchester School*, Sept. 1976.
Neuberger, Henry, *From the Dole Queue to the Sweatshop*, Low Pay Unit, London, 1984.
—— *Unemployment: Are Wages to Blame?* Low Pay Unit, London, 1984.
New York University, *Conference on Labor 1983*, New York, 1983.
Nickell, S., 'Trade Unions and the Position of Women in the Industrial Wage Structure', *BJIR*. 15(3), 1977.
Nossiter, Bernard D., *Britain: A Future that Works*, André Deutsch, London, 1978.
Oi, W., 'Labor as a Quasi-Fixed Factor', *Journal of Political Economy*, 70, 1962.
Okun, A. M., *Prices and Quantities: A Microeconomic Analysis*, Blackwell, Oxford, 1981.
Parker, Hermione, *The Moral Hazard of Social Benefit*, IEA Research Monograph 37, Institute of Economic Affairs, London, 1982.
Parkin, J. M. and Sumner, M. T., *Incomes Policy and Inflation*, University of Manchester Press, Manchester, 1972.

Parkin, Michael, 'The UK Evidence on the Causes of Inflation', in *Inflation and the Unions*, IEA Readings in Political Economy 6, Institute of Economic Affairs, London, 1972.
Parsley, C. J., 'Labor Unions and Wages: A Survey', *Journal of Economic Literature*, 18, March, 1980.
Pencavel, J., 'Relative Wages and Trade Unions in the UK', *Economica*, May 1974.
Phelps, E. S., 'Money Wage Dynamics and Labor Market Equilibrium', *Journal of Political Economy*, 76, 1967.
—— et al., *Microeconomic Foundations of Employment and Inflation Theory*, Macmillan, London, 1970.
Phillips, A. W., The Relation between Unemployment and the Rate of Change of Money Wage Rates in the United Kingdom, 1861-1957, *Economica*, Nov. 1958.
Pond, Chris and Winyard, Steve, *The Case for a National Minimum Wage*, Low Pay Unit, London, 1983.
Price, Robert and Bain, George Sayers, 'Union Growth in Britain: Retrospect and Prospect', *BJIR*. 21, March 1983.
Purvis, Douglas D., 'Monetarism: A Review', *Canadian Journal of Economics*, 13, 1980.
Rees, Albert, *The Economics of Work and Pay*, Harper & Row, New York, 1973.
Richardson, G. B., *Information and Investment*, Oxford University Press, Oxford, 1960.
Rima, Ingrid, 'Whatever Happened to the Concept of Involuntary Unemployment?' *International Journal of Social Economics*, 11(3/4), 1984.
Robinson, Derek, 'Wage Rates, Wage Income and Wages Policy', *Bulletin of the Oxford University Institute of Statistics*, 25(1), 1963.
—— *Non-wage Incomes and Prices Policy*, OECD, Paris, 1966.
—— *Wage Drift, Fringe Benefits and Manpower Distribution*, OECD, Paris, 1968.
—— (ed.), *Local Labour Markets and Wage Structures*, Gower Press, London, 1970.
—— 'Labour Market Policies', in *The Labour Government's Economic Record: 1964-1970*, W. Beckerman (ed.), Duckworth, London, 1972.
—— 'Differentials and Incomes Policy', *Industrial Relations Journal*, Spring 1973.
—— 'Government Pay Policy', in *The Economic System in the UK*, 3rd edn., Derek Morris, Oxford, 1985.
—— 'Trade Union Growth and Industrial Disputes: Comments', in Richard E. Caves and Lawrence B. Krause (eds.), *Britain's Economic Performance*, Brookings Institute, Washington, DC, 1980.
—— and Mayhew, Ken (eds.), *Pay Policies for the Future*, Oxford University Press, Oxford, 1983.
Rosen, S., 'Unionism and the Occupational Wage Structure in the United States', *International Economic Review*, 11, 1970.
Rosewell, Bridget and Robinson, Derek, 'Reliability of Vacancy Statistics', *BOUIES*. 42, 1980.

Ross, A. M., *Trade Union Wage Policy*, University of California Press, Berkeley, Calif., 1948.
Rowthorn, Bob, 'Conflict, Inflation and Money', *Cambridge Journal of Economics*, 1, 1977.
Sapsford, David, *Labour Market Economics*, Allen & Unwin, London, 1981.
Sargan, J. D., 'Wages and Prices in the United Kingdom: A Study in Econometric Methodology', in P. E. Hart, G. Mills, and J. K. Whitaker (eds.), *Econometric Analysis for National Economic Planning*, Butterworth, London, 1964.
—— 'A Model of Wage-Price Inflation', *Review of Economic Studies*, 47, 1980.
Sargent, T. J. and Wallace, N., 'Rational Expectations and the Optimal Money Instruments and the Optimal Money Supply Rule', *Journal of Political Economy*, 83, 1975.
—— 'Rational Expectations and the Theory of Economic Policy', *Journal of Monetary Economics*, 2, 1976.
Sharp, Hugh, 'Working in a Wages Council Industry', *Employment Gazette*, Nov. 1978.
Shaw, E. R., *The London Money Market*, Heinemann, London, 1981.
Smith, Adam, *An Inquiry into the Nature and Causes of the Wealth of Nations*, ed. Edwin Cannan (1976), University of Chicago Press, Chicago, Ill., 1976.
Smith, David C., 'Incomes Policy, in R. E. Caves *et al.*, *Britain's Economic Prospects*, Allen & Unwin, London, 1968.
Stewart, Mark B., *Relative Earnings and Individual Union Membership in the UK*, Centre for Labour Economics, Discussion Paper 110, London School of Economics, London, 1981.
Taylor, Robert, *The Fifth Estate: Britain's Unions in the Modern World*, revised edn., Pan Books, London, 1980.
Thirlwall, A. P. (ed.), *Keynes as a Policy Adviser*, Macmillan, London, 1982.
—— 'What are Estimates of the Natural Rate of Unemployment Measuring?' *Bulletin of the Oxford University Institute of Economics and Statistics*, 45(2), May 1983.
Treasury, HM., *'Cash Limits, Pay and the Public Expenditure Process'*, Note for the Megaw Committee, Jan. 1982.
Trevithick, J. A. and Mulvey, C., *The Economics of Inflation*, Martin Robertson, London, 1975.
Ulman, Lloyd, 'Report on the Conference', *Collective Bargaining and Government Policies*, OECD, Paris, 1979.
—— 'Unions, Economists and Incomes Policy', in Joseph Pechman and N. J. Simler, *Economics in the Public Service*, W. W. Norton and Company, Inc., New York, 1982.
Walters, Alan, *Economists and the British Economy*, IEA Occasional Paper 54, Institute of Economic Affairs, London, 1978.
Weekes, Brian, Mellish, Michael, Dickens, Linda, and Lloyd, John, *Industrial Relations and the Limits of Law*, Blackwell, Oxford, 1975.
Wells, William, *The Relative Pay and Employment of Young People*, Department of Employment, Research Paper 42, London, 1983.

Wood, John B., *How Much Unemployment?*, IEA Research Monograph 28, Institute of Economic Affairs, London, 1972.
—— *How Little Unemployment?*, Hobart Paper 65, Institute of Economic Affairs, London, 1975.
Worswick, G. D. N. (ed.), *The Concept and Measurement of Involuntary Unemployment*, Allen & Unwin, London, 1976.
Wren-Lewis, S., *A Model of Private Sector Earnings Behaviour*, Government Economic Service Working Paper 57 (Treasury Working Paper 23), HM Treasury, London, 1982.

Index

acceptable labour supply (ALS) 106, 111–12, 136–42, 283
  see also job requirements
Addison, J. T. 213, 240
arbitration in public sector pay negotiations 427–8
assembly line production 101–2
assets, demand for money and 27–8
Atkinson, A. B. 120, 255–6

banks and money supply control 38–41
Batstone, E. 204
Beenstock, M. 353
Beveridge, W. H. 13
Blackburn, R. M. and Mann, M. 132, 136
Blanchflower, D. 213
Brittan, S. 343, 409, 453
Brown, G. *et al.* 400
Bruno, M. and Sachs, J. 348
Buckland, R. and Davies, E. W. 453
Burkitt, B. and Bowers, D. 213
Butler, D. and Kavanagh, D. 435

Canada: money supply control 41
capital costs *v.* labour costs 85
Casson, M. 156, 158, 187
Chicago School of Monetarism *see* Friedman
City University Business School 353
Clark, C. 213
Clegg Commission 429
closed shops 205–6, 207–8, 434–6
collective bargaining *see* trade unions
Community Industry 250
Community Programme 250
comparability element in wage determination 72–3, 199–201
  abolition in Civil Service pay 428–9
  collective bargaining and 322, 324
Confederation of British Industry
  on trade union power 402
  on Wages Councils 439–40
Conservative Government *see* Heath Government; Thatcher Government
consumption: and income expectations 47–9, 56
cost-of-living adjustment agreements in wage settlements 161
credit:
  creditworthiness 40
  policy 10, 11, 14
cycles, business: and the Natural Rate of Unemployment 298

Daniel, W. W. 253
Deakin, B. M. and Pratten, C. F. 391, 392
demand:
  employment effects 23, 102–4, 108, 329
    demand deficient unemployment 234–7
    demand management policies 10–11, 13
      in counter-inflationary policies 467–8, 469–70
      dissatisfaction with 11–13, 14
      in restoration of Natural Rate of Unemployment 352
    Natural Rate of Unemployment 360–1
    trade union distortion 329–30
  income and 47–9
    permanent income 56, 58, 61
  inflation effect 275–80
  money *see under* money
disabled in unemployment statistics 246, 247, 248, 251–2
Dunlop, J. T. 195, 201

economies of scale 23
  worker attitudes and 101–2
economy: structural change and new occupations 168, 231
educational system and unemployment 378–80
effort-input in Job Requirements 100–2, 215–17
employers:
  decisions and uncertainties:
    demand changes 104–5, 275–80
    marginal revenue product 100–2
    redundancies 377–8
    see also labour: demand for
  and trade unions 209–11, 220
Employment Acts (1980 & 1982) 431–6
employment levels:
  fluctuations preferred to wage fluctuations 92–9
  full:
    definitions 23
    expectations and response 98–9
    general policy objective 13, 415
    over-full 222–3

employment levels (*cont.*)
  health and safety legislation and 86
  high: political belief and commitment 263-4
  inflation, trade-off with:
    exception 279-80
    Phillips curve 260-5
      expectations-augmented 266-75
        weaknesses in application 280-6
      short-run 265-6, 275-9
  Quantity Theory and 21-4
  trade unions and 215-17, 222
  see also labour; Natural Rate of Unemployment; unemployment
Employment Protection Act (1975) 431-2
Enterprise Allowance Scheme 250, 392
environmental protection 86
equilibrium:
  economy 18-19
  firm 85
  labour market *see under* labour market
exchange rates 7-8, 13
expectations:
  income 50-1
    permanent income 51-4
      and consumption 47-9
      effects 54-8
      influencing 59-63
      revision 149
  role in Monetarist explanation of inflation 289-95
    adaptive expectations 295-6
      expectations-augmented Phillips curve 266-75, 341-2
      Monetarist development 275-80
      money supply change requirement 303-5
      behaviour change requirement 308-12
      rational expectations hypothesis 297-303
        in a counter-inflationary policy 462-5
      monetary targets and 305-8
        example 417-20
      and trade unions 316-18
  trade unions' *see under* trade unions

Fair Wages Resolution (1946) 438-9
fairness in pay, notions of:
  comparability 72-3, 199-201
    collective bargaining and 322, 324
  input related 183
  internal differentials 184-5
fiscal policy:
  cases for use of 352, 468
  criticisms 12
Fisher equation 18-21
  labour market implications 21-30
Fothergill, S. and Gudgin, G. 398
Friedman, Milton 3, 14
  on consumption and permanent income 48-9, 51-2
  on demand for money 27-9, 36, 37, 38
  on employment and the labour market
    Natural Rate of Unemployment 343, 349-50
      determinants 350-1
      estimation difficulties 352
      and unemployment insurance 369
    Phillips curve 266, 274
    real wages and supply and demand for labour 146, 342
    trade unions 211, 214, 335
  on the inflationary process 275-80
Friedman, Milton and Friedman, R. 390, 399
Friedman, Milton and Schwartz, A. 20, 25

Garside, W. R. 260
geographical mobility 133, 169, 393-4
  housing policy and 170-2, 359-60, 452-3
    effect on Natural Rate of Unemployment 394-7
  reasons for advocating 173-4
  regional policies and 397-8
  structural change and 232
  wage levels and 186-7
Gilmour, Sir Ian 416
global Monetarism 7
government:
  and closed occupations 167-8
  economic policies *see* demand: management policies; incomes policies; inflation: counter-inflationary policies; Monetarism; Thatcher Government
  as employer *see* public sector
  Heath Government 176n4, 332
  Labour Government 14, 223, 335
  and minimum wage levels 241-2, 398-402, 438-42
  and permanent income expectations 59-63
  spending 8, 13, 42
    see also Public Sector Borrowing Requirement
  and trade unions 222-4, 402-3
  training responsibilities 389-90, 391, 446-7
    Special Employment and Training Measures 249-50, 391-2, 442-3
      effects on unemployment levels 364, 444
  and unemployment 223
    official statistics 244-56
    see also Natural Rate of Unemployment: areas of influence
Gradualist School of Monetarism 7, 290-1
  see also Laidler
Greenhalgh, C. A. *et al.* 348

Griffiths, B. 212, 217-18
Grubb, D. *et al.* 348
Gummer, John:
  on closed shops 205
  on Wages Councils 440

Hayek, F. A.:
  on wages and employment levels 190, 390
  and trade unions 223, 331, 332
health and safety legislation 86
Heath Government 176n4, 332
Hendry, D. F. 3, 25
  and Ericsson, N. R. 20, 25
Hicks, J. R. 13, 265
House of Commons Expenditure Committee report (1974) 14-15
housing: costs and policies 302
  and geographical mobility 170-2, 359-60, 452-3
  effect on Natural Rate of Unemployment 394-7
Howe, Sir Geoffrey:
  on effectiveness of monetary targets 307, 308, 309-10
  and current inflation control 465
  and trade unions 332
  and velocity of circulation 26
human capital 27-8, 50-1

implicit contract theory 92-9
income:
  and creditworthiness 40
  permanent 51-4
    and consumption 47-9
    effects 54-8
    influencing 59-63
    revision 149
  and the unemployed 449-50
incomes policies:
  as counter-inflationary policy 468, 469-70
    advantages 478-80
    collective bargaining freedom restrictions 477-8
    methods and results 471-4
  Heath Government's 176n4
  Keynesian view 193
  Monetarist view 193, 333
  political attitudes and practice 14, 415
Industrial Relations Act (1971) 332, 405-6
Industrial Training Boards 92
inflation:
  causes (in Monetarist theory)
    money supply increase 2
    and expectations 289-96
      see also Rational Expectations Hypothesis
    short-run inflation/unemployment trade-off 275-80

  trade unions 211-15, 222-3, 348-9
constant rate:
  and Natural Rate of Unemployment 341-3
  and non-accelerating inflation rate of unemployment 343-4
control:
  demand-management policies 467-8, 469-70
  incomes policies 468, 469-74
    advantages 478-80
    trade unions and 477-8
  Monetarist policy 6, 460-2, 471-4
    adaptive expectations theory 303-5
    limitations 465-7, 475-6
    practical requirements 308-12, 462-5
    Rational Expectations Hypothesis 305-8
  real wages and 470-1
  structural policies 468
    housing policy 170-2, 359-60, 452-3
    industrial relations policy 222-3, 332, 402-3, 405-6
    Thatcher Government legislation 430-8
  regional policy 397-8
information:
  labour market 178-9, 184, 383-7
  role in Rational Expectations Hypothesis 297, 301-2
Institute of Economic Affairs 416
interest rates:
  interaction with Public Sector Borrowing Requirement and money supply 8, 41-3
  as policy tool 10, 14
  undesirability 6, 10, 38, 40-1
International Labour Organisation Conventions 438-9
international Monetarism 7
International Monetary Fund 14

Jay, Peter 333, 334
Job Centres 378, 385-6
Job Release Scheme 250
Job Requirements 69-70
  defined as occupation 76
  defined by employer 77, 78-9
    acceptable labour supply 106, 136-42, 283
    and internal labour market 82-3
    personal qualities 80-2
  and effort-input 100-2, 215-17
  and the individual 119
    evaluation 128-32
    selection 126-7, 132-6
job search theory 148-53
  criticisms 153-6
  and frictional unemployment 230-1

Job Splitting Scheme 250
Joseph, Sir Keith 311-12, 332, 416

Kay, J. A. et al. 374
Keynes, J. M.:
  categorization of unemployed 229
  concept of demand deficient
    unemployment 234-7
  on speculative demand for money 38
Keynesians:
  demand-management policies 10-11, 13
    in counter-inflationary policies 467-8,
      469-70
  dissatisfaction with 11-13, 14
  labour market views and policies 193, 346
  and Monetarism 2, 20
King, Tom 440
Knowles, K. G. J. C. and Winsten,
  C. B. 260

Labour Force Survey (1981) 250, 251
Labour Government:
  prices and incomes policies 14
  and trade unions 223, 335
labour market:
  demand:
    marginal analysis *see* marginal
      productivity analysis
    recruitment
      costs and benefits 88-91
      internal *v.* external labour market
        82-3, 206-7
      overtime alternative 105-8
    specification *see* Job Requirements;
      occupations
  equilibrium 345-50
    clearing concept 5, 15-16, 177-9
      in theory of inflation 275-80
        criticism 280-6
        wage rigidities 182-8, 318-25, 357-8
        see also trade unions
    full employment and 23
    product market equilibrium and 361-4
    Walrasian equilibrium 179-82
    see also Natural Rate of Unemployment;
      Phillips curve
  information 178-9, 184, 383-7
  local 172-4
  supply:
    acceptability 106, 111-12, 136-42, 283
      see also Job Requirements
    excess 268-9
      see also unemployment
    expansion without wage increase 282-5
    internal 82-3, 105-8, 122-5
    labour force composition 378-80
    labour force and occupational
      participation decisions

  income-leisure trade-off 112-15
  job net advantages 128-32
  job search theory 148-56
  labour force participation rate 380-1
  occupational choices 132-6
    see also Reservation wage
  trade unions and 205-7, 209-10
    see also geographical mobility; occupational
      mobility; training
Labour Standard 13
Laidler, D.:
  on expectations 290-1, 299, 306
  on money, demand for 4, 25-6, 40
  on money supply 41, 188
  on Natural Rate of Unemployment 351,
    387
  and demand-management policies 352
Lawson, Nigel: Monetarist policies 43
  monetary targets 417, 418-19, 420
  public expenditure 422, 429
  Thatcher Government and 223, 415-16
    industry and employment 216, 217, 332
    labour market functioning 431
    profit margins 361
    unemployment 469
Layard, R. et al. 212
Layard R. and Nickell, S. 234, 353, 377, 410
lay-off and rehiring of labour 95-7, 99, 157,
  377-8
leisure-income trade-off 112-15
Lekachman, Robert 479
Lewis, H. G. 212
liquidity 38, 39
Liverpool Research Group 353
local authorities expenditure, Thatcher
  Government and 424-6
Lowry, Pat 224
Lucas, R. E. and Rapping, L. A. 150, 153,
  347, 348
Lucas-Sargent aggregate supply equation
  292-3

McCormick, H. 172, 396
MacDougall, D. 262
MacKay, D. I. et al. 140, 148
Manpower Services Commission:
  Job Centres 378, 385-6
  training initiatives 389-90, 391, 446-7
marginal productivity analysis 65-75,
  83-6
  distortions in labour productivity
    implicit contracts 92-9
    overmanning 215-17
    see also trade unions
  non-homogeneity of labour and 86-92
  uncertainties in 99-105
Martin, J. and Roberts, C. 117
Mayhew, K. 201, 210, 325

Medium Term Financial Strategy (Thatcher Government) 417-20
Metcalf, D. 212, 399, 400
Middleton, Sir Peter E. 307, 309
Miller, R. and Wood, J. B. 253, 396-7, 399-400
Minford, A. P. L.:
  on rational expectations 291
  on trade unions and wages 214-18, 222, 282, 332
  on voluntary unemployment 120, 242, 243-4
mobility see geographical mobility; occupational mobility
Monetarism:
  basic concepts and associated ideas 1-2, 4-6, 16
    Quantity Theory 18-21
    see also money
  development and acceptance of theories 3, 13-15
  expectations theories see under expectations
  inflation (casues and control) see inflation
  labour market issues:
    demand-management policies 352
    expectations augmented Phillips curve 266-75
    short-run inflation/unemployment trade-off 275-80
    reservation wage influences:
      housing policy 170-2
      unemployment benefits 119-22
    trade unions 209, 211-12, 214-15, 217, 222-3, 430
    voluntary unemployment 240-4
    see also Natural Rate of Unemployment
  political policies 8-9
    see also Thatcher Government
  schools of see Gradualist School; New Classical School
  see also Friedman, Milton
monetary targets 305-8
  response 308-12
  Thatcher Government's 417-20
money:
  demand for:
    interest elasticity of, controlling 39-41
    government and 41-3
    Monetarists and the Quantity Theory and 20, 36-7
      variables in function 24-30
    speculative requirements 38
    transactions requirements 37
      and conception of permanent income 59-60, 62-3
  Quantity Theory 18-21
    labour market implications 21-30
  supply:

control:
  banks and 38-41
  demand-management techniques 10
  difficulties 43-4
  interest rates and 39-41
    Public Sector Borrowing Requirement and 41-5
  Monetarist position 4, 7-8, 10
  Thatcher Government and 417-22
  definitions 33-6
and inflation:
  expectations analysis 289-95
    adaptive expectations 295-6, 303-5
    Rational Expectations Hypothesis 297-303
    monetary targets and response 305-12
and unemployment:
  long-term relationship 187-8
  short-term relationship 275-80
mortgages and political policies 40, 452-3
Mulvey, C. and Abowd, J. M. 212

National Health Service, privatization of services 453-4
National Insurance contributions and unemployment 410
nationalized industries, external financing limits 424
Natural Rate of Unemployment (NRU) 279, 341-3, 349-50
  and aggregate demand 360-1
  areas of influence:
    employment decisions:
      labour force composition and participation 378-81
        see also labour market: supply
      lay-offs 95-7, 99, 157, 377-8
      quit-rate 377
      Unemployment Benefits 369-77
        see also Reservation wage
    expectations-augmented Phillips curve shift 406-9
      see also Phillips curve
    geographical mismatch 393-4
      housing policy 394-7
      regional policies 397-8
      see also geographical mobility
    labour market information and functioning 178-9, 184, 383-7
    minimum wage levels, statutory 398-402, 438-42
    public sector employment 403-5
      see also public sector
    real wages 409-10
      see also wages
    trade union power 402-3
      see also trade unions

Natural Rate of Unemployment (*cont.*)
  and demand-management policies 352
  determinants 350-1, 354-60
  and labour market equilibrium 345-50, 361-4
  measurement 364-6
    difficulties 352-3
    UK estimates 353
  and Non-accelerating Inflation Rate of Unemployment (NAIRU) 343-4
  usefulness of concept 367, 368
net advantages of job concept 128-32
New Classical School of Monetarism:
  counter-inflationary policy 6-7
    rational expectations basis & monetary targets 188, 291, 305-8
      labour market implications 319-20, 347
    rejection 462-3
  see also Minford; Rational Expectations Hypothesis
Non-accelerating Inflation Rate of Unemployment (NAIRU) 343-4
  and collective bargaining 345-6, 347
  usefulness 367
Nossiter, B. D. 216

occupational mobility 167-9
  barriers:
    closed occupations 111-12
    skills mismatch 358-9, 387-91
      structural change 231-4
  decisions 135-6
  downward 238-9
  economic benefits 377
  internal upward mobility 82-3, 138-9
  see also geographical mobility
occupations:
  boundaries and definitions 75-8, 111-12
  choice of 132-4
    net advantages of jobs 128-32
      occupational reservation wage 126-7, 134-5
  demand, employers *see* Job Requirements
  see also occupational mobility
overmanning in industry 216
overtime 105-8

Parker, Hermione 381-2
Parkin, J. M. 212
Parkin, J. M. *et al.* 353
part-time working 114
Phelps, E. S. *et al.* 345, 348
Phillips curve 260-6
  criticism 260-1, 264-5
  expectations-augmented 266-75
    and short-run inflation/unemployment trade-off 275-80
    weaknesses 280-6
picketing 206, 432-3
Pond, C. 442
Price, R. and Bain, G. S. 219
product real wage 84
productivity *see* marginal productivity analysis
productivity agreement 106
public sector:
  privatization and job cut-backs 422, 453-5
  wage settlements 403-5
    cash limits and guidelines 320, 423-4
    influence on private sector 224
    negotiations 426-30
Public Sector Borrowing Requirement
  policy of reduction 8
    Thatcher Government 417, 421, 422-3, 453
  relationship with interest rates and money supply 41-2

Quantity Theory of Money 18-21
  labour market implications 21-30
  velocity of circulation and 22, 24-6
quit-rate, labour 377

Rational Expectations Hypothesis (REH) 297-303
  in a counter-inflationary policy 462-5
  monetary targets and 305-8
    example 417-20
  and trade unions 316-18
recruitment of personnel
  acceptable labour 106, 111-12, 136-42, 283
  costs 88-9
  internal *v.* external labour market 82-3, 90-1
  overtime alternative 105-8
  see also Job Requirements
redundancy 95-7, 99, 157, 377-8
  Redundancy Payments Act (1965) 405-6
regional policies 397-8
rent allowance *see* housing policy
replacement ratio 369-75
  effect on unemployment level 377
  and employment decisions 119-20, 158, 255-6, 369
  voluntary unemployment 242
reservation wage 115
  determinants 118-19, 356-60
    Unemployment Benefit level 119-21
    influencing 381-3, 450-1
  and labour force participation 115-18
  occupational/job reservation wage 126-7, 134-5
    determinants 356-60
  real 146-7, 153
    housing policy and 170-1, 394-6

revision 156-8
retention reservation wage 122-5
  real 157-67
  revision 148-51
Richardson, Gordon
  on monetary policy 307-8
  on pay negotiations 326-7
Rima, I. 153, 166
Robinson, D. (references to previous works)
  collective bargaining 323
  counter-inflationary policies 467, 471, 478
  labour supply 76, 118, 282, 380
    and wages 148
  and Mayhew, K. 200
Rosewall, B. and Robinson, D. 232
Ross, A. M. 194-5, 201
Rowthorn, B. 345

St. John-Stevas, Norman
  on Conservative Monetarism 416
Sargent, T. J. 410
security of employment:
  and revision of reservation wage 157
semi-skilled workers 79
  study by Blackburn & Mann 132, 136
  trade union effect on wages 212-13
Sharp, H. 399
Smith, Adam:
  on division and specialization of labour 74
  on local labour markets 173
  on net advantages of jobs 128-31
social security benefits *see* housing; Supplementary Benefits; Unemployment Benefits
Special Employment and Training Measures 249-50, 391-2, 442-3
  effects on unemployment levels 364, 444
  Manpower Services Commission on Requirements 446-7
strikes:
  legislation 402-3
    ballots 436
  rationale 206, 207, 220, 221
  withholding tax refunds from strikers 451
structural change and unemployment 231-4
Sumner, M. T. 353
Sunday working 441
Supplementary Benefits
  recipients 249, 400
    the unemployed 448
  and reservation wage/replacement ratio 119-21, 371, 372

taxation:
  fiscal policy 12, 352, 468
  and strikers 451
  and the unemployed 448-51
Tebbit, Norman
  on closed shops 435

on unemployment statistics 248
on wage settlements 211, 401-2, 443, 444-5
technology, new, and new occupations 168
structural unemployment 231-4
Temporary Employment Subsidy 391, 392
Thatcher Government:
  housing policy 452-3
  inflation control 462
  and local authority spending 424-6
  Monetarism, commitment to 415-17
  money supply control 417-22
  private sector wages, reducing 438-45
  public expenditure control 422-30
    public sector reduction 453-5
  trade union legislation 430-8
  on training 446-7
  on unemployment and benefits 447-51
Trade Union Act (1984) 436-7, 438
trade unions:
  ballots 436
  closed shops 205-6, 207-8, 434-6
  effects 202-3
    employment levels 215-17, 222
    for members 203-5
    labour market 193-4, 318-25, 462-3
    wage levels 211-15
  expectations 325-8, 336-7
    and aspirations 316-18
    influencing 332-5
    in counter-inflationary policies 471-4
    and labour market clearing rigidities 318-25, 462-3
  Germany 328
  government and 222-4, 332, 402-3, 405-6
    Thatcher Government legislation 430-8
  Keynesian view 193
  leadership 436, 437-8
  Monetarist views 209, 211-12, 214-15, 217, 222-3, 430
  objectives 194-6
    and individual members objectives 196-8
    wage claims/settlements 191-4
      comparability 72-3, 199-201, 322, 324
      influences 324-5
      real wage increases 57-8, 202, 328-32
  political funds 436
  power 206-9, 335-6
    bilateral monopoly situation 209-11
    decrease 12, 332-3
    measurement 217-19, 221-2
    militancy 219-21
    see also strikes
  and public sector pay negotiations 426-30
Trades Union Congress 224
training:

training (*cont.*)
  choice of occupation and 128, 133
  employer's costs and benefits 87-92, 106
  government responsibilities 389-90, 391, 446-7
    Special Employment and Training Measures 249-50, 391-2, 442-3
      effects on employment levels 364, 444
Training in Industry (Scheme) 250

Ulman, L. 471
uncertainties:
  employers' 99-105
  in job search 155-6
unemployment:
  categorization 228-9, 251-2
  demand-deficient 234-7, 268-9
    frictional 230-1, 353
      determinants 354-8
      job search theory 148-53
    seasonal 229-30
    structural 231-4
    unemployment individuals 229
    voluntary or involuntary 237-8, 254-6, 374-7
      concept of reasonableness 238-40
      Monetarists on 240-4
  and economically inactive 118
  employers' attitudes towards 140, 386
  fear of, and inflation control 60-1, 330-1
  and inflation *see under* employment levels
  influencing *see* Natural Rate of Unemployment: areas of influence
  measurement
  surveys 244-5
  UK official statistics 245-6
    changes of count method (1982 & 1983) 245-9
    relation to Natural Rate of Unemployment 364-5, 380-1
    validity of count queried 250-4
    see also Special Employment and Training Measures
  Natural Rate of *see* Natural Rate of Unemployment
  political acceptability 223
  social issues 120-1, 478-80
  youth 443-5
    educational system and 378-80
Unemployment Benefits:
  and employment/unemployment decisions 119
  absolute level of benefits and 369, 373-4, 375
  benefits/income ratio *see* replacement ratio
  Thatcher Government on 447-51
  and voluntary or involuntary unemployment 374-7

Union Membership Agreement (closed shop) 205-6, 207-8, 434-6

vacancies, job
  advertisement 383-7
  in job search theory 154-7
  and voluntary or involuntary unemployment 238-40
velocity of circulation in Quantity Theory 22, 24-6

Waddington, David 444
wages:
  determination by market forces 177-9, 356-7
  and aggregate demand 329-30
  marginal analysis 65-75, 83-6
    non-homogeneity of labour and 86-92
    uncertainties in 99-105
  and money supply 303-5
    monetary targets 305-12
  rigidities 182-8, 318-25, 357-8
    collective bargaining *see* trade unions
    fairness and comparability concepts 72-3, 103-5, 199-201, 322, 324
    government intervention
      minimum wage legislation 241-2, 398-402, 438-42
    see also incomes policies
  supply side *see* labour market: supply
  Walrasian equilibrium 179-82
  differentials, internal 72, 184-5
  and expectations 289-90
  and inflation *see* inflation
  low, attitudes towards 118-19, 243-4, 383, 441-2
  money wages
    reduction resistance 166, 182-3, 234-5
      implicit contract theory 92-9
    relative 183-7
  product real wage 84
  real 84, 146-8
    individual's conception of own 300-3
    labour market responses 160-7, 182, 234-6
    see also Phillips curve
Wages Councils 399-402, 439-42
Walrasian equilibrium 179-82
Walters, Alan 15, 188
wealth:
  Friedman on 27-9, 37
  human capital component 37, 50-1
  see also income
wives, working 116-17, 380
Wood, J. B. 396
work ethic 120-1
working conditions 86, 101, 129, 382
Wren-Lewis, S. 29-30

Young Workers Scheme 442-3, 444
    effect on unemployment statistics 249-50
youth:
    unemployment 443-5
        educational system and 378-80

wages protection removed 439, 440
see also Special Employment and Training Measures
Youth Training Scheme 391, 446, 447
    numbers covered 250